OISHINBO

A la Carte

Vegetables

Story by **Tetsu Kariya**
Art by **Akira Hanasaki**

OISHINBO
A la Carte

Vegetables

The recipes on this and the following page are for the dishes "Asparagus Grilled *Kabayaki*-style" and "Asparagus with Walnut Dressing" which appear in the story "The Breath of Spring" on page 183.

Kabayaki is a cooking method usually reserved for cooking fish and is most closely associated with grilled eel. But this method can also be used for a variety of vegetables. In essence, the ingredient is continually coated with a *tare* sauce made from soy sauce, sake, *mirin*, and sugar while being grilled on a charcoal brassier.

The walnut and miso dressing creates a nice counterpoint in flavor, and both dishes bring out the refreshing taste of asparagus.

Note: The bamboo skewers—which are about half as long as regular wooden skewers—can be found in Asian food stores or gourmet cook shops. Of course, if you can't find them, any kind of smaller decorative skewer can be used, but don't use plastic ones, as they'll melt on the grill.

◆Ingredient/Item List

Asparagus Grilled Kabayaki-style
10 asparagus stalks
Tare sauce:
1/2 cup soy sauce
1/2 cup mirin (sweet rice wine)
1/2 cup sake
Sansho (Japanese pepper) or Sichuan pepper

Asparagus with Walnut Dressing
10 asparagus stalks
1/4 cup walnuts
1/4 cup white miso
1/4 cup dashi broth
1 teaspoon salt

Asparagus with Walnut Dressing

1

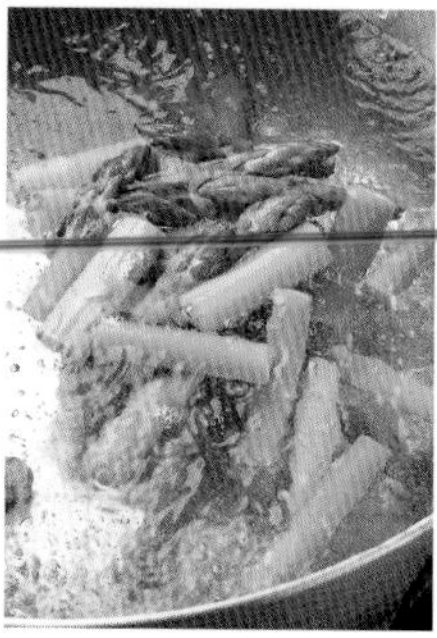

Rinse and dry the asparagus. Trim off the tough part at the base of the stalk and the scales along the side. Cut the stalks into 2-inch lengths, place them in a pot with hot water and a dash of salt and bring to a boil.

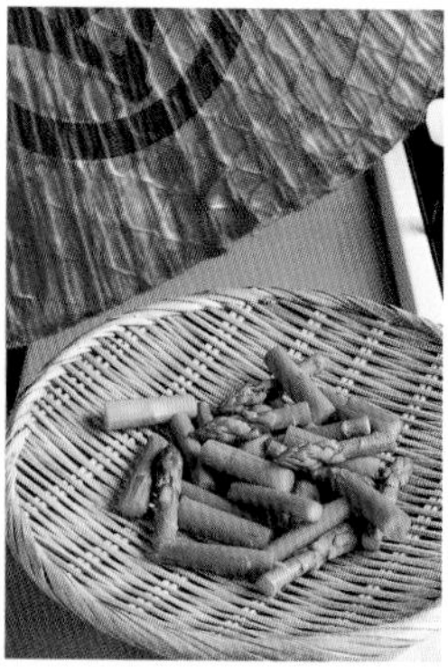

2

Before the asparagus gets too soft, remove them from the pan and place them on a strainer to cool. Fan them to cool quickly and prevent overcooking.

Note: The asparagus needs be boiled only briefly and then quickly cooled, or they become mushy. Rinsing them with cool water can make them watery, so the recommended method is to cool by fanning them, letting air instead of water reduce the temperature.

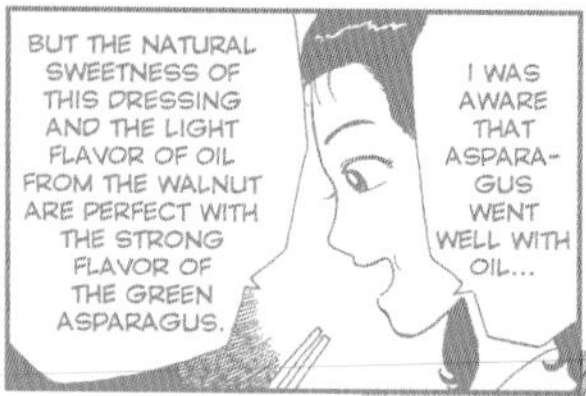
I WAS AWARE THAT ASPARA-GUS WENT WELL WITH OIL...
BUT THE NATURAL SWEETNESS OF THIS DRESSING AND THE LIGHT FLAVOR OF OIL FROM THE WALNUT ARE PERFECT WITH THE STRONG FLAVOR OF THE GREEN ASPARAGUS.

3

Grind the walnuts with a mortar and pestle or food processor. Put in a mixing bowl and stir in the miso and the dashi. Arrange the asparagus on a dish and spoon the dressing over the stalks.

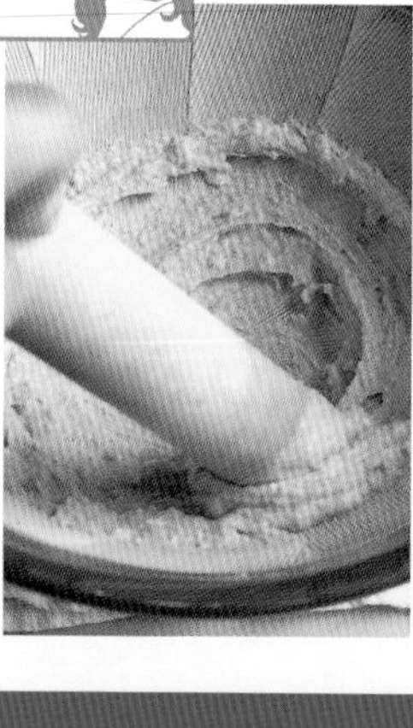

Asparagus Grilled *Kabayaki*-style

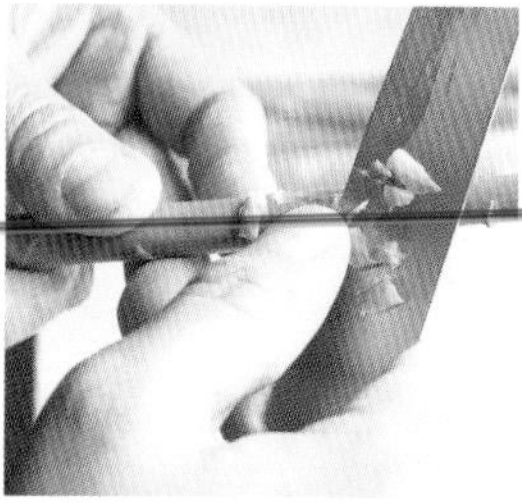

1

Rinse and dry the asparagus. Trim off the tough part at the base of the stalk and the scales along the side.

2

Line five stalks of asparagus neatly in a row and skewer them with two bamboo skewers.

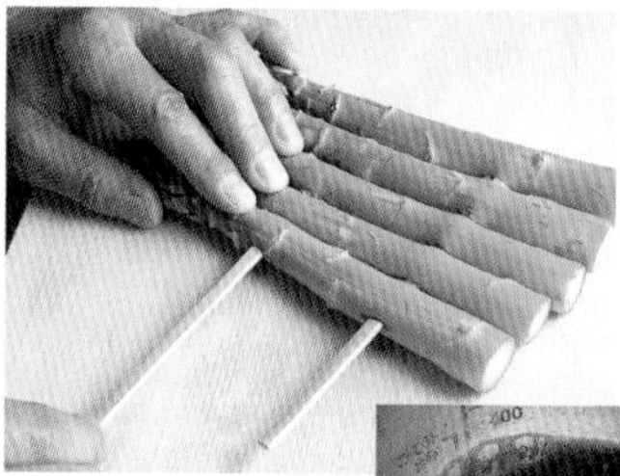

3

For the tare sauce, combine the soy sauce, mirin and sake in a small saucepan and bring to a light boil.

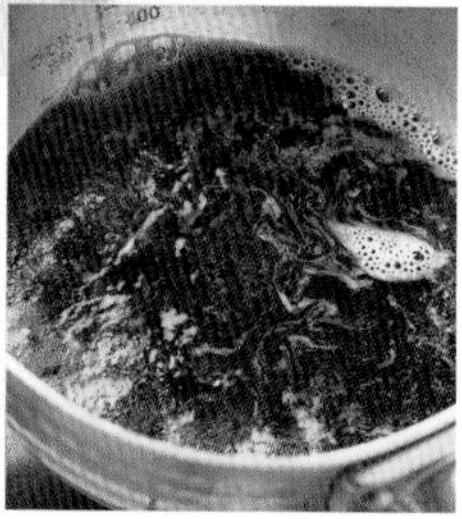

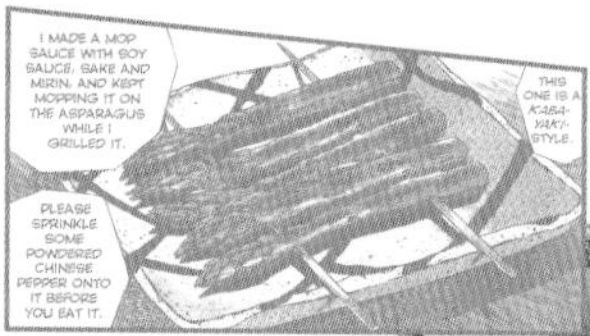
THIS ONE IS A KABA-YAKI-STYLE.
I MADE A MOP SAUCE WITH SOY SAUCE, SAKE AND MIRIN, AND KEPT MOPPING IT ON THE ASPARAGUS WHILE I GRILLED IT.
PLEASE SPRINKLE SOME POWDERED CHINESE PEPPER ONTO IT BEFORE YOU EAT IT.

4

Place the asparagus skewers on a heated grill. A charcoal *hibachi* grill is most suitable for the size of the dish, but any grill can be used. In a pinch, they can even be fried in a regular skillet.

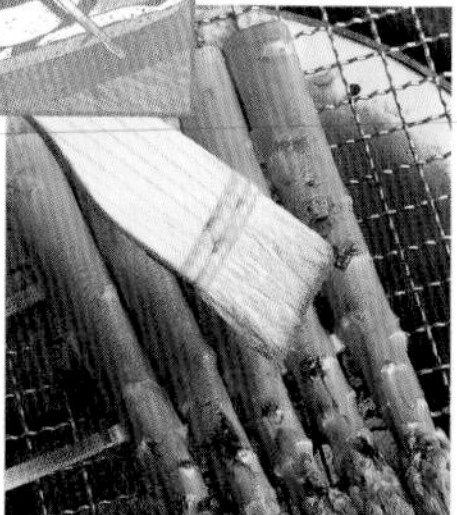

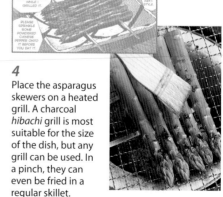

As the skewers grill, brush the asparagus with the tare sauce several times to make sure the flavor soaks in. When done, sprinkle with the sansho pepper to taste and serve.

Contents

Characters and Story Summary

Yamaoka Shirō
The (anti-?)hero of the series, he's a journalist for the *Tōzai News* placed in charge of the Ultimate Menu project

Kaibara Yūzan
A prominent artist, as well as founder and director of The Gourmet Club, he's Yamaoka's father and rival

Kurita Yūko
Yamaoka's partner on the Ultimate Menu project and later his wife

Ōhara Daizō
Publisher of the *Tōzai News*

Koizumi Kyōichi
Executive editor of the *Tōzai News*

Tanimura Hideo
Director of *Tōzai's* Arts & Culture department

Tomii Tomio
Deputy director under Tanimura

Tōyama Tōjin
A famed ceramicist and
gourmet

Kyōgoku Mantarō
A wealthy businessman
and gourmet

Futaki Mariko
A coworker of Yamaoka and
Kurita's at the paper

Okaboshi Seiichi
Chef/owner of Yamaoka's
local hangout

Nakagawa Tokuo
Head chef at the Gourmet Club

As part of the celebrations for its 100th anniversary, the publishers of the *Tōzai News* have commissioned the creation of the "Ultimate Menu," a model meal embodying the pinnacle of Japanese cuisine. This all-important task has been entrusted to Yamaoka, an inveterate cynic who possesses zero initiative—but also an incredibly refined palate and an encyclopedic knowledge of food.

Yamaoka was trained from a young age by his father, Kaibara, a man widely revered for his sense of taste and feared for his ferocious temper. Father-son relations are strained, to say the least, and degenerate even further after Kaibara agrees to head the "Supreme Menu" project of the *Teito Times*, rival paper to the *Tōzai News*.

As Yamaoka and Kurita go about conducting the research for the Ultimate Menu, they're helped along by their boss, the avuncular Tanimura, and sometimes helped and sometimes stymied by the excitable Tomii. Kyōgoku and Tōyama, two stalwarts always up for a good meal, are frequent companions, as are coworkers Mitani and Tabata. And at the end of the day you can usually find them at Okaboshi's, planning the next step of their grand culinary adventure!

FIRST COURSE

VEGETABLE SHOWDOWN! (PART ONE)

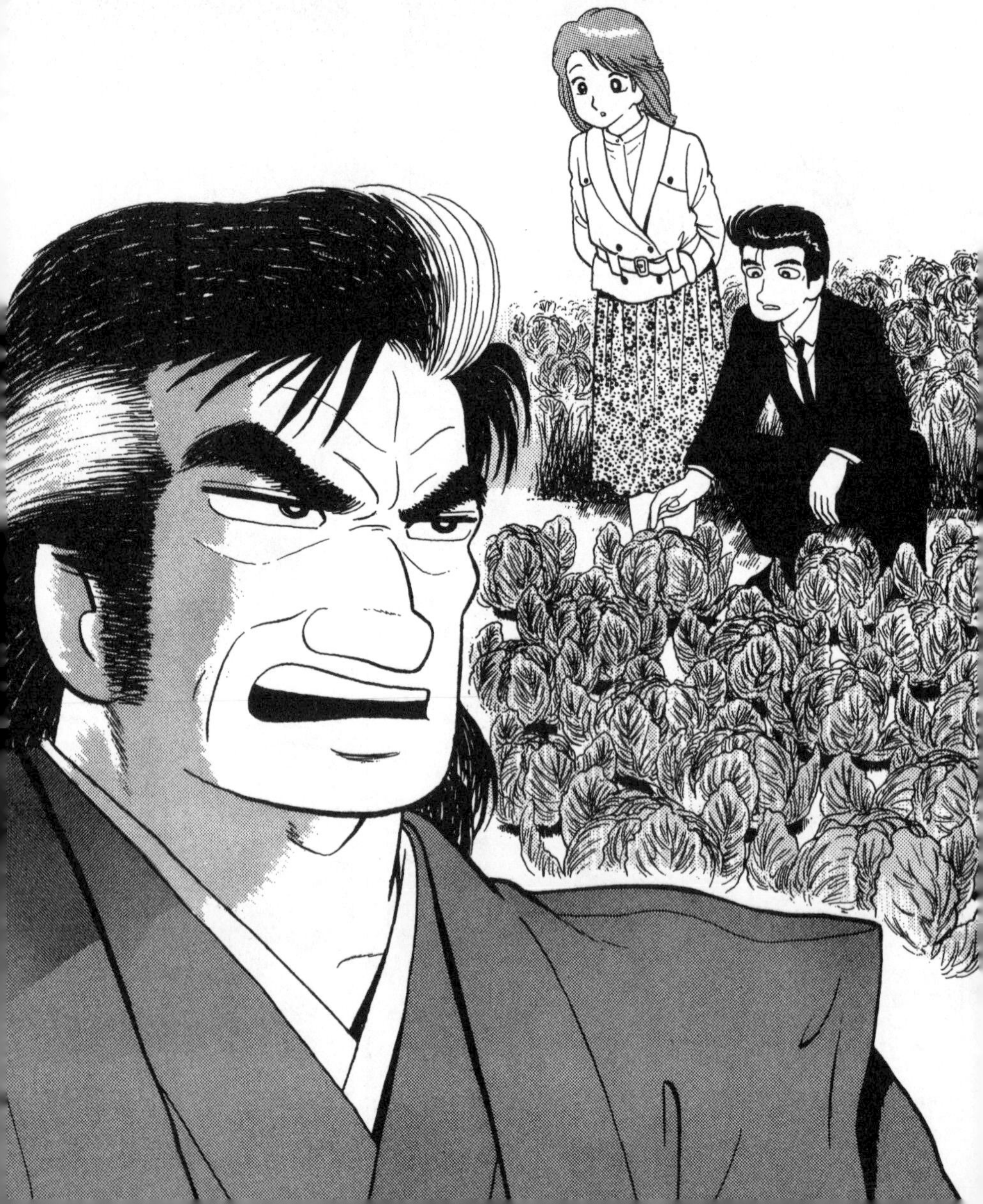

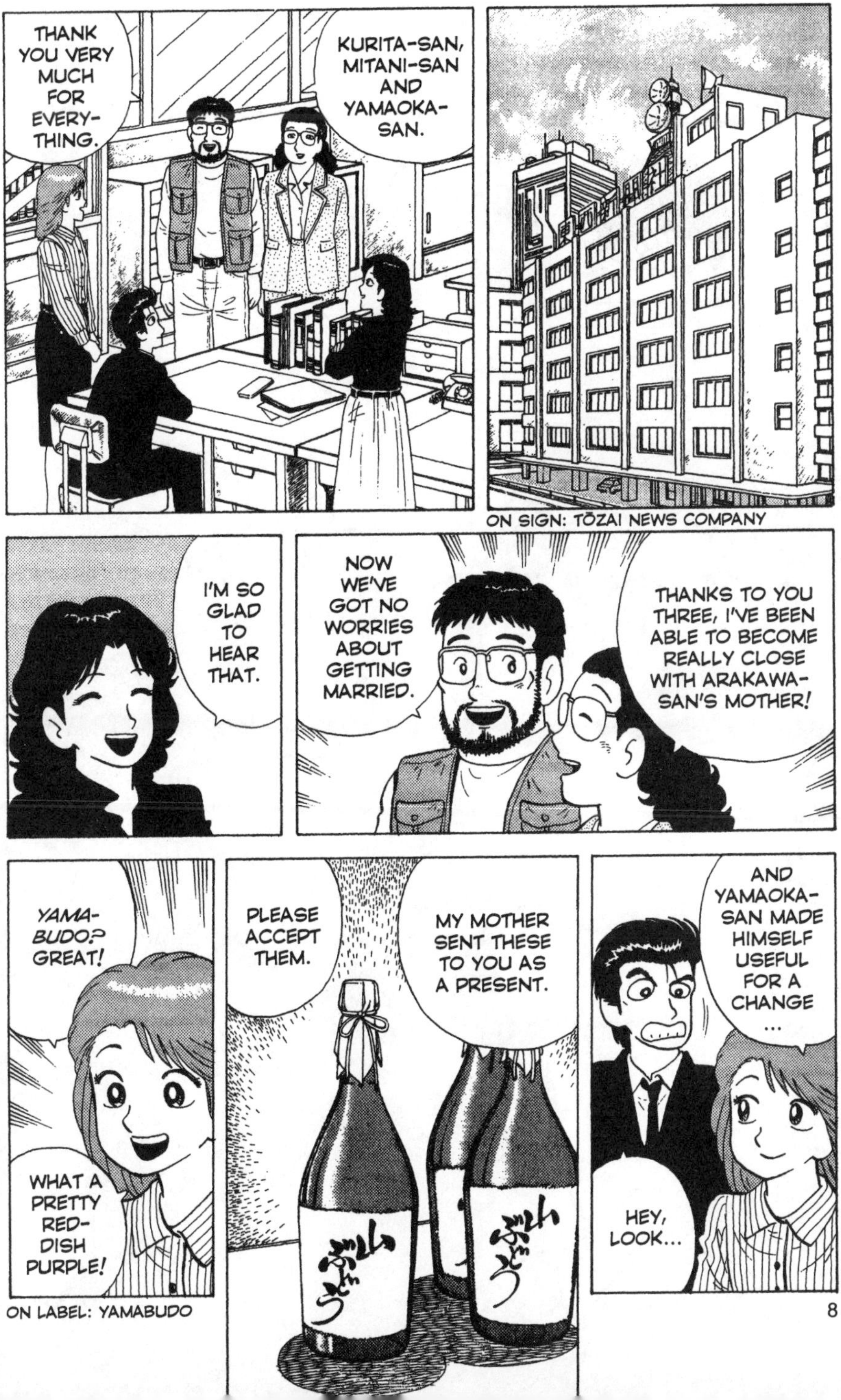
KURITA-SAN, MITANI-SAN AND YAMAOKA-SAN.
THANK YOU VERY MUCH FOR EVERYTHING.
THANKS TO YOU THREE, I'VE BEEN ABLE TO BECOME REALLY CLOSE WITH ARAKAWA-SAN'S MOTHER!
NOW WE'VE GOT NO WORRIES ABOUT GETTING MARRIED.
I'M SO GLAD TO HEAR THAT.
AND YAMAOKA-SAN MADE HIMSELF USEFUL FOR A CHANGE ...
HEY, LOOK...
MY MOTHER SENT THESE TO YOU AS A PRESENT.
PLEASE ACCEPT THEM.
YAMA-BUDO? GREAT!
WHAT A PRETTY RED-DISH PURPLE!

ON SIGN: TŌZAI NEWS COMPANY

ON LABEL: YAMABUDO

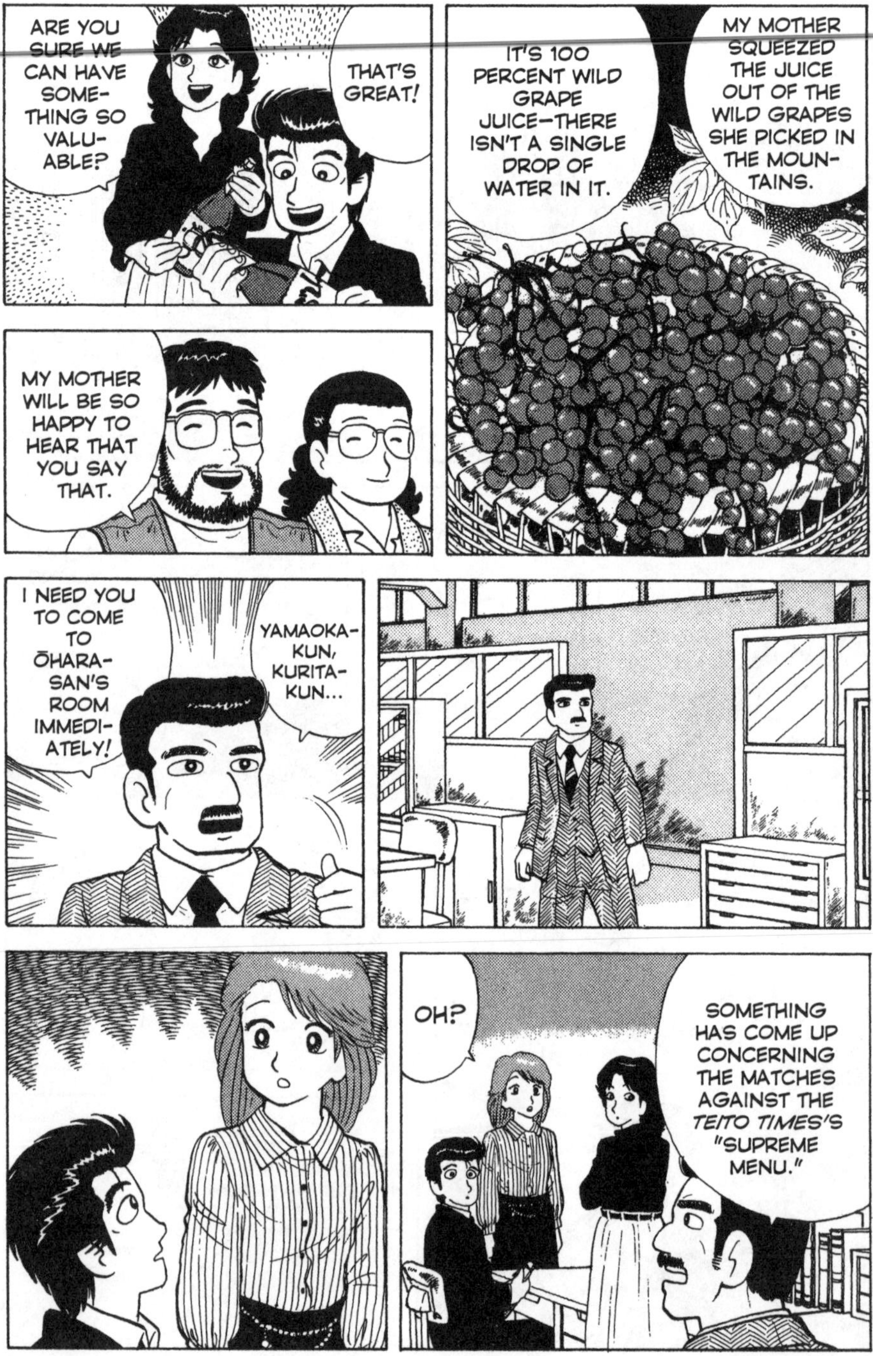
MY MOTHER SQUEEZED THE JUICE OUT OF THE WILD GRAPES SHE PICKED IN THE MOUNTAINS.
IT'S 100 PERCENT WILD GRAPE JUICE—THERE ISN'T A SINGLE DROP OF WATER IN IT.
THAT'S GREAT!
ARE YOU SURE WE CAN HAVE SOMETHING SO VALUABLE?
MY MOTHER WILL BE SO HAPPY TO HEAR THAT YOU SAY THAT.
YAMAOKA-KUN, KURITA-KUN...
I NEED YOU TO COME TO ŌHARA-SAN'S ROOM IMMEDIATELY!
SOMETHING HAS COME UP CONCERNING THE MATCHES AGAINST THE *TEITO TIMES*'S "SUPREME MENU."
OH?

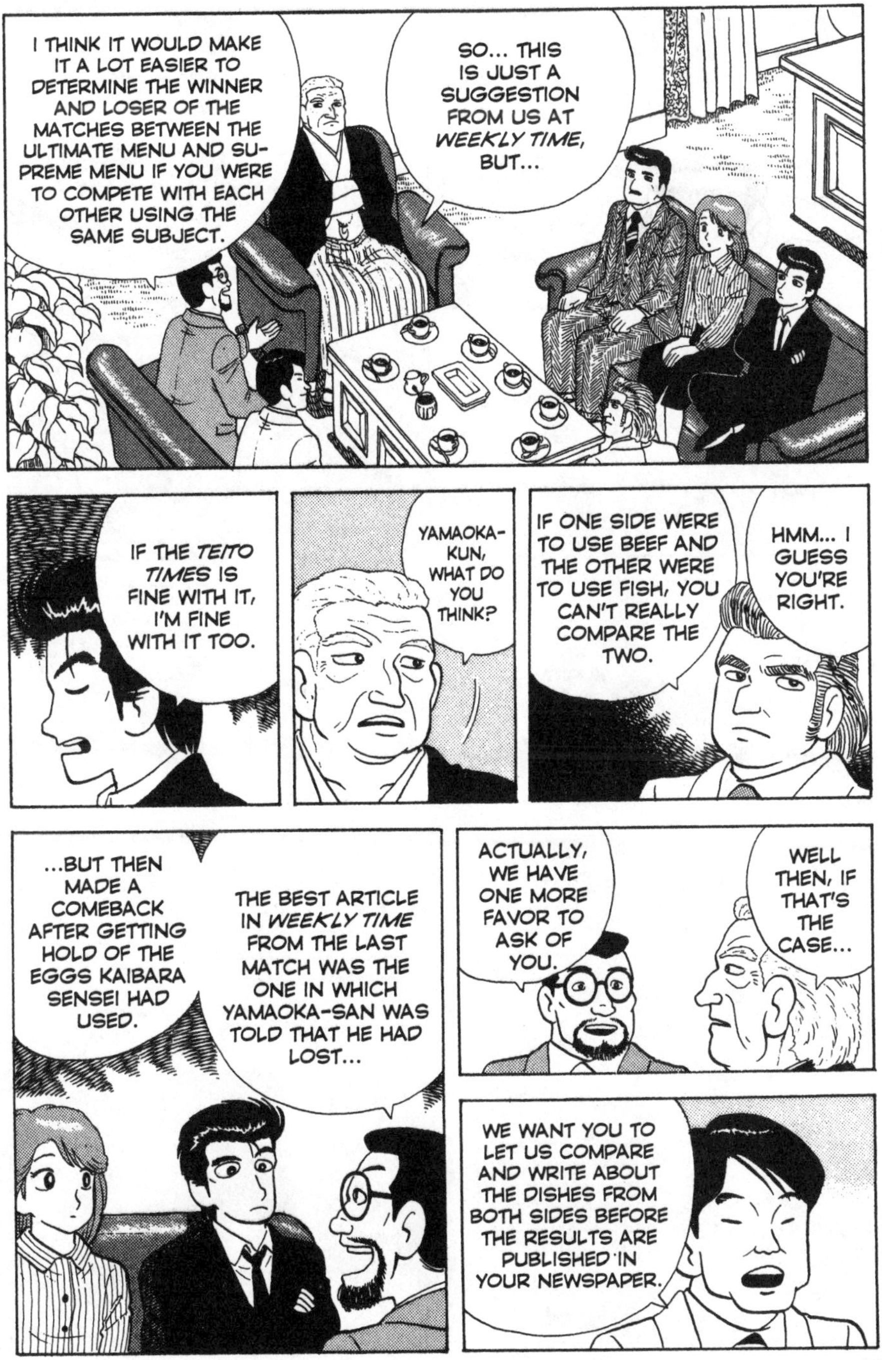
SO... THIS IS JUST A SUGGESTION FROM US AT *WEEKLY TIME*, BUT...
I THINK IT WOULD MAKE IT A LOT EASIER TO DETERMINE THE WINNER AND LOSER OF THE MATCHES BETWEEN THE ULTIMATE MENU AND SUPREME MENU IF YOU WERE TO COMPETE WITH EACH OTHER USING THE SAME SUBJECT.
HMM... I GUESS YOU'RE RIGHT.
IF ONE SIDE WERE TO USE BEEF AND THE OTHER WERE TO USE FISH, YOU CAN'T REALLY COMPARE THE TWO.
YAMAOKA-KUN, WHAT DO YOU THINK?
IF THE *TEITO TIMES* IS FINE WITH IT, I'M FINE WITH IT TOO.
WELL THEN, IF THAT'S THE CASE...
ACTUALLY, WE HAVE ONE MORE FAVOR TO ASK OF YOU.
WE WANT YOU TO LET US COMPARE AND WRITE ABOUT THE DISHES FROM BOTH SIDES BEFORE THE RESULTS ARE PUBLISHED IN YOUR NEWSPAPER.
THE BEST ARTICLE IN *WEEKLY TIME* FROM THE LAST MATCH WAS THE ONE IN WHICH YAMAOKA-SAN WAS TOLD THAT HE HAD LOST...
...BUT THEN MADE A COMEBACK AFTER GETTING HOLD OF THE EGGS KAIBARA SENSEI HAD USED.

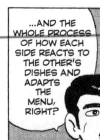

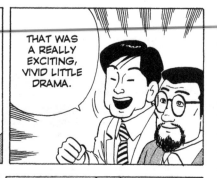

THAT WAS A REALLY EXCITING, VIVID LITTLE DRAMA.
I SEE... NOT JUST A SIMPLE COMPARISON OF THE DISHES— YOU WANT TO WRITE ABOUT THE EXCHANGES BETWEEN THE TEAMS...
...AND THE WHOLE PROCESS OF HOW EACH SIDE REACTS TO THE OTHER'S DISHES AND ADAPTS THE MENU, RIGHT?
THAT'S RIGHT. THE "TRUFFLE EGG" WAS CREATED OUT OF JUST SUCH AN EXCHANGE BETWEEN THE ULTIMATE AND THE SUPREME LAST TIME.
AND I BELIEVE THAT IT WOULD HELP BOTH SIDES A LOT IN REVISING THE DISHES IN THEIR MENUS.
WELL... IT DEPENDS ON WHAT YAMAOKA THINKS.
I'M OKAY WITH IT.
ARE YOU SURE? THINGS MAY NOT TURN OUT AS WELL AS THEY DID LAST TIME, YOU KNOW!
NO PROBLEM. JUST LEAVE IT TO ME!
THIS IS GOING TO BE TOUGH FOR YOU, YAMAOKA.
WELL, I'LL LIVE WITH IT IF YOU'RE GOING TO JACK UP MY BONUS IN RETURN.
THEN IF YOU LOSE...
YOUR BONUS GOES TO *ZERO!*

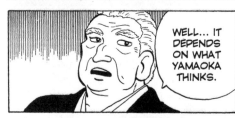

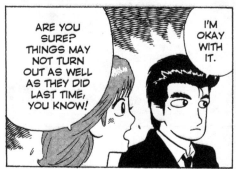

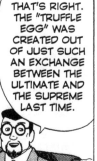

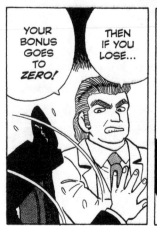

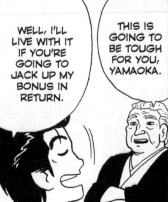

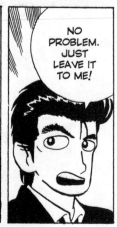

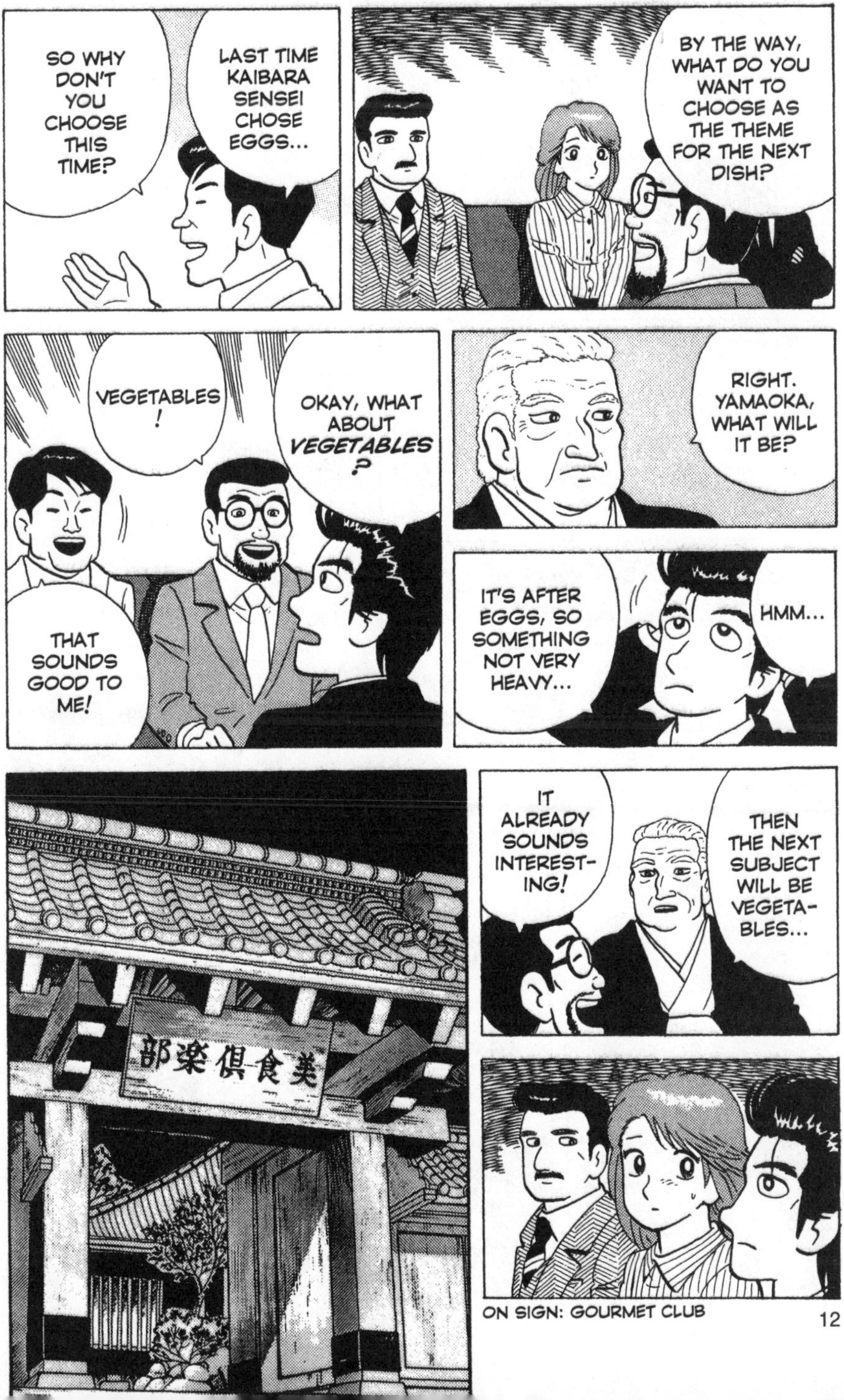
BY THE WAY, WHAT DO YOU WANT TO CHOOSE AS THE THEME FOR THE NEXT DISH?
LAST TIME KAIBARA SENSEI CHOSE EGGS...
SO WHY DON'T YOU CHOOSE THIS TIME?
RIGHT. YAMAOKA, WHAT WILL IT BE?
HMM...
IT'S AFTER EGGS, SO SOMETHING NOT VERY HEAVY...
OKAY, WHAT ABOUT *VEGETABLES*?
VEGETABLES!
THAT SOUNDS GOOD TO ME!
THEN THE NEXT SUBJECT WILL BE VEGETA-BLES...
IT ALREADY SOUNDS INTEREST-ING!
美食倶楽部

ON SIGN: GOURMET CLUB

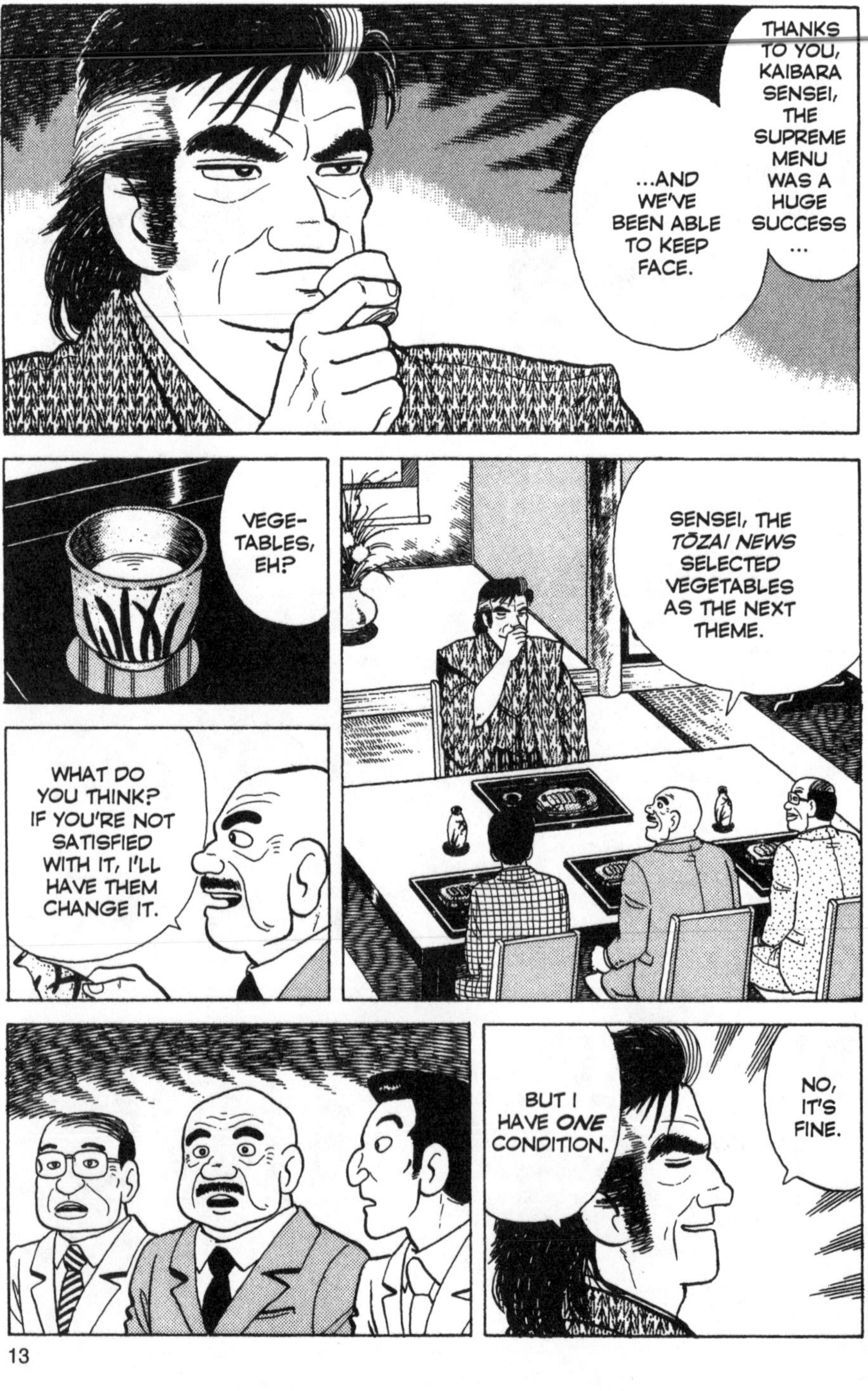
THANKS TO YOU, KAIBARA SENSEI, THE SUPREME MENU WAS A HUGE SUCCESS ...
...AND WE'VE BEEN ABLE TO KEEP FACE.
SENSEI, THE *TŌZAI NEWS* SELECTED VEGETABLES AS THE NEXT THEME.
VEGE-TABLES, EH?
WHAT DO YOU THINK? IF YOU'RE NOT SATISFIED WITH IT, I'LL HAVE THEM CHANGE IT.
NO, IT'S FINE.
BUT I HAVE *ONE* CONDITION.

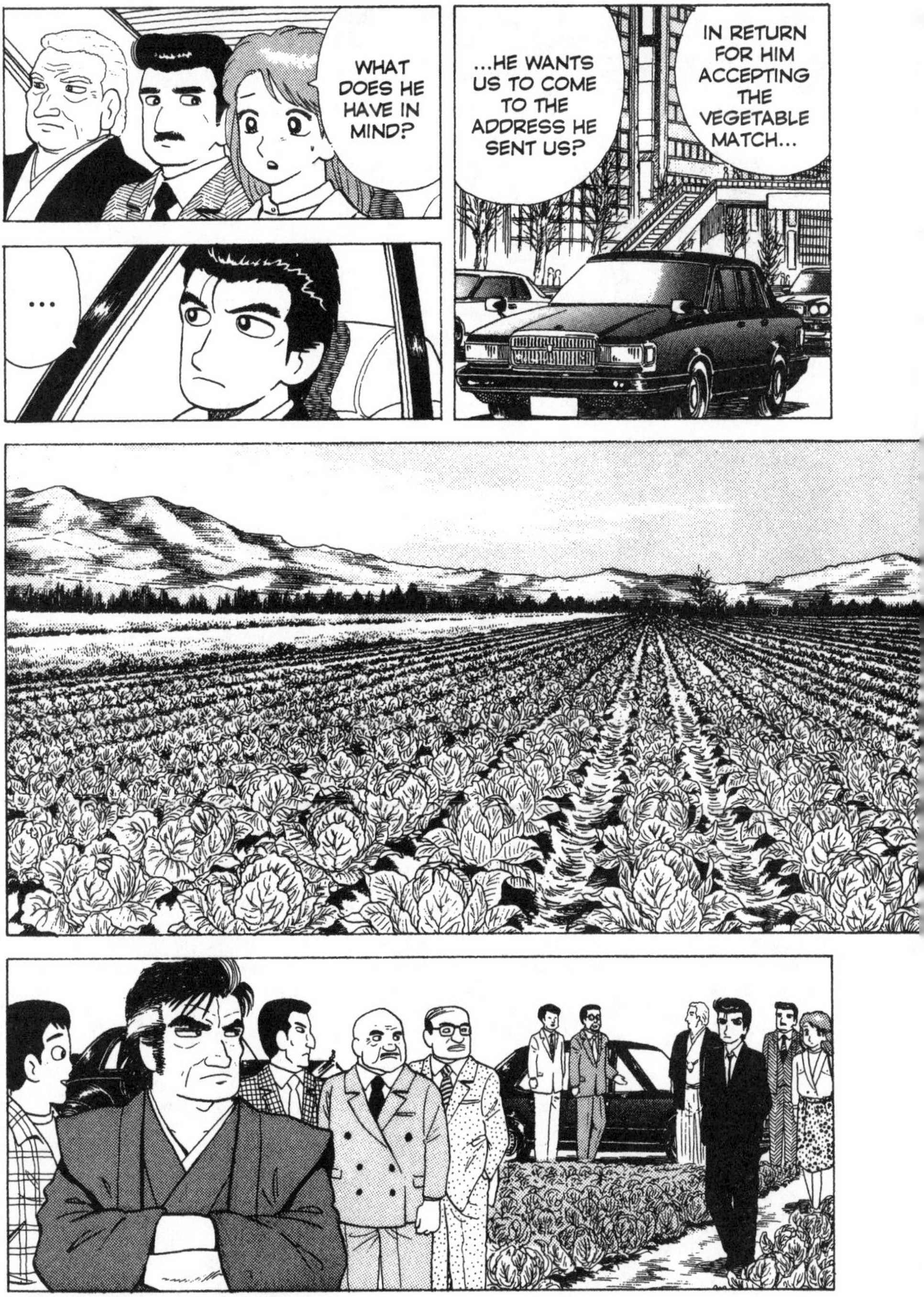
IN RETURN FOR HIM ACCEPTING THE VEGETABLE MATCH...
...HE WANTS US TO COME TO THE ADDRESS HE SENT US?
WHAT DOES HE HAVE IN MIND?
...

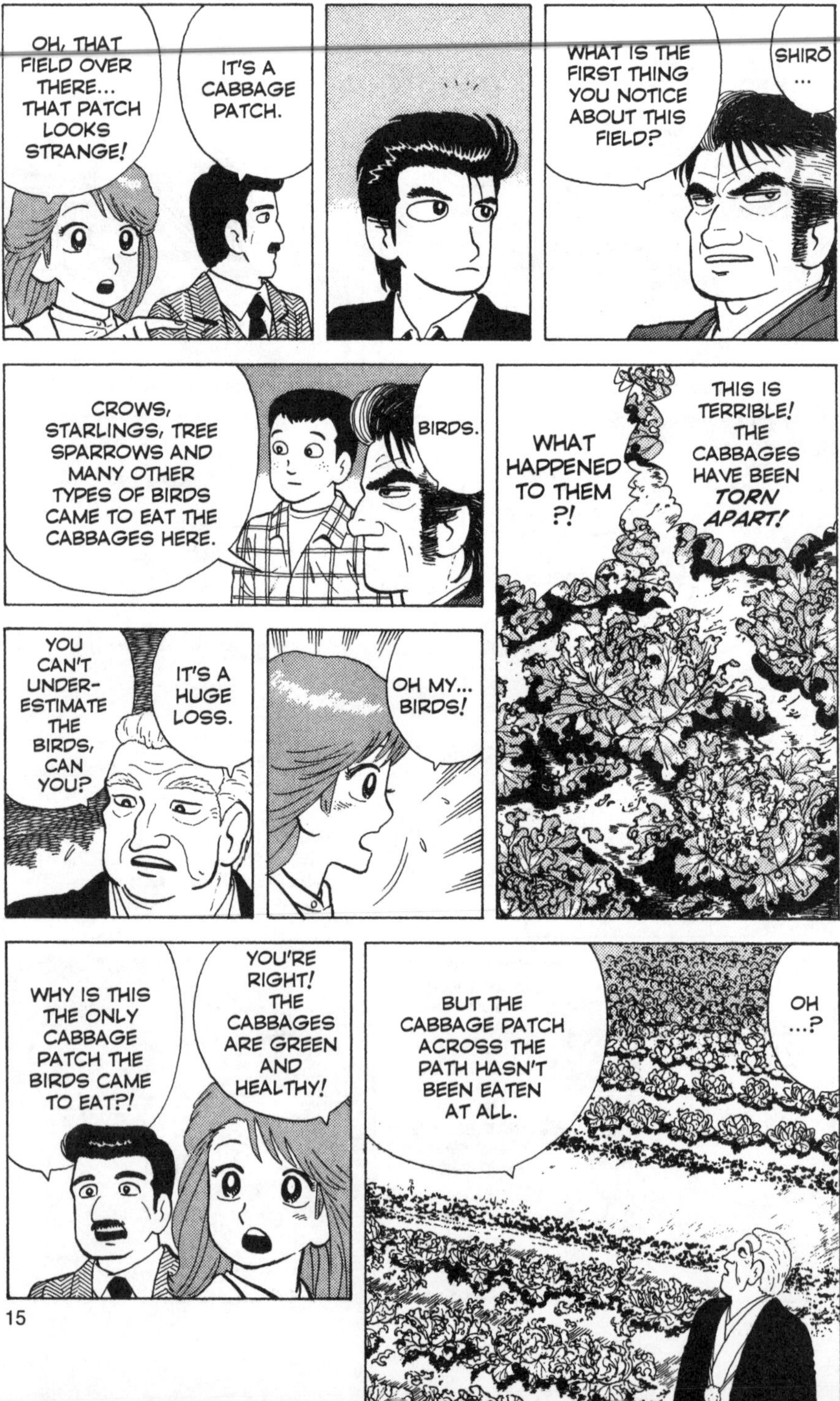
SHIRŌ...
WHAT IS THE FIRST THING YOU NOTICE ABOUT THIS FIELD?
IT'S A CABBAGE PATCH.
OH, THAT FIELD OVER THERE... THAT PATCH LOOKS STRANGE!
THIS IS TERRIBLE! THE CABBAGES HAVE BEEN *TORN APART!*
WHAT HAPPENED TO THEM ?!
BIRDS.
CROWS, STARLINGS, TREE SPARROWS AND MANY OTHER TYPES OF BIRDS CAME TO EAT THE CABBAGES HERE.
OH MY... BIRDS!
IT'S A HUGE LOSS.
YOU CAN'T UNDER-ESTIMATE THE BIRDS, CAN YOU?
OH ...?
BUT THE CABBAGE PATCH ACROSS THE PATH HASN'T BEEN EATEN AT ALL.
YOU'RE RIGHT! THE CABBAGES ARE GREEN AND HEALTHY!
WHY IS THIS THE ONLY CABBAGE PATCH THE BIRDS CAME TO EAT?!

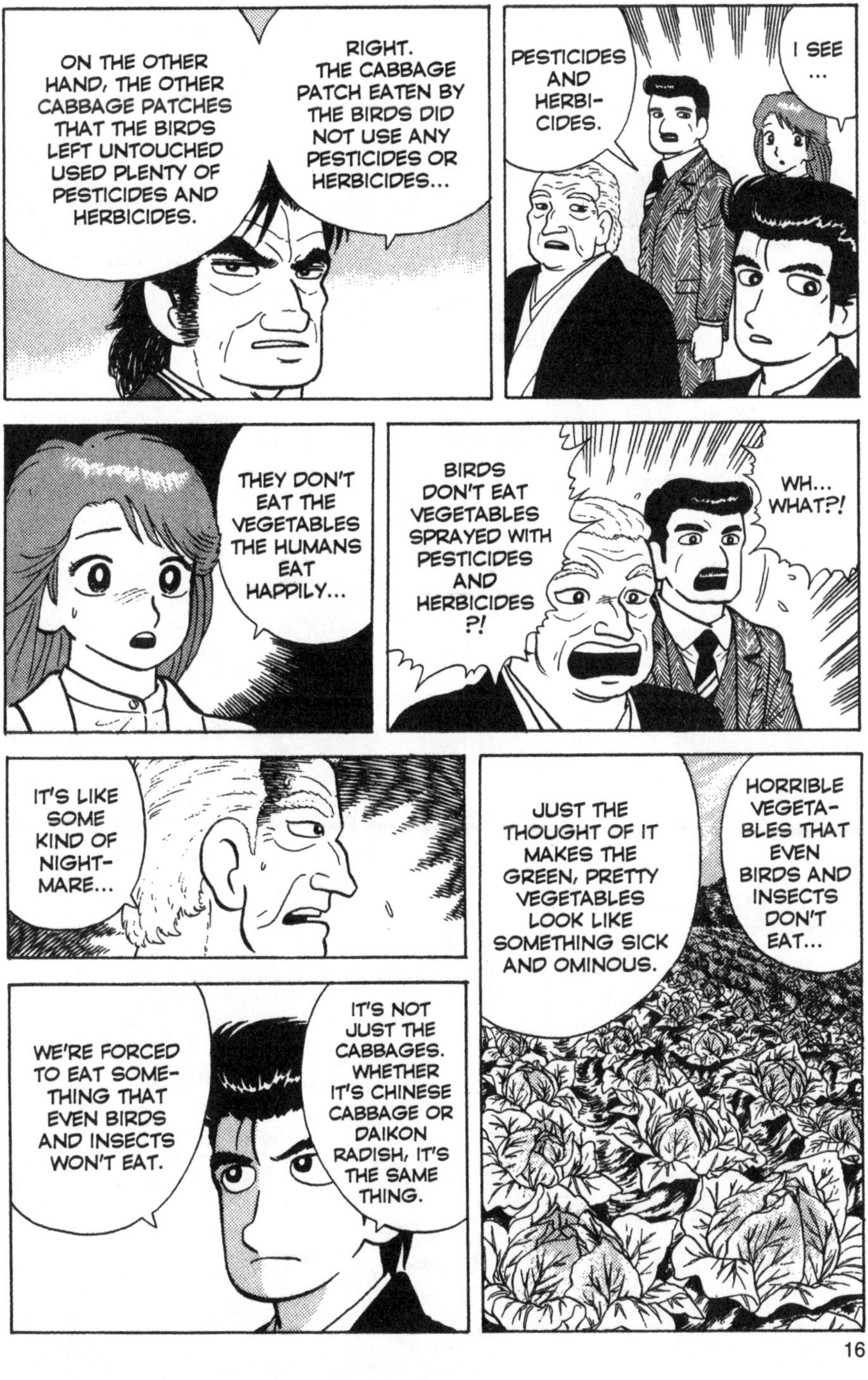
I SEE ...
PESTICIDES AND HERBI-CIDES.
RIGHT. THE CABBAGE PATCH EATEN BY THE BIRDS DID NOT USE ANY PESTICIDES OR HERBICIDES...
ON THE OTHER HAND, THE OTHER CABBAGE PATCHES THAT THE BIRDS LEFT UNTOUCHED USED PLENTY OF PESTICIDES AND HERBICIDES.
WH... WHAT?!
BIRDS DON'T EAT VEGETABLES SPRAYED WITH PESTICIDES AND HERBICIDES ?!
THEY DON'T EAT THE VEGETABLES THE HUMANS EAT HAPPILY...
HORRIBLE VEGETA-BLES THAT EVEN BIRDS AND INSECTS DON'T EAT...
JUST THE THOUGHT OF IT MAKES THE GREEN, PRETTY VEGETABLES LOOK LIKE SOMETHING SICK AND OMINOUS.
IT'S LIKE SOME KIND OF NIGHT-MARE...
IT'S NOT JUST THE CABBAGES. WHETHER IT'S CHINESE CABBAGE OR DAIKON RADISH, IT'S THE SAME THING.
WE'RE FORCED TO EAT SOME-THING THAT EVEN BIRDS AND INSECTS WON'T EAT.

OH, THAT FIELD OVER THERE ...

THERE'S A NET ALL AROUND IT.

THAT IS WHAT SAVES US.

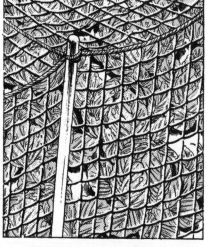

YES, SIR.

RYŌ- ZŌ.

LOOK, THEY'VE GOT SOME WORM- HOLES.

THEN THAT MEANS ...

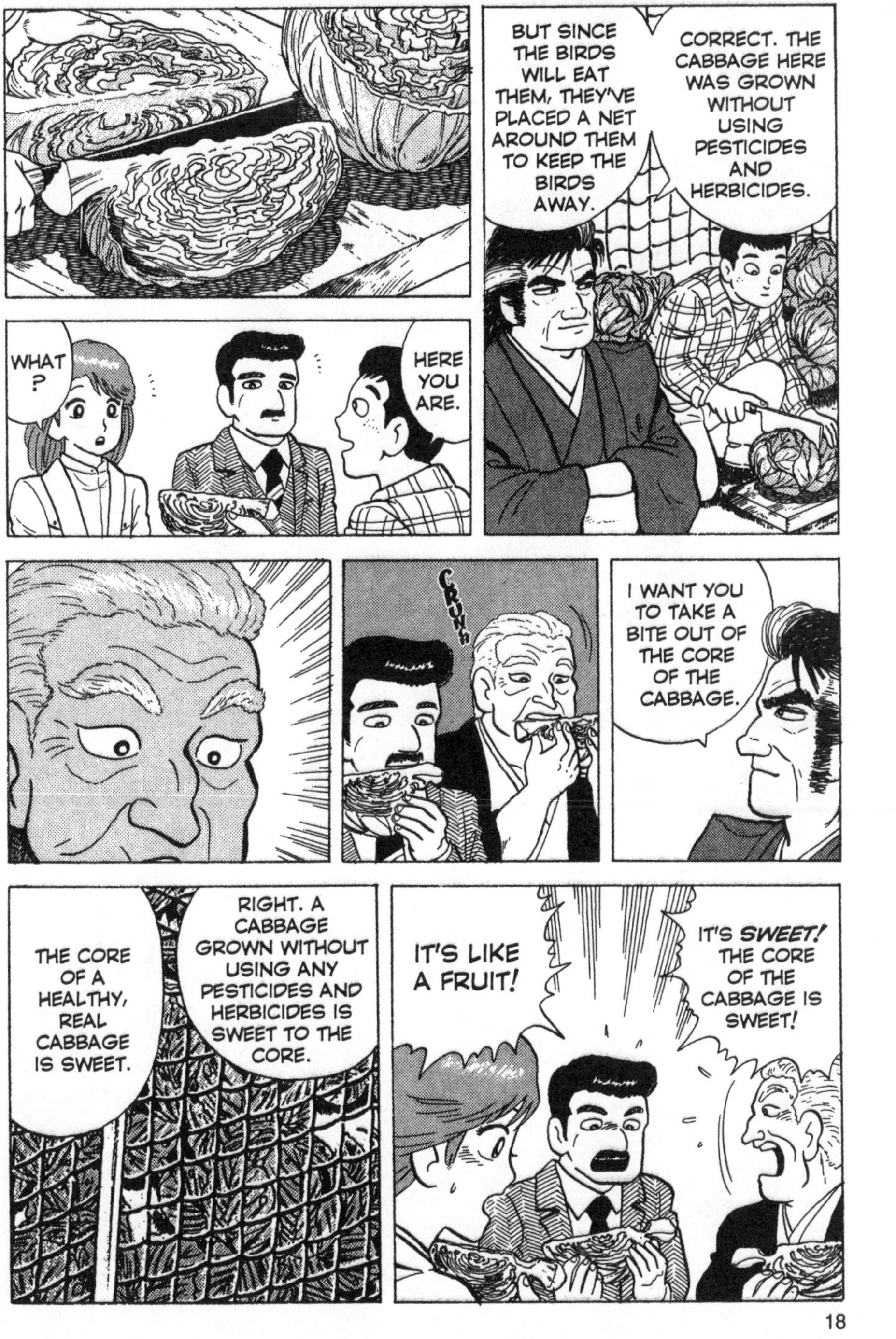
CORRECT. THE CABBAGE HERE WAS GROWN WITHOUT USING PESTICIDES AND HERBICIDES.
BUT SINCE THE BIRDS WILL EAT THEM, THEY'VE PLACED A NET AROUND THEM TO KEEP THE BIRDS AWAY.
HERE YOU ARE.
WHAT ?
I WANT YOU TO TAKE A BITE OUT OF THE CORE OF THE CABBAGE.
CRUNCH
IT'S *SWEET!* THE CORE OF THE CABBAGE IS SWEET!
IT'S LIKE A FRUIT!
RIGHT. A CABBAGE GROWN WITHOUT USING ANY PESTICIDES AND HERBICIDES IS SWEET TO THE CORE.
THE CORE OF A HEALTHY, REAL CABBAGE IS SWEET.

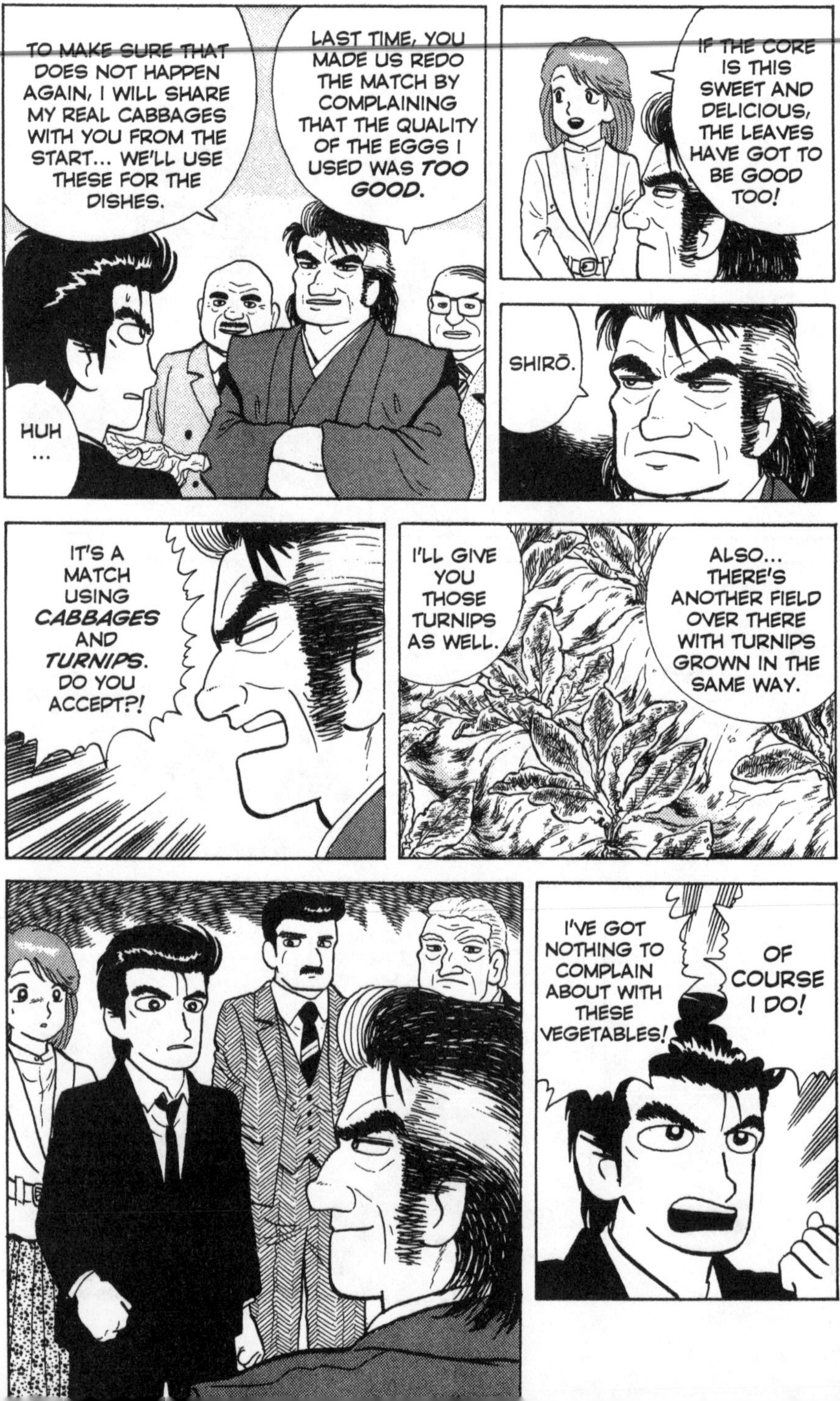
IF THE CORE IS THIS SWEET AND DELICIOUS, THE LEAVES HAVE GOT TO BE GOOD TOO!
SHIRŌ.
LAST TIME, YOU MADE US REDO THE MATCH BY COMPLAINING THAT THE QUALITY OF THE EGGS I USED WAS *TOO GOOD*.
TO MAKE SURE THAT DOES NOT HAPPEN AGAIN, I WILL SHARE MY REAL CABBAGES WITH YOU FROM THE START... WE'LL USE THESE FOR THE DISHES.
HUH ...
ALSO... THERE'S ANOTHER FIELD OVER THERE WITH TURNIPS GROWN IN THE SAME WAY.
I'LL GIVE YOU THOSE TURNIPS AS WELL.
IT'S A MATCH USING *CABBAGES* AND *TURNIPS*. DO YOU ACCEPT?!
OF COURSE I DO!
I'VE GOT NOTHING TO COMPLAIN ABOUT WITH THESE VEGETABLES!

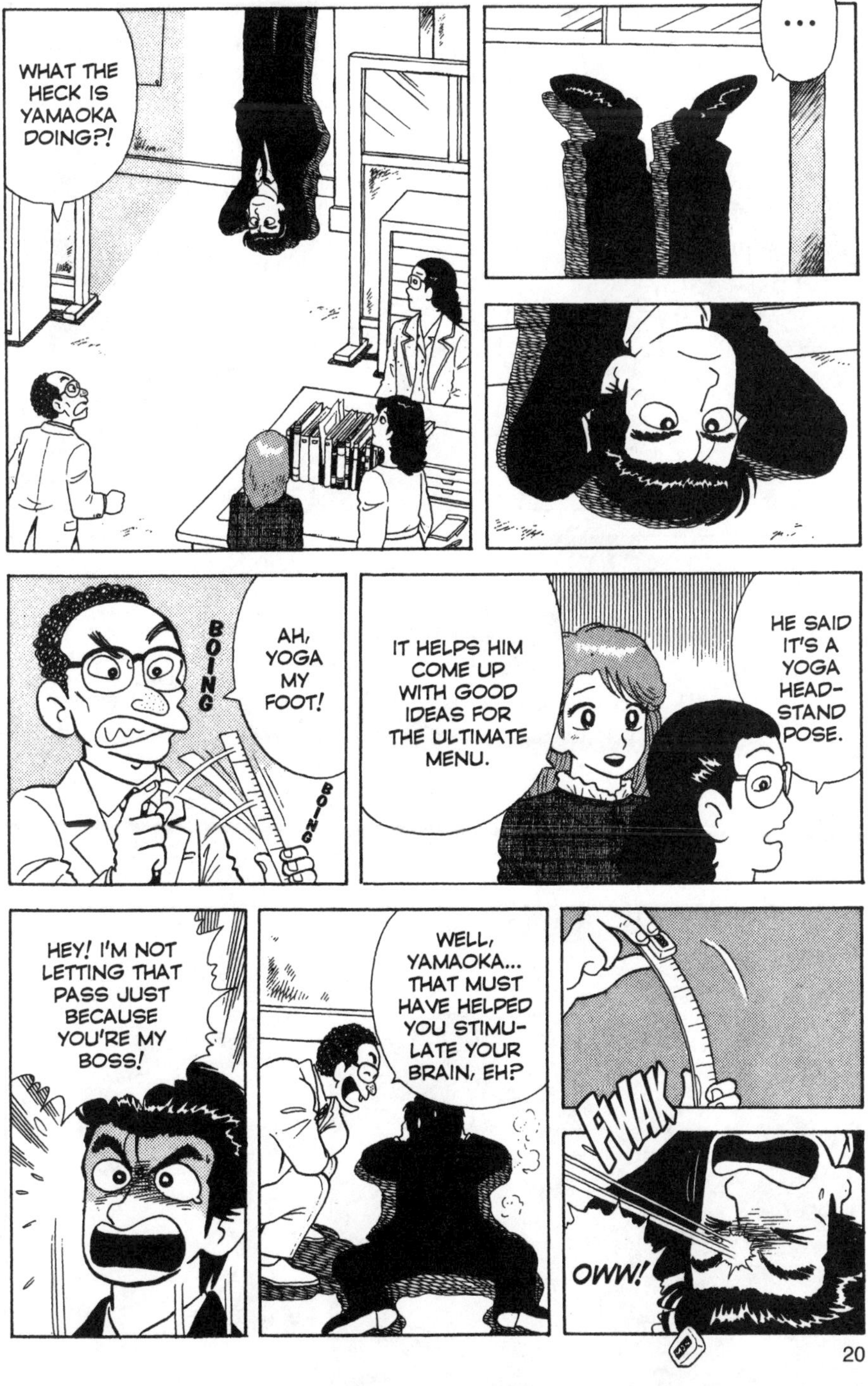
...
WHAT THE HECK IS YAMAOKA DOING?!
HE SAID IT'S A YOGA HEAD-STAND POSE.
IT HELPS HIM COME UP WITH GOOD IDEAS FOR THE ULTIMATE MENU.
AH, YOGA MY FOOT!
BOING
BOING
FWAK
OWW!
WELL, YAMAOKA... THAT MUST HAVE HELPED YOU STIMULATE YOUR BRAIN, EH?
HEY! I'M NOT LETTING THAT PASS JUST BECAUSE YOU'RE MY BOSS!

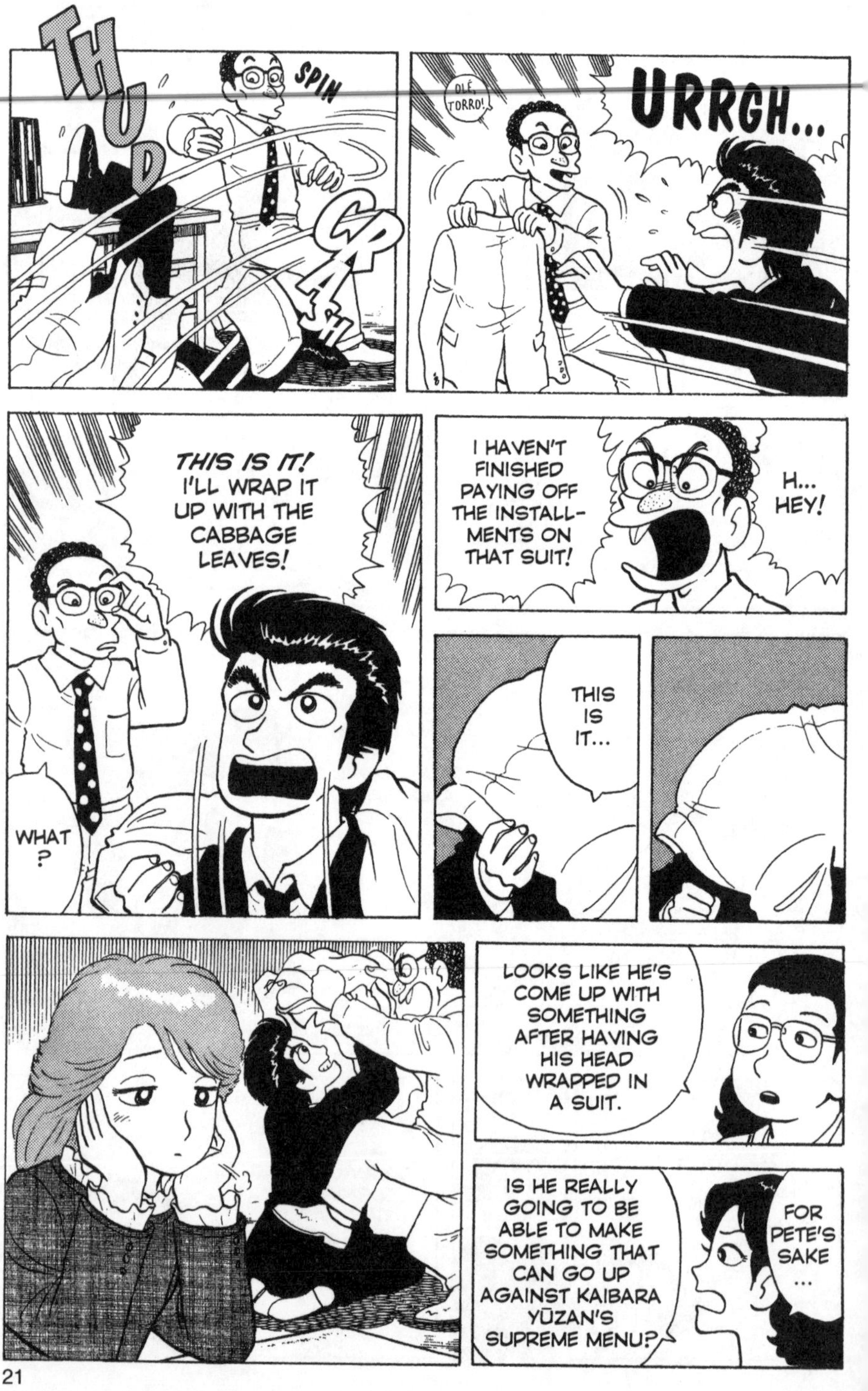
URRGH...
OLÉ, TORRO!
SPIN
THUD
CRASH
H... HEY!
I HAVEN'T FINISHED PAYING OFF THE INSTALLMENTS ON THAT SUIT!
THIS IS IT...
THIS IS IT! I'LL WRAP IT UP WITH THE CABBAGE LEAVES!
WHAT?
LOOKS LIKE HE'S COME UP WITH SOMETHING AFTER HAVING HIS HEAD WRAPPED IN A SUIT.
FOR PETE'S SAKE...
IS HE REALLY GOING TO BE ABLE TO MAKE SOMETHING THAT CAN GO UP AGAINST KAIBARA YŪZAN'S SUPREME MENU?

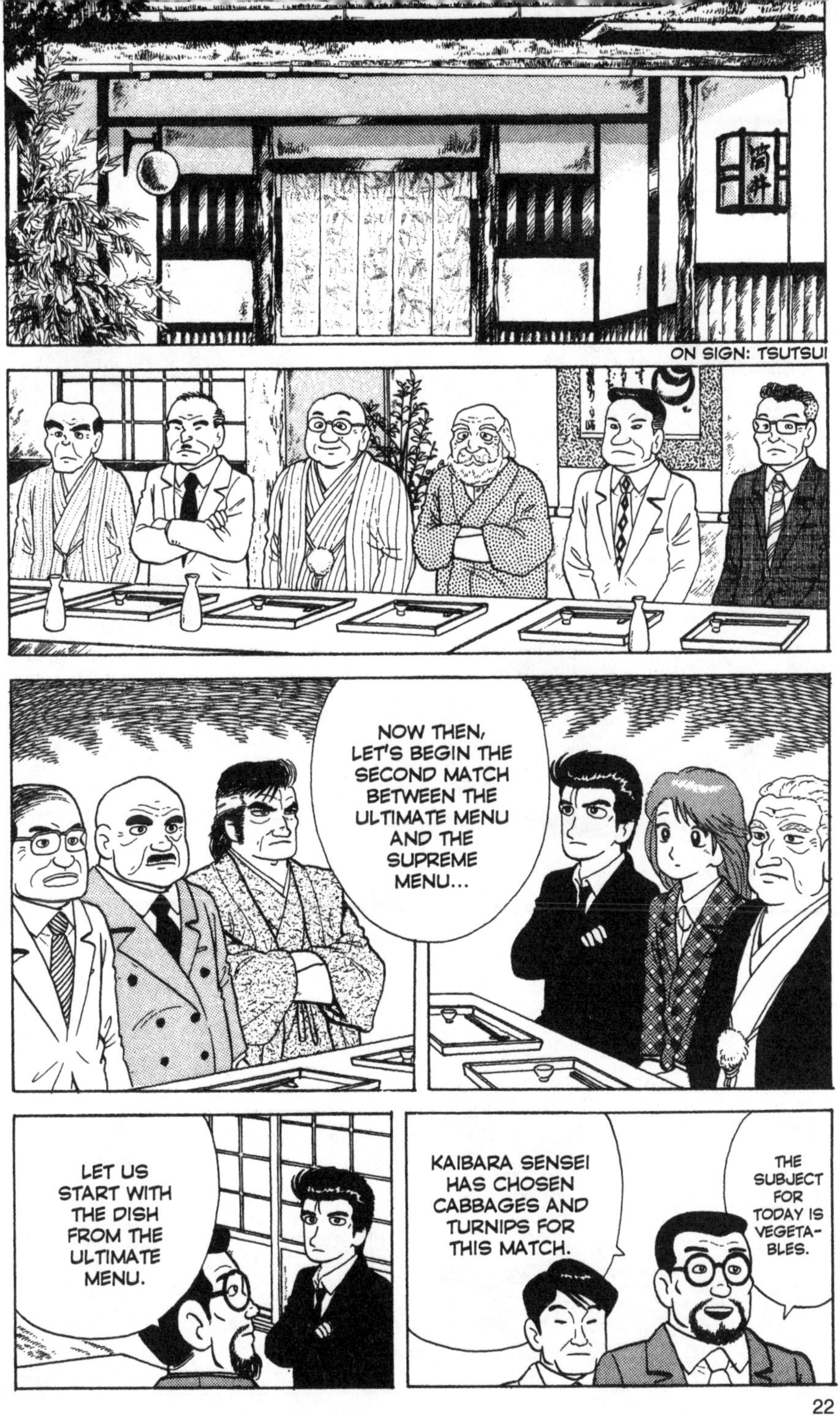
ON SIGN: TSUTSUI
NOW THEN, LET'S BEGIN THE SECOND MATCH BETWEEN THE ULTIMATE MENU AND THE SUPREME MENU...
THE SUBJECT FOR TODAY IS VEGETA-BLES.
KAIBARA SENSEI HAS CHOSEN CABBAGES AND TURNIPS FOR THIS MATCH.
LET US START WITH THE DISH FROM THE ULTIMATE MENU.

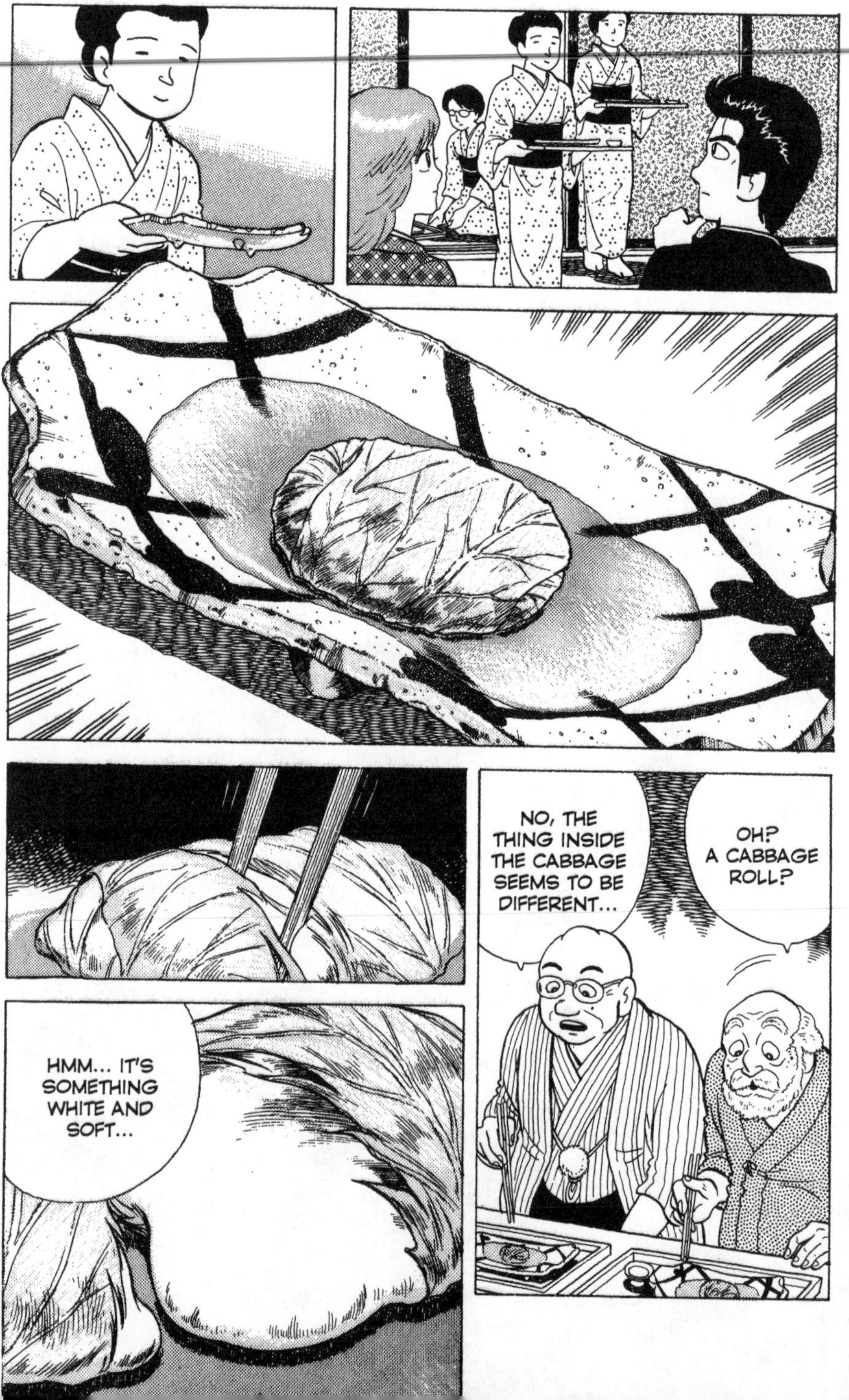
OH? A CABBAGE ROLL?
NO, THE THING INSIDE THE CABBAGE SEEMS TO BE DIFFERENT...
HMM... IT'S SOMETHING WHITE AND SOFT...

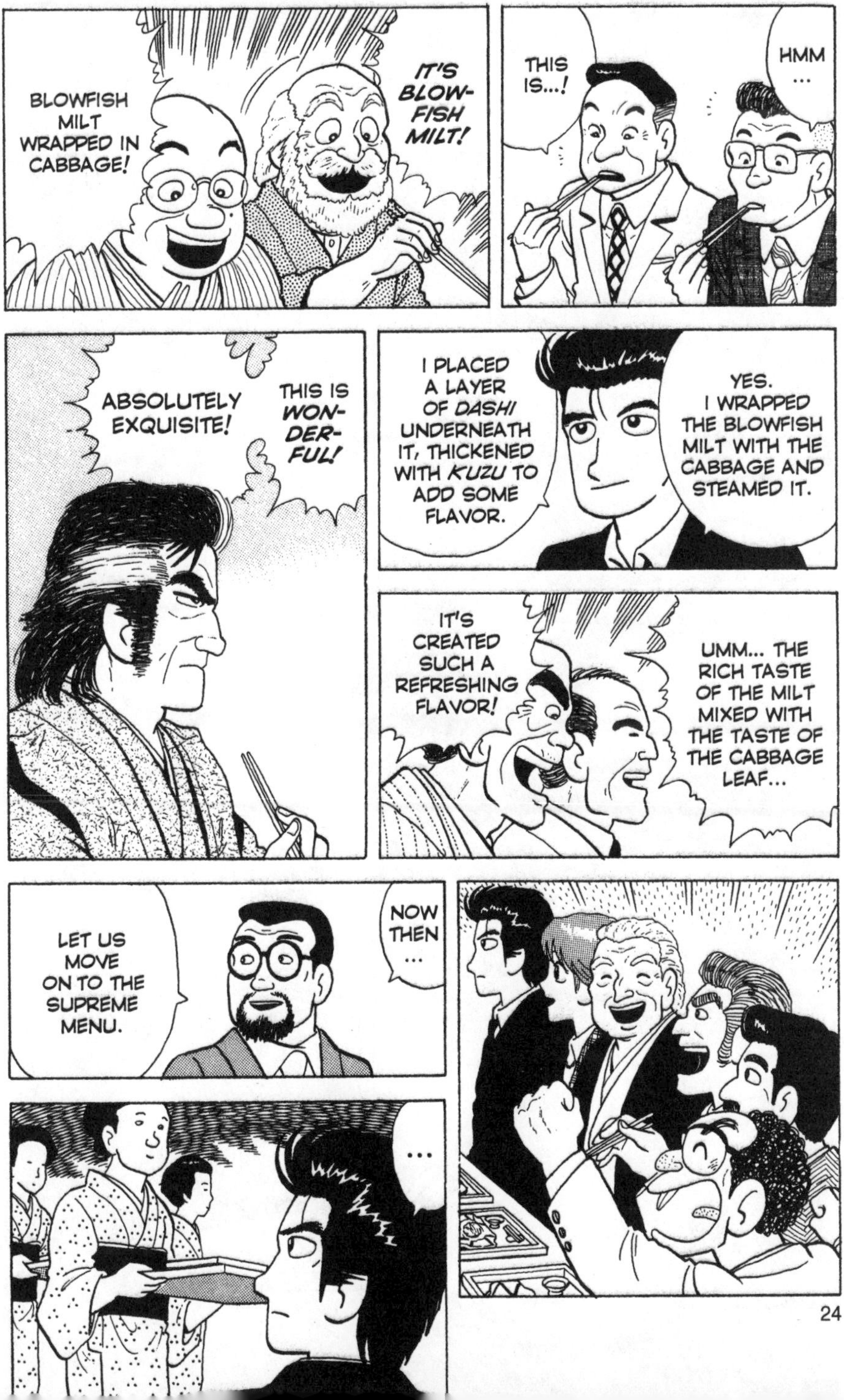
HMM ...
THIS IS...!
IT'S BLOW-FISH MILT!
BLOWFISH MILT WRAPPED IN CABBAGE!
YES. I WRAPPED THE BLOWFISH MILT WITH THE CABBAGE AND STEAMED IT.
I PLACED A LAYER OF DASHI UNDERNEATH IT, THICKENED WITH KUZU TO ADD SOME FLAVOR.
UMM... THE RICH TASTE OF THE MILT MIXED WITH THE TASTE OF THE CABBAGE LEAF...
IT'S CREATED SUCH A REFRESHING FLAVOR!
THIS IS WON-DER-FUL!
ABSOLUTELY EXQUISITE!
NOW THEN ...
LET US MOVE ON TO THE SUPREME MENU.
...

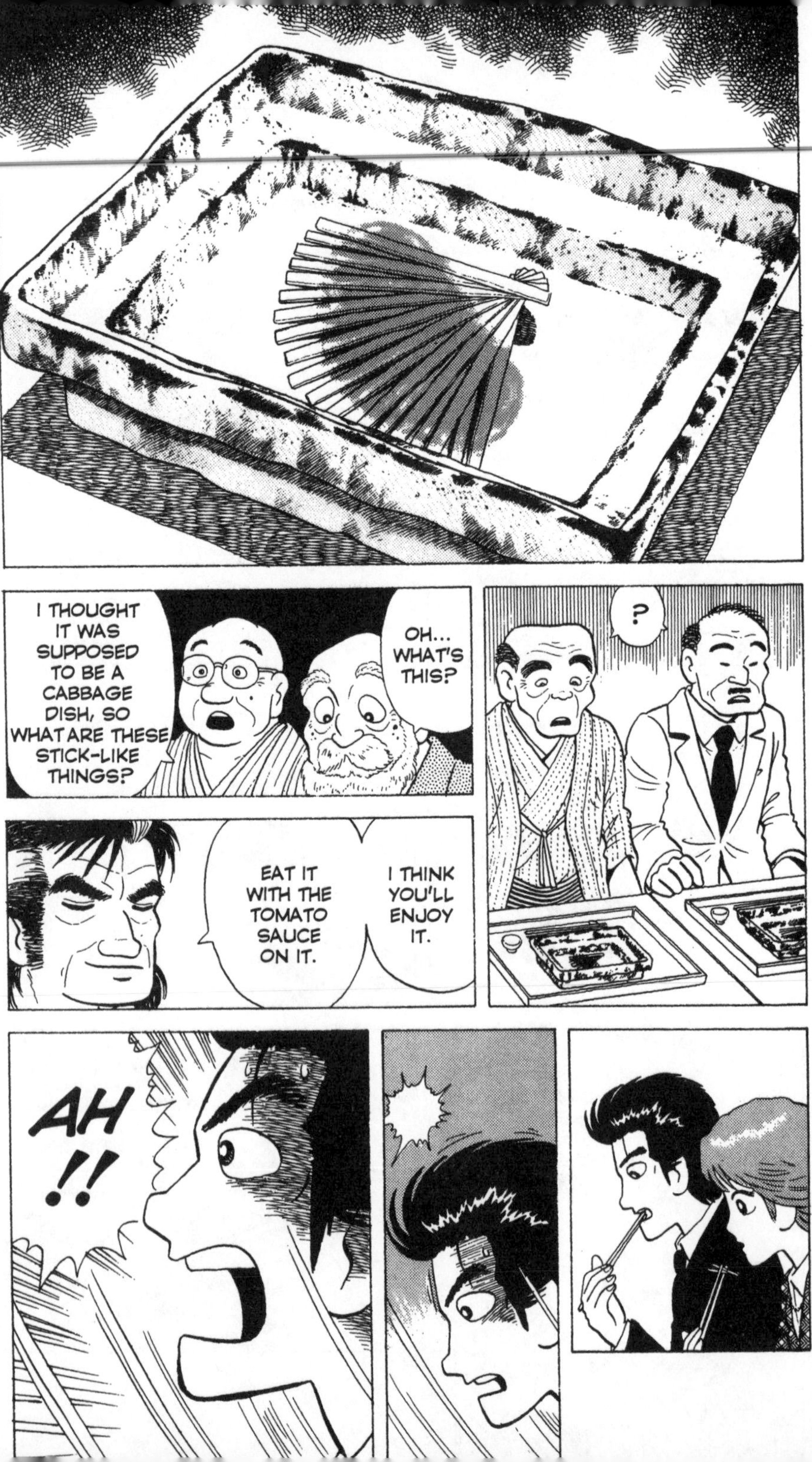
?
OH... WHAT'S THIS?
I THOUGHT IT WAS SUPPOSED TO BE A CABBAGE DISH, SO WHAT ARE THESE STICK-LIKE THINGS?
I THINK YOU'LL ENJOY IT.
EAT IT WITH THE TOMATO SAUCE ON IT.
AH!!

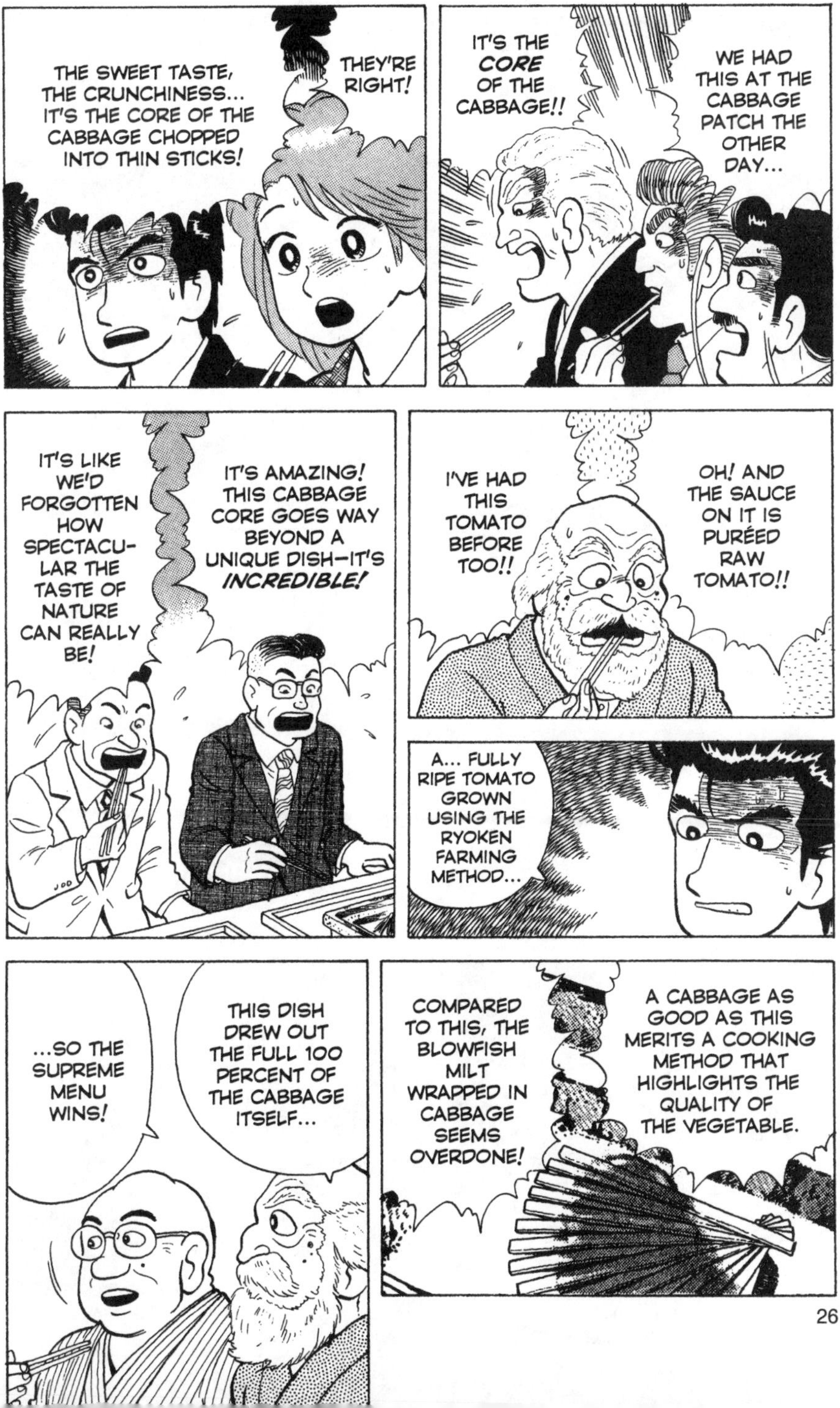
WE HAD THIS AT THE CABBAGE PATCH THE OTHER DAY...
IT'S THE *CORE* OF THE CABBAGE!!
THEY'RE RIGHT!
THE SWEET TASTE, THE CRUNCHINESS... IT'S THE CORE OF THE CABBAGE CHOPPED INTO THIN STICKS!
OH! AND THE SAUCE ON IT IS PURÉED RAW TOMATO!!
I'VE HAD THIS TOMATO BEFORE TOO!!
A... FULLY RIPE TOMATO GROWN USING THE RYOKEN FARMING METHOD...
IT'S AMAZING! THIS CABBAGE CORE GOES WAY BEYOND A UNIQUE DISH—IT'S *INCREDIBLE!*
IT'S LIKE WE'D FORGOTTEN HOW SPECTACU-LAR THE TASTE OF NATURE CAN REALLY BE!
A CABBAGE AS GOOD AS THIS MERITS A COOKING METHOD THAT HIGHLIGHTS THE QUALITY OF THE VEGETABLE.
COMPARED TO THIS, THE BLOWFISH MILT WRAPPED IN CABBAGE SEEMS OVERDONE!
THIS DISH DREW OUT THE FULL 100 PERCENT OF THE CABBAGE ITSELF...
...SO THE SUPREME MENU WINS!

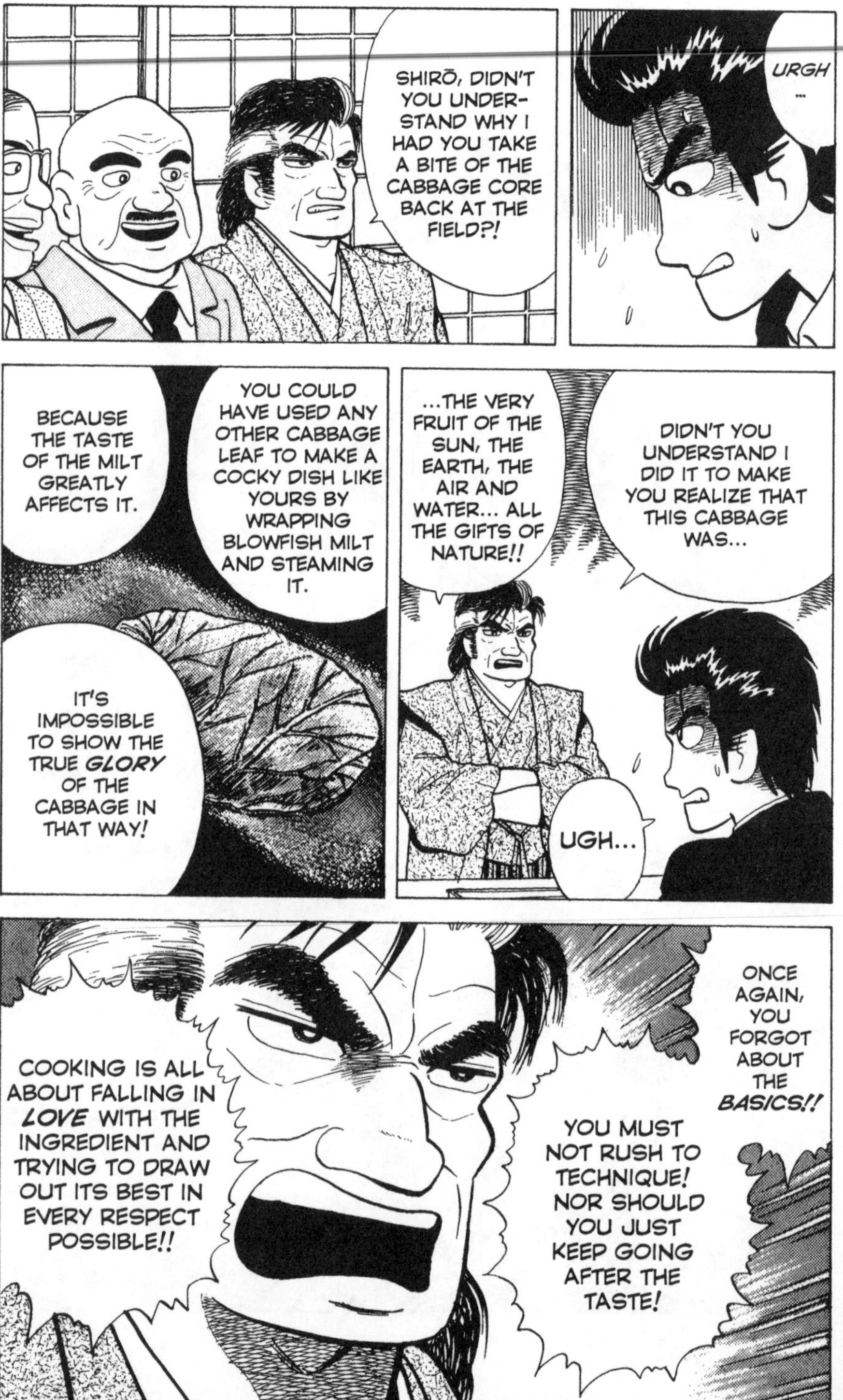
URGH ...
SHIRŌ, DIDN'T YOU UNDERSTAND WHY I HAD YOU TAKE A BITE OF THE CABBAGE CORE BACK AT THE FIELD?!
DIDN'T YOU UNDERSTAND I DID IT TO MAKE YOU REALIZE THAT THIS CABBAGE WAS...
...THE VERY FRUIT OF THE SUN, THE EARTH, THE AIR AND WATER... ALL THE GIFTS OF NATURE!!
UGH...
YOU COULD HAVE USED ANY OTHER CABBAGE LEAF TO MAKE A COCKY DISH LIKE YOURS BY WRAPPING BLOWFISH MILT AND STEAMING IT.
BECAUSE THE TASTE OF THE MILT GREATLY AFFECTS IT.
IT'S IMPOSSIBLE TO SHOW THE TRUE *GLORY* OF THE CABBAGE IN THAT WAY!
ONCE AGAIN, YOU FORGOT ABOUT THE *BASICS!!*
YOU MUST NOT RUSH TO TECHNIQUE! NOR SHOULD YOU JUST KEEP GOING AFTER THE TASTE!
COOKING IS ALL ABOUT FALLING IN *LOVE* WITH THE INGREDIENT AND TRYING TO DRAW OUT ITS BEST IN EVERY RESPECT POSSIBLE!!

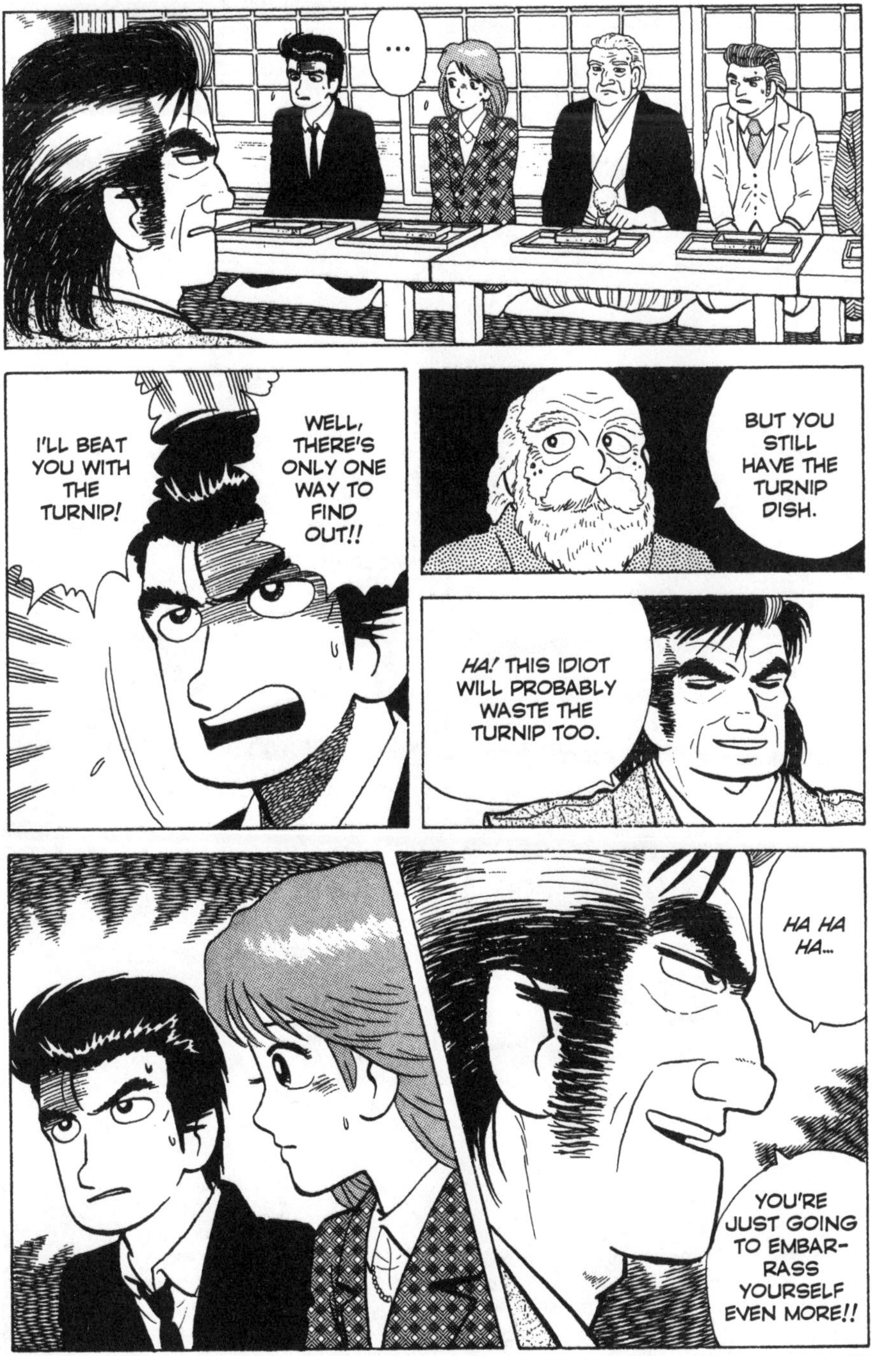
...
BUT YOU STILL HAVE THE TURNIP DISH.
HA! THIS IDIOT WILL PROBABLY WASTE THE TURNIP TOO.
WELL, THERE'S ONLY ONE WAY TO FIND OUT!!
I'LL BEAT YOU WITH THE TURNIP!
HA HA HA...
YOU'RE JUST GOING TO EMBAR-RASS YOURSELF EVEN MORE!!

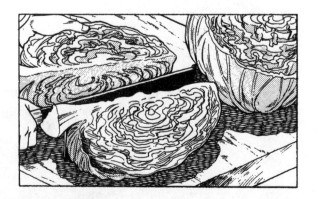

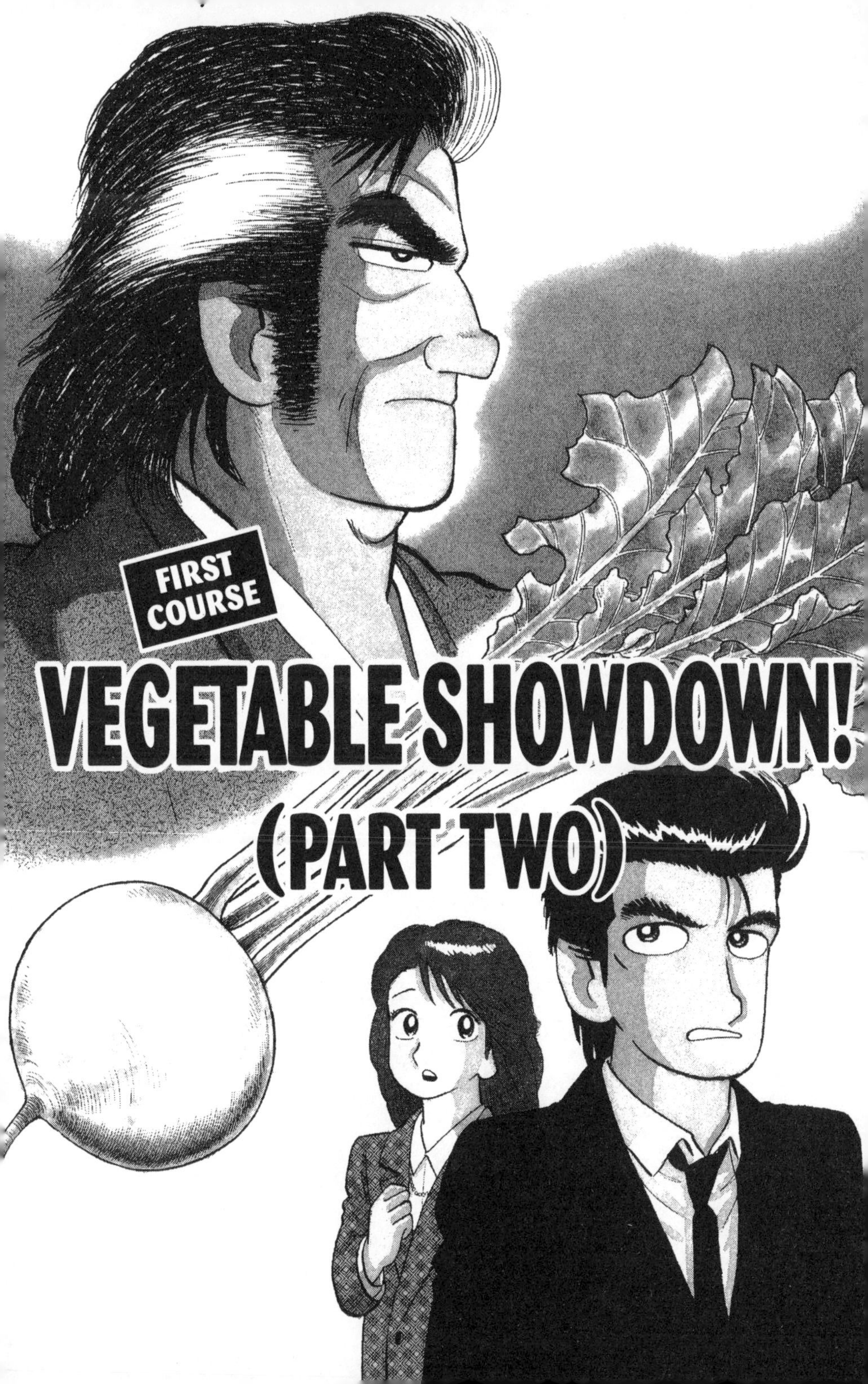
FIRST COURSE
VEGETABLE SHOWDOWN!
(PART TWO)

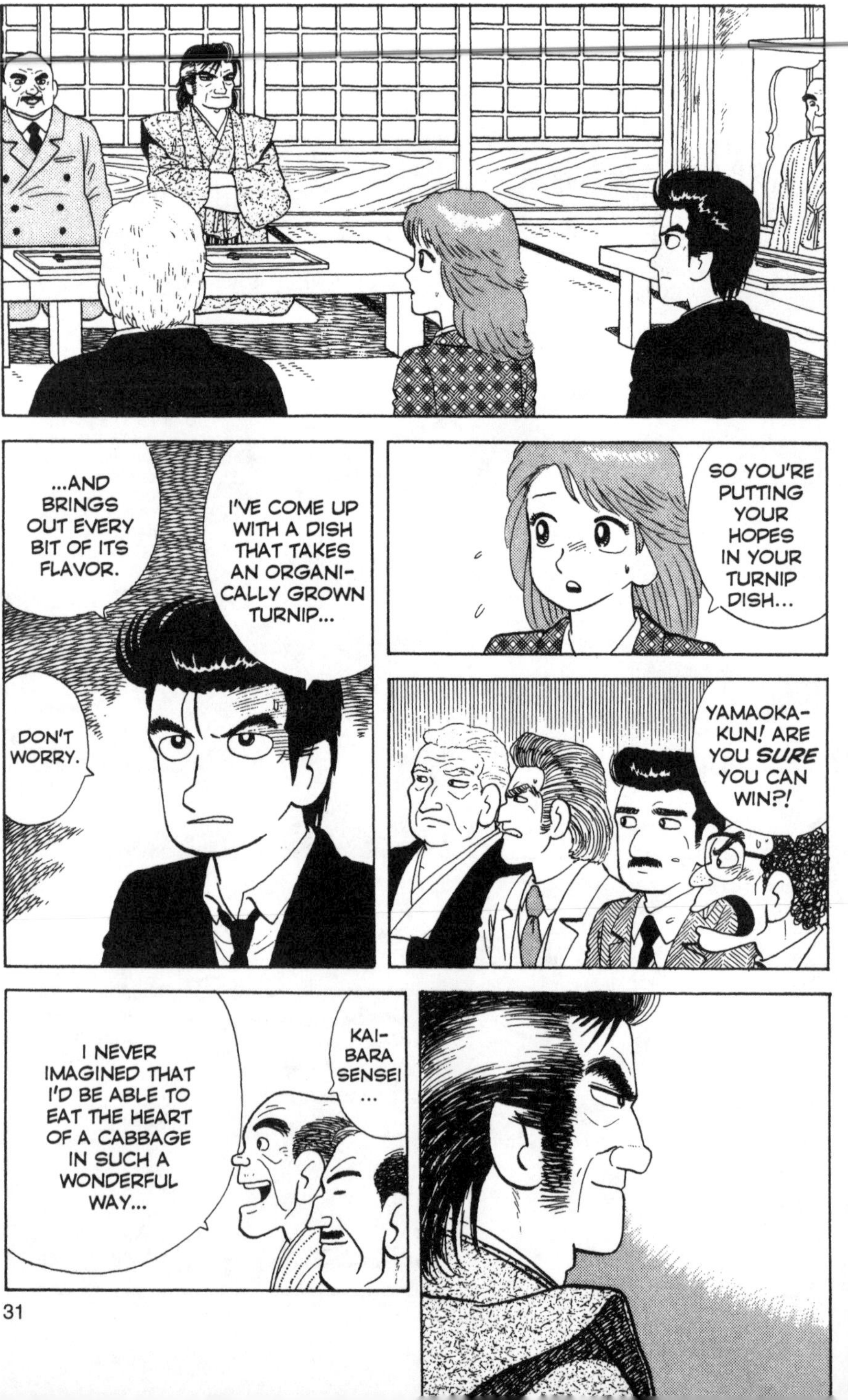
SO YOU'RE PUTTING YOUR HOPES IN YOUR TURNIP DISH...
YAMAOKA-KUN! ARE YOU *SURE* YOU CAN WIN?!
I'VE COME UP WITH A DISH THAT TAKES AN ORGANI-CALLY GROWN TURNIP...
...AND BRINGS OUT EVERY BIT OF ITS FLAVOR.
DON'T WORRY.
KAI-BARA SENSEI ...
I NEVER IMAGINED THAT I'D BE ABLE TO EAT THE HEART OF A CABBAGE IN SUCH A WONDERFUL WAY...

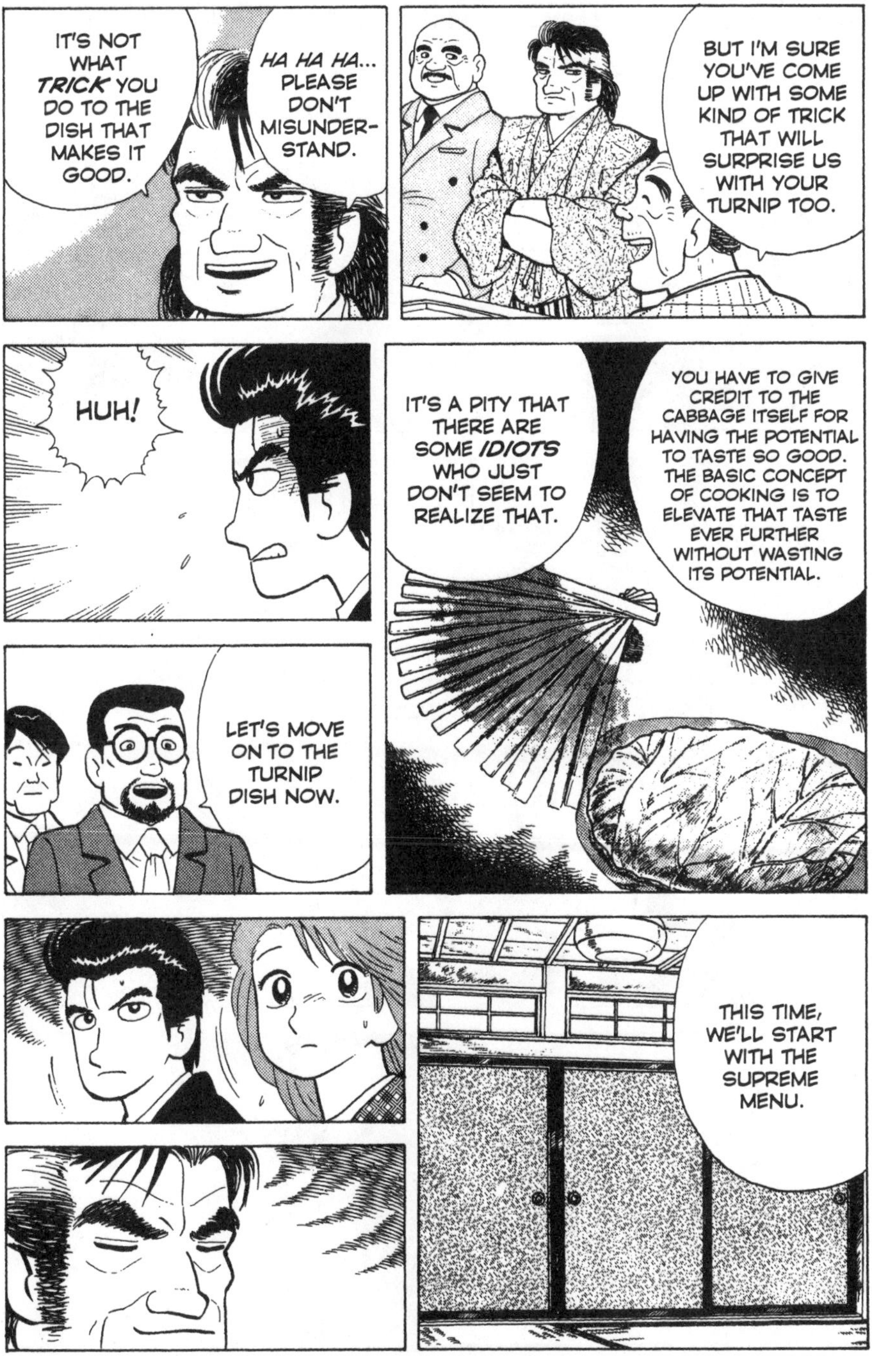
BUT I'M SURE YOU'VE COME UP WITH SOME KIND OF TRICK THAT WILL SURPRISE US WITH YOUR TURNIP TOO.
HA HA HA... PLEASE DON'T MISUNDERSTAND.
IT'S NOT WHAT *TRICK* YOU DO TO THE DISH THAT MAKES IT GOOD.
YOU HAVE TO GIVE CREDIT TO THE CABBAGE ITSELF FOR HAVING THE POTENTIAL TO TASTE SO GOOD. THE BASIC CONCEPT OF COOKING IS TO ELEVATE THAT TASTE EVER FURTHER WITHOUT WASTING ITS POTENTIAL.
IT'S A PITY THAT THERE ARE SOME *IDIOTS* WHO JUST DON'T SEEM TO REALIZE THAT.
HUH!
LET'S MOVE ON TO THE TURNIP DISH NOW.
THIS TIME, WE'LL START WITH THE SUPREME MENU.

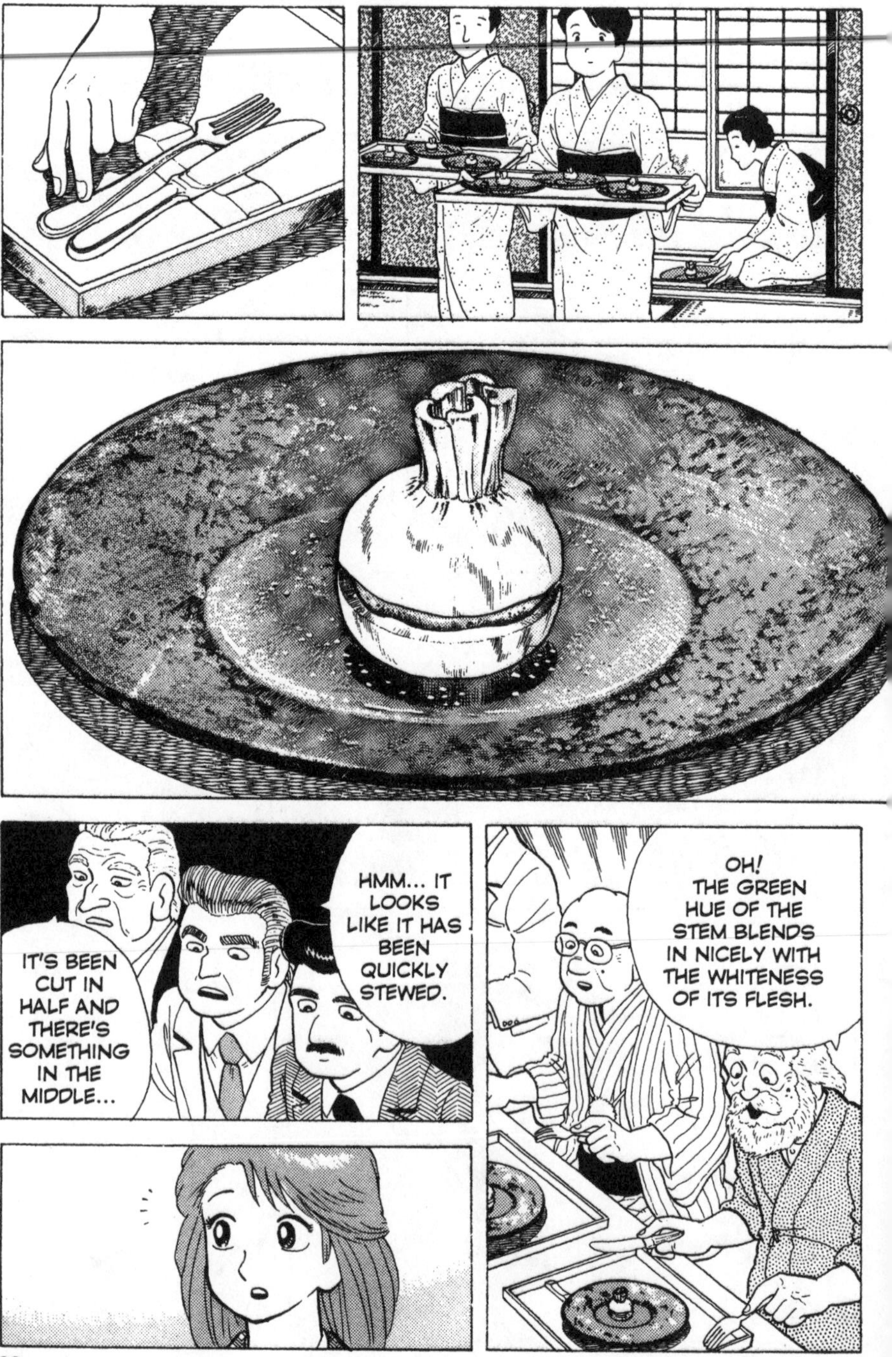
OH! THE GREEN HUE OF THE STEM BLENDS IN NICELY WITH THE WHITENESS OF ITS FLESH.
HMM... IT LOOKS LIKE IT HAS BEEN QUICKLY STEWED.
IT'S BEEN CUT IN HALF AND THERE'S SOMETHING IN THE MIDDLE...

EH... NOTHING ...

WHAT'S THE MATTER, YAMA-OKA-SAN?

...

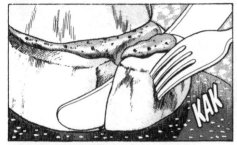

KAK

I CAN'T... QUITE PUT IT INTO WORDS!

HA... HA!

OOH !!

AH...

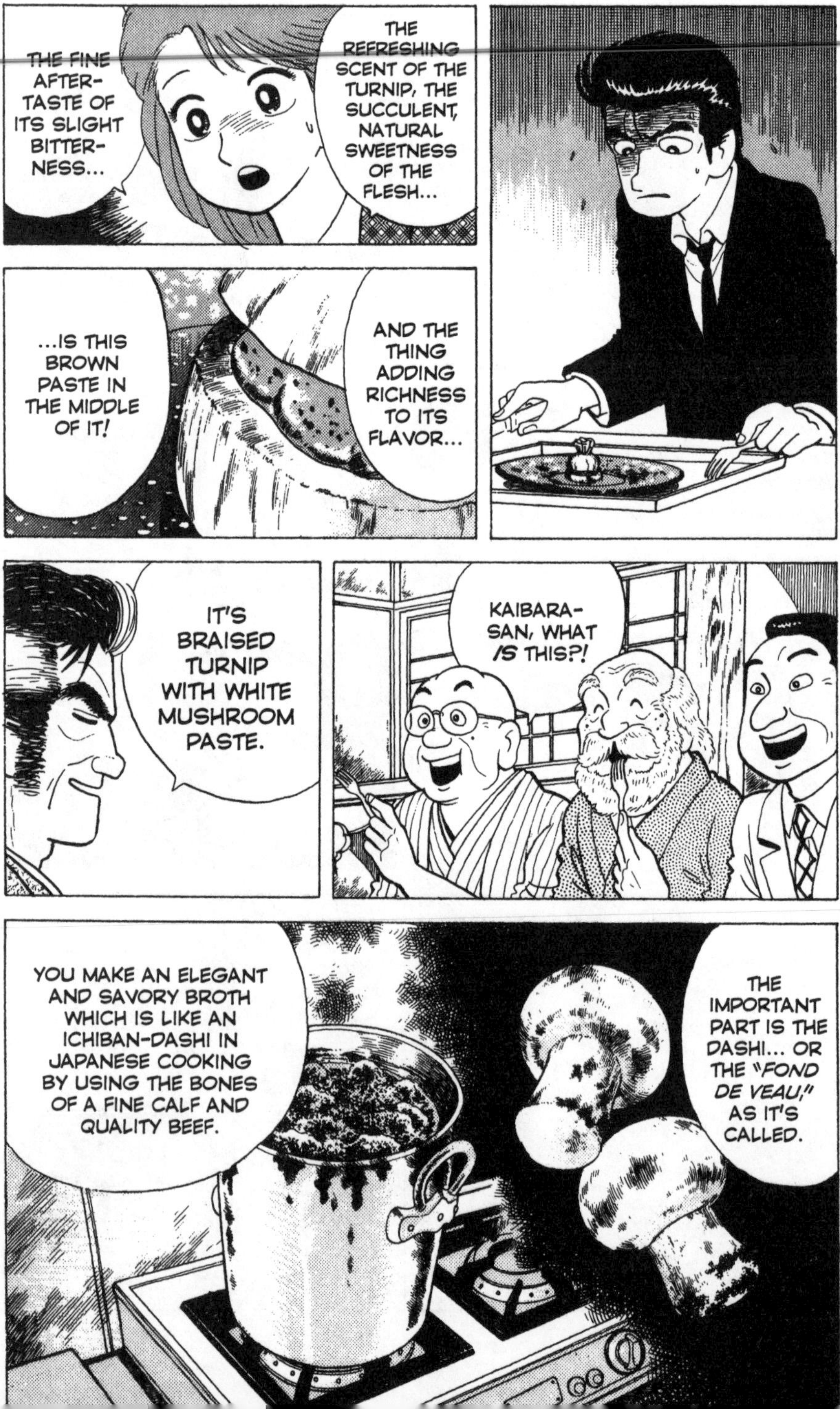
THE REFRESHING SCENT OF THE TURNIP, THE SUCCULENT, NATURAL SWEETNESS OF THE FLESH...
THE FINE AFTER-TASTE OF ITS SLIGHT BITTER-NESS...
AND THE THING ADDING RICHNESS TO ITS FLAVOR...
...IS THIS BROWN PASTE IN THE MIDDLE OF IT!
KAIBARA-SAN, WHAT *IS* THIS?!
IT'S BRAISED TURNIP WITH WHITE MUSHROOM PASTE.
THE IMPORTANT PART IS THE DASHI... OR THE "*FOND DE VEAU,*" AS IT'S CALLED.
YOU MAKE AN ELEGANT AND SAVORY BROTH WHICH IS LIKE AN ICHIBAN-DASHI IN JAPANESE COOKING BY USING THE BONES OF A FINE CALF AND QUALITY BEEF.

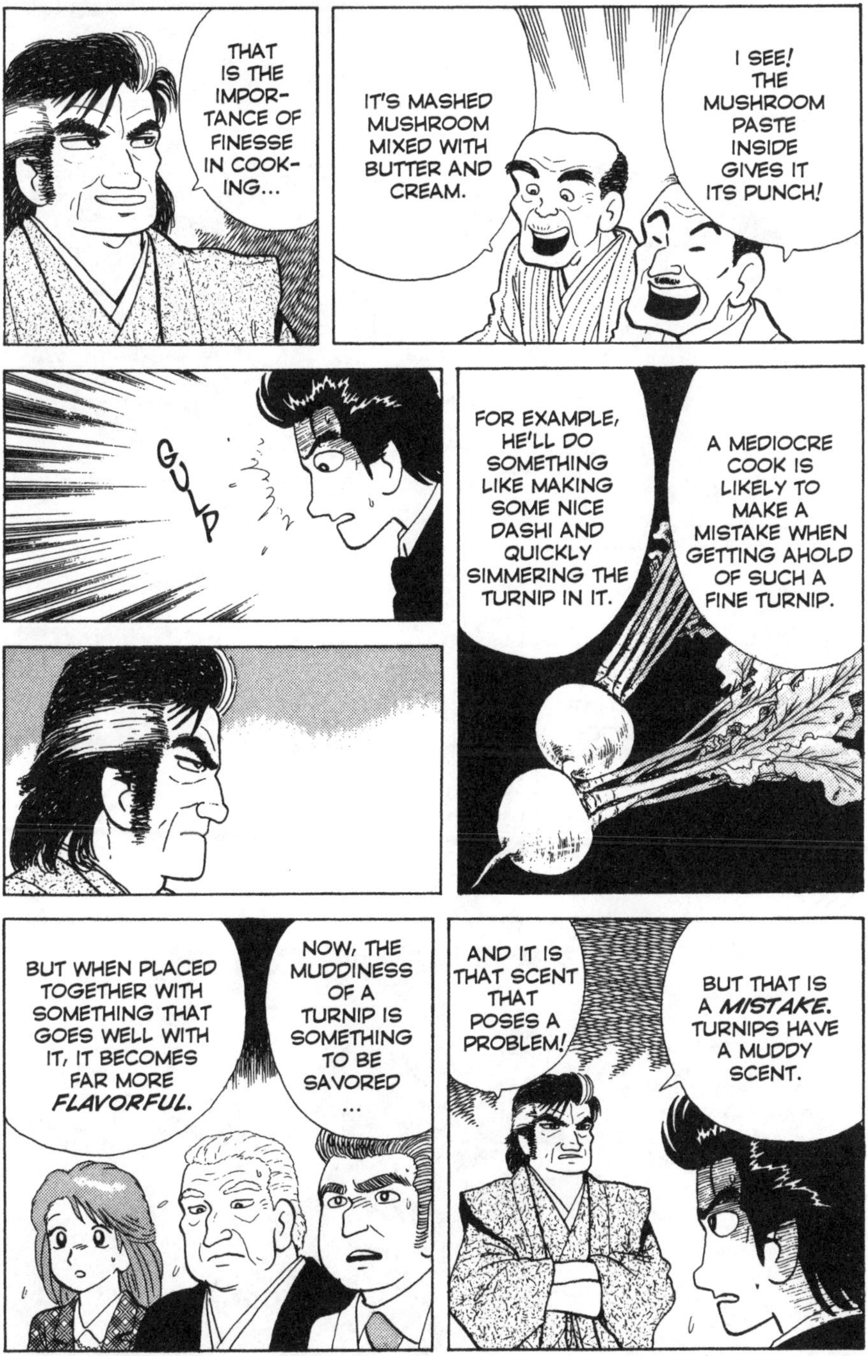
I SEE! THE MUSHROOM PASTE INSIDE GIVES IT ITS PUNCH!
IT'S MASHED MUSHROOM MIXED WITH BUTTER AND CREAM.
THAT IS THE IMPORTANCE OF FINESSE IN COOKING...
A MEDIOCRE COOK IS LIKELY TO MAKE A MISTAKE WHEN GETTING AHOLD OF SUCH A FINE TURNIP.
FOR EXAMPLE, HE'LL DO SOMETHING LIKE MAKING SOME NICE DASHI AND QUICKLY SIMMERING THE TURNIP IN IT.
GULP
BUT THAT IS A *MISTAKE.* TURNIPS HAVE A MUDDY SCENT.
AND IT IS THAT SCENT THAT POSES A PROBLEM!
NOW, THE MUDDINESS OF A TURNIP IS SOMETHING TO BE SAVORED ...
BUT WHEN PLACED TOGETHER WITH SOMETHING THAT GOES WELL WITH IT, IT BECOMES FAR MORE ***FLAVORFUL.***

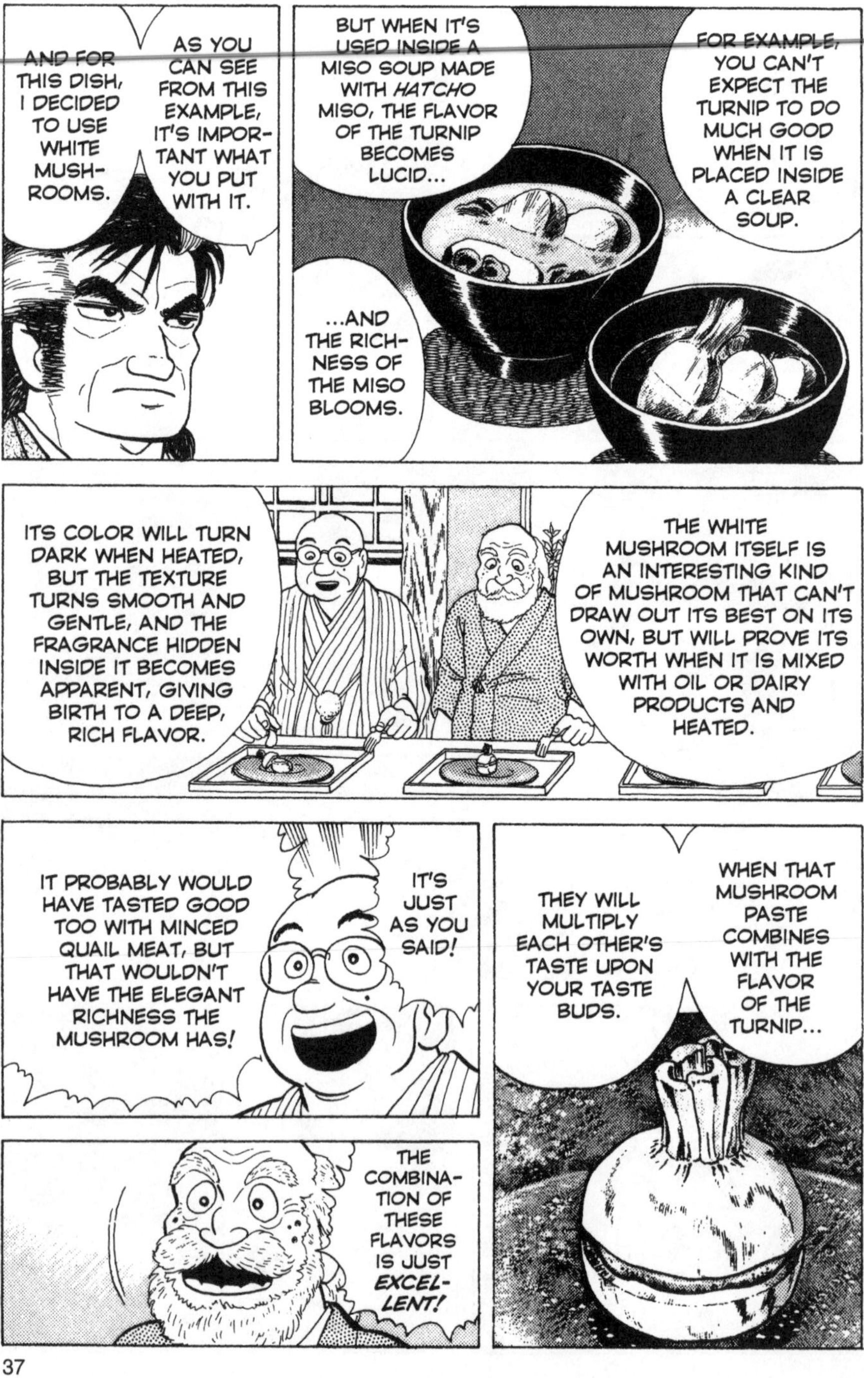
FOR EXAMPLE, YOU CAN'T EXPECT THE TURNIP TO DO MUCH GOOD WHEN IT IS PLACED INSIDE A CLEAR SOUP.
BUT WHEN IT'S USED INSIDE A MISO SOUP MADE WITH *HATCHO* MISO, THE FLAVOR OF THE TURNIP BECOMES LUCID...
...AND THE RICHNESS OF THE MISO BLOOMS.
AS YOU CAN SEE FROM THIS EXAMPLE, IT'S IMPORTANT WHAT YOU PUT WITH IT.
AND FOR THIS DISH, I DECIDED TO USE WHITE MUSHROOMS.
THE WHITE MUSHROOM ITSELF IS AN INTERESTING KIND OF MUSHROOM THAT CAN'T DRAW OUT ITS BEST ON ITS OWN, BUT WILL PROVE ITS WORTH WHEN IT IS MIXED WITH OIL OR DAIRY PRODUCTS AND HEATED.
ITS COLOR WILL TURN DARK WHEN HEATED, BUT THE TEXTURE TURNS SMOOTH AND GENTLE, AND THE FRAGRANCE HIDDEN INSIDE IT BECOMES APPARENT, GIVING BIRTH TO A DEEP, RICH FLAVOR.
WHEN THAT MUSHROOM PASTE COMBINES WITH THE FLAVOR OF THE TURNIP...
THEY WILL MULTIPLY EACH OTHER'S TASTE UPON YOUR TASTE BUDS.
IT'S JUST AS YOU SAID!
IT PROBABLY WOULD HAVE TASTED GOOD TOO WITH MINCED QUAIL MEAT, BUT THAT WOULDN'T HAVE THE ELEGANT RICHNESS THE MUSHROOM HAS!
THE COMBINATION OF THESE FLAVORS IS JUST *EXCELLENT!*

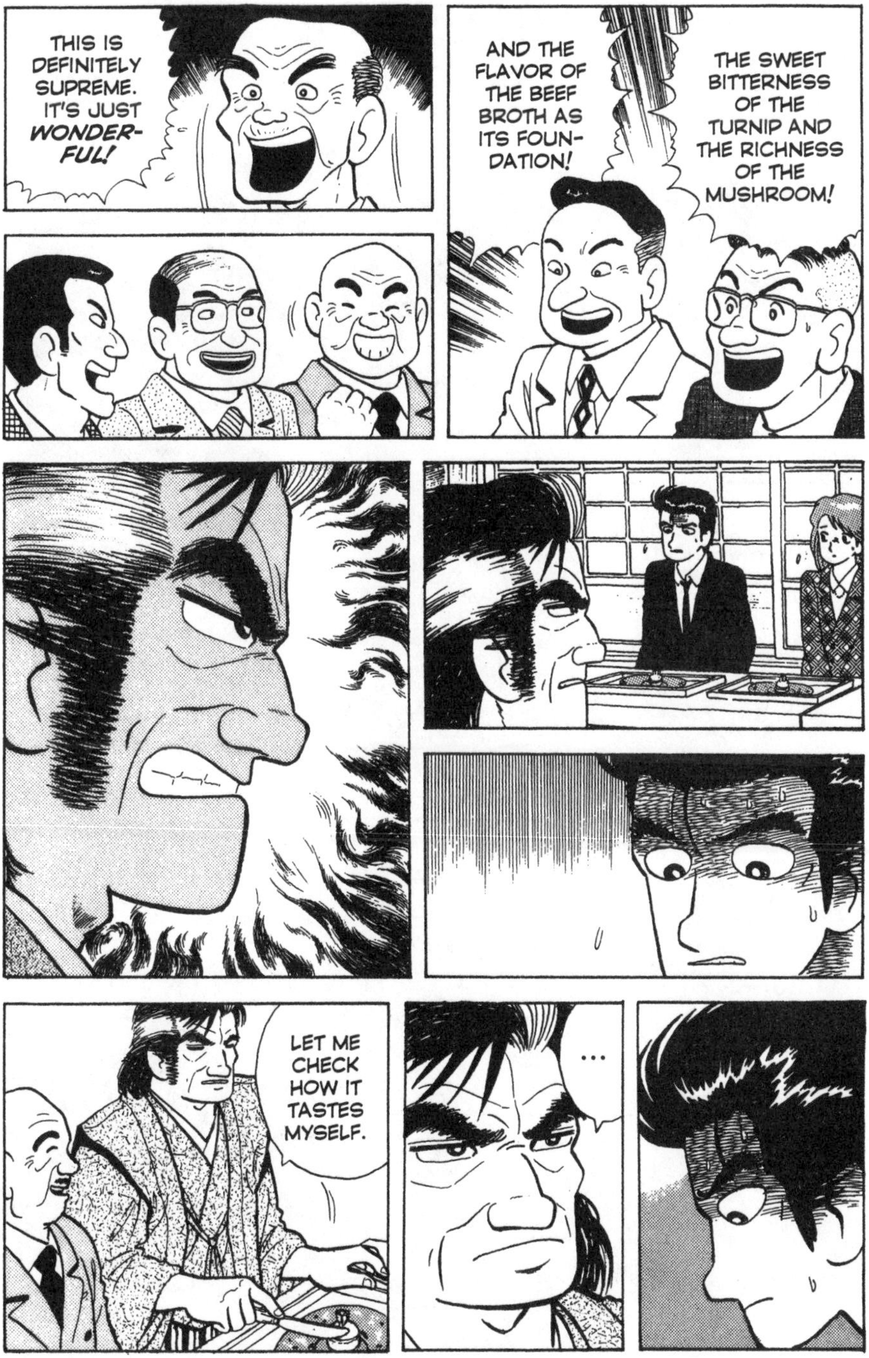
THE SWEET BITTERNESS OF THE TURNIP AND THE RICHNESS OF THE MUSHROOM!
AND THE FLAVOR OF THE BEEF BROTH AS ITS FOUNDATION!
THIS IS DEFINITELY SUPREME. IT'S JUST *WONDERFUL!*
...
LET ME CHECK HOW IT TASTES MYSELF.

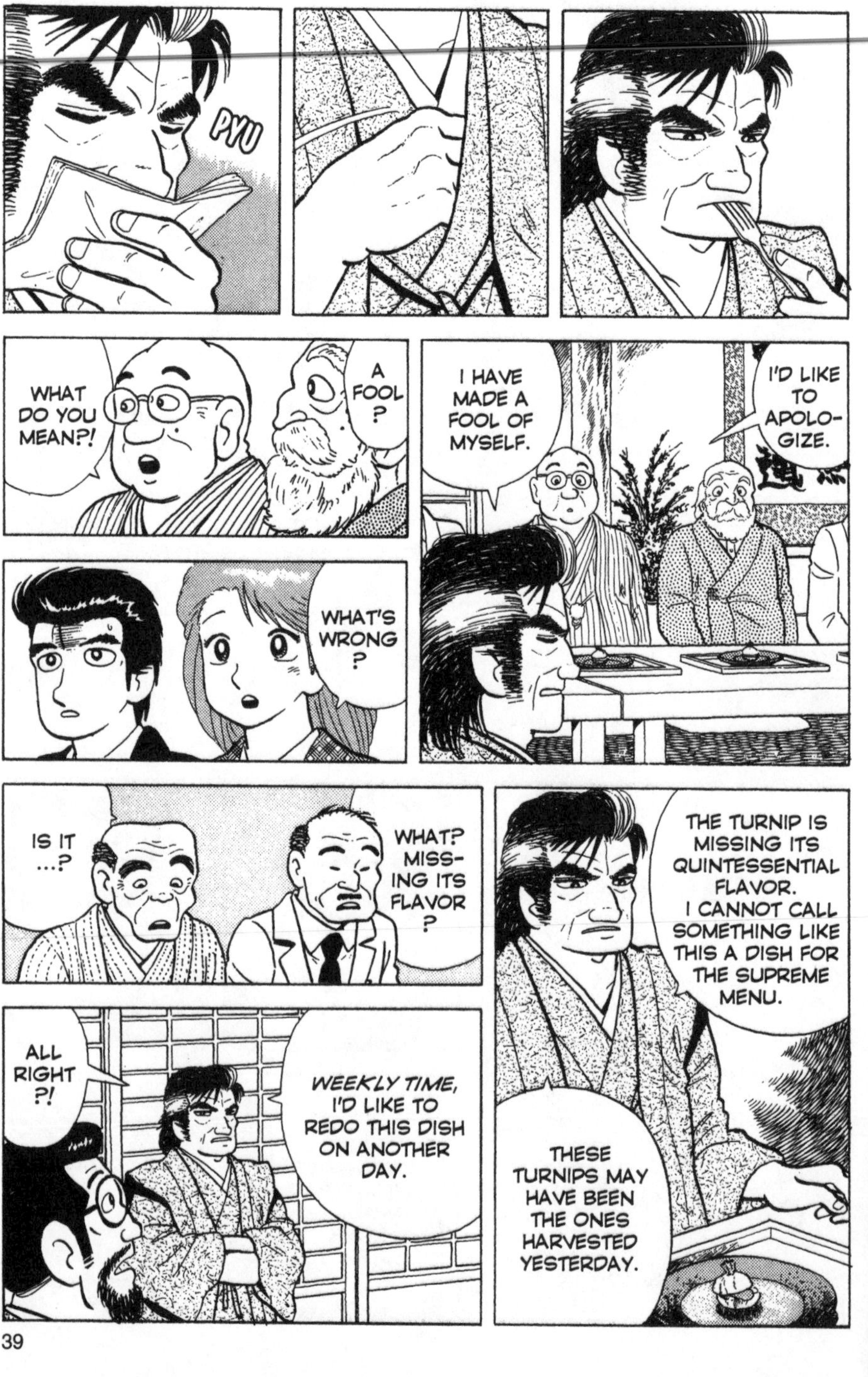
PYU
I'D LIKE TO APOLOGIZE.
I HAVE MADE A FOOL OF MYSELF.
A FOOL?
WHAT DO YOU MEAN?!
WHAT'S WRONG?
THE TURNIP IS MISSING ITS QUINTESSENTIAL FLAVOR. I CANNOT CALL SOMETHING LIKE THIS A DISH FOR THE SUPREME MENU.
THESE TURNIPS MAY HAVE BEEN THE ONES HARVESTED YESTERDAY.
WHAT? MISSING ITS FLAVOR?
IS IT ...?
WEEKLY TIME, I'D LIKE TO REDO THIS DISH ON ANOTHER DAY.
ALL RIGHT?!

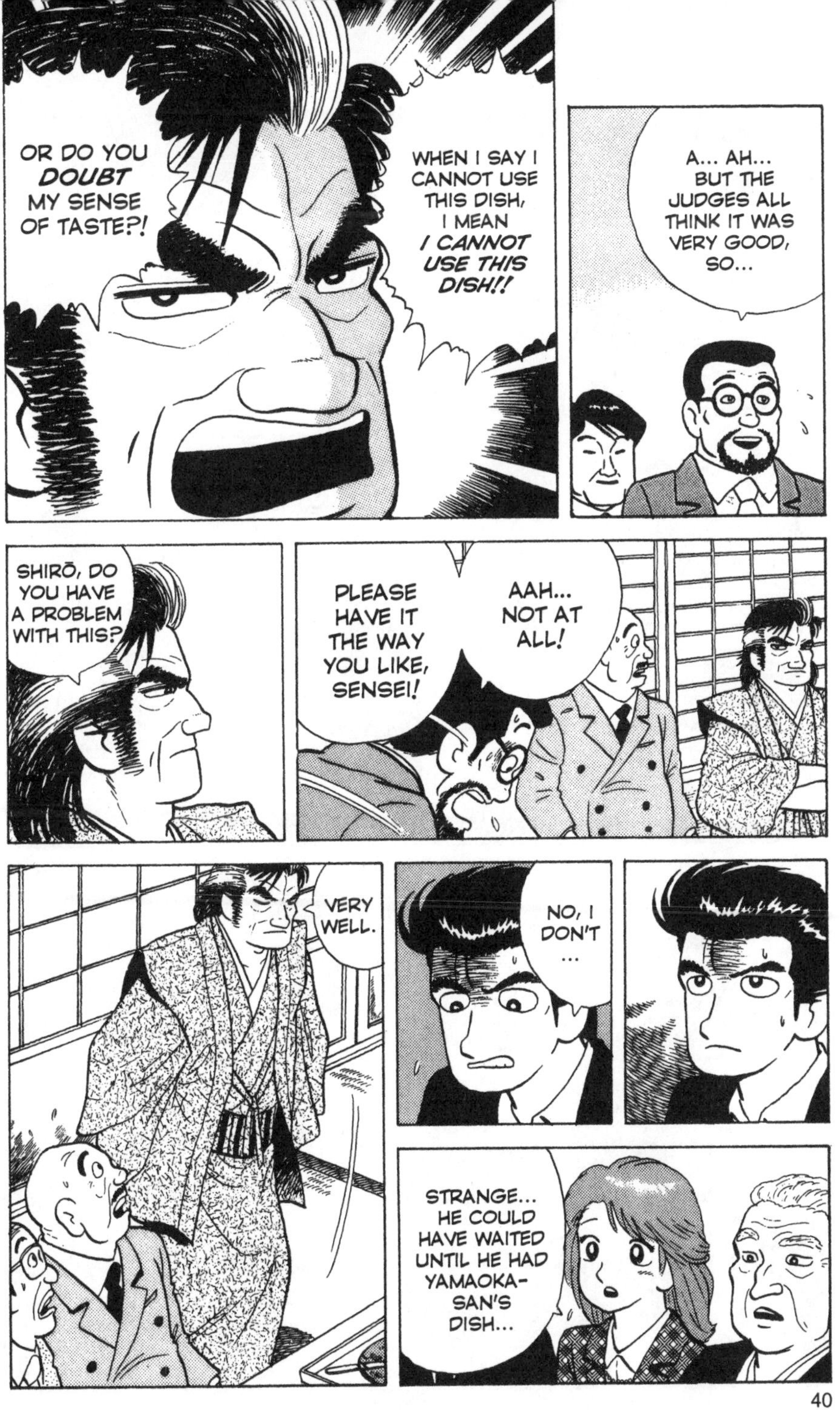
A... AH... BUT THE JUDGES ALL THINK IT WAS VERY GOOD, SO...
WHEN I SAY I CANNOT USE THIS DISH, I MEAN *I CANNOT USE THIS DISH!!*
OR DO YOU *DOUBT* MY SENSE OF TASTE?!
AAH... NOT AT ALL!
PLEASE HAVE IT THE WAY YOU LIKE, SENSEI!
SHIRŌ, DO YOU HAVE A PROBLEM WITH THIS?
NO, I DON'T ...
STRANGE... HE COULD HAVE WAITED UNTIL HE HAD YAMAOKA-SAN'S DISH...
VERY WELL.

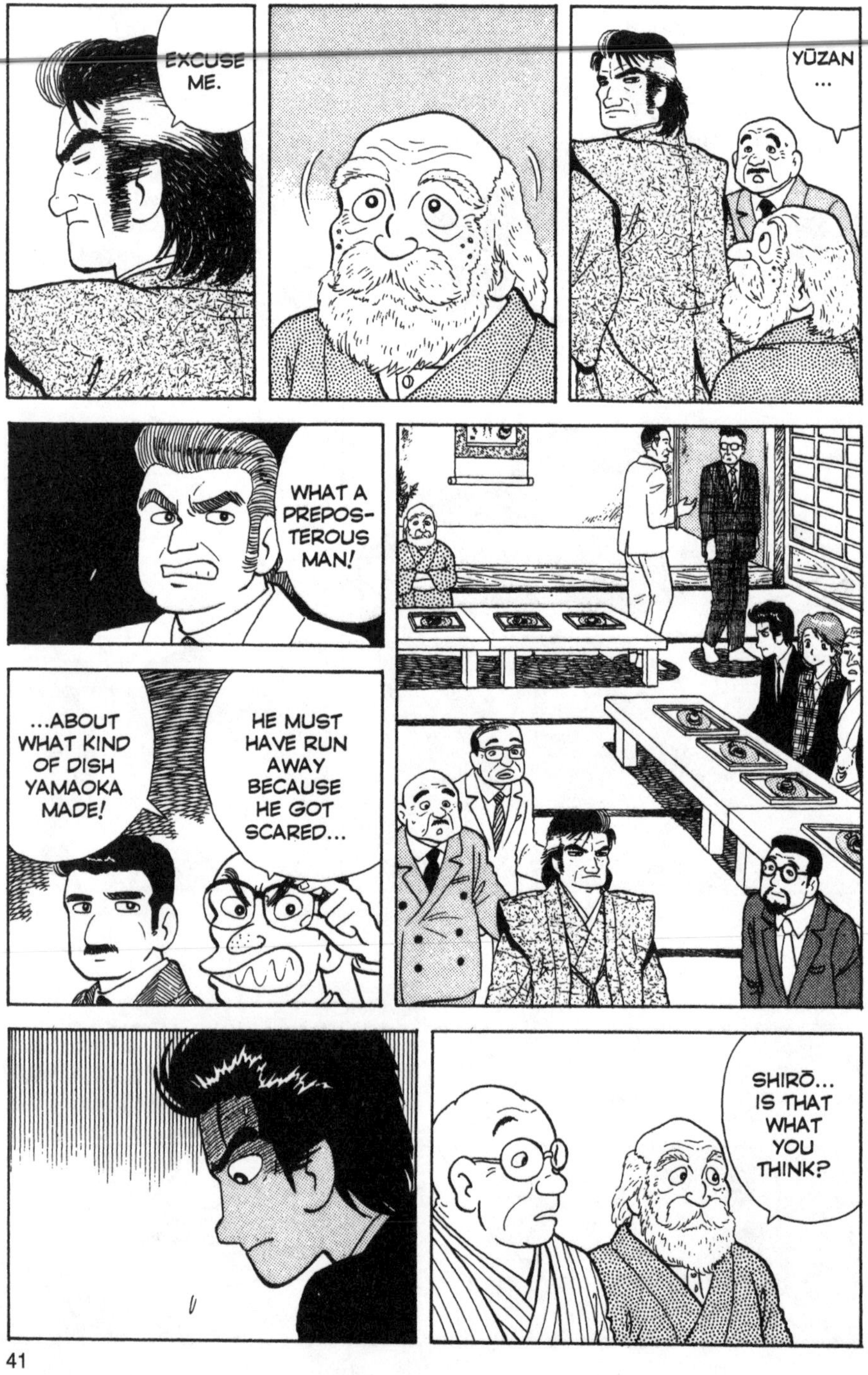
YŪZAN ...
EXCUSE ME.
WHAT A PREPOS-TEROUS MAN!
HE MUST HAVE RUN AWAY BECAUSE HE GOT SCARED...
...ABOUT WHAT KIND OF DISH YAMAOKA MADE!
SHIRŌ... IS THAT WHAT YOU THINK?

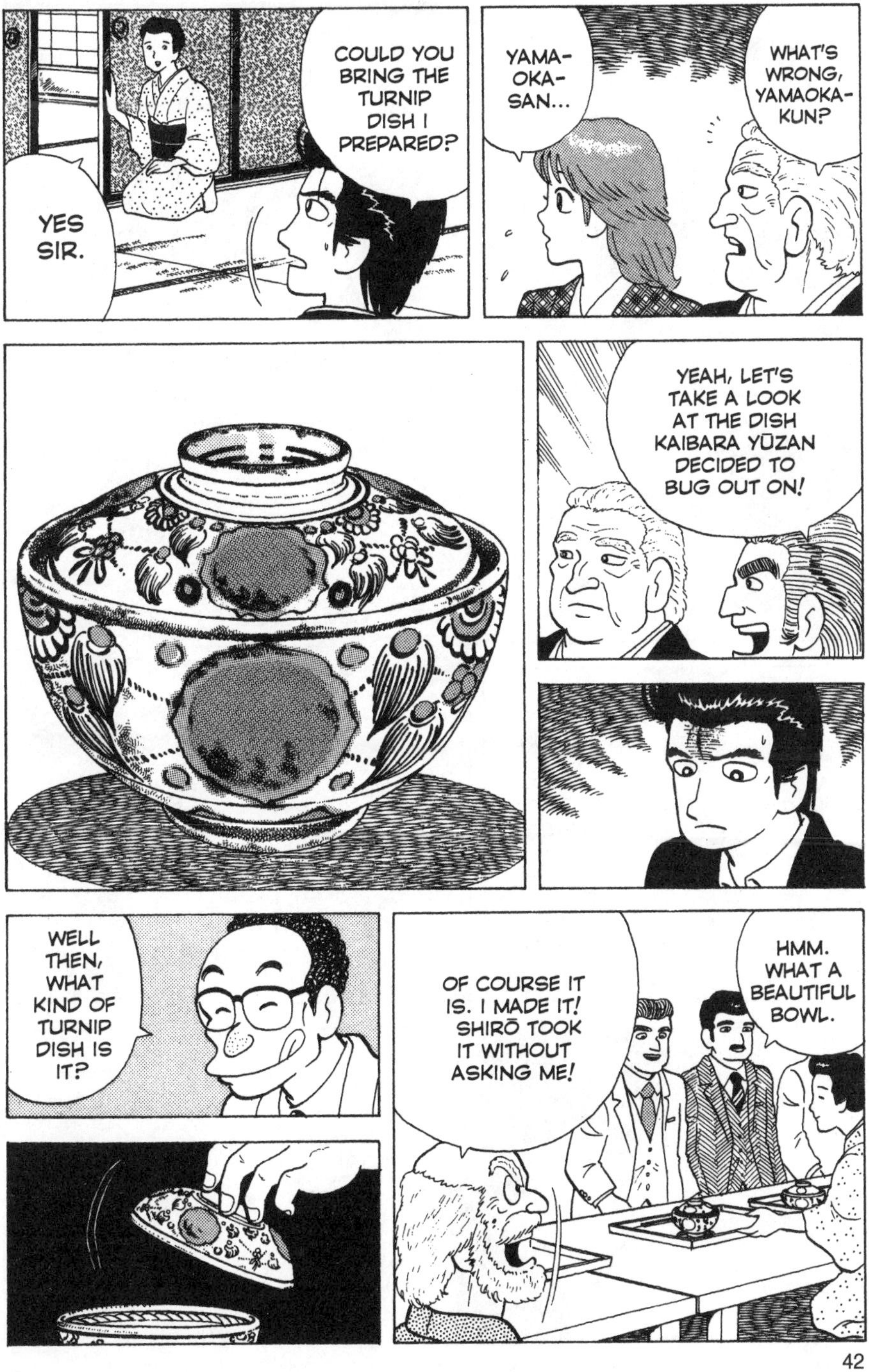
WHAT'S WRONG, YAMAOKA-KUN?
YAMA-OKA-SAN...
COULD YOU BRING THE TURNIP DISH I PREPARED?
YES SIR.
YEAH, LET'S TAKE A LOOK AT THE DISH KAIBARA YŪZAN DECIDED TO BUG OUT ON!
HMM. WHAT A BEAUTIFUL BOWL.
OF COURSE IT IS. I MADE IT! SHIRŌ TOOK IT WITHOUT ASKING ME!
WELL THEN, WHAT KIND OF TURNIP DISH IS IT?

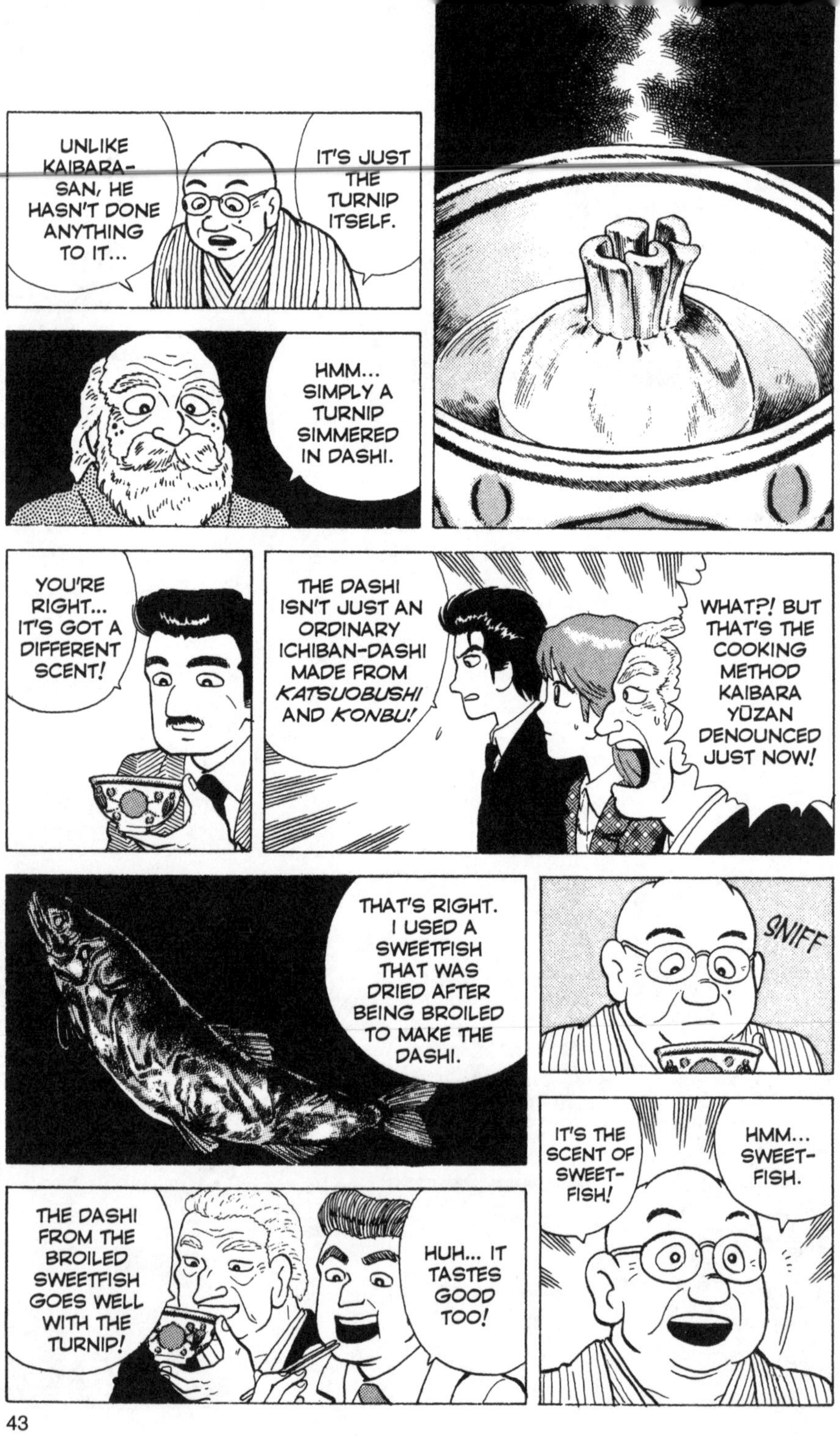
IT'S JUST THE TURNIP ITSELF.
UNLIKE KAIBARA-SAN, HE HASN'T DONE ANYTHING TO IT...
HMM... SIMPLY A TURNIP SIMMERED IN DASHI.
WHAT?! BUT THAT'S THE COOKING METHOD KAIBARA YŪZAN DENOUNCED JUST NOW!
THE DASHI ISN'T JUST AN ORDINARY ICHIBAN-DASHI MADE FROM *KATSUOBUSHI* AND *KONBU!*
YOU'RE RIGHT... IT'S GOT A DIFFERENT SCENT!
SNIFF
HMM... SWEET-FISH.
IT'S THE SCENT OF SWEET-FISH!
THAT'S RIGHT. I USED A SWEETFISH THAT WAS DRIED AFTER BEING BROILED TO MAKE THE DASHI.
HUH... IT TASTES GOOD TOO!
THE DASHI FROM THE BROILED SWEETFISH GOES WELL WITH THE TURNIP!

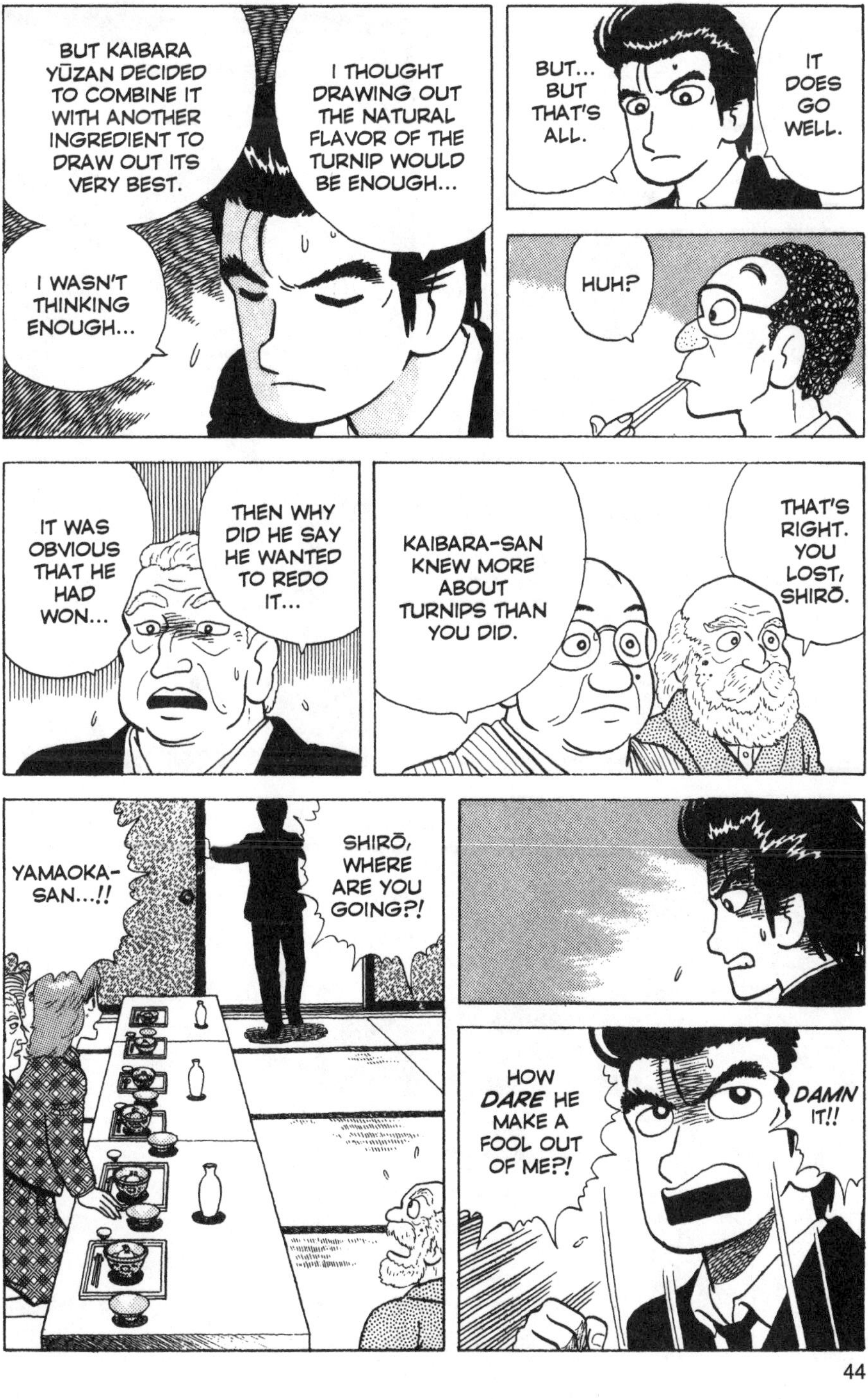

IT DOES GO WELL.
BUT... BUT THAT'S ALL.
HUH?
I THOUGHT DRAWING OUT THE NATURAL FLAVOR OF THE TURNIP WOULD BE ENOUGH...
BUT KAIBARA YŪZAN DECIDED TO COMBINE IT WITH ANOTHER INGREDIENT TO DRAW OUT ITS VERY BEST.
I WASN'T THINKING ENOUGH...
THAT'S RIGHT. YOU LOST, SHIRŌ.
KAIBARA-SAN KNEW MORE ABOUT TURNIPS THAN YOU DID.
THEN WHY DID HE SAY HE WANTED TO REDO IT...
IT WAS OBVIOUS THAT HE HAD WON...
DAMN IT!!
HOW DARE HE MAKE A FOOL OUT OF ME?!
SHIRŌ, WHERE ARE YOU GOING?!
YAMAOKA-SAN...!!

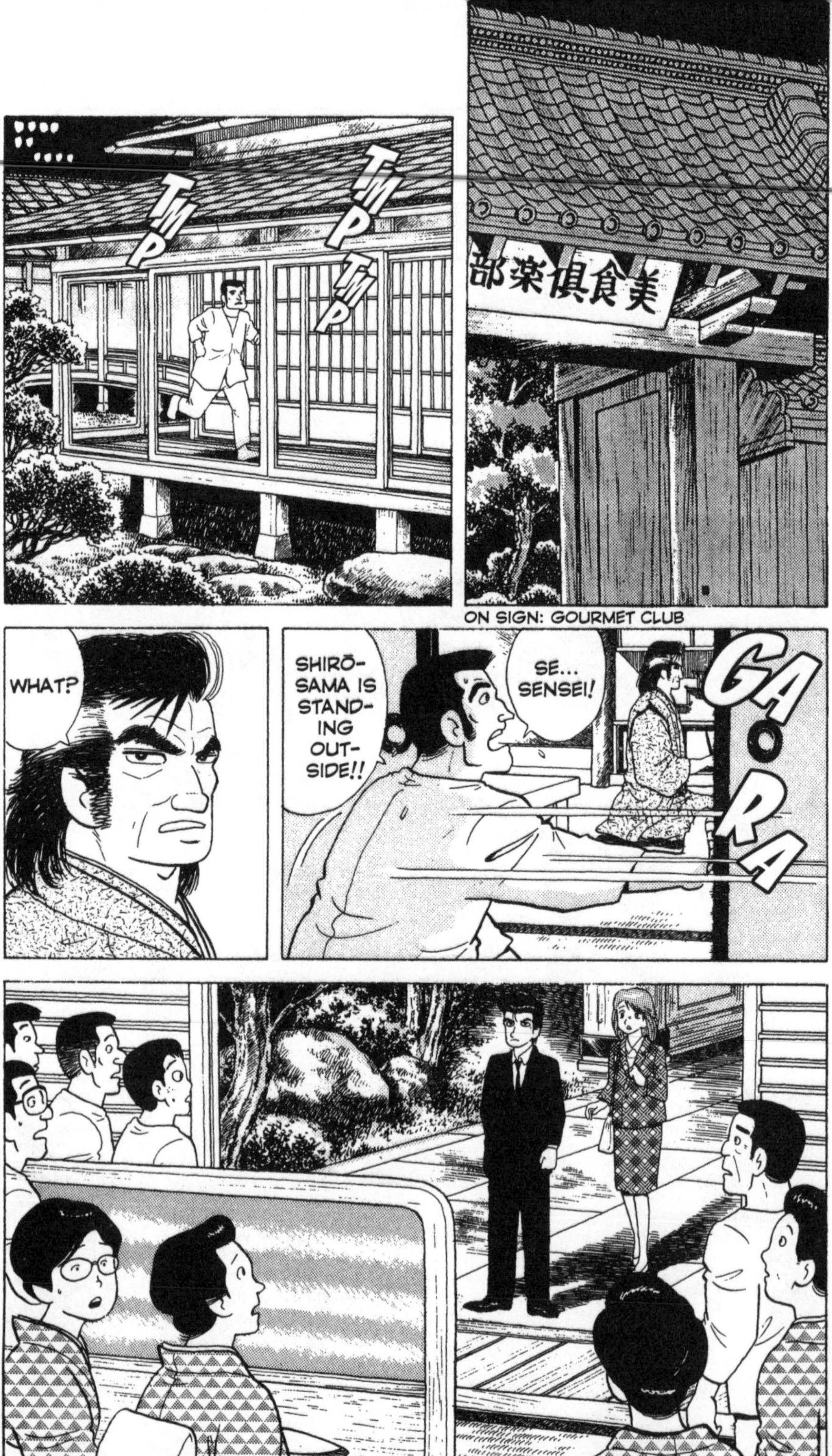
美食倶楽部
ON SIGN: GOURMET CLUB
TMP
TMP
TMP
GA
RA
SE... SENSEI!
SHIRŌ-SAMA IS STANDING OUTSIDE!!
WHAT?

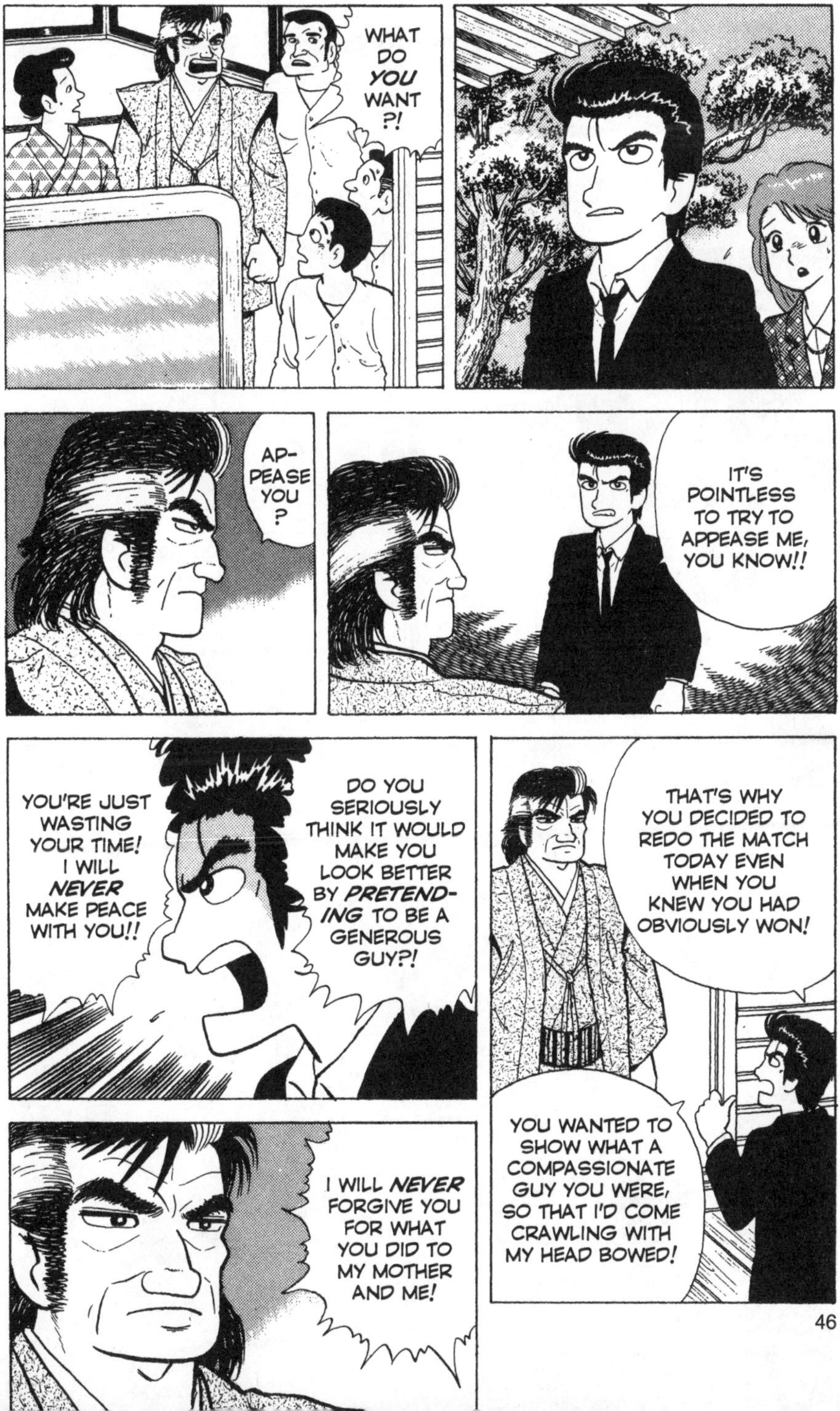
WHAT DO *YOU* WANT ?!
IT'S POINTLESS TO TRY TO APPEASE ME, YOU KNOW!!
AP-PEASE YOU ?
THAT'S WHY YOU DECIDED TO REDO THE MATCH TODAY EVEN WHEN YOU KNEW YOU HAD OBVIOUSLY WON!
YOU WANTED TO SHOW WHAT A COMPASSIONATE GUY YOU WERE, SO THAT I'D COME CRAWLING WITH MY HEAD BOWED!
DO YOU SERIOUSLY THINK IT WOULD MAKE YOU LOOK BETTER BY *PRETEND-ING* TO BE A GENEROUS GUY?!
YOU'RE JUST WASTING YOUR TIME! I WILL *NEVER* MAKE PEACE WITH YOU!!
I WILL *NEVER* FORGIVE YOU FOR WHAT YOU DID TO MY MOTHER AND ME!

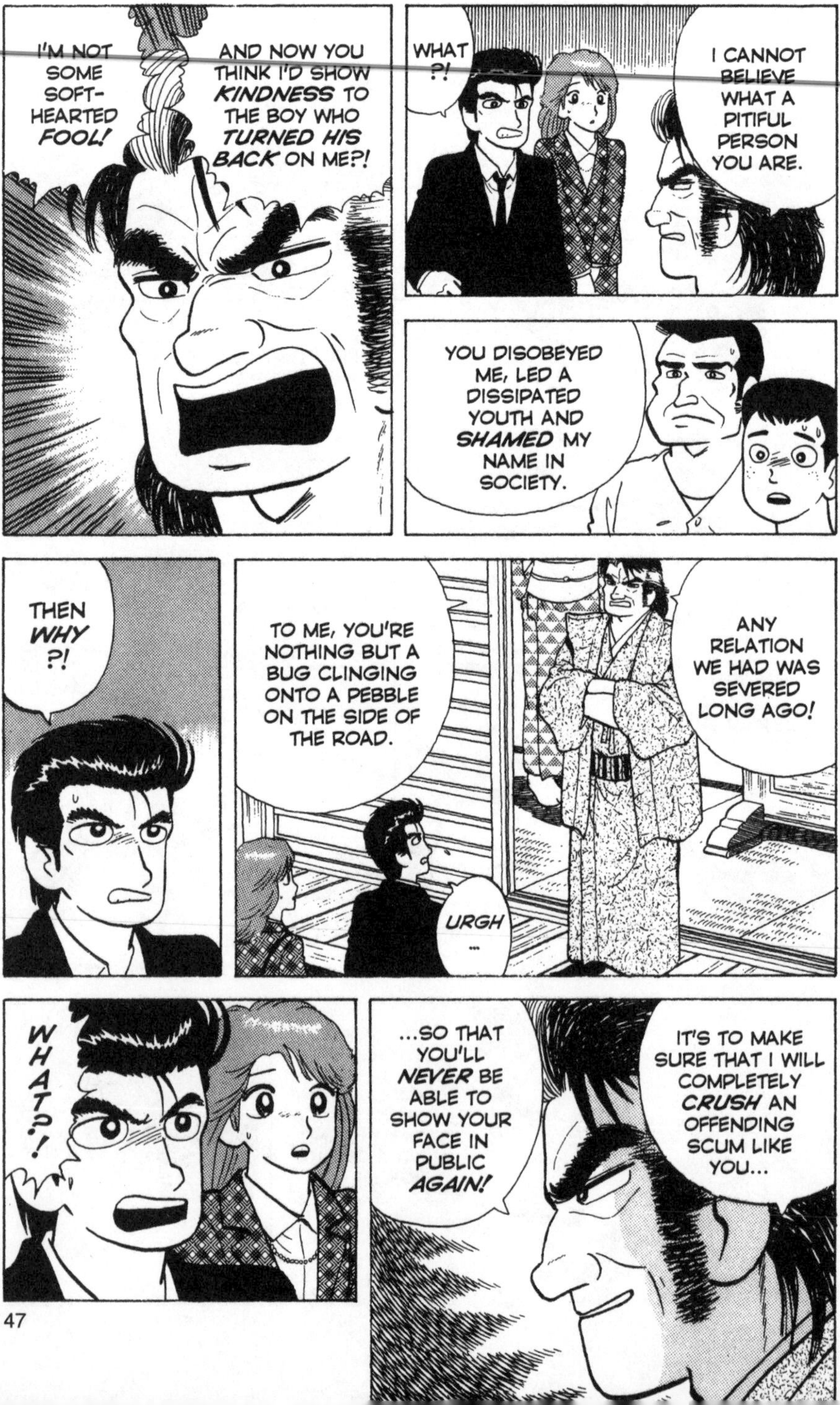

I CANNOT BELIEVE WHAT A PITIFUL PERSON YOU ARE.
WHAT ?!
YOU DISOBEYED ME, LED A DISSIPATED YOUTH AND SHAMED MY NAME IN SOCIETY.
AND NOW YOU THINK I'D SHOW KINDNESS TO THE BOY WHO TURNED HIS BACK ON ME?!
I'M NOT SOME SOFT-HEARTED FOOL!
ANY RELATION WE HAD WAS SEVERED LONG AGO!
TO ME, YOU'RE NOTHING BUT A BUG CLINGING ONTO A PEBBLE ON THE SIDE OF THE ROAD.
URGH ...
THEN WHY ?!
IT'S TO MAKE SURE THAT I WILL COMPLETELY CRUSH AN OFFENDING SCUM LIKE YOU...
...SO THAT YOU'LL NEVER BE ABLE TO SHOW YOUR FACE IN PUBLIC AGAIN!
WHAT?!

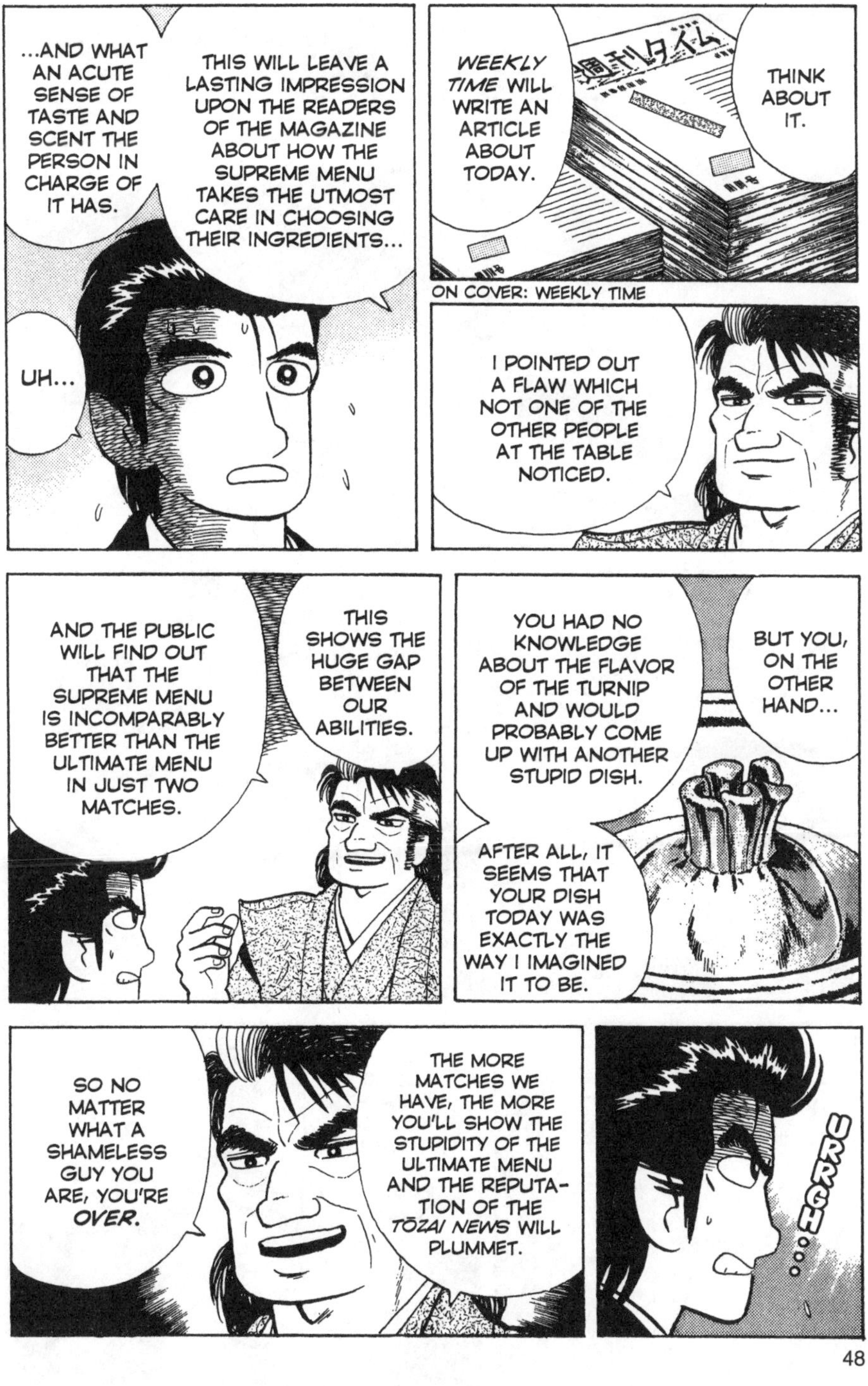
THINK ABOUT IT.
WEEKLY TIME WILL WRITE AN ARTICLE ABOUT TODAY.
ON COVER: WEEKLY TIME
I POINTED OUT A FLAW WHICH NOT ONE OF THE OTHER PEOPLE AT THE TABLE NOTICED.
THIS WILL LEAVE A LASTING IMPRESSION UPON THE READERS OF THE MAGAZINE ABOUT HOW THE SUPREME MENU TAKES THE UTMOST CARE IN CHOOSING THEIR INGREDIENTS...
...AND WHAT AN ACUTE SENSE OF TASTE AND SCENT THE PERSON IN CHARGE OF IT HAS.
UH...
BUT YOU, ON THE OTHER HAND...
YOU HAD NO KNOWLEDGE ABOUT THE FLAVOR OF THE TURNIP AND WOULD PROBABLY COME UP WITH ANOTHER STUPID DISH.
AFTER ALL, IT SEEMS THAT YOUR DISH TODAY WAS EXACTLY THE WAY I IMAGINED IT TO BE.
THIS SHOWS THE HUGE GAP BETWEEN OUR ABILITIES.
AND THE PUBLIC WILL FIND OUT THAT THE SUPREME MENU IS INCOMPARABLY BETTER THAN THE ULTIMATE MENU IN JUST TWO MATCHES.
URRGH...
THE MORE MATCHES WE HAVE, THE MORE YOU'LL SHOW THE STUPIDITY OF THE ULTIMATE MENU AND THE REPUTATION OF THE *TŌZAI NEWS* WILL PLUMMET.
SO NO MATTER WHAT A SHAMELESS GUY YOU ARE, YOU'RE ***OVER***.

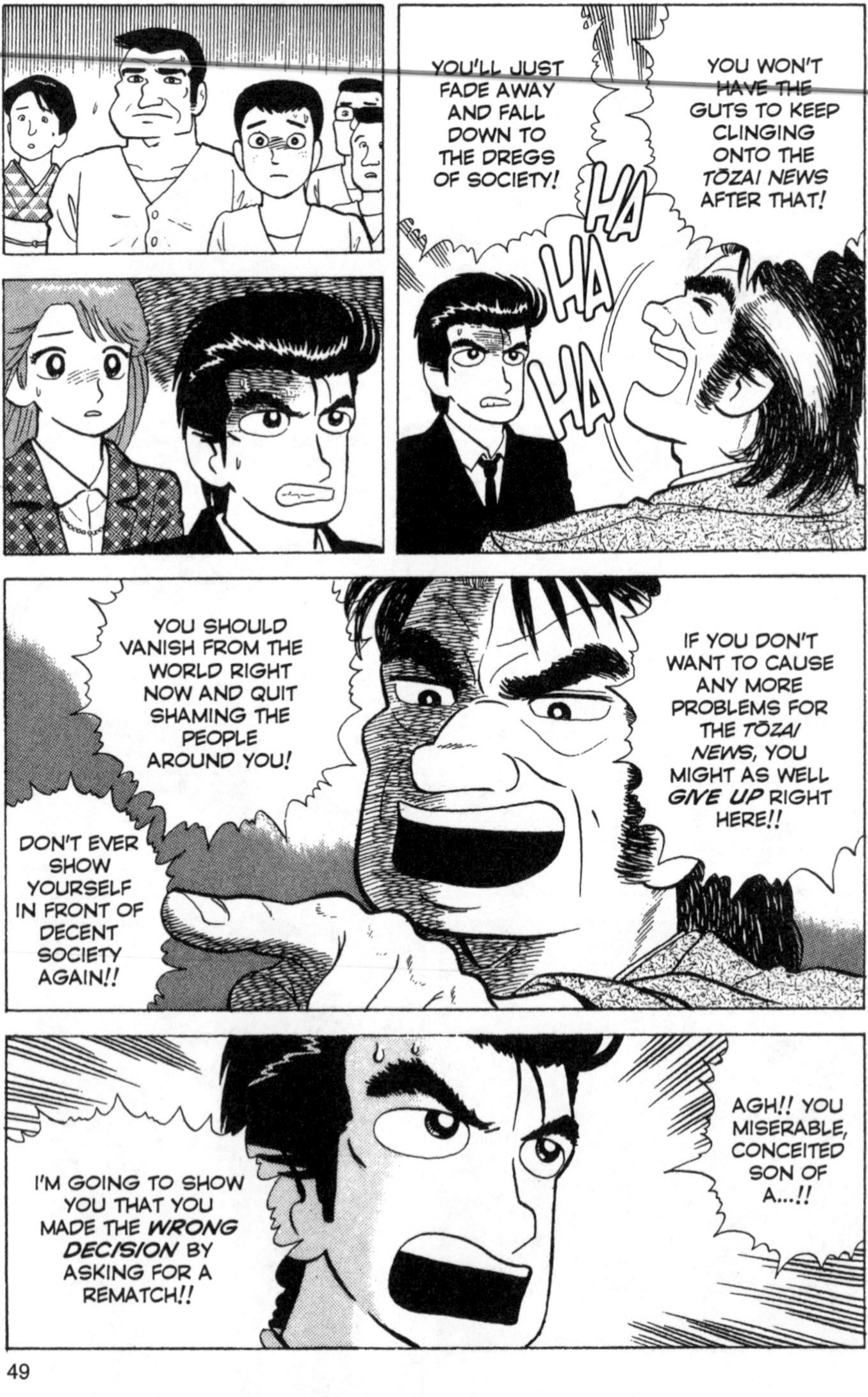
YOU WON'T HAVE THE GUTS TO KEEP CLINGING ONTO THE *TŌZAI NEWS* AFTER THAT!
YOU'LL JUST FADE AWAY AND FALL DOWN TO THE DREGS OF SOCIETY!
HA HA HA
IF YOU DON'T WANT TO CAUSE ANY MORE PROBLEMS FOR THE *TŌZAI NEWS*, YOU MIGHT AS WELL ***GIVE UP*** RIGHT HERE!!
YOU SHOULD VANISH FROM THE WORLD RIGHT NOW AND QUIT SHAMING THE PEOPLE AROUND YOU!
DON'T EVER SHOW YOURSELF IN FRONT OF DECENT SOCIETY AGAIN!!
AGH!! YOU MISERABLE, CONCEITED SON OF A...!!
I'M GOING TO SHOW YOU THAT YOU MADE THE ***WRONG DECISION*** BY ASKING FOR A REMATCH!!

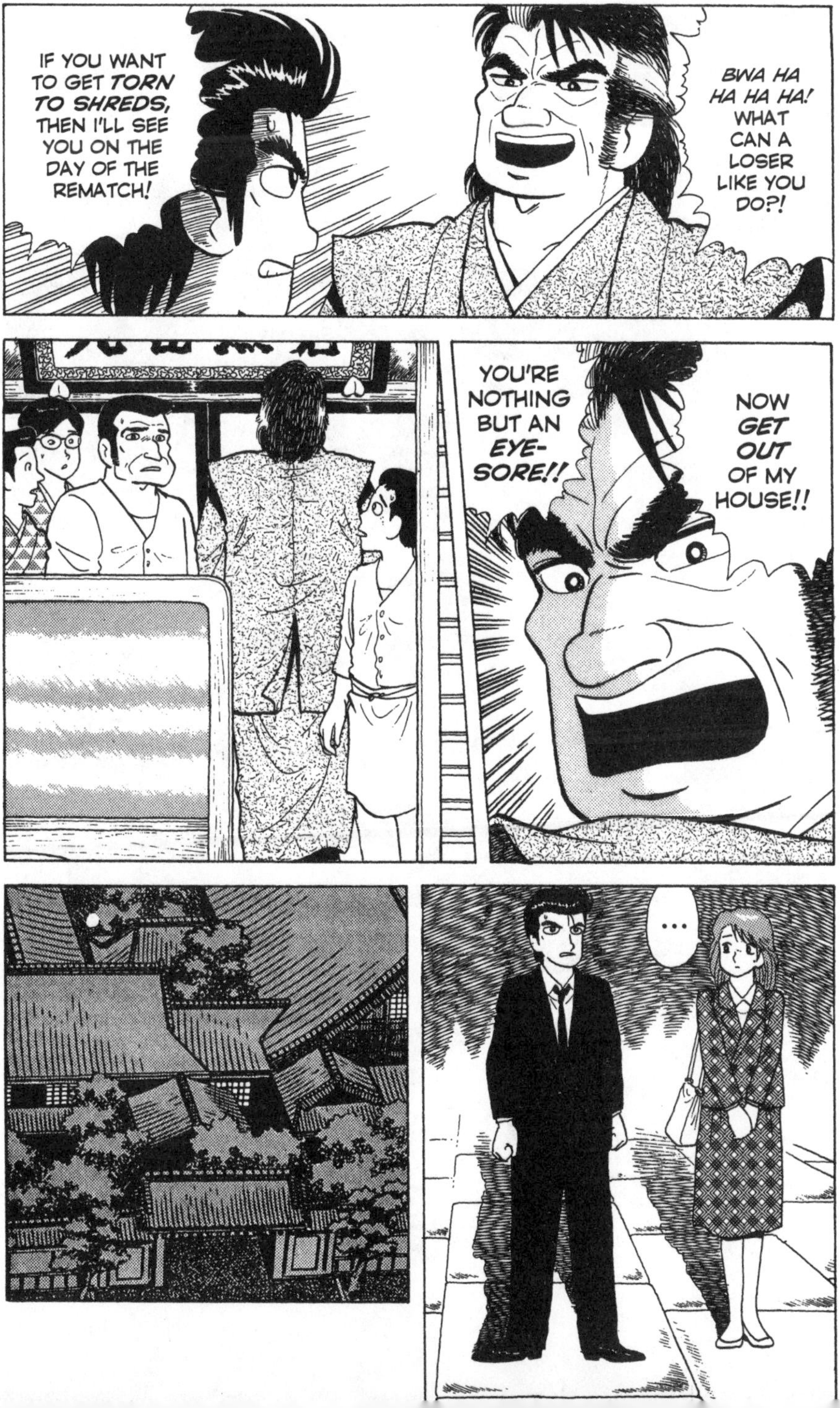
BWA HA HA HA HA! WHAT CAN A LOSER LIKE YOU DO?!
IF YOU WANT TO GET *TORN TO SHREDS,* THEN I'LL SEE YOU ON THE DAY OF THE REMATCH!
NOW *GET OUT* OF MY HOUSE!!
YOU'RE NOTHING BUT AN *EYE-SORE!!*
...

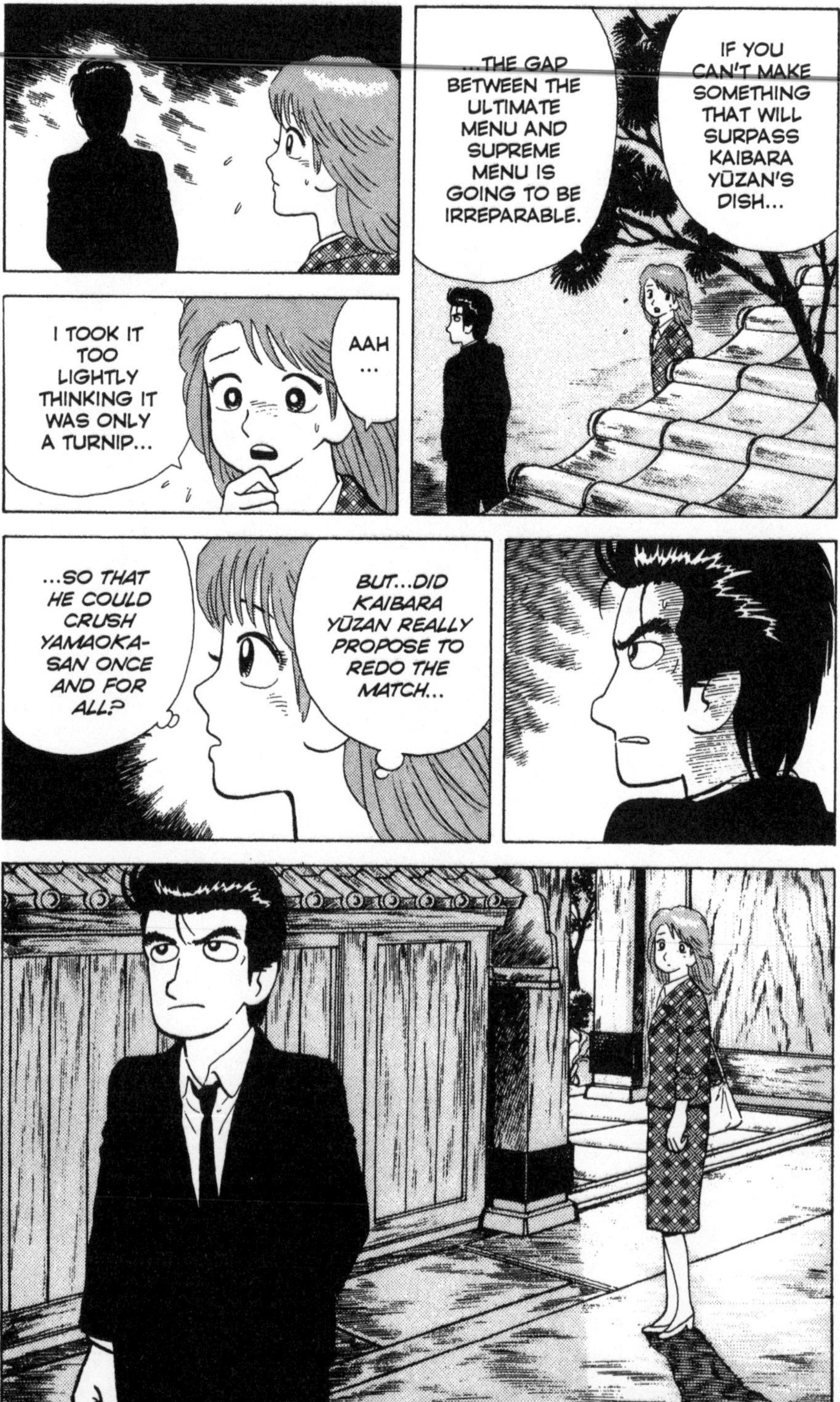
IF YOU CAN'T MAKE SOMETHING THAT WILL SURPASS KAIBARA YŪZAN'S DISH...
...THE GAP BETWEEN THE ULTIMATE MENU AND SUPREME MENU IS GOING TO BE IRREPARABLE.
AAH ...
I TOOK IT TOO LIGHTLY THINKING IT WAS ONLY A TURNIP...
BUT...DID KAIBARA YŪZAN REALLY PROPOSE TO REDO THE MATCH...
...SO THAT HE COULD CRUSH YAMAOKA-SAN ONCE AND FOR ALL?

O-I-S-H-I-N-B-O

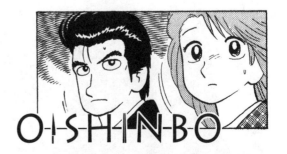

FIRST COURSE

VEGETABLE SHOWDOWN! (PART THREE)

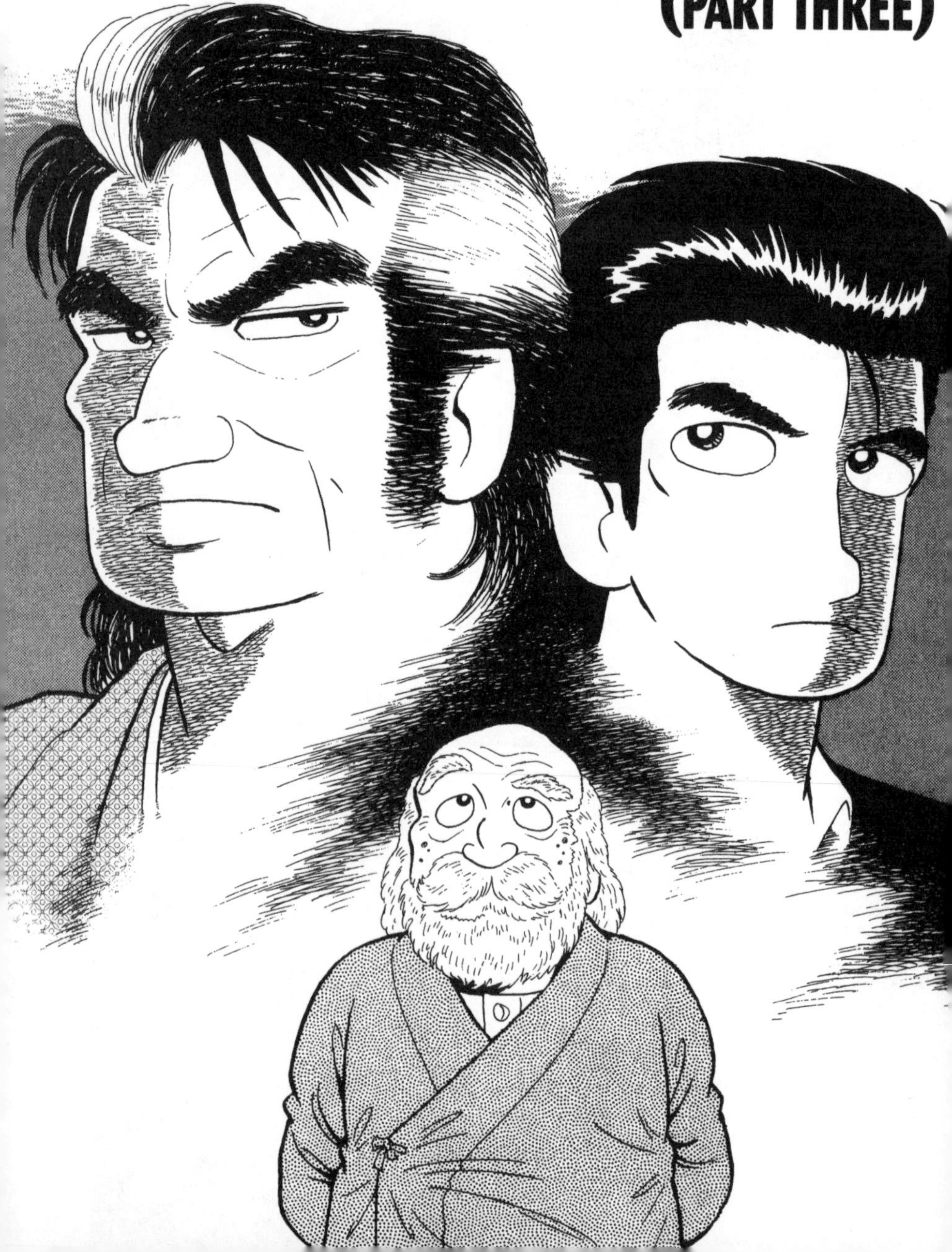

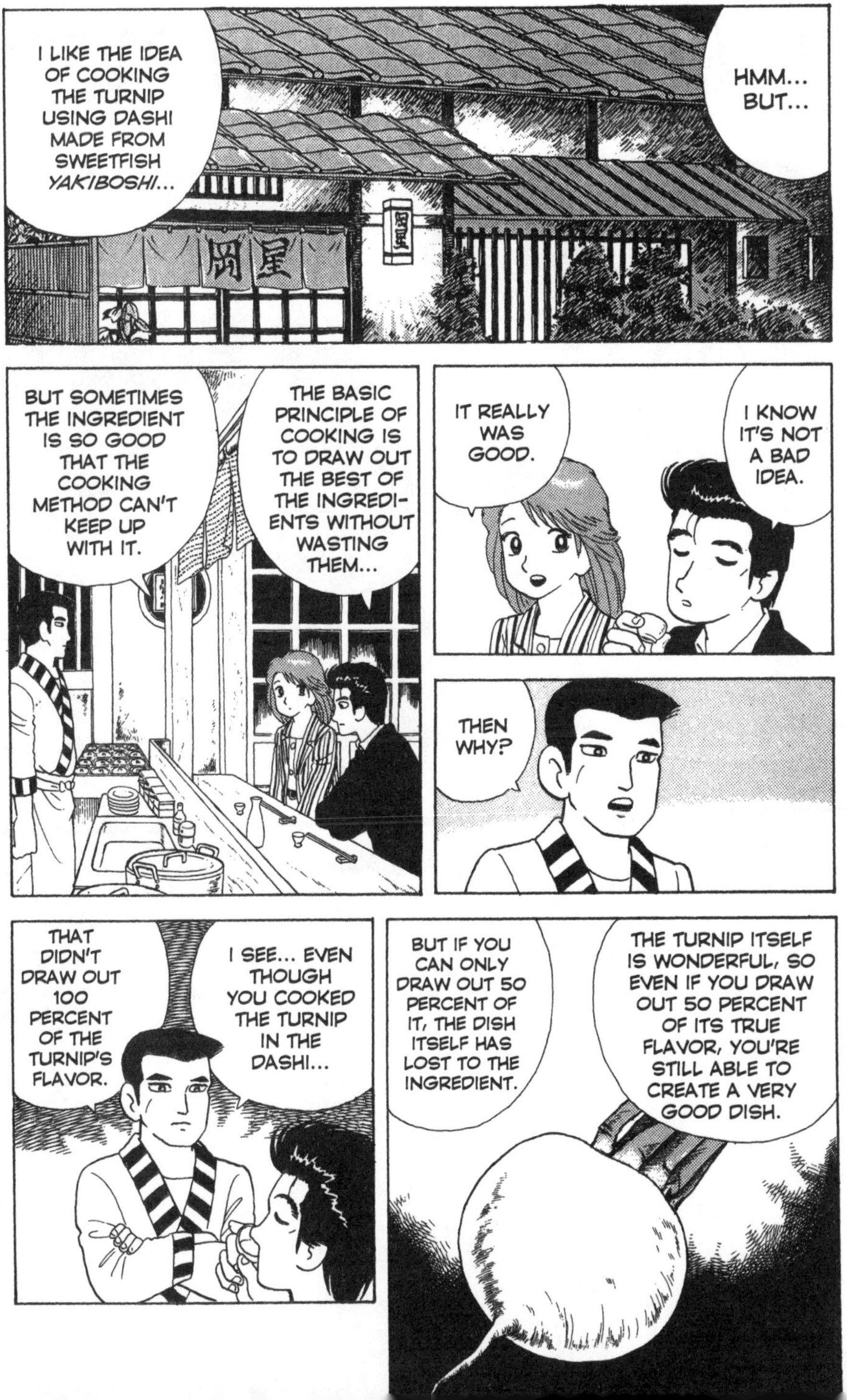
HMM... BUT...
I LIKE THE IDEA OF COOKING THE TURNIP USING DASHI MADE FROM SWEETFISH *YAKIBOSHI*...
岡星
I KNOW IT'S NOT A BAD IDEA.
IT REALLY WAS GOOD.
THEN WHY?
THE BASIC PRINCIPLE OF COOKING IS TO DRAW OUT THE BEST OF THE INGREDIENTS WITHOUT WASTING THEM...
BUT SOMETIMES THE INGREDIENT IS SO GOOD THAT THE COOKING METHOD CAN'T KEEP UP WITH IT.
THE TURNIP ITSELF IS WONDERFUL, SO EVEN IF YOU DRAW OUT 50 PERCENT OF ITS TRUE FLAVOR, YOU'RE STILL ABLE TO CREATE A VERY GOOD DISH.
BUT IF YOU CAN ONLY DRAW OUT 50 PERCENT OF IT, THE DISH ITSELF HAS LOST TO THE INGREDIENT.
I SEE... EVEN THOUGH YOU COOKED THE TURNIP IN THE DASHI...
THAT DIDN'T DRAW OUT 100 PERCENT OF THE TURNIP'S FLAVOR.

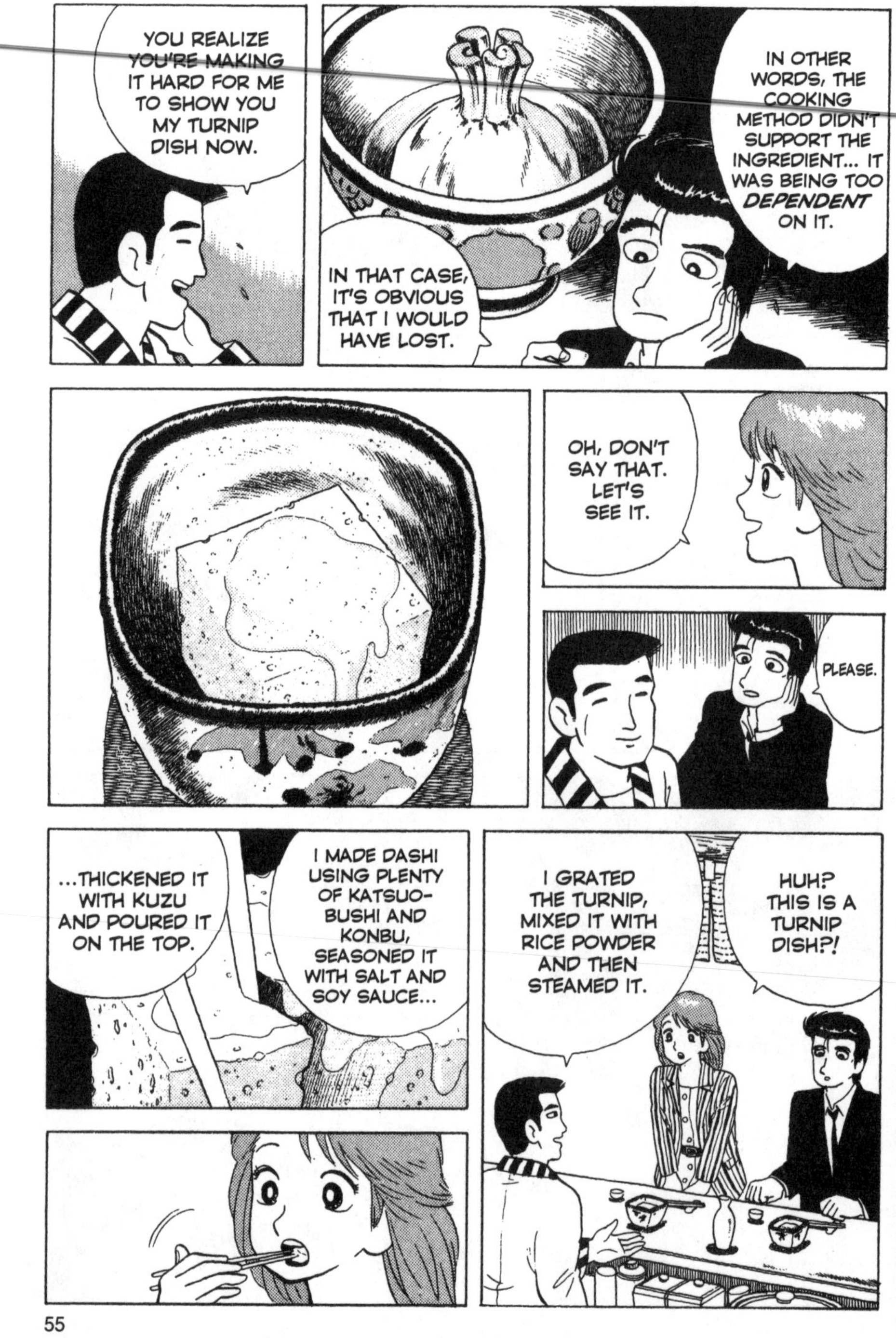
IN OTHER WORDS, THE COOKING METHOD DIDN'T SUPPORT THE INGREDIENT... IT WAS BEING TOO *DEPENDENT* ON IT.
IN THAT CASE, IT'S OBVIOUS THAT I WOULD HAVE LOST.
YOU REALIZE YOU'RE MAKING IT HARD FOR ME TO SHOW YOU MY TURNIP DISH NOW.
OH, DON'T SAY THAT. LET'S SEE IT.
PLEASE.
HUH? THIS IS A TURNIP DISH?!
I GRATED THE TURNIP, MIXED IT WITH RICE POWDER AND THEN STEAMED IT.
I MADE DASHI USING PLENTY OF KATSUO-BUSHI AND KONBU, SEASONED IT WITH SALT AND SOY SAUCE...
...THICKENED IT WITH KUZU AND POURED IT ON THE TOP.

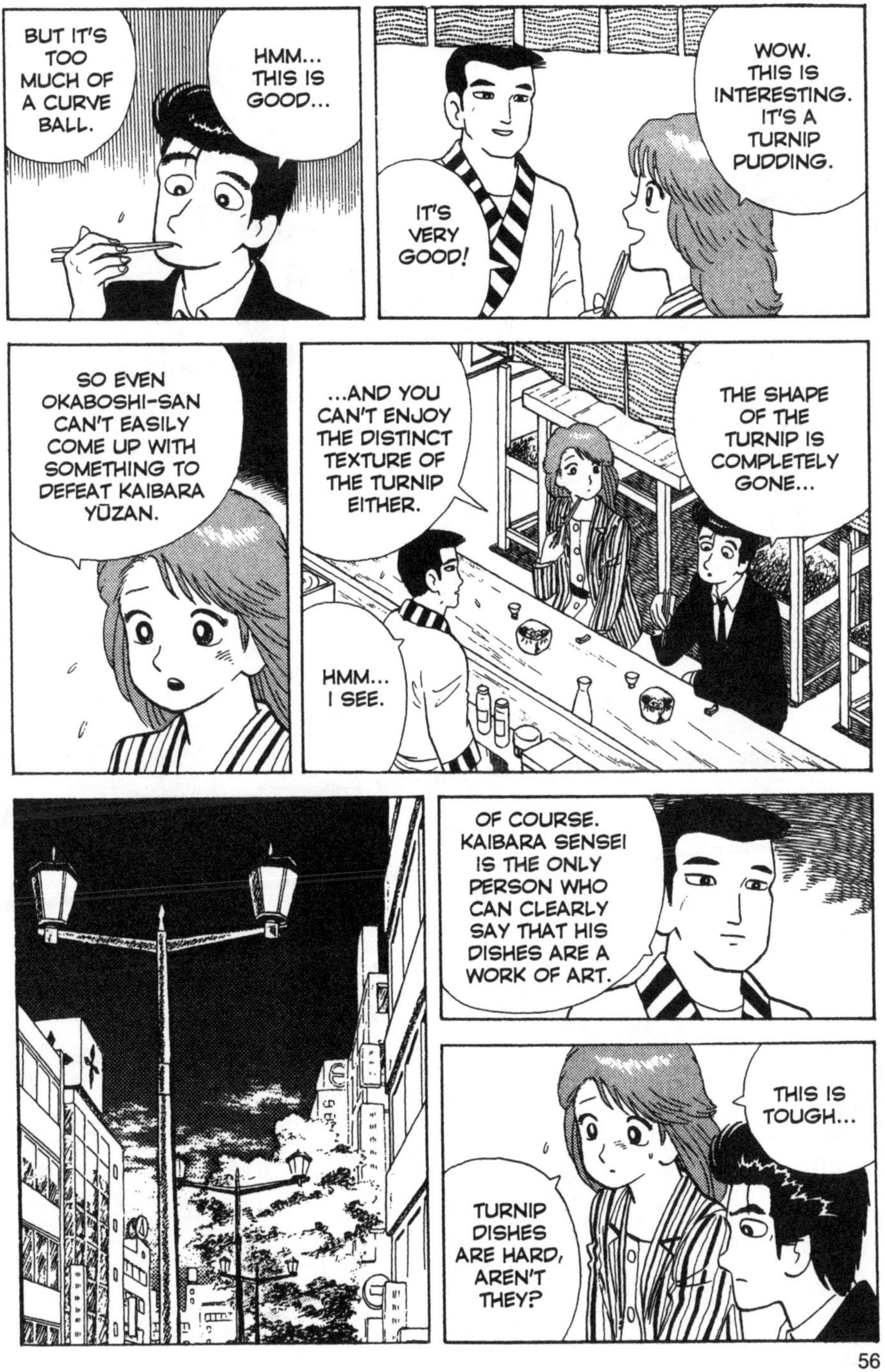
WOW. THIS IS INTERESTING. IT'S A TURNIP PUDDING.
IT'S VERY GOOD!
HMM... THIS IS GOOD...
BUT IT'S TOO MUCH OF A CURVE BALL.
THE SHAPE OF THE TURNIP IS COMPLETELY GONE...
...AND YOU CAN'T ENJOY THE DISTINCT TEXTURE OF THE TURNIP EITHER.
HMM... I SEE.
SO EVEN OKABOSHI-SAN CAN'T EASILY COME UP WITH SOMETHING TO DEFEAT KAIBARA YŪZAN.
OF COURSE. KAIBARA SENSEI IS THE ONLY PERSON WHO CAN CLEARLY SAY THAT HIS DISHES ARE A WORK OF ART.
THIS IS TOUGH...
TURNIP DISHES ARE HARD, AREN'T THEY?

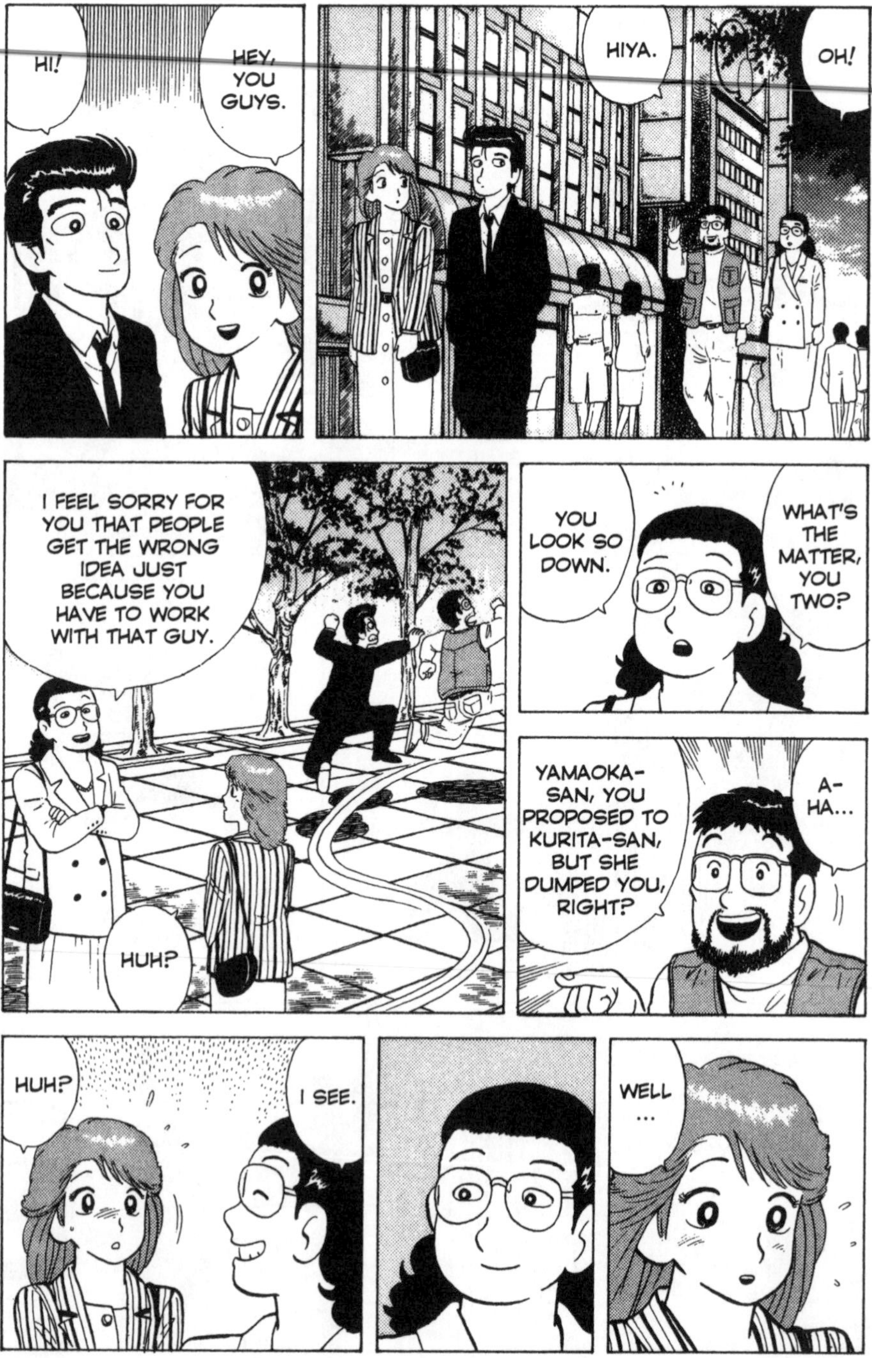
OH!
HIYA.
HEY, YOU GUYS.
HI!
WHAT'S THE MATTER, YOU TWO?
YOU LOOK SO DOWN.
A-HA...
YAMAOKA-SAN, YOU PROPOSED TO KURITA-SAN, BUT SHE DUMPED YOU, RIGHT?
I FEEL SORRY FOR YOU THAT PEOPLE GET THE WRONG IDEA JUST BECAUSE YOU HAVE TO WORK WITH THAT GUY.
HUH?
WELL ...
I SEE.
HUH?

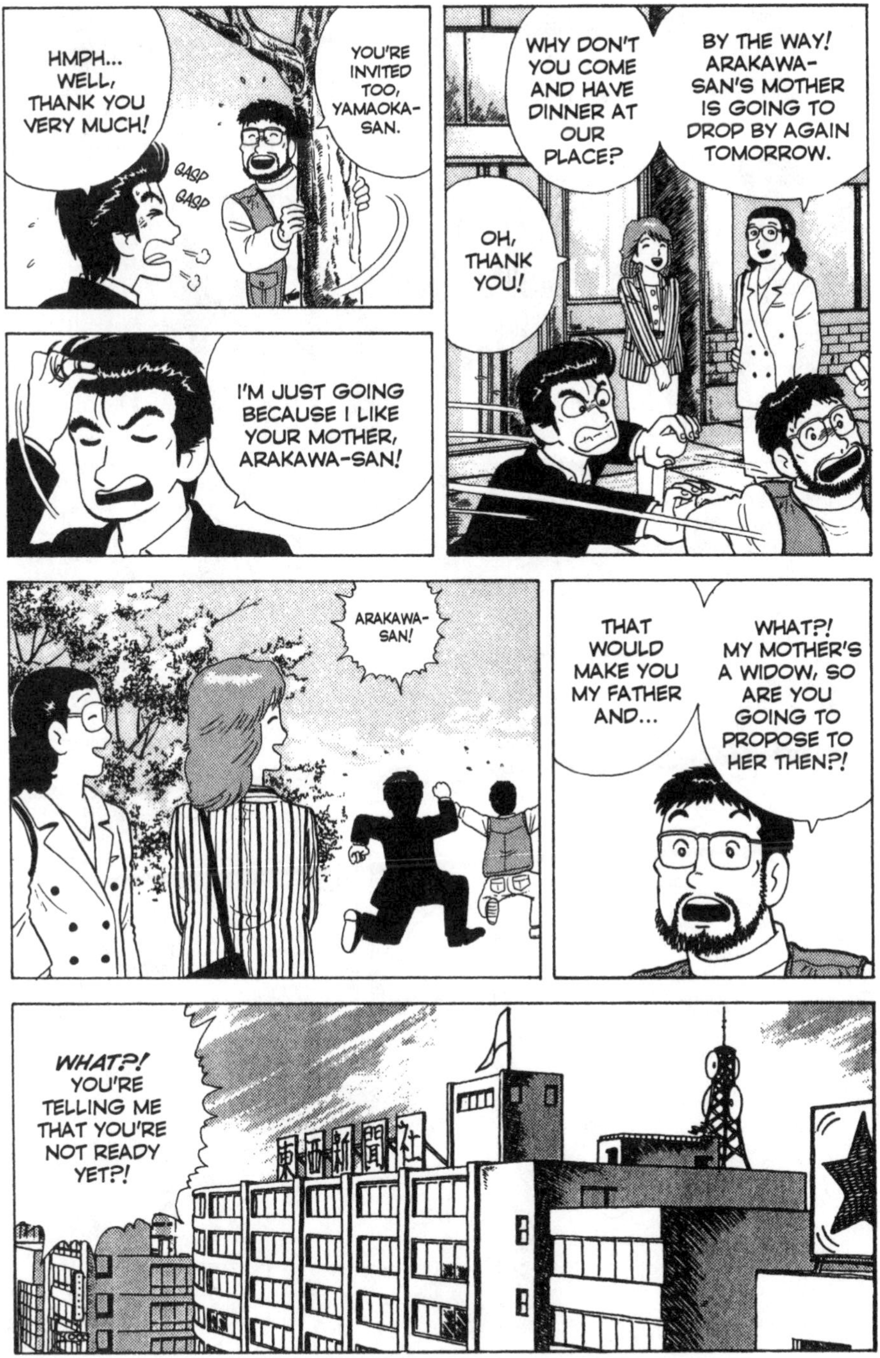
BY THE WAY! ARAKAWA-SAN'S MOTHER IS GOING TO DROP BY AGAIN TOMORROW.
WHY DON'T YOU COME AND HAVE DINNER AT OUR PLACE?
OH, THANK YOU!
YOU'RE INVITED TOO, YAMAOKA-SAN.
HMPH... WELL, THANK YOU VERY MUCH!
GASP GASP
I'M JUST GOING BECAUSE I LIKE YOUR MOTHER, ARAKAWA-SAN!
WHAT?! MY MOTHER'S A WIDOW, SO ARE YOU GOING TO PROPOSE TO HER THEN?!
THAT WOULD MAKE YOU MY FATHER AND...
ARAKAWA-SAN!
東西新聞社
WHAT?! YOU'RE TELLING ME THAT YOU'RE NOT READY YET?!

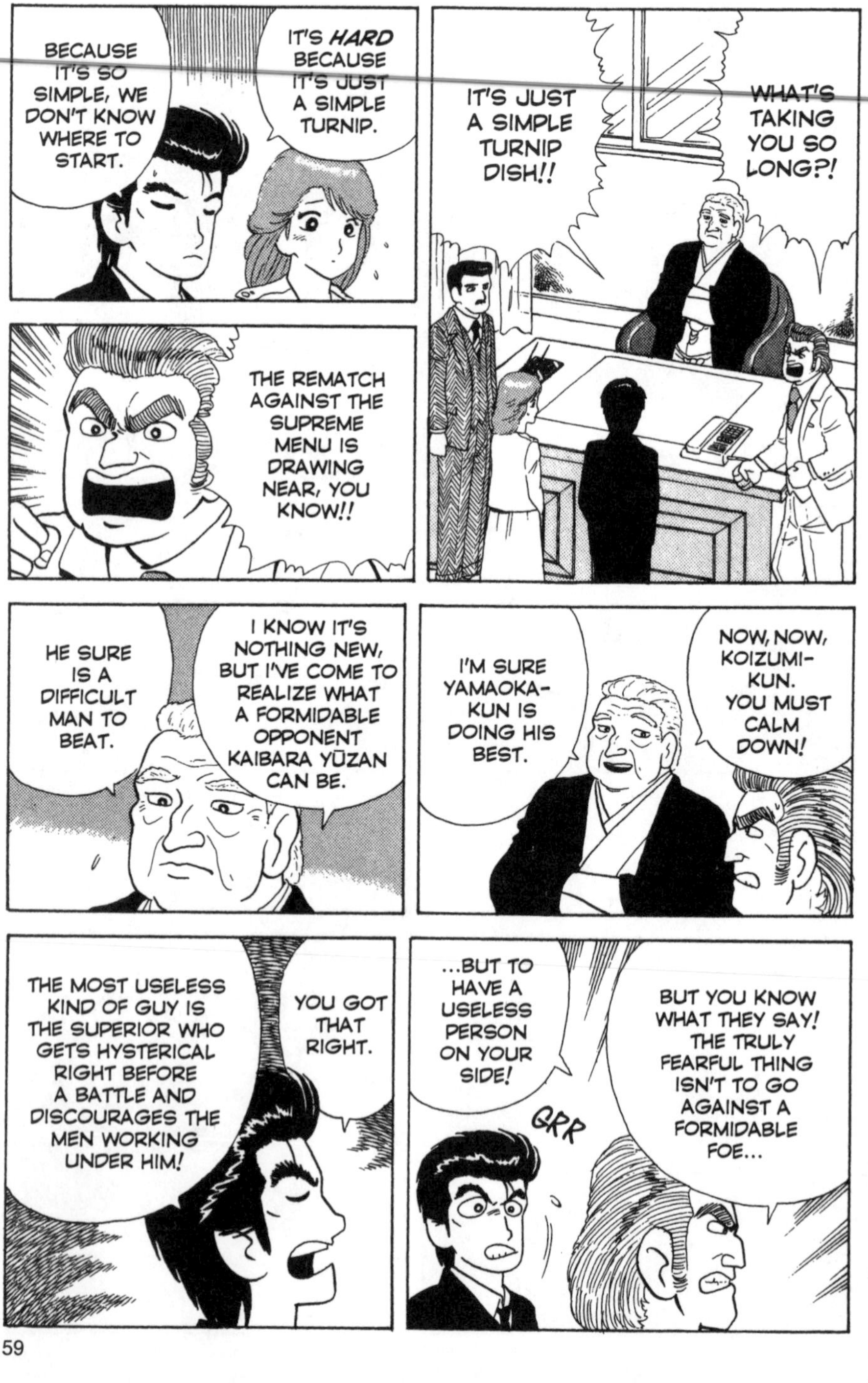
WHAT'S TAKING YOU SO LONG?!
IT'S JUST A SIMPLE TURNIP DISH!!
IT'S HARD BECAUSE IT'S JUST A SIMPLE TURNIP.
BECAUSE IT'S SO SIMPLE, WE DON'T KNOW WHERE TO START.
THE REMATCH AGAINST THE SUPREME MENU IS DRAWING NEAR, YOU KNOW!!
NOW, NOW, KOIZUMI-KUN. YOU MUST CALM DOWN!
I'M SURE YAMAOKA-KUN IS DOING HIS BEST.
I KNOW IT'S NOTHING NEW, BUT I'VE COME TO REALIZE WHAT A FORMIDABLE OPPONENT KAIBARA YŪZAN CAN BE.
HE SURE IS A DIFFICULT MAN TO BEAT.
BUT YOU KNOW WHAT THEY SAY! THE TRULY FEARFUL THING ISN'T TO GO AGAINST A FORMIDABLE FOE...
...BUT TO HAVE A USELESS PERSON ON YOUR SIDE!
GRR
YOU GOT THAT RIGHT.
THE MOST USELESS KIND OF GUY IS THE SUPERIOR WHO GETS HYSTERICAL RIGHT BEFORE A BATTLE AND DISCOURAGES THE MEN WORKING UNDER HIM!

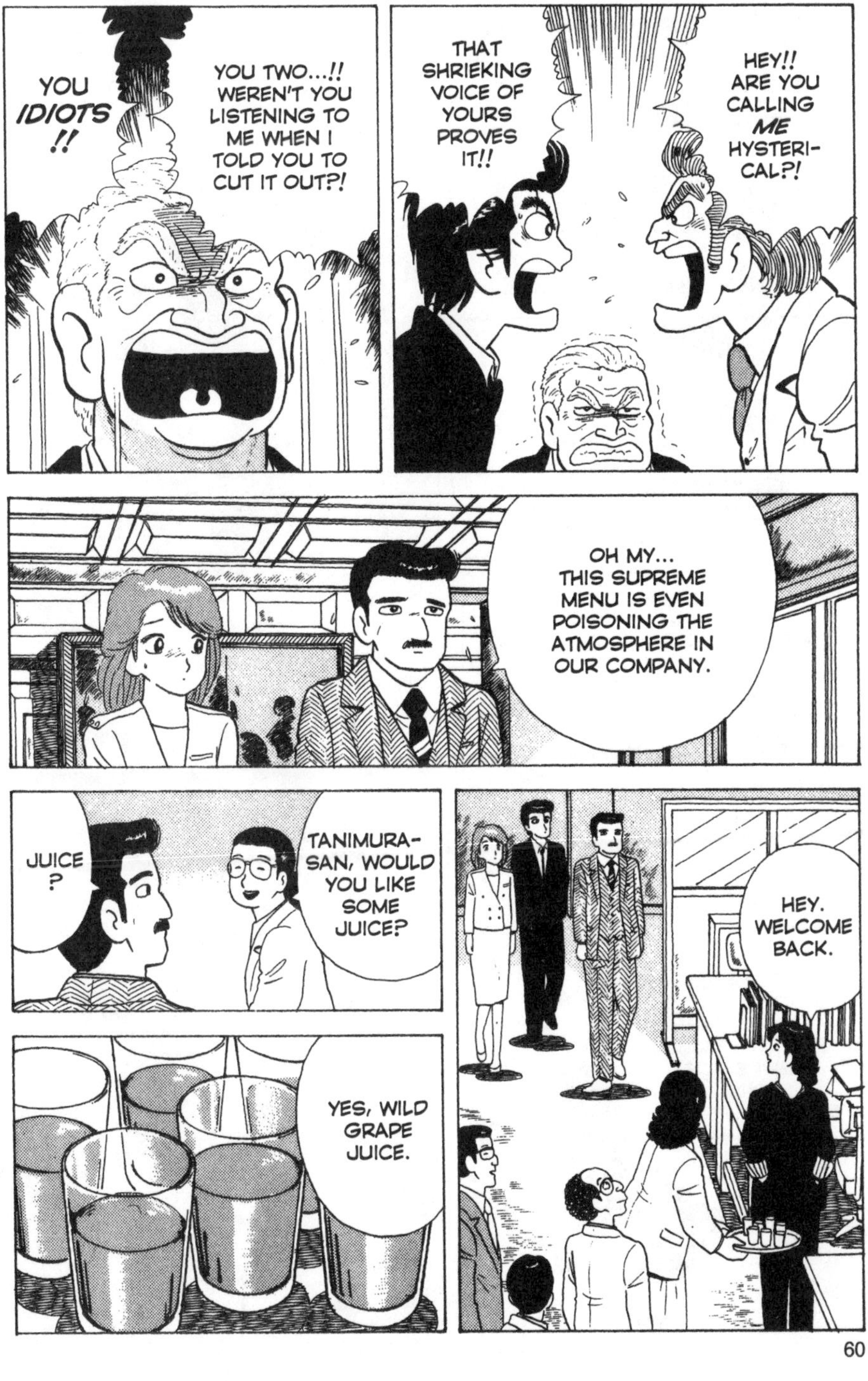

HEY!! ARE YOU CALLING *ME* HYSTERI-CAL?!
THAT SHRIEKING VOICE OF YOURS PROVES IT!!
YOU TWO...!! WEREN'T YOU LISTENING TO ME WHEN I TOLD YOU TO CUT IT OUT?!
YOU *IDIOTS* !!
OH MY... THIS SUPREME MENU IS EVEN POISONING THE ATMOSPHERE IN OUR COMPANY.
HEY. WELCOME BACK.
TANIMURA-SAN, WOULD YOU LIKE SOME JUICE?
JUICE?
YES, WILD GRAPE JUICE.

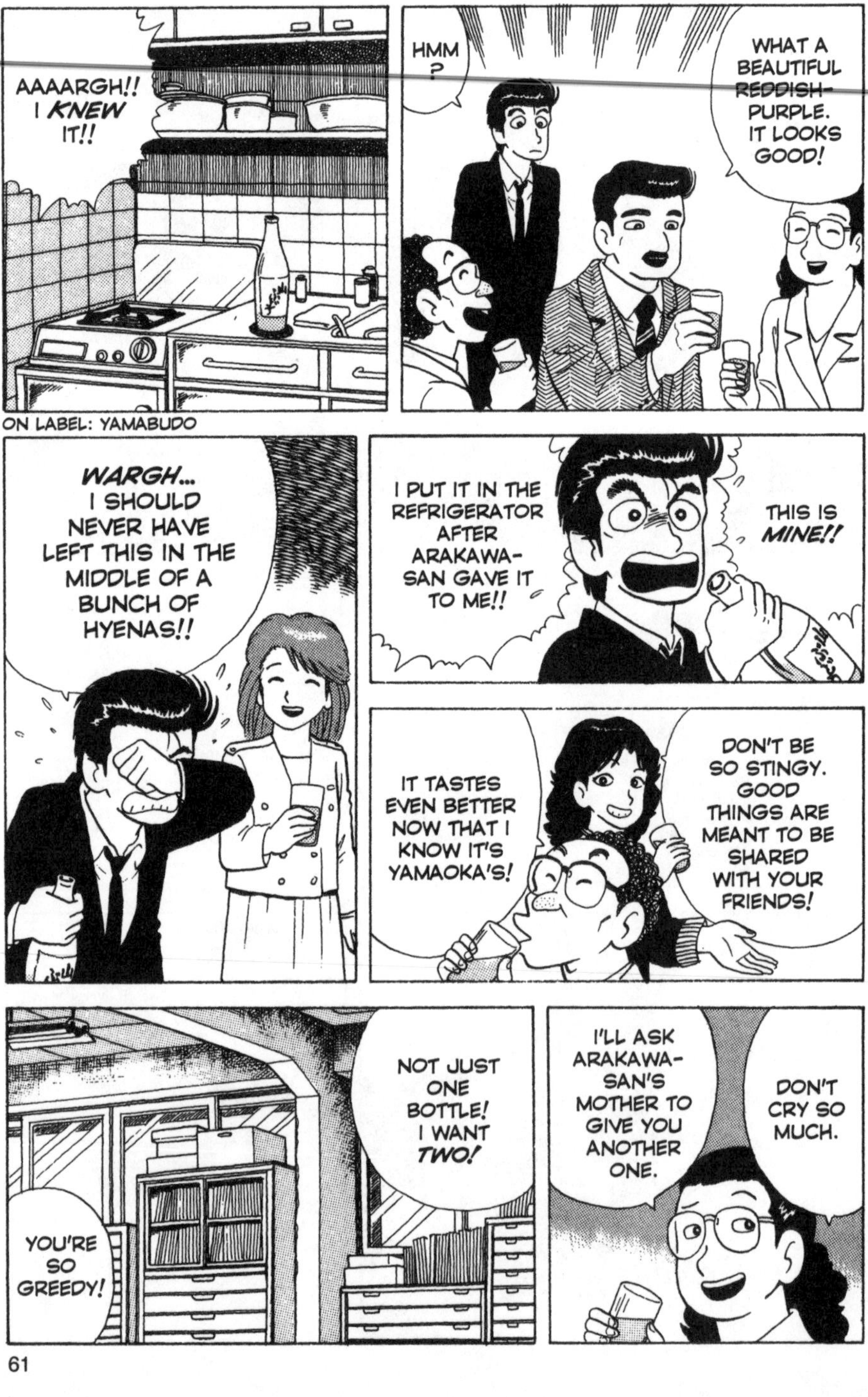
WHAT A BEAUTIFUL REDDISH-PURPLE. IT LOOKS GOOD!
HMM ?
AAAARGH!! I KNEW IT!!
THIS IS MINE!!
I PUT IT IN THE REFRIGERATOR AFTER ARAKAWA-SAN GAVE IT TO ME!!
DON'T BE SO STINGY. GOOD THINGS ARE MEANT TO BE SHARED WITH YOUR FRIENDS!
IT TASTES EVEN BETTER NOW THAT I KNOW IT'S YAMAOKA'S!
WARGH... I SHOULD NEVER HAVE LEFT THIS IN THE MIDDLE OF A BUNCH OF HYENAS!!
DON'T CRY SO MUCH.
I'LL ASK ARAKAWA-SAN'S MOTHER TO GIVE YOU ANOTHER ONE.
NOT JUST ONE BOTTLE! I WANT TWO!
YOU'RE SO GREEDY!
ON LABEL: YAMABUDO

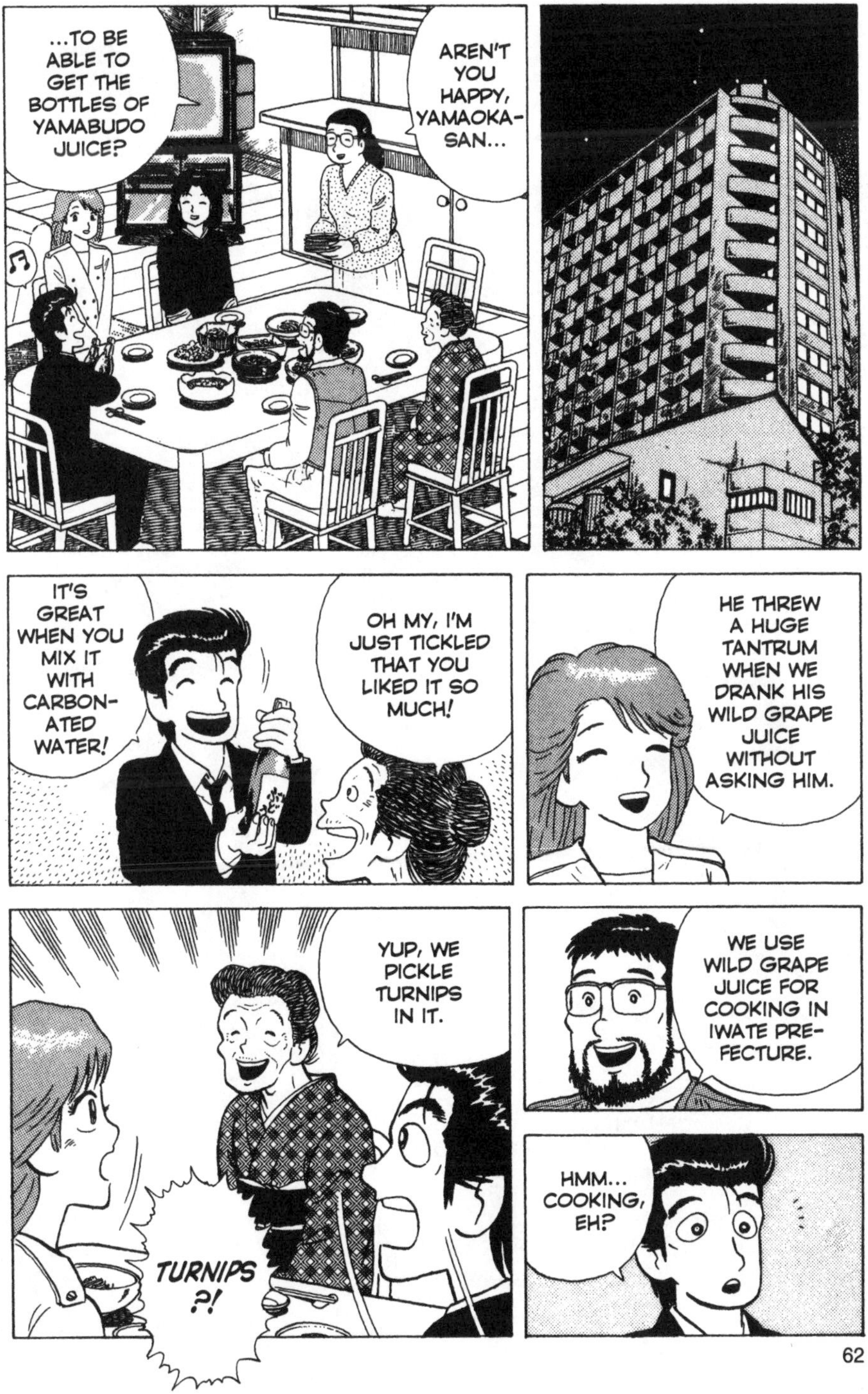

AREN'T YOU HAPPY, YAMAOKA-SAN...
...TO BE ABLE TO GET THE BOTTLES OF YAMABUDO JUICE?
HE THREW A HUGE TANTRUM WHEN WE DRANK HIS WILD GRAPE JUICE WITHOUT ASKING HIM.
OH MY, I'M JUST TICKLED THAT YOU LIKED IT SO MUCH!
IT'S GREAT WHEN YOU MIX IT WITH CARBON-ATED WATER!
WE USE WILD GRAPE JUICE FOR COOKING IN IWATE PRE-FECTURE.
HMM... COOKING, EH?
YUP, WE PICKLE TURNIPS IN IT.
TURNIPS ?!

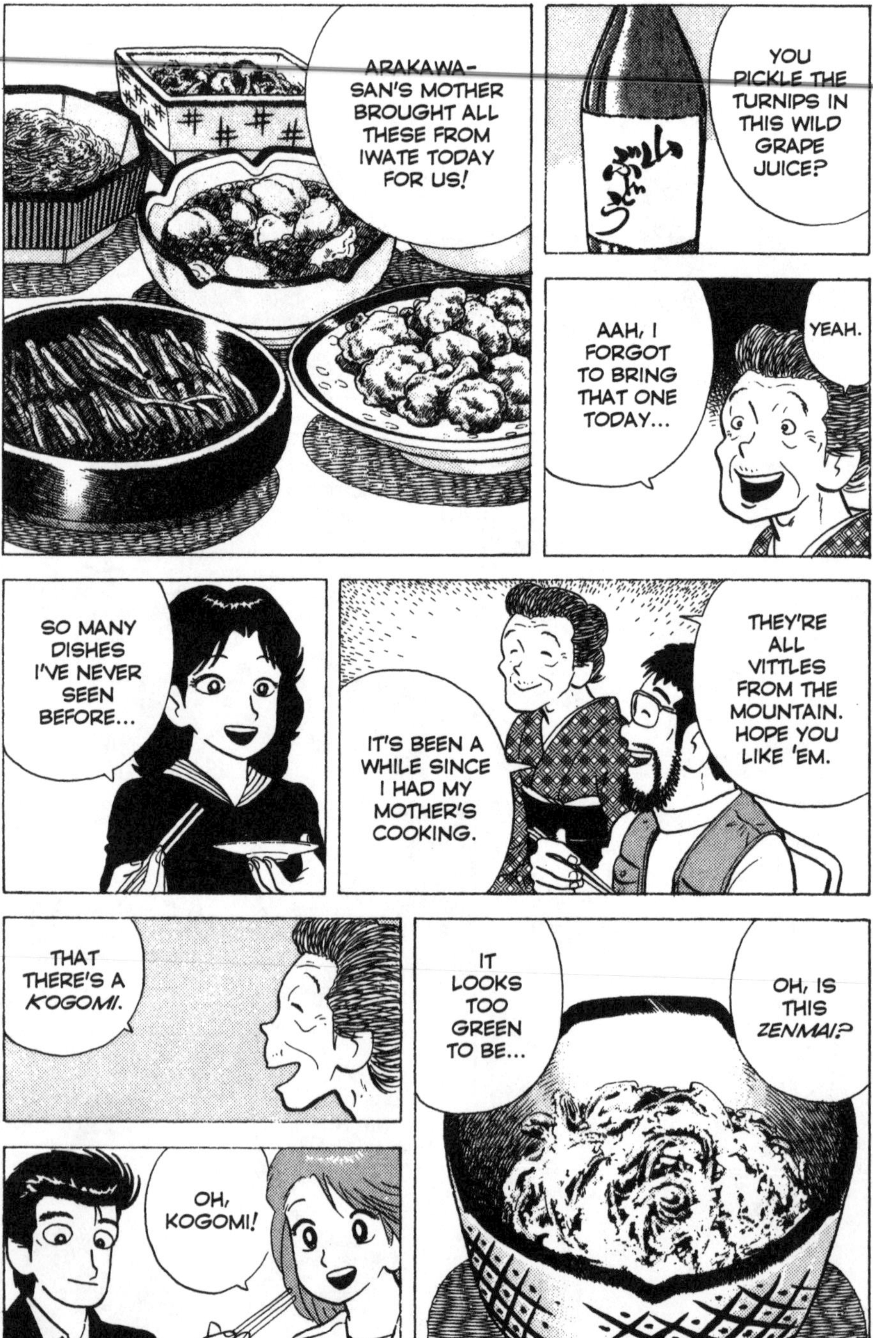
YOU PICKLE THE TURNIPS IN THIS WILD GRAPE JUICE?
YEAH.
AAH, I FORGOT TO BRING THAT ONE TODAY...
ARAKAWA-SAN'S MOTHER BROUGHT ALL THESE FROM IWATE TODAY FOR US!
THEY'RE ALL VITTLES FROM THE MOUNTAIN. HOPE YOU LIKE 'EM.
IT'S BEEN A WHILE SINCE I HAD MY MOTHER'S COOKING.
SO MANY DISHES I'VE NEVER SEEN BEFORE...
OH, IS THIS *ZENMAI*?
IT LOOKS TOO GREEN TO BE...
THAT THERE'S A *KOGOMI*.
OH, KOGOMI!

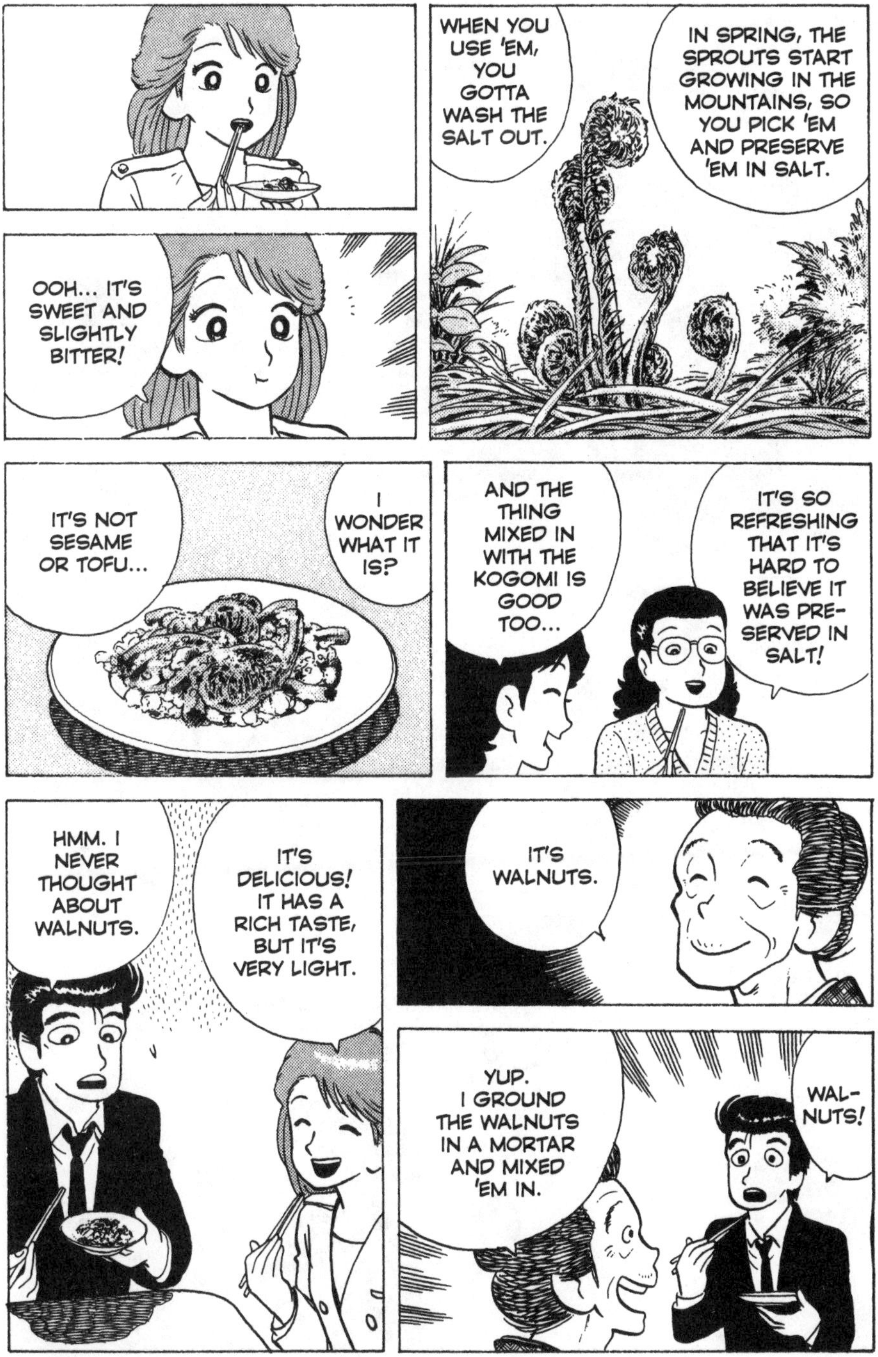
IN SPRING, THE SPROUTS START GROWING IN THE MOUNTAINS, SO YOU PICK 'EM AND PRESERVE 'EM IN SALT.
WHEN YOU USE 'EM, YOU GOTTA WASH THE SALT OUT.
OOH... IT'S SWEET AND SLIGHTLY BITTER!
IT'S SO REFRESHING THAT IT'S HARD TO BELIEVE IT WAS PRE-SERVED IN SALT!
AND THE THING MIXED IN WITH THE KOGOMI IS GOOD TOO...
I WONDER WHAT IT IS?
IT'S NOT SESAME OR TOFU...
IT'S WALNUTS.
WAL-NUTS!
YUP. I GROUND THE WALNUTS IN A MORTAR AND MIXED 'EM IN.
IT'S DELICIOUS! IT HAS A RICH TASTE, BUT IT'S VERY LIGHT.
HMM. I NEVER THOUGHT ABOUT WALNUTS.

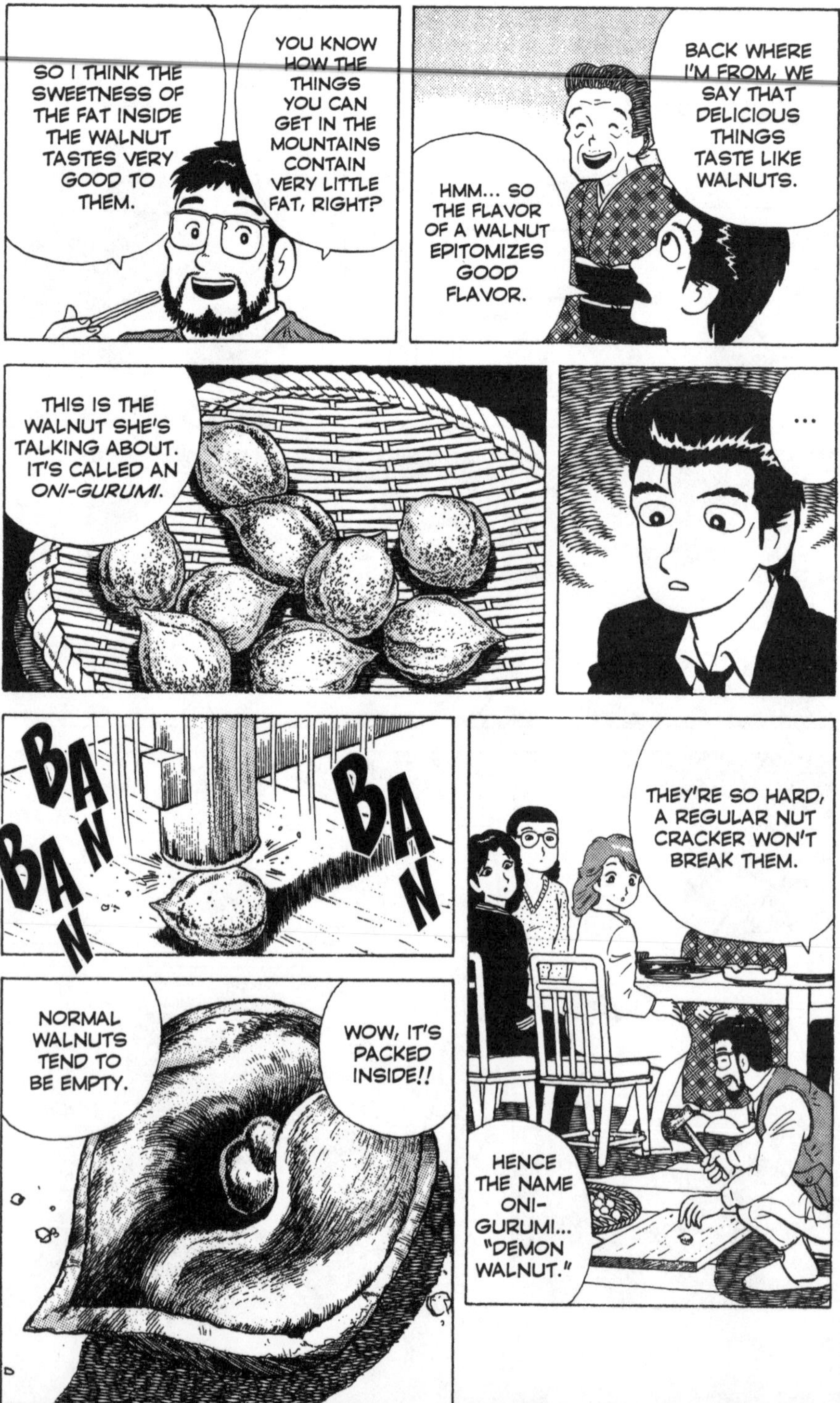
BACK WHERE I'M FROM, WE SAY THAT DELICIOUS THINGS TASTE LIKE WALNUTS.
HMM... SO THE FLAVOR OF A WALNUT EPITOMIZES GOOD FLAVOR.
YOU KNOW HOW THE THINGS YOU CAN GET IN THE MOUNTAINS CONTAIN VERY LITTLE FAT, RIGHT?
SO I THINK THE SWEETNESS OF THE FAT INSIDE THE WALNUT TASTES VERY GOOD TO THEM.
...
THIS IS THE WALNUT SHE'S TALKING ABOUT. IT'S CALLED AN *ONI-GURUMI*.
THEY'RE SO HARD, A REGULAR NUT CRACKER WON'T BREAK THEM.
HENCE THE NAME ONI-GURUMI... "DEMON WALNUT."
BABAN
BABAN
WOW, IT'S PACKED INSIDE!!
NORMAL WALNUTS TEND TO BE EMPTY.

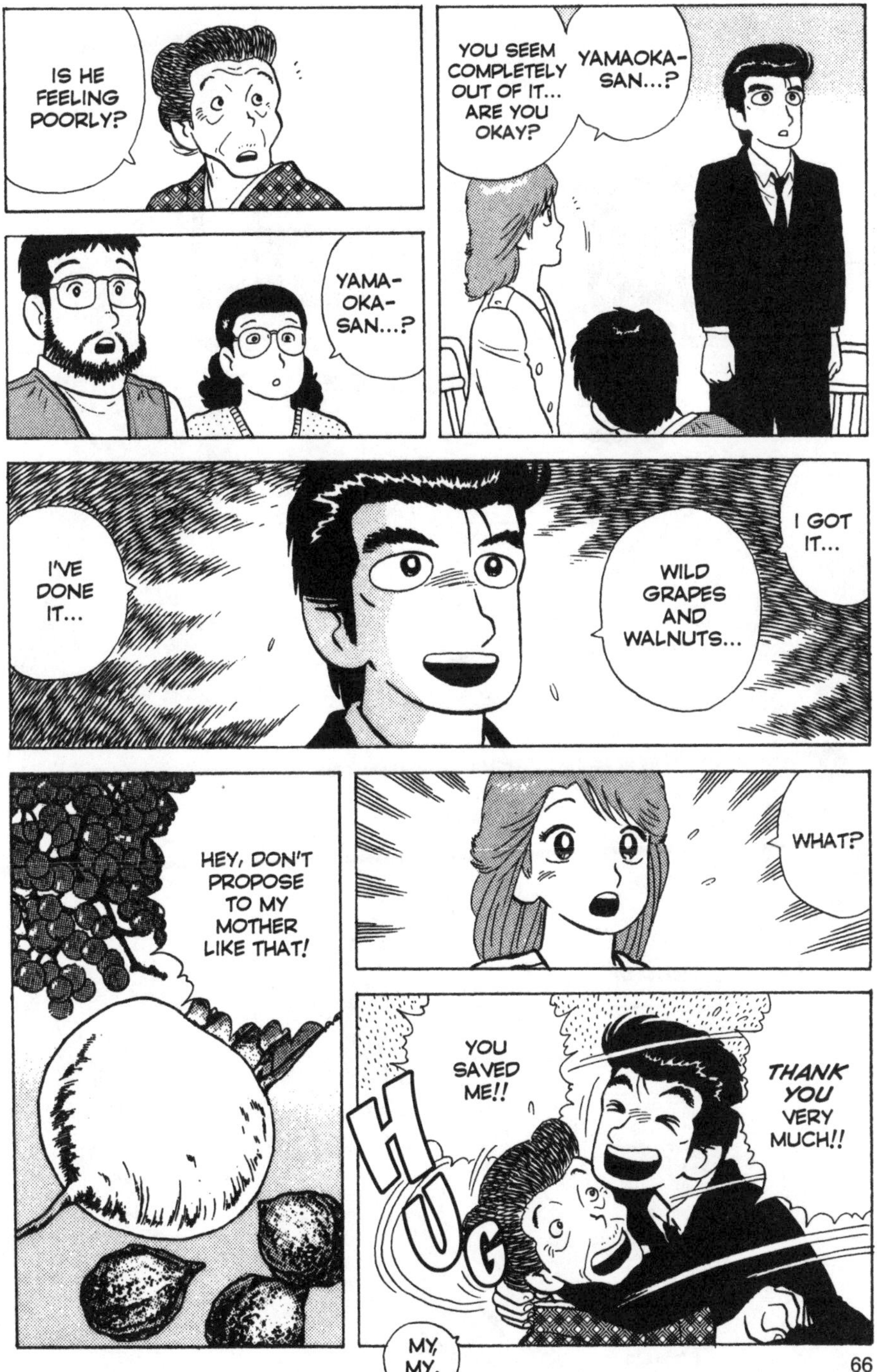
YAMAOKA-SAN...?
YOU SEEM COMPLETELY OUT OF IT... ARE YOU OKAY?
IS HE FEELING POORLY?
YAMA-OKA-SAN...?
I GOT IT...
WILD GRAPES AND WALNUTS...
I'VE DONE IT...
WHAT?
THANK YOU VERY MUCH!!
YOU SAVED ME!!
HUG
MY, MY.
HEY, DON'T PROPOSE TO MY MOTHER LIKE THAT!

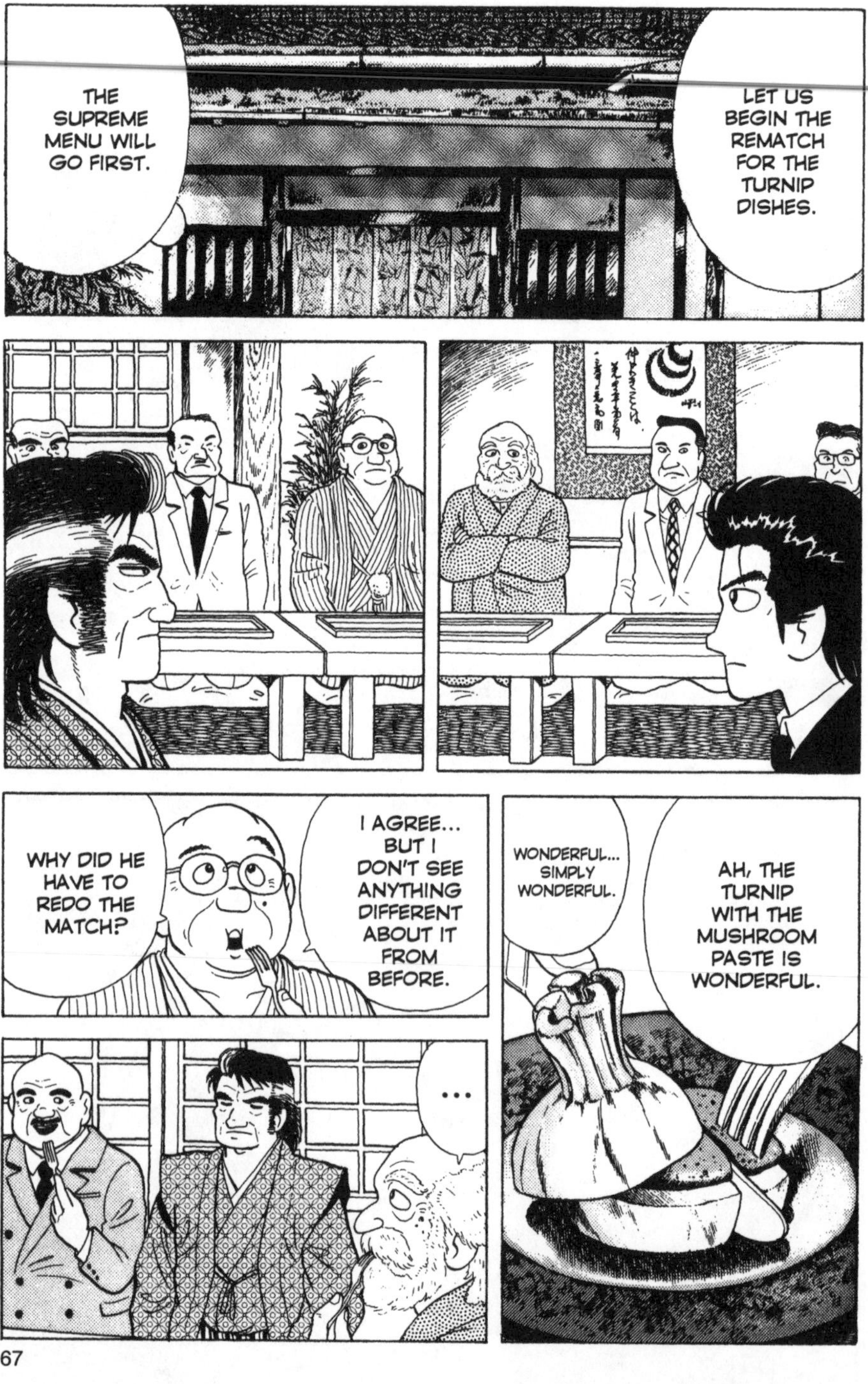
LET US BEGIN THE REMATCH FOR THE TURNIP DISHES.
THE SUPREME MENU WILL GO FIRST.
AH, THE TURNIP WITH THE MUSHROOM PASTE IS WONDERFUL.
WONDERFUL... SIMPLY WONDERFUL.
I AGREE... BUT I DON'T SEE ANYTHING DIFFERENT ABOUT IT FROM BEFORE.
WHY DID HE HAVE TO REDO THE MATCH?
...

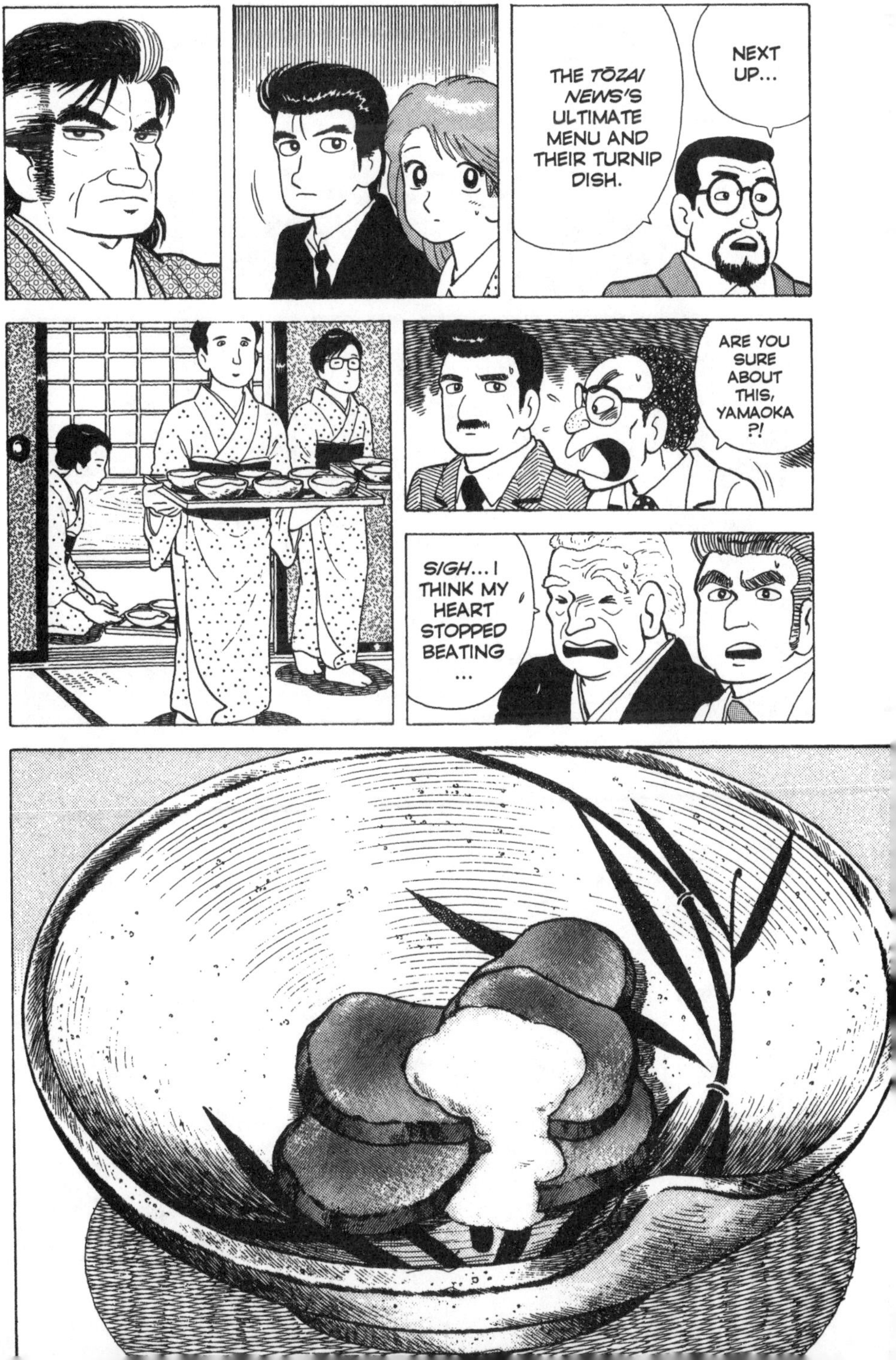
NEXT UP...
THE *TŌZAI NEWS*'S ULTIMATE MENU AND THEIR TURNIP DISH.
ARE YOU SURE ABOUT THIS, YAMAOKA?!
SIGH... I THINK MY HEART STOPPED BEATING...

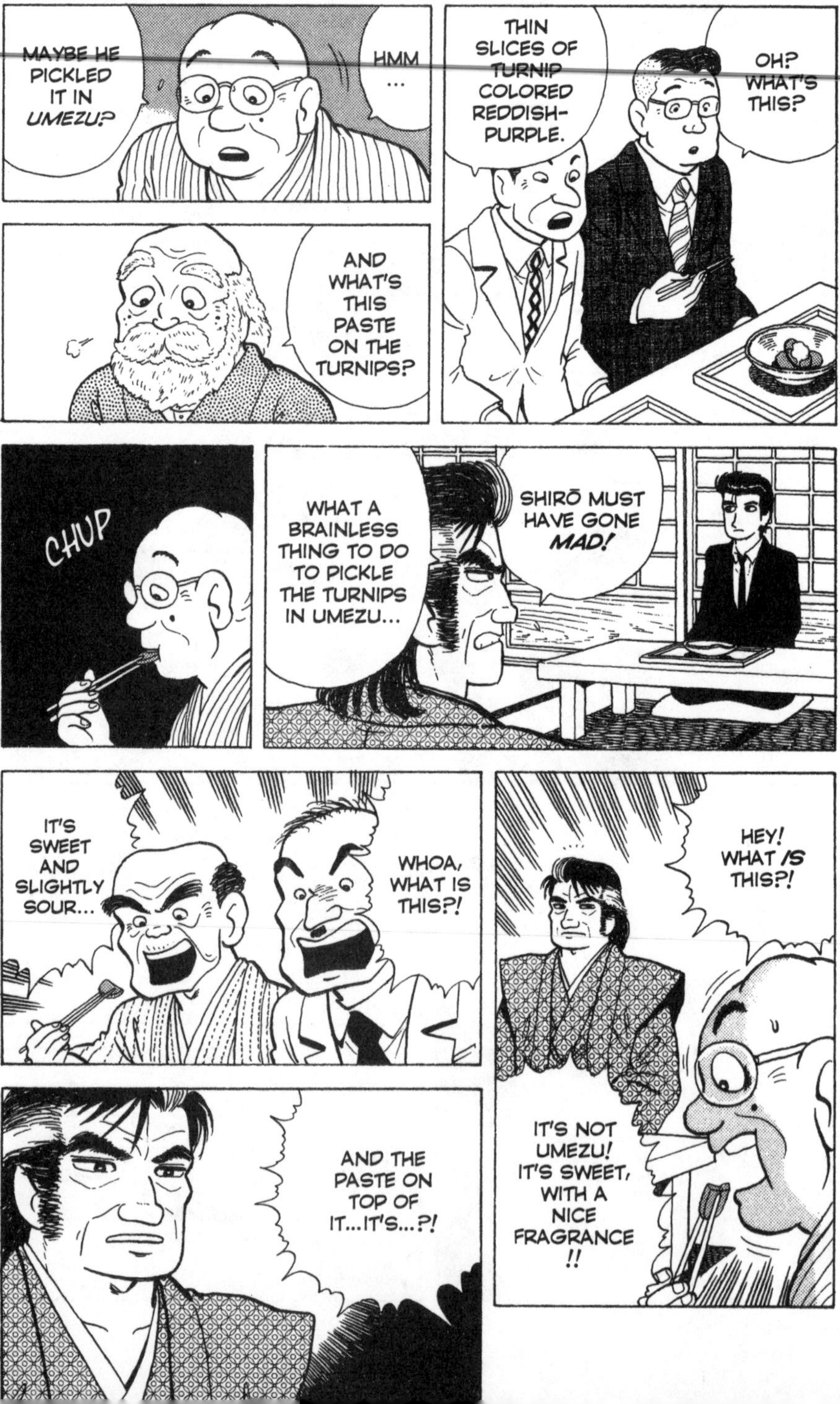
OH? WHAT'S THIS?
THIN SLICES OF TURNIP COLORED REDDISH-PURPLE.
HMM ...
MAYBE HE PICKLED IT IN *UMEZU?*
AND WHAT'S THIS PASTE ON THE TURNIPS?
SHIRŌ MUST HAVE GONE *MAD!*
WHAT A BRAINLESS THING TO DO TO PICKLE THE TURNIPS IN UMEZU...
CHUP
HEY! WHAT *IS* THIS?!
IT'S NOT UMEZU! IT'S SWEET, WITH A NICE FRAGRANCE !!
WHOA, WHAT IS THIS?!
IT'S SWEET AND SLIGHTLY SOUR...
AND THE PASTE ON TOP OF IT...IT'S...?!

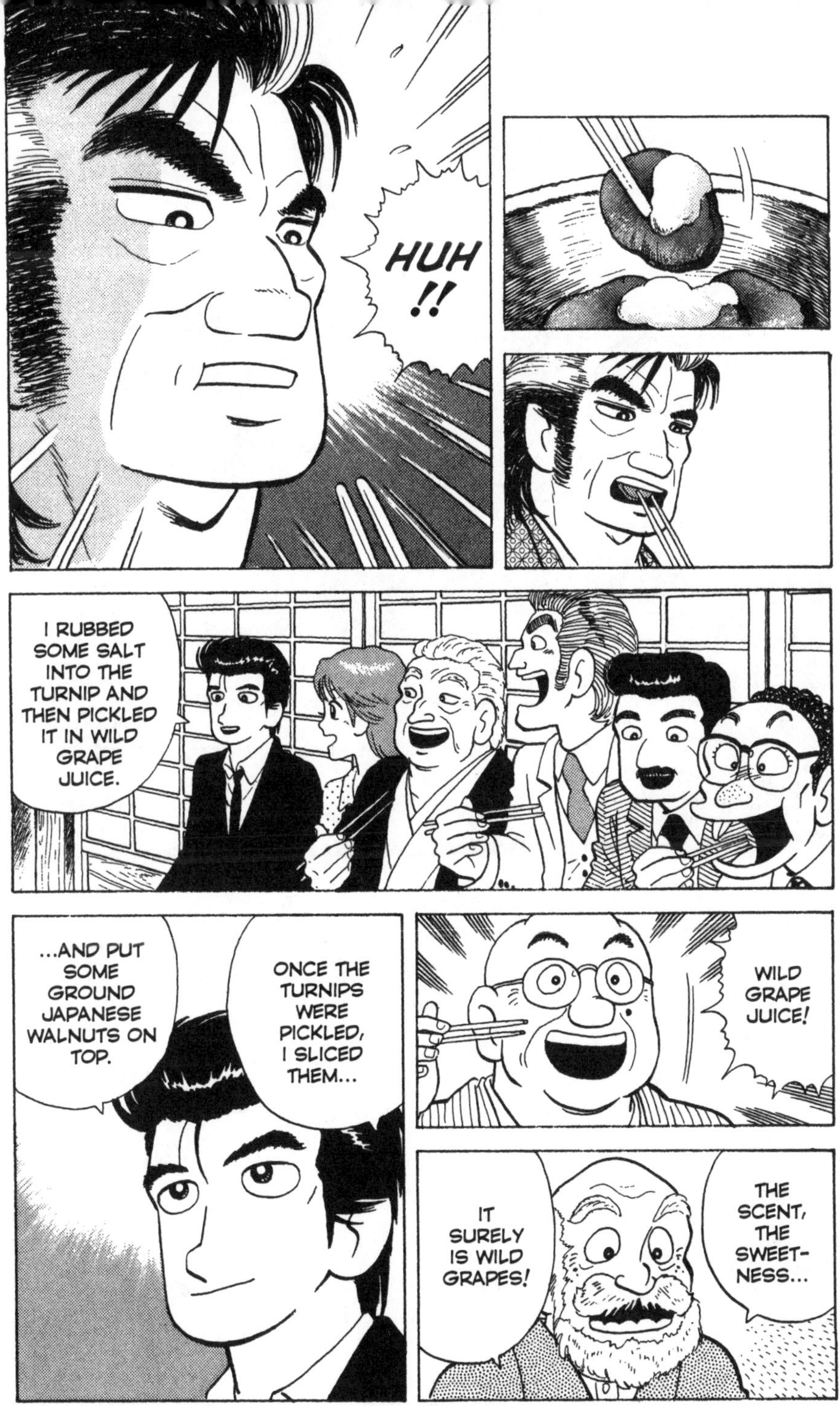
HUH!!
I RUBBED SOME SALT INTO THE TURNIP AND THEN PICKLED IT IN WILD GRAPE JUICE.
WILD GRAPE JUICE!
THE SCENT, THE SWEET-NESS...
IT SURELY IS WILD GRAPES!
ONCE THE TURNIPS WERE PICKLED, I SLICED THEM...
...AND PUT SOME GROUND JAPANESE WALNUTS ON TOP.

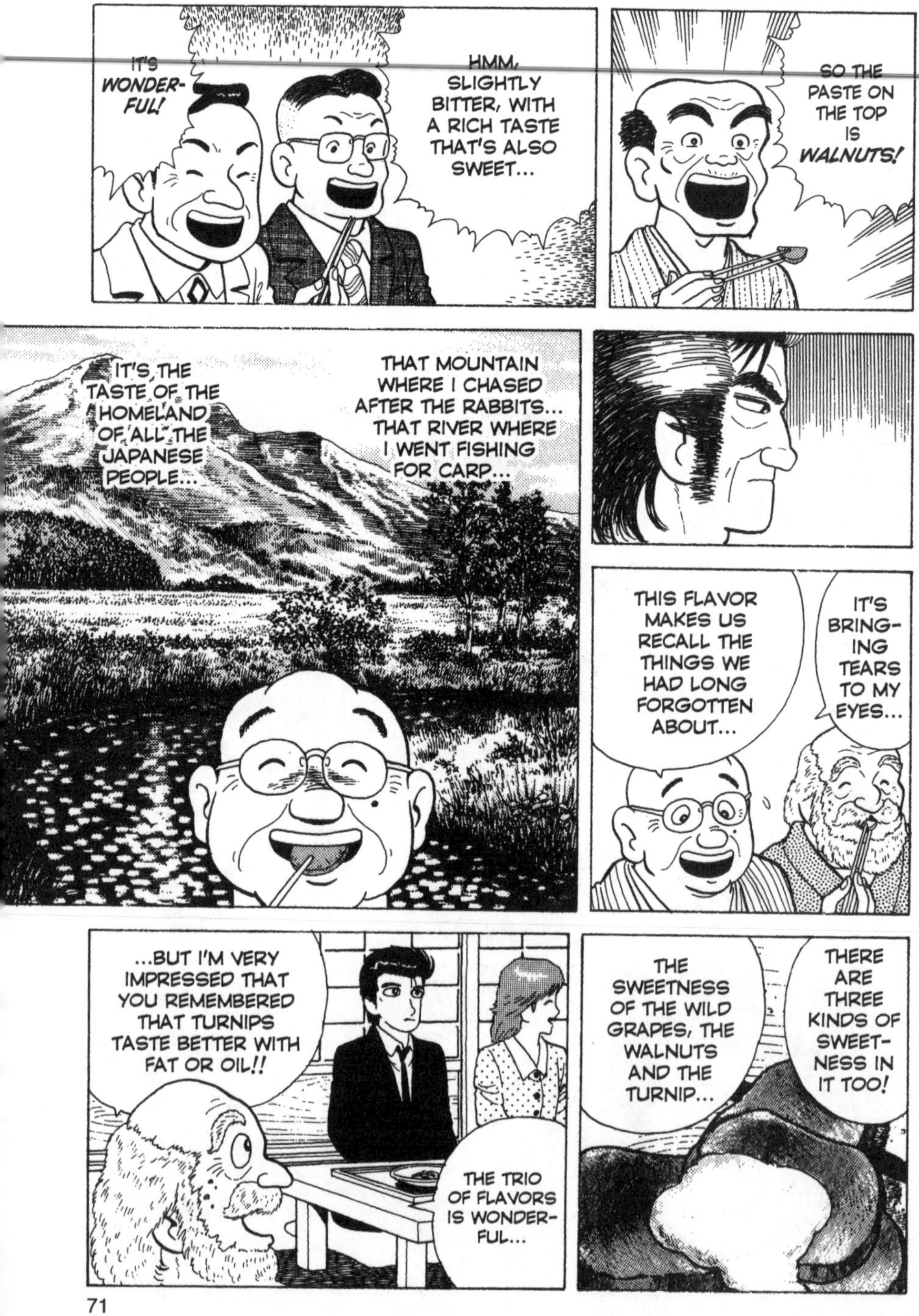
SO THE PASTE ON THE TOP IS *WALNUTS!*
HMM, SLIGHTLY BITTER, WITH A RICH TASTE THAT'S ALSO SWEET...
IT'S *WONDERFUL!*
IT'S BRINGING TEARS TO MY EYES...
THIS FLAVOR MAKES US RECALL THE THINGS WE HAD LONG FORGOTTEN ABOUT...
THAT MOUNTAIN WHERE I CHASED AFTER THE RABBITS... THAT RIVER WHERE I WENT FISHING FOR CARP...
IT'S THE TASTE OF THE HOMELAND OF ALL THE JAPANESE PEOPLE...
THERE ARE THREE KINDS OF SWEETNESS IN IT TOO!
THE SWEETNESS OF THE WILD GRAPES, THE WALNUTS AND THE TURNIP...
THE TRIO OF FLAVORS IS WONDERFUL...
...BUT I'M VERY IMPRESSED THAT YOU REMEMBERED THAT TURNIPS TASTE BETTER WITH FAT OR OIL!!

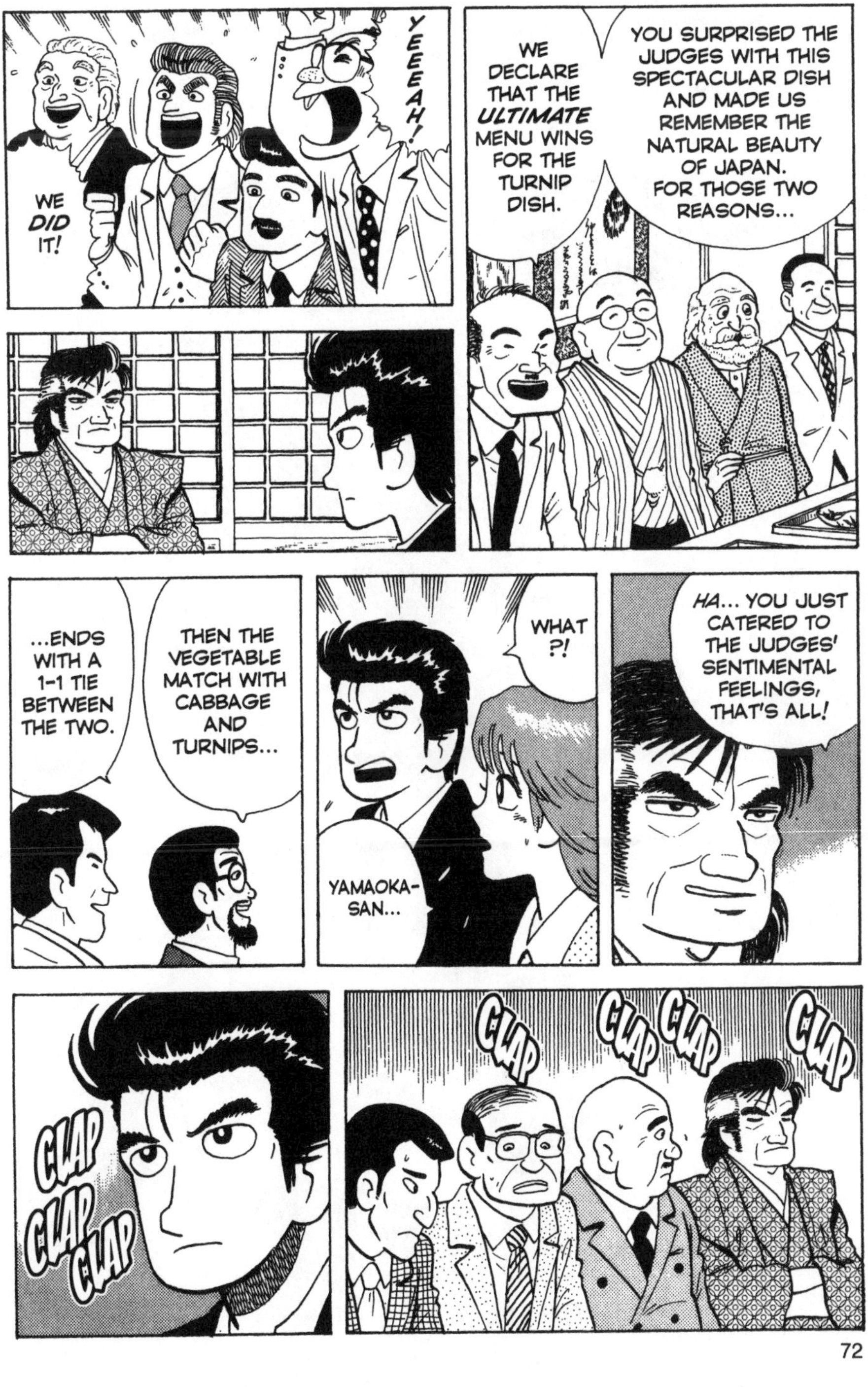
YOU SURPRISED THE JUDGES WITH THIS SPECTACULAR DISH AND MADE US REMEMBER THE NATURAL BEAUTY OF JAPAN. FOR THOSE TWO REASONS...
WE DECLARE THAT THE *ULTIMATE* MENU WINS FOR THE TURNIP DISH.
YEEEEAH!
WE *DID* IT!
HA... YOU JUST CATERED TO THE JUDGES' SENTIMENTAL FEELINGS, THAT'S ALL!
WHAT ?!
YAMAOKA-SAN...
THEN THE VEGETABLE MATCH WITH CABBAGE AND TURNIPS...
...ENDS WITH A 1-1 TIE BETWEEN THE TWO.
CLAP
CLAP
CLAP
CLAP
CLAP
CLAP
CLAP

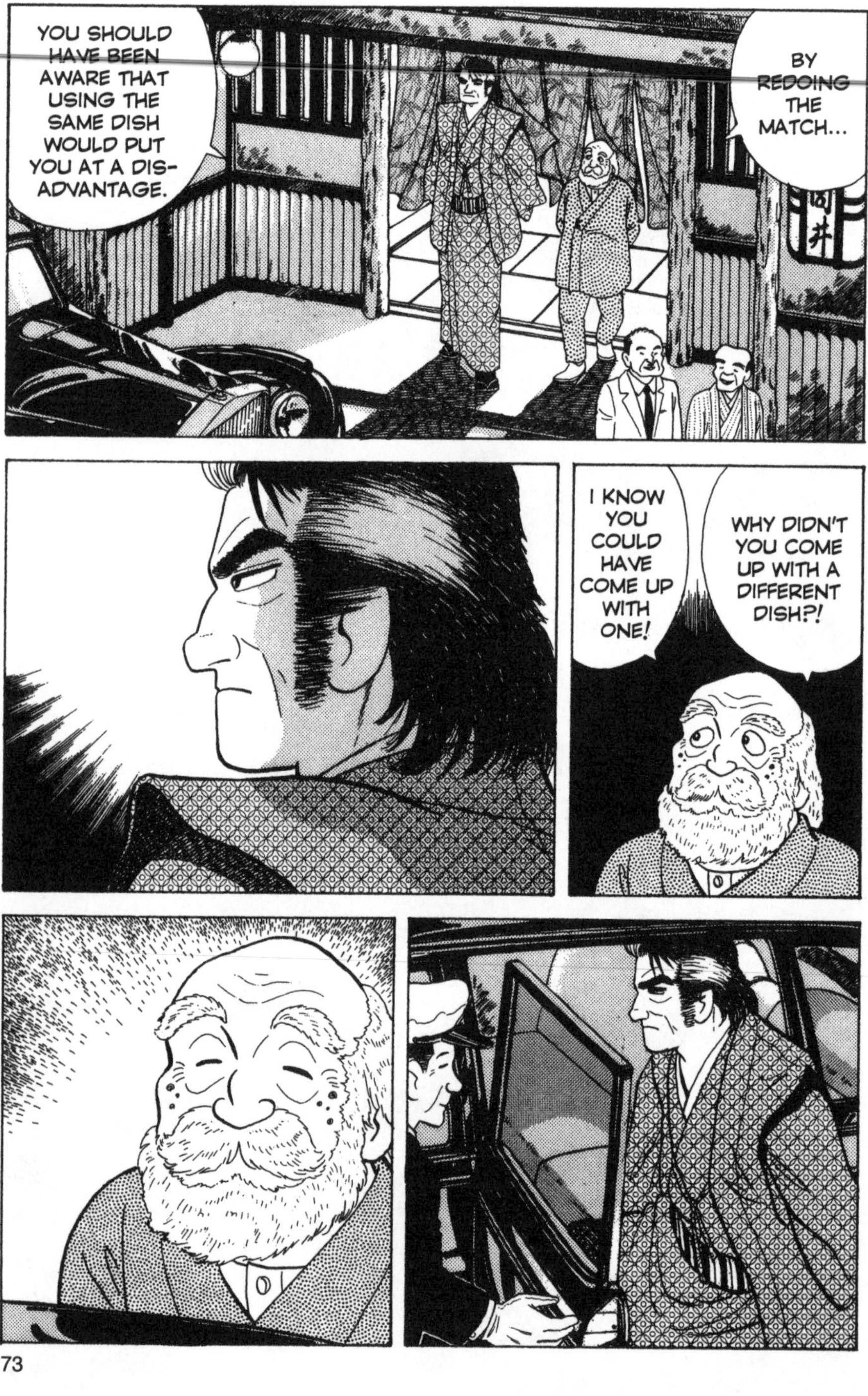
BY REDOING THE MATCH...
YOU SHOULD HAVE BEEN AWARE THAT USING THE SAME DISH WOULD PUT YOU AT A DIS-ADVANTAGE.
WHY DIDN'T YOU COME UP WITH A DIFFERENT DISH?!
I KNOW YOU COULD HAVE COME UP WITH ONE!

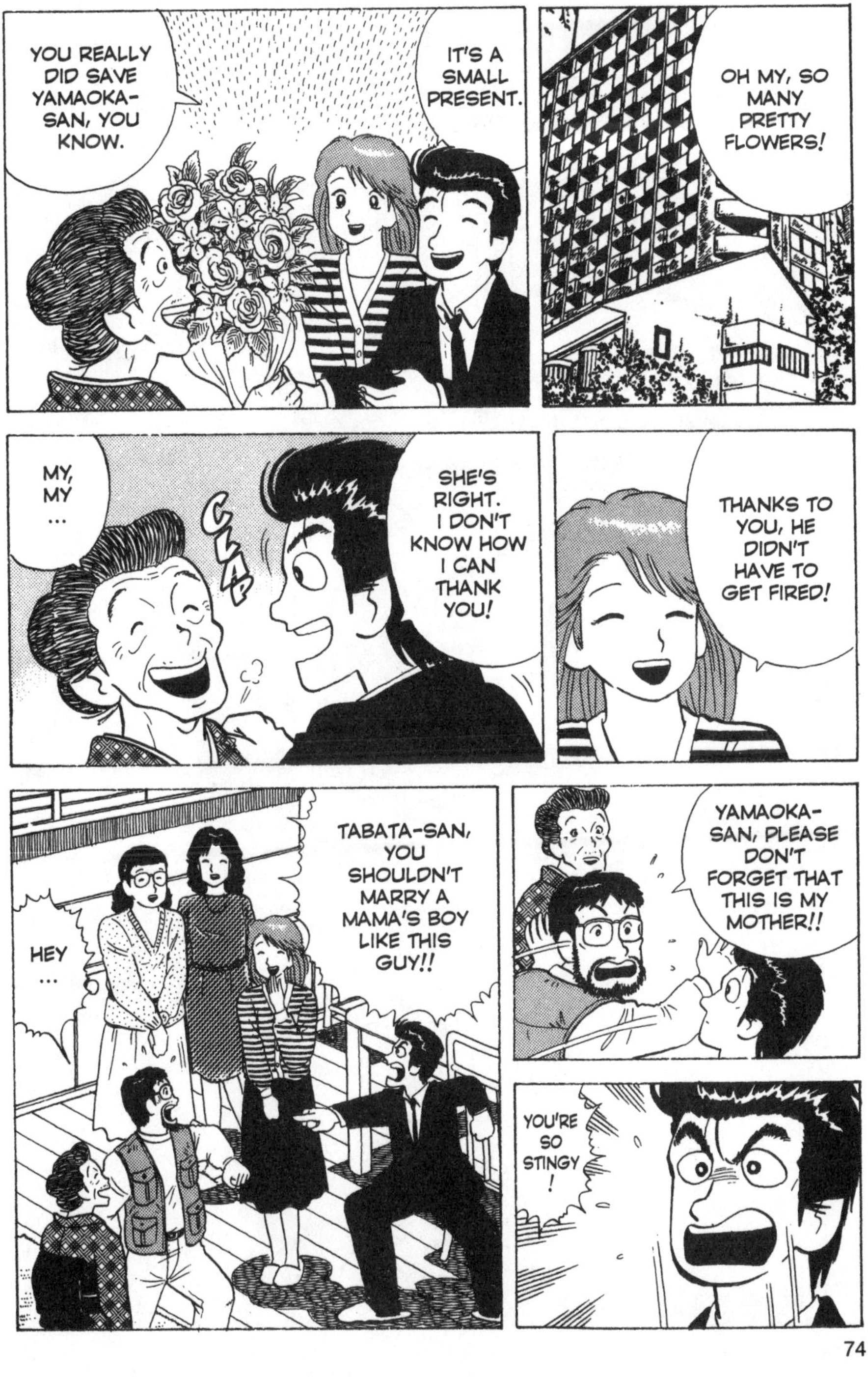
OH MY, SO MANY PRETTY FLOWERS!
IT'S A SMALL PRESENT.
YOU REALLY DID SAVE YAMAOKA-SAN, YOU KNOW.
THANKS TO YOU, HE DIDN'T HAVE TO GET FIRED!
SHE'S RIGHT. I DON'T KNOW HOW I CAN THANK YOU!
CLAP
MY, MY ...
YAMAOKA-SAN, PLEASE DON'T FORGET THAT THIS IS MY MOTHER!!
YOU'RE SO STINGY!
TABATA-SAN, YOU SHOULDN'T MARRY A MAMA'S BOY LIKE THIS GUY!!
HEY ...

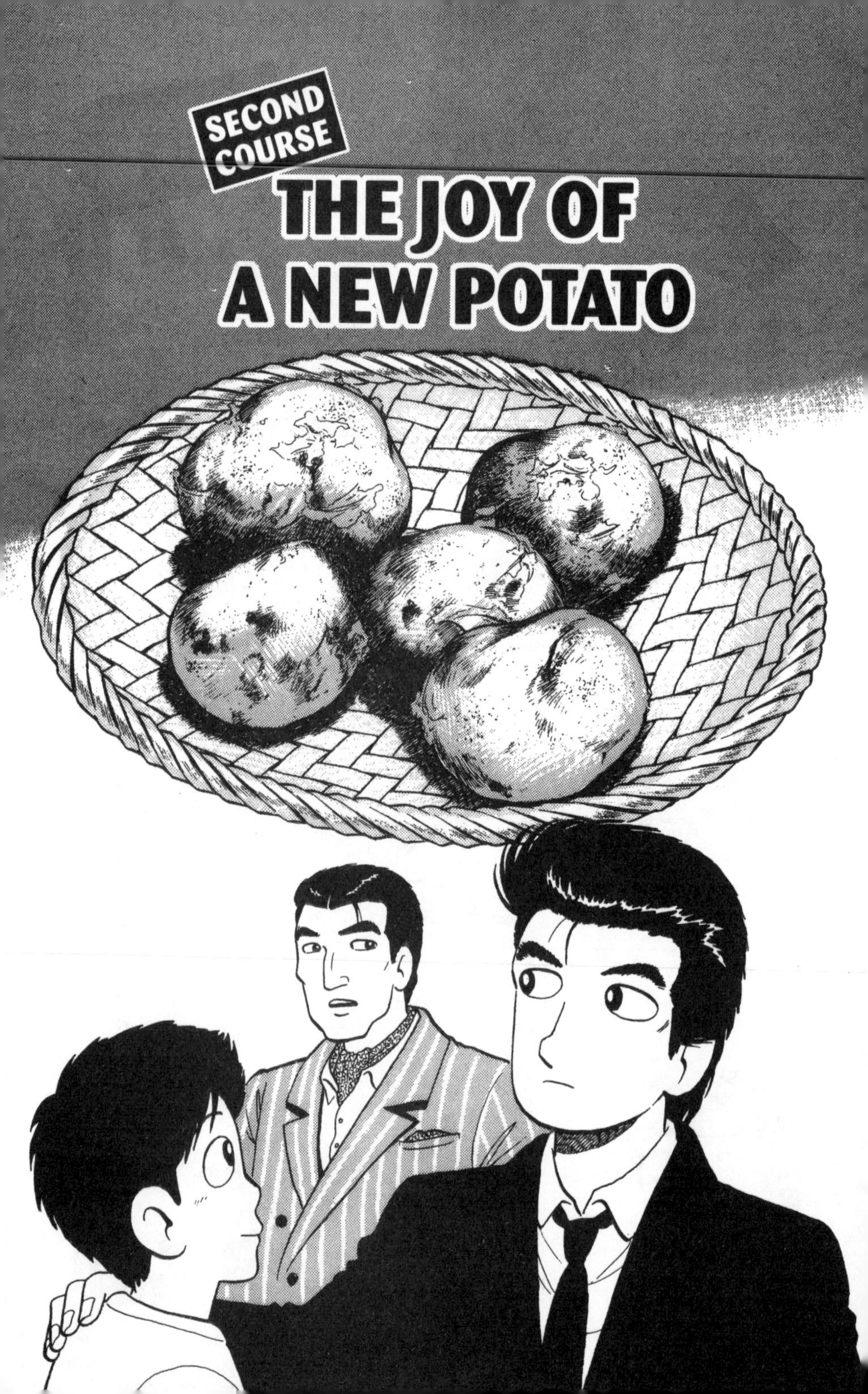
SECOND COURSE
THE JOY OF A NEW POTATO

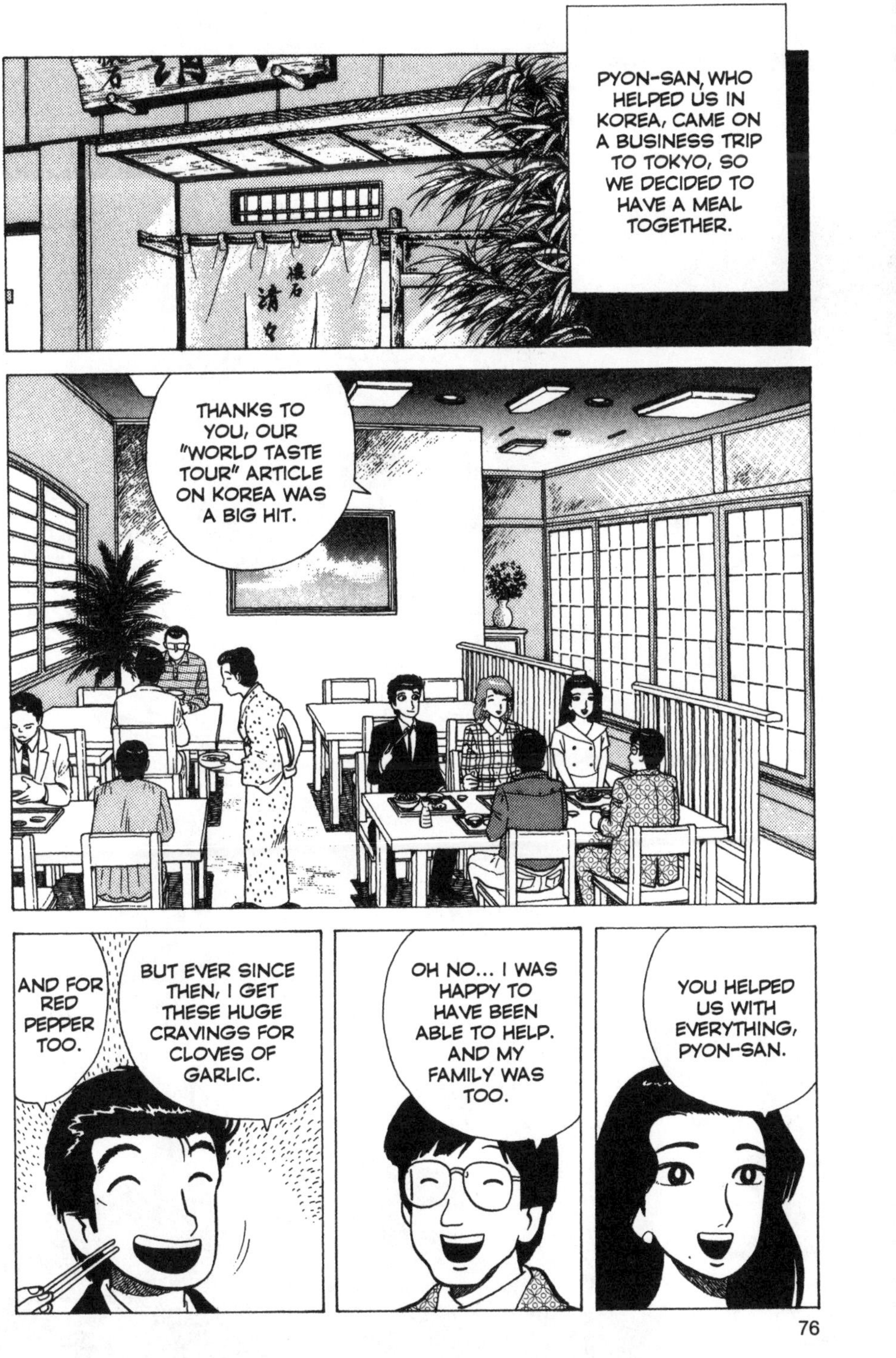
PYON-SAN, WHO HELPED US IN KOREA, CAME ON A BUSINESS TRIP TO TOKYO, SO WE DECIDED TO HAVE A MEAL TOGETHER.
THANKS TO YOU, OUR "WORLD TASTE TOUR" ARTICLE ON KOREA WAS A BIG HIT.
YOU HELPED US WITH EVERYTHING, PYON-SAN.
OH NO... I WAS HAPPY TO HAVE BEEN ABLE TO HELP. AND MY FAMILY WAS TOO.
BUT EVER SINCE THEN, I GET THESE HUGE CRAVINGS FOR CLOVES OF GARLIC.
AND FOR RED PEPPER TOO.

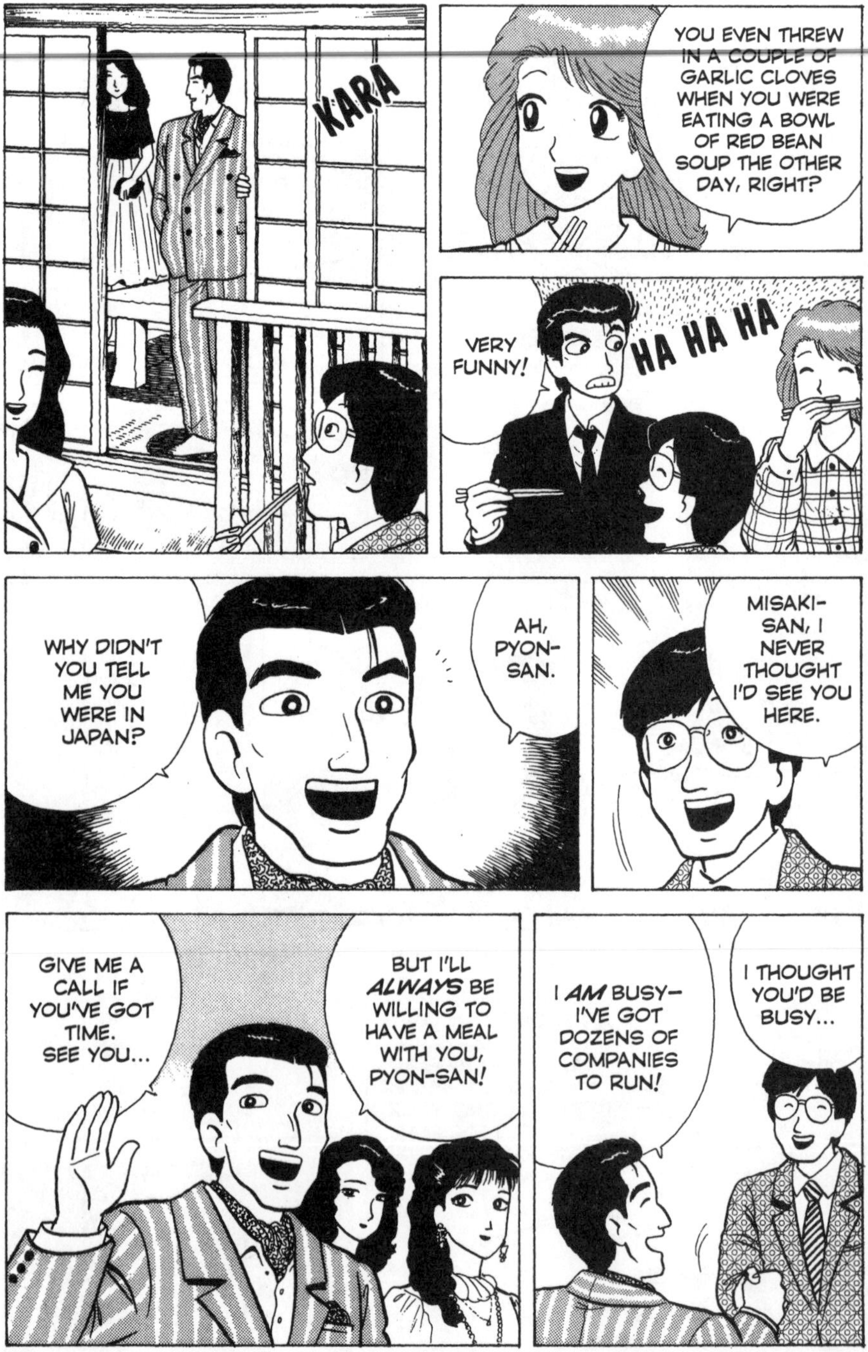
YOU EVEN THREW IN A COUPLE OF GARLIC CLOVES WHEN YOU WERE EATING A BOWL OF RED BEAN SOUP THE OTHER DAY, RIGHT?
HA HA HA
VERY FUNNY!
KARA
MISAKI-SAN, I NEVER THOUGHT I'D SEE YOU HERE.
AH, PYON-SAN.
WHY DIDN'T YOU TELL ME YOU WERE IN JAPAN?
I THOUGHT YOU'D BE BUSY...
I *AM* BUSY— I'VE GOT DOZENS OF COMPANIES TO RUN!
BUT I'LL *ALWAYS* BE WILLING TO HAVE A MEAL WITH YOU, PYON-SAN!
GIVE ME A CALL IF YOU'VE GOT TIME. SEE YOU...

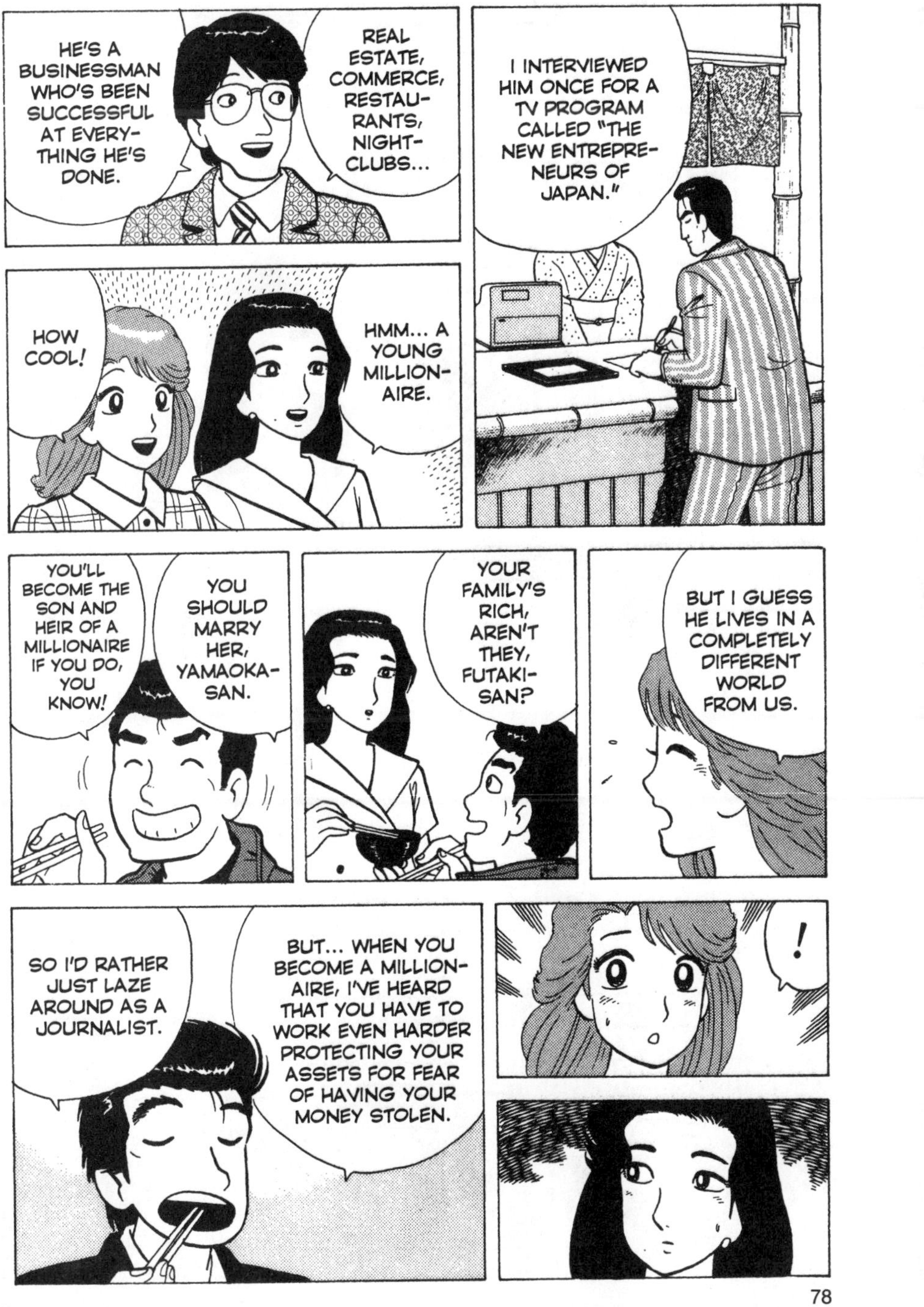
I INTERVIEWED HIM ONCE FOR A TV PROGRAM CALLED "THE NEW ENTREPRENEURS OF JAPAN."
REAL ESTATE, COMMERCE, RESTAURANTS, NIGHTCLUBS...
HE'S A BUSINESSMAN WHO'S BEEN SUCCESSFUL AT EVERYTHING HE'S DONE.
HMM... A YOUNG MILLIONAIRE.
HOW COOL!
BUT I GUESS HE LIVES IN A COMPLETELY DIFFERENT WORLD FROM US.
YOUR FAMILY'S RICH, AREN'T THEY, FUTAKI-SAN?
YOU SHOULD MARRY HER, YAMAOKA-SAN.
YOU'LL BECOME THE SON AND HEIR OF A MILLIONAIRE IF YOU DO, YOU KNOW!
!
BUT... WHEN YOU BECOME A MILLIONAIRE, I'VE HEARD THAT YOU HAVE TO WORK EVEN HARDER PROTECTING YOUR ASSETS FOR FEAR OF HAVING YOUR MONEY STOLEN.
SO I'D RATHER JUST LAZE AROUND AS A JOURNALIST.

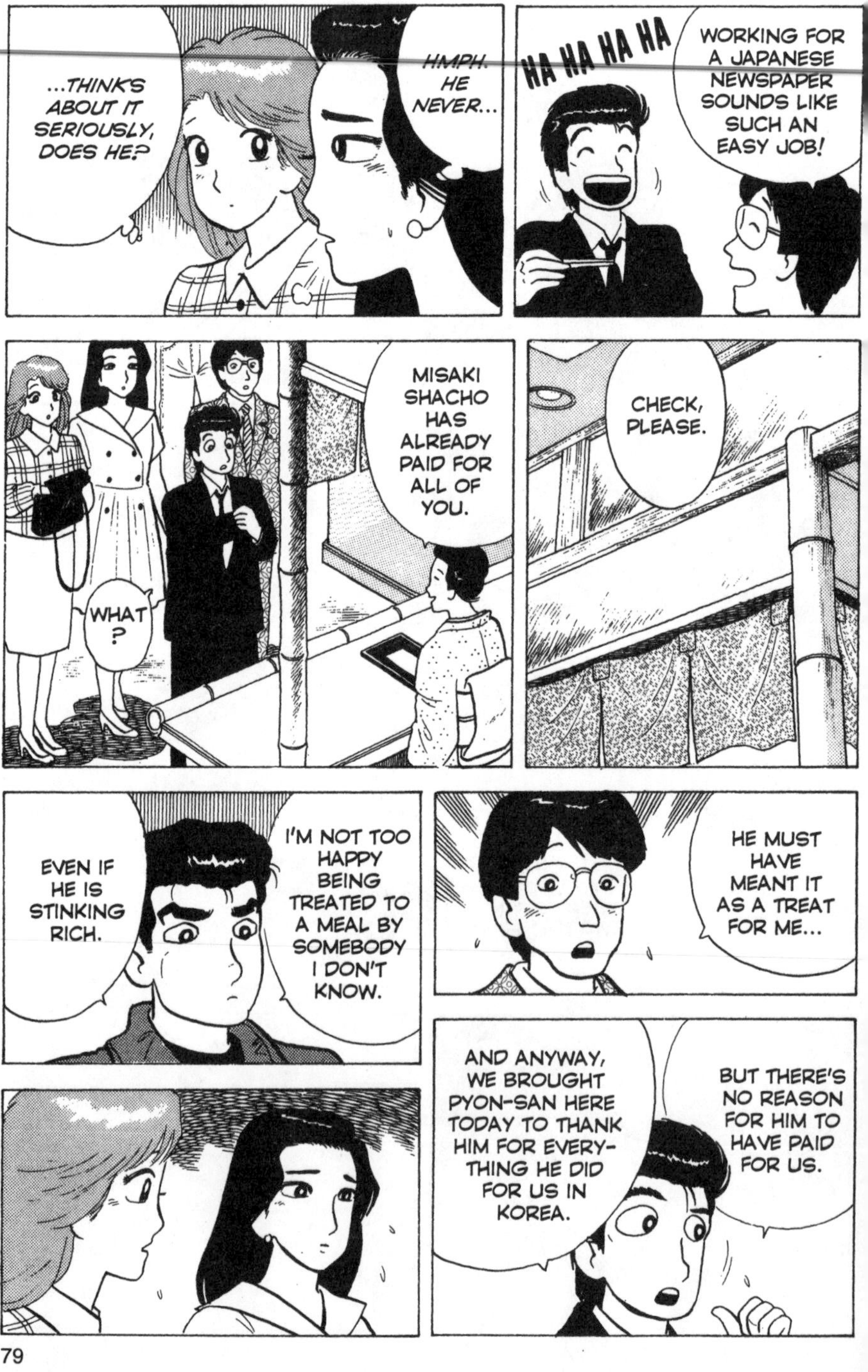
WORKING FOR A JAPANESE NEWSPAPER SOUNDS LIKE SUCH AN EASY JOB!
HA HA HA HA
HMPH. HE NEVER...
...THINKS ABOUT IT SERIOUSLY, DOES HE?
CHECK, PLEASE.
MISAKI SHACHO HAS ALREADY PAID FOR ALL OF YOU.
WHAT?
HE MUST HAVE MEANT IT AS A TREAT FOR ME...
I'M NOT TOO HAPPY BEING TREATED TO A MEAL BY SOMEBODY I DON'T KNOW.
EVEN IF HE IS STINKING RICH.
BUT THERE'S NO REASON FOR HIM TO HAVE PAID FOR US.
AND ANYWAY, WE BROUGHT PYON-SAN HERE TODAY TO THANK HIM FOR EVERYTHING HE DID FOR US IN KOREA.

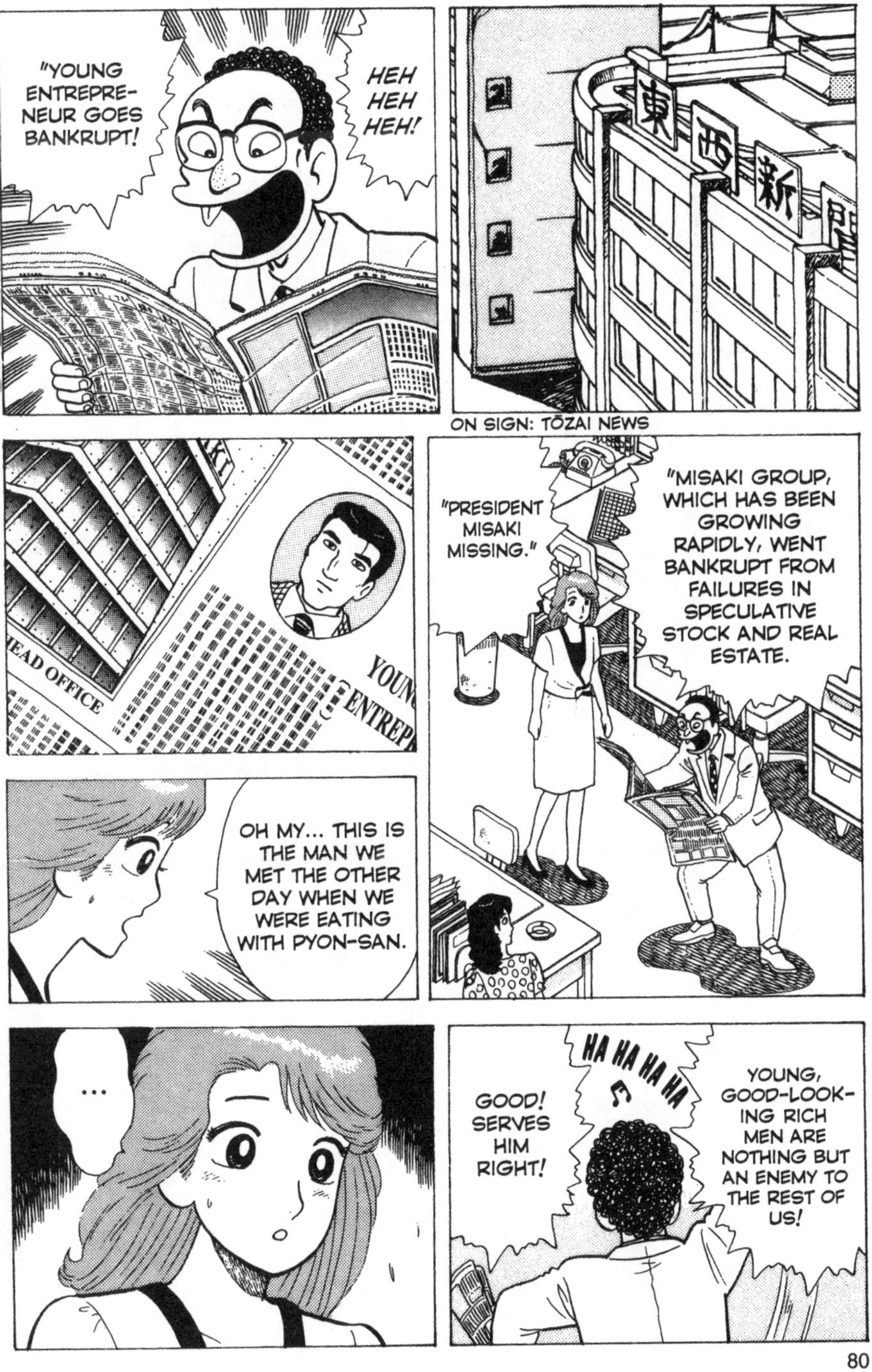
ON SIGN: TŌZAI NEWS
"YOUNG ENTREPRE-NEUR GOES BANKRUPT!
HEH HEH HEH!
"MISAKI GROUP, WHICH HAS BEEN GROWING RAPIDLY, WENT BANKRUPT FROM FAILURES IN SPECULATIVE STOCK AND REAL ESTATE.
"PRESIDENT MISAKI MISSING."
OH MY... THIS IS THE MAN WE MET THE OTHER DAY WHEN WE WERE EATING WITH PYON-SAN.
HA HA HA HA
YOUNG, GOOD-LOOKING RICH MEN ARE NOTHING BUT AN ENEMY TO THE REST OF US!
GOOD! SERVES HIM RIGHT!
...

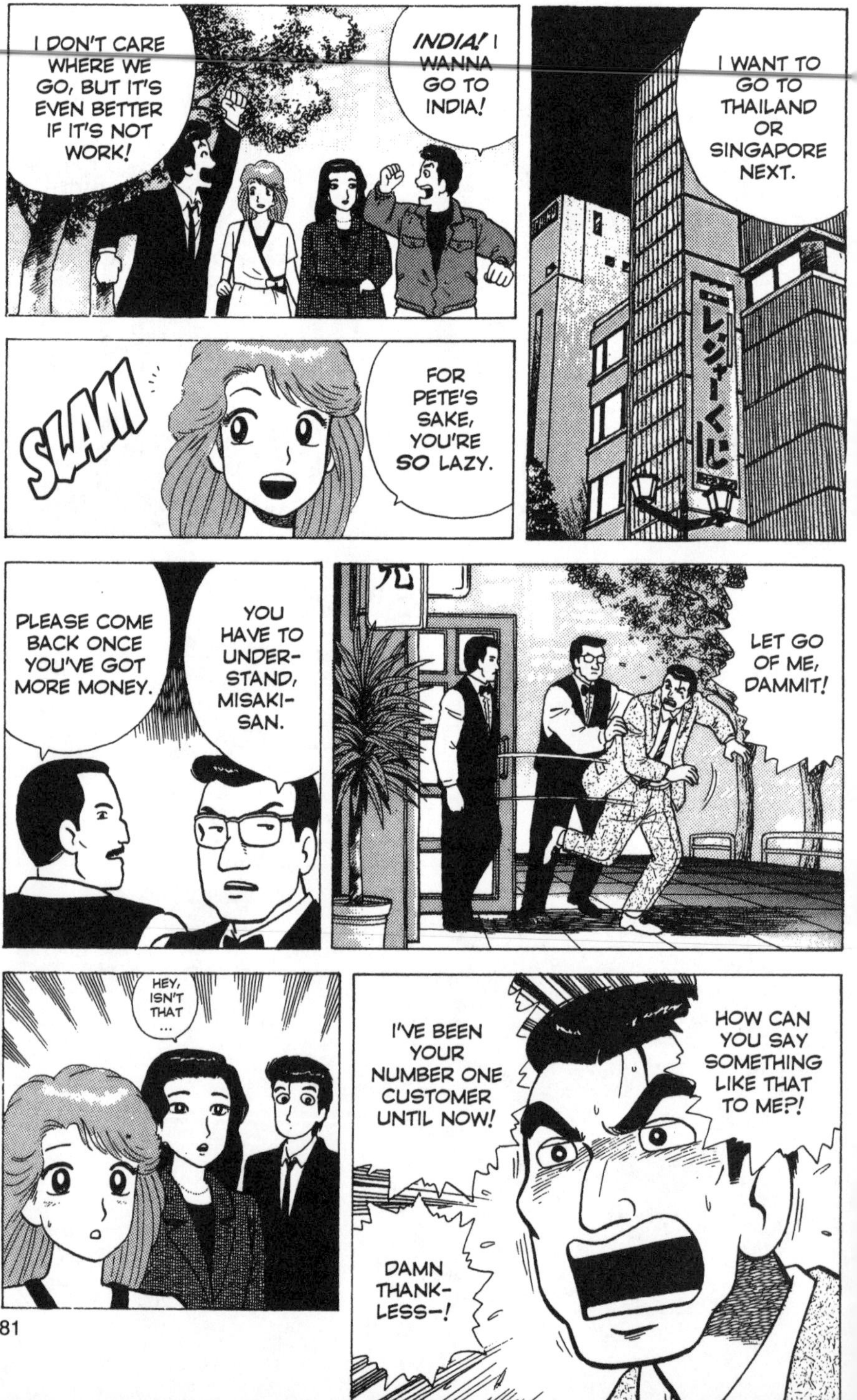
I WANT TO GO TO THAILAND OR SINGAPORE NEXT.
レジャーくじ
INDIA! I WANNA GO TO INDIA!
I DON'T CARE WHERE WE GO, BUT IT'S EVEN BETTER IF IT'S NOT WORK!
FOR PETE'S SAKE, YOU'RE SO LAZY.
SLAM
LET GO OF ME, DAMMIT!
YOU HAVE TO UNDERSTAND, MISAKI-SAN.
PLEASE COME BACK ONCE YOU'VE GOT MORE MONEY.
HOW CAN YOU SAY SOMETHING LIKE THAT TO ME?!
I'VE BEEN YOUR NUMBER ONE CUSTOMER UNTIL NOW!
DAMN THANKLESS—!
HEY, ISN'T THAT ...

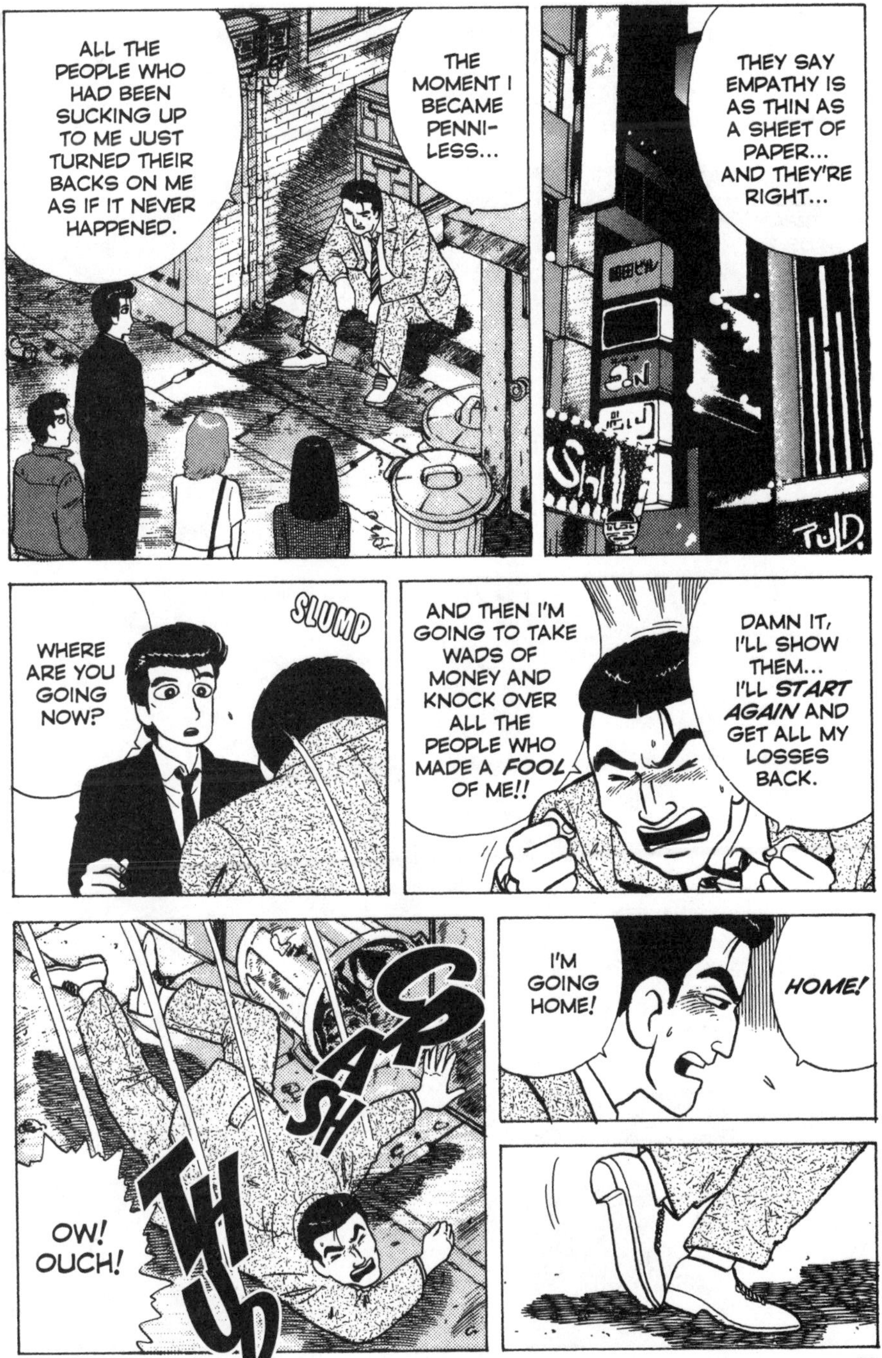
THEY SAY EMPATHY IS AS THIN AS A SHEET OF PAPER... AND THEY'RE RIGHT...
THE MOMENT I BECAME PENNI- LESS...
ALL THE PEOPLE WHO HAD BEEN SUCKING UP TO ME JUST TURNED THEIR BACKS ON ME AS IF IT NEVER HAPPENED.
DAMN IT, I'LL SHOW THEM... I'LL *START AGAIN* AND GET ALL MY LOSSES BACK.
AND THEN I'M GOING TO TAKE WADS OF MONEY AND KNOCK OVER ALL THE PEOPLE WHO MADE A *FOOL* OF ME!!
SLUMP
WHERE ARE YOU GOING NOW?
I'M GOING HOME!
HOME!
CRASH
THUD
OW! OUCH!

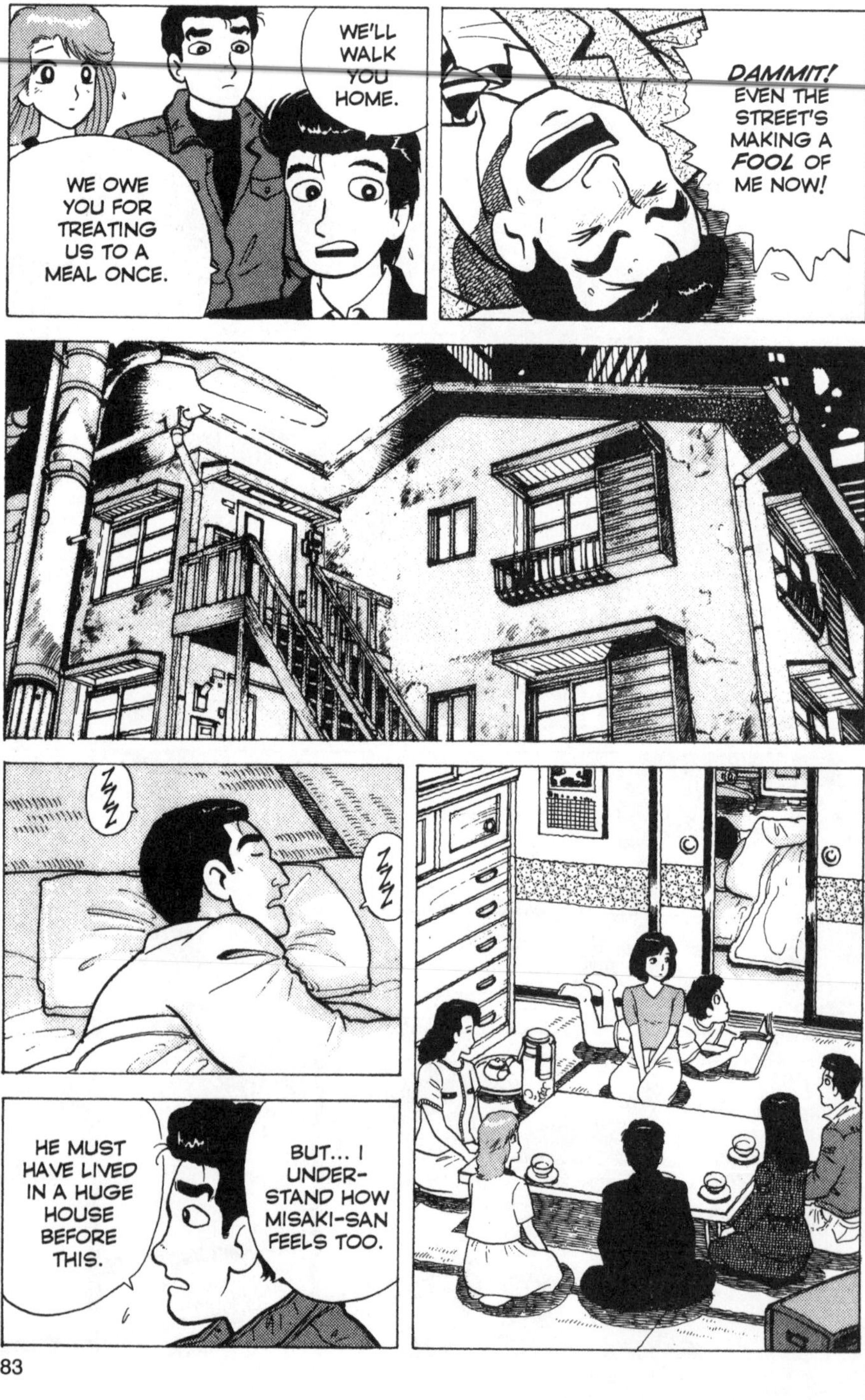
DAMMIT! EVEN THE STREET'S MAKING A FOOL OF ME NOW!
WE'LL WALK YOU HOME.
WE OWE YOU FOR TREATING US TO A MEAL ONCE.
ZZZ
ZZZ
BUT... I UNDER-STAND HOW MISAKI-SAN FEELS TOO.
HE MUST HAVE LIVED IN A HUGE HOUSE BEFORE THIS.

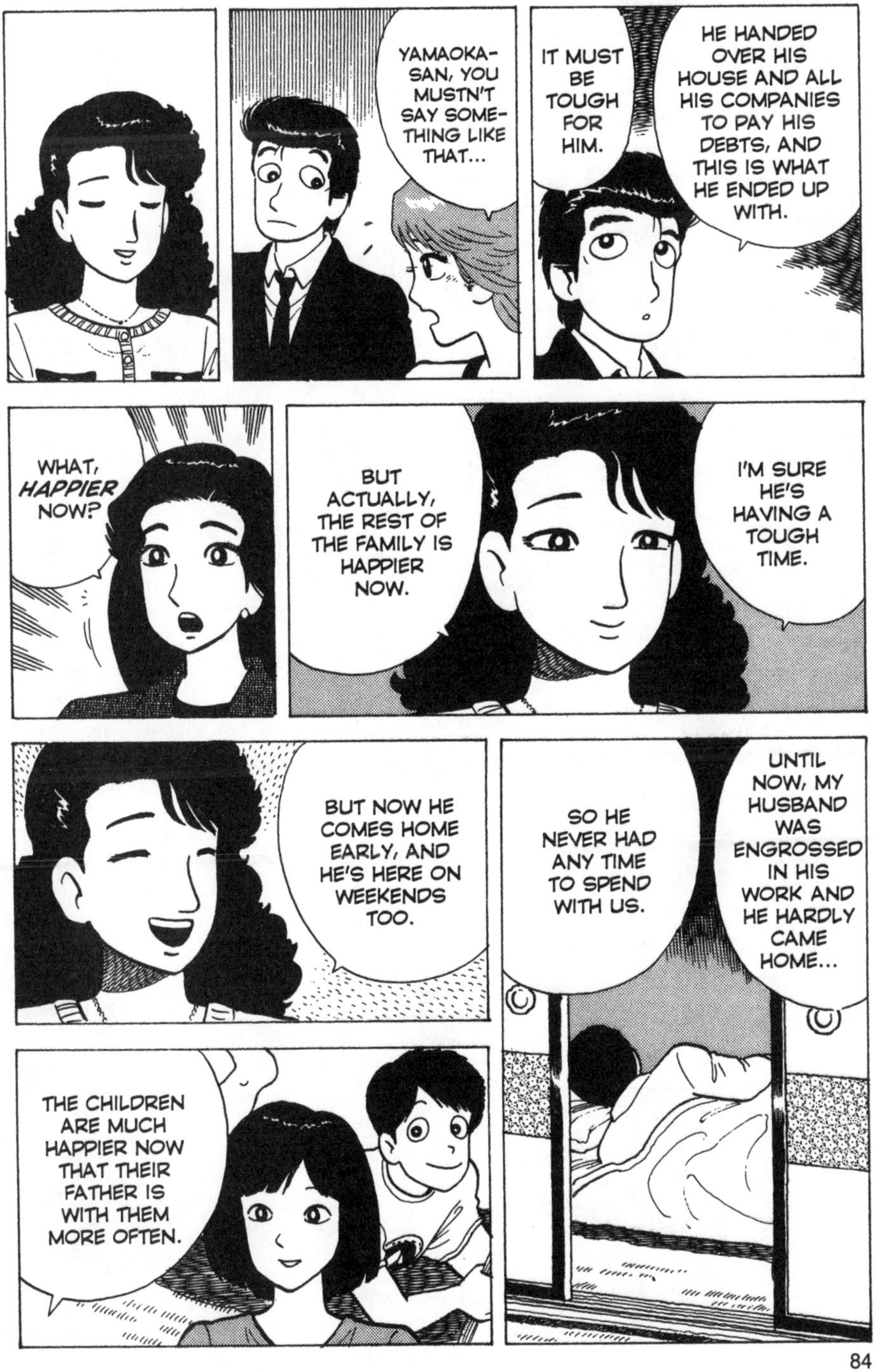
HE HANDED OVER HIS HOUSE AND ALL HIS COMPANIES TO PAY HIS DEBTS, AND THIS IS WHAT HE ENDED UP WITH.
IT MUST BE TOUGH FOR HIM.
YAMAOKA-SAN, YOU MUSTN'T SAY SOMETHING LIKE THAT...
I'M SURE HE'S HAVING A TOUGH TIME.
BUT ACTUALLY, THE REST OF THE FAMILY IS HAPPIER NOW.
WHAT, *HAPPIER* NOW?
UNTIL NOW, MY HUSBAND WAS ENGROSSED IN HIS WORK AND HE HARDLY CAME HOME...
SO HE NEVER HAD ANY TIME TO SPEND WITH US.
BUT NOW HE COMES HOME EARLY, AND HE'S HERE ON WEEKENDS TOO.
THE CHILDREN ARE MUCH HAPPIER NOW THAT THEIR FATHER IS WITH THEM MORE OFTEN.

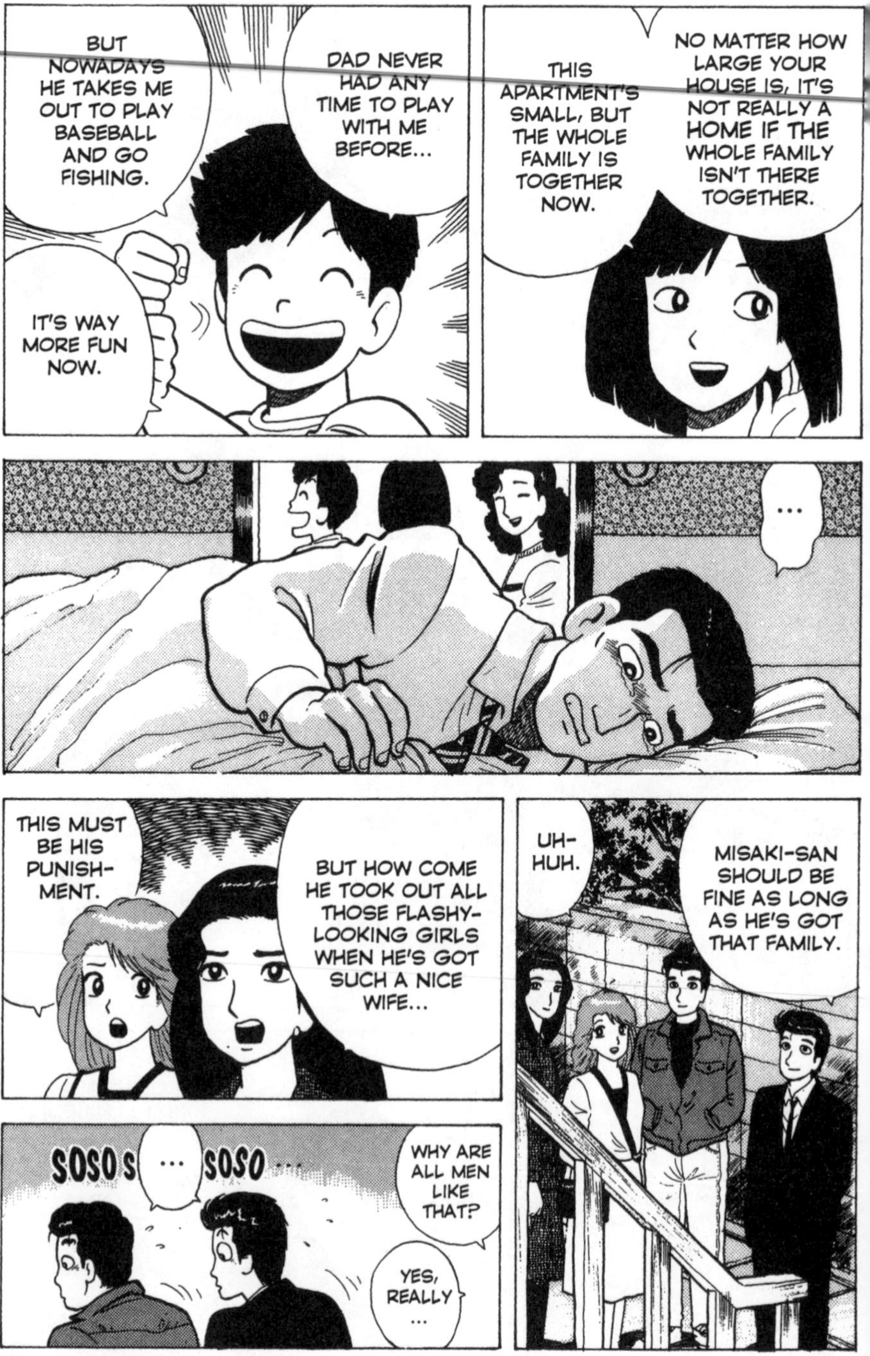
NO MATTER HOW LARGE YOUR HOUSE IS, IT'S NOT REALLY A HOME IF THE WHOLE FAMILY ISN'T THERE TOGETHER.
THIS APARTMENT'S SMALL, BUT THE WHOLE FAMILY IS TOGETHER NOW.
DAD NEVER HAD ANY TIME TO PLAY WITH ME BEFORE...
BUT NOWADAYS HE TAKES ME OUT TO PLAY BASEBALL AND GO FISHING.
IT'S WAY MORE FUN NOW.
...
MISAKI-SAN SHOULD BE FINE AS LONG AS HE'S GOT THAT FAMILY.
UH-HUH.
BUT HOW COME HE TOOK OUT ALL THOSE FLASHY-LOOKING GIRLS WHEN HE'S GOT SUCH A NICE WIFE...
THIS MUST BE HIS PUNISHMENT.
WHY ARE ALL MEN LIKE THAT?
YES, REALLY...
SOSO s
...
SOSO ...

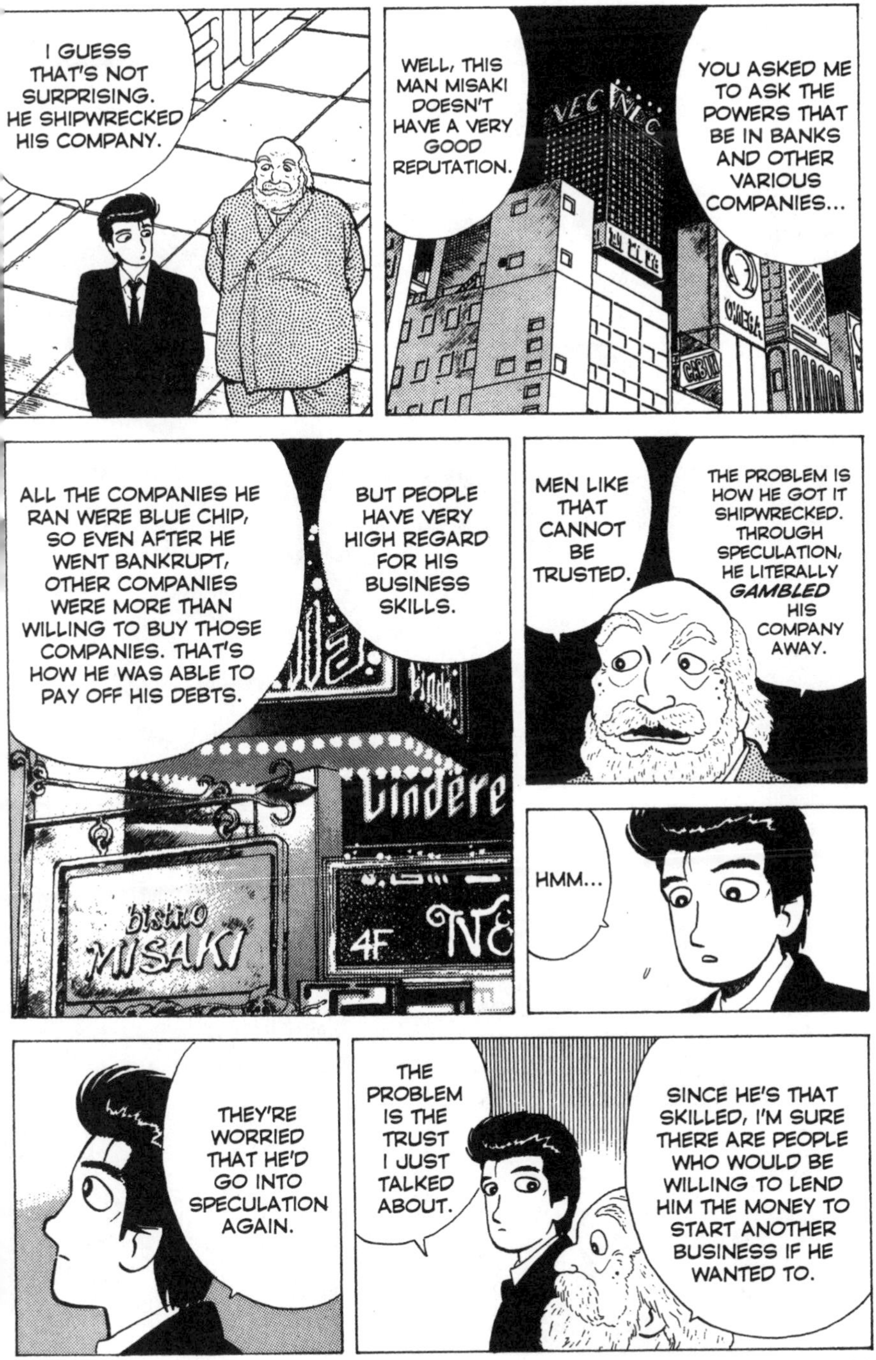
YOU ASKED ME TO ASK THE POWERS THAT BE IN BANKS AND OTHER VARIOUS COMPANIES...
WELL, THIS MAN MISAKI DOESN'T HAVE A VERY GOOD REPUTATION.
OMEGA
I GUESS THAT'S NOT SURPRISING. HE SHIPWRECKED HIS COMPANY.
THE PROBLEM IS HOW HE GOT IT SHIPWRECKED. THROUGH SPECULATION, HE LITERALLY ***GAMBLED*** HIS COMPANY AWAY.
MEN LIKE THAT CANNOT BE TRUSTED.
HMM...
BUT PEOPLE HAVE VERY HIGH REGARD FOR HIS BUSINESS SKILLS.
ALL THE COMPANIES HE RAN WERE BLUE CHIP, SO EVEN AFTER HE WENT BANKRUPT, OTHER COMPANIES WERE MORE THAN WILLING TO BUY THOSE COMPANIES. THAT'S HOW HE WAS ABLE TO PAY OFF HIS DEBTS.
bistro MISAKI
4F
SINCE HE'S THAT SKILLED, I'M SURE THERE ARE PEOPLE WHO WOULD BE WILLING TO LEND HIM THE MONEY TO START ANOTHER BUSINESS IF HE WANTED TO.
THE PROBLEM IS THE TRUST I JUST TALKED ABOUT.
THEY'RE WORRIED THAT HE'D GO INTO SPECULATION AGAIN.

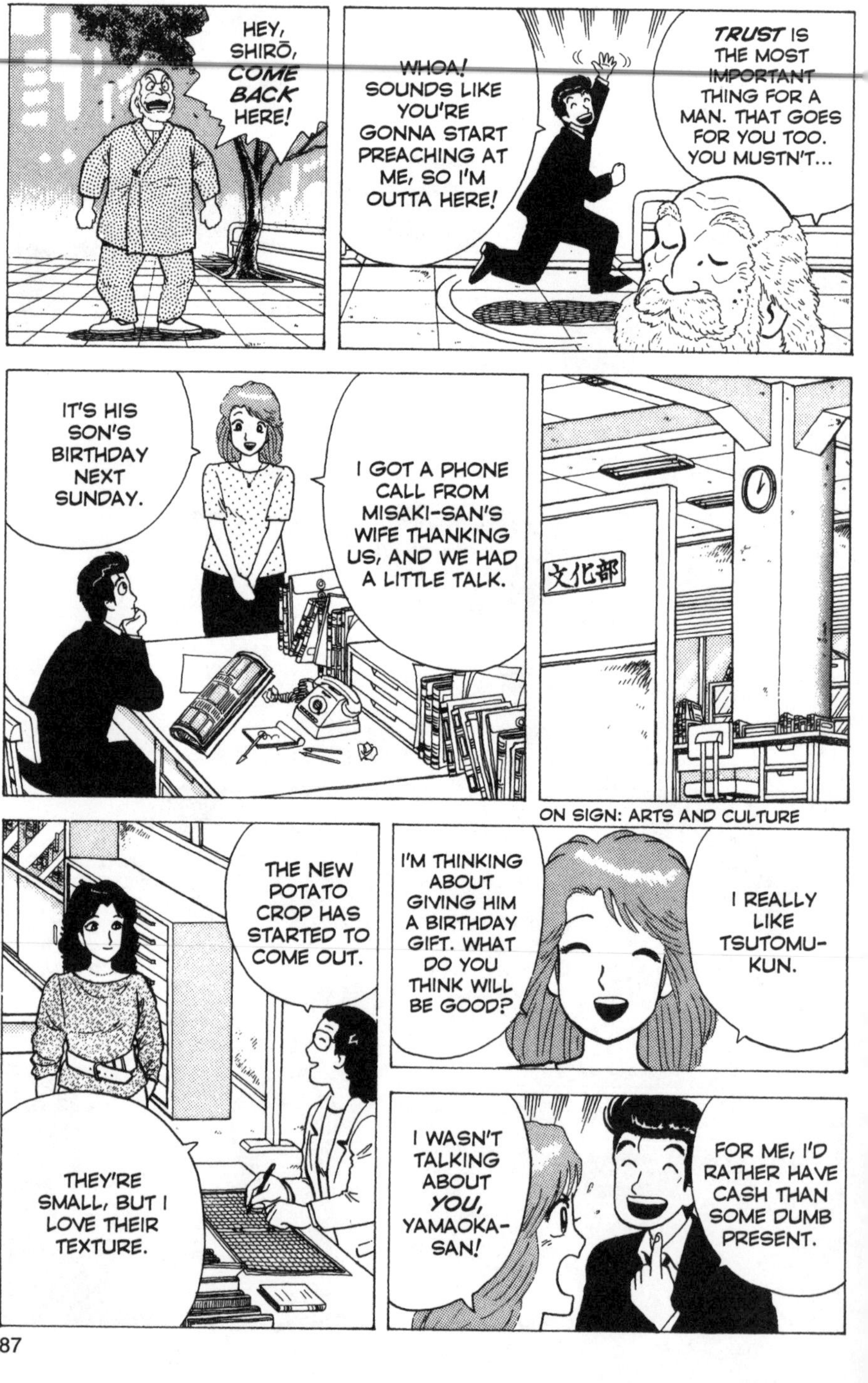
TRUST IS THE MOST IMPORTANT THING FOR A MAN. THAT GOES FOR YOU TOO. YOU MUSTN'T...
WHOA! SOUNDS LIKE YOU'RE GONNA START PREACHING AT ME, SO I'M OUTTA HERE!
HEY, SHIRŌ, COME BACK HERE!
文化部
I GOT A PHONE CALL FROM MISAKI-SAN'S WIFE THANKING US, AND WE HAD A LITTLE TALK.
IT'S HIS SON'S BIRTHDAY NEXT SUNDAY.
I REALLY LIKE TSUTOMU-KUN.
I'M THINKING ABOUT GIVING HIM A BIRTHDAY GIFT. WHAT DO YOU THINK WILL BE GOOD?
FOR ME, I'D RATHER HAVE CASH THAN SOME DUMB PRESENT.
I WASN'T TALKING ABOUT YOU, YAMAOKA-SAN!
THE NEW POTATO CROP HAS STARTED TO COME OUT.
THEY'RE SMALL, BUT I LOVE THEIR TEXTURE.
ON SIGN: ARTS AND CULTURE

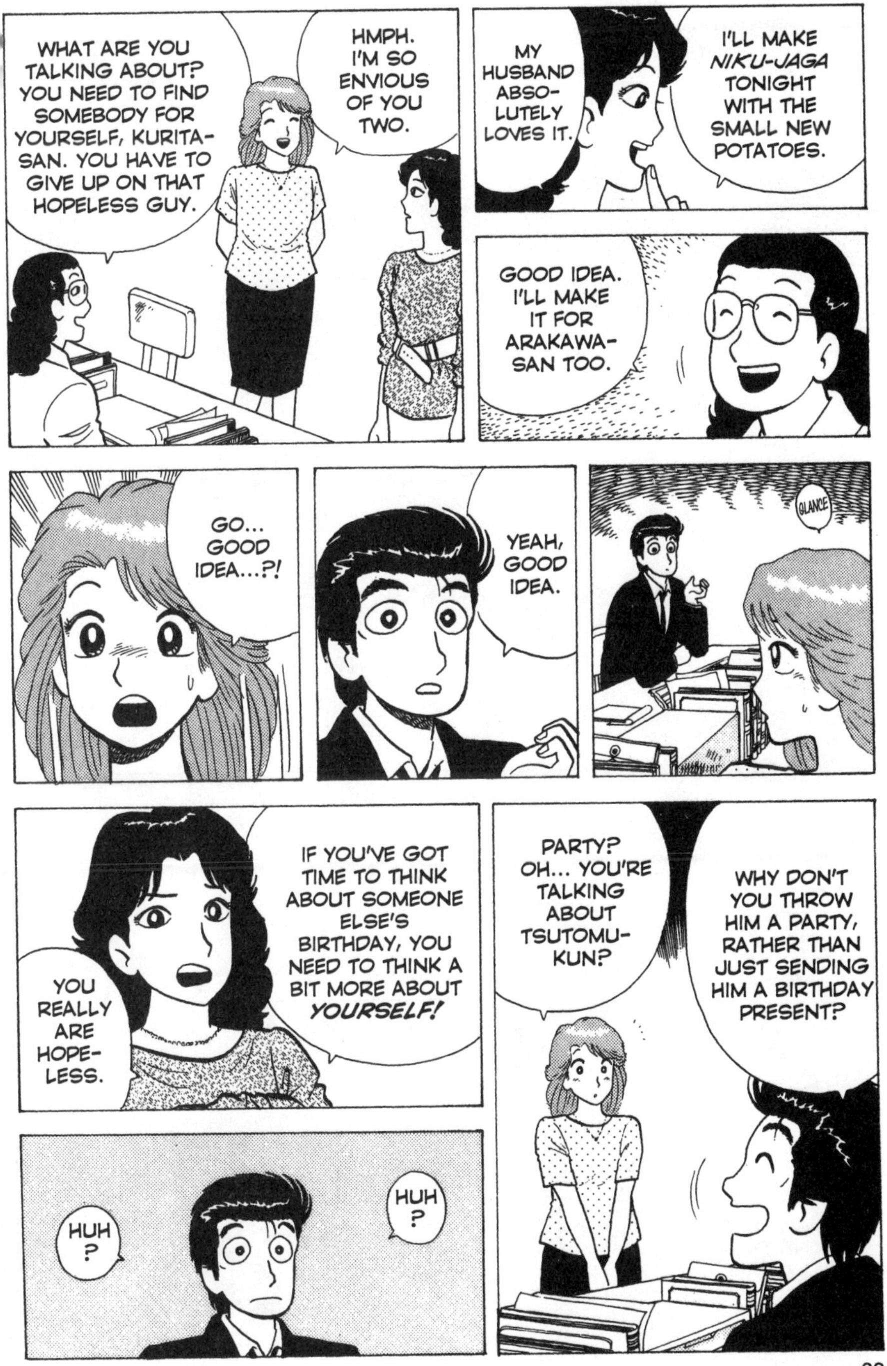
I'LL MAKE *NIKU-JAGA* TONIGHT WITH THE SMALL NEW POTATOES.
MY HUSBAND ABSO-LUTELY LOVES IT.
GOOD IDEA. I'LL MAKE IT FOR ARAKAWA-SAN TOO.
HMPH. I'M SO ENVIOUS OF YOU TWO.
WHAT ARE YOU TALKING ABOUT? YOU NEED TO FIND SOMEBODY FOR YOURSELF, KURITA-SAN. YOU HAVE TO GIVE UP ON THAT HOPELESS GUY.
GLANCE
YEAH, GOOD IDEA.
GO... GOOD IDEA...?!
WHY DON'T YOU THROW HIM A PARTY, RATHER THAN JUST SENDING HIM A BIRTHDAY PRESENT?
PARTY? OH... YOU'RE TALKING ABOUT TSUTOMU-KUN?
IF YOU'VE GOT TIME TO THINK ABOUT SOMEONE ELSE'S BIRTHDAY, YOU NEED TO THINK A BIT MORE ABOUT *YOURSELF!*
YOU REALLY ARE HOPE-LESS.
HUH?
HUH?

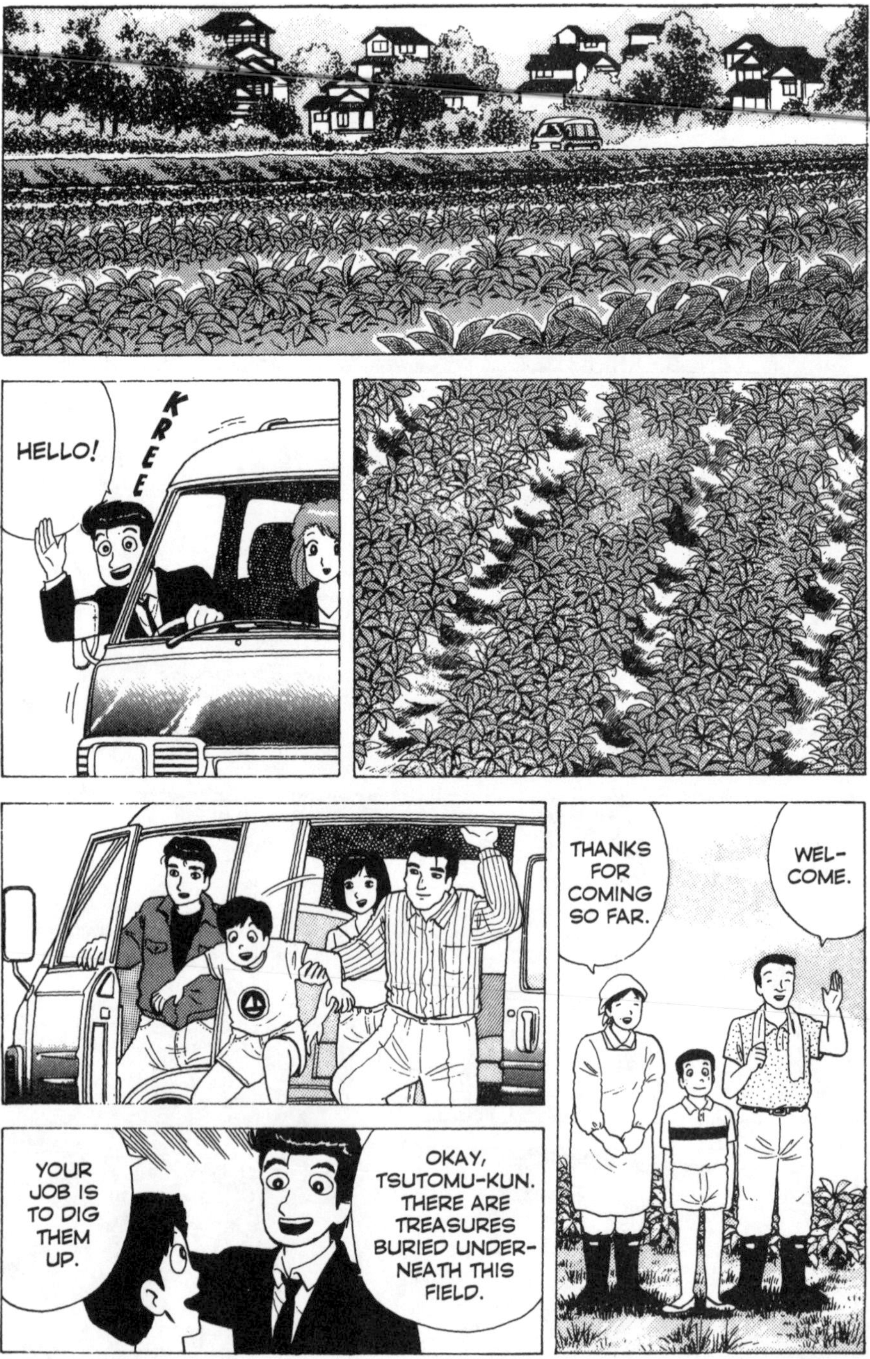
HELLO!
KREE
WEL-COME.
THANKS FOR COMING SO FAR.
OKAY, TSUTOMU-KUN. THERE ARE TREASURES BURIED UNDER-NEATH THIS FIELD.
YOUR JOB IS TO DIG THEM UP.

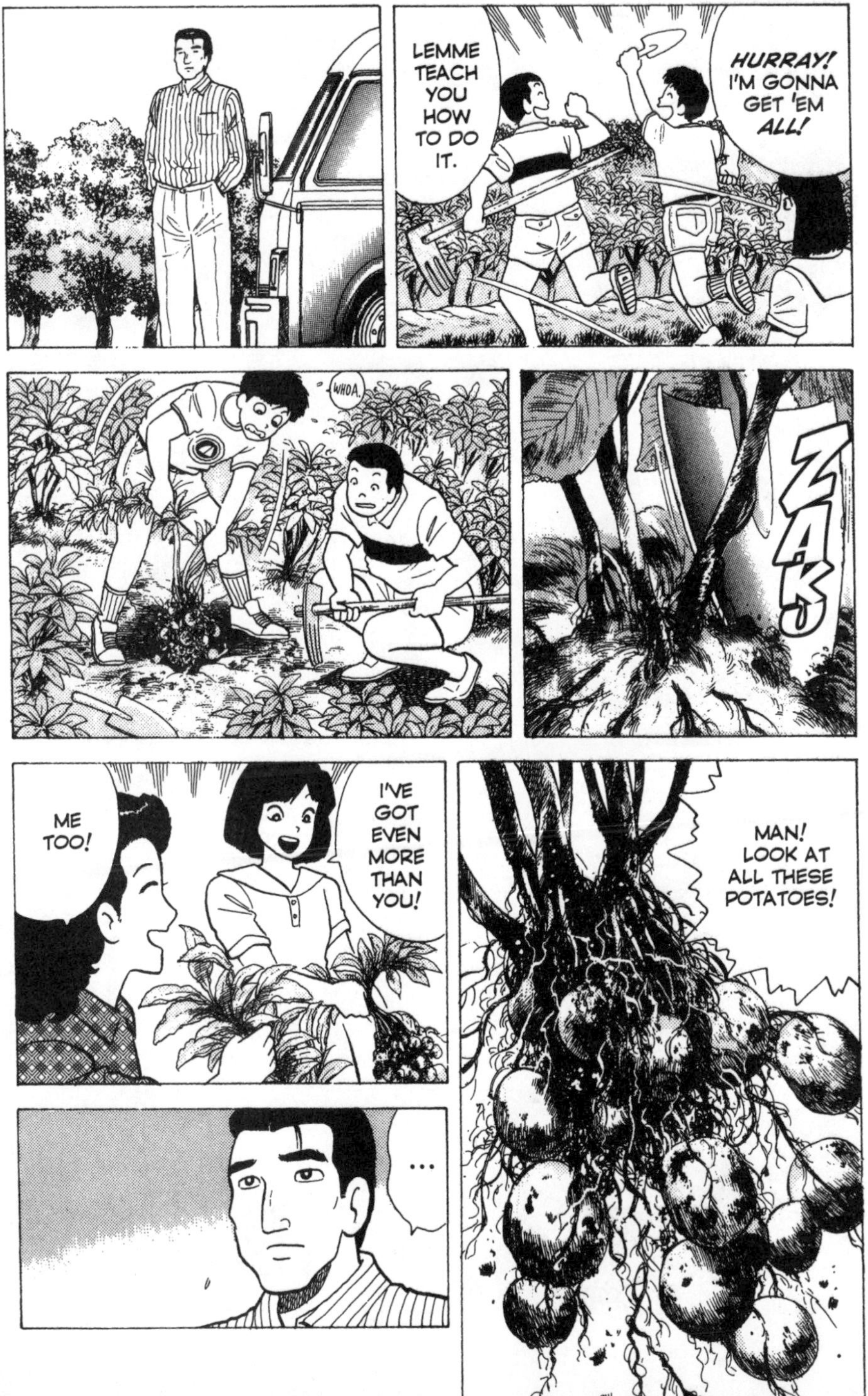

HURRAY! I'M GONNA GET 'EM ALL!
LEMME TEACH YOU HOW TO DO IT.
ZAKU
WHOA.
MAN! LOOK AT ALL THESE POTATOES!
I'VE GOT EVEN MORE THAN YOU!
ME TOO!
...

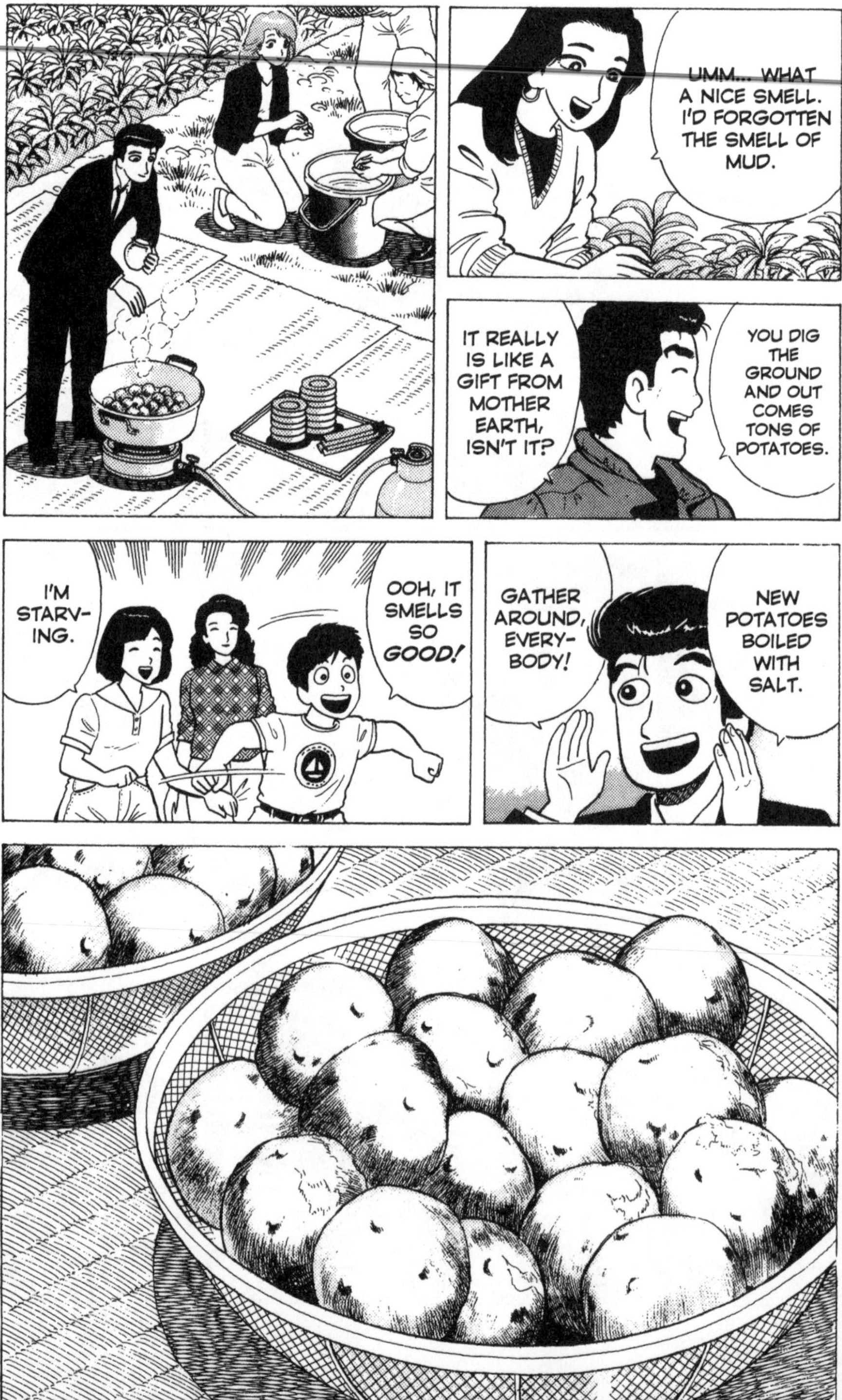
UMM... WHAT A NICE SMELL. I'D FORGOTTEN THE SMELL OF MUD.
YOU DIG THE GROUND AND OUT COMES TONS OF POTATOES.
IT REALLY IS LIKE A GIFT FROM MOTHER EARTH, ISN'T IT?
NEW POTATOES BOILED WITH SALT.
GATHER AROUND, EVERY-BODY!
OOH, IT SMELLS SO *GOOD!*
I'M STARV-ING.

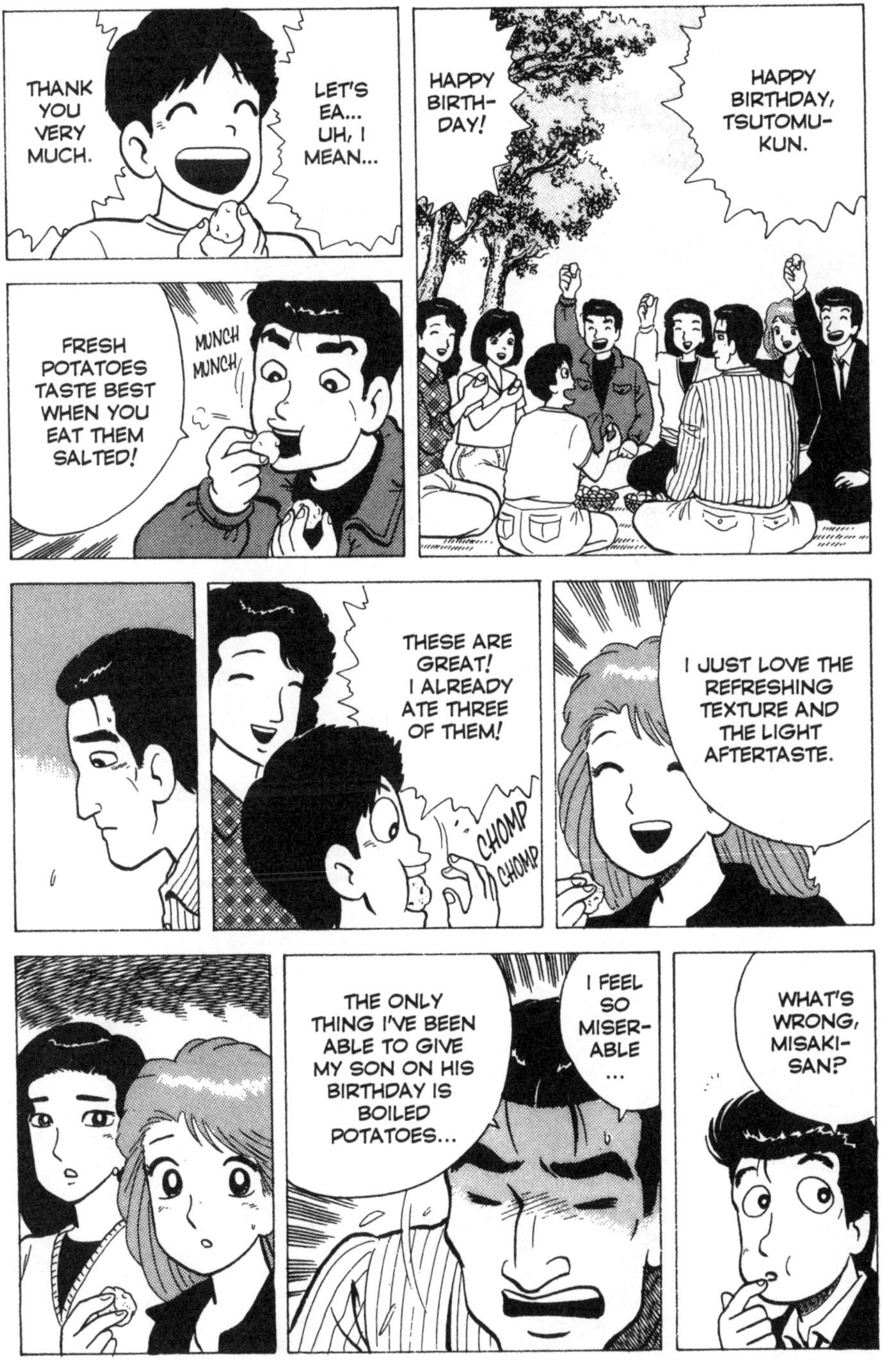
HAPPY BIRTHDAY, TSUTOMU-KUN.
HAPPY BIRTH-DAY!
LET'S EA... UH, I MEAN...
THANK YOU VERY MUCH.
MUNCH MUNCH
FRESH POTATOES TASTE BEST WHEN YOU EAT THEM SALTED!
I JUST LOVE THE REFRESHING TEXTURE AND THE LIGHT AFTERTASTE.
THESE ARE GREAT! I ALREADY ATE THREE OF THEM!
CHOMP CHOMP
WHAT'S WRONG, MISAKI-SAN?
I FEEL SO MISER-ABLE ...
THE ONLY THING I'VE BEEN ABLE TO GIVE MY SON ON HIS BIRTHDAY IS BOILED POTATOES...

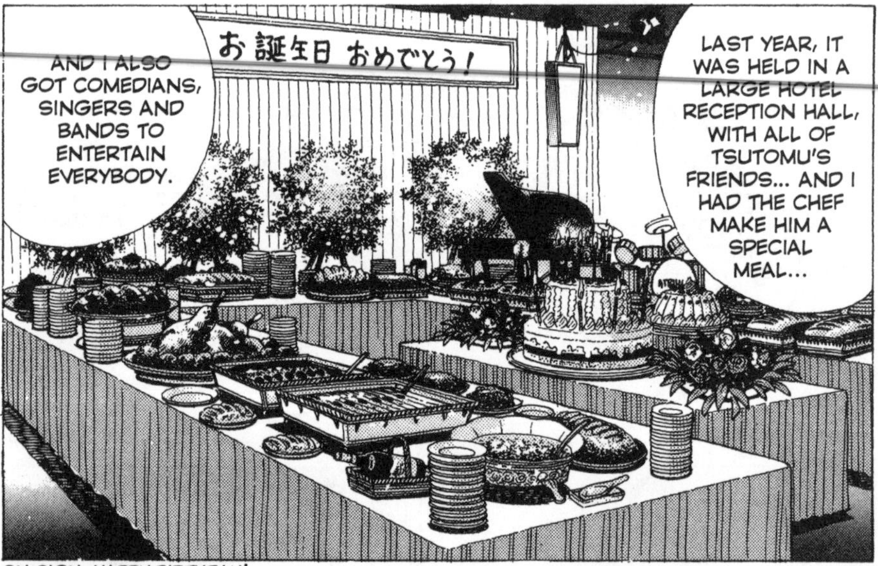
お誕生日 おめでとう!
LAST YEAR, IT WAS HELD IN A LARGE HOTEL RECEPTION HALL, WITH ALL OF TSUTOMU'S FRIENDS... AND I HAD THE CHEF MAKE HIM A SPECIAL MEAL...
AND I ALSO GOT COMEDIANS, SINGERS AND BANDS TO ENTERTAIN EVERYBODY.
ON SIGN: HAPPY BIRTHDAY!

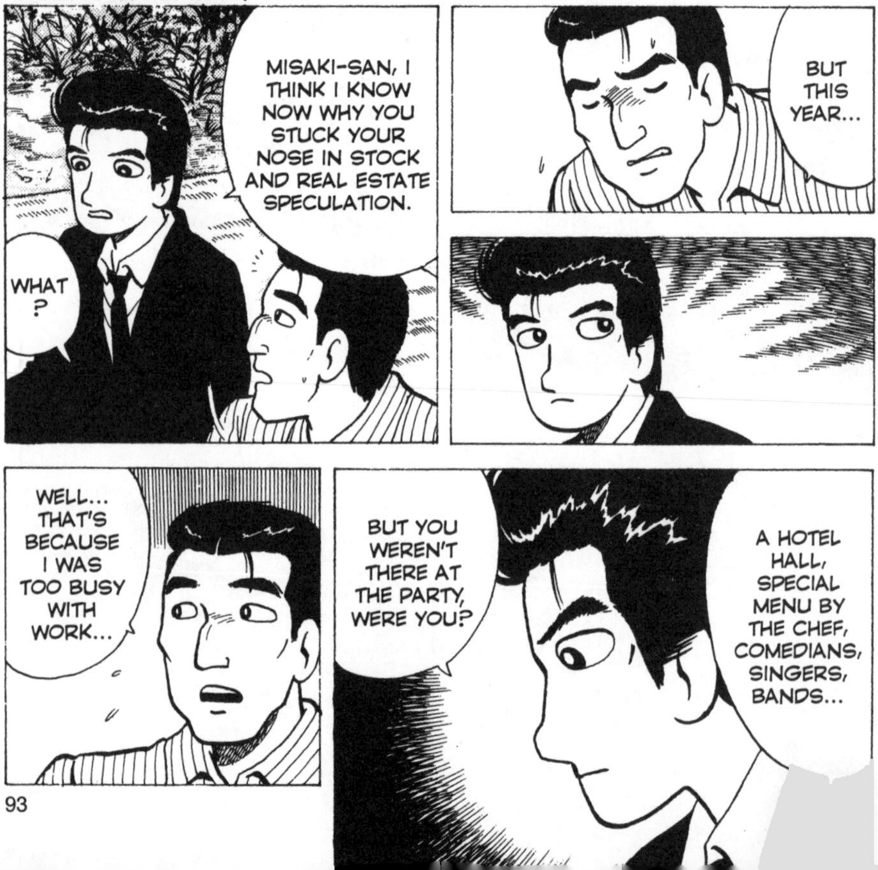
BUT THIS YEAR...
MISAKI-SAN, I THINK I KNOW NOW WHY YOU STUCK YOUR NOSE IN STOCK AND REAL ESTATE SPECULATION.
WHAT?
A HOTEL HALL, SPECIAL MENU BY THE CHEF, COMEDIANS, SINGERS, BANDS...
BUT YOU WEREN'T THERE AT THE PARTY, WERE YOU?
WELL... THAT'S BECAUSE I WAS TOO BUSY WITH WORK...

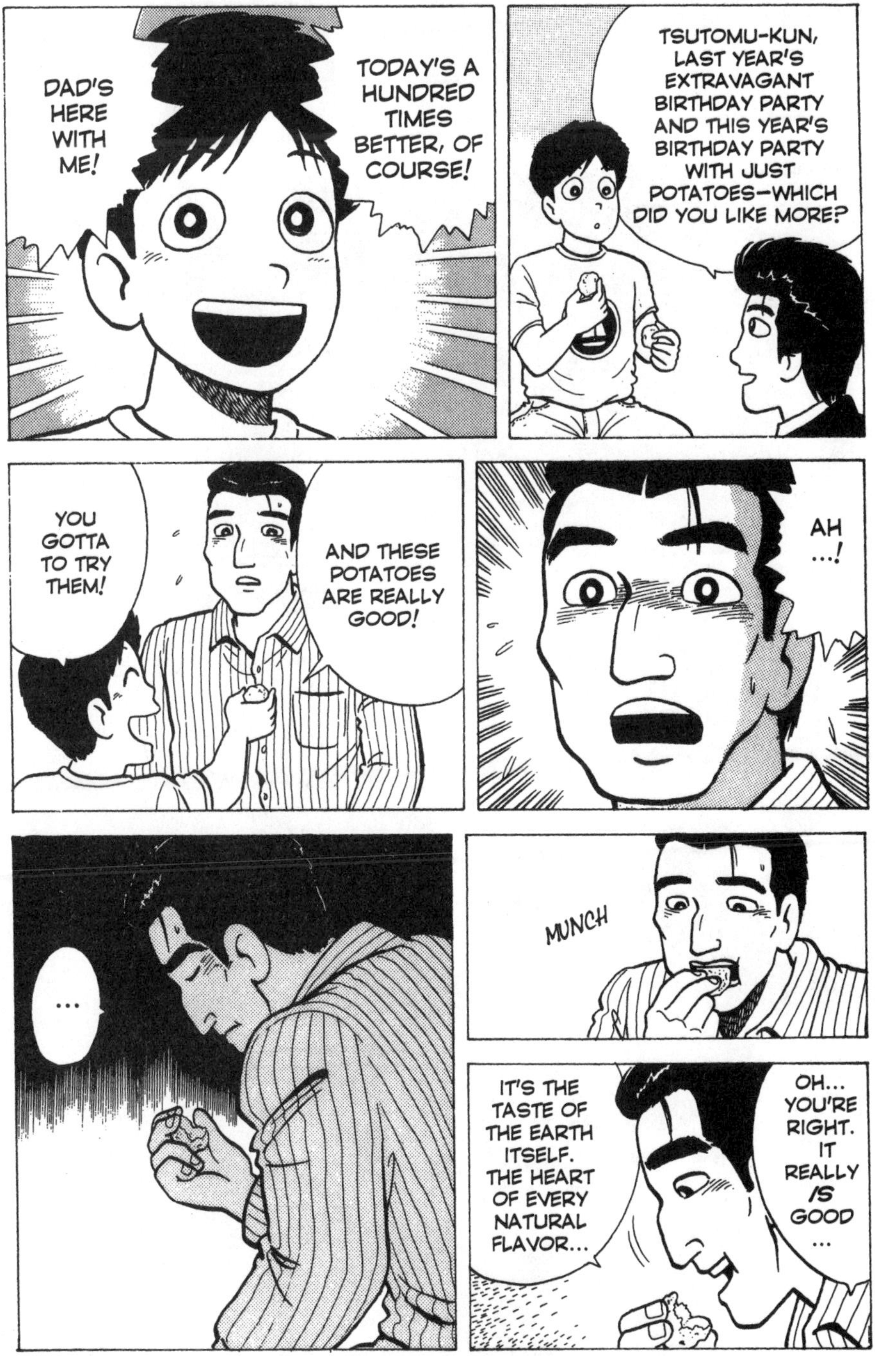
TSUTOMU-KUN, LAST YEAR'S EXTRAVAGANT BIRTHDAY PARTY AND THIS YEAR'S BIRTHDAY PARTY WITH JUST POTATOES—WHICH DID YOU LIKE MORE?
TODAY'S A HUNDRED TIMES BETTER, OF COURSE!
DAD'S HERE WITH ME!
AH ...!
AND THESE POTATOES ARE REALLY GOOD!
YOU GOTTA TO TRY THEM!
MUNCH
OH... YOU'RE RIGHT. IT REALLY *IS* GOOD ...
IT'S THE TASTE OF THE EARTH ITSELF. THE HEART OF EVERY NATURAL FLAVOR...
...

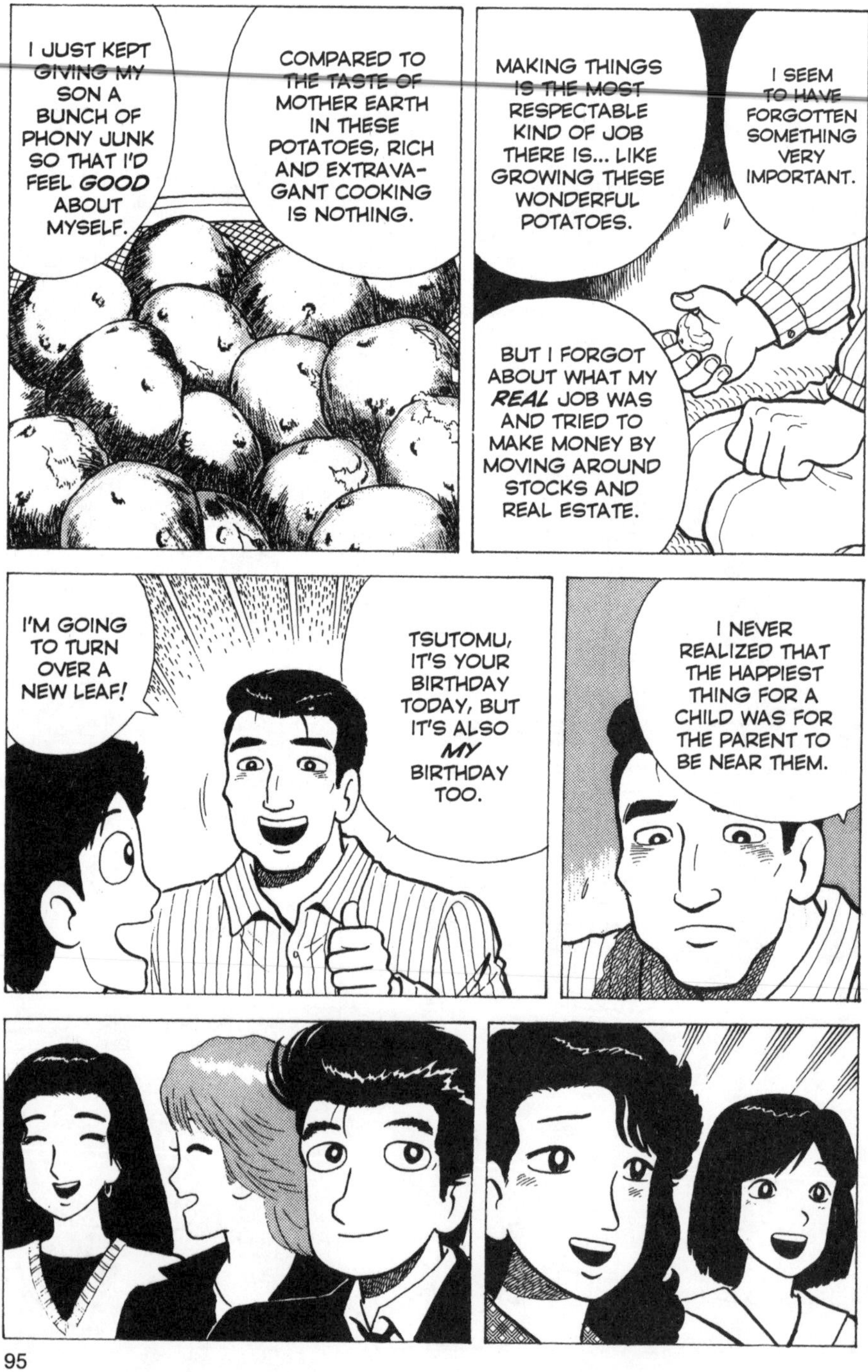
I SEEM TO HAVE FORGOTTEN SOMETHING VERY IMPORTANT.
MAKING THINGS IS THE MOST RESPECTABLE KIND OF JOB THERE IS... LIKE GROWING THESE WONDERFUL POTATOES.
BUT I FORGOT ABOUT WHAT MY *REAL* JOB WAS AND TRIED TO MAKE MONEY BY MOVING AROUND STOCKS AND REAL ESTATE.
COMPARED TO THE TASTE OF MOTHER EARTH IN THESE POTATOES, RICH AND EXTRAVA-GANT COOKING IS NOTHING.
I JUST KEPT GIVING MY SON A BUNCH OF PHONY JUNK SO THAT I'D FEEL *GOOD* ABOUT MYSELF.
I NEVER REALIZED THAT THE HAPPIEST THING FOR A CHILD WAS FOR THE PARENT TO BE NEAR THEM.
TSUTOMU, IT'S YOUR BIRTHDAY TODAY, BUT IT'S ALSO *MY* BIRTHDAY TOO.
I'M GOING TO TURN OVER A NEW LEAF!

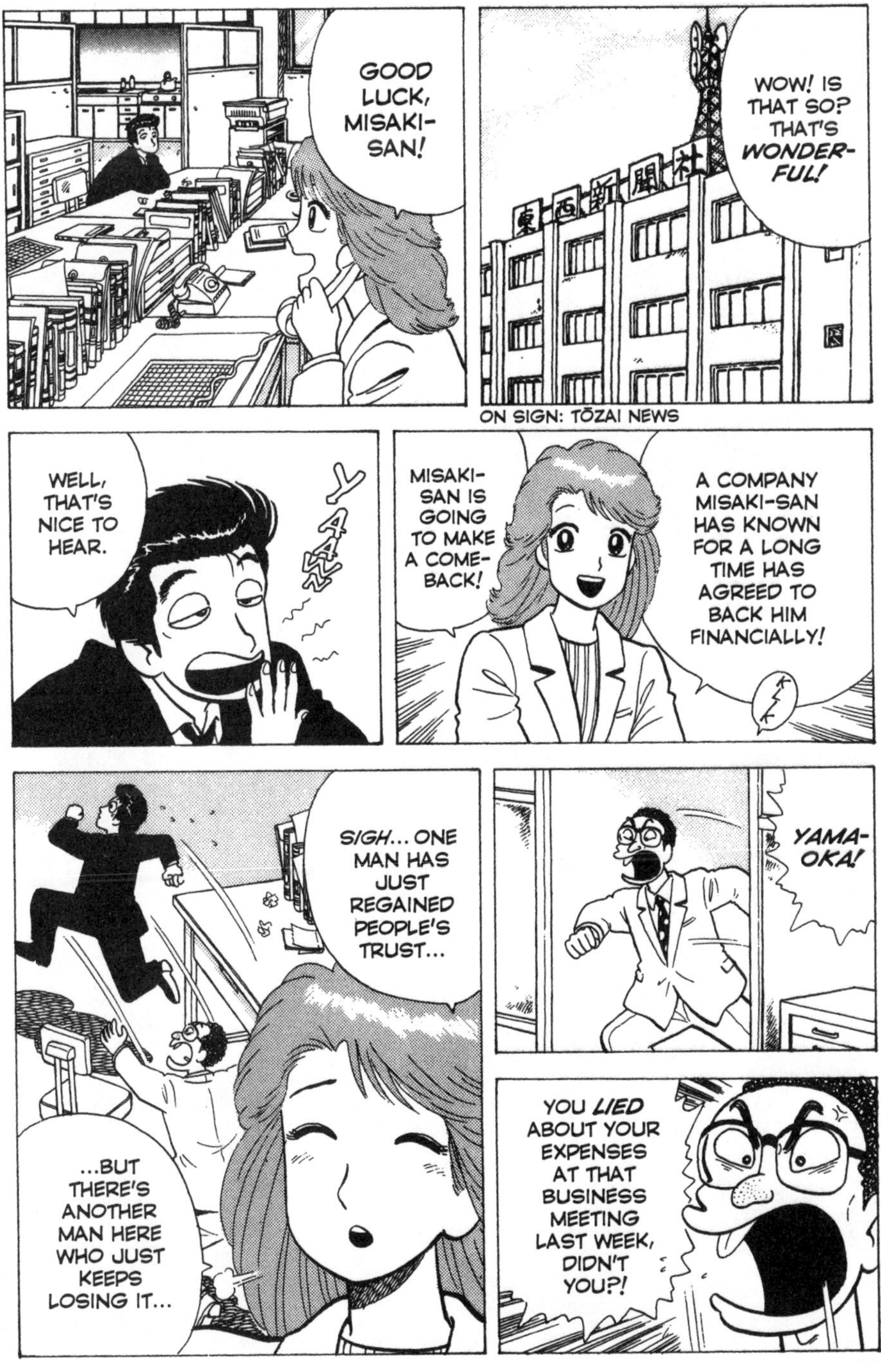
WOW! IS THAT SO? THAT'S *WONDERFUL!*
ON SIGN: TŌZAI NEWS
GOOD LUCK, MISAKI-SAN!
A COMPANY MISAKI-SAN HAS KNOWN FOR A LONG TIME HAS AGREED TO BACK HIM FINANCIALLY!
MISAKI-SAN IS GOING TO MAKE A COME-BACK!
WELL, THAT'S NICE TO HEAR.
YAAWN
YAMA-OKA!
YOU *LIED* ABOUT YOUR EXPENSES AT THAT BUSINESS MEETING LAST WEEK, DIDN'T YOU?!
SIGH... ONE MAN HAS JUST REGAINED PEOPLE'S TRUST...
...BUT THERE'S ANOTHER MAN HERE WHO JUST KEEPS LOSING IT...

Author commentary

Oishinbo Day-by-Day

Tetsu Kariya

The connection between hotpots and vegetables.

The "Hotpot Demon King" dominates the hotpot with cooking chopsticks!!

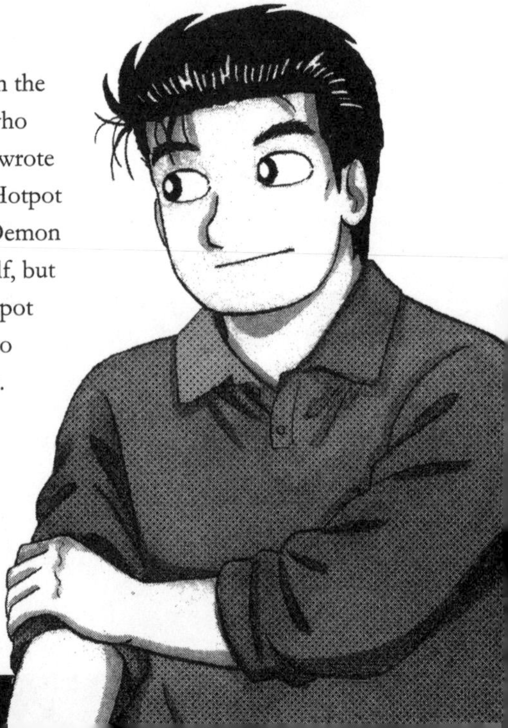

I've written several times elsewhere in the *Oishinbo* series about my friend "A" who lives in Okinawa. In a recent entry, I wrote about how A has gone past being a Hotpot Boss and has turned into a Hotpot Demon King. I showed the entry to A himself, but just the other day, A became the Hotpot Demon King again, so I've decided to write about it here out of frustration.

I've known A since 1969, and A is the kind of guy who wants to manage every little thing when it comes to a gathering of

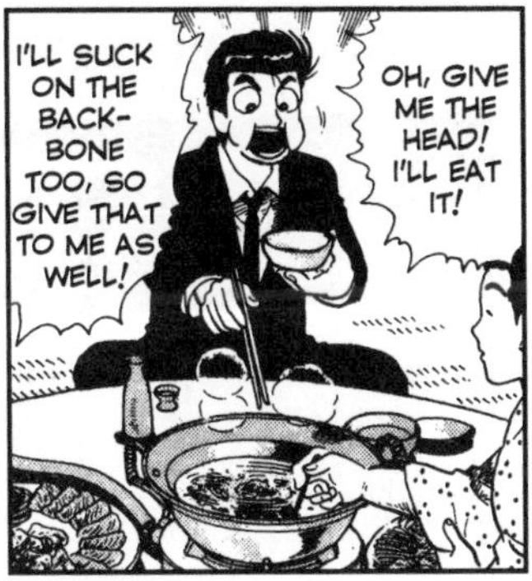
OH, GIVE ME THE HEAD! I'LL EAT IT!
I'LL SUCK ON THE BACK-BONE TOO, SO GIVE THAT TO ME AS WELL!

friends. When it comes to the hotpot, he won't let anybody touch it. He'll stand right next to the pot with a pair of cooking chopsticks in hand to exercise full control of it. All we're allowed to do is eat it the way A allows us to. That's why I call A the Hotpot Demon King.

So this time, I decided to come up with a plan. It was going to be a large gathering of 15 people, so I got two pots ready and said to A, "Look, you're free to do anything with that pot. But this pot is mine. I'll take care of this one."

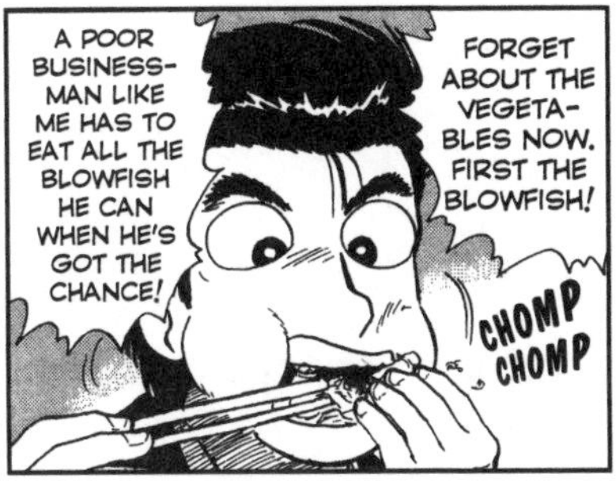
FORGET ABOUT THE VEGETA-BLES NOW. FIRST THE BLOWFISH!
A POOR BUSINESS-MAN LIKE ME HAS TO EAT ALL THE BLOWFISH HE CAN WHEN HE'S GOT THE CHANCE!
CHOMP CHOMP

I was surprised A agreed to this arrangement so easily. The hotpot was Pork *Shabu-shabu*. First I poured in konbu dashi and sweet potato *shochu* of about half the amount of the dashi, along with a lot of thick slices of ginger. I also added soy sauce to the broth for flavoring. Into each of our small bowls, I poured some of the broth and a little more soy sauce and ground a lot of sesame on top to get them ready.

Next, I placed the extremely thinly sliced pork into the broth just long enough for the meat to become slightly pink, then drew it out and placed it in my bowl before throwing it into my mouth. Delicious. There are those who think that you must cook pork thoroughly, but that is a mistake. You must not cook it too much. Once the meat goes past being pink, the texture becomes bad, and its flavor is lost too. It is the best when it is still slightly pink.

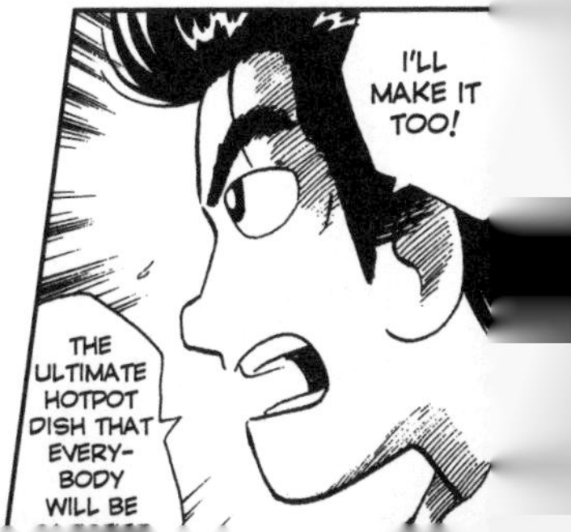
I'LL MAKE IT TOO!
THE ULTIMATE HOTPOT DISH THAT EVERY-BODY WILL BE

Whether it be pork shabu-shabu or beef sukiyaki, I want to eat the meat. To me, the green onions, Chinese cabbage, shiitake mushrooms and other vegetables can be left until the end. I don't even mind if they're never put into the hotpot at all. I just want to eat the meat.

And, since I had stationed A at a different pot, I would be able to eat all the meat I wanted. Or so I thought.

The Hotpot Demon King started to throw loads of vegetables into the pot that was supposed to be mine.

But when I looked up, there stood A next to my pot with his dreaded cooking chopsticks in hand. I immediately told him, "Hey, A, you're supposed to be in charge of the other pot. Leave this pot alone," but A said outright, "Oh no, I'm done taking care of that pot over there. I'll take care of this pot now." I begged him, "Please, you don't have to take care of this one."

> **"Look, you're free to do anything with that pot. But this pot is mine. I'll take care of this one."**

But the Hotpot Demon King had no ears for the wailing of the weak. A started to throw loads of vegetables into the pot that was supposed to be mine. In went the green onions, the Chinese cabbage, the shiitake mushrooms and even the tofu. And with a wicked smile upon his face, he said, "The vegetables suck up all the flavor from the meat and become really good, you know." "Yeah, I know that. But if you put in so many vegetables, there won't be any space left to cook the meat."

But A took no notice of my plea. My pot that had been commandeered by A was now filled with vegetables, and my dream of eating all the meat I wanted had once

again been shattered. I ended up eating just an ordinary pork hotpot. Once the Demon King gets his hands on something, you can't do anything about it.

Now, you may think I don't like vegetables after reading this story, but that's not true. Whenever I'm extremely tired, I suddenly get the urge to

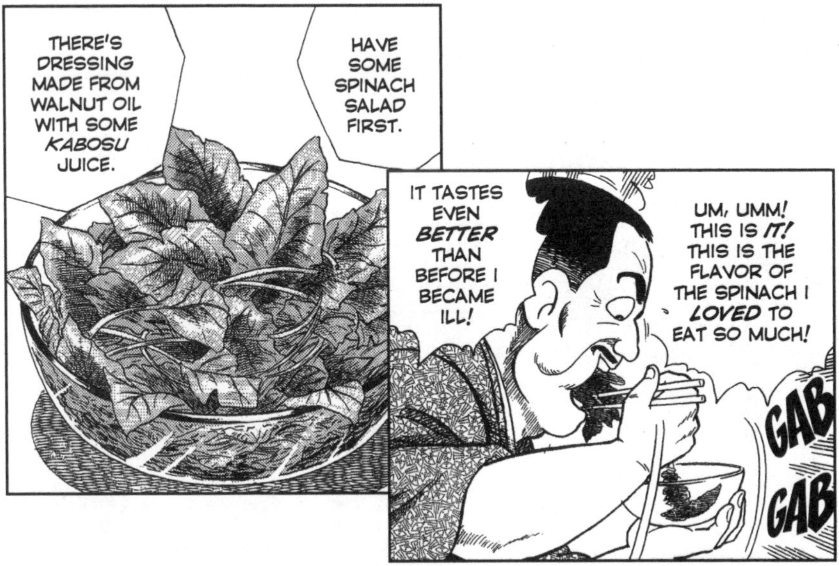
HAVE SOME SPINACH SALAD FIRST.
THERE'S DRESSING MADE FROM WALNUT OIL WITH SOME *KABOSU* JUICE.
UM, UMM! THIS IS *IT!* THIS IS THE FLAVOR OF THE SPINACH I *LOVED* TO EAT SO MUCH!
IT TASTES EVEN *BETTER* THAN BEFORE I BECAME ILL!
GAB
GAB

eat vegetables. One time, I ate a large bowl of salad without raising my head or pausing to breathe. When I am exhausted, I want to eat vegetables that have a strong taste. Bitter vegetables taste even better, since it feels like they'll get rid of all the bad things inside your body. When eating a salad of arugula and ripe tomatoes covered with balsamic vinegar and heaped with grated parmesan cheese, I can just feel my blood running clean.

I simply want to eat a lot of meat before putting the vegetables into the pot, that's all. Demon King A, you've got to understand that.

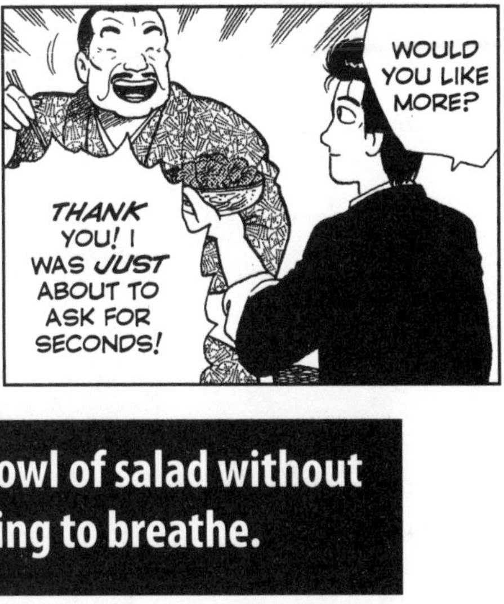
WOULD YOU LIKE MORE?
THANK YOU! I WAS *JUST* ABOUT TO ASK FOR SECONDS!

One time, I ate a large bowl of salad without raising my head or pausing to breathe.

THE BEAN SPROUT KID

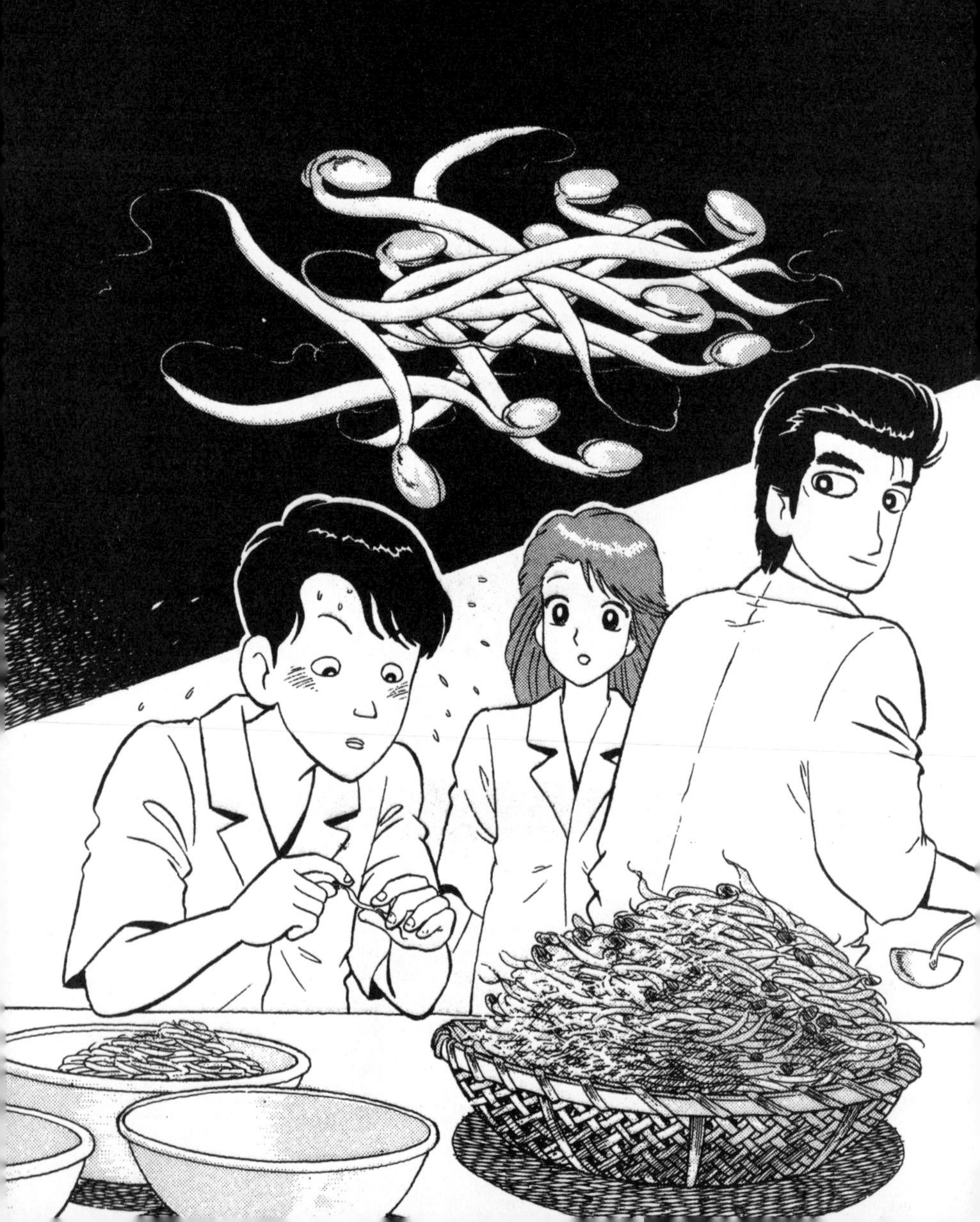

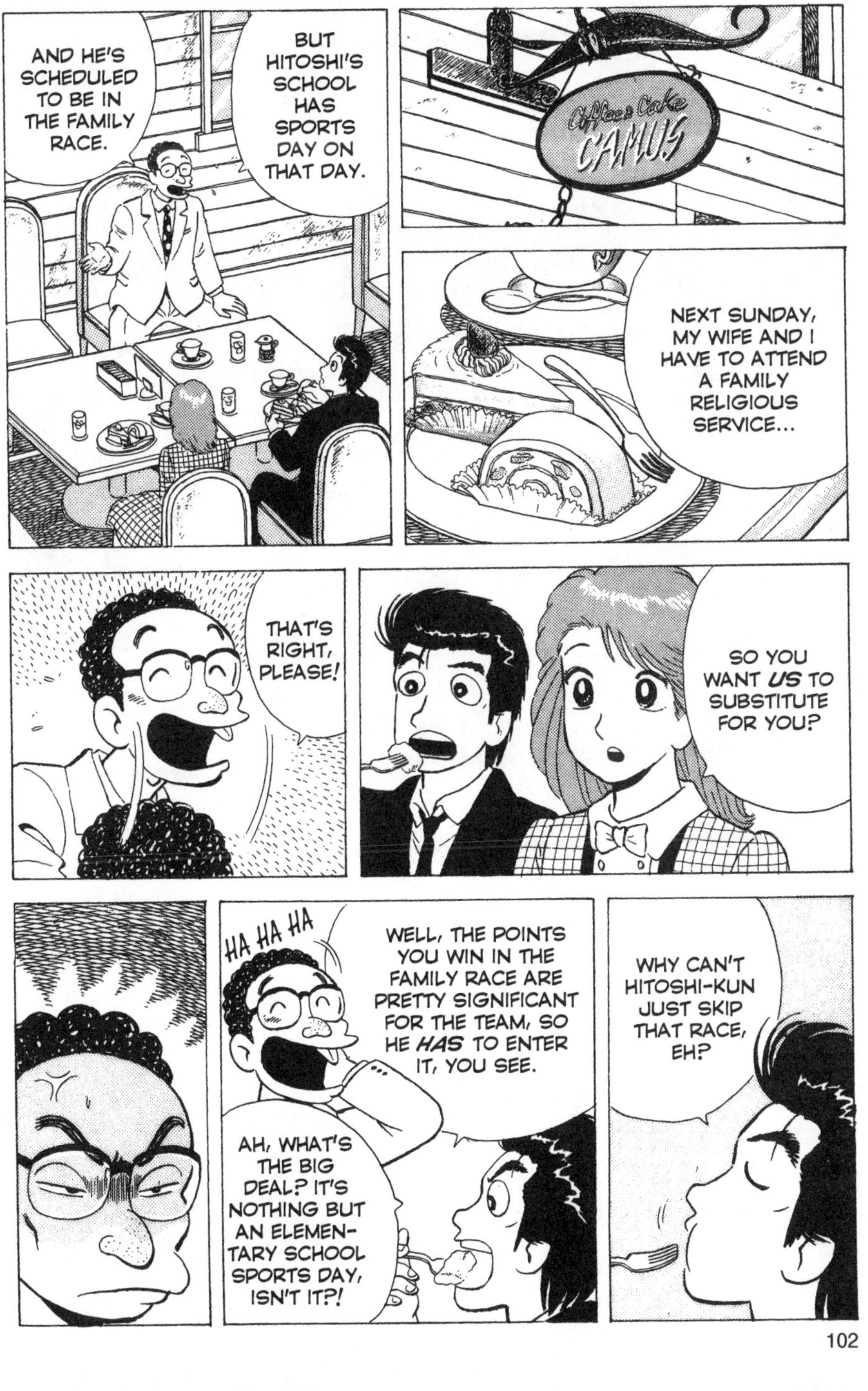
Coffee & Cake
CAMUS
NEXT SUNDAY, MY WIFE AND I HAVE TO ATTEND A FAMILY RELIGIOUS SERVICE...
BUT HITOSHI'S SCHOOL HAS SPORTS DAY ON THAT DAY.
AND HE'S SCHEDULED TO BE IN THE FAMILY RACE.
SO YOU WANT *US* TO SUBSTITUTE FOR YOU?
THAT'S RIGHT, PLEASE!
WHY CAN'T HITOSHI-KUN JUST SKIP THAT RACE, EH?
HA HA HA
WELL, THE POINTS YOU WIN IN THE FAMILY RACE ARE PRETTY SIGNIFICANT FOR THE TEAM, SO HE *HAS* TO ENTER IT, YOU SEE.
AH, WHAT'S THE BIG DEAL? IT'S NOTHING BUT AN ELEMENTARY SCHOOL SPORTS DAY, ISN'T IT?!

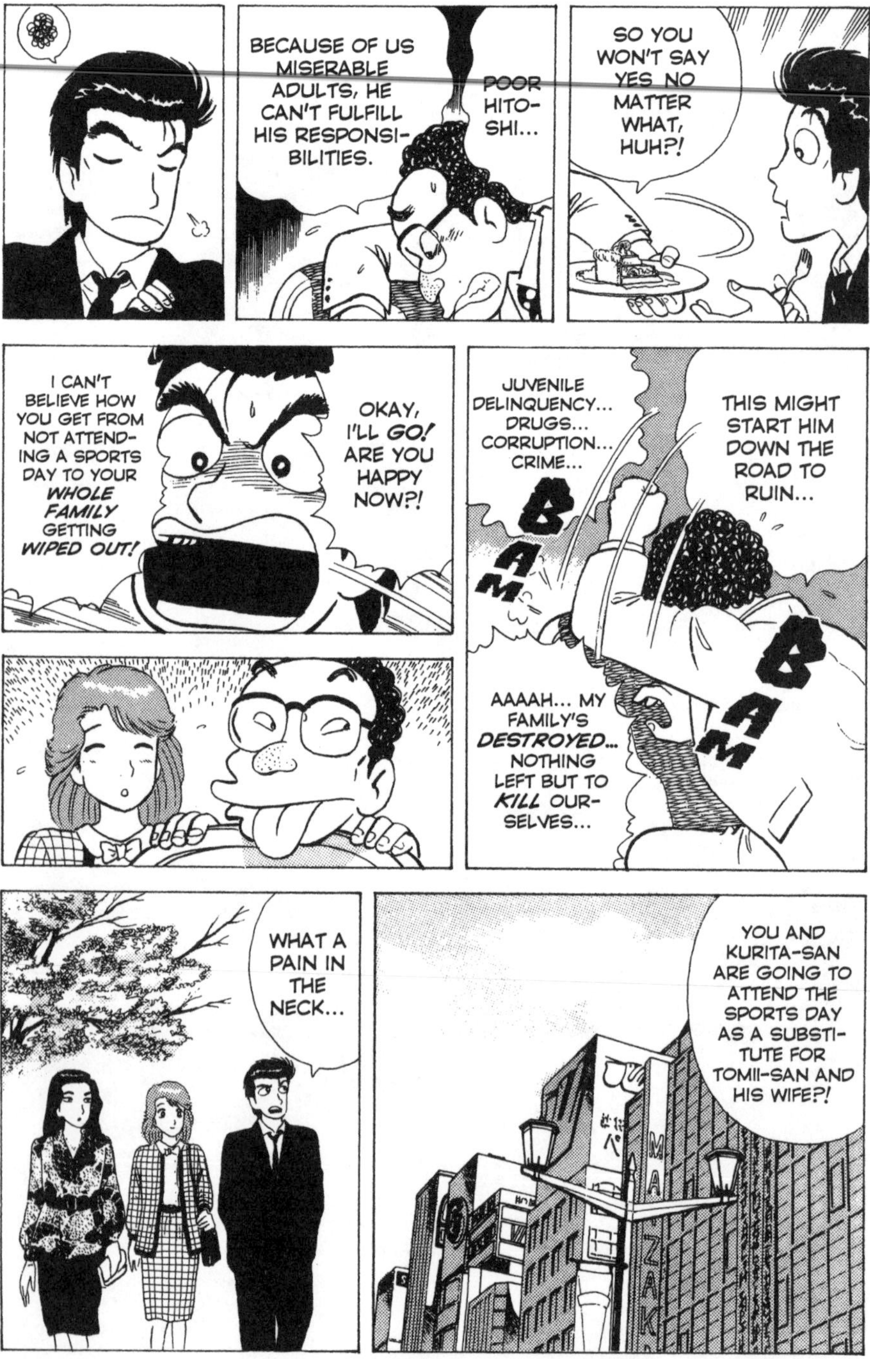
SO YOU WON'T SAY YES NO MATTER WHAT, HUH?!
POOR HITO-SHI...
BECAUSE OF US MISERABLE ADULTS, HE CAN'T FULFILL HIS RESPONSI-BILITIES.
THIS MIGHT START HIM DOWN THE ROAD TO RUIN...
JUVENILE DELINQUENCY... DRUGS... CORRUPTION... CRIME...
BAM
BAM
AAAAH... MY FAMILY'S DESTROYED... NOTHING LEFT BUT TO KILL OUR-SELVES...
OKAY, I'LL GO! ARE YOU HAPPY NOW?!
I CAN'T BELIEVE HOW YOU GET FROM NOT ATTEND-ING A SPORTS DAY TO YOUR WHOLE FAMILY GETTING WIPED OUT!
YOU AND KURITA-SAN ARE GOING TO ATTEND THE SPORTS DAY AS A SUBSTI-TUTE FOR TOMII-SAN AND HIS WIFE?!
WHAT A PAIN IN THE NECK...

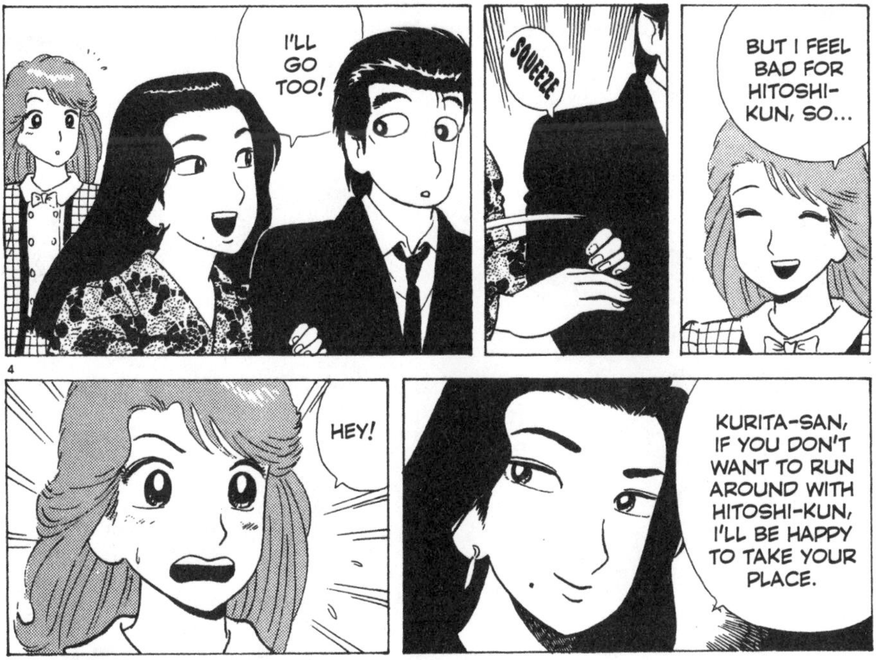
BUT I FEEL BAD FOR HITOSHI-KUN, SO...
SQUEEZE
I'LL GO TOO!
KURITA-SAN, IF YOU DON'T WANT TO RUN AROUND WITH HITOSHI-KUN, I'LL BE HAPPY TO TAKE YOUR PLACE.
HEY!

ON SIGN: SHINTO NO. 3 ELEMENTARY SCHOOL

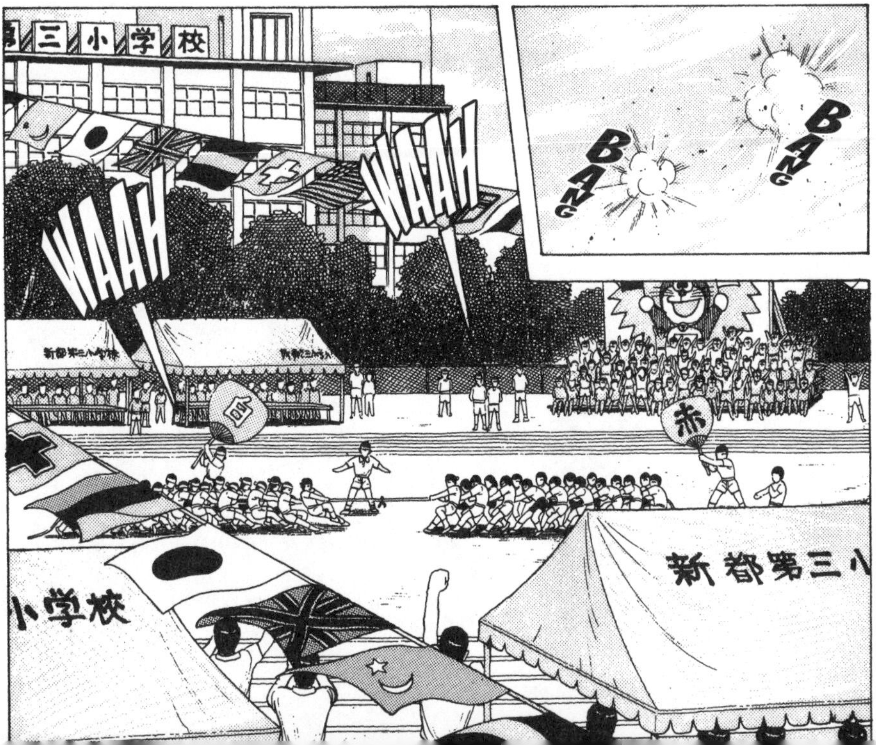
BANG
BANG
WAAH
WAAH

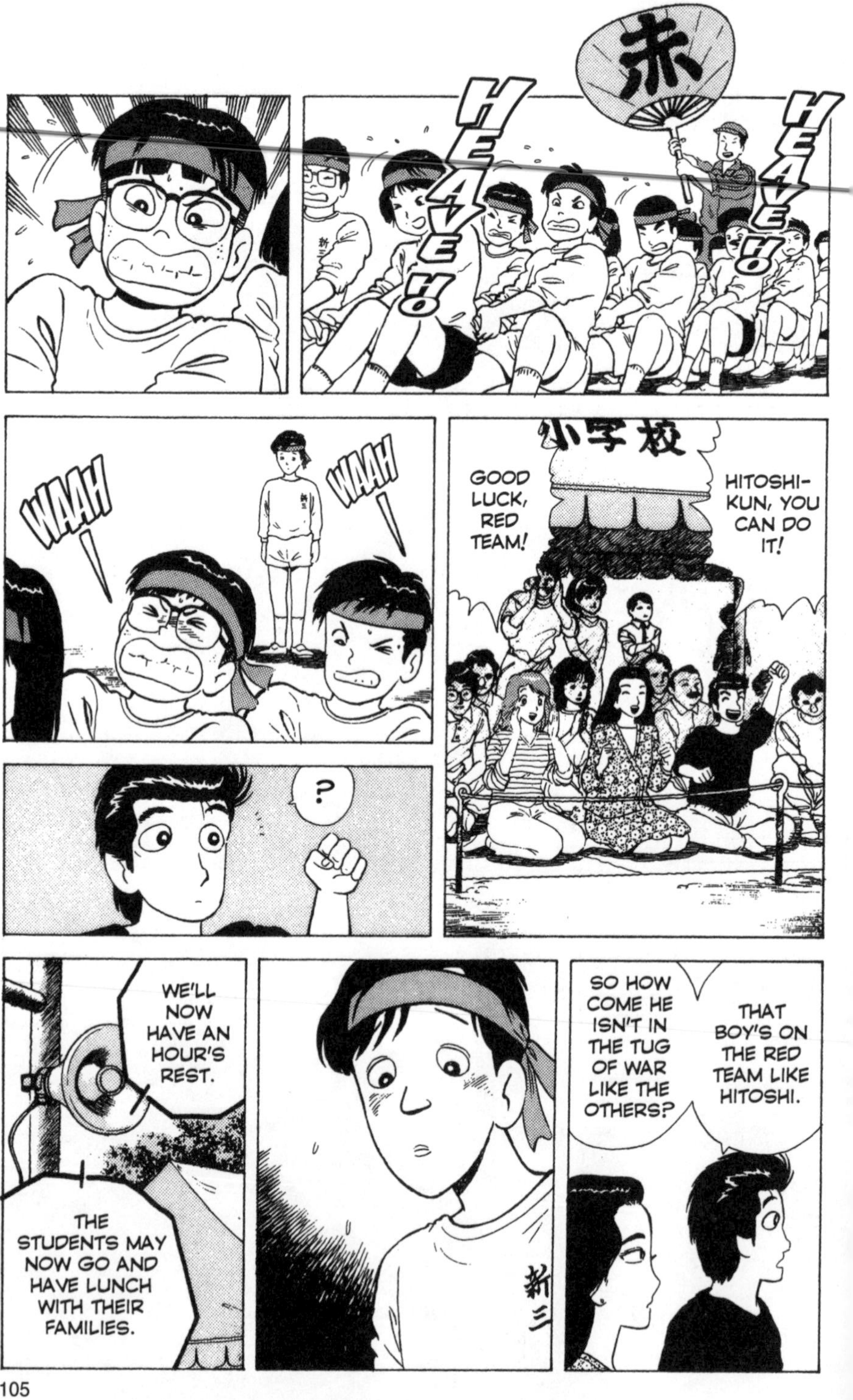
赤
HEAVE HO
HEAVE HO
小学校
HITOSHI-KUN, YOU CAN DO IT!
GOOD LUCK, RED TEAM!
WAAH
WAAH
?
THAT BOY'S ON THE RED TEAM LIKE HITOSHI.
SO HOW COME HE ISN'T IN THE TUG OF WAR LIKE THE OTHERS?
WE'LL NOW HAVE AN HOUR'S REST.
THE STUDENTS MAY NOW GO AND HAVE LUNCH WITH THEIR FAMILIES.

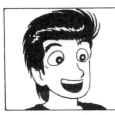

WHOA, I'M HUNGRY!
YOU'RE DOING REALLY WELL, HITOSHI-KUN.
YOU WON THE TUG OF WAR, SO AT THIS RATE THE RED TEAM MAY WIN TODAY.
THE RED TEAM WILL *DEFINITELY* WIN!
HITOSHI-KUN, I MADE THIS MYSELF. EAT AS MUCH AS YOU WANT.
YOU TOO, YAMAOKA-SAN.
I BROUGHT A FEAST FOR BOTH OF YOU.
OH MY... A STACKING LUNCH BOX!
YUM! LET'S DIG IN!!

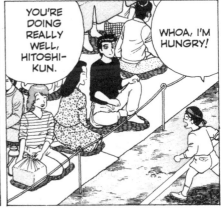

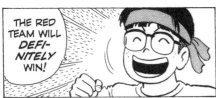

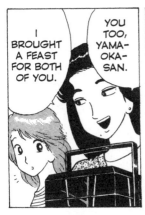

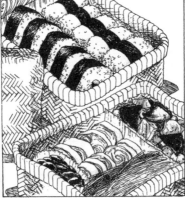

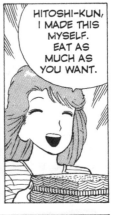

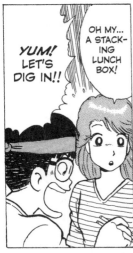

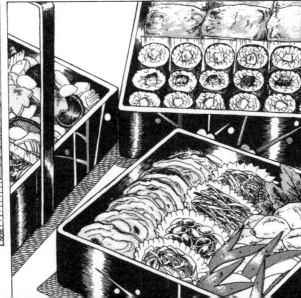

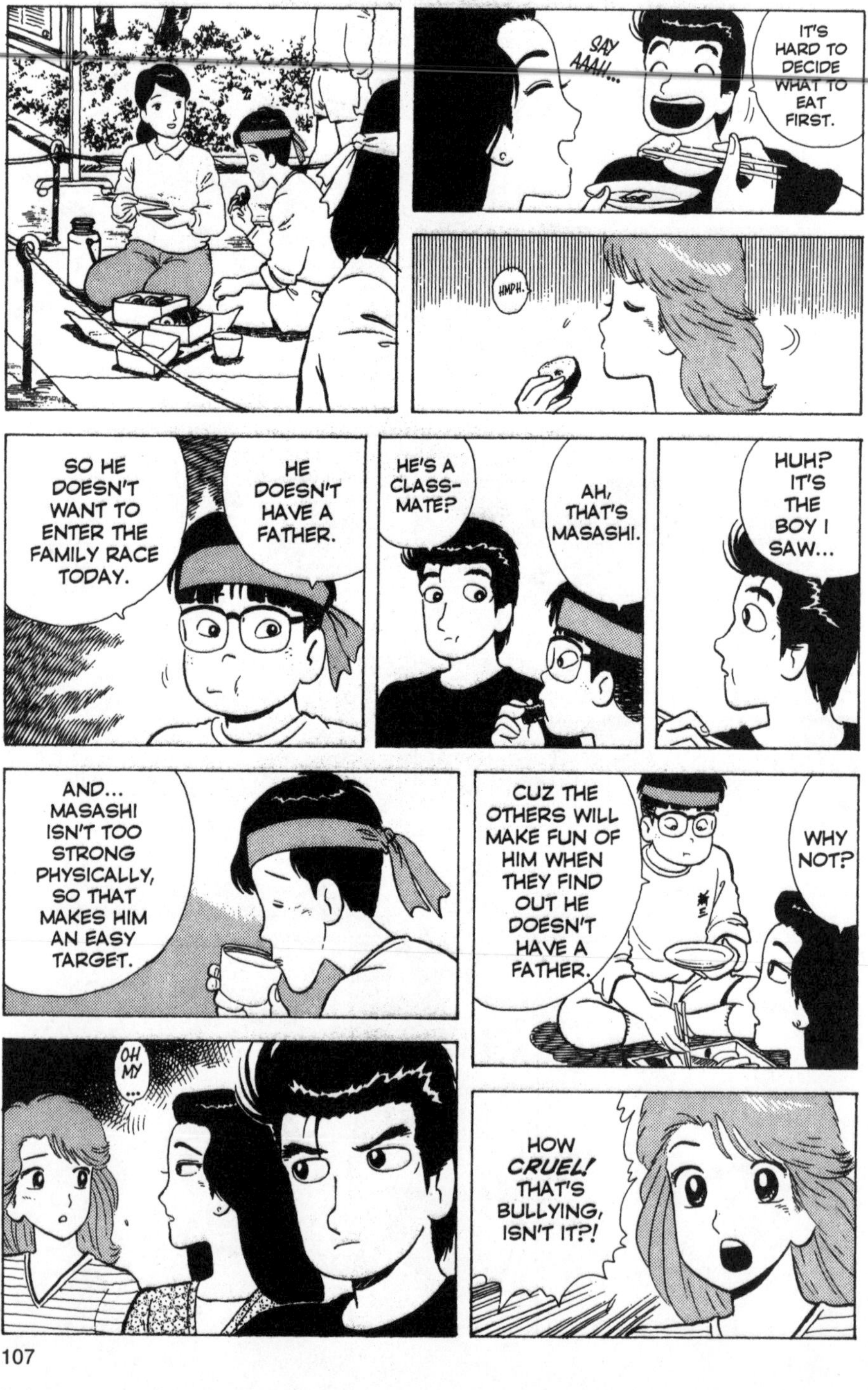
IT'S HARD TO DECIDE WHAT TO EAT FIRST.
SAY AAAH...
HMPH.
HUH? IT'S THE BOY I SAW...
AH, THAT'S MASASHI.
HE'S A CLASSMATE?
HE DOESN'T HAVE A FATHER.
SO HE DOESN'T WANT TO ENTER THE FAMILY RACE TODAY.
WHY NOT?
CUZ THE OTHERS WILL MAKE FUN OF HIM WHEN THEY FIND OUT HE DOESN'T HAVE A FATHER.
AND... MASASHI ISN'T TOO STRONG PHYSICALLY, SO THAT MAKES HIM AN EASY TARGET.
HOW *CRUEL!* THAT'S BULLYING, ISN'T IT?!
OH MY...

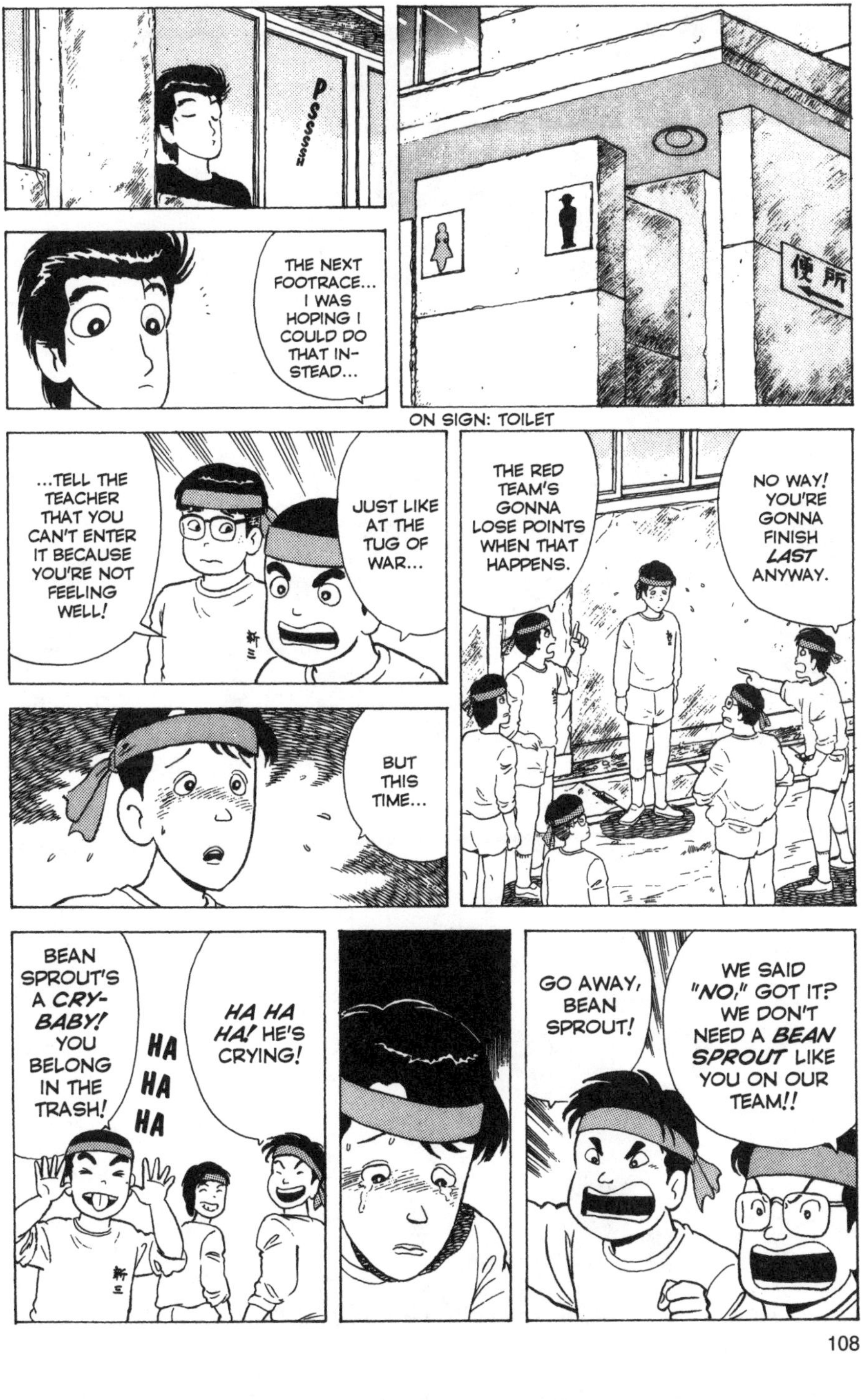
便所
THE NEXT FOOTRACE... I WAS HOPING I COULD DO THAT INSTEAD...
ON SIGN: TOILET
NO WAY! YOU'RE GONNA FINISH *LAST* ANYWAY.
THE RED TEAM'S GONNA LOSE POINTS WHEN THAT HAPPENS.
JUST LIKE AT THE TUG OF WAR...
...TELL THE TEACHER THAT YOU CAN'T ENTER IT BECAUSE YOU'RE NOT FEELING WELL!
BUT THIS TIME...
WE SAID "*NO*," GOT IT? WE DON'T NEED A *BEAN SPROUT* LIKE YOU ON OUR TEAM!!
GO AWAY, BEAN SPROUT!
HA HA HA! HE'S CRYING!
HA HA HA
BEAN SPROUT'S A *CRY-BABY!* YOU BELONG IN THE TRASH!

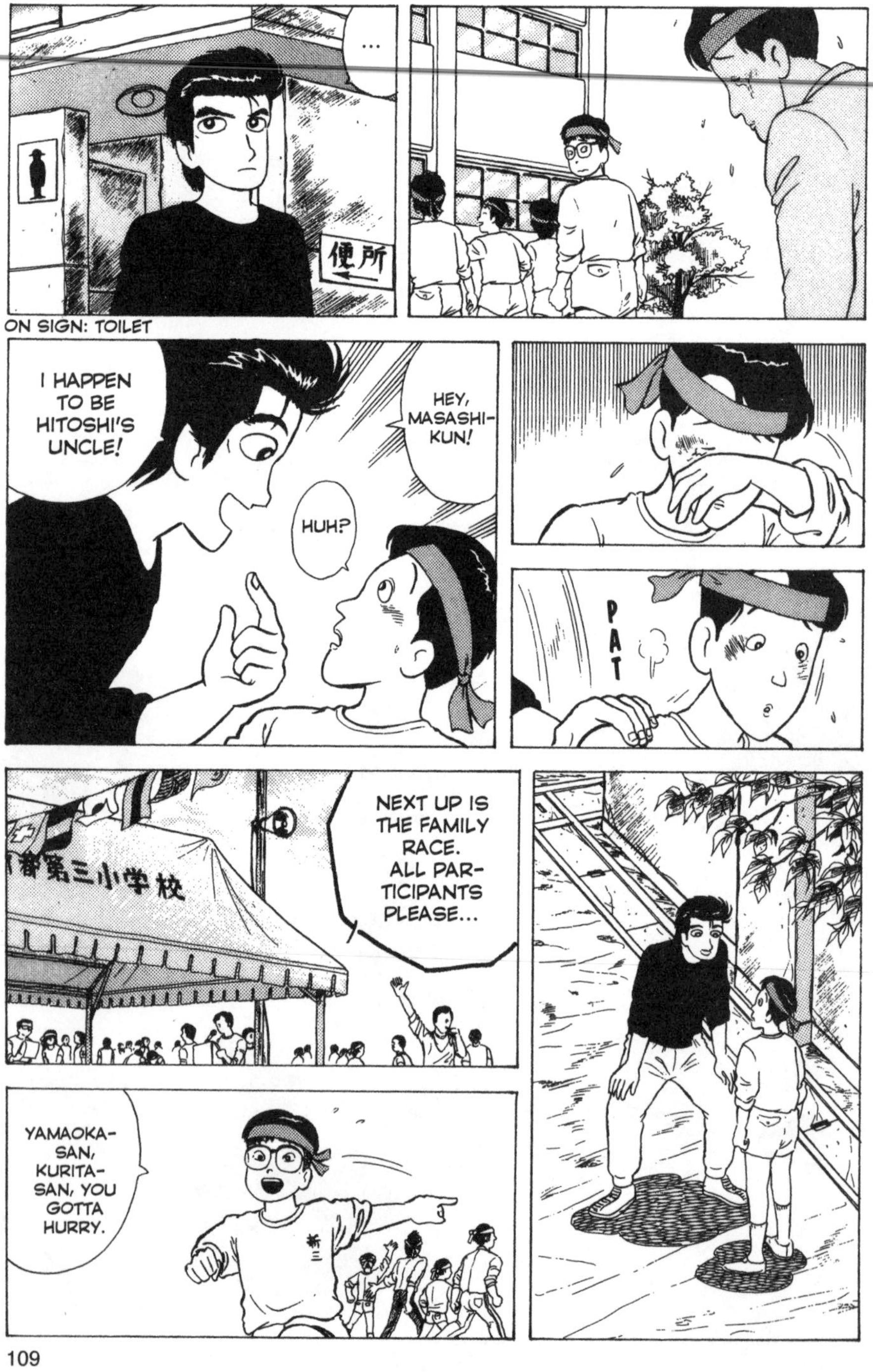
...
便所
ON SIGN: TOILET
PAT
HEY, MASASHI-KUN!
HUH?
I HAPPEN TO BE HITOSHI'S UNCLE!
NEXT UP IS THE FAMILY RACE. ALL PARTICIPANTS PLEASE...
YAMAOKA-SAN, KURITA-SAN, YOU GOTTA HURRY.

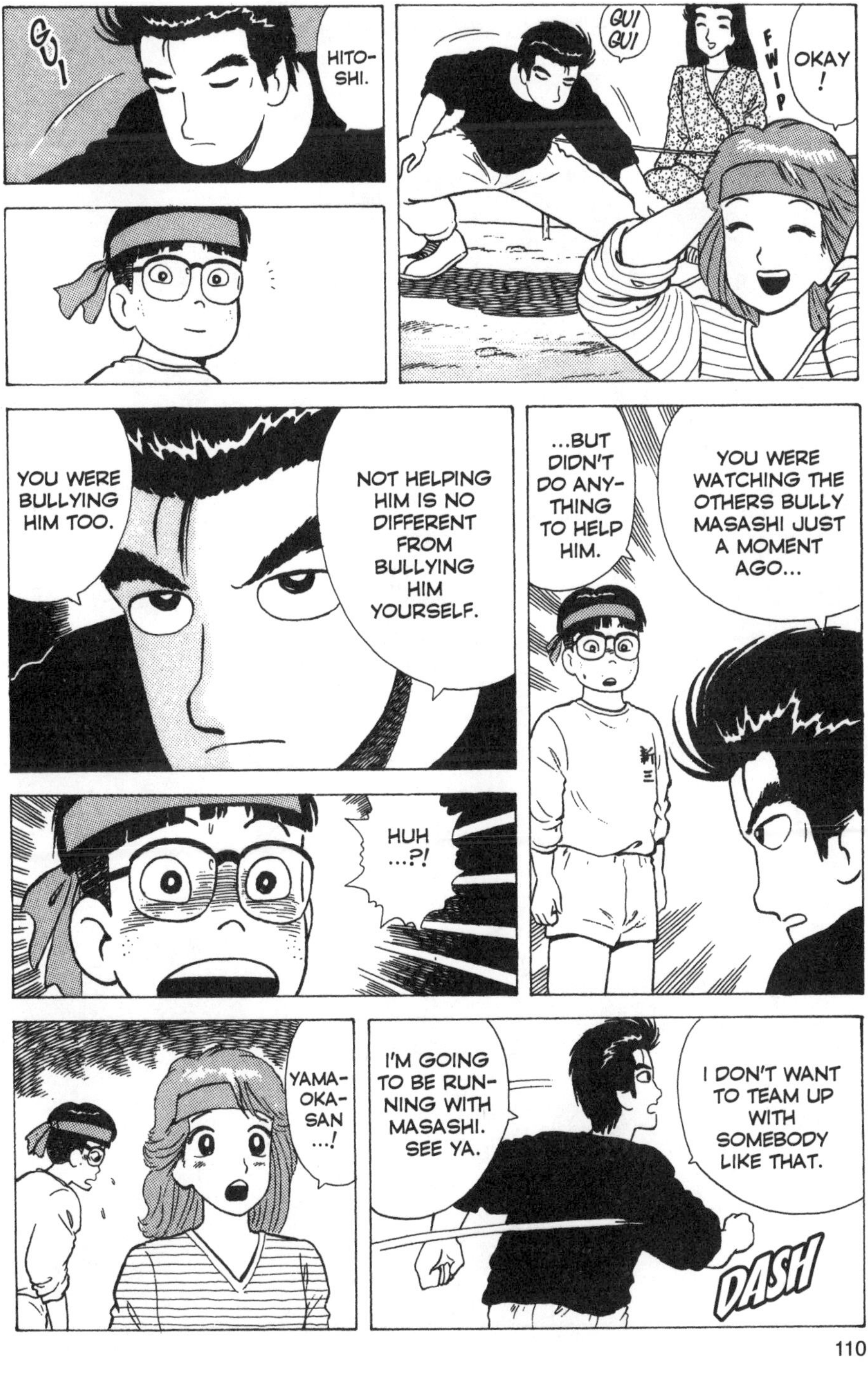
OKAY!
FWIP
GUI GUI
HITOSHI.
GUI
YOU WERE WATCHING THE OTHERS BULLY MASASHI JUST A MOMENT AGO...
...BUT DIDN'T DO ANYTHING TO HELP HIM.
NOT HELPING HIM IS NO DIFFERENT FROM BULLYING HIM YOURSELF.
YOU WERE BULLYING HIM TOO.
HUH ...?!
I DON'T WANT TO TEAM UP WITH SOMEBODY LIKE THAT.
I'M GOING TO BE RUNNING WITH MASASHI. SEE YA.
DASH
YAMAOKA-SAN ...!

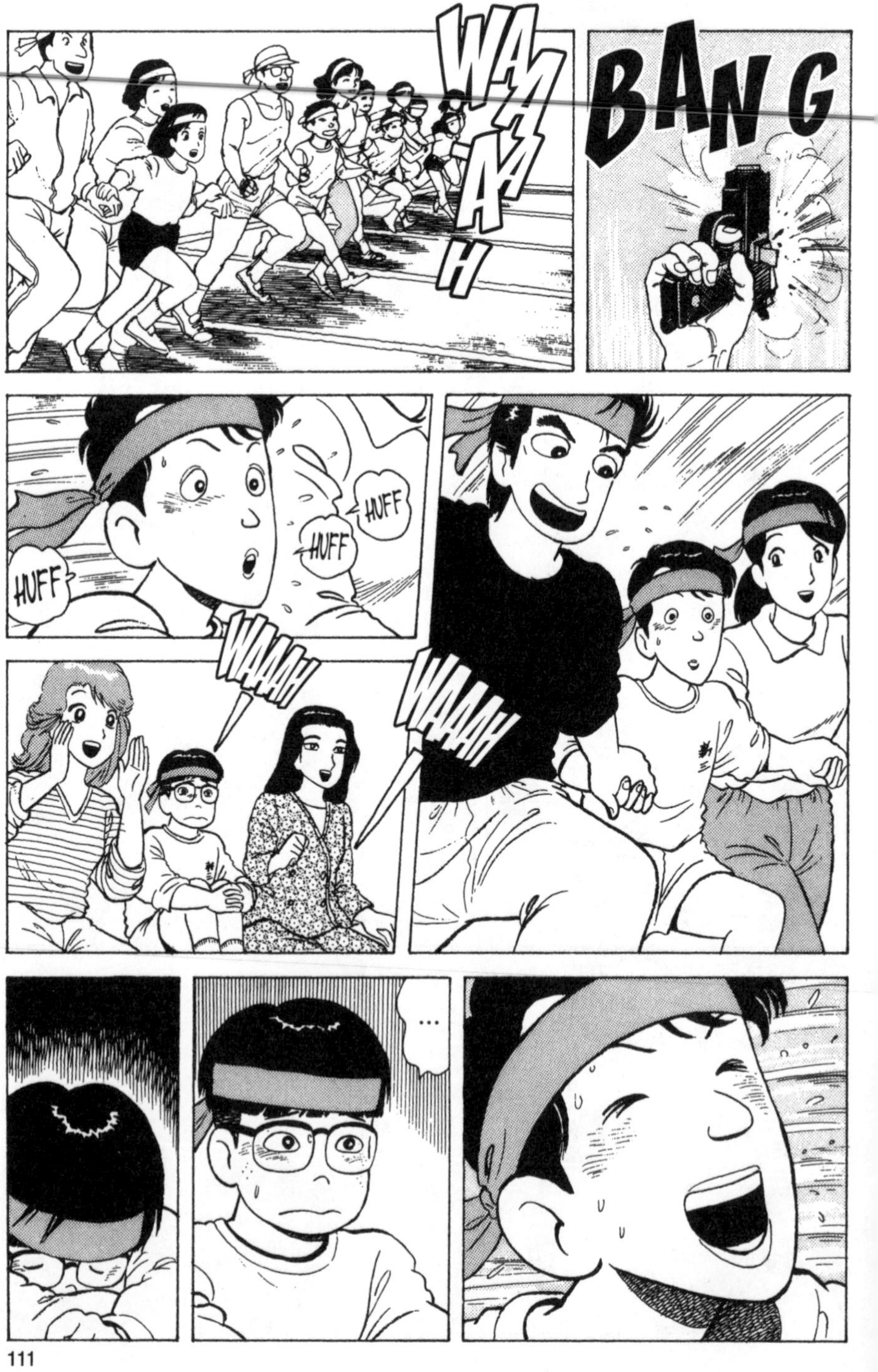

BANG
WAAAAAH
HUFF
HUFF
HUFF
WAAAH
WAAAH
...

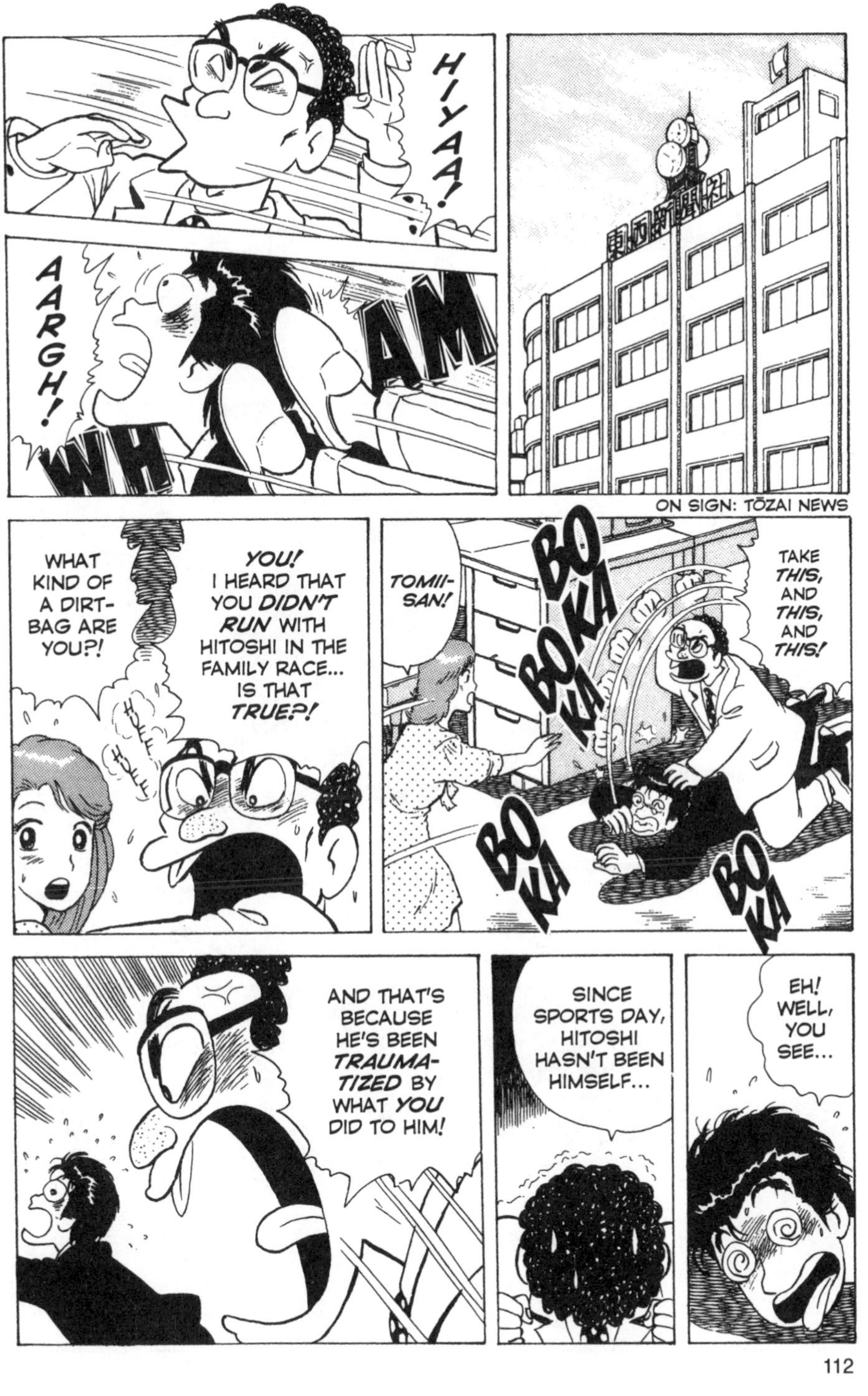
ON SIGN: TŌZAI NEWS
HIYAAA!
AARGH!
WHAM
TAKE THIS, AND THIS, AND THIS!
TOMII-SAN!
BOKA BOKA BOKA BOKA BOKA
YOU! I HEARD THAT YOU DIDN'T RUN WITH HITOSHI IN THE FAMILY RACE... IS THAT TRUE?!
WHAT KIND OF A DIRT-BAG ARE YOU?!
HUFF HUFF
EH! WELL, YOU SEE...
SINCE SPORTS DAY, HITOSHI HASN'T BEEN HIMSELF...
AND THAT'S BECAUSE HE'S BEEN TRAUMATIZED BY WHAT YOU DID TO HIM!

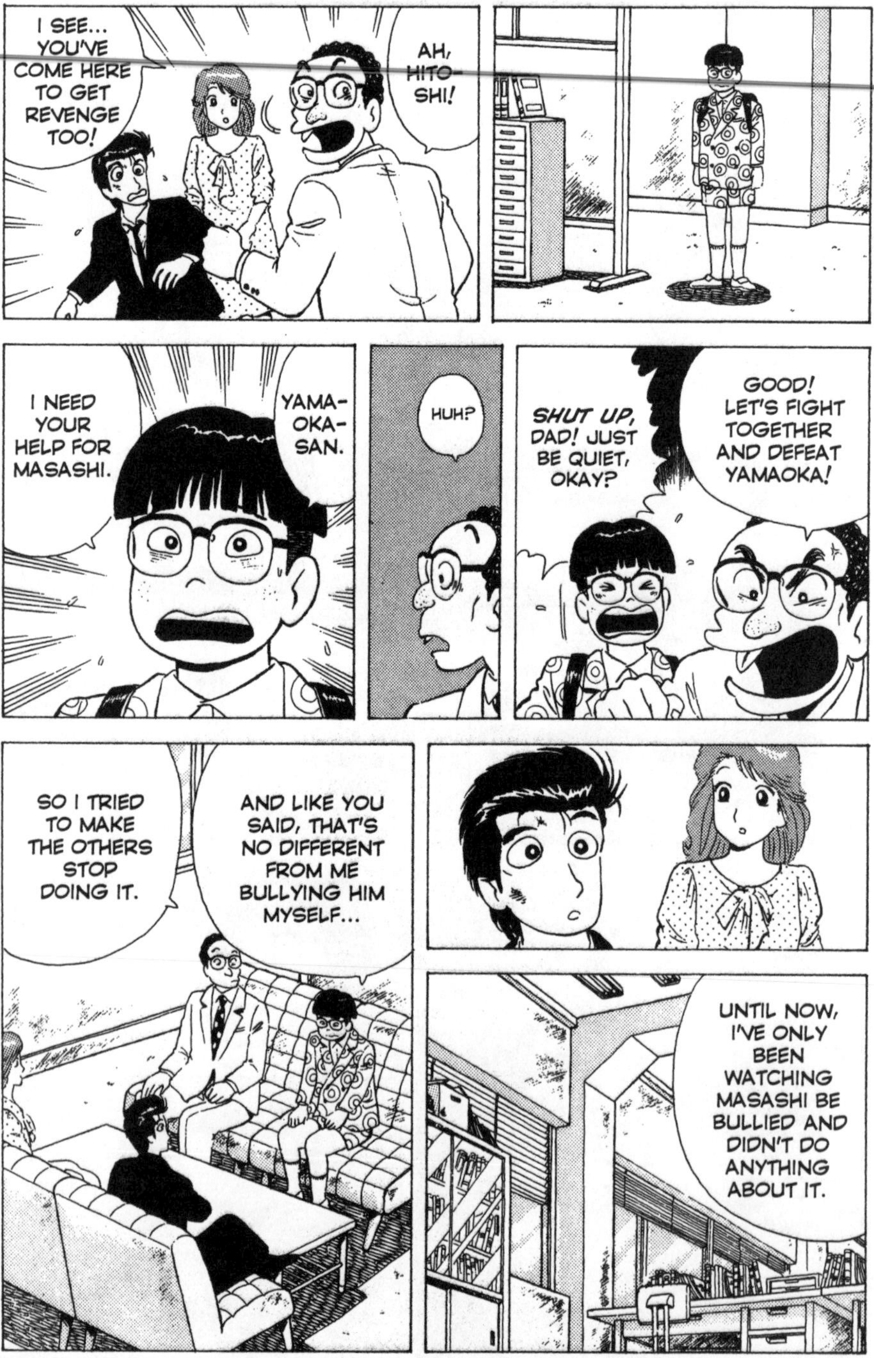
AH, HITO-SHI!
I SEE... YOU'VE COME HERE TO GET REVENGE TOO!
GOOD! LET'S FIGHT TOGETHER AND DEFEAT YAMAOKA!
SHUT UP, DAD! JUST BE QUIET, OKAY?
HUH?
YAMA-OKA-SAN.
I NEED YOUR HELP FOR MASASHI.
UNTIL NOW, I'VE ONLY BEEN WATCHING MASASHI BE BULLIED AND DIDN'T DO ANYTHING ABOUT IT.
AND LIKE YOU SAID, THAT'S NO DIFFERENT FROM ME BULLYING HIM MYSELF...
SO I TRIED TO MAKE THE OTHERS STOP DOING IT.

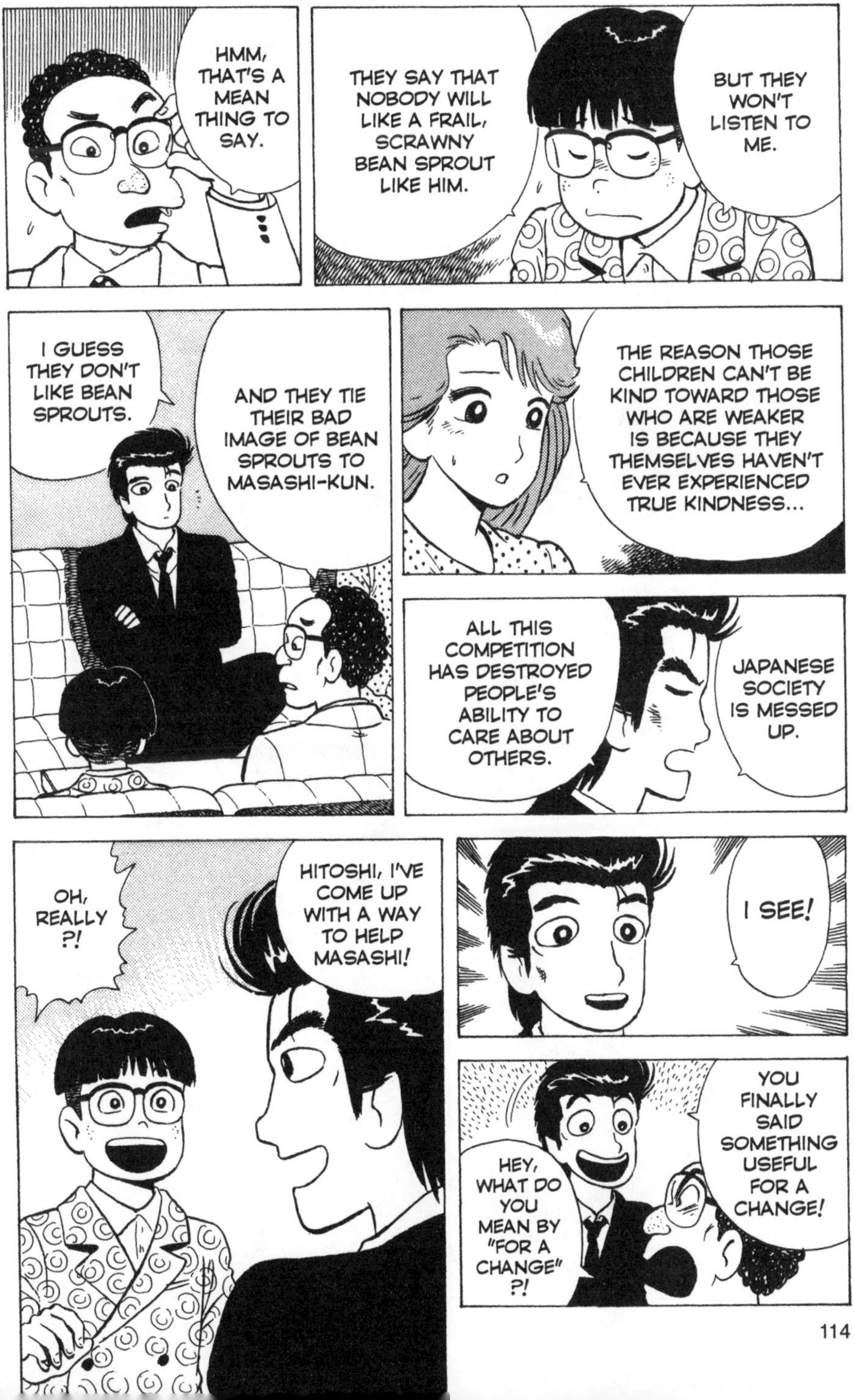

BUT THEY WON'T LISTEN TO ME.
THEY SAY THAT NOBODY WILL LIKE A FRAIL, SCRAWNY BEAN SPROUT LIKE HIM.
HMM, THAT'S A MEAN THING TO SAY.
THE REASON THOSE CHILDREN CAN'T BE KIND TOWARD THOSE WHO ARE WEAKER IS BECAUSE THEY THEMSELVES HAVEN'T EVER EXPERIENCED TRUE KINDNESS...
JAPANESE SOCIETY IS MESSED UP.
ALL THIS COMPETITION HAS DESTROYED PEOPLE'S ABILITY TO CARE ABOUT OTHERS.
I GUESS THEY DON'T LIKE BEAN SPROUTS.
AND THEY TIE THEIR BAD IMAGE OF BEAN SPROUTS TO MASASHI-KUN.
I SEE!
YOU FINALLY SAID SOMETHING USEFUL FOR A CHANGE!
HEY, WHAT DO YOU MEAN BY "FOR A CHANGE" ?!
HITOSHI, I'VE COME UP WITH A WAY TO HELP MASASHI!
OH, REALLY ?!

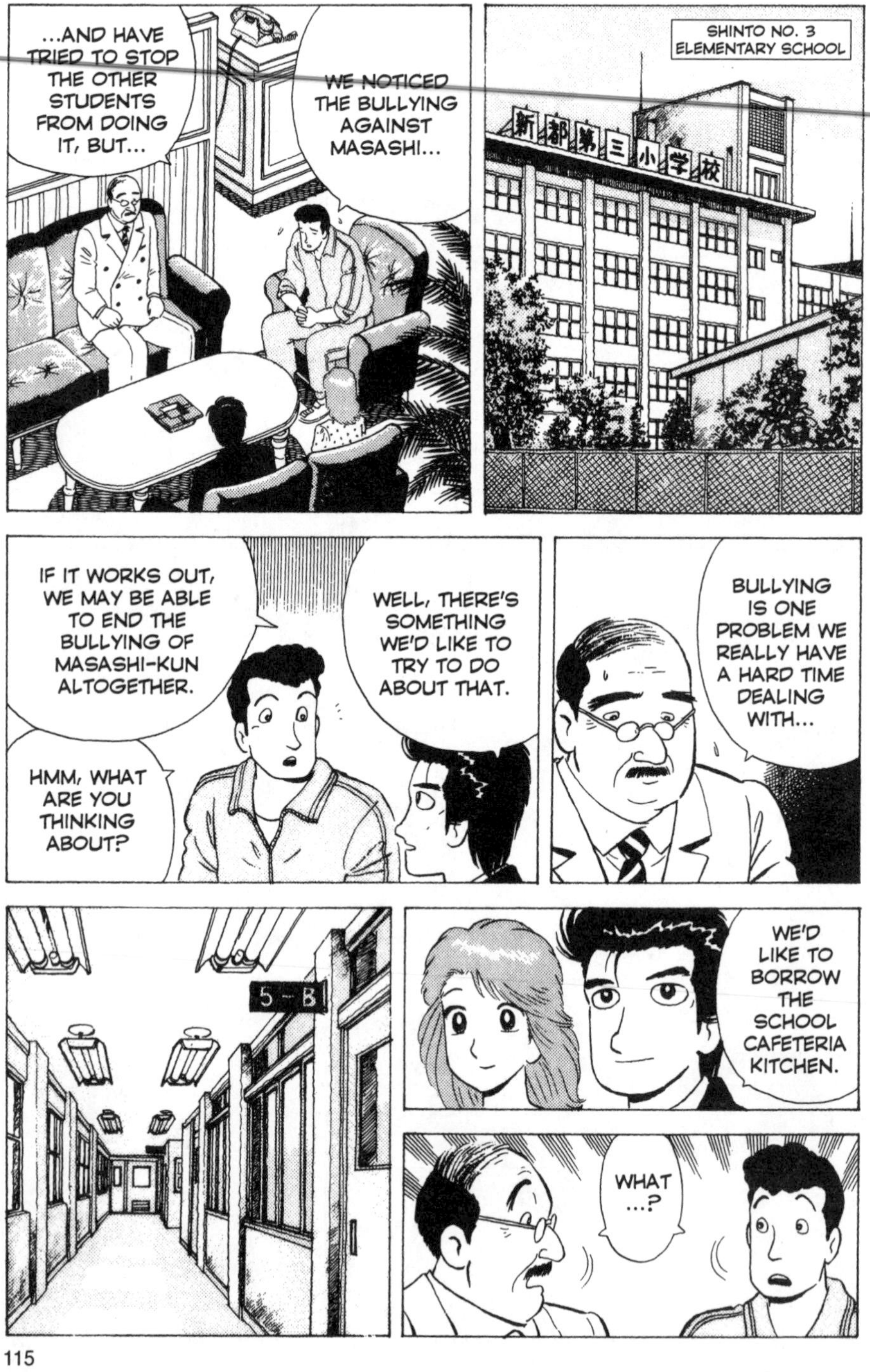
SHINTO NO. 3 ELEMENTARY SCHOOL
新都第三小学校
WE NOTICED THE BULLYING AGAINST MASASHI...
...AND HAVE TRIED TO STOP THE OTHER STUDENTS FROM DOING IT, BUT...
BULLYING IS ONE PROBLEM WE REALLY HAVE A HARD TIME DEALING WITH...
WELL, THERE'S SOMETHING WE'D LIKE TO TRY TO DO ABOUT THAT.
IF IT WORKS OUT, WE MAY BE ABLE TO END THE BULLYING OF MASASHI-KUN ALTOGETHER.
HMM, WHAT ARE YOU THINKING ABOUT?
WE'D LIKE TO BORROW THE SCHOOL CAFETERIA KITCHEN.
WHAT ...?
5-B

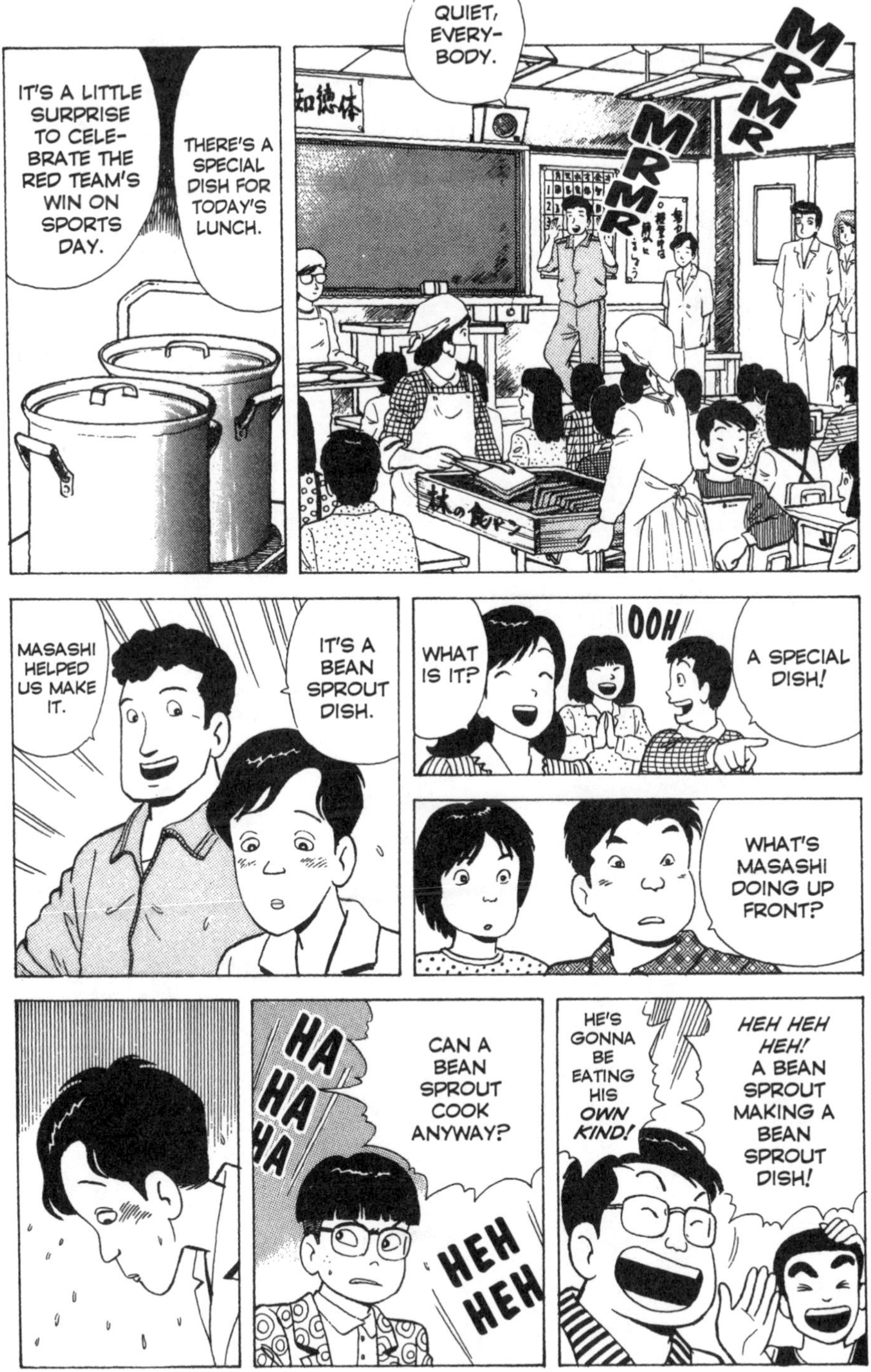
MRMR
MRMR
QUIET, EVERYBODY.
THERE'S A SPECIAL DISH FOR TODAY'S LUNCH.
IT'S A LITTLE SURPRISE TO CELEBRATE THE RED TEAM'S WIN ON SPORTS DAY.
A SPECIAL DISH!
OOH
WHAT IS IT?
WHAT'S MASASHI DOING UP FRONT?
IT'S A BEAN SPROUT DISH.
MASASHI HELPED US MAKE IT.
HEH HEH HEH! A BEAN SPROUT MAKING A BEAN SPROUT DISH!
HE'S GONNA BE EATING HIS *OWN KIND!*
CAN A BEAN SPROUT COOK ANYWAY?
HA HA HA
HEH HEH

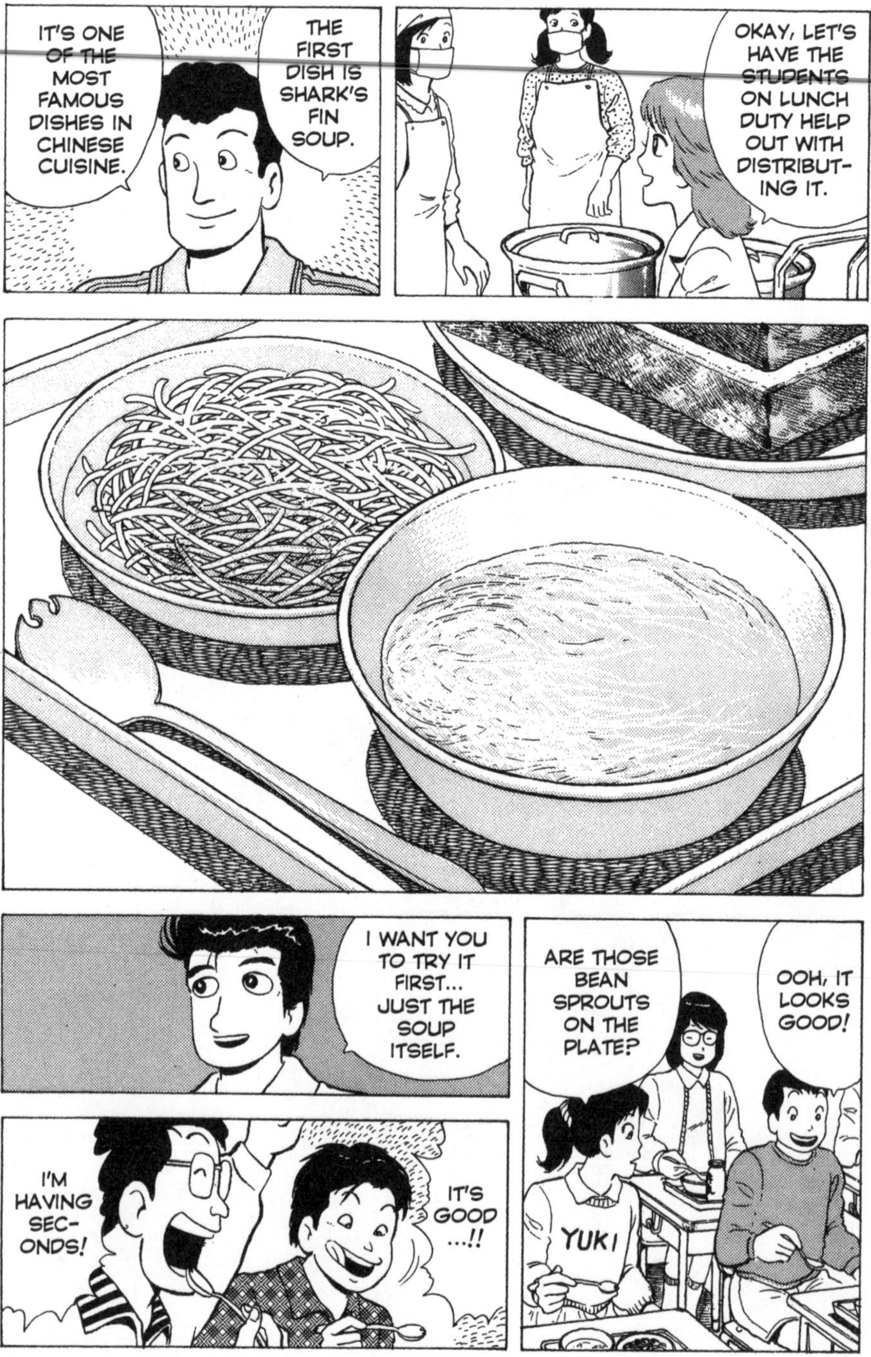
OKAY, LET'S HAVE THE STUDENTS ON LUNCH DUTY HELP OUT WITH DISTRIBUT-ING IT.
THE FIRST DISH IS SHARK'S FIN SOUP.
IT'S ONE OF THE MOST FAMOUS DISHES IN CHINESE CUISINE.
OOH, IT LOOKS GOOD!
ARE THOSE BEAN SPROUTS ON THE PLATE?
YUKI
I WANT YOU TO TRY IT FIRST... JUST THE SOUP ITSELF.
IT'S GOOD ...!!
I'M HAVING SEC-ONDS!

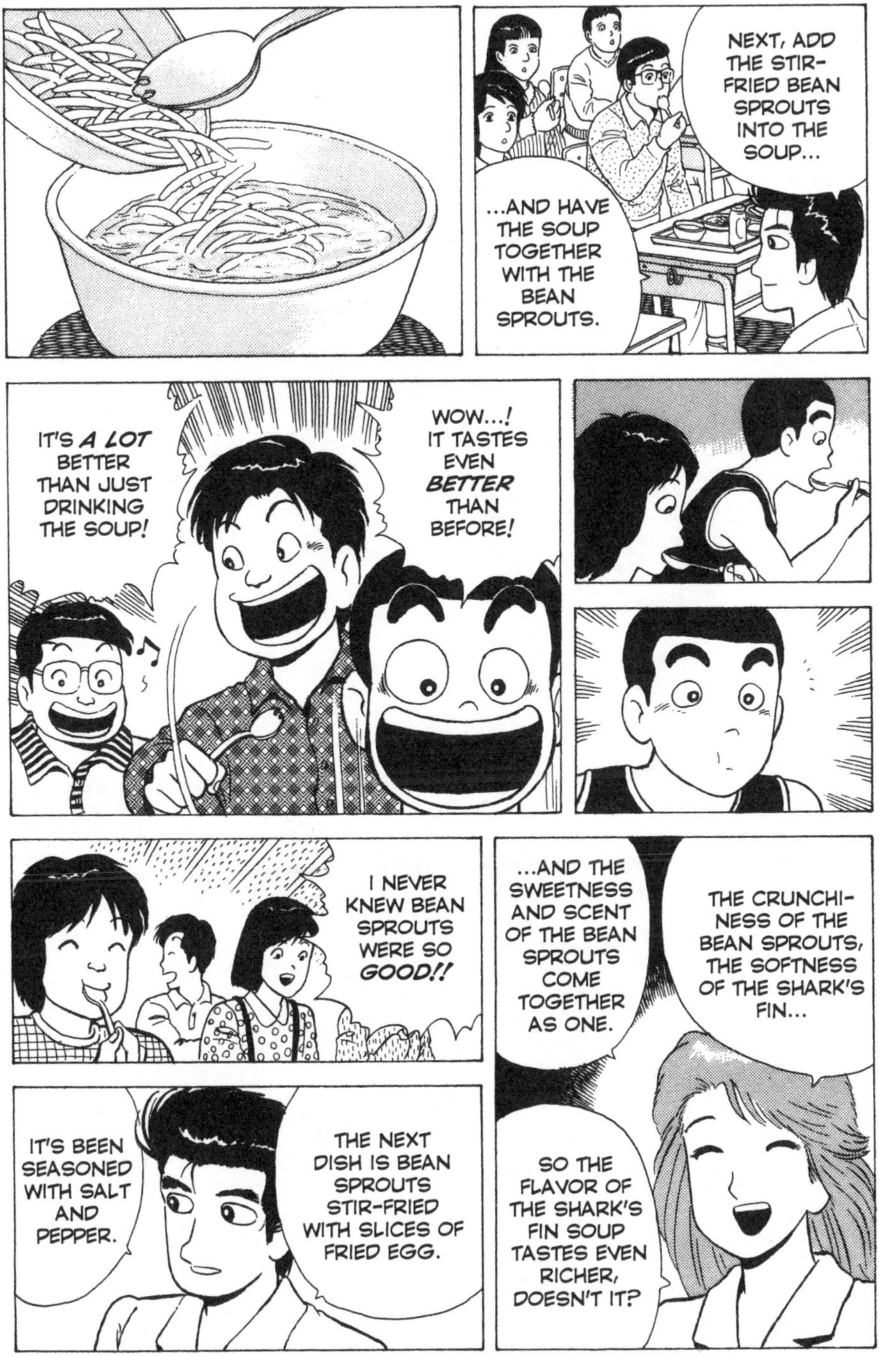

NEXT, ADD THE STIR-FRIED BEAN SPROUTS INTO THE SOUP...
...AND HAVE THE SOUP TOGETHER WITH THE BEAN SPROUTS.
WOW...! IT TASTES EVEN *BETTER* THAN BEFORE!
IT'S *A LOT* BETTER THAN JUST DRINKING THE SOUP!
THE CRUNCHI-NESS OF THE BEAN SPROUTS, THE SOFTNESS OF THE SHARK'S FIN...
...AND THE SWEETNESS AND SCENT OF THE BEAN SPROUTS COME TOGETHER AS ONE.
SO THE FLAVOR OF THE SHARK'S FIN SOUP TASTES EVEN RICHER, DOESN'T IT?
I NEVER KNEW BEAN SPROUTS WERE SO *GOOD!!*
THE NEXT DISH IS BEAN SPROUTS STIR-FRIED WITH SLICES OF FRIED EGG.
IT'S BEEN SEASONED WITH SALT AND PEPPER.

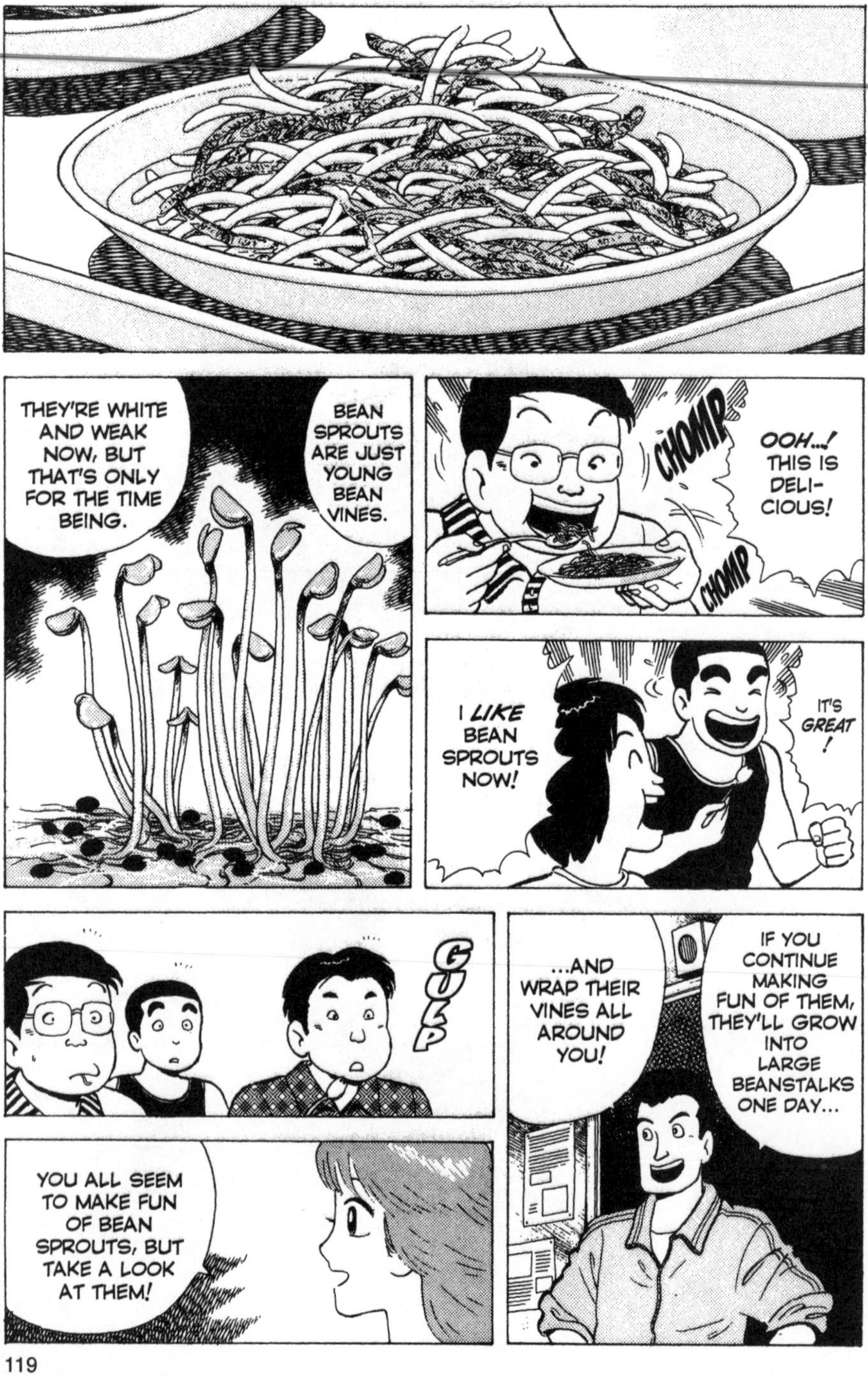
OOH...! THIS IS DELI-CIOUS!
CHOMP
CHOMP
IT'S GREAT!
I LIKE BEAN SPROUTS NOW!
BEAN SPROUTS ARE JUST YOUNG BEAN VINES.
THEY'RE WHITE AND WEAK NOW, BUT THAT'S ONLY FOR THE TIME BEING.
IF YOU CONTINUE MAKING FUN OF THEM, THEY'LL GROW INTO LARGE BEANSTALKS ONE DAY...
...AND WRAP THEIR VINES ALL AROUND YOU!
GULP
YOU ALL SEEM TO MAKE FUN OF BEAN SPROUTS, BUT TAKE A LOOK AT THEM!

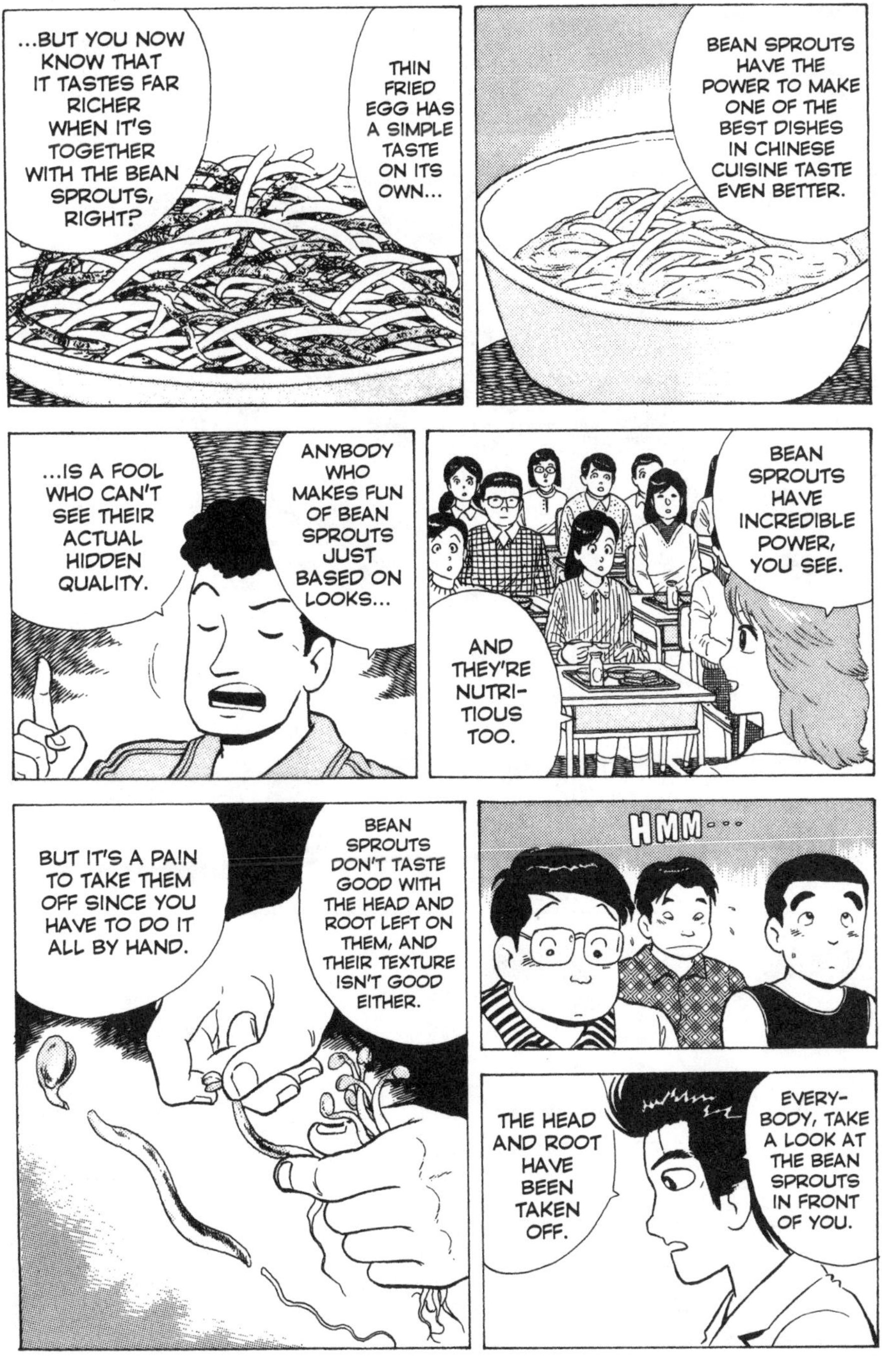
BEAN SPROUTS HAVE THE POWER TO MAKE ONE OF THE BEST DISHES IN CHINESE CUISINE TASTE EVEN BETTER.
THIN FRIED EGG HAS A SIMPLE TASTE ON ITS OWN...
...BUT YOU NOW KNOW THAT IT TASTES FAR RICHER WHEN IT'S TOGETHER WITH THE BEAN SPROUTS, RIGHT?
BEAN SPROUTS HAVE INCREDIBLE POWER, YOU SEE.
AND THEY'RE NUTRITIOUS TOO.
ANYBODY WHO MAKES FUN OF BEAN SPROUTS JUST BASED ON LOOKS...
...IS A FOOL WHO CAN'T SEE THEIR ACTUAL HIDDEN QUALITY.
HMM...
EVERYBODY, TAKE A LOOK AT THE BEAN SPROUTS IN FRONT OF YOU.
THE HEAD AND ROOT HAVE BEEN TAKEN OFF.
BEAN SPROUTS DON'T TASTE GOOD WITH THE HEAD AND ROOT LEFT ON THEM, AND THEIR TEXTURE ISN'T GOOD EITHER.
BUT IT'S A PAIN TO TAKE THEM OFF SINCE YOU HAVE TO DO IT ALL BY HAND.

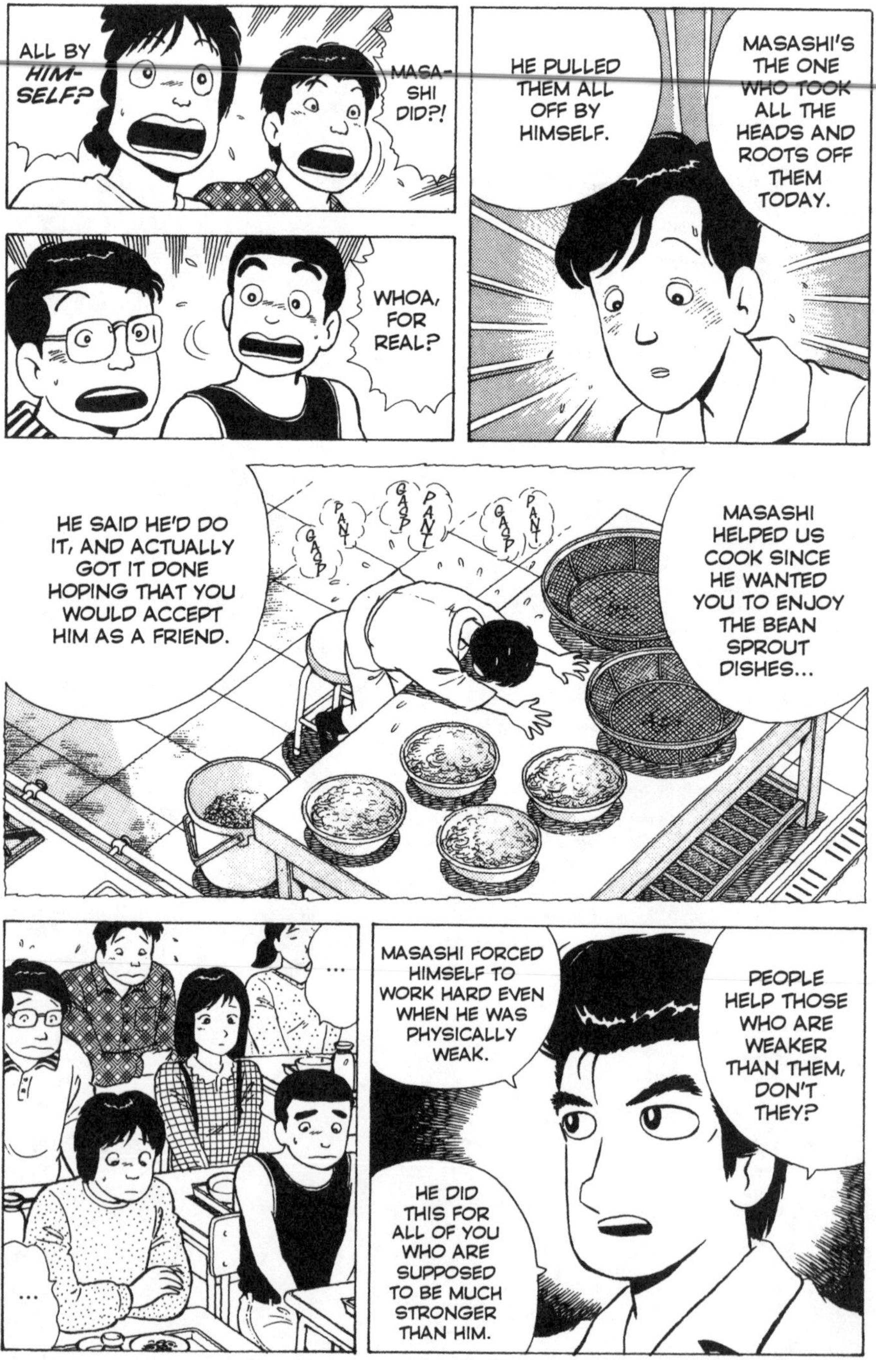
MASASHI'S THE ONE WHO TOOK ALL THE HEADS AND ROOTS OFF THEM TODAY.
HE PULLED THEM ALL OFF BY HIMSELF.
MASASHI DID?!
ALL BY HIMSELF?
WHOA, FOR REAL?
MASASHI HELPED US COOK SINCE HE WANTED YOU TO ENJOY THE BEAN SPROUT DISHES...
HE SAID HE'D DO IT, AND ACTUALLY GOT IT DONE HOPING THAT YOU WOULD ACCEPT HIM AS A FRIEND.
PANT
GASP
PANT
GASP
PANT
GASP
PEOPLE HELP THOSE WHO ARE WEAKER THAN THEM, DON'T THEY?
MASASHI FORCED HIMSELF TO WORK HARD EVEN WHEN HE WAS PHYSICALLY WEAK.
HE DID THIS FOR ALL OF YOU WHO ARE SUPPOSED TO BE MUCH STRONGER THAN HIM.
...
...

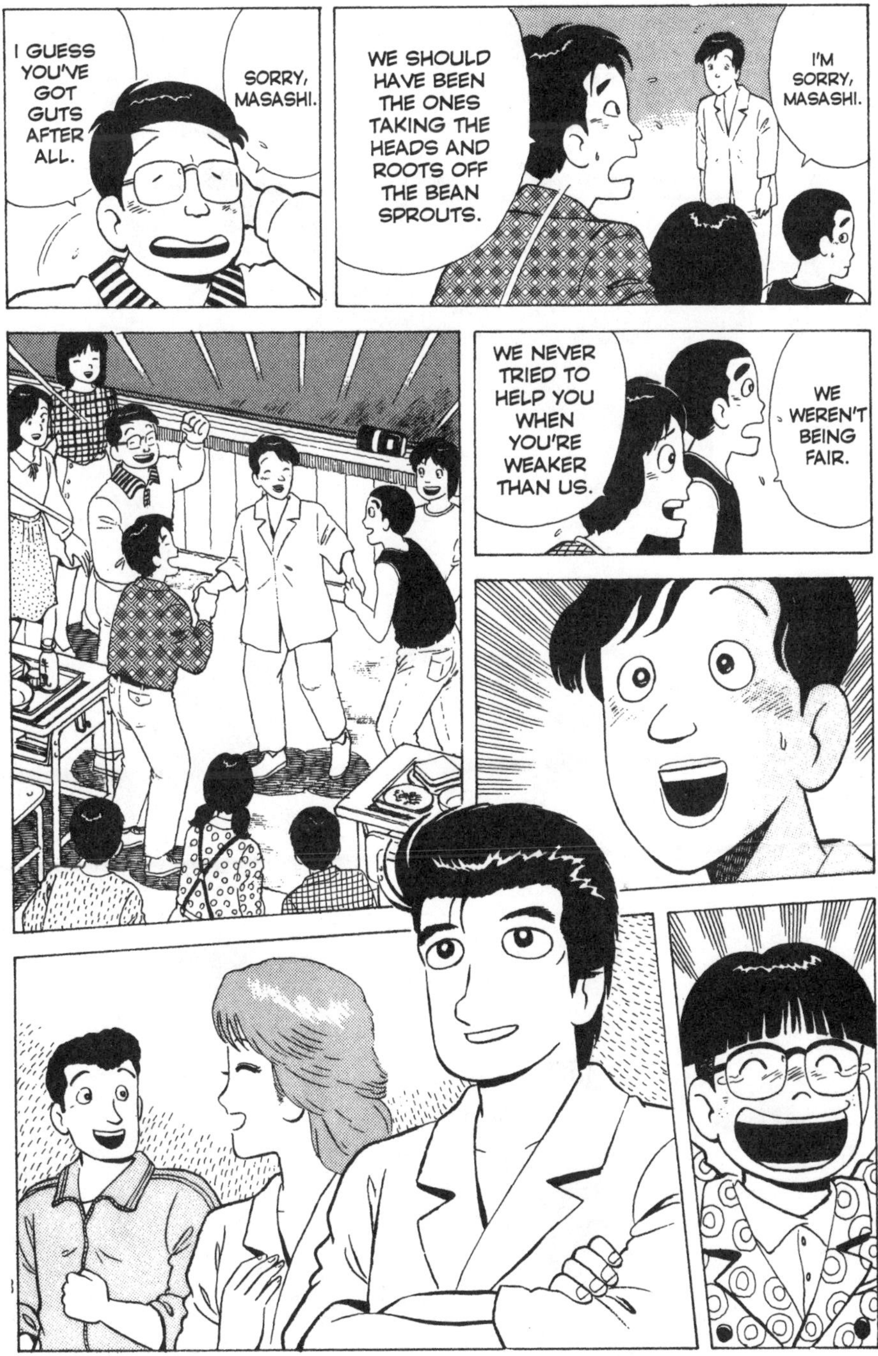
I'M SORRY, MASASHI.
WE SHOULD HAVE BEEN THE ONES TAKING THE HEADS AND ROOTS OFF THE BEAN SPROUTS.
SORRY, MASASHI.
I GUESS YOU'VE GOT GUTS AFTER ALL.
WE WEREN'T BEING FAIR.
WE NEVER TRIED TO HELP YOU WHEN YOU'RE WEAKER THAN US.

FOURTH COURSE

GOOD EGGPLANT, BAD EGGPLANT

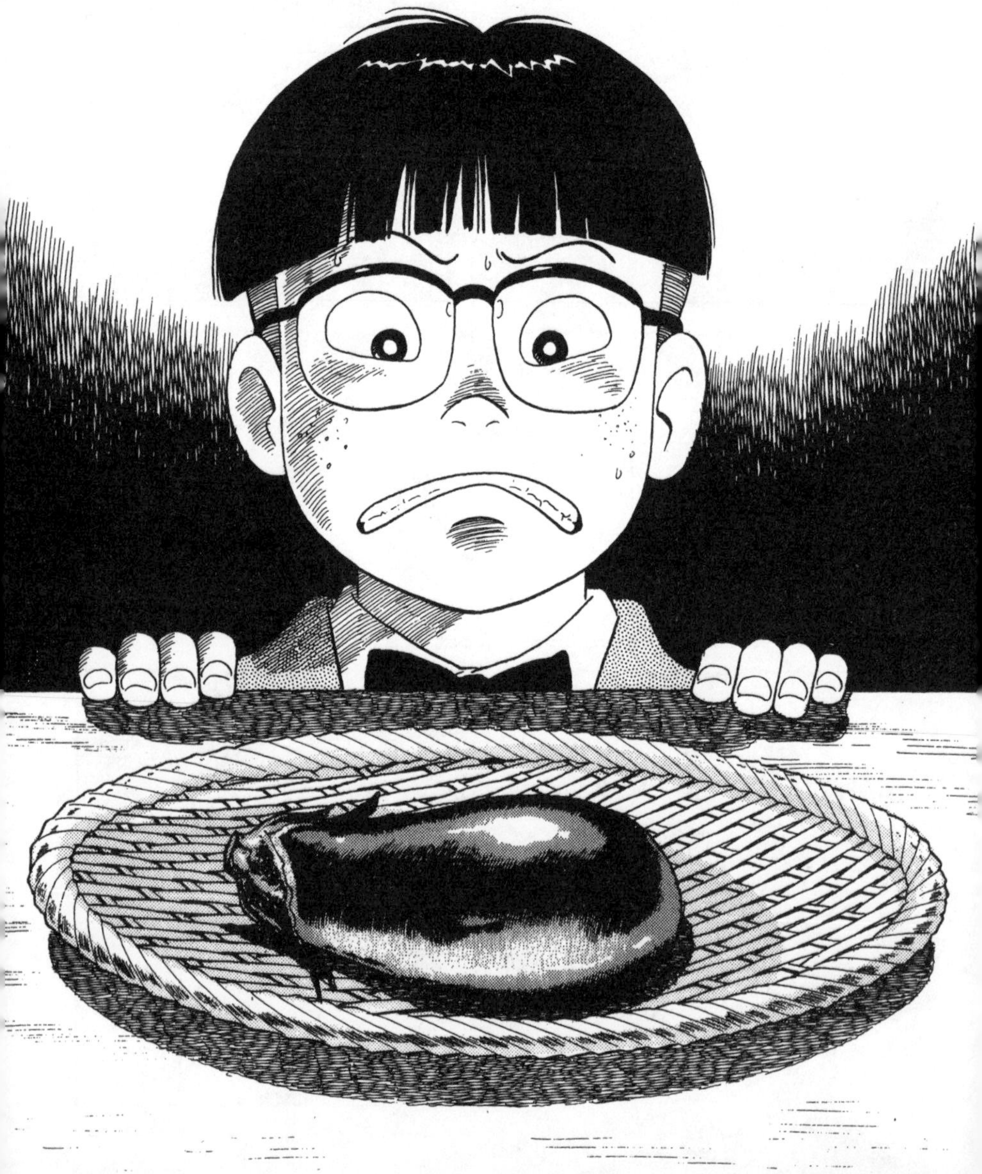

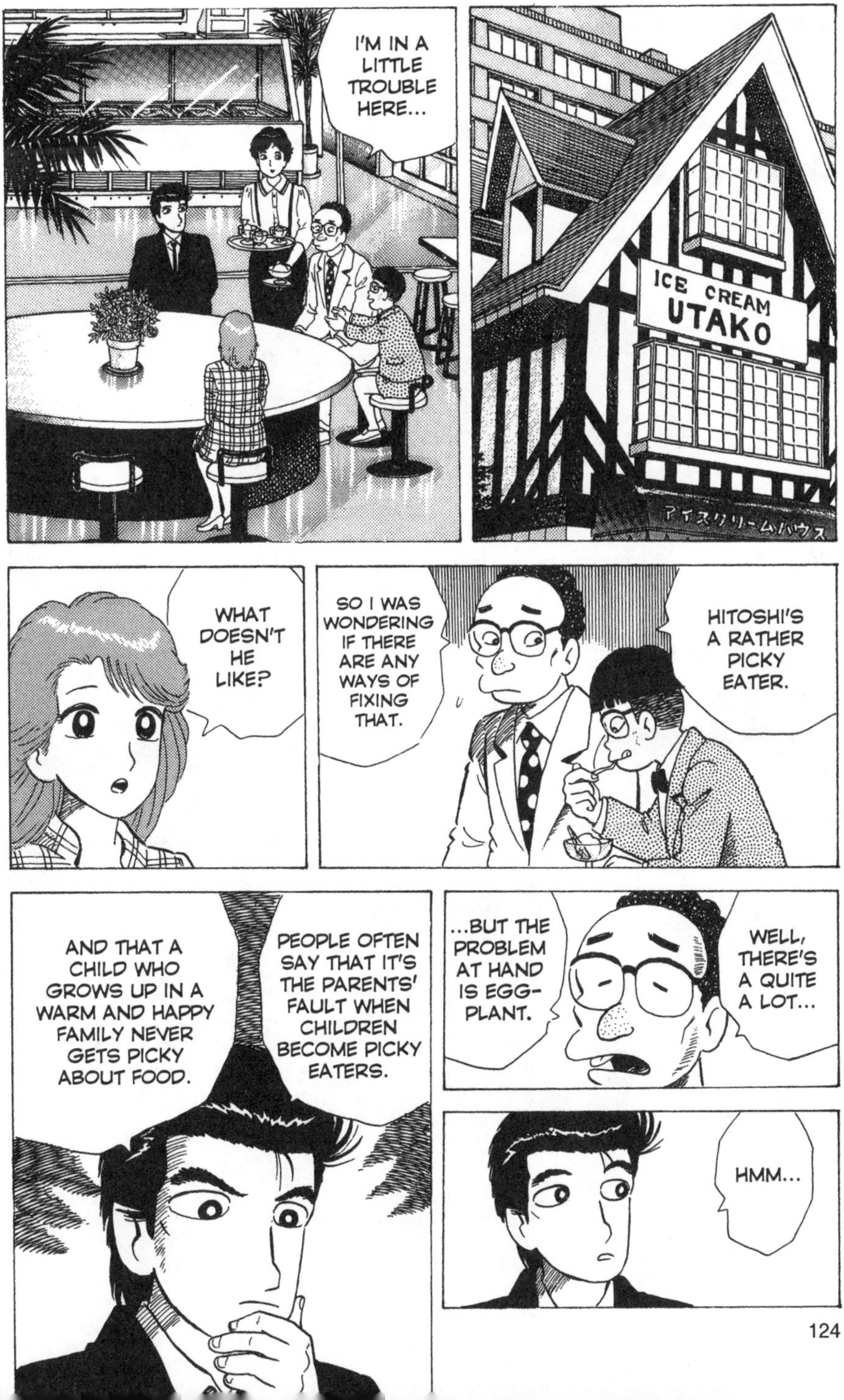
ICE CREAM
UTAKO
アイスクリームハウス
I'M IN A LITTLE TROUBLE HERE...
HITOSHI'S A RATHER PICKY EATER.
SO I WAS WONDERING IF THERE ARE ANY WAYS OF FIXING THAT.
WHAT DOESN'T HE LIKE?
WELL, THERE'S A QUITE A LOT...
...BUT THE PROBLEM AT HAND IS EGG-PLANT.
HMM...
PEOPLE OFTEN SAY THAT IT'S THE PARENTS' FAULT WHEN CHILDREN BECOME PICKY EATERS.
AND THAT A CHILD WHO GROWS UP IN A WARM AND HAPPY FAMILY NEVER GETS PICKY ABOUT FOOD.

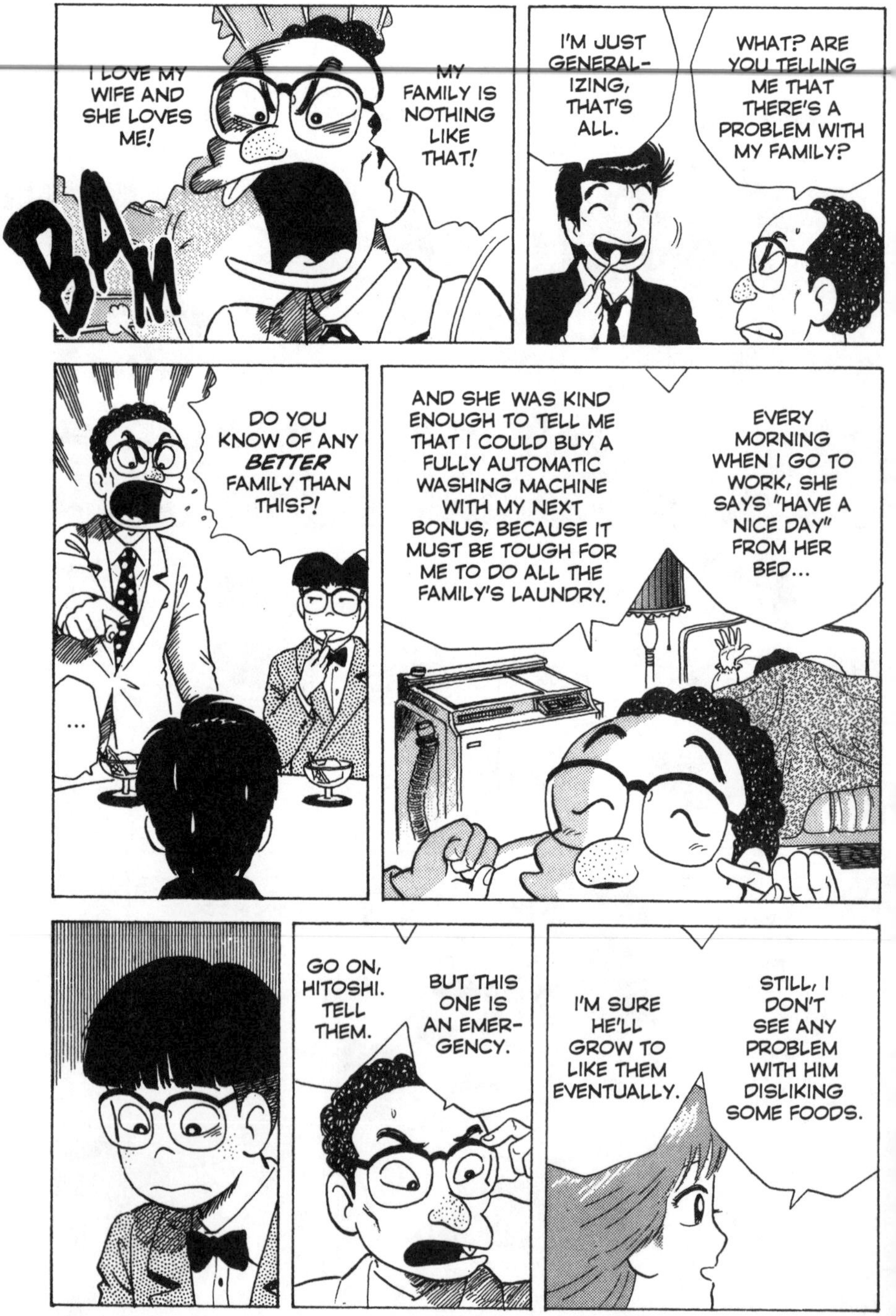
WHAT? ARE YOU TELLING ME THAT THERE'S A PROBLEM WITH MY FAMILY?
I'M JUST GENERAL-IZING, THAT'S ALL.
MY FAMILY IS NOTHING LIKE THAT!
I LOVE MY WIFE AND SHE LOVES ME!
BAM
EVERY MORNING WHEN I GO TO WORK, SHE SAYS "HAVE A NICE DAY" FROM HER BED...
AND SHE WAS KIND ENOUGH TO TELL ME THAT I COULD BUY A FULLY AUTOMATIC WASHING MACHINE WITH MY NEXT BONUS, BECAUSE IT MUST BE TOUGH FOR ME TO DO ALL THE FAMILY'S LAUNDRY.
DO YOU KNOW OF ANY *BETTER* FAMILY THAN THIS?!
...
STILL, I DON'T SEE ANY PROBLEM WITH HIM DISLIKING SOME FOODS.
I'M SURE HE'LL GROW TO LIKE THEM EVENTUALLY.
BUT THIS ONE IS AN EMER-GENCY.
GO ON, HITOSHI. TELL THEM.

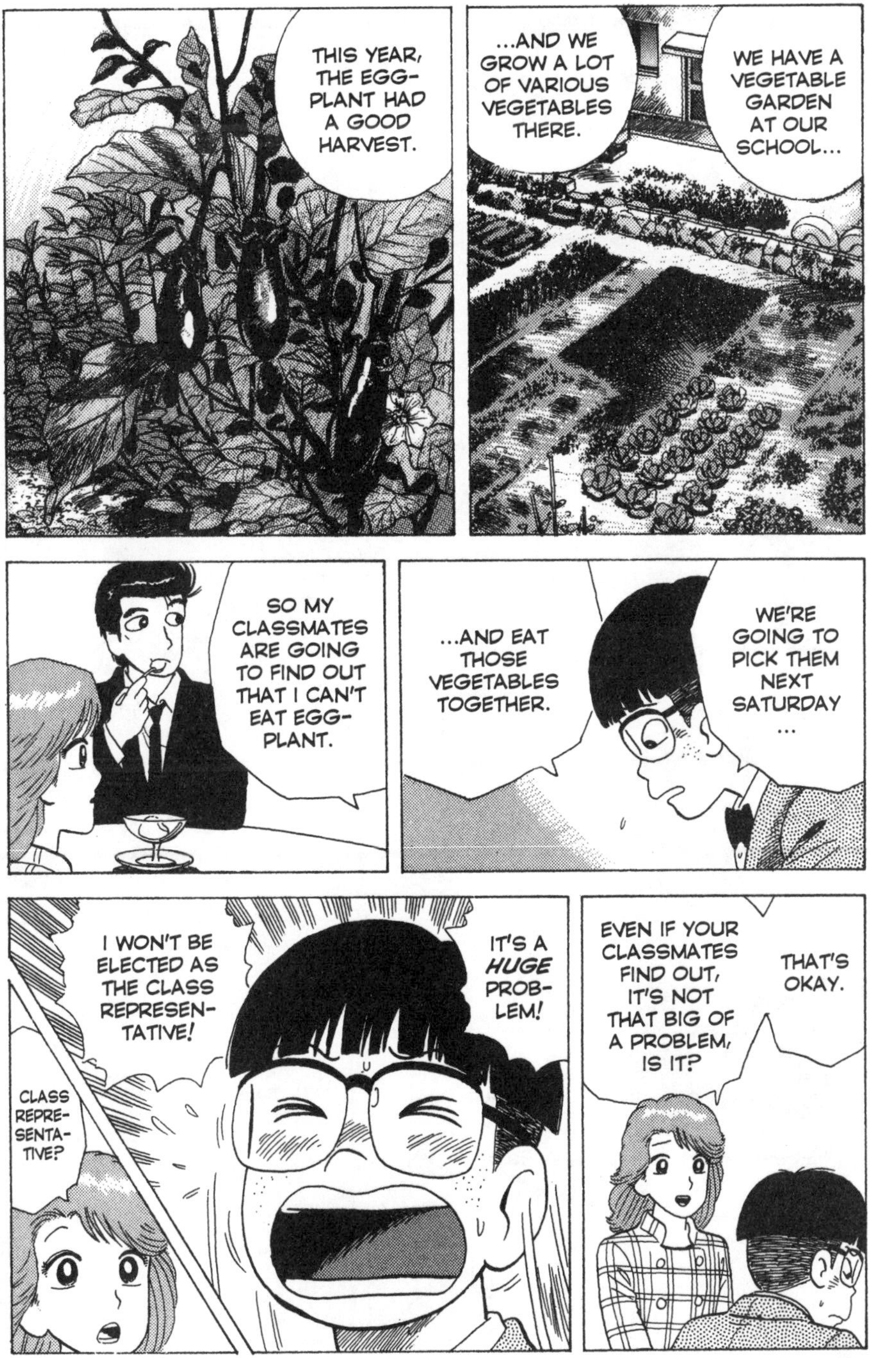
WE HAVE A VEGETABLE GARDEN AT OUR SCHOOL...
...AND WE GROW A LOT OF VARIOUS VEGETABLES THERE.
THIS YEAR, THE EGG-PLANT HAD A GOOD HARVEST.
WE'RE GOING TO PICK THEM NEXT SATURDAY ...
...AND EAT THOSE VEGETABLES TOGETHER.
SO MY CLASSMATES ARE GOING TO FIND OUT THAT I CAN'T EAT EGG-PLANT.
EVEN IF YOUR CLASSMATES FIND OUT, IT'S NOT THAT BIG OF A PROBLEM, IS IT?
THAT'S OKAY.
IT'S A *HUGE* PROB-LEM!
I WON'T BE ELECTED AS THE CLASS REPRESEN-TATIVE!
CLASS REPRE-SENTA-TIVE?

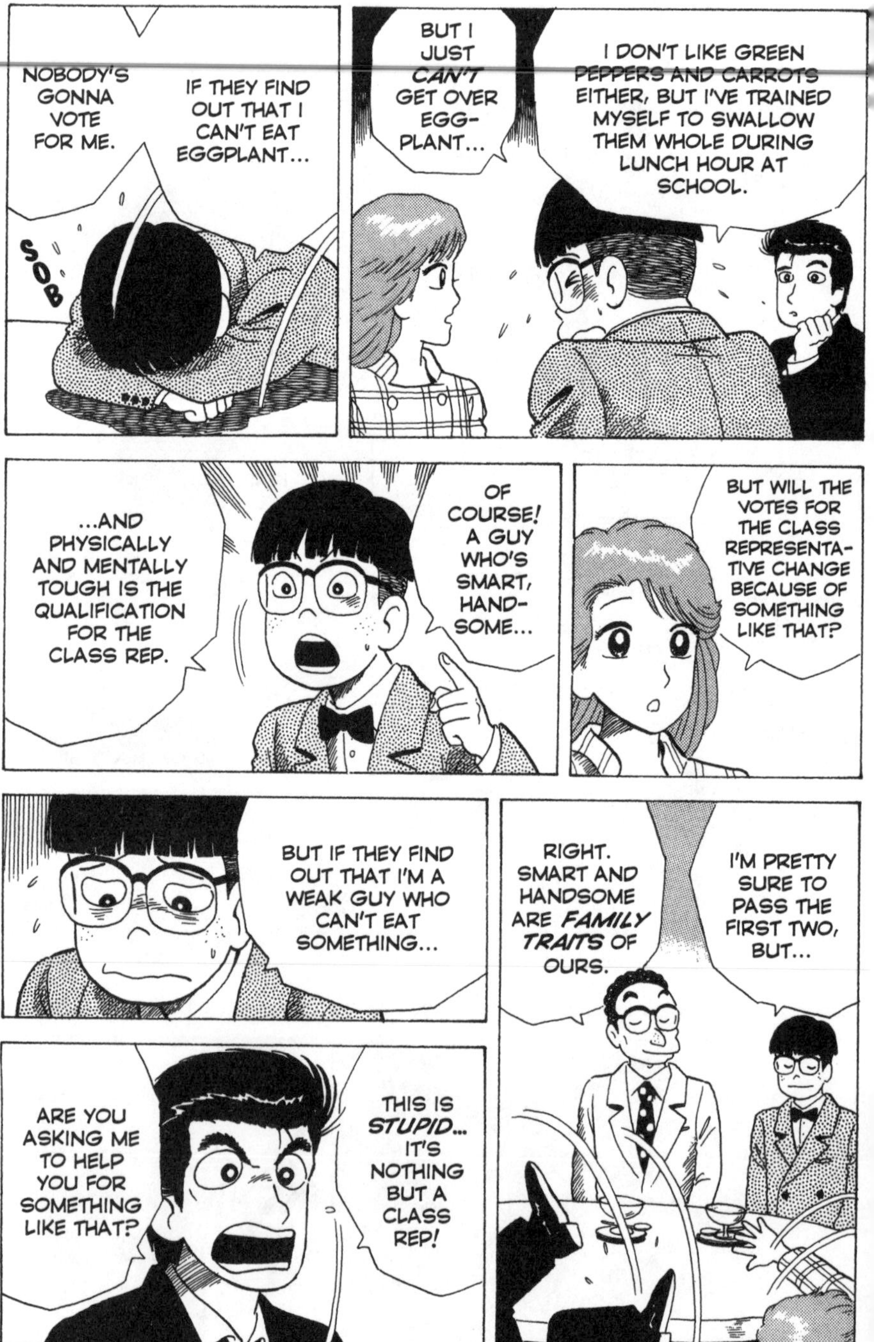
I DON'T LIKE GREEN PEPPERS AND CARROTS EITHER, BUT I'VE TRAINED MYSELF TO SWALLOW THEM WHOLE DURING LUNCH HOUR AT SCHOOL.
BUT I JUST *CAN'T* GET OVER EGG-PLANT...
IF THEY FIND OUT THAT I CAN'T EAT EGGPLANT...
NOBODY'S GONNA VOTE FOR ME.
SOB
BUT WILL THE VOTES FOR THE CLASS REPRESENTA-TIVE CHANGE BECAUSE OF SOMETHING LIKE THAT?
OF COURSE! A GUY WHO'S SMART, HAND-SOME...
...AND PHYSICALLY AND MENTALLY TOUGH IS THE QUALIFICATION FOR THE CLASS REP.
I'M PRETTY SURE TO PASS THE FIRST TWO, BUT...
RIGHT. SMART AND HANDSOME ARE *FAMILY TRAITS* OF OURS.
BUT IF THEY FIND OUT THAT I'M A WEAK GUY WHO CAN'T EAT SOMETHING...
THIS IS *STUPID*... IT'S NOTHING BUT A CLASS REP!
ARE YOU ASKING ME TO HELP YOU FOR SOMETHING LIKE THAT?

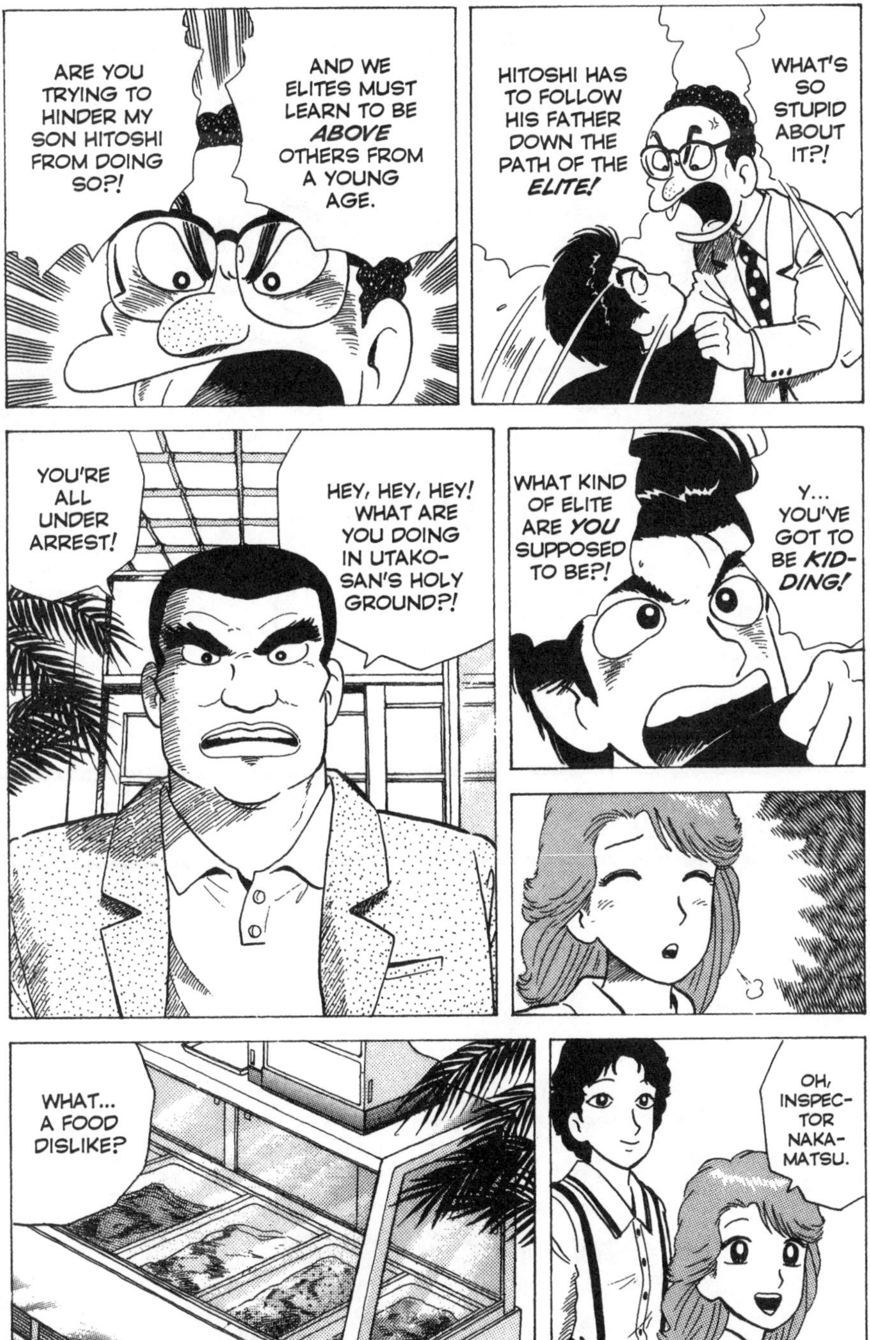
WHAT'S SO STUPID ABOUT IT?!
HITOSHI HAS TO FOLLOW HIS FATHER DOWN THE PATH OF THE *ELITE!*
AND WE ELITES MUST LEARN TO BE *ABOVE* OTHERS FROM A YOUNG AGE.
ARE YOU TRYING TO HINDER MY SON HITOSHI FROM DOING SO?!
Y... YOU'VE GOT TO BE *KID-DING!*
WHAT KIND OF ELITE ARE *YOU* SUPPOSED TO BE?!
HEY, HEY, HEY! WHAT ARE YOU DOING IN UTAKO-SAN'S HOLY GROUND?!
YOU'RE ALL UNDER ARREST!
OH, INSPECTOR NAKAMATSU.
WHAT... A FOOD DISLIKE?

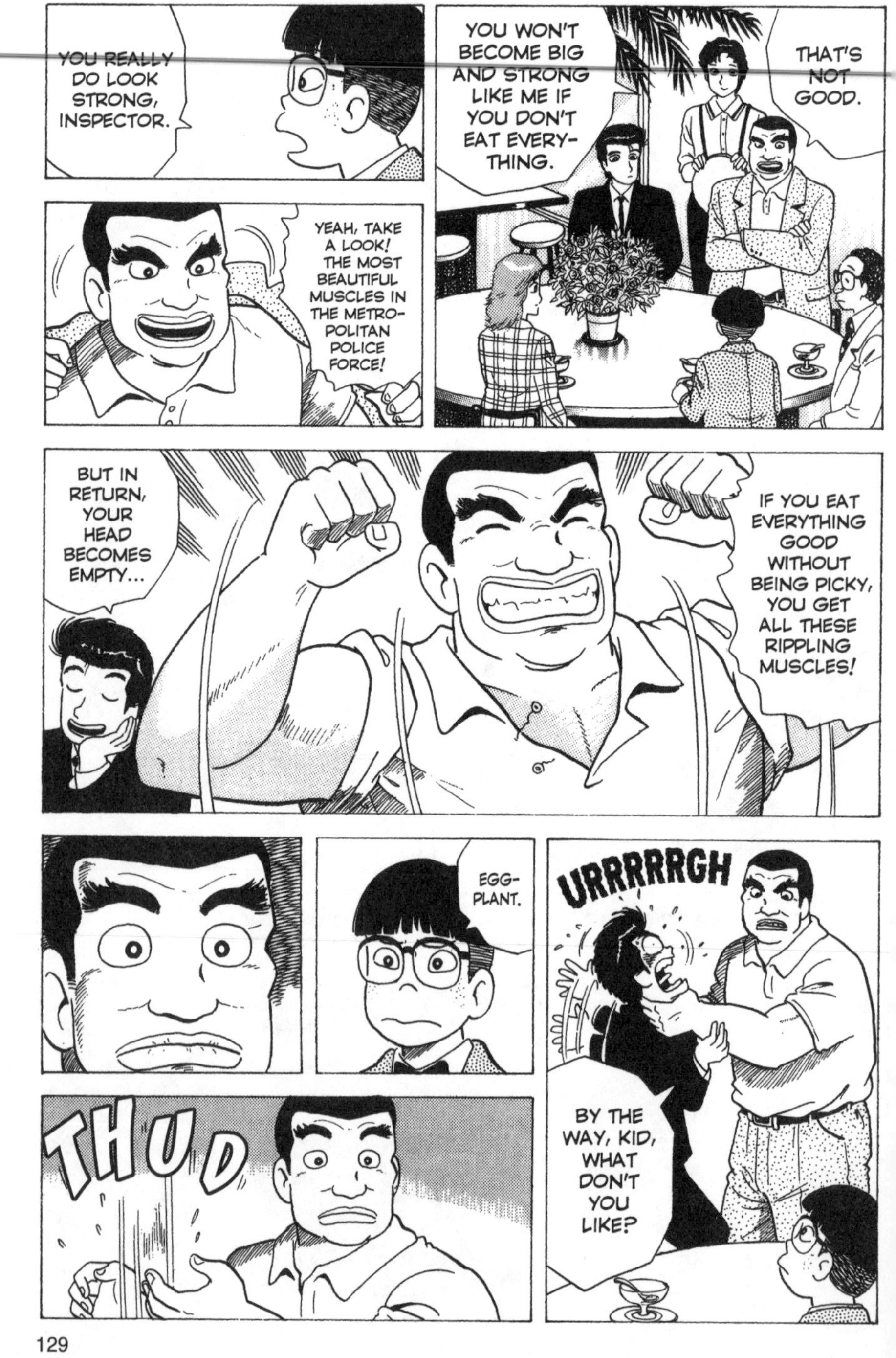
THAT'S NOT GOOD.
YOU WON'T BECOME BIG AND STRONG LIKE ME IF YOU DON'T EAT EVERY-THING.
YOU REALLY DO LOOK STRONG, INSPECTOR.
YEAH, TAKE A LOOK! THE MOST BEAUTIFUL MUSCLES IN THE METRO-POLITAN POLICE FORCE!
IF YOU EAT EVERYTHING GOOD WITHOUT BEING PICKY, YOU GET ALL THESE RIPPLING MUSCLES!
BUT IN RETURN, YOUR HEAD BECOMES EMPTY...
URRRRRGH
BY THE WAY, KID, WHAT DON'T YOU LIKE?
EGG-PLANT.
THUD

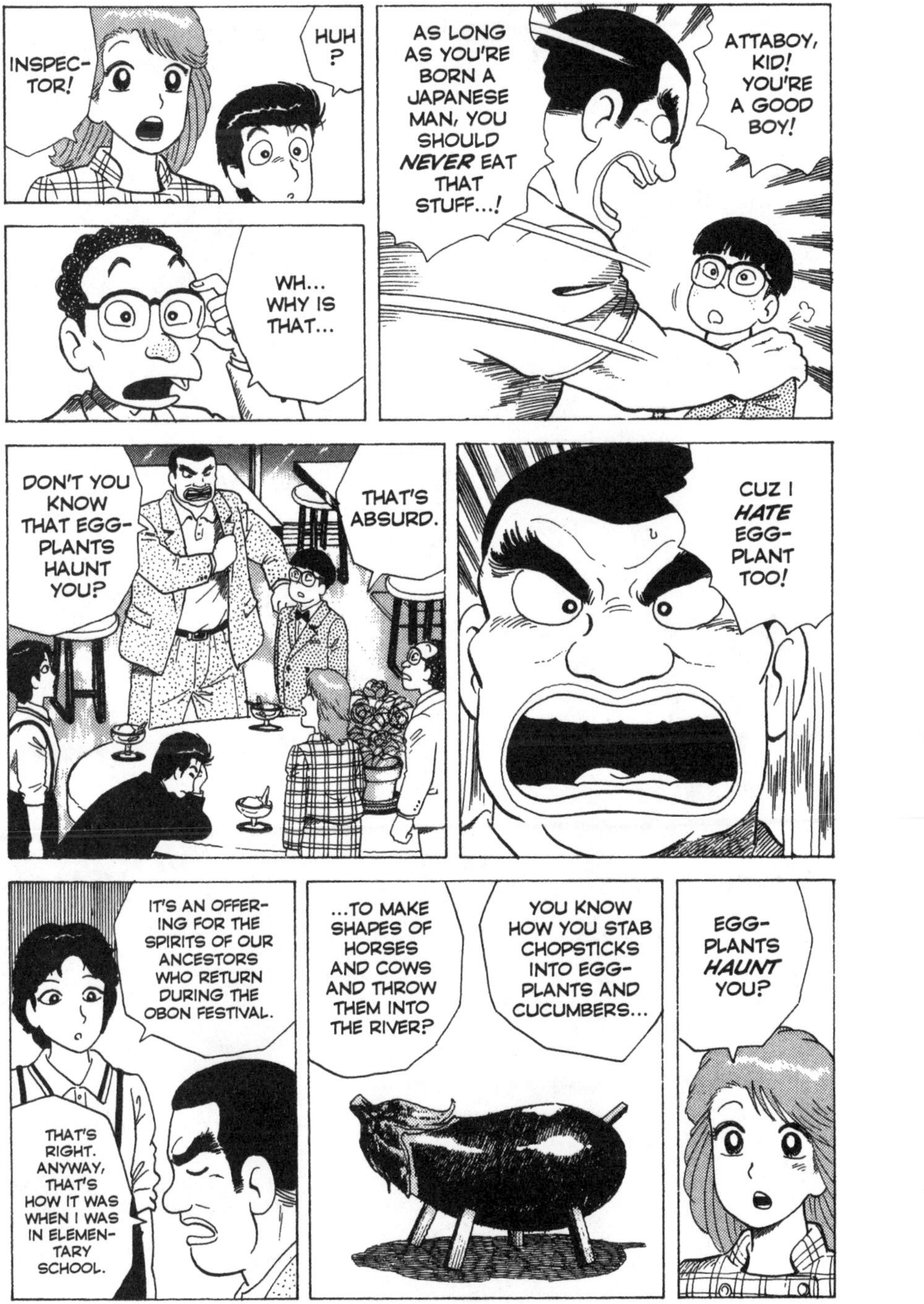
ATTABOY, KID! YOU'RE A GOOD BOY!
AS LONG AS YOU'RE BORN A JAPANESE MAN, YOU SHOULD *NEVER* EAT THAT STUFF...!
HUH ?
INSPEC-TOR!
WH... WHY IS THAT...
CUZ I *HATE* EGG-PLANT TOO!
THAT'S ABSURD.
DON'T YOU KNOW THAT EGG-PLANTS HAUNT YOU?
EGG-PLANTS *HAUNT* YOU?
YOU KNOW HOW YOU STAB CHOPSTICKS INTO EGG-PLANTS AND CUCUMBERS...
...TO MAKE SHAPES OF HORSES AND COWS AND THROW THEM INTO THE RIVER?
IT'S AN OFFER-ING FOR THE SPIRITS OF OUR ANCESTORS WHO RETURN DURING THE OBON FESTIVAL.
THAT'S RIGHT. ANYWAY, THAT'S HOW IT WAS WHEN I WAS IN ELEMEN-TARY SCHOOL.

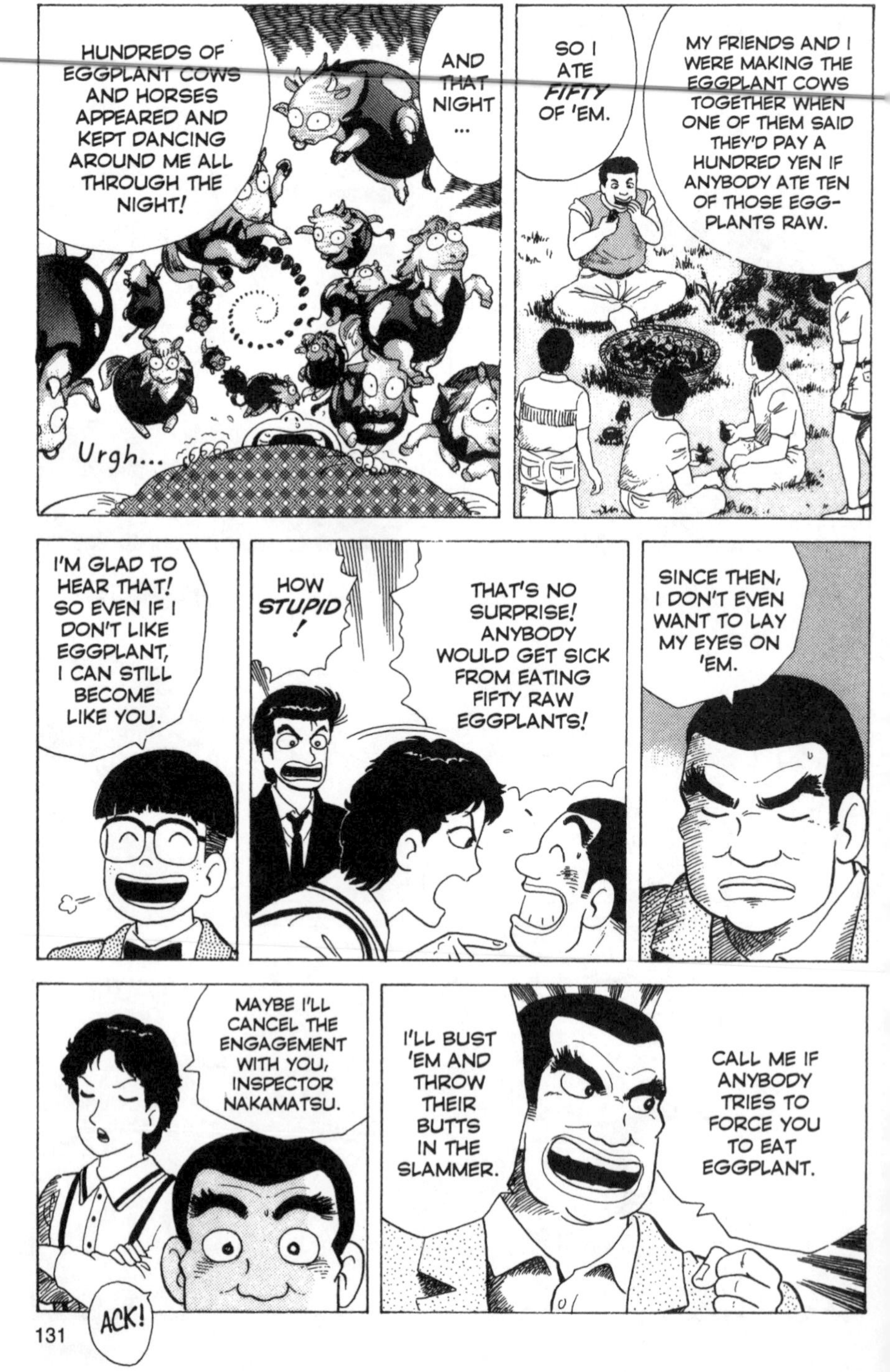
MY FRIENDS AND I WERE MAKING THE EGGPLANT COWS TOGETHER WHEN ONE OF THEM SAID THEY'D PAY A HUNDRED YEN IF ANYBODY ATE TEN OF THOSE EGG-PLANTS RAW.
SO I ATE *FIFTY* OF 'EM.
AND THAT NIGHT ...
HUNDREDS OF EGGPLANT COWS AND HORSES APPEARED AND KEPT DANCING AROUND ME ALL THROUGH THE NIGHT!
Urgh...
SINCE THEN, I DON'T EVEN WANT TO LAY MY EYES ON 'EM.
THAT'S NO SURPRISE! ANYBODY WOULD GET SICK FROM EATING FIFTY RAW EGGPLANTS!
HOW *STUPID*!
I'M GLAD TO HEAR THAT! SO EVEN IF I DON'T LIKE EGGPLANT, I CAN STILL BECOME LIKE YOU.
CALL ME IF ANYBODY TRIES TO FORCE YOU TO EAT EGGPLANT.
I'LL BUST 'EM AND THROW THEIR BUTTS IN THE SLAMMER.
MAYBE I'LL CANCEL THE ENGAGEMENT WITH YOU, INSPECTOR NAKAMATSU.
ACK!

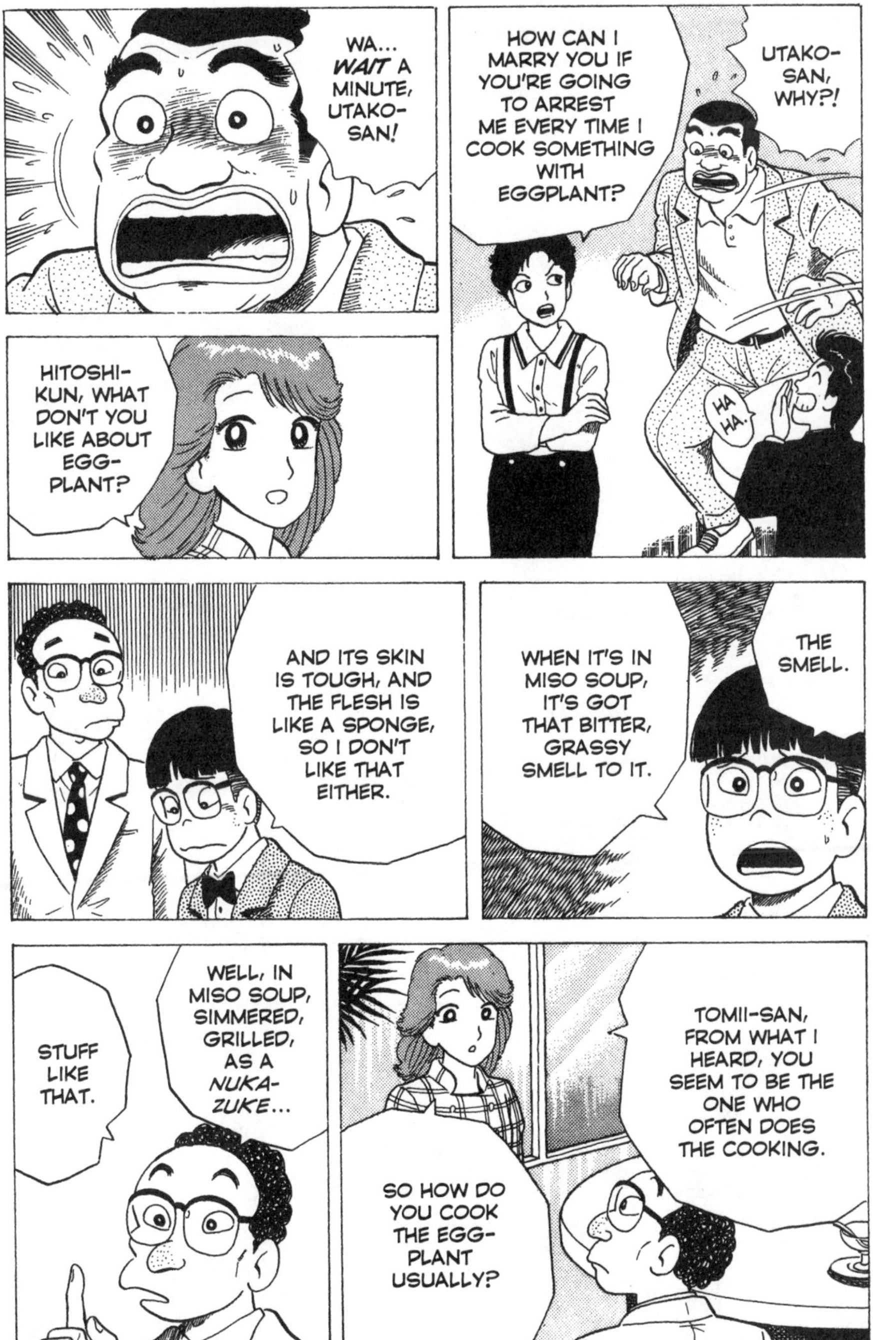
UTAKO-SAN, WHY?!
HOW CAN I MARRY YOU IF YOU'RE GOING TO ARREST ME EVERY TIME I COOK SOMETHING WITH EGGPLANT?
HA HA.
WA... *WAIT* A MINUTE, UTAKO-SAN!
HITOSHI-KUN, WHAT DON'T YOU LIKE ABOUT EGG-PLANT?
THE SMELL.
WHEN IT'S IN MISO SOUP, IT'S GOT THAT BITTER, GRASSY SMELL TO IT.
AND ITS SKIN IS TOUGH, AND THE FLESH IS LIKE A SPONGE, SO I DON'T LIKE THAT EITHER.
TOMII-SAN, FROM WHAT I HEARD, YOU SEEM TO BE THE ONE WHO OFTEN DOES THE COOKING.
SO HOW DO YOU COOK THE EGG-PLANT USUALLY?
WELL, IN MISO SOUP, SIMMERED, GRILLED, AS A *NUKA-ZUKE*...
STUFF LIKE THAT.

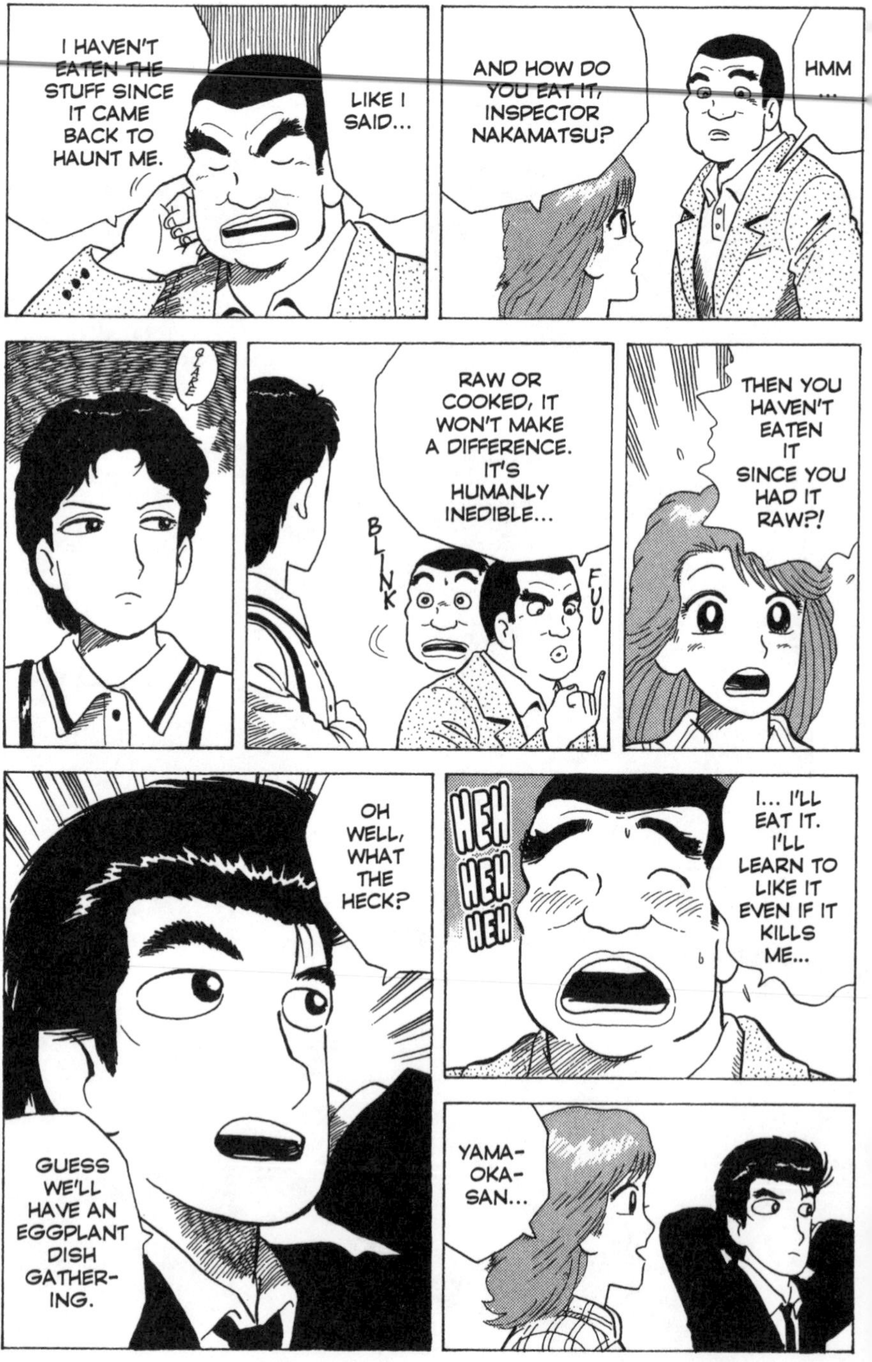
HMM ...
AND HOW DO YOU EAT IT, INSPECTOR NAKAMATSU?
LIKE I SAID...
I HAVEN'T EATEN THE STUFF SINCE IT CAME BACK TO HAUNT ME.
THEN YOU HAVEN'T EATEN IT SINCE YOU HAD IT RAW?!
FUU
RAW OR COOKED, IT WON'T MAKE A DIFFERENCE. IT'S HUMANLY INEDIBLE...
BLINK
GLARE
I... I'LL EAT IT. I'LL LEARN TO LIKE IT EVEN IF IT KILLS ME...
HEH HEH HEH
YAMA-OKA-SAN...
OH WELL, WHAT THE HECK?
GUESS WE'LL HAVE AN EGGPLANT DISH GATHER-ING.

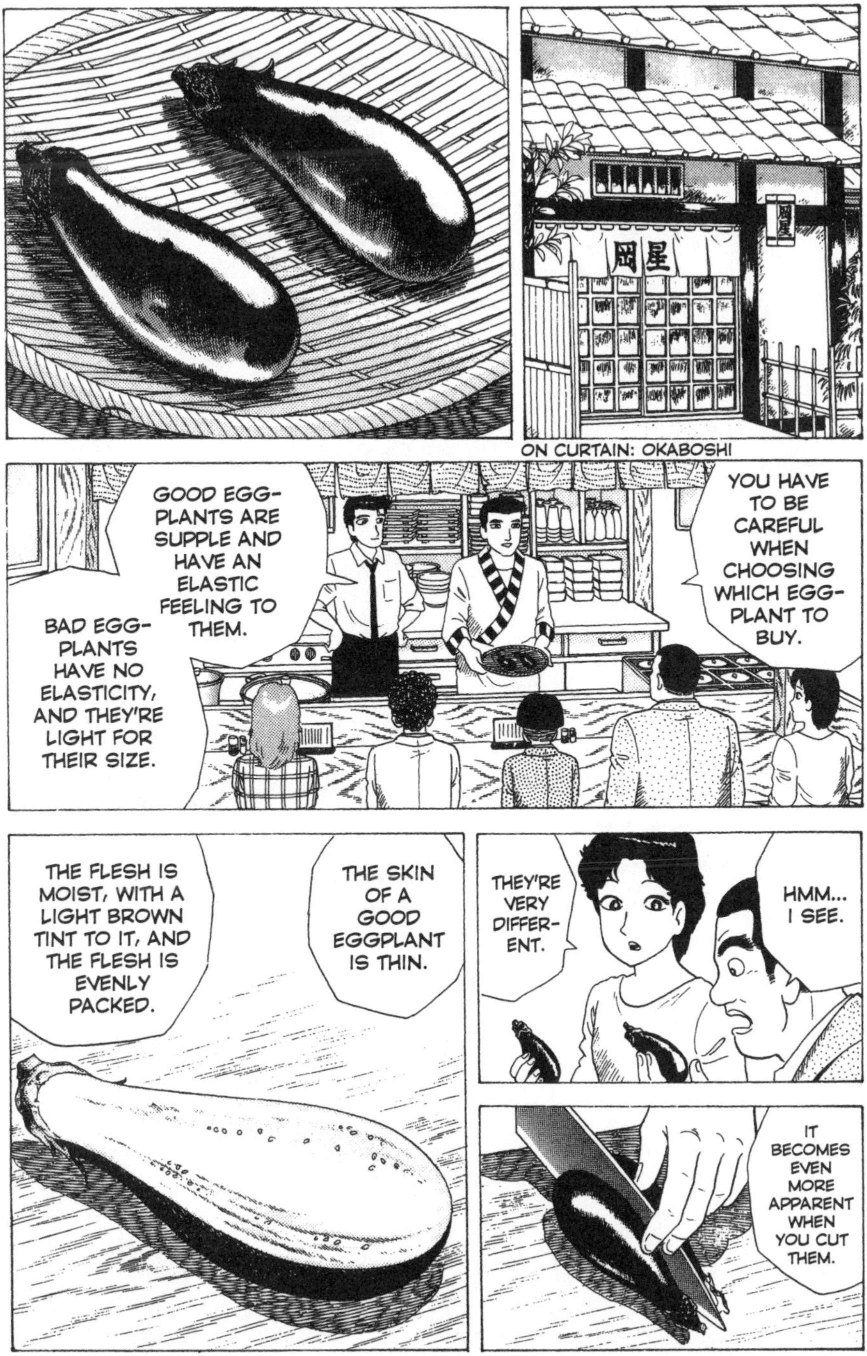
ON CURTAIN: OKABOSHI
YOU HAVE TO BE CAREFUL WHEN CHOOSING WHICH EGG-PLANT TO BUY.
GOOD EGG-PLANTS ARE SUPPLE AND HAVE AN ELASTIC FEELING TO THEM.
BAD EGG-PLANTS HAVE NO ELASTICITY, AND THEY'RE LIGHT FOR THEIR SIZE.
HMM... I SEE.
THEY'RE VERY DIFFER-ENT.
IT BECOMES EVEN MORE APPARENT WHEN YOU CUT THEM.
THE SKIN OF A GOOD EGGPLANT IS THIN.
THE FLESH IS MOIST, WITH A LIGHT BROWN TINT TO IT, AND THE FLESH IS EVENLY PACKED.

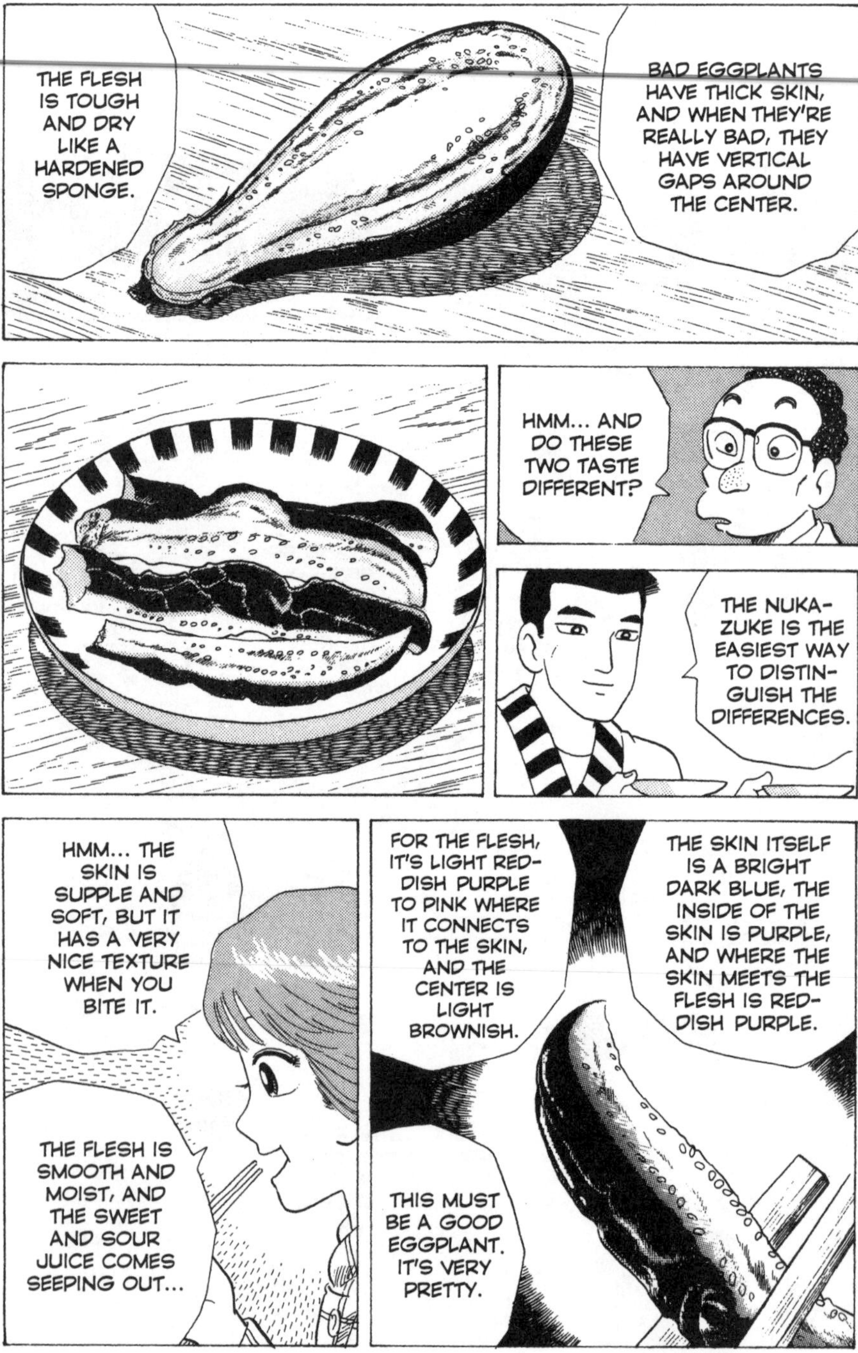
BAD EGGPLANTS HAVE THICK SKIN, AND WHEN THEY'RE REALLY BAD, THEY HAVE VERTICAL GAPS AROUND THE CENTER.
THE FLESH IS TOUGH AND DRY LIKE A HARDENED SPONGE.
HMM... AND DO THESE TWO TASTE DIFFERENT?
THE NUKA-ZUKE IS THE EASIEST WAY TO DISTINGUISH THE DIFFERENCES.
THE SKIN ITSELF IS A BRIGHT DARK BLUE, THE INSIDE OF THE SKIN IS PURPLE, AND WHERE THE SKIN MEETS THE FLESH IS REDDISH PURPLE.
FOR THE FLESH, IT'S LIGHT REDDISH PURPLE TO PINK WHERE IT CONNECTS TO THE SKIN, AND THE CENTER IS LIGHT BROWNISH.
THIS MUST BE A GOOD EGGPLANT. IT'S VERY PRETTY.
HMM... THE SKIN IS SUPPLE AND SOFT, BUT IT HAS A VERY NICE TEXTURE WHEN YOU BITE IT.
THE FLESH IS SMOOTH AND MOIST, AND THE SWEET AND SOUR JUICE COMES SEEPING OUT...

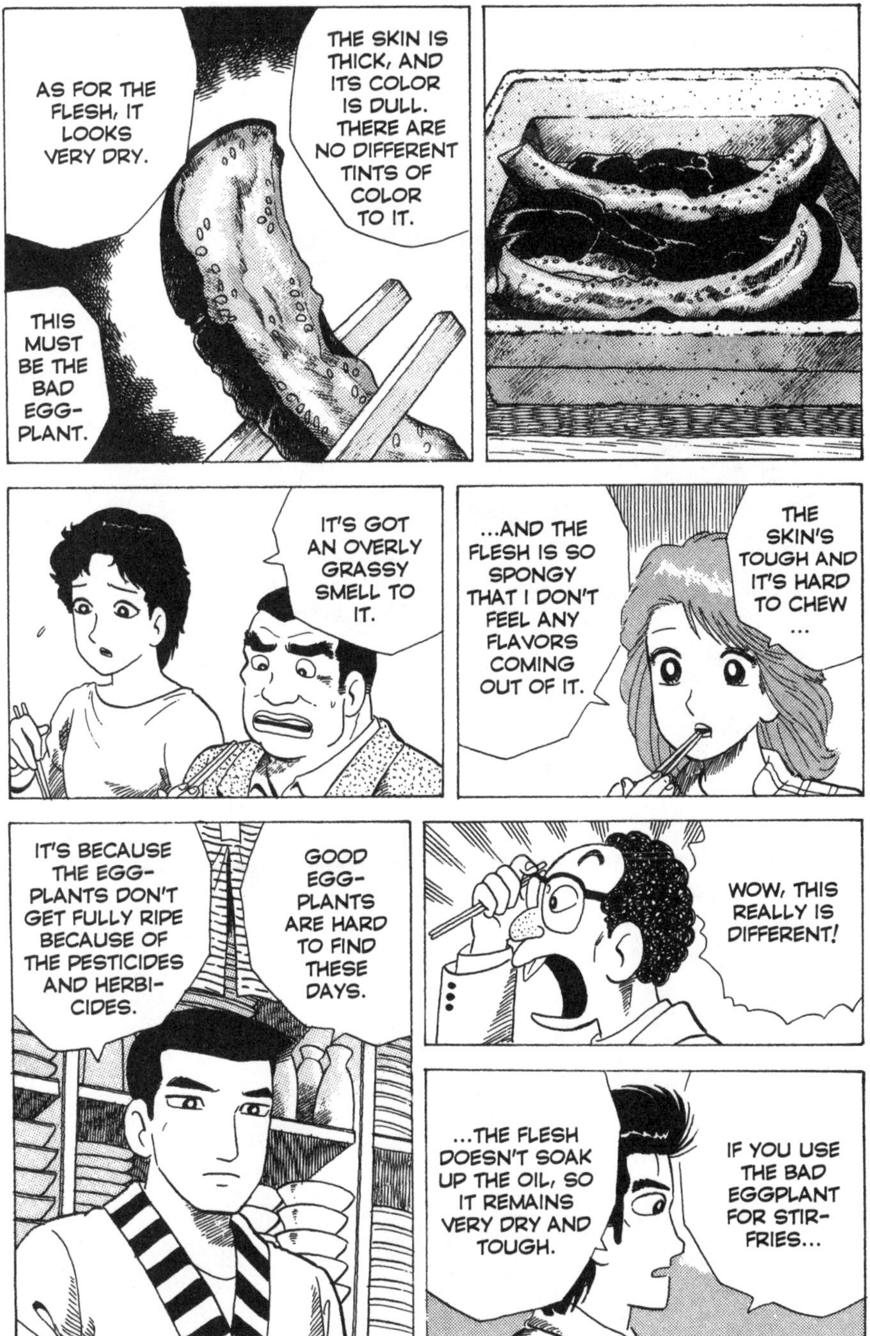
THE SKIN IS THICK, AND ITS COLOR IS DULL. THERE ARE NO DIFFERENT TINTS OF COLOR TO IT.
AS FOR THE FLESH, IT LOOKS VERY DRY.
THIS MUST BE THE BAD EGG-PLANT.
THE SKIN'S TOUGH AND IT'S HARD TO CHEW ...
...AND THE FLESH IS SO SPONGY THAT I DON'T FEEL ANY FLAVORS COMING OUT OF IT.
IT'S GOT AN OVERLY GRASSY SMELL TO IT.
WOW, THIS REALLY IS DIFFERENT!
IF YOU USE THE BAD EGGPLANT FOR STIR-FRIES...
...THE FLESH DOESN'T SOAK UP THE OIL, SO IT REMAINS VERY DRY AND TOUGH.
GOOD EGG-PLANTS ARE HARD TO FIND THESE DAYS.
IT'S BECAUSE THE EGG-PLANTS DON'T GET FULLY RIPE BECAUSE OF THE PESTICIDES AND HERBI-CIDES.

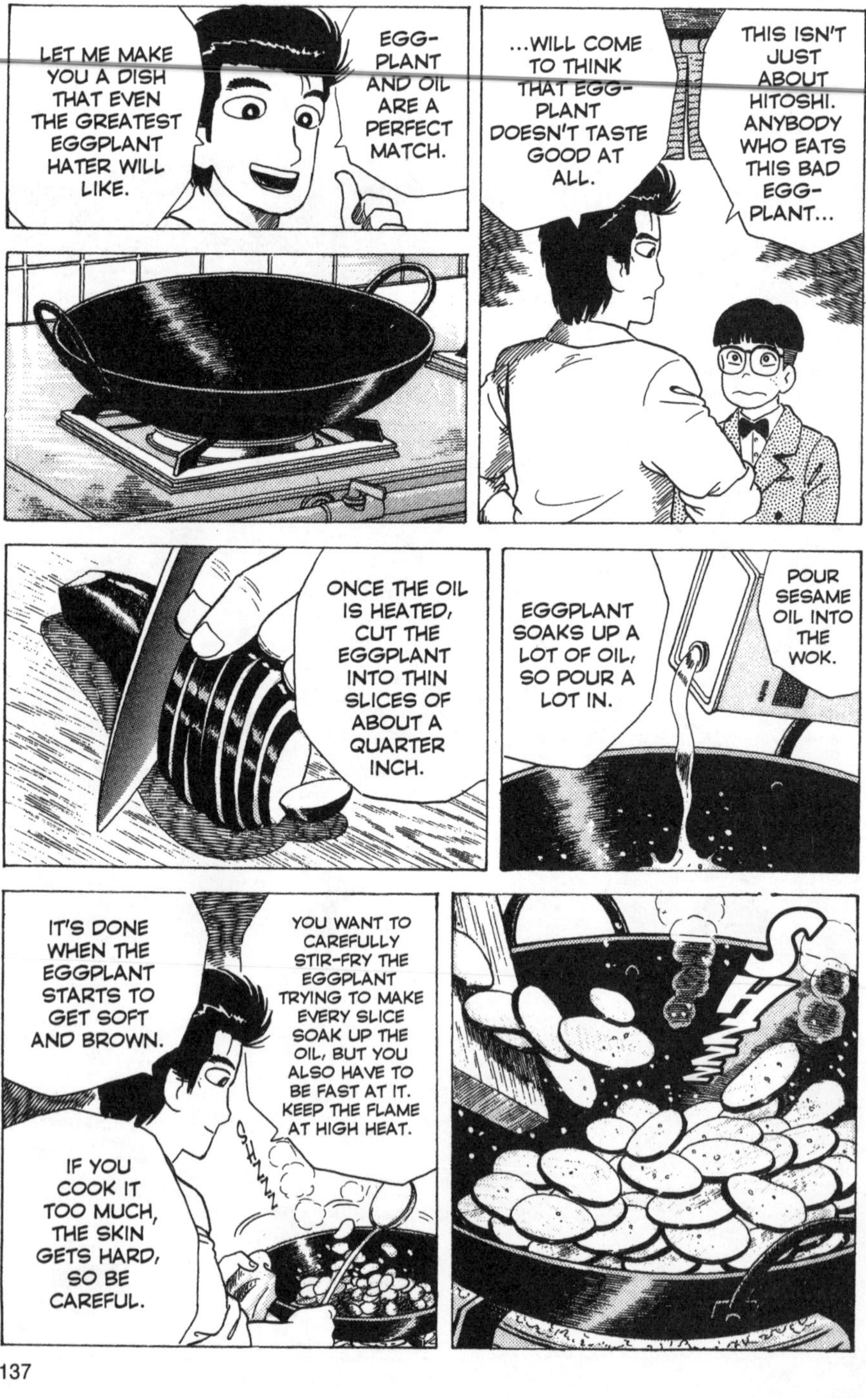
THIS ISN'T JUST ABOUT HITOSHI. ANYBODY WHO EATS THIS BAD EGG-PLANT...
...WILL COME TO THINK THAT EGG-PLANT DOESN'T TASTE GOOD AT ALL.
EGG-PLANT AND OIL ARE A PERFECT MATCH.
LET ME MAKE YOU A DISH THAT EVEN THE GREATEST EGGPLANT HATER WILL LIKE.
POUR SESAME OIL INTO THE WOK.
EGGPLANT SOAKS UP A LOT OF OIL, SO POUR A LOT IN.
ONCE THE OIL IS HEATED, CUT THE EGGPLANT INTO THIN SLICES OF ABOUT A QUARTER INCH.
YOU WANT TO CAREFULLY STIR-FRY THE EGGPLANT TRYING TO MAKE EVERY SLICE SOAK UP THE OIL, BUT YOU ALSO HAVE TO BE FAST AT IT. KEEP THE FLAME AT HIGH HEAT.
IT'S DONE WHEN THE EGGPLANT STARTS TO GET SOFT AND BROWN.
IF YOU COOK IT TOO MUCH, THE SKIN GETS HARD, SO BE CAREFUL.

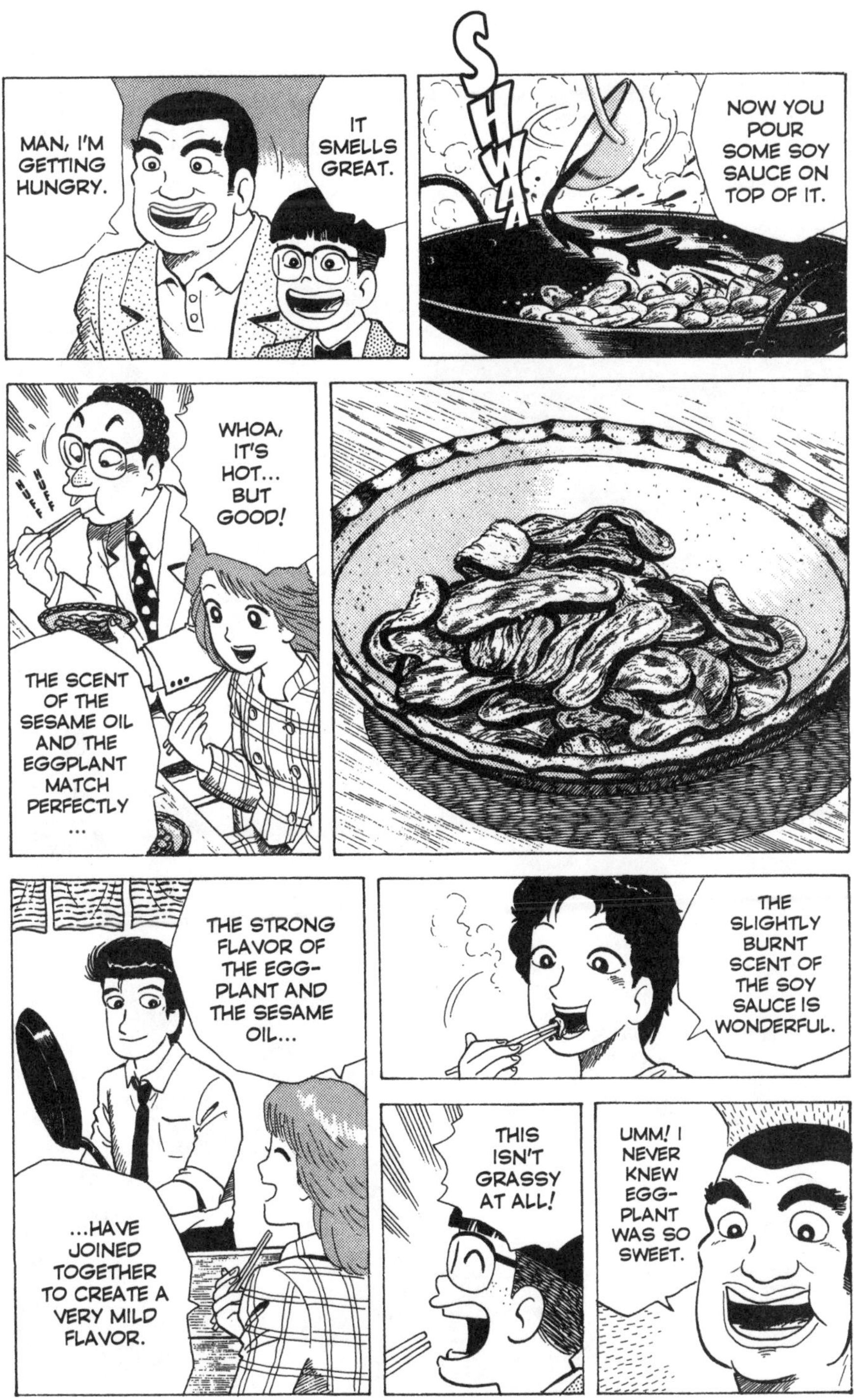
SHWA
NOW YOU POUR SOME SOY SAUCE ON TOP OF IT.
IT SMELLS GREAT.
MAN, I'M GETTING HUNGRY.
WHOA, IT'S HOT... BUT GOOD!
HUFF HUFF
...
THE SCENT OF THE SESAME OIL AND THE EGGPLANT MATCH PERFECTLY ...
THE SLIGHTLY BURNT SCENT OF THE SOY SAUCE IS WONDERFUL.
UMM! I NEVER KNEW EGGPLANT WAS SO SWEET.
THIS ISN'T GRASSY AT ALL!
THE STRONG FLAVOR OF THE EGGPLANT AND THE SESAME OIL...
...HAVE JOINED TOGETHER TO CREATE A VERY MILD FLAVOR.

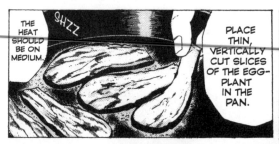

NEXT, POUR SOME MILD-TASTING PEANUT OIL...
...UNTIL THERE'S A THIN COAT OF OIL COVERING THE ENTIRE PAN.
PLACE THIN, VERTICALLY CUT SLICES OF THE EGG-PLANT IN THE PAN.
SHZZ
THE HEAT SHOULD BE ON MEDIUM.
YOU DON'T NEED TO LET IT SOAK UP AS MUCH OIL AS YOU DID IN THE LAST DISH.
TURN THE EGGPLANT OVER, AND IT'S DONE WHEN THE FLESH BECOMES LIGHT BROWN.
SPRINKLE SOME GROUND GINGER ONTO IT, AND POUR SOME SOY SAUCE ON JUST BEFORE EATING IT.
OH! THIS TASTES DIFFER-ENT!
THE FLESH IS VERY SOFT AND MELTS IN YOUR MOUTH...
THE SWEET-NESS OF THE EGG-PLANT IS REALLY NICE!
AND THE SKIN IS SOFT AND GOOD TOO!

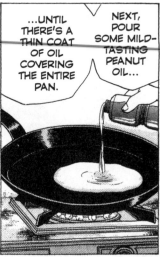

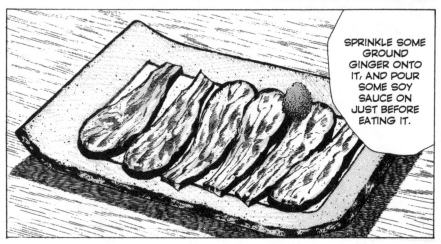

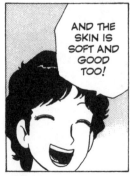

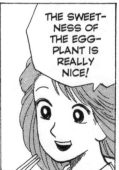

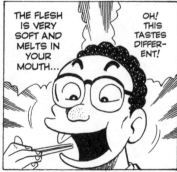

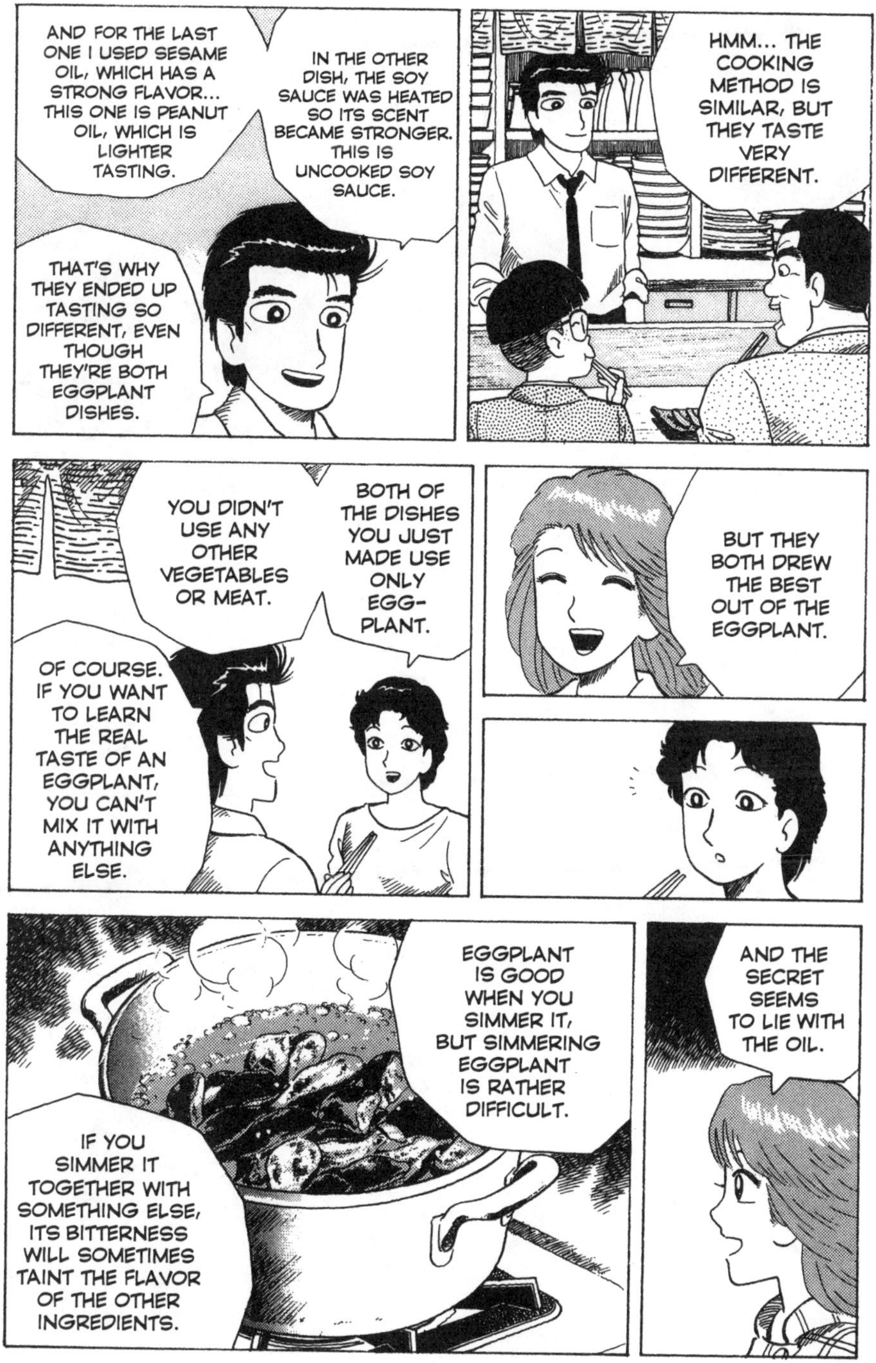
HMM... THE COOKING METHOD IS SIMILAR, BUT THEY TASTE VERY DIFFERENT.
IN THE OTHER DISH, THE SOY SAUCE WAS HEATED SO ITS SCENT BECAME STRONGER. THIS IS UNCOOKED SOY SAUCE.
AND FOR THE LAST ONE I USED SESAME OIL, WHICH HAS A STRONG FLAVOR... THIS ONE IS PEANUT OIL, WHICH IS LIGHTER TASTING.
THAT'S WHY THEY ENDED UP TASTING SO DIFFERENT, EVEN THOUGH THEY'RE BOTH EGGPLANT DISHES.
BUT THEY BOTH DREW THE BEST OUT OF THE EGGPLANT.
BOTH OF THE DISHES YOU JUST MADE USE ONLY EGG-PLANT.
YOU DIDN'T USE ANY OTHER VEGETABLES OR MEAT.
OF COURSE. IF YOU WANT TO LEARN THE REAL TASTE OF AN EGGPLANT, YOU CAN'T MIX IT WITH ANYTHING ELSE.
AND THE SECRET SEEMS TO LIE WITH THE OIL.
EGGPLANT IS GOOD WHEN YOU SIMMER IT, BUT SIMMERING EGGPLANT IS RATHER DIFFICULT.
IF YOU SIMMER IT TOGETHER WITH SOMETHING ELSE, ITS BITTERNESS WILL SOMETIMES TAINT THE FLAVOR OF THE OTHER INGREDIENTS.

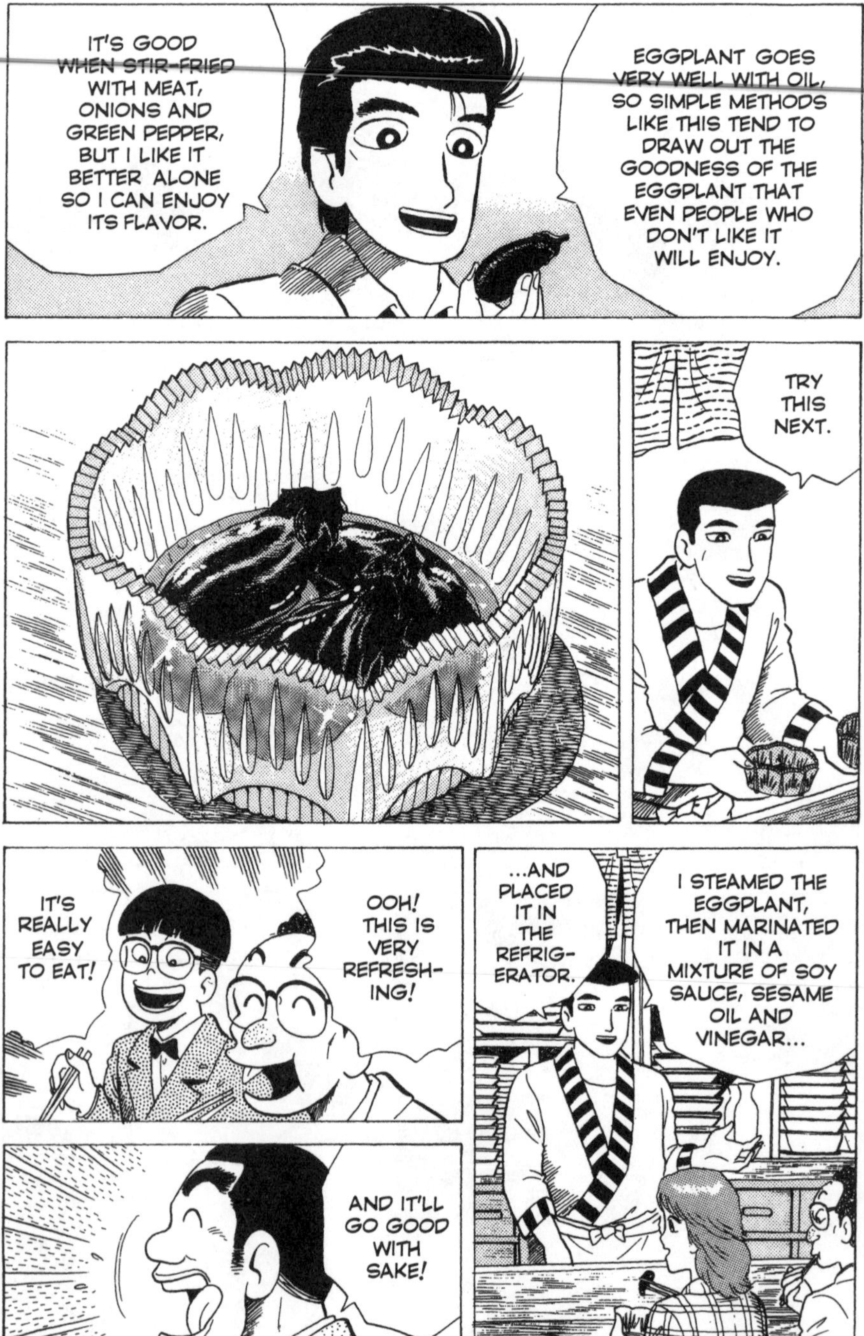
EGGPLANT GOES VERY WELL WITH OIL, SO SIMPLE METHODS LIKE THIS TEND TO DRAW OUT THE GOODNESS OF THE EGGPLANT THAT EVEN PEOPLE WHO DON'T LIKE IT WILL ENJOY.
IT'S GOOD WHEN STIR-FRIED WITH MEAT, ONIONS AND GREEN PEPPER, BUT I LIKE IT BETTER ALONE SO I CAN ENJOY ITS FLAVOR.
TRY THIS NEXT.
I STEAMED THE EGGPLANT, THEN MARINATED IT IN A MIXTURE OF SOY SAUCE, SESAME OIL AND VINEGAR...
...AND PLACED IT IN THE REFRIG-ERATOR.
OOH! THIS IS VERY REFRESH-ING!
IT'S REALLY EASY TO EAT!
AND IT'LL GO GOOD WITH SAKE!

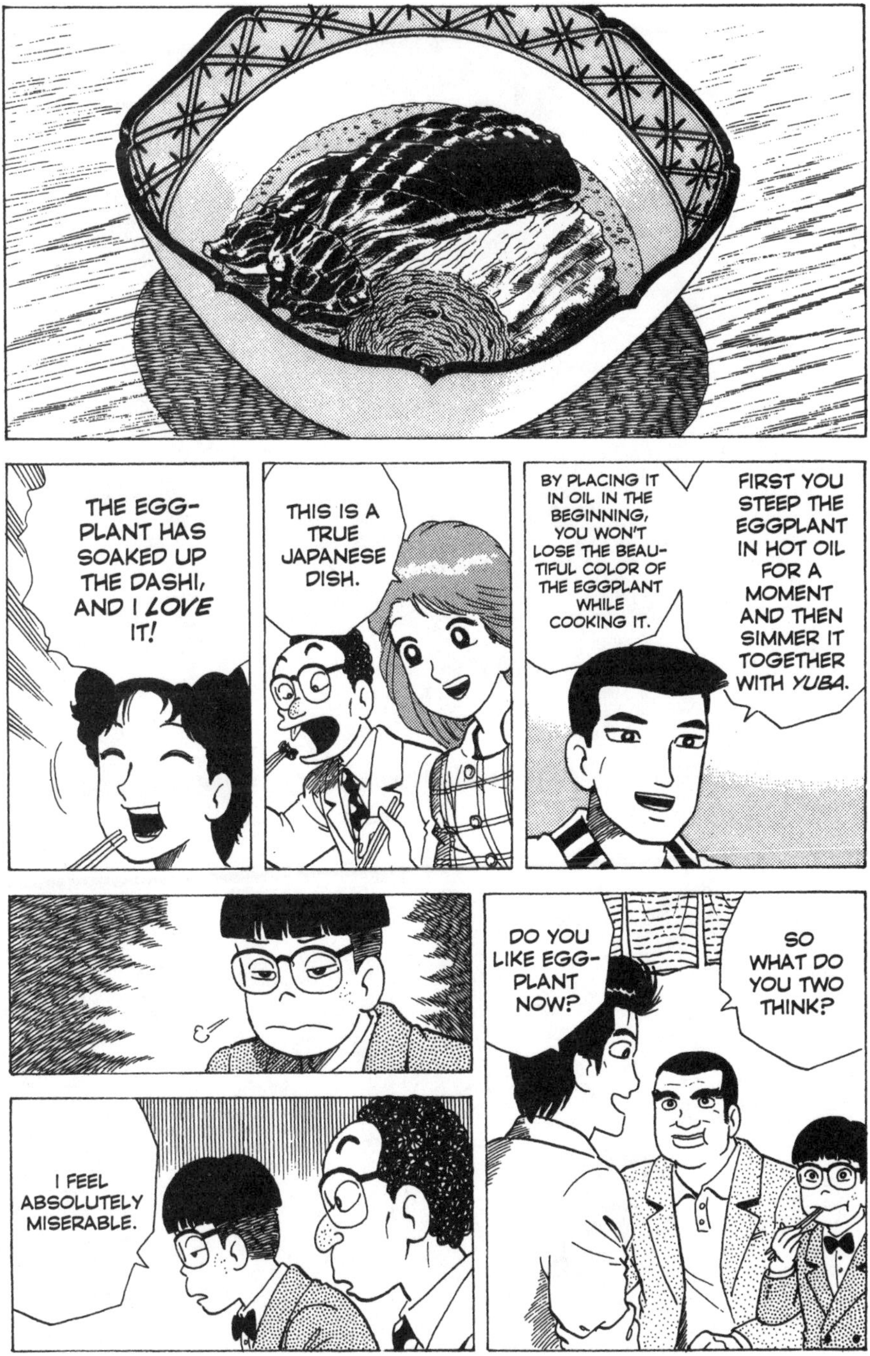
FIRST YOU STEEP THE EGGPLANT IN HOT OIL FOR A MOMENT AND THEN SIMMER IT TOGETHER WITH *YUBA*.
BY PLACING IT IN OIL IN THE BEGINNING, YOU WON'T LOSE THE BEAU-TIFUL COLOR OF THE EGGPLANT WHILE COOKING IT.
THIS IS A TRUE JAPANESE DISH.
THE EGG-PLANT HAS SOAKED UP THE DASHI, AND I *LOVE* IT!
SO WHAT DO YOU TWO THINK?
DO YOU LIKE EGG-PLANT NOW?
I FEEL ABSOLUTELY MISERABLE.

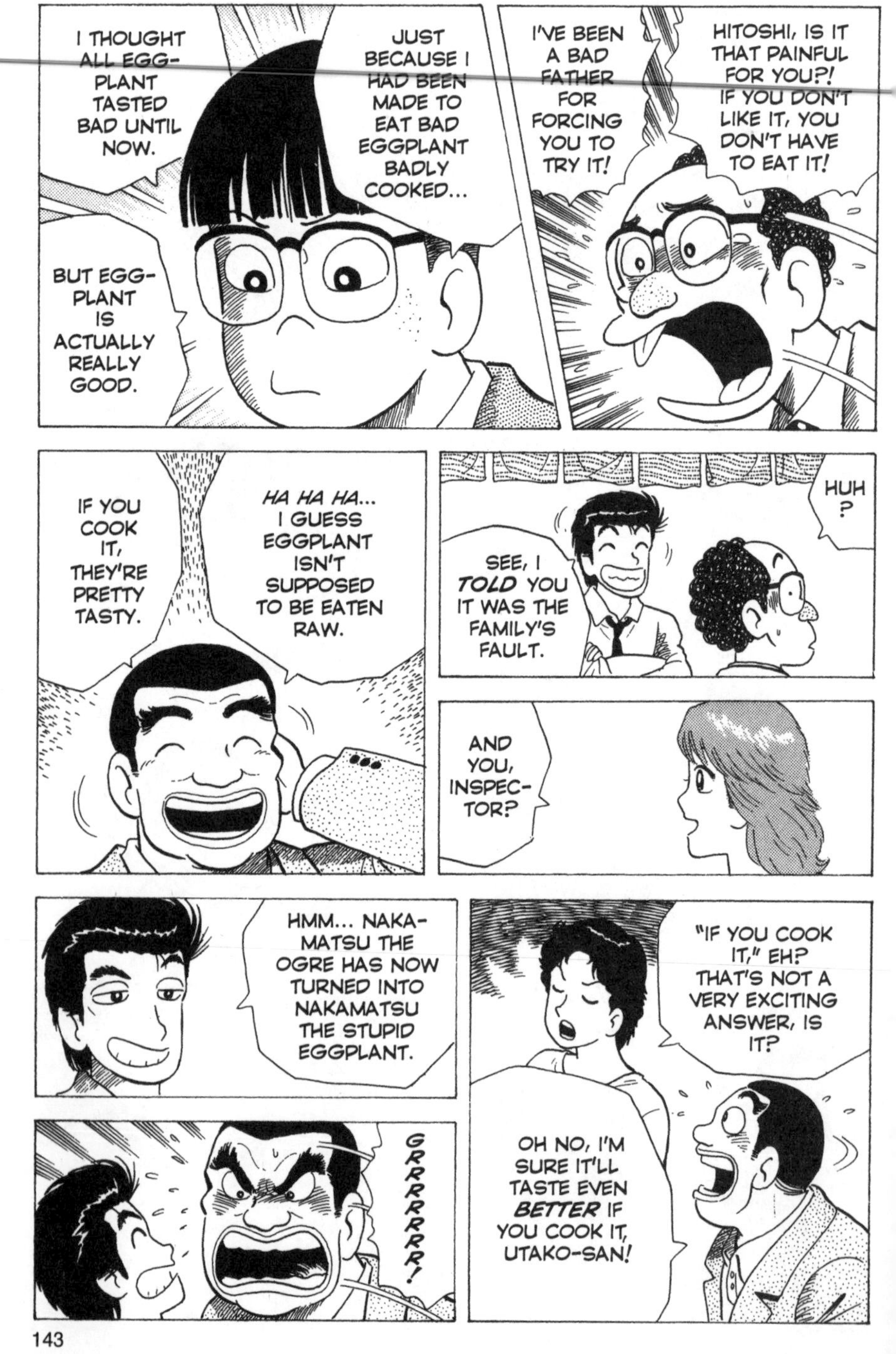
HITOSHI, IS IT THAT PAINFUL FOR YOU?! IF YOU DON'T LIKE IT, YOU DON'T HAVE TO EAT IT!
I'VE BEEN A BAD FATHER FOR FORCING YOU TO TRY IT!
JUST BECAUSE I HAD BEEN MADE TO EAT BAD EGGPLANT BADLY COOKED...
I THOUGHT ALL EGG-PLANT TASTED BAD UNTIL NOW.
BUT EGG-PLANT IS ACTUALLY REALLY GOOD.
HUH?
SEE, I *TOLD* YOU IT WAS THE FAMILY'S FAULT.
AND YOU, INSPEC-TOR?
HA HA HA... I GUESS EGGPLANT ISN'T SUPPOSED TO BE EATEN RAW.
IF YOU COOK IT, THEY'RE PRETTY TASTY.
"IF YOU COOK IT," EH? THAT'S NOT A VERY EXCITING ANSWER, IS IT?
OH NO, I'M SURE IT'LL TASTE EVEN *BETTER* IF YOU COOK IT, UTAKO-SAN!
HMM... NAKA-MATSU THE OGRE HAS NOW TURNED INTO NAKAMATSU THE STUPID EGGPLANT.
GRRRRRRR!

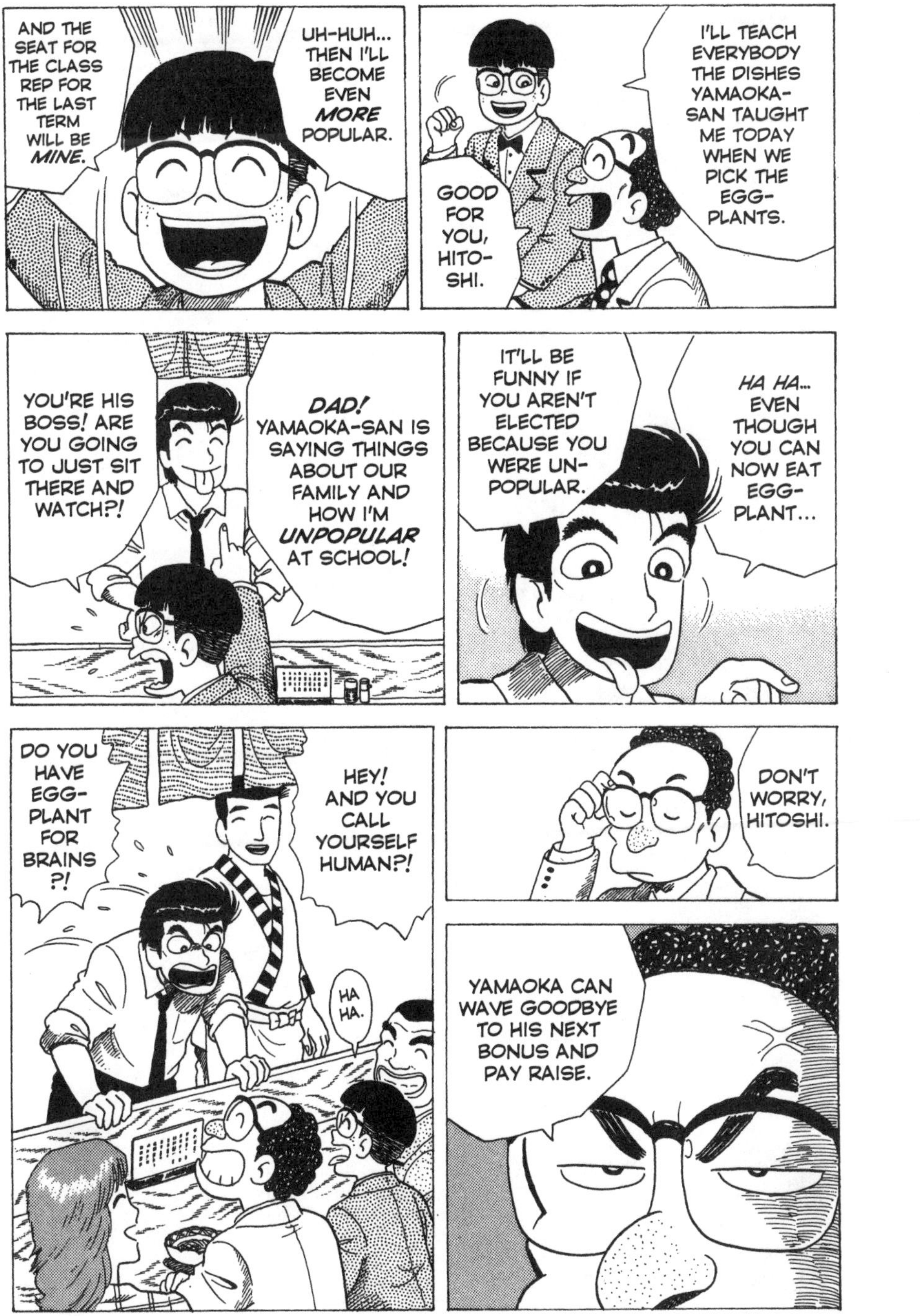
I'LL TEACH EVERYBODY THE DISHES YAMAOKA-SAN TAUGHT ME TODAY WHEN WE PICK THE EGG-PLANTS.
GOOD FOR YOU, HITO-SHI.
UH-HUH... THEN I'LL BECOME EVEN MORE POPULAR.
AND THE SEAT FOR THE CLASS REP FOR THE LAST TERM WILL BE MINE.
HA HA... EVEN THOUGH YOU CAN NOW EAT EGG-PLANT...
IT'LL BE FUNNY IF YOU AREN'T ELECTED BECAUSE YOU WERE UN-POPULAR.
DAD! YAMAOKA-SAN IS SAYING THINGS ABOUT OUR FAMILY AND HOW I'M UNPOPULAR AT SCHOOL!
YOU'RE HIS BOSS! ARE YOU GOING TO JUST SIT THERE AND WATCH?!
DON'T WORRY, HITOSHI.
YAMAOKA CAN WAVE GOODBYE TO HIS NEXT BONUS AND PAY RAISE.
HEY! AND YOU CALL YOURSELF HUMAN?!
DO YOU HAVE EGG-PLANT FOR BRAINS ?!
HA HA.

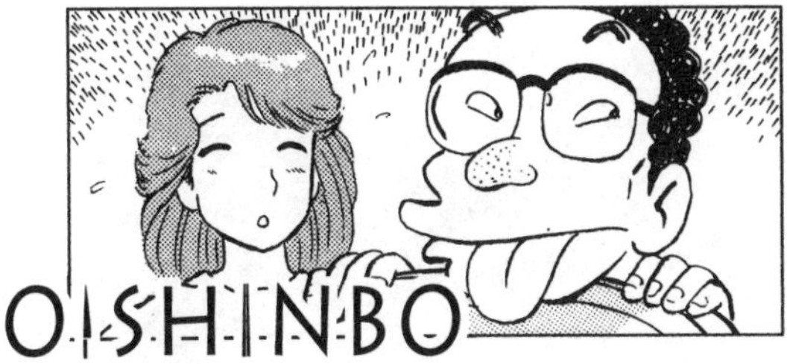
OISHINBO

FIFTH COURSE

THE STORY OF VEGETABLES, NOW AND THEN

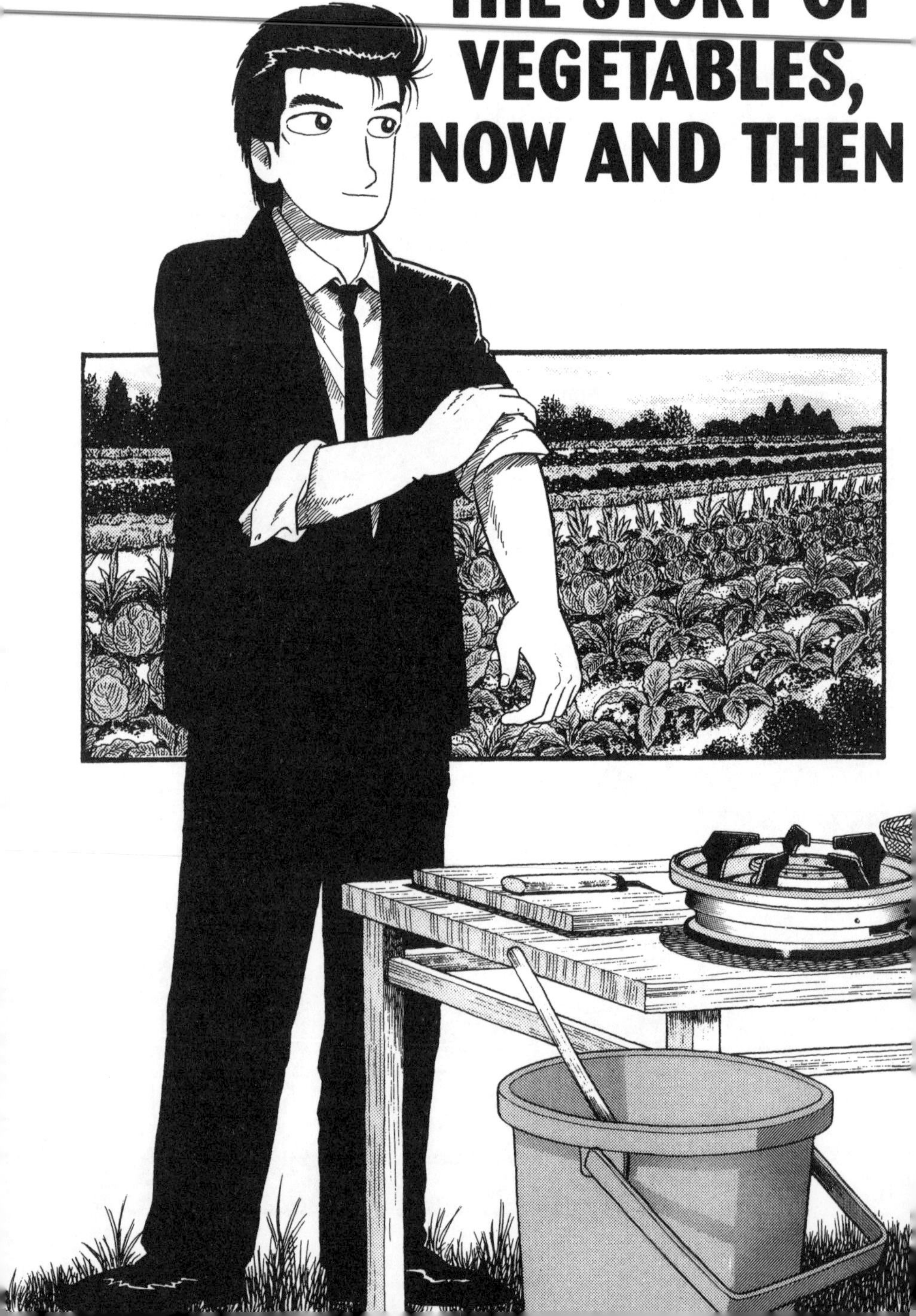

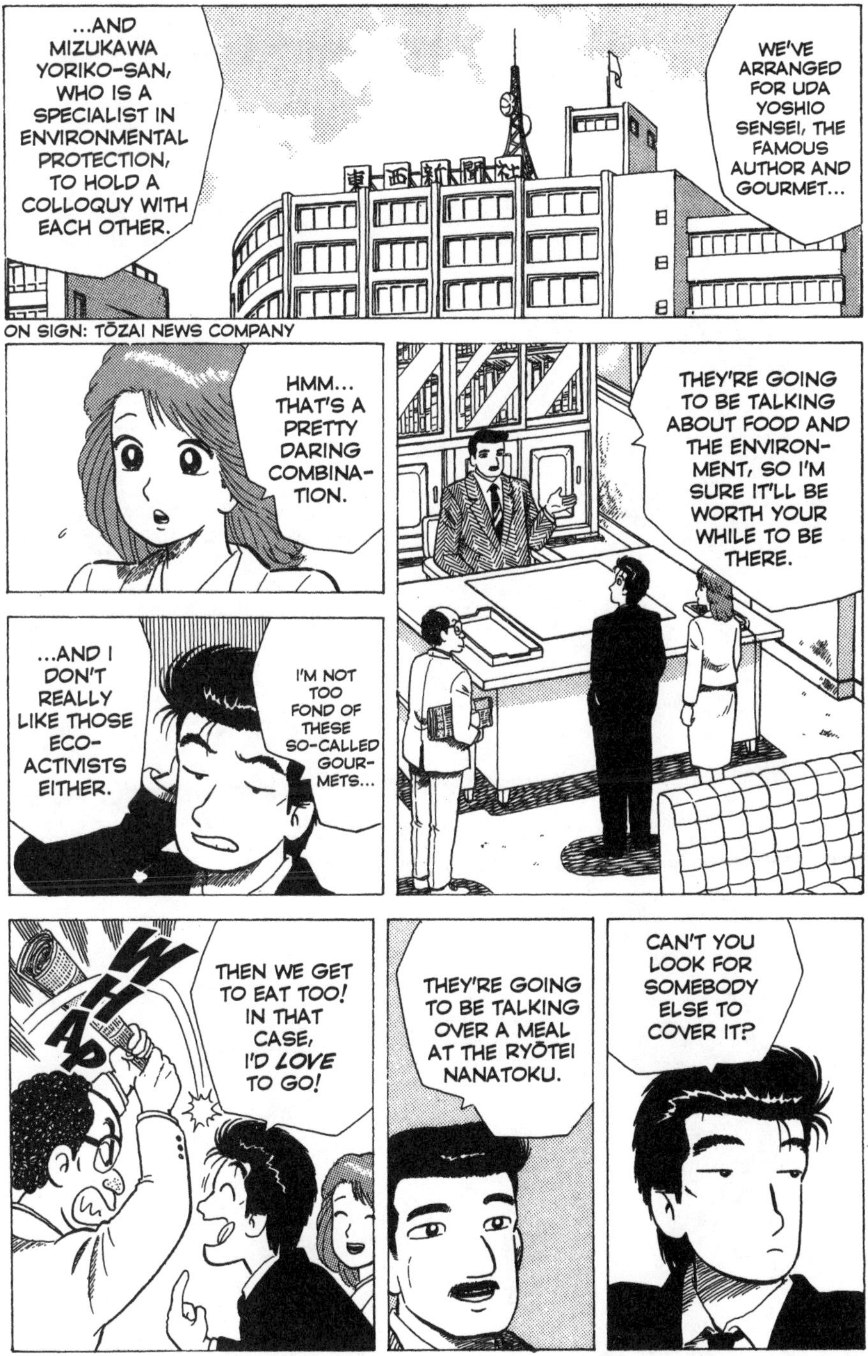
WE'VE ARRANGED FOR UDA YOSHIO SENSEI, THE FAMOUS AUTHOR AND GOURMET...
...AND MIZUKAWA YORIKO-SAN, WHO IS A SPECIALIST IN ENVIRONMENTAL PROTECTION, TO HOLD A COLLOQUY WITH EACH OTHER.
ON SIGN: TŌZAI NEWS COMPANY
THEY'RE GOING TO BE TALKING ABOUT FOOD AND THE ENVIRONMENT, SO I'M SURE IT'LL BE WORTH YOUR WHILE TO BE THERE.
HMM... THAT'S A PRETTY DARING COMBINATION.
I'M NOT TOO FOND OF THESE SO-CALLED GOURMETS...
...AND I DON'T REALLY LIKE THOSE ECO-ACTIVISTS EITHER.
CAN'T YOU LOOK FOR SOMEBODY ELSE TO COVER IT?
THEY'RE GOING TO BE TALKING OVER A MEAL AT THE RYŌTEI NANATOKU.
THEN WE GET TO EAT TOO! IN THAT CASE, I'D *LOVE* TO GO!
WHAP

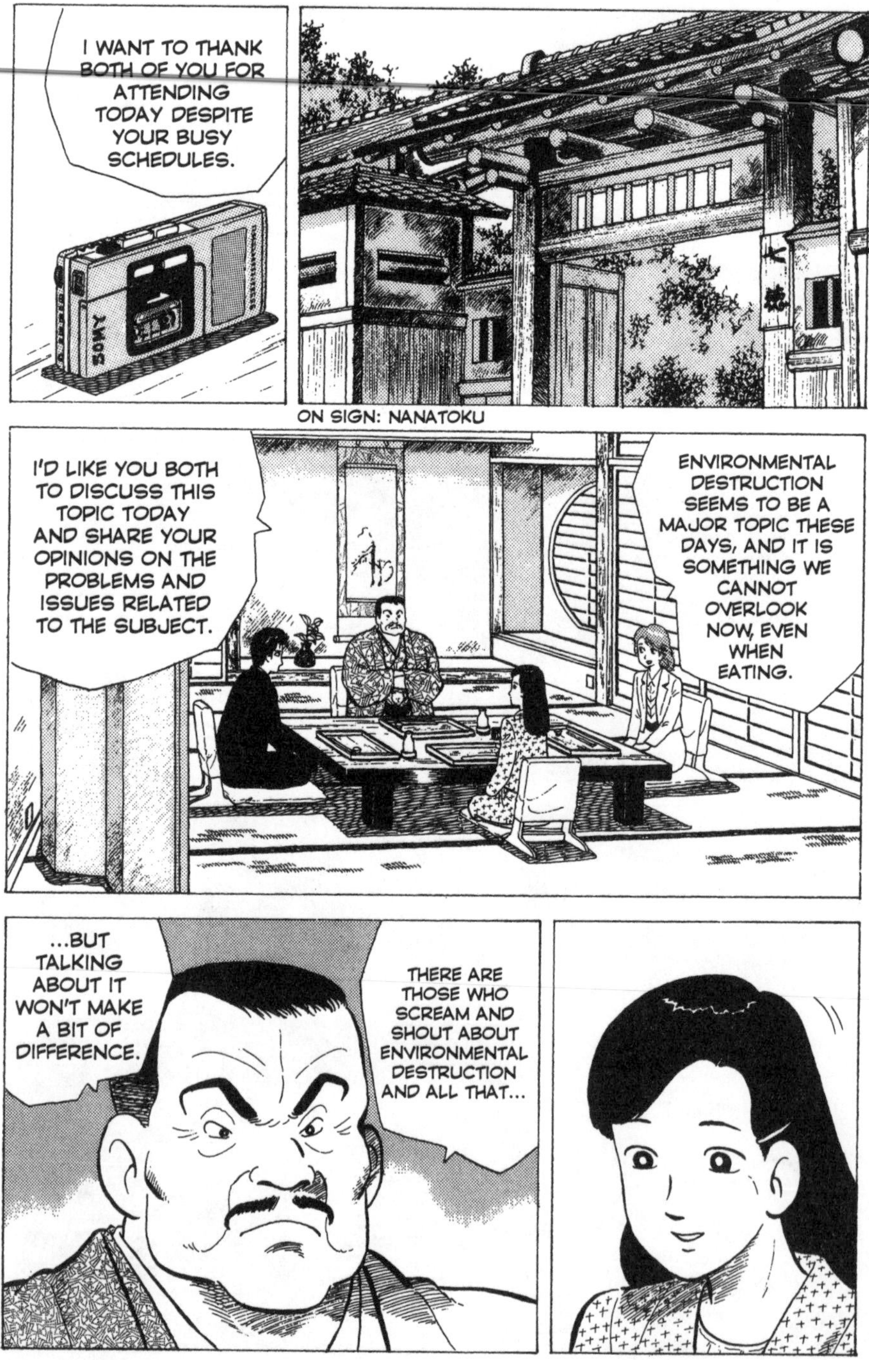
ON SIGN: NANATOKU
I WANT TO THANK BOTH OF YOU FOR ATTENDING TODAY DESPITE YOUR BUSY SCHEDULES.
ENVIRONMENTAL DESTRUCTION SEEMS TO BE A MAJOR TOPIC THESE DAYS, AND IT IS SOMETHING WE CANNOT OVERLOOK NOW, EVEN WHEN EATING.
I'D LIKE YOU BOTH TO DISCUSS THIS TOPIC TODAY AND SHARE YOUR OPINIONS ON THE PROBLEMS AND ISSUES RELATED TO THE SUBJECT.
THERE ARE THOSE WHO SCREAM AND SHOUT ABOUT ENVIRONMENTAL DESTRUCTION AND ALL THAT...
...BUT TALKING ABOUT IT WON'T MAKE A BIT OF DIFFERENCE.

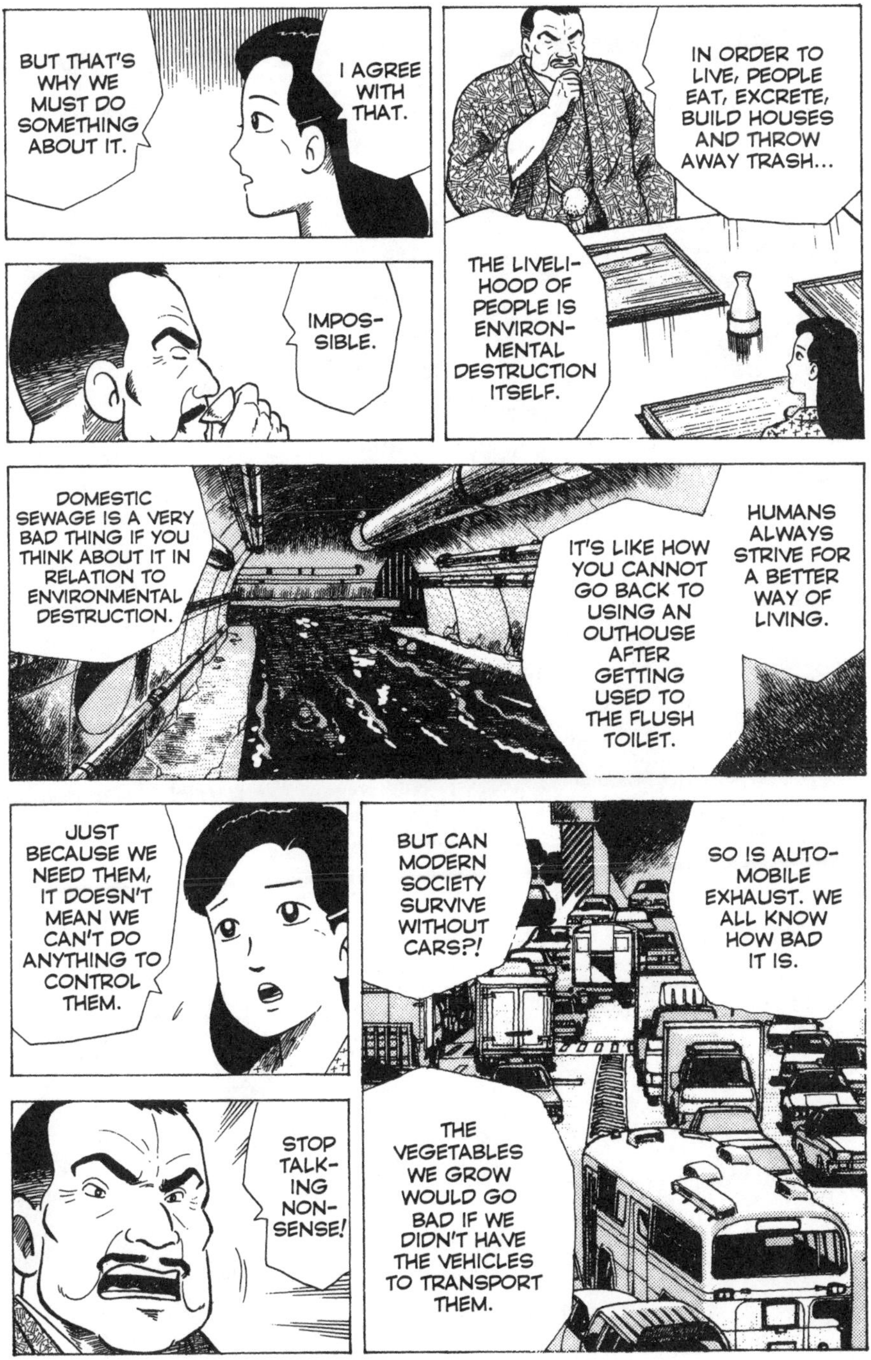
IN ORDER TO LIVE, PEOPLE EAT, EXCRETE, BUILD HOUSES AND THROW AWAY TRASH...
THE LIVELIHOOD OF PEOPLE IS ENVIRONMENTAL DESTRUCTION ITSELF.
I AGREE WITH THAT.
BUT THAT'S WHY WE MUST DO SOMETHING ABOUT IT.
IMPOSSIBLE.
HUMANS ALWAYS STRIVE FOR A BETTER WAY OF LIVING.
IT'S LIKE HOW YOU CANNOT GO BACK TO USING AN OUTHOUSE AFTER GETTING USED TO THE FLUSH TOILET.
DOMESTIC SEWAGE IS A VERY BAD THING IF YOU THINK ABOUT IT IN RELATION TO ENVIRONMENTAL DESTRUCTION.
SO IS AUTOMOBILE EXHAUST. WE ALL KNOW HOW BAD IT IS.
BUT CAN MODERN SOCIETY SURVIVE WITHOUT CARS?!
THE VEGETABLES WE GROW WOULD GO BAD IF WE DIDN'T HAVE THE VEHICLES TO TRANSPORT THEM.
JUST BECAUSE WE NEED THEM, IT DOESN'T MEAN WE CAN'T DO ANYTHING TO CONTROL THEM.
STOP TALKING NONSENSE!

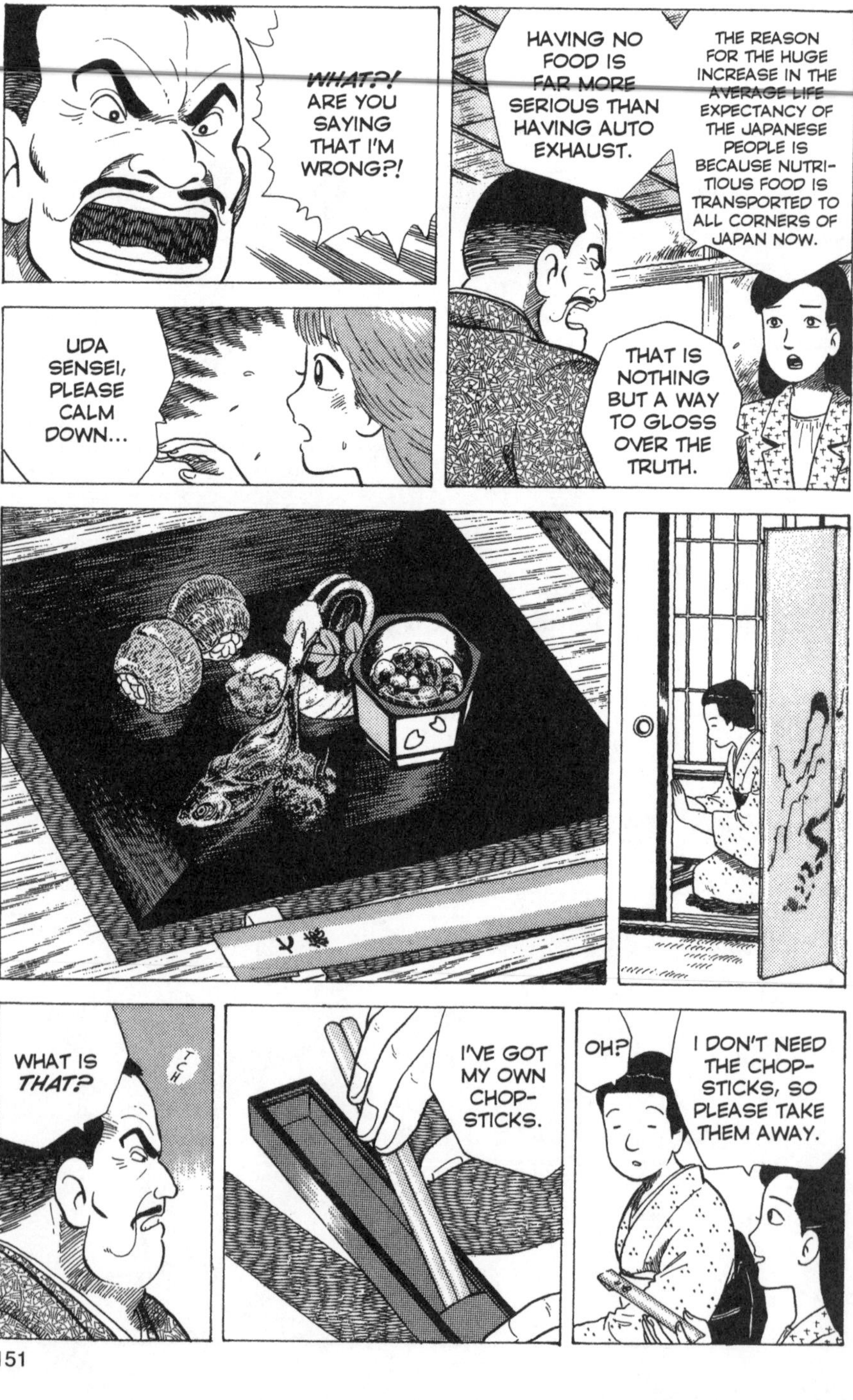
THE REASON FOR THE HUGE INCREASE IN THE AVERAGE LIFE EXPECTANCY OF THE JAPANESE PEOPLE IS BECAUSE NUTRITIOUS FOOD IS TRANSPORTED TO ALL CORNERS OF JAPAN NOW.
HAVING NO FOOD IS FAR MORE SERIOUS THAN HAVING AUTO EXHAUST.
THAT IS NOTHING BUT A WAY TO GLOSS OVER THE TRUTH.
WHAT?! ARE YOU SAYING THAT I'M WRONG?!
UDA SENSEI, PLEASE CALM DOWN...
I DON'T NEED THE CHOPSTICKS, SO PLEASE TAKE THEM AWAY.
OH?
I'VE GOT MY OWN CHOPSTICKS.
WHAT IS *THAT?*
TCH

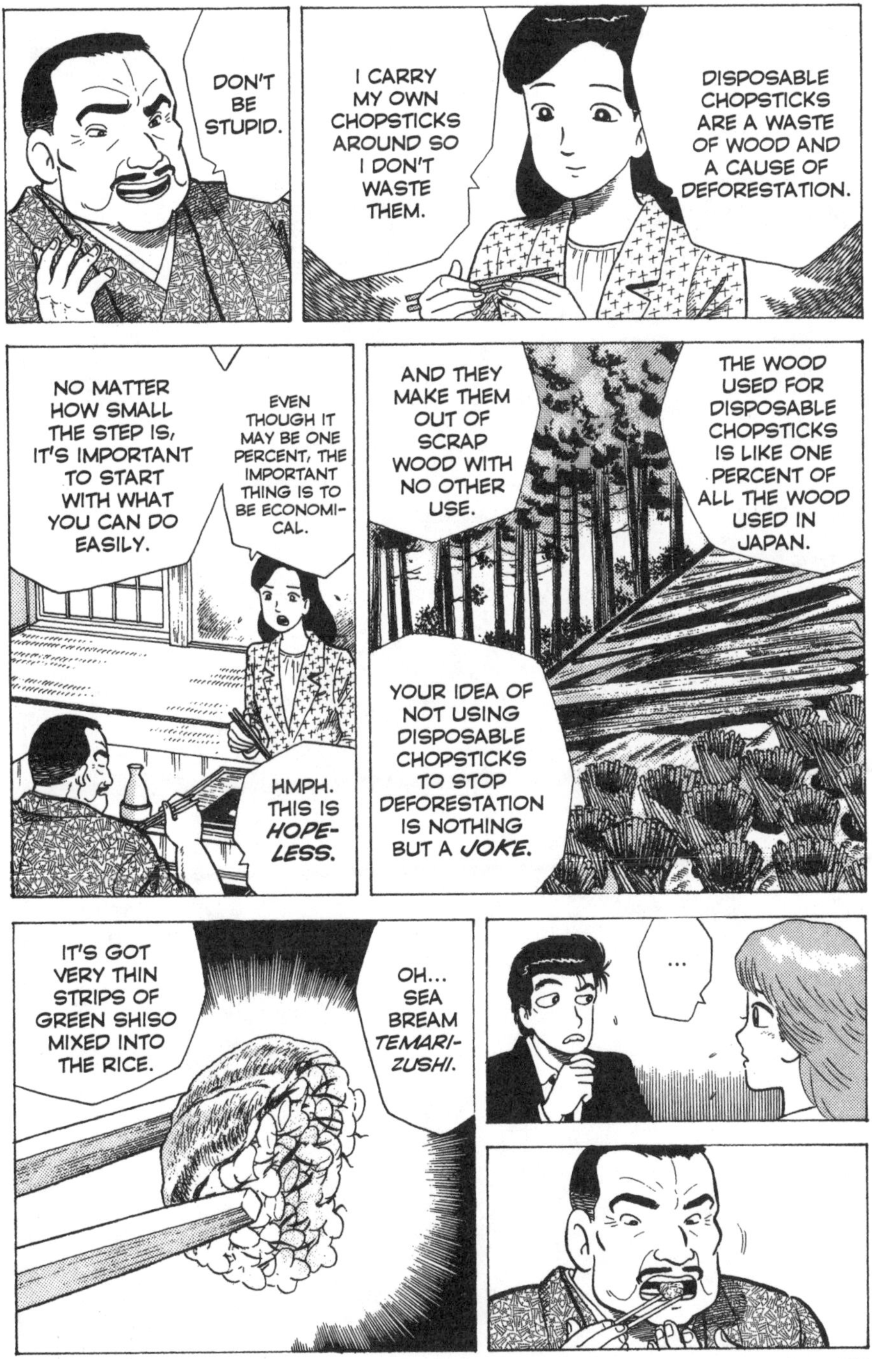
DISPOSABLE CHOPSTICKS ARE A WASTE OF WOOD AND A CAUSE OF DEFORESTATION.
I CARRY MY OWN CHOPSTICKS AROUND SO I DON'T WASTE THEM.
DON'T BE STUPID.
THE WOOD USED FOR DISPOSABLE CHOPSTICKS IS LIKE ONE PERCENT OF ALL THE WOOD USED IN JAPAN.
AND THEY MAKE THEM OUT OF SCRAP WOOD WITH NO OTHER USE.
YOUR IDEA OF NOT USING DISPOSABLE CHOPSTICKS TO STOP DEFORESTATION IS NOTHING BUT A *JOKE.*
EVEN THOUGH IT MAY BE ONE PERCENT, THE IMPORTANT THING IS TO BE ECONOMICAL.
NO MATTER HOW SMALL THE STEP IS, IT'S IMPORTANT TO START WITH WHAT YOU CAN DO EASILY.
HMPH. THIS IS *HOPELESS.*
...
OH... SEA BREAM *TEMARI-ZUSHI.*
IT'S GOT VERY THIN STRIPS OF GREEN SHISO MIXED INTO THE RICE.

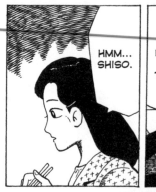

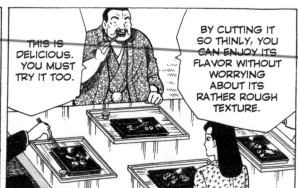

BY CUTTING IT SO THINLY, YOU CAN ENJOY ITS FLAVOR WITHOUT WORRYING ABOUT ITS RATHER ROUGH TEXTURE.
THIS IS DELICIOUS. YOU MUST TRY IT TOO.
HMM... SHISO.
DO YOU GROW YOUR OWN GREEN SHISO AT YOUR PLACE?
OR IS THERE A FARM THAT GROWS THESE ORGANICALLY THAT YOU BUY FROM...
THEN I'M VERY SORRY, BUT I MUST REFRAIN FROM EATING THIS.
NO... IT WOULD BE TOO MUCH WORK FOR US TO DO THAT, SO WE JUST BUY THEM AT THE MARKETPLACE.
WHY?
THE GREEN SHISO OUT IN THE MARKET IS GROWN USING TONS OF PESTICIDE TO MAKE SURE THEY HAVE NO WORM HOLES AND TO GROW THEM ALL TO THE SAME SIZE.
BUT IF YOU WASH THEM WITH WATER, THEY BECOME WRINKLY. SO THEY ARE ALL SHIPPED OUT WITHOUT BEING WASHED.
AND PEOPLE USING THE GREEN SHISO FOR A DISH WILL ALSO USE THEM WITHOUT WASHING THEM TO MAKE THEM LOOK CRISP EVEN WHEN THERE IS A THICK LAYER OF PESTICIDES LEFT ON THEM.
SO EATING A GREEN SHISO FROM THE MARKETPLACE IS LIKE EATING THE PESTICIDE ITSELF.

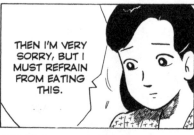

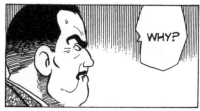

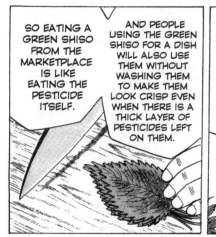

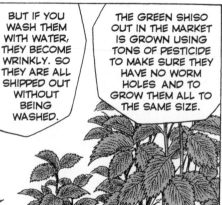

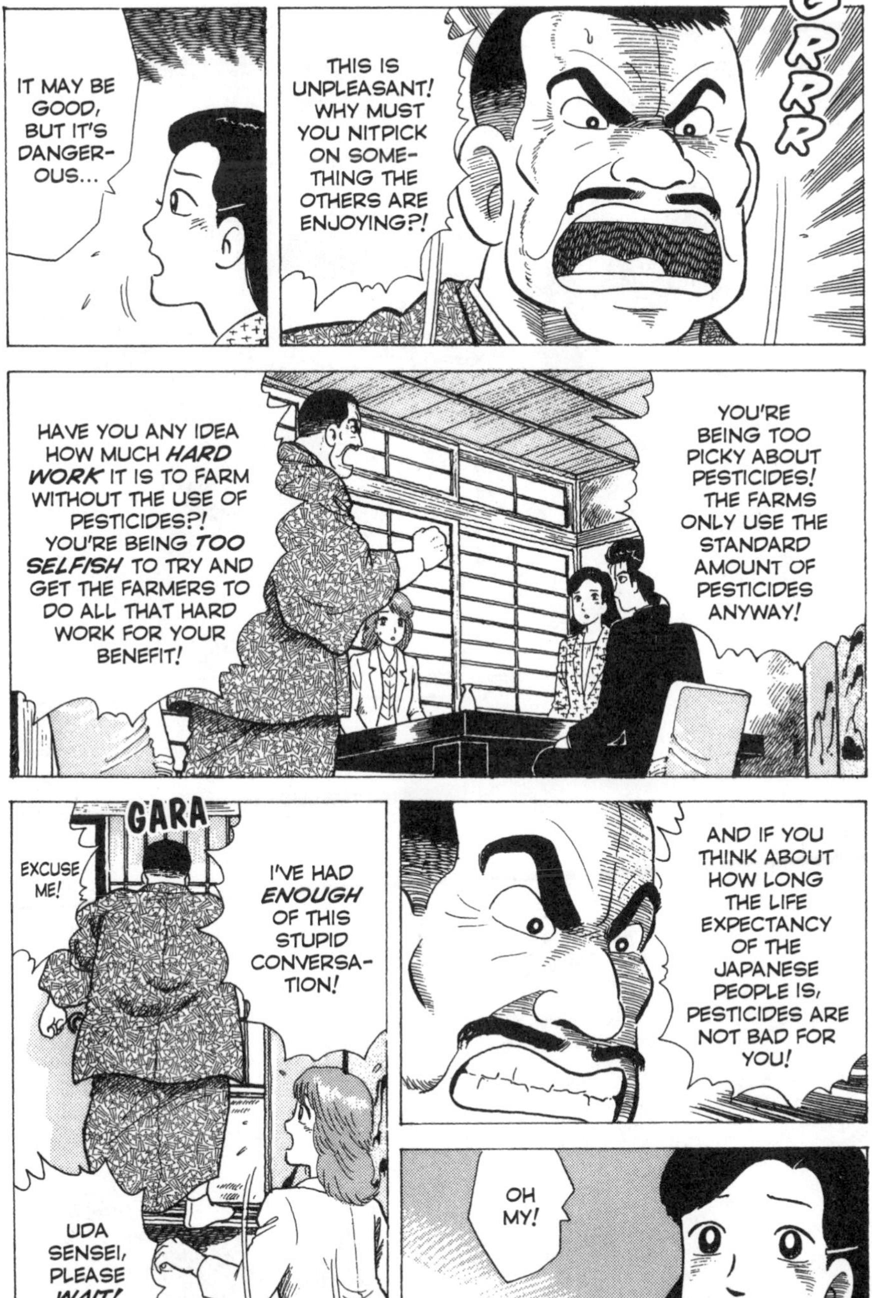
GRRR
THIS IS UNPLEASANT! WHY MUST YOU NITPICK ON SOMETHING THE OTHERS ARE ENJOYING?!
IT MAY BE GOOD, BUT IT'S DANGEROUS...
YOU'RE BEING TOO PICKY ABOUT PESTICIDES! THE FARMS ONLY USE THE STANDARD AMOUNT OF PESTICIDES ANYWAY!
HAVE YOU ANY IDEA HOW MUCH HARD WORK IT IS TO FARM WITHOUT THE USE OF PESTICIDES?! YOU'RE BEING TOO SELFISH TO TRY AND GET THE FARMERS TO DO ALL THAT HARD WORK FOR YOUR BENEFIT!
AND IF YOU THINK ABOUT HOW LONG THE LIFE EXPECTANCY OF THE JAPANESE PEOPLE IS, PESTICIDES ARE NOT BAD FOR YOU!
OH MY!
GARA
I'VE HAD ENOUGH OF THIS STUPID CONVERSATION!
EXCUSE ME!
UDA SENSEI, PLEASE WAIT!

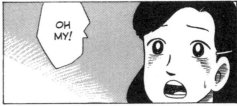

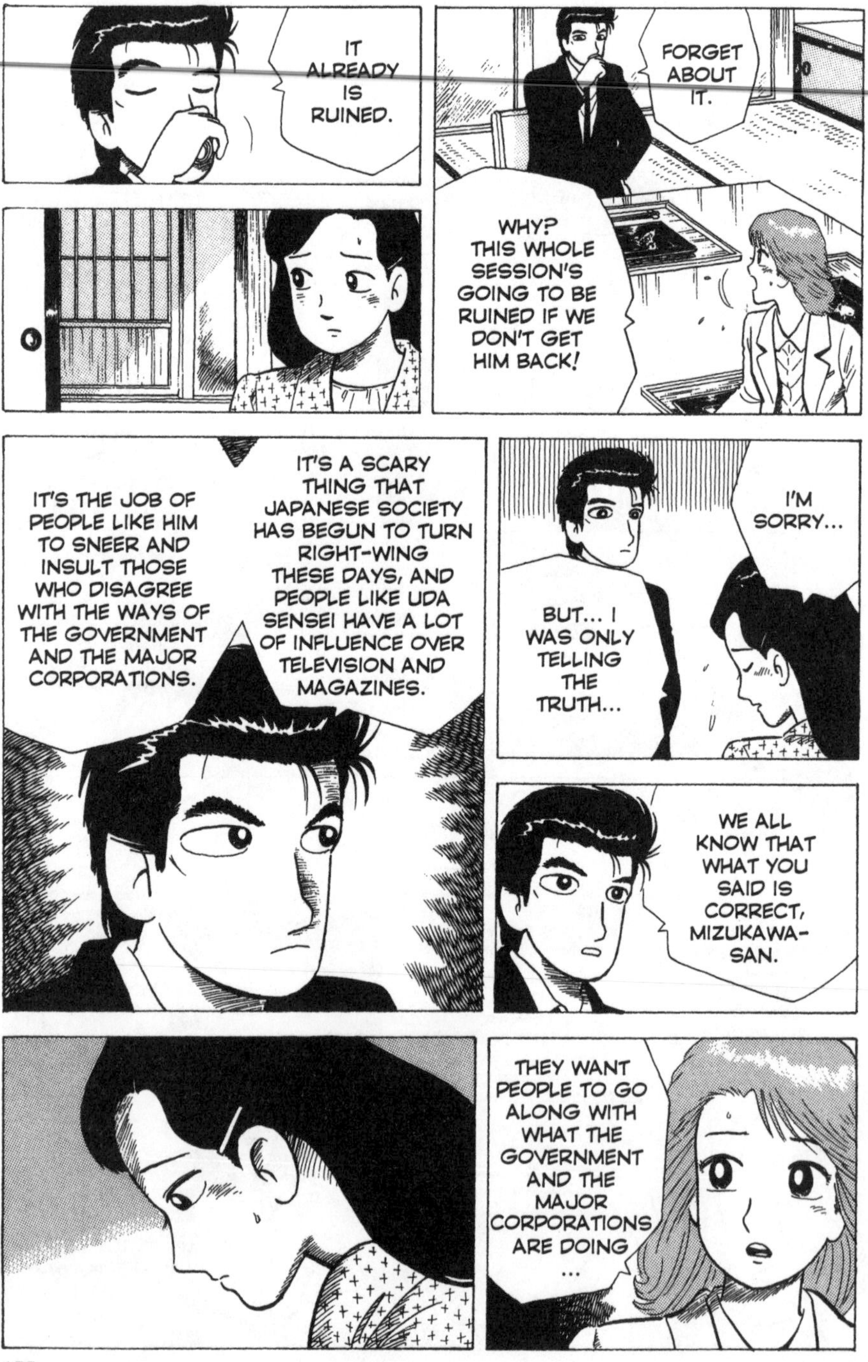
FORGET ABOUT IT.
WHY? THIS WHOLE SESSION'S GOING TO BE RUINED IF WE DON'T GET HIM BACK!
IT ALREADY IS RUINED.
I'M SORRY...
BUT... I WAS ONLY TELLING THE TRUTH...
WE ALL KNOW THAT WHAT YOU SAID IS CORRECT, MIZUKAWA-SAN.
IT'S A SCARY THING THAT JAPANESE SOCIETY HAS BEGUN TO TURN RIGHT-WING THESE DAYS, AND PEOPLE LIKE UDA SENSEI HAVE A LOT OF INFLUENCE OVER TELEVISION AND MAGAZINES.
IT'S THE JOB OF PEOPLE LIKE HIM TO SNEER AND INSULT THOSE WHO DISAGREE WITH THE WAYS OF THE GOVERNMENT AND THE MAJOR CORPORATIONS.
THEY WANT PEOPLE TO GO ALONG WITH WHAT THE GOVERNMENT AND THE MAJOR CORPORATIONS ARE DOING ...

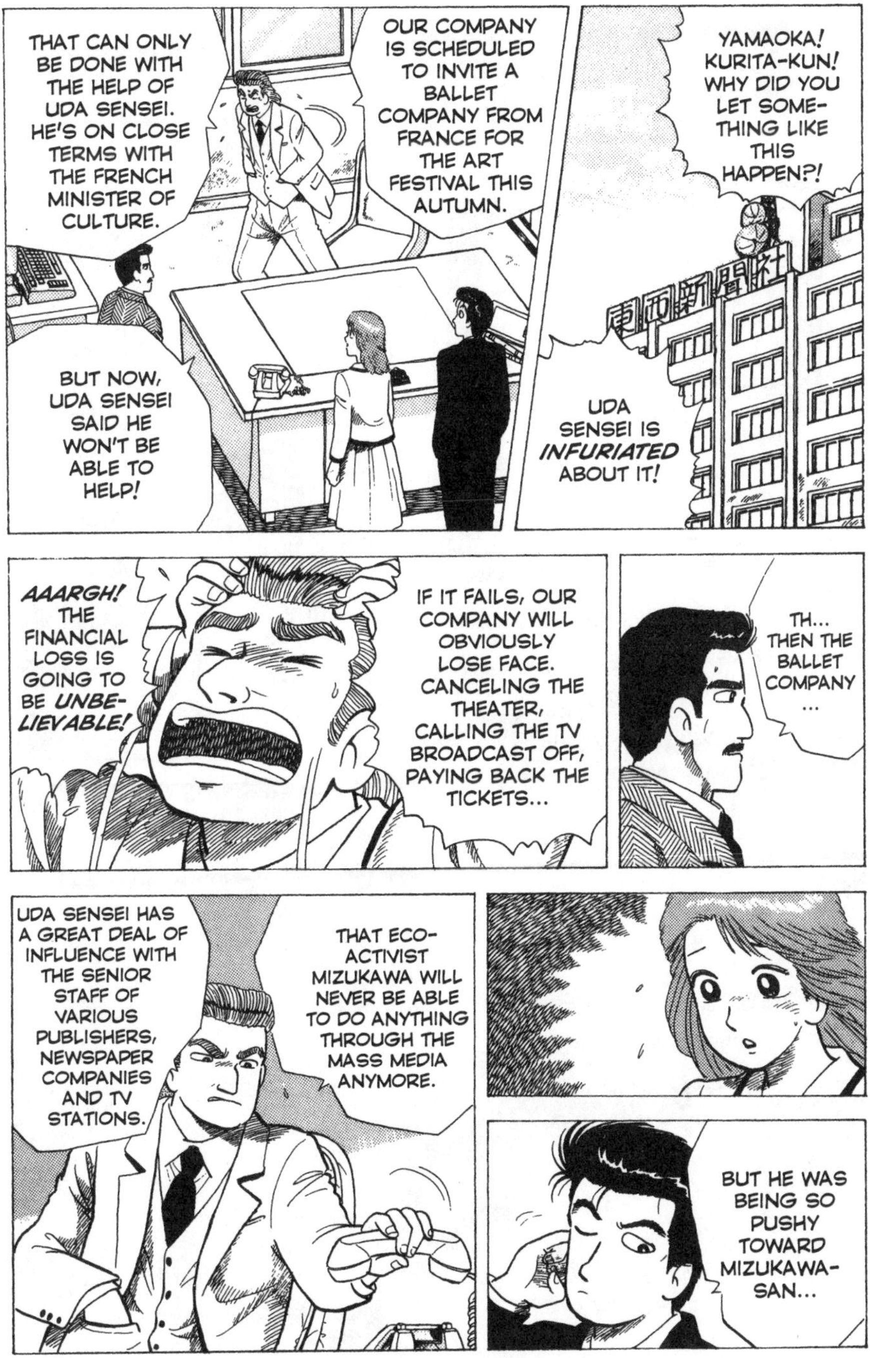
YAMAOKA! KURITA-KUN! WHY DID YOU LET SOME-THING LIKE THIS HAPPEN?!
東西新聞社
UDA SENSEI IS *INFURIATED* ABOUT IT!
OUR COMPANY IS SCHEDULED TO INVITE A BALLET COMPANY FROM FRANCE FOR THE ART FESTIVAL THIS AUTUMN.
THAT CAN ONLY BE DONE WITH THE HELP OF UDA SENSEI. HE'S ON CLOSE TERMS WITH THE FRENCH MINISTER OF CULTURE.
BUT NOW, UDA SENSEI SAID HE WON'T BE ABLE TO HELP!
TH... THEN THE BALLET COMPANY ...
IF IT FAILS, OUR COMPANY WILL OBVIOUSLY LOSE FACE. CANCELING THE THEATER, CALLING THE TV BROADCAST OFF, PAYING BACK THE TICKETS...
AAARGH! THE FINANCIAL LOSS IS GOING TO BE *UNBE-LIEVABLE!*
BUT HE WAS BEING SO PUSHY TOWARD MIZUKAWA-SAN...
THAT ECO-ACTIVIST MIZUKAWA WILL NEVER BE ABLE TO DO ANYTHING THROUGH THE MASS MEDIA ANYMORE.
UDA SENSEI HAS A GREAT DEAL OF INFLUENCE WITH THE SENIOR STAFF OF VARIOUS PUBLISHERS, NEWSPAPER COMPANIES AND TV STATIONS.

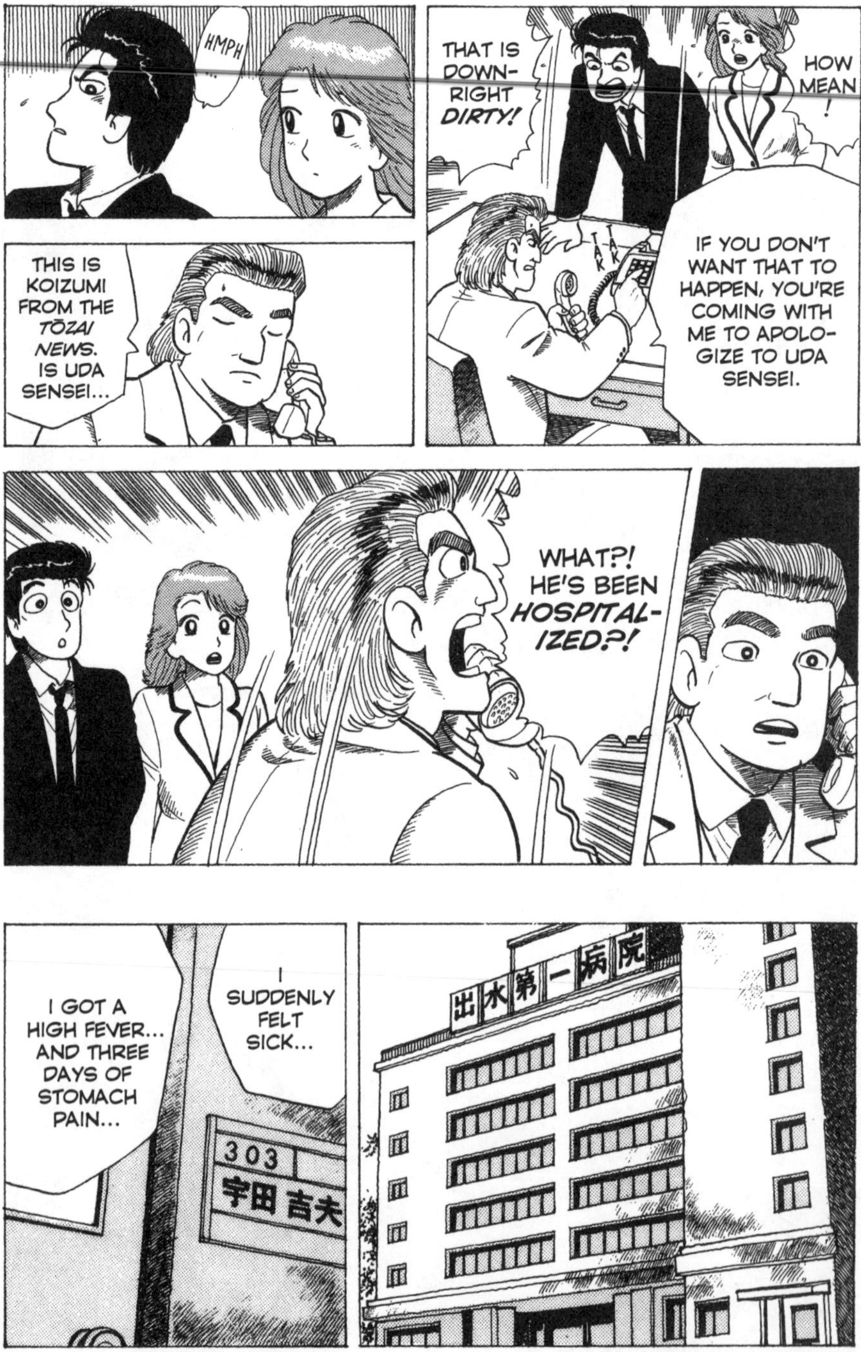
HOW MEAN!
THAT IS DOWN-RIGHT *DIRTY!*
TAK TAK
IF YOU DON'T WANT THAT TO HAPPEN, YOU'RE COMING WITH ME TO APOLO-GIZE TO UDA SENSEI.
HMPH...
THIS IS KOIZUMI FROM THE *TŌZAI NEWS.* IS UDA SENSEI...
WHAT?! HE'S BEEN ***HOSPITAL-IZED?!***
出水第一病院
I SUDDENLY FELT SICK...
I GOT A HIGH FEVER... AND THREE DAYS OF STOMACH PAIN...
303
宇田吉夫

NAME LABEL: UDA YOSHIO

ON SIGN: DEMIZU DAI-ICHI HOSPITAL

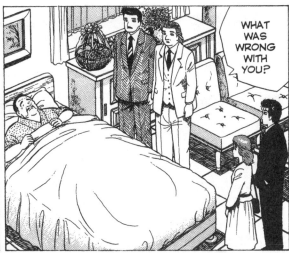

WHAT WAS WRONG WITH YOU?
IT TURNS OUT THAT THE DOCTORS COULDN'T TELL.
THEY'VE DONE ALL SORTS OF EXAMINATIONS, BUT THEY COULDN'T FIND ANYTHING WRONG WITH ME.
THEY COULDN'T FIND ANYTHING ...
BUT THAT IS A LOT BETTER THAN FINDING SOMETHING WRONG.
THE DOCTOR SAID I CAN BE DISCHARGED ANYTIME I WANT TO, BUT I FEEL UNEASY ABOUT IT.
I WONDER.
I'M SO GLAD UDA SENSEI HAS CHANGED HIS MIND.
HE HAS AGREED TO HELP US ABOUT THE BALLET COMPANY AS HE PROMISED.
TAXI

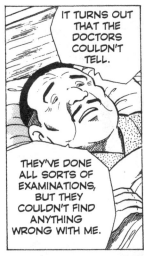

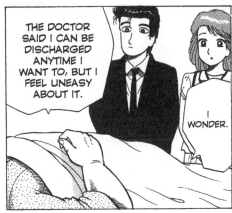

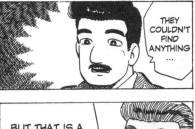

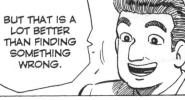

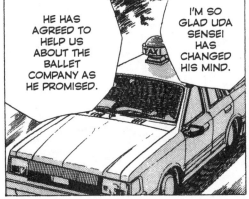

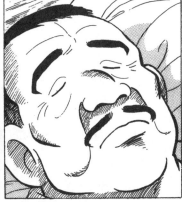

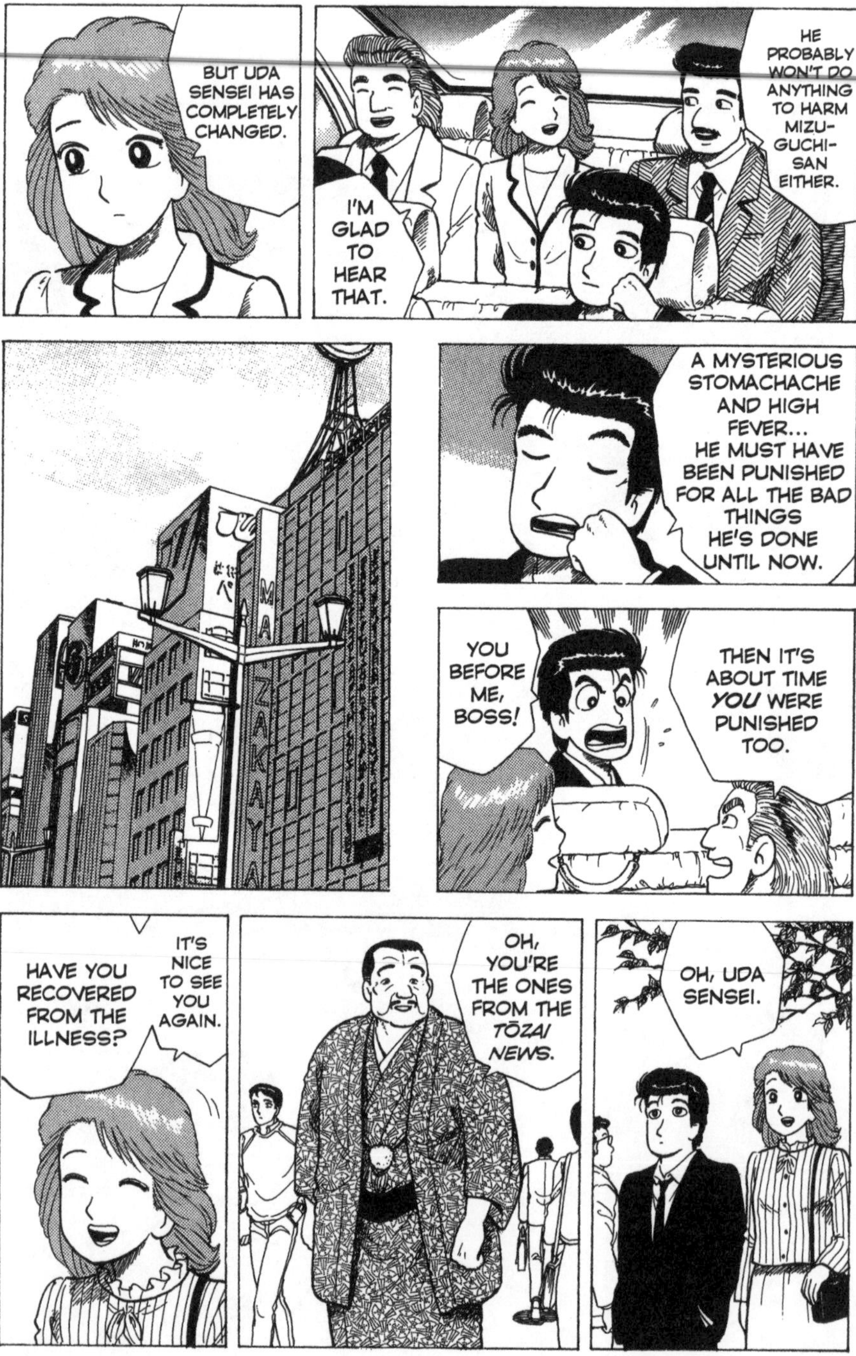
HE PROBABLY WON'T DO ANYTHING TO HARM MIZUGUCHI-SAN EITHER.
I'M GLAD TO HEAR THAT.
BUT UDA SENSEI HAS COMPLETELY CHANGED.
A MYSTERIOUS STOMACHACHE AND HIGH FEVER... HE MUST HAVE BEEN PUNISHED FOR ALL THE BAD THINGS HE'S DONE UNTIL NOW.
THEN IT'S ABOUT TIME *YOU* WERE PUNISHED TOO.
YOU BEFORE ME, BOSS!
OH, UDA SENSEI.
OH, YOU'RE THE ONES FROM THE *TŌZAI NEWS*.
IT'S NICE TO SEE YOU AGAIN.
HAVE YOU RECOVERED FROM THE ILLNESS?

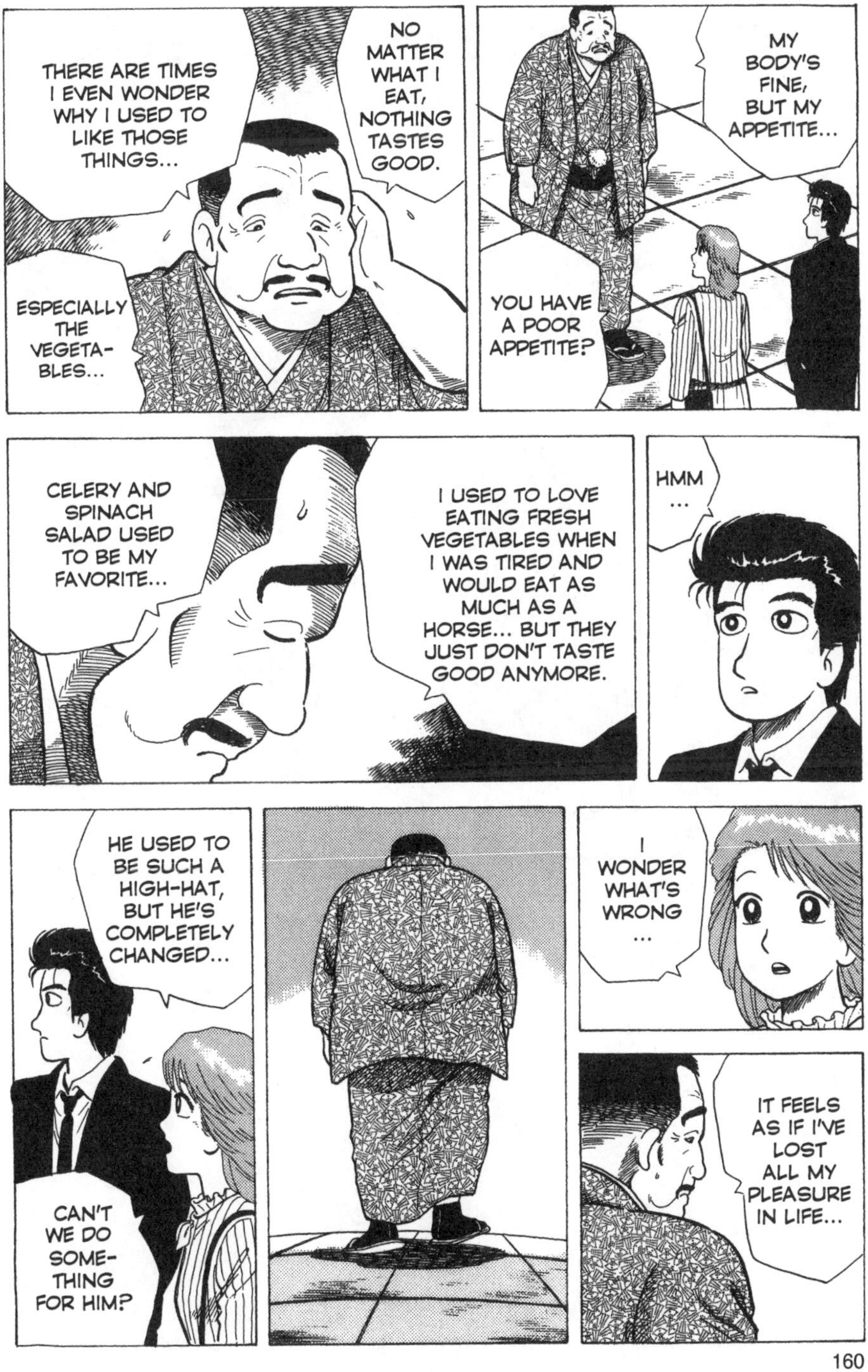
MY BODY'S FINE, BUT MY APPETITE...
YOU HAVE A POOR APPETITE?
NO MATTER WHAT I EAT, NOTHING TASTES GOOD.
THERE ARE TIMES I EVEN WONDER WHY I USED TO LIKE THOSE THINGS...
ESPECIALLY THE VEGETA-BLES...
HMM ...
I USED TO LOVE EATING FRESH VEGETABLES WHEN I WAS TIRED AND WOULD EAT AS MUCH AS A HORSE... BUT THEY JUST DON'T TASTE GOOD ANYMORE.
CELERY AND SPINACH SALAD USED TO BE MY FAVORITE...
I WONDER WHAT'S WRONG ...
IT FEELS AS IF I'VE LOST ALL MY PLEASURE IN LIFE...
HE USED TO BE SUCH A HIGH-HAT, BUT HE'S COMPLETELY CHANGED...
CAN'T WE DO SOME-THING FOR HIM?

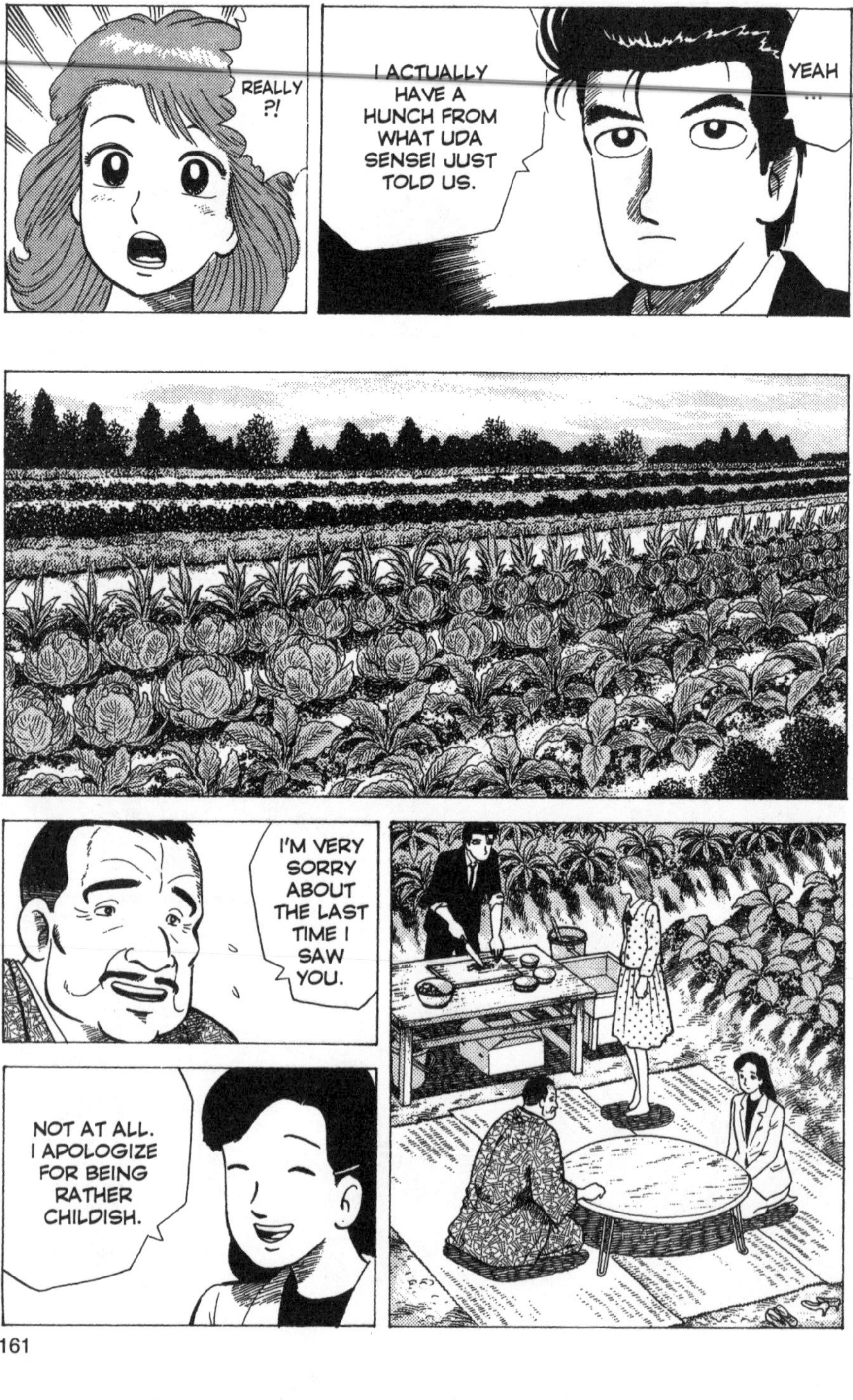
YEAH ...
I ACTUALLY HAVE A HUNCH FROM WHAT UDA SENSEI JUST TOLD US.
REALLY ?!
I'M VERY SORRY ABOUT THE LAST TIME I SAW YOU.
NOT AT ALL. I APOLOGIZE FOR BEING RATHER CHILDISH.

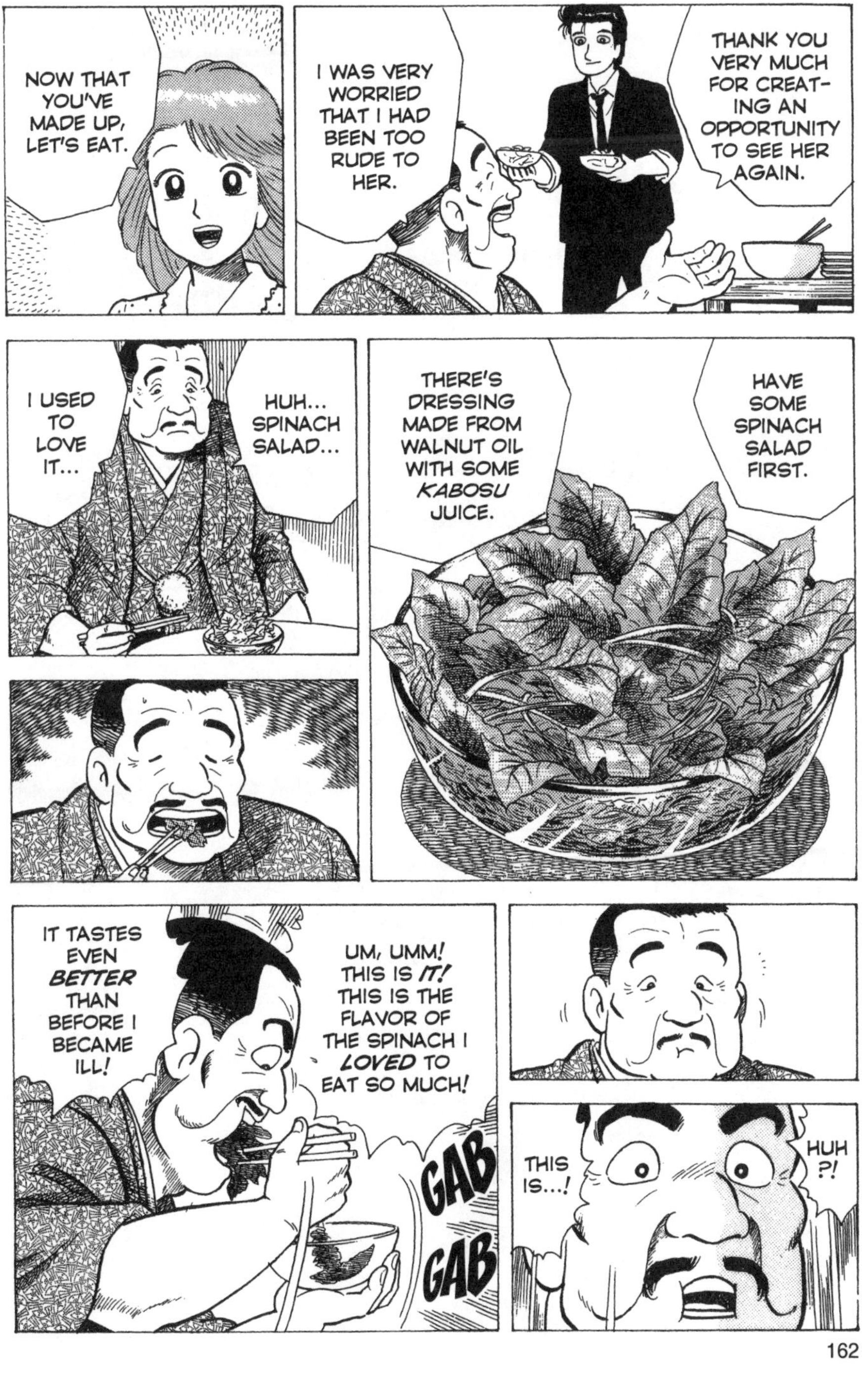
THANK YOU VERY MUCH FOR CREATING AN OPPORTUNITY TO SEE HER AGAIN.
I WAS VERY WORRIED THAT I HAD BEEN TOO RUDE TO HER.
NOW THAT YOU'VE MADE UP, LET'S EAT.
HAVE SOME SPINACH SALAD FIRST.
THERE'S DRESSING MADE FROM WALNUT OIL WITH SOME *KABOSU* JUICE.
HUH... SPINACH SALAD...
I USED TO LOVE IT...
HUH ?!
THIS IS...!
UM, UMM! THIS IS *IT!* THIS IS THE FLAVOR OF THE SPINACH I *LOVED* TO EAT SO MUCH!
IT TASTES EVEN ***BETTER*** THAN BEFORE I BECAME ILL!
GAB
GAB

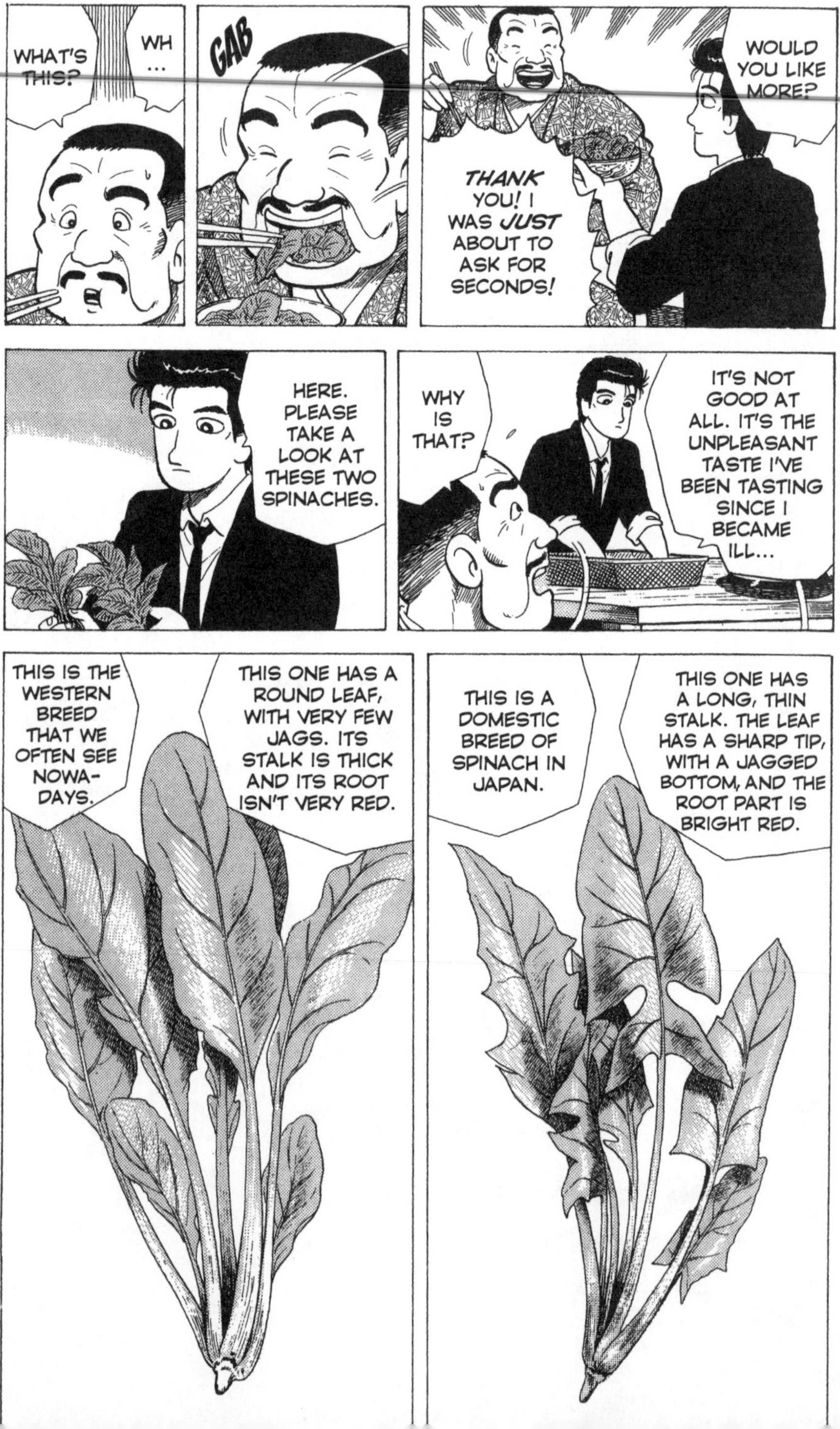
WOULD YOU LIKE MORE?
THANK YOU! I WAS JUST ABOUT TO ASK FOR SECONDS!
GAB
WH ...
WHAT'S THIS?
IT'S NOT GOOD AT ALL. IT'S THE UNPLEASANT TASTE I'VE BEEN TASTING SINCE I BECAME ILL...
WHY IS THAT?
HERE. PLEASE TAKE A LOOK AT THESE TWO SPINACHES.
THIS ONE HAS A LONG, THIN STALK. THE LEAF HAS A SHARP TIP, WITH A JAGGED BOTTOM, AND THE ROOT PART IS BRIGHT RED.
THIS IS A DOMESTIC BREED OF SPINACH IN JAPAN.
THIS ONE HAS A ROUND LEAF, WITH VERY FEW JAGS. ITS STALK IS THICK AND ITS ROOT ISN'T VERY RED.
THIS IS THE WESTERN BREED THAT WE OFTEN SEE NOWADAYS.

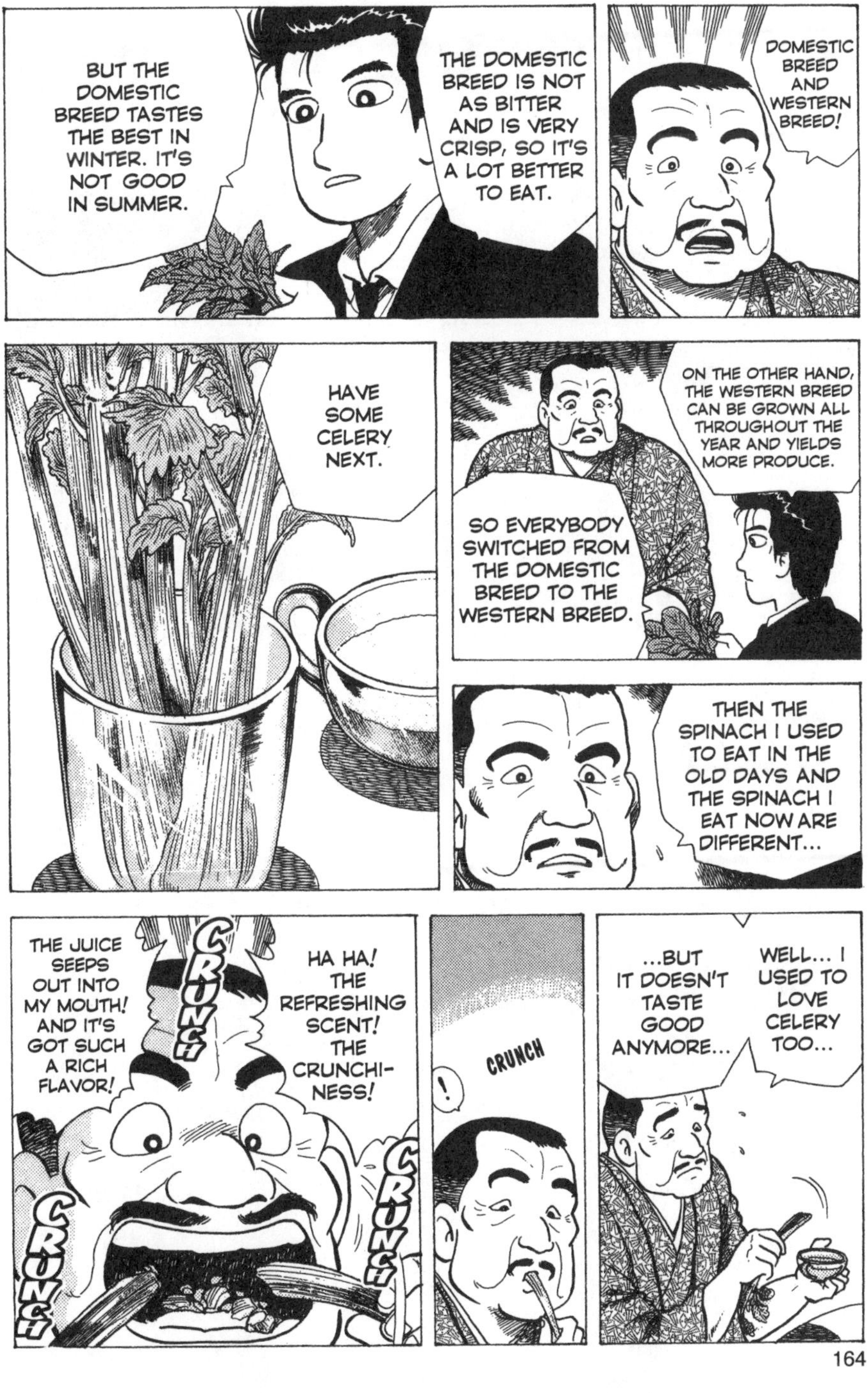
DOMESTIC BREED AND WESTERN BREED!
THE DOMESTIC BREED IS NOT AS BITTER AND IS VERY CRISP, SO IT'S A LOT BETTER TO EAT.
BUT THE DOMESTIC BREED TASTES THE BEST IN WINTER. IT'S NOT GOOD IN SUMMER.
ON THE OTHER HAND, THE WESTERN BREED CAN BE GROWN ALL THROUGHOUT THE YEAR AND YIELDS MORE PRODUCE.
SO EVERYBODY SWITCHED FROM THE DOMESTIC BREED TO THE WESTERN BREED.
THEN THE SPINACH I USED TO EAT IN THE OLD DAYS AND THE SPINACH I EAT NOW ARE DIFFERENT...
HAVE SOME CELERY NEXT.
WELL... I USED TO LOVE CELERY TOO...
...BUT IT DOESN'T TASTE GOOD ANYMORE...
CRUNCH
!
CRUNCH
HA HA! THE REFRESHING SCENT! THE CRUNCHINESS!
CRUNCH
THE JUICE SEEPS OUT INTO MY MOUTH! AND IT'S GOT SUCH A RICH FLAVOR!
CRUNCH

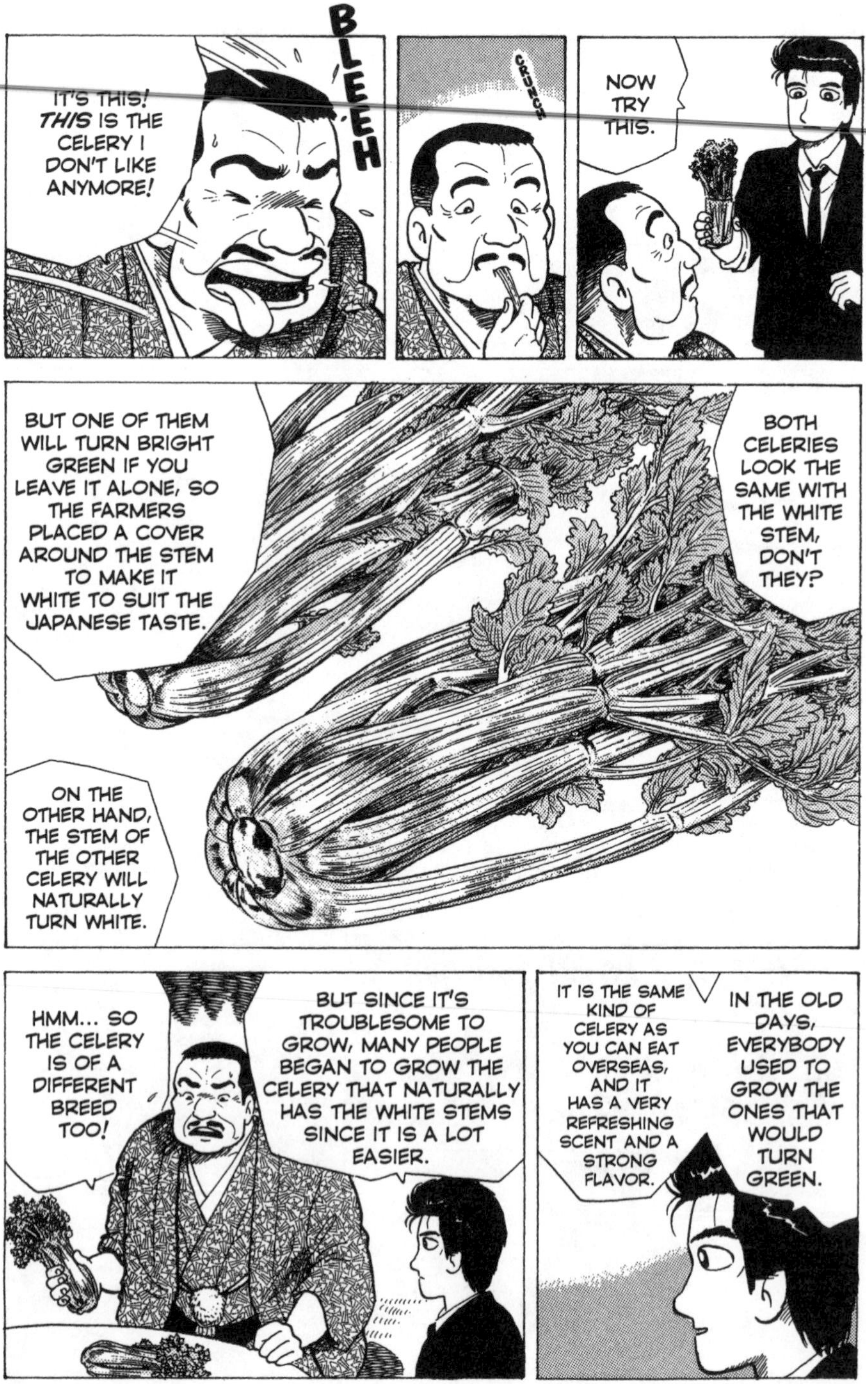
NOW TRY THIS.
CRUNCH
BLEEH
IT'S THIS! *THIS* IS THE CELERY I DON'T LIKE ANYMORE!
BOTH CELERIES LOOK THE SAME WITH THE WHITE STEM, DON'T THEY?
BUT ONE OF THEM WILL TURN BRIGHT GREEN IF YOU LEAVE IT ALONE, SO THE FARMERS PLACED A COVER AROUND THE STEM TO MAKE IT WHITE TO SUIT THE JAPANESE TASTE.
ON THE OTHER HAND, THE STEM OF THE OTHER CELERY WILL NATURALLY TURN WHITE.
IN THE OLD DAYS, EVERYBODY USED TO GROW THE ONES THAT WOULD TURN GREEN.
IT IS THE SAME KIND OF CELERY AS YOU CAN EAT OVERSEAS, AND IT HAS A VERY REFRESHING SCENT AND A STRONG FLAVOR.
BUT SINCE IT'S TROUBLESOME TO GROW, MANY PEOPLE BEGAN TO GROW THE CELERY THAT NATURALLY HAS THE WHITE STEMS SINCE IT IS A LOT EASIER.
HMM... SO THE CELERY IS OF A DIFFERENT BREED TOO!

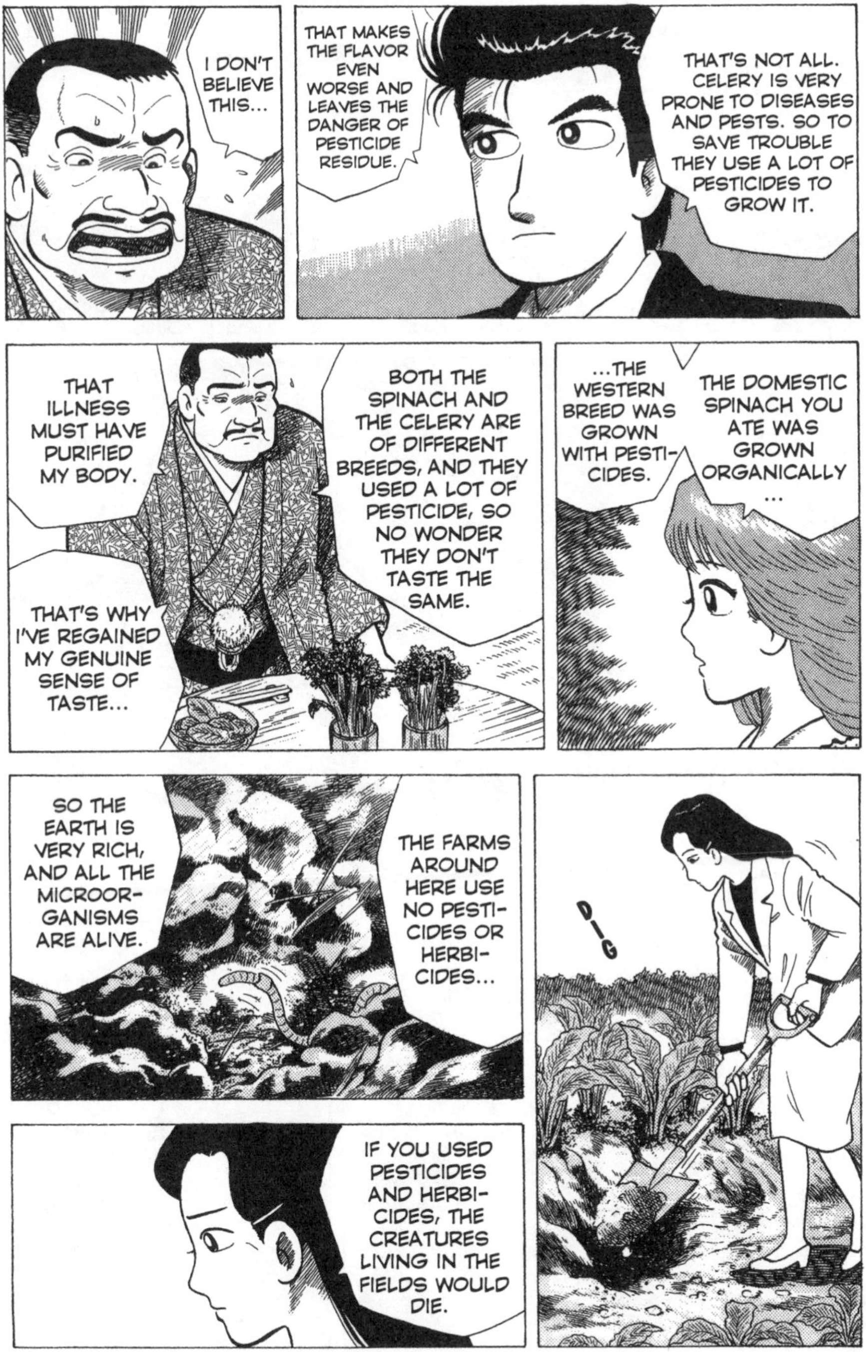

THAT'S NOT ALL. CELERY IS VERY PRONE TO DISEASES AND PESTS. SO TO SAVE TROUBLE THEY USE A LOT OF PESTICIDES TO GROW IT.
THAT MAKES THE FLAVOR EVEN WORSE AND LEAVES THE DANGER OF PESTICIDE RESIDUE.
I DON'T BELIEVE THIS...
THE DOMESTIC SPINACH YOU ATE WAS GROWN ORGANICALLY ...
...THE WESTERN BREED WAS GROWN WITH PESTI-CIDES.
BOTH THE SPINACH AND THE CELERY ARE OF DIFFERENT BREEDS, AND THEY USED A LOT OF PESTICIDE, SO NO WONDER THEY DON'T TASTE THE SAME.
THAT ILLNESS MUST HAVE PURIFIED MY BODY.
THAT'S WHY I'VE REGAINED MY GENUINE SENSE OF TASTE...
DIG
THE FARMS AROUND HERE USE NO PESTI-CIDES OR HERBI-CIDES...
SO THE EARTH IS VERY RICH, AND ALL THE MICROOR-GANISMS ARE ALIVE.
IF YOU USED PESTICIDES AND HERBI-CIDES, THE CREATURES LIVING IN THE FIELDS WOULD DIE.

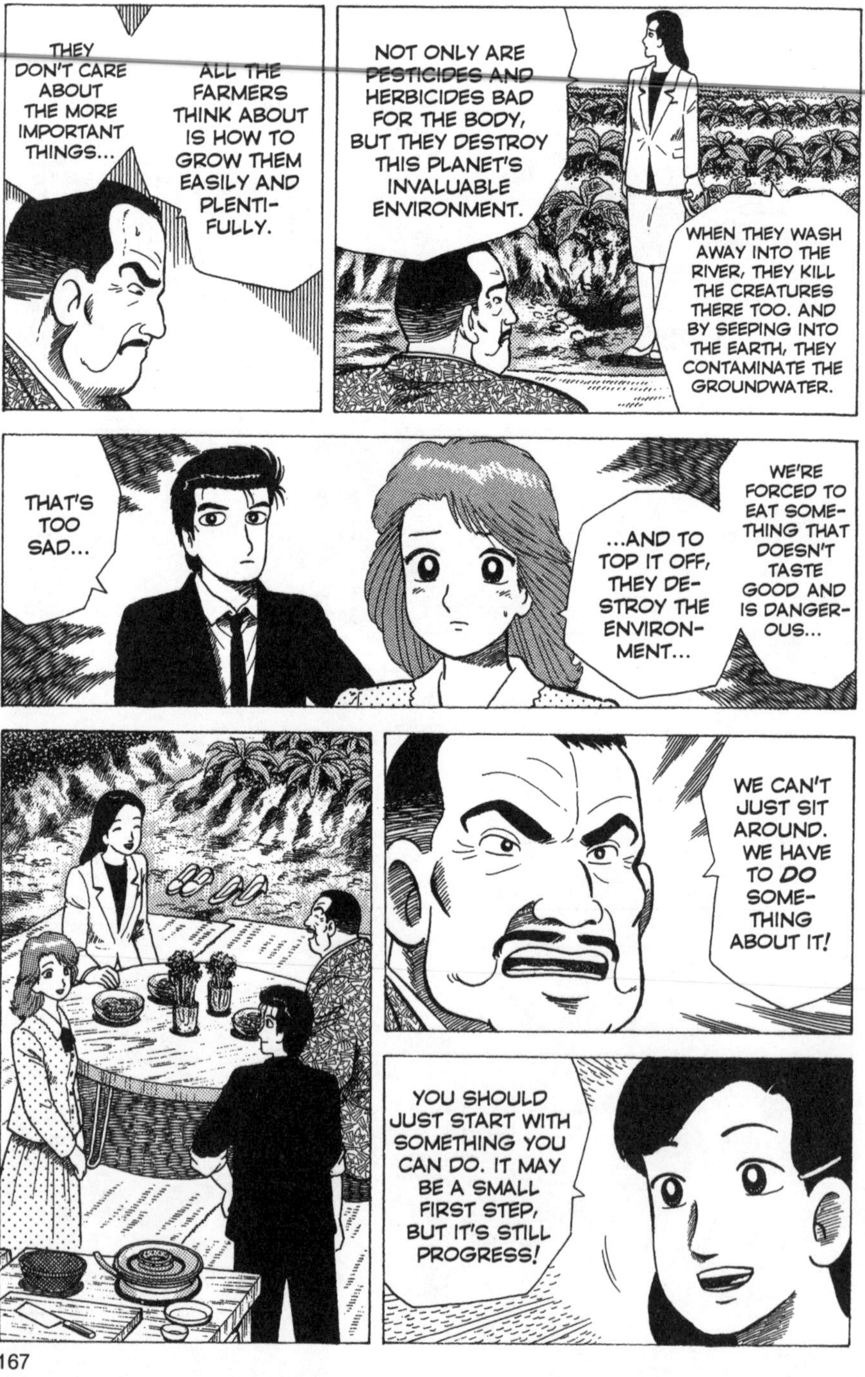
NOT ONLY ARE PESTICIDES AND HERBICIDES BAD FOR THE BODY, BUT THEY DESTROY THIS PLANET'S INVALUABLE ENVIRONMENT.
WHEN THEY WASH AWAY INTO THE RIVER, THEY KILL THE CREATURES THERE TOO. AND BY SEEPING INTO THE EARTH, THEY CONTAMINATE THE GROUNDWATER.
ALL THE FARMERS THINK ABOUT IS HOW TO GROW THEM EASILY AND PLENTI-FULLY.
THEY DON'T CARE ABOUT THE MORE IMPORTANT THINGS...
WE'RE FORCED TO EAT SOME-THING THAT DOESN'T TASTE GOOD AND IS DANGER-OUS...
...AND TO TOP IT OFF, THEY DE-STROY THE ENVIRON-MENT...
THAT'S TOO SAD...
WE CAN'T JUST SIT AROUND. WE HAVE TO *DO* SOME-THING ABOUT IT!
YOU SHOULD JUST START WITH SOMETHING YOU CAN DO. IT MAY BE A SMALL FIRST STEP, BUT IT'S STILL PROGRESS!

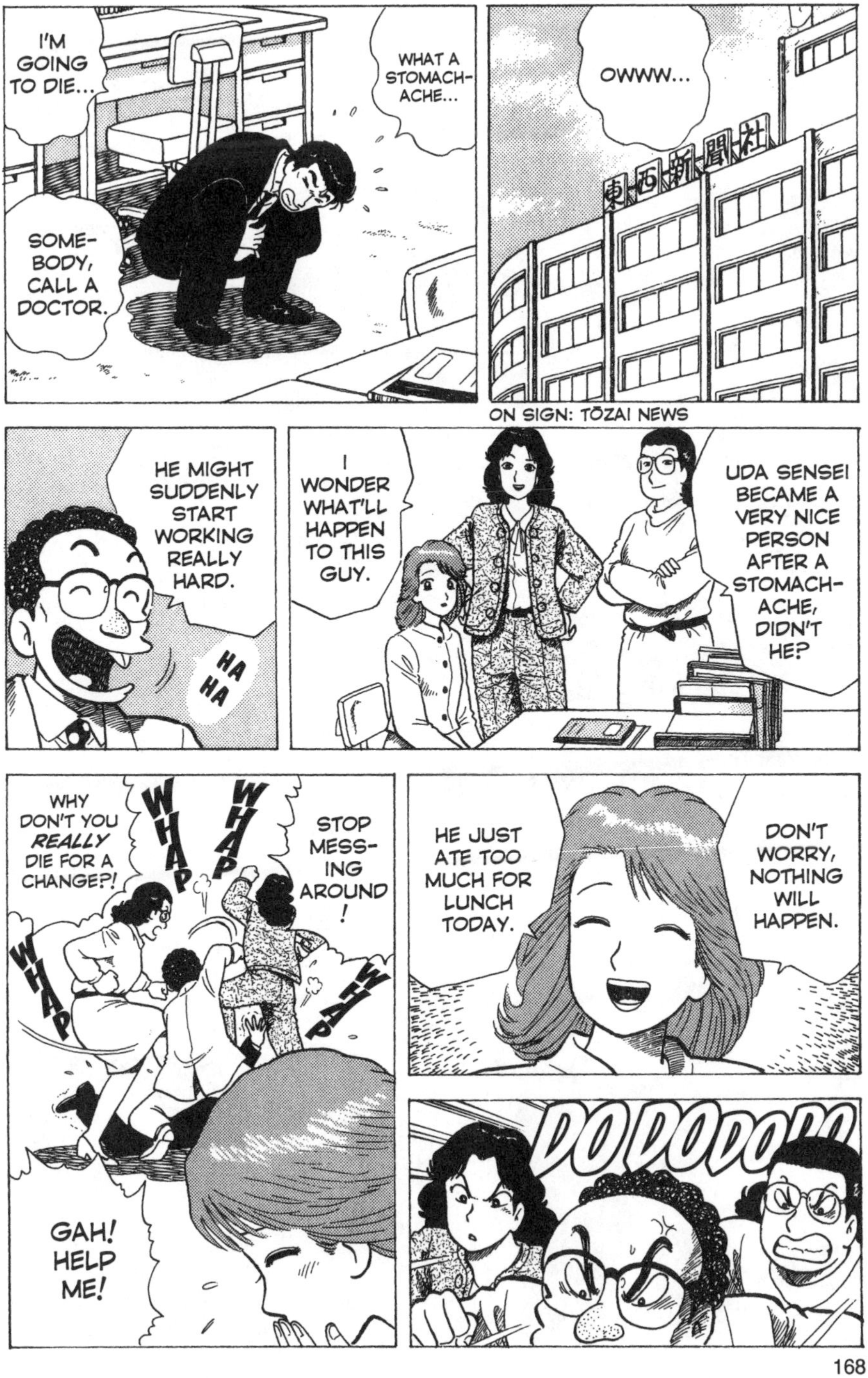
OWWW...
ON SIGN: TŌZAI NEWS
WHAT A STOMACH-ACHE...
I'M GOING TO DIE...
SOME-BODY, CALL A DOCTOR.
UDA SENSEI BECAME A VERY NICE PERSON AFTER A STOMACH-ACHE, DIDN'T HE?
I WONDER WHAT'LL HAPPEN TO THIS GUY.
HE MIGHT SUDDENLY START WORKING REALLY HARD.
HA HA
DON'T WORRY, NOTHING WILL HAPPEN.
HE JUST ATE TOO MUCH FOR LUNCH TODAY.
DODODODO
STOP MESS-ING AROUND!
WHAP
WHAP
WHY DON'T YOU *REALLY* DIE FOR A CHANGE?!
WHAP
WHAP
GAH! HELP ME!

SIXTH COURSE

THE BREATH OF SPRING

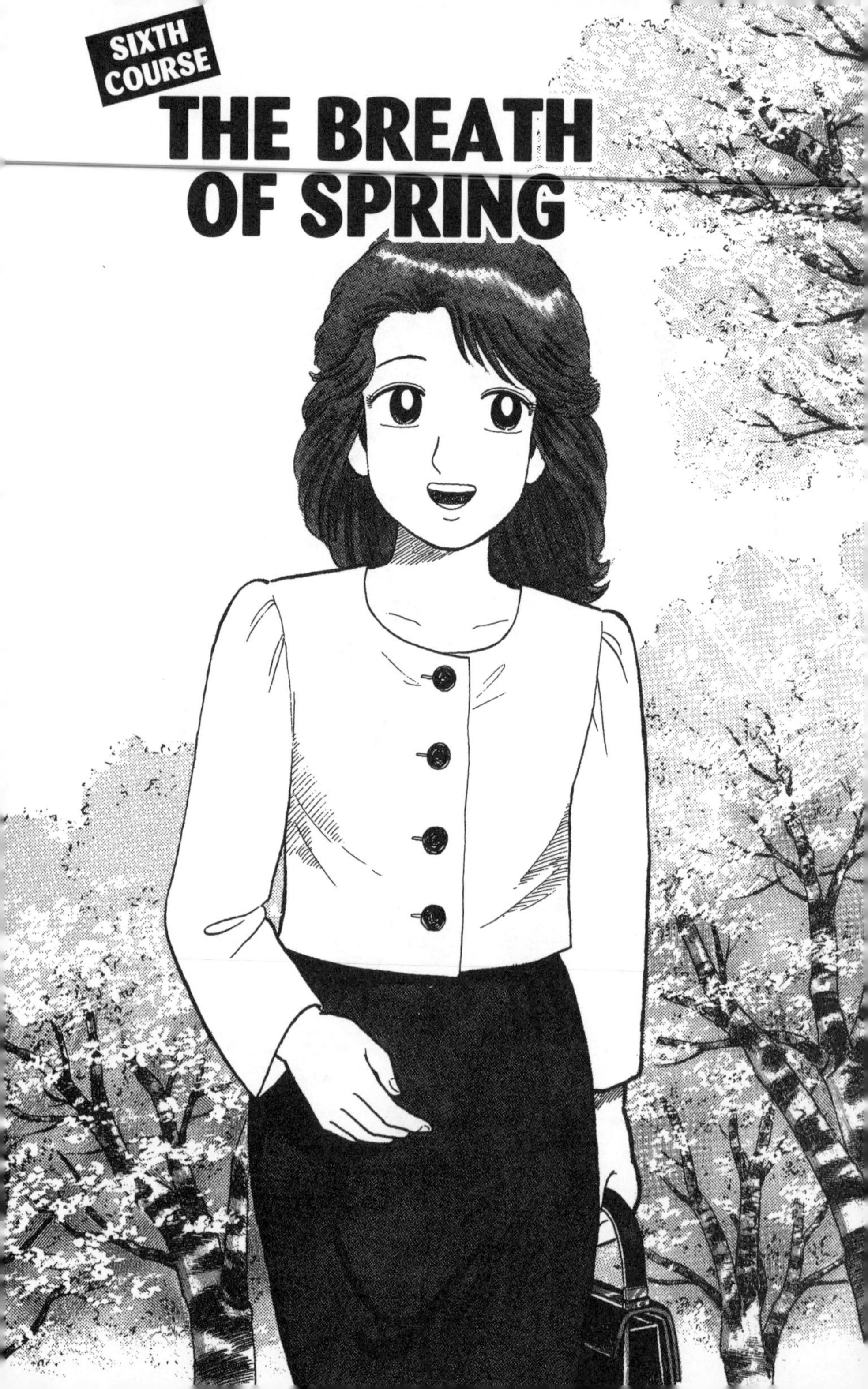

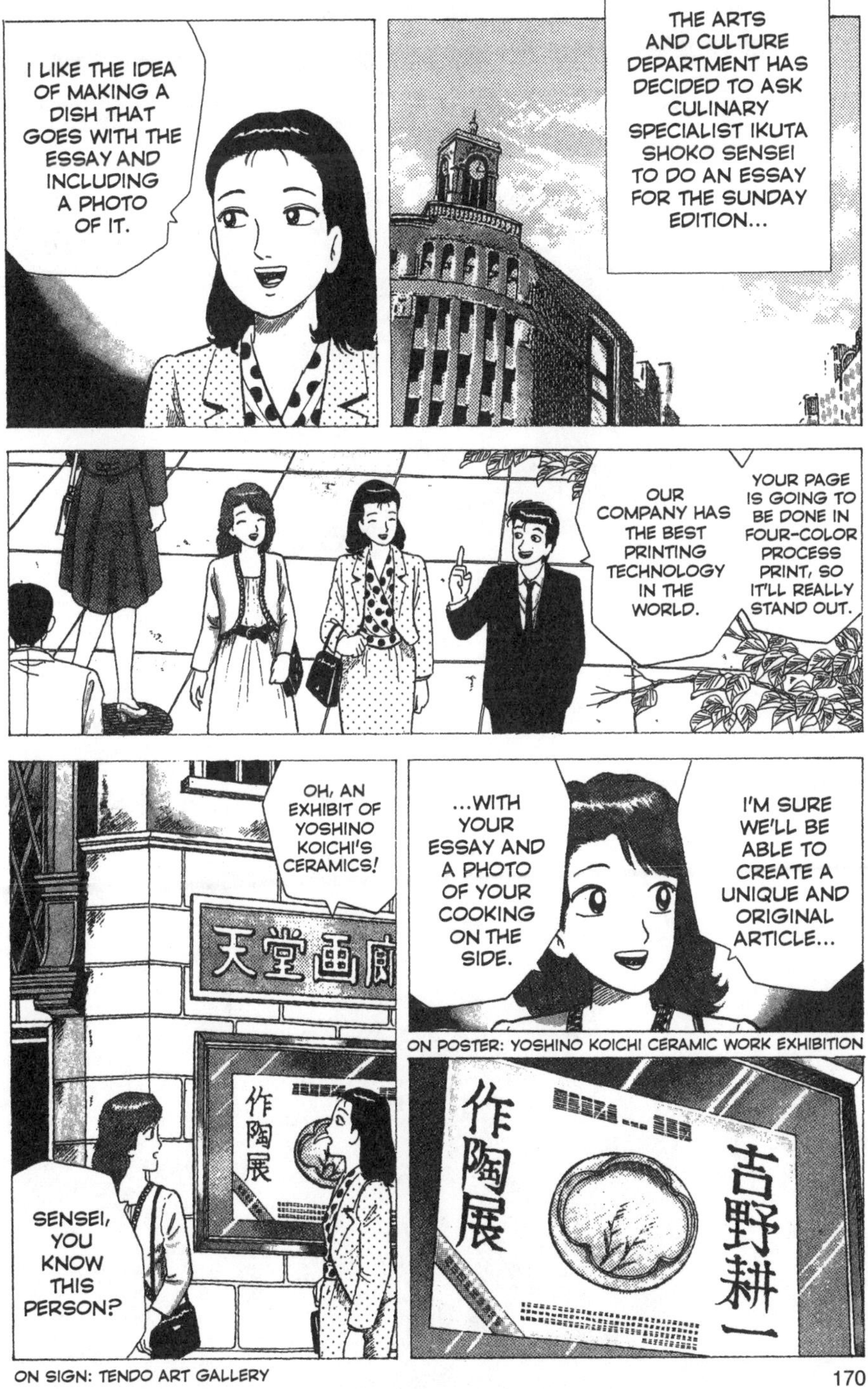
THE ARTS AND CULTURE DEPARTMENT HAS DECIDED TO ASK CULINARY SPECIALIST IKUTA SHOKO SENSEI TO DO AN ESSAY FOR THE SUNDAY EDITION...
I LIKE THE IDEA OF MAKING A DISH THAT GOES WITH THE ESSAY AND INCLUDING A PHOTO OF IT.
YOUR PAGE IS GOING TO BE DONE IN FOUR-COLOR PROCESS PRINT, SO IT'LL REALLY STAND OUT.
OUR COMPANY HAS THE BEST PRINTING TECHNOLOGY IN THE WORLD.
I'M SURE WE'LL BE ABLE TO CREATE A UNIQUE AND ORIGINAL ARTICLE...
...WITH YOUR ESSAY AND A PHOTO OF YOUR COOKING ON THE SIDE.
吉野耕一
作陶展
天堂画廊
OH, AN EXHIBIT OF YOSHINO KOICHI'S CERAMICS!
SENSEI, YOU KNOW THIS PERSON?

ON POSTER: YOSHINO KOICHI CERAMIC WORK EXHIBITION

ON SIGN: TENDO ART GALLERY

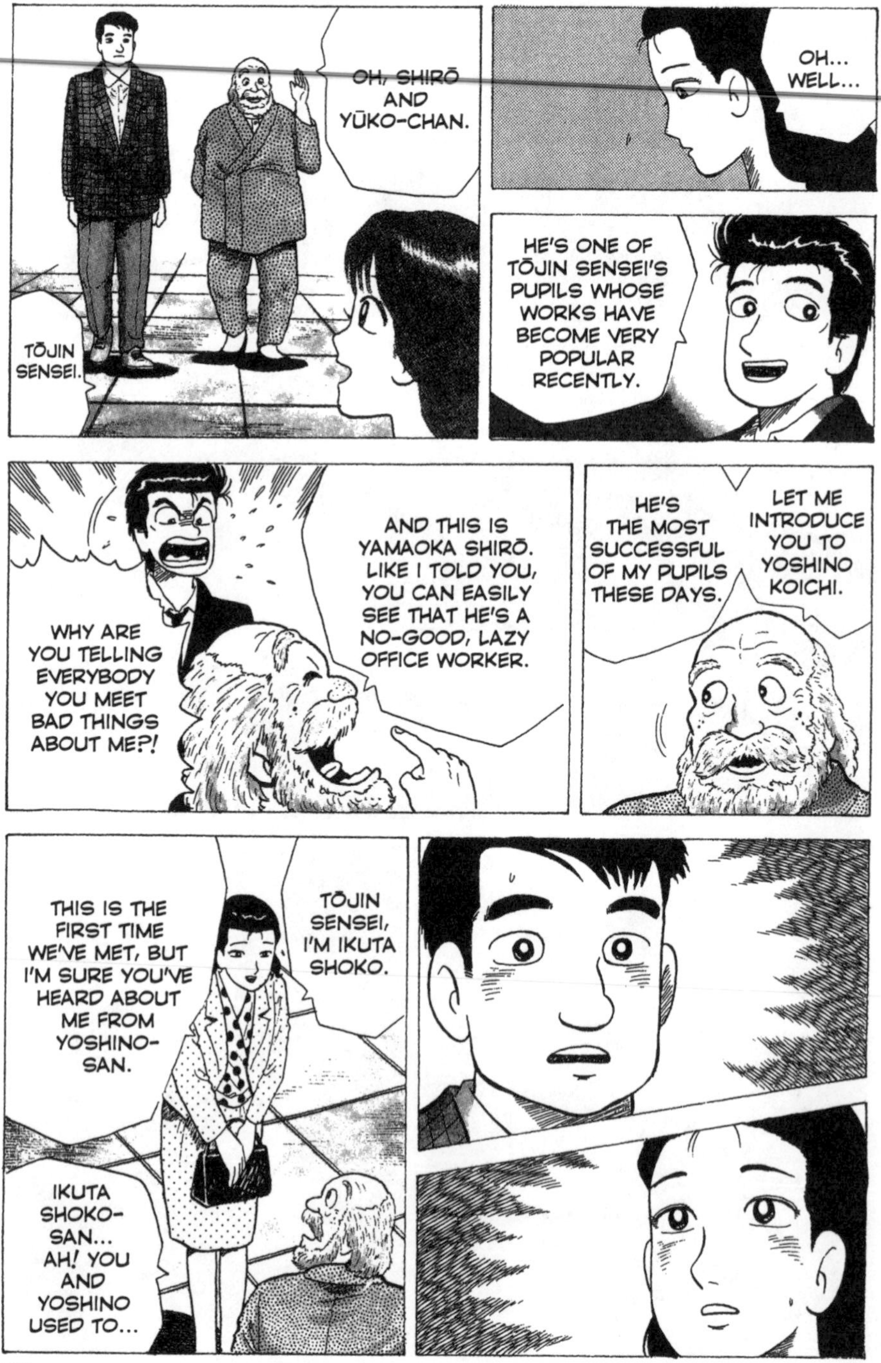
OH... WELL...
HE'S ONE OF TŌJIN SENSEI'S PUPILS WHOSE WORKS HAVE BECOME VERY POPULAR RECENTLY.
OH, SHIRŌ AND YŪKO-CHAN.
TŌJIN SENSEI.
LET ME INTRODUCE YOU TO YOSHINO KOICHI.
HE'S THE MOST SUCCESSFUL OF MY PUPILS THESE DAYS.
AND THIS IS YAMAOKA SHIRŌ. LIKE I TOLD YOU, YOU CAN EASILY SEE THAT HE'S A NO-GOOD, LAZY OFFICE WORKER.
WHY ARE YOU TELLING EVERYBODY YOU MEET BAD THINGS ABOUT ME?!
TŌJIN SENSEI, I'M IKUTA SHOKO.
THIS IS THE FIRST TIME WE'VE MET, BUT I'M SURE YOU'VE HEARD ABOUT ME FROM YOSHINO-SAN.
IKUTA SHOKO-SAN... AH! YOU AND YOSHINO USED TO...

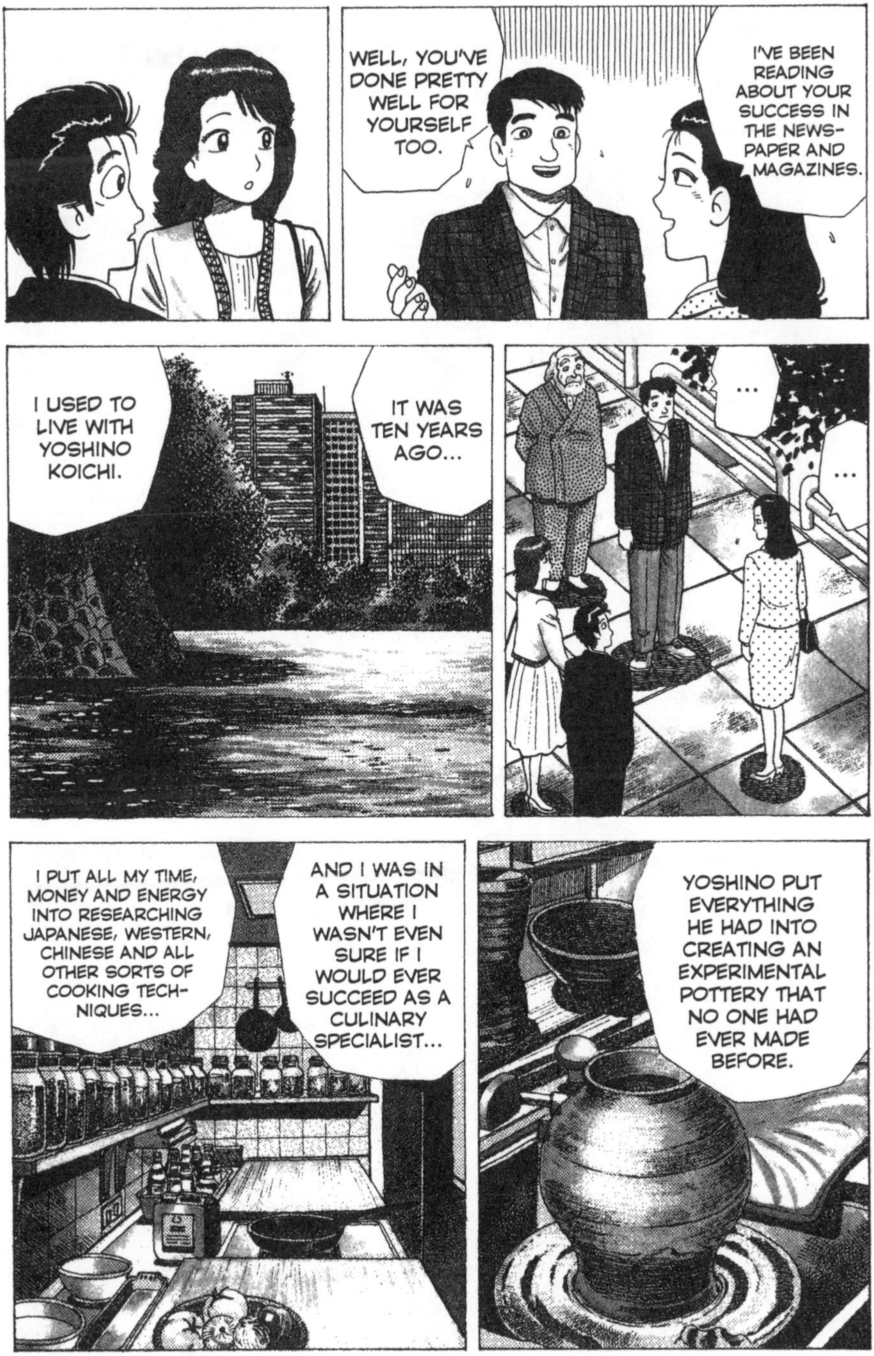
I'VE BEEN READING ABOUT YOUR SUCCESS IN THE NEWS-PAPER AND MAGAZINES.
WELL, YOU'VE DONE PRETTY WELL FOR YOURSELF TOO.
...
...
IT WAS TEN YEARS AGO...
I USED TO LIVE WITH YOSHINO KOICHI.
YOSHINO PUT EVERYTHING HE HAD INTO CREATING AN EXPERIMENTAL POTTERY THAT NO ONE HAD EVER MADE BEFORE.
I PUT ALL MY TIME, MONEY AND ENERGY INTO RESEARCHING JAPANESE, WESTERN, CHINESE AND ALL OTHER SORTS OF COOKING TECH-NIQUES...
AND I WAS IN A SITUATION WHERE I WASN'T EVEN SURE IF I WOULD EVER SUCCEED AS A CULINARY SPECIALIST...

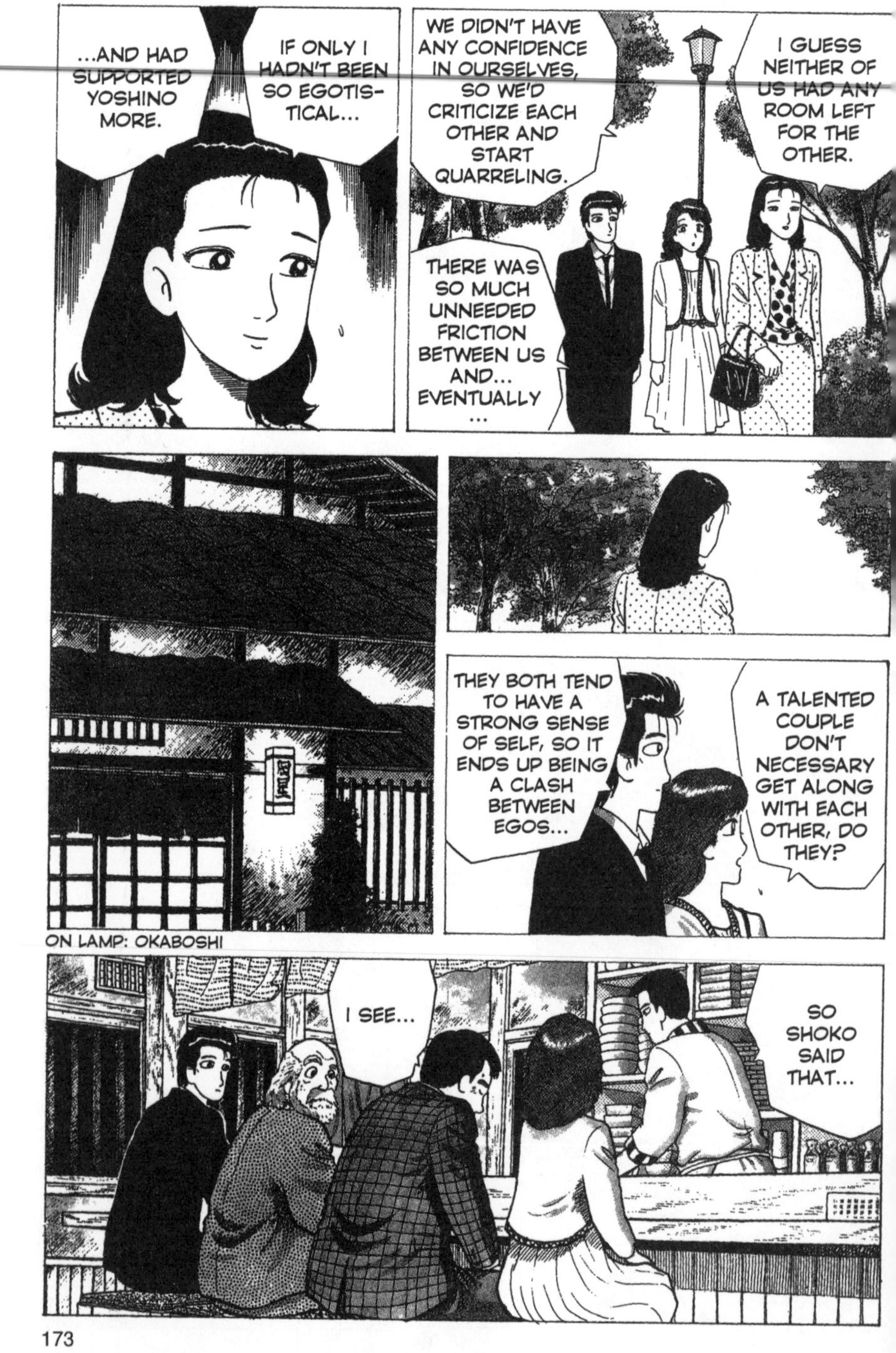
I GUESS NEITHER OF US HAD ANY ROOM LEFT FOR THE OTHER.
WE DIDN'T HAVE ANY CONFIDENCE IN OURSELVES, SO WE'D CRITICIZE EACH OTHER AND START QUARRELING.
THERE WAS SO MUCH UNNEEDED FRICTION BETWEEN US AND... EVENTUALLY ...
IF ONLY I HADN'T BEEN SO EGOTISTICAL...
...AND HAD SUPPORTED YOSHINO MORE.
A TALENTED COUPLE DON'T NECESSARY GET ALONG WITH EACH OTHER, DO THEY?
THEY BOTH TEND TO HAVE A STRONG SENSE OF SELF, SO IT ENDS UP BEING A CLASH BETWEEN EGOS...
ON LAMP: OKABOSHI
SO SHOKO SAID THAT...
I SEE...

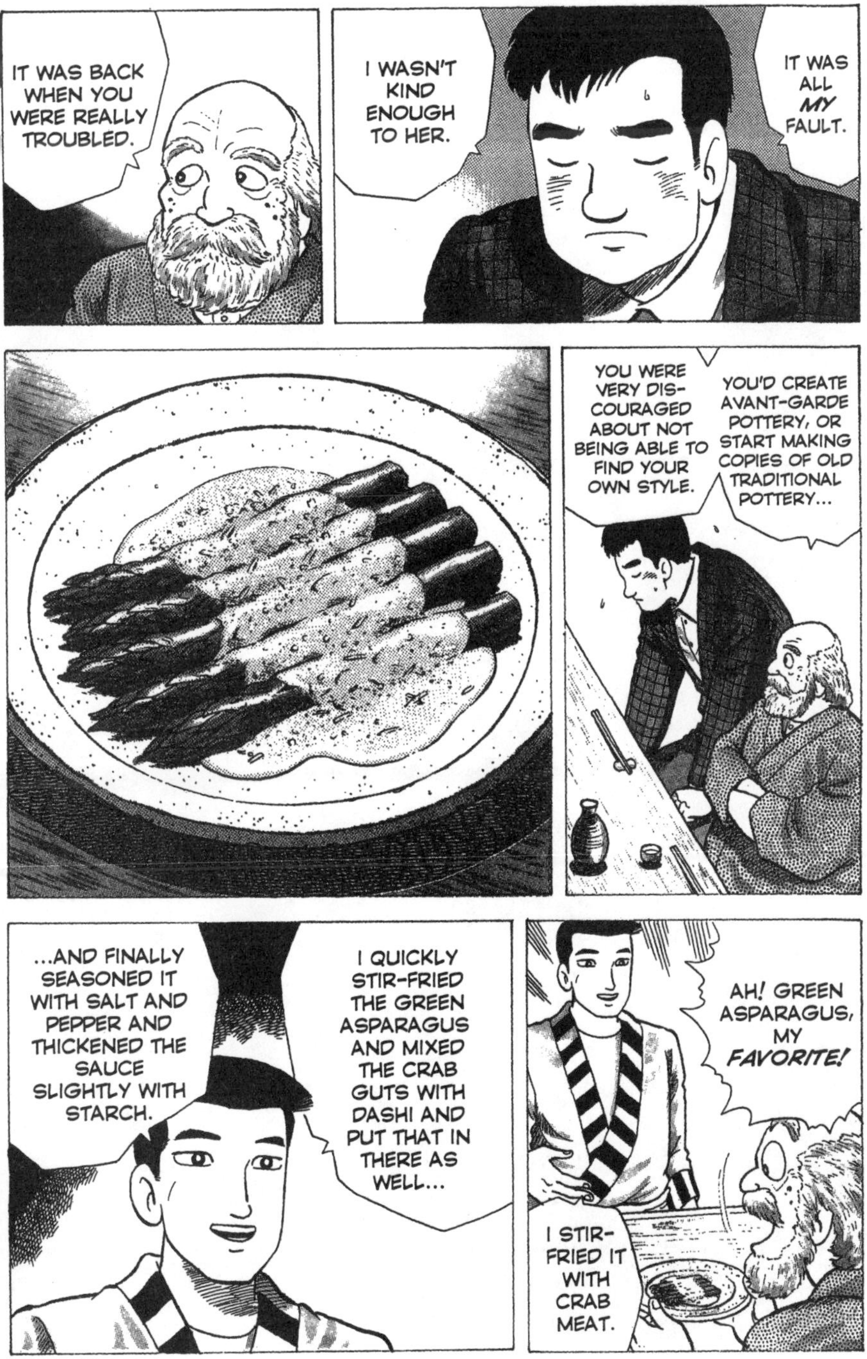
IT WAS ALL *MY* FAULT.
I WASN'T KIND ENOUGH TO HER.
IT WAS BACK WHEN YOU WERE REALLY TROUBLED.
YOU WERE VERY DIS-COURAGED ABOUT NOT BEING ABLE TO FIND YOUR OWN STYLE.
YOU'D CREATE AVANT-GARDE POTTERY, OR START MAKING COPIES OF OLD TRADITIONAL POTTERY...
AH! GREEN ASPARAGUS, MY *FAVORITE!*
I STIR-FRIED IT WITH CRAB MEAT.
I QUICKLY STIR-FRIED THE GREEN ASPARAGUS AND MIXED THE CRAB GUTS WITH DASHI AND PUT THAT IN THERE AS WELL...
...AND FINALLY SEASONED IT WITH SALT AND PEPPER AND THICKENED THE SAUCE SLIGHTLY WITH STARCH.

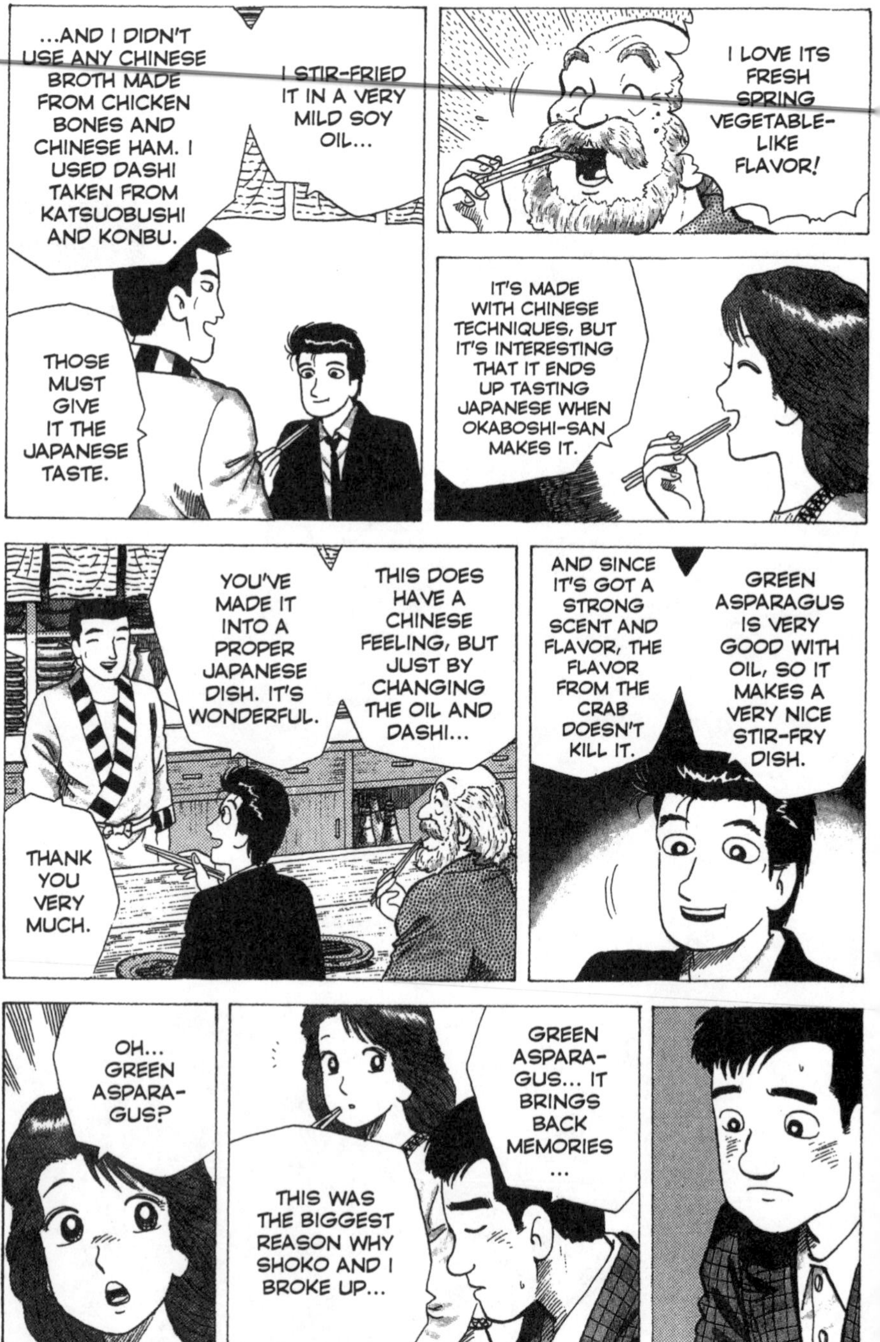
I LOVE ITS FRESH SPRING VEGETABLE-LIKE FLAVOR!
IT'S MADE WITH CHINESE TECHNIQUES, BUT IT'S INTERESTING THAT IT ENDS UP TASTING JAPANESE WHEN OKABOSHI-SAN MAKES IT.
I STIR-FRIED IT IN A VERY MILD SOY OIL...
...AND I DIDN'T USE ANY CHINESE BROTH MADE FROM CHICKEN BONES AND CHINESE HAM. I USED DASHI TAKEN FROM KATSUOBUSHI AND KONBU.
THOSE MUST GIVE IT THE JAPANESE TASTE.
GREEN ASPARAGUS IS VERY GOOD WITH OIL, SO IT MAKES A VERY NICE STIR-FRY DISH.
AND SINCE IT'S GOT A STRONG SCENT AND FLAVOR, THE FLAVOR FROM THE CRAB DOESN'T KILL IT.
THIS DOES HAVE A CHINESE FEELING, BUT JUST BY CHANGING THE OIL AND DASHI...
YOU'VE MADE IT INTO A PROPER JAPANESE DISH. IT'S WONDERFUL.
THANK YOU VERY MUCH.
GREEN ASPARAGUS... IT BRINGS BACK MEMORIES ...
THIS WAS THE BIGGEST REASON WHY SHOKO AND I BROKE UP...
OH... GREEN ASPARAGUS?

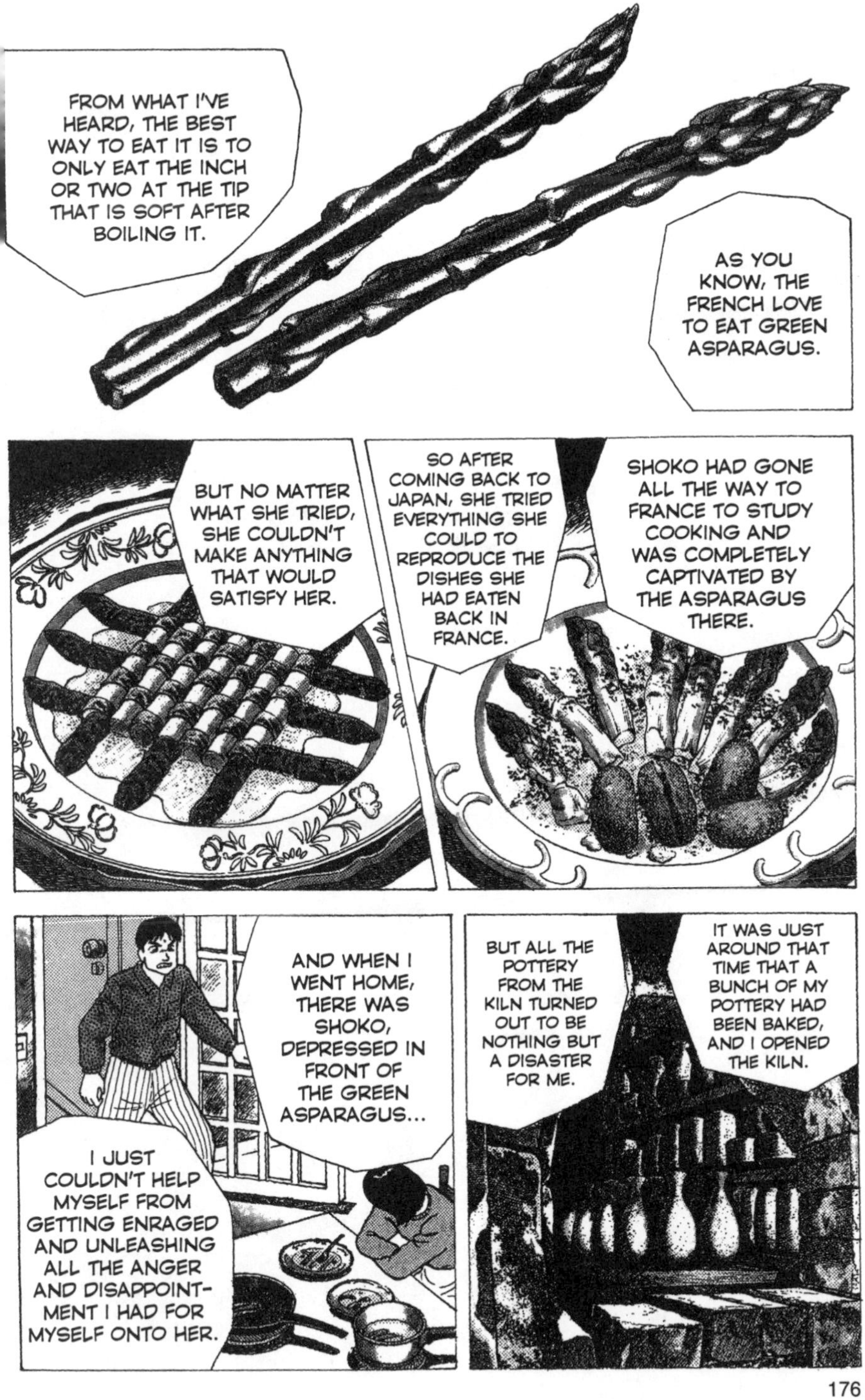
AS YOU KNOW, THE FRENCH LOVE TO EAT GREEN ASPARAGUS.
FROM WHAT I'VE HEARD, THE BEST WAY TO EAT IT IS TO ONLY EAT THE INCH OR TWO AT THE TIP THAT IS SOFT AFTER BOILING IT.
SHOKO HAD GONE ALL THE WAY TO FRANCE TO STUDY COOKING AND WAS COMPLETELY CAPTIVATED BY THE ASPARAGUS THERE.
SO AFTER COMING BACK TO JAPAN, SHE TRIED EVERYTHING SHE COULD TO REPRODUCE THE DISHES SHE HAD EATEN BACK IN FRANCE.
BUT NO MATTER WHAT SHE TRIED, SHE COULDN'T MAKE ANYTHING THAT WOULD SATISFY HER.
IT WAS JUST AROUND THAT TIME THAT A BUNCH OF MY POTTERY HAD BEEN BAKED, AND I OPENED THE KILN.
BUT ALL THE POTTERY FROM THE KILN TURNED OUT TO BE NOTHING BUT A DISASTER FOR ME.
AND WHEN I WENT HOME, THERE WAS SHOKO, DEPRESSED IN FRONT OF THE GREEN ASPARAGUS...
I JUST COULDN'T HELP MYSELF FROM GETTING ENRAGED AND UNLEASHING ALL THE ANGER AND DISAPPOINTMENT I HAD FOR MYSELF ONTO HER.

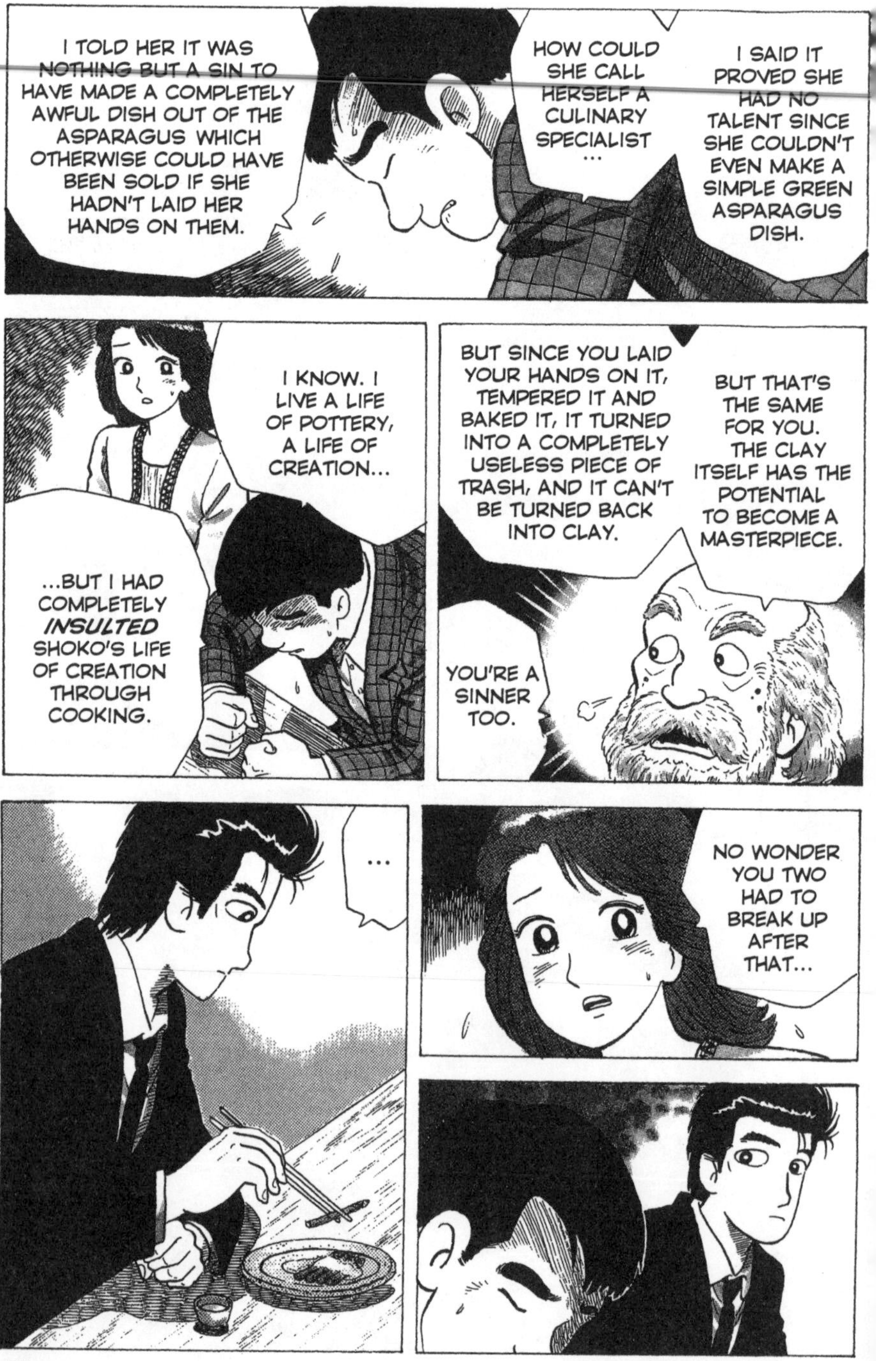
I SAID IT PROVED SHE HAD NO TALENT SINCE SHE COULDN'T EVEN MAKE A SIMPLE GREEN ASPARAGUS DISH.
HOW COULD SHE CALL HERSELF A CULINARY SPECIALIST ...
I TOLD HER IT WAS NOTHING BUT A SIN TO HAVE MADE A COMPLETELY AWFUL DISH OUT OF THE ASPARAGUS WHICH OTHERWISE COULD HAVE BEEN SOLD IF SHE HADN'T LAID HER HANDS ON THEM.
BUT THAT'S THE SAME FOR YOU. THE CLAY ITSELF HAS THE POTENTIAL TO BECOME A MASTERPIECE.
BUT SINCE YOU LAID YOUR HANDS ON IT, TEMPERED IT AND BAKED IT, IT TURNED INTO A COMPLETELY USELESS PIECE OF TRASH, AND IT CAN'T BE TURNED BACK INTO CLAY.
YOU'RE A SINNER TOO.
I KNOW. I LIVE A LIFE OF POTTERY, A LIFE OF CREATION...
...BUT I HAD COMPLETELY *INSULTED* SHOKO'S LIFE OF CREATION THROUGH COOKING.
NO WONDER YOU TWO HAD TO BREAK UP AFTER THAT...
...

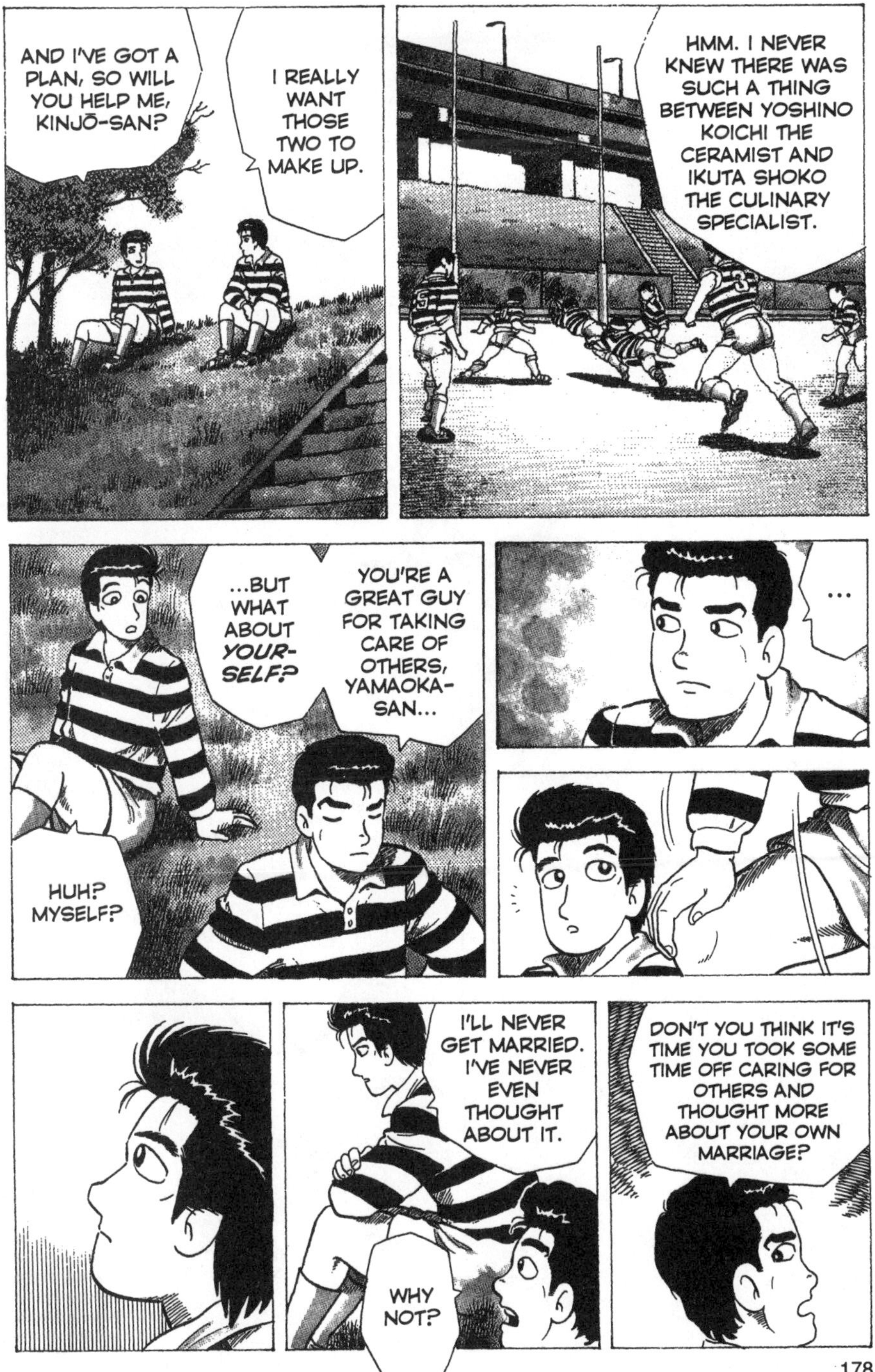
HMM. I NEVER KNEW THERE WAS SUCH A THING BETWEEN YOSHINO KOICHI THE CERAMIST AND IKUTA SHOKO THE CULINARY SPECIALIST.
I REALLY WANT THOSE TWO TO MAKE UP.
AND I'VE GOT A PLAN, SO WILL YOU HELP ME, KINJŌ-SAN?
...
YOU'RE A GREAT GUY FOR TAKING CARE OF OTHERS, YAMAOKA-SAN...
...BUT WHAT ABOUT *YOURSELF?*
HUH? MYSELF?
DON'T YOU THINK IT'S TIME YOU TOOK SOME TIME OFF CARING FOR OTHERS AND THOUGHT MORE ABOUT YOUR OWN MARRIAGE?
I'LL NEVER GET MARRIED. I'VE NEVER EVEN THOUGHT ABOUT IT.
WHY NOT?

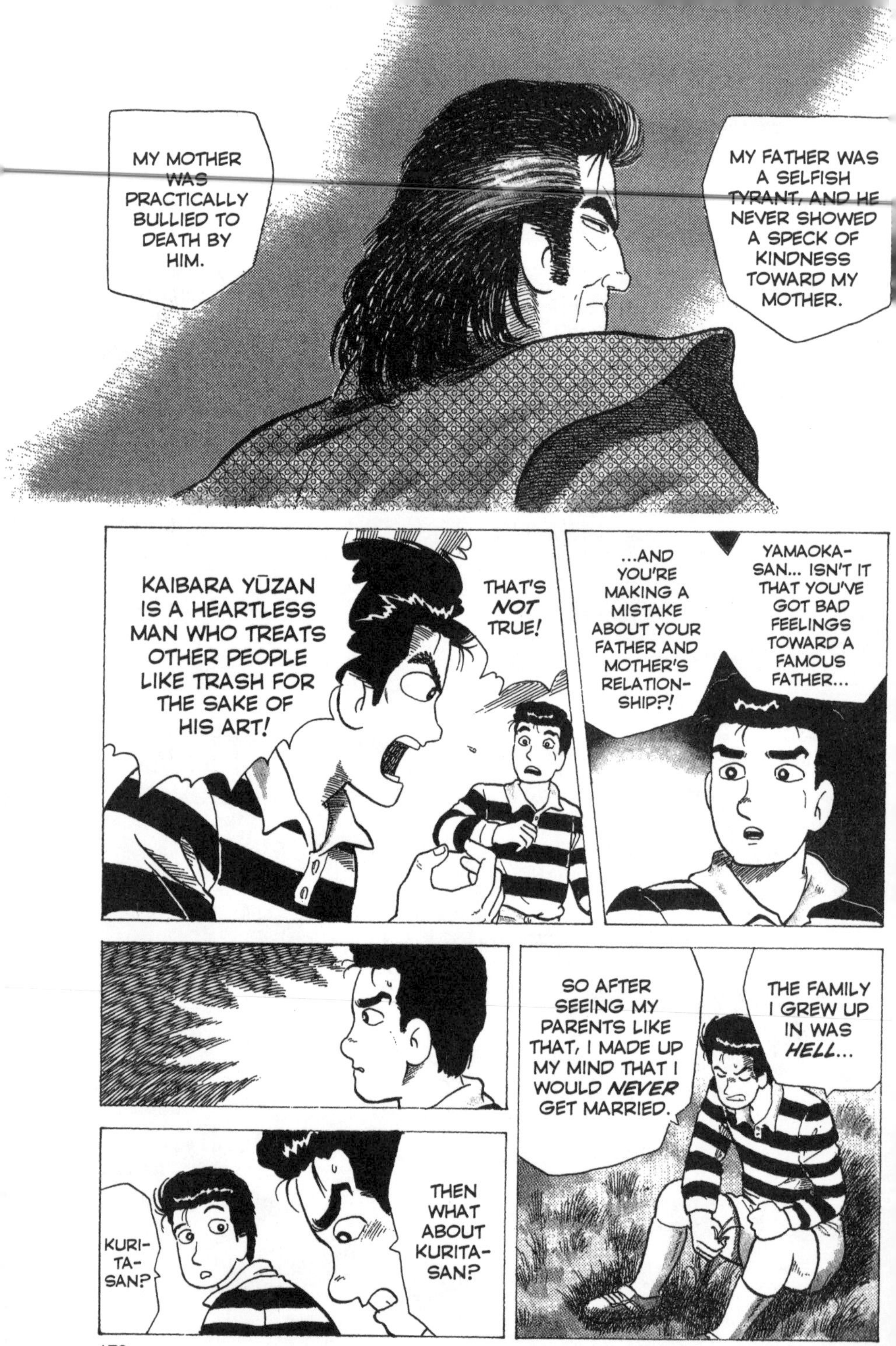

MY FATHER WAS A SELFISH TYRANT, AND HE NEVER SHOWED A SPECK OF KINDNESS TOWARD MY MOTHER.
MY MOTHER WAS PRACTICALLY BULLIED TO DEATH BY HIM.
YAMAOKA-SAN... ISN'T IT THAT YOU'VE GOT BAD FEELINGS TOWARD A FAMOUS FATHER...
...AND YOU'RE MAKING A MISTAKE ABOUT YOUR FATHER AND MOTHER'S RELATIONSHIP?!
THAT'S *NOT* TRUE!
KAIBARA YŪZAN IS A HEARTLESS MAN WHO TREATS OTHER PEOPLE LIKE TRASH FOR THE SAKE OF HIS ART!
THE FAMILY I GREW UP IN WAS *HELL*...
SO AFTER SEEING MY PARENTS LIKE THAT, I MADE UP MY MIND THAT I WOULD *NEVER* GET MARRIED.
THEN WHAT ABOUT KURITA-SAN?
KURITA-SAN?

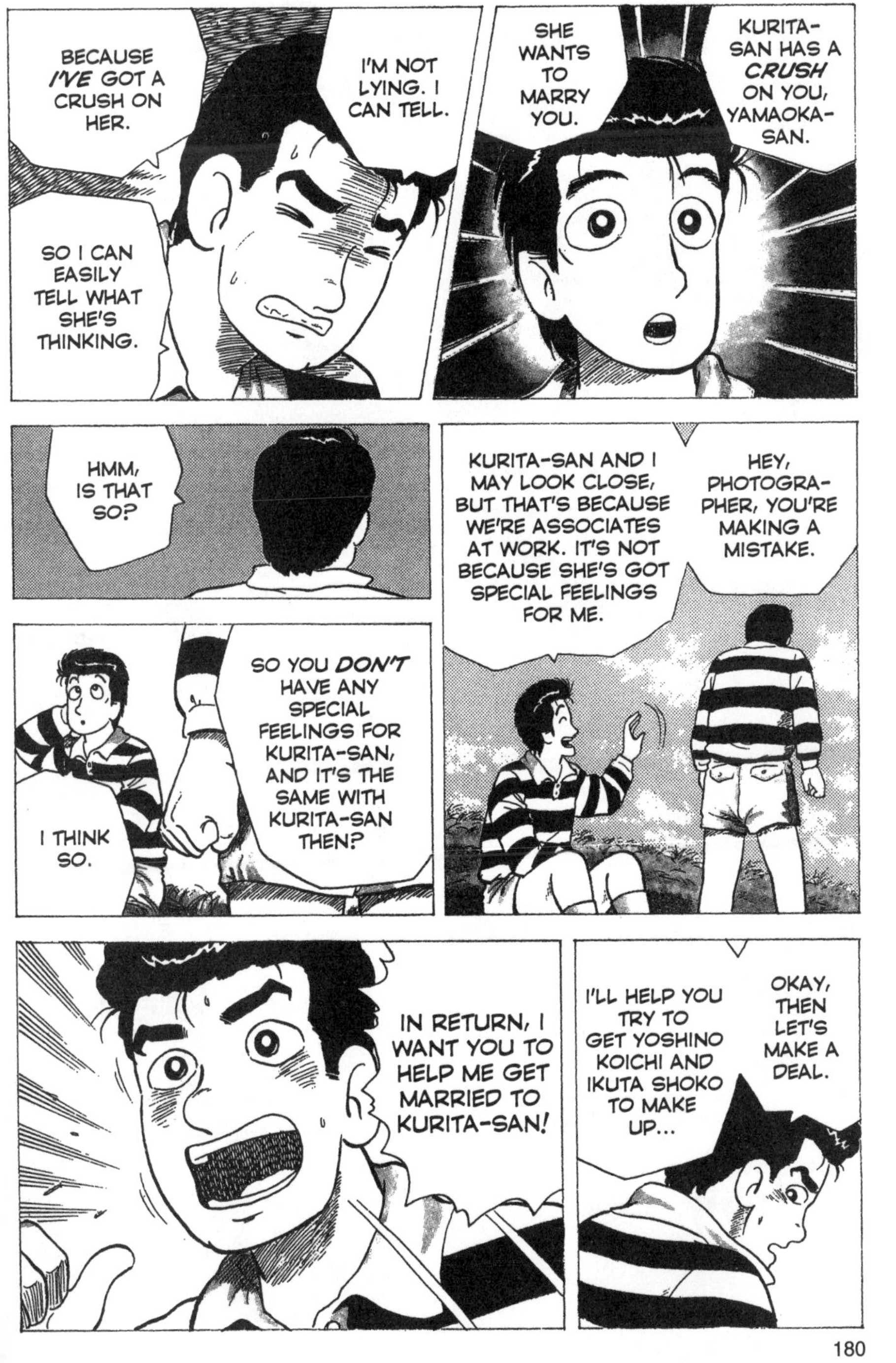
KURITA-SAN HAS A CRUSH ON YOU, YAMAOKA-SAN.
SHE WANTS TO MARRY YOU.
I'M NOT LYING. I CAN TELL.
BECAUSE I'VE GOT A CRUSH ON HER.
SO I CAN EASILY TELL WHAT SHE'S THINKING.
HEY, PHOTOGRAPHER, YOU'RE MAKING A MISTAKE.
KURITA-SAN AND I MAY LOOK CLOSE, BUT THAT'S BECAUSE WE'RE ASSOCIATES AT WORK. IT'S NOT BECAUSE SHE'S GOT SPECIAL FEELINGS FOR ME.
HMM, IS THAT SO?
SO YOU DON'T HAVE ANY SPECIAL FEELINGS FOR KURITA-SAN, AND IT'S THE SAME WITH KURITA-SAN THEN?
I THINK SO.
OKAY, THEN LET'S MAKE A DEAL.
I'LL HELP YOU TRY TO GET YOSHINO KOICHI AND IKUTA SHOKO TO MAKE UP...
IN RETURN, I WANT YOU TO HELP ME GET MARRIED TO KURITA-SAN!

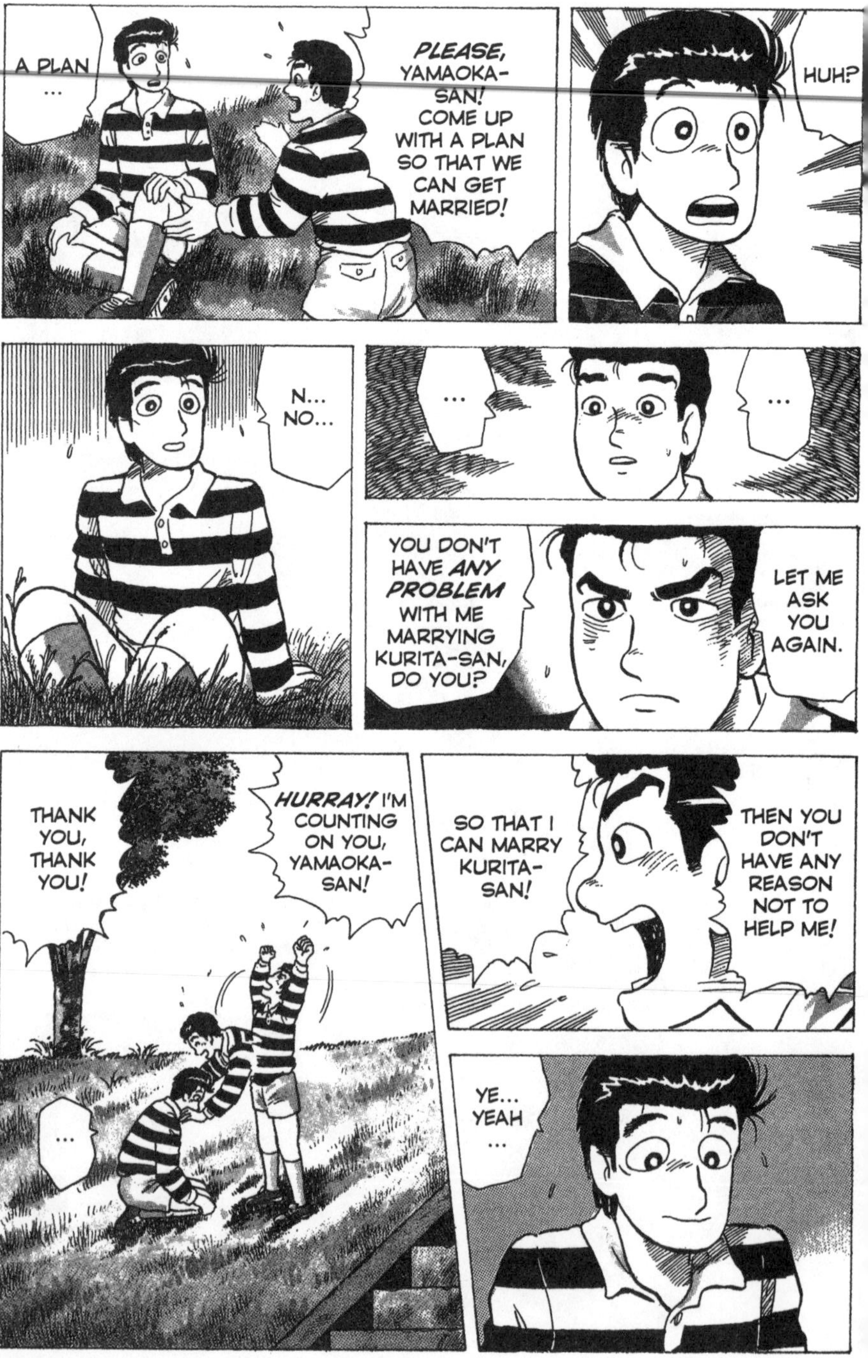
HUH?
PLEASE, YAMAOKA-SAN! COME UP WITH A PLAN SO THAT WE CAN GET MARRIED!
A PLAN ...
...
...
LET ME ASK YOU AGAIN.
YOU DON'T HAVE ANY PROBLEM WITH ME MARRYING KURITA-SAN, DO YOU?
N... NO...
THEN YOU DON'T HAVE ANY REASON NOT TO HELP ME!
SO THAT I CAN MARRY KURITA-SAN!
YE... YEAH ...
HURRAY! I'M COUNTING ON YOU, YAMAOKA-SAN!
THANK YOU, THANK YOU!
...

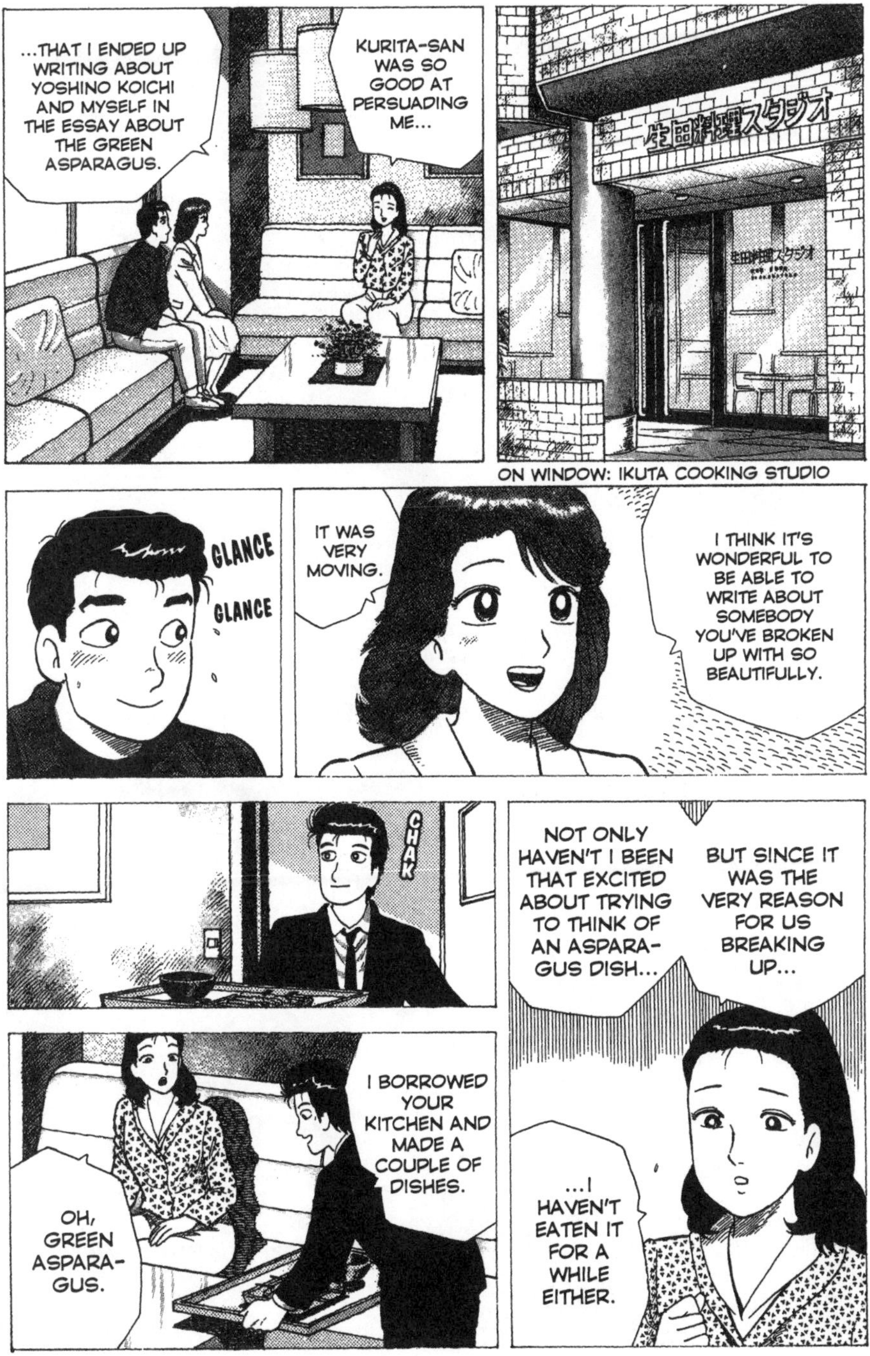
ON WINDOW: IKUTA COOKING STUDIO
KURITA-SAN WAS SO GOOD AT PERSUADING ME...
...THAT I ENDED UP WRITING ABOUT YOSHINO KOICHI AND MYSELF IN THE ESSAY ABOUT THE GREEN ASPARAGUS.
I THINK IT'S WONDERFUL TO BE ABLE TO WRITE ABOUT SOMEBODY YOU'VE BROKEN UP WITH SO BEAUTIFULLY.
IT WAS VERY MOVING.
GLANCE
GLANCE
NOT ONLY HAVEN'T I BEEN THAT EXCITED ABOUT TRYING TO THINK OF AN ASPARA-GUS DISH...
BUT SINCE IT WAS THE VERY REASON FOR US BREAKING UP...
...I HAVEN'T EATEN IT FOR A WHILE EITHER.
CHAK
I BORROWED YOUR KITCHEN AND MADE A COUPLE OF DISHES.
OH, GREEN ASPARA-GUS.

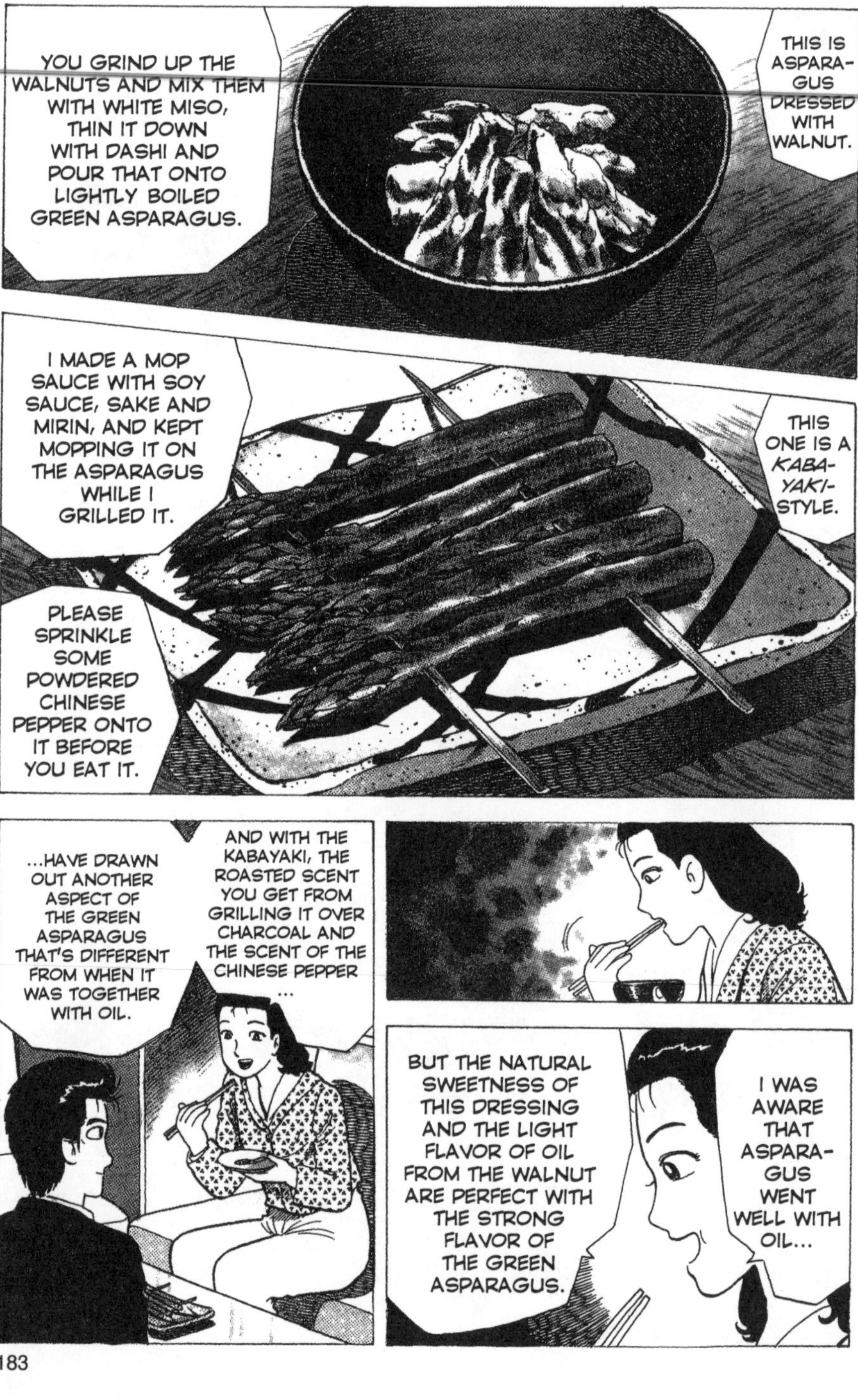
THIS IS ASPARAGUS DRESSED WITH WALNUT.
YOU GRIND UP THE WALNUTS AND MIX THEM WITH WHITE MISO, THIN IT DOWN WITH DASHI AND POUR THAT ONTO LIGHTLY BOILED GREEN ASPARAGUS.
THIS ONE IS A *KABAYAKI*-STYLE.
I MADE A MOP SAUCE WITH SOY SAUCE, SAKE AND MIRIN, AND KEPT MOPPING IT ON THE ASPARAGUS WHILE I GRILLED IT.
PLEASE SPRINKLE SOME POWDERED CHINESE PEPPER ONTO IT BEFORE YOU EAT IT.
I WAS AWARE THAT ASPARAGUS WENT WELL WITH OIL...
BUT THE NATURAL SWEETNESS OF THIS DRESSING AND THE LIGHT FLAVOR OF OIL FROM THE WALNUT ARE PERFECT WITH THE STRONG FLAVOR OF THE GREEN ASPARAGUS.
AND WITH THE KABAYAKI, THE ROASTED SCENT YOU GET FROM GRILLING IT OVER CHARCOAL AND THE SCENT OF THE CHINESE PEPPER ...
...HAVE DRAWN OUT ANOTHER ASPECT OF THE GREEN ASPARAGUS THAT'S DIFFERENT FROM WHEN IT WAS TOGETHER WITH OIL.

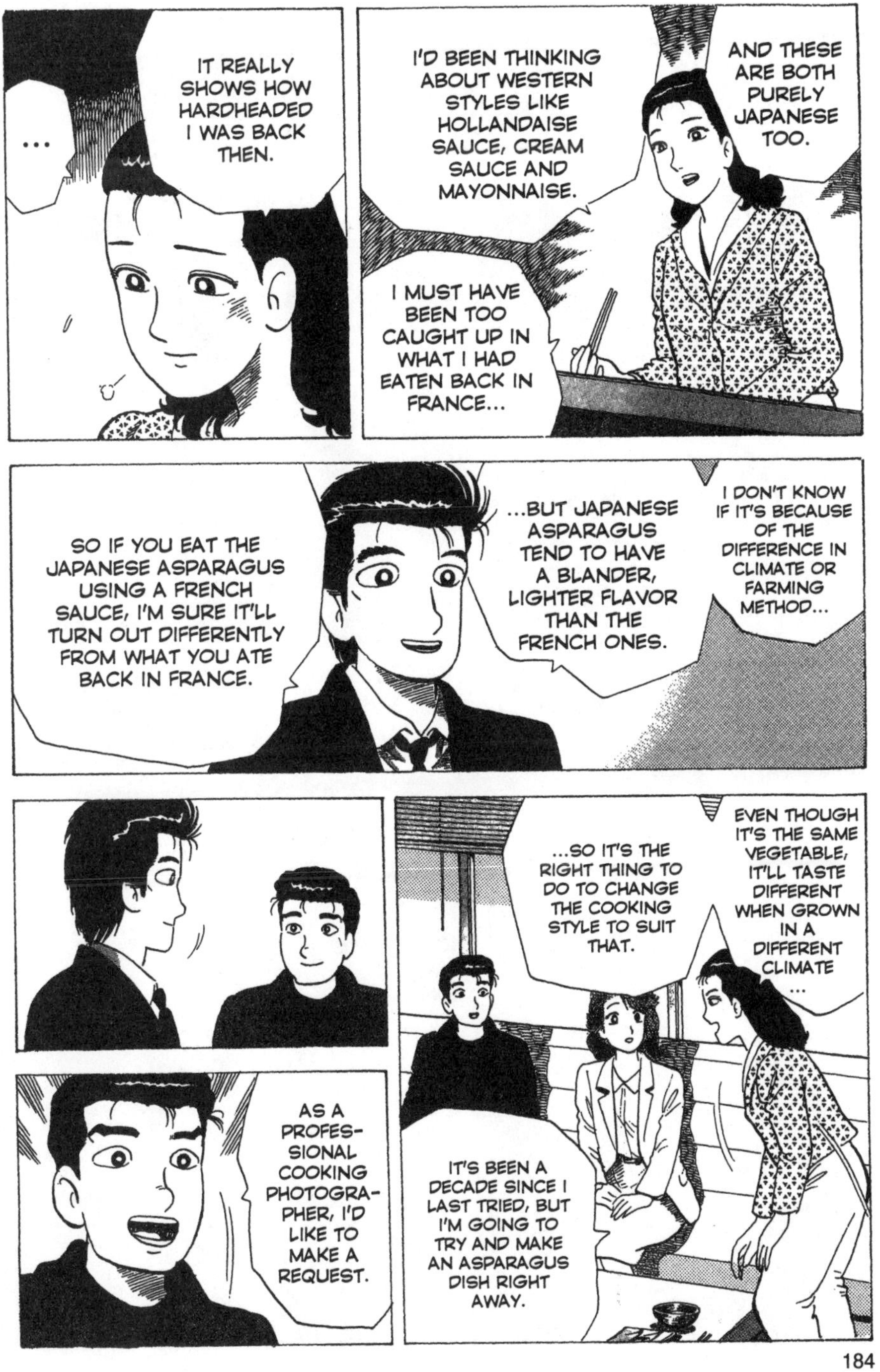
AND THESE ARE BOTH PURELY JAPANESE TOO.
I'D BEEN THINKING ABOUT WESTERN STYLES LIKE HOLLANDAISE SAUCE, CREAM SAUCE AND MAYONNAISE.
I MUST HAVE BEEN TOO CAUGHT UP IN WHAT I HAD EATEN BACK IN FRANCE...
IT REALLY SHOWS HOW HARDHEADED I WAS BACK THEN.
...
I DON'T KNOW IF IT'S BECAUSE OF THE DIFFERENCE IN CLIMATE OR FARMING METHOD...
...BUT JAPANESE ASPARAGUS TEND TO HAVE A BLANDER, LIGHTER FLAVOR THAN THE FRENCH ONES.
SO IF YOU EAT THE JAPANESE ASPARAGUS USING A FRENCH SAUCE, I'M SURE IT'LL TURN OUT DIFFERENTLY FROM WHAT YOU ATE BACK IN FRANCE.
EVEN THOUGH IT'S THE SAME VEGETABLE, IT'LL TASTE DIFFERENT WHEN GROWN IN A DIFFERENT CLIMATE ...
...SO IT'S THE RIGHT THING TO DO TO CHANGE THE COOKING STYLE TO SUIT THAT.
IT'S BEEN A DECADE SINCE I LAST TRIED, BUT I'M GOING TO TRY AND MAKE AN ASPARAGUS DISH RIGHT AWAY.
AS A PROFESSIONAL COOKING PHOTOGRAPHER, I'D LIKE TO MAKE A REQUEST.

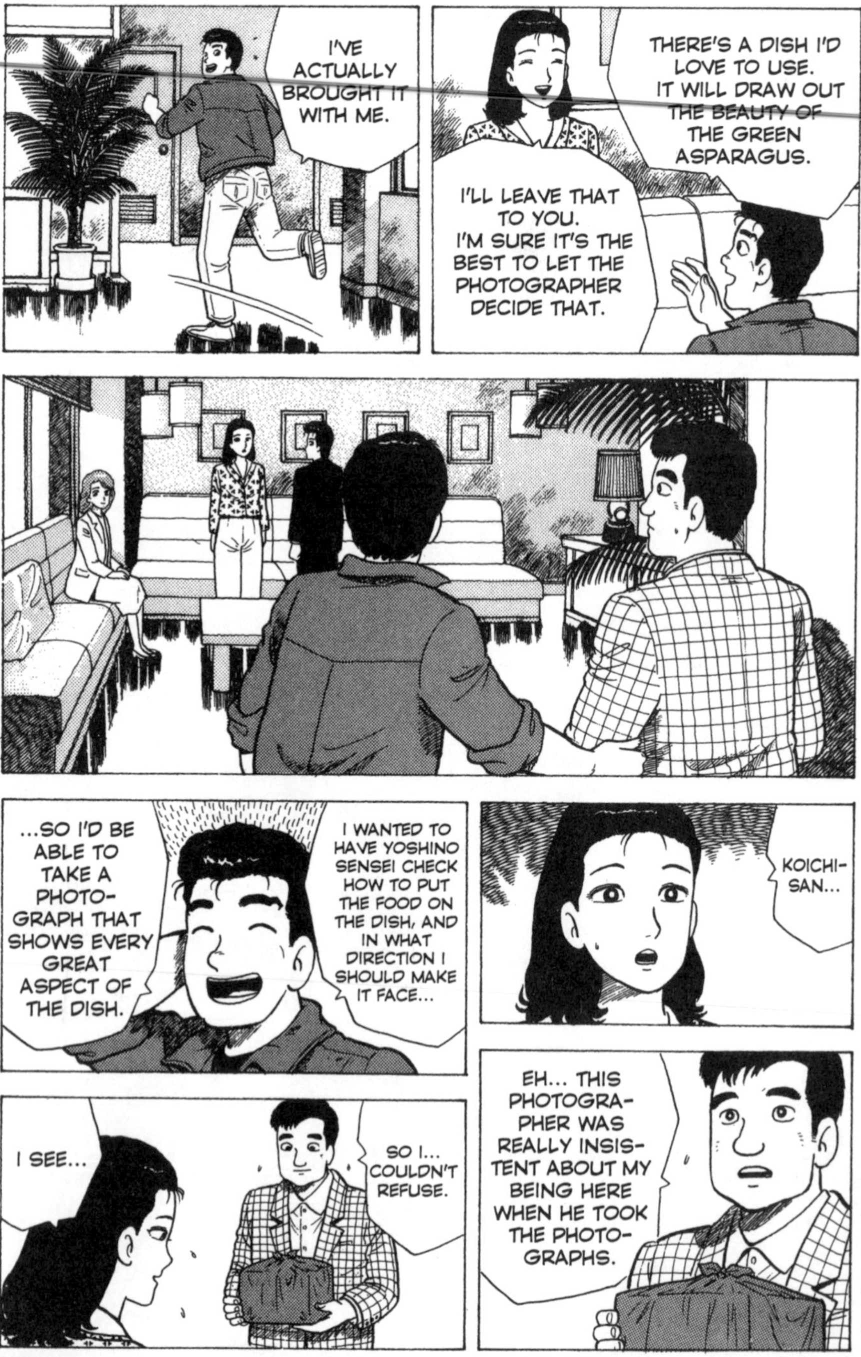
THERE'S A DISH I'D LOVE TO USE. IT WILL DRAW OUT THE BEAUTY OF THE GREEN ASPARAGUS.
I'LL LEAVE THAT TO YOU. I'M SURE IT'S THE BEST TO LET THE PHOTOGRAPHER DECIDE THAT.
I'VE ACTUALLY BROUGHT IT WITH ME.
KOICHI-SAN...
I WANTED TO HAVE YOSHINO SENSEI CHECK HOW TO PUT THE FOOD ON THE DISH, AND IN WHAT DIRECTION I SHOULD MAKE IT FACE...
...SO I'D BE ABLE TO TAKE A PHOTOGRAPH THAT SHOWS EVERY GREAT ASPECT OF THE DISH.
EH... THIS PHOTOGRAPHER WAS REALLY INSISTENT ABOUT MY BEING HERE WHEN HE TOOK THE PHOTOGRAPHS.
SO I... COULDN'T REFUSE.
I SEE...

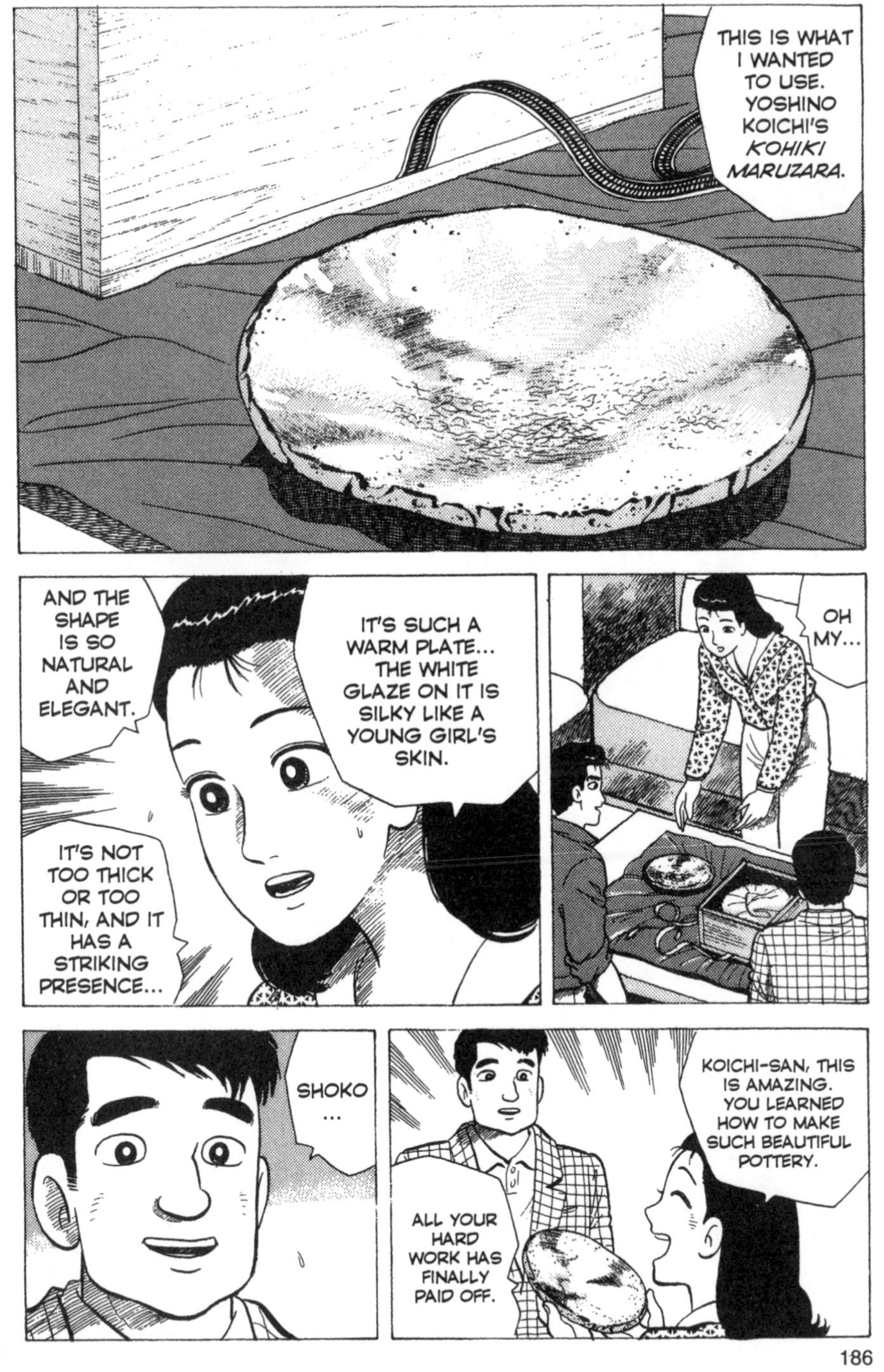
THIS IS WHAT I WANTED TO USE. YOSHINO KOICHI'S *KOHIKI MARUZARA*.
OH MY...
IT'S SUCH A WARM PLATE... THE WHITE GLAZE ON IT IS SILKY LIKE A YOUNG GIRL'S SKIN.
AND THE SHAPE IS SO NATURAL AND ELEGANT.
IT'S NOT TOO THICK OR TOO THIN, AND IT HAS A STRIKING PRESENCE...
KOICHI-SAN, THIS IS AMAZING. YOU LEARNED HOW TO MAKE SUCH BEAUTIFUL POTTERY.
ALL YOUR HARD WORK HAS FINALLY PAID OFF.
SHOKO ...

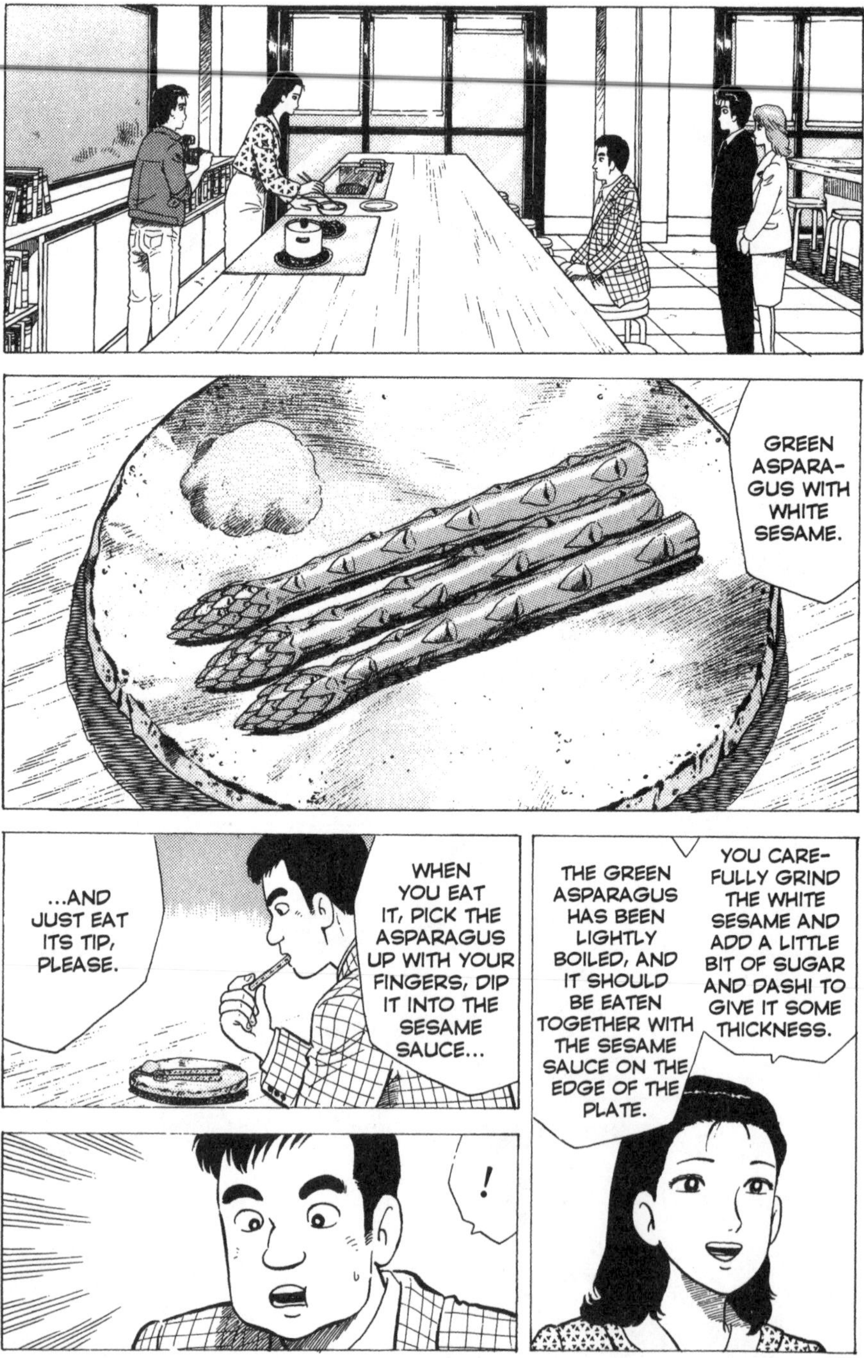
GREEN ASPARAGUS WITH WHITE SESAME.
YOU CAREFULLY GRIND THE WHITE SESAME AND ADD A LITTLE BIT OF SUGAR AND DASHI TO GIVE IT SOME THICKNESS.
THE GREEN ASPARAGUS HAS BEEN LIGHTLY BOILED, AND IT SHOULD BE EATEN TOGETHER WITH THE SESAME SAUCE ON THE EDGE OF THE PLATE.
WHEN YOU EAT IT, PICK THE ASPARAGUS UP WITH YOUR FINGERS, DIP IT INTO THE SESAME SAUCE...
...AND JUST EAT ITS TIP, PLEASE.
!

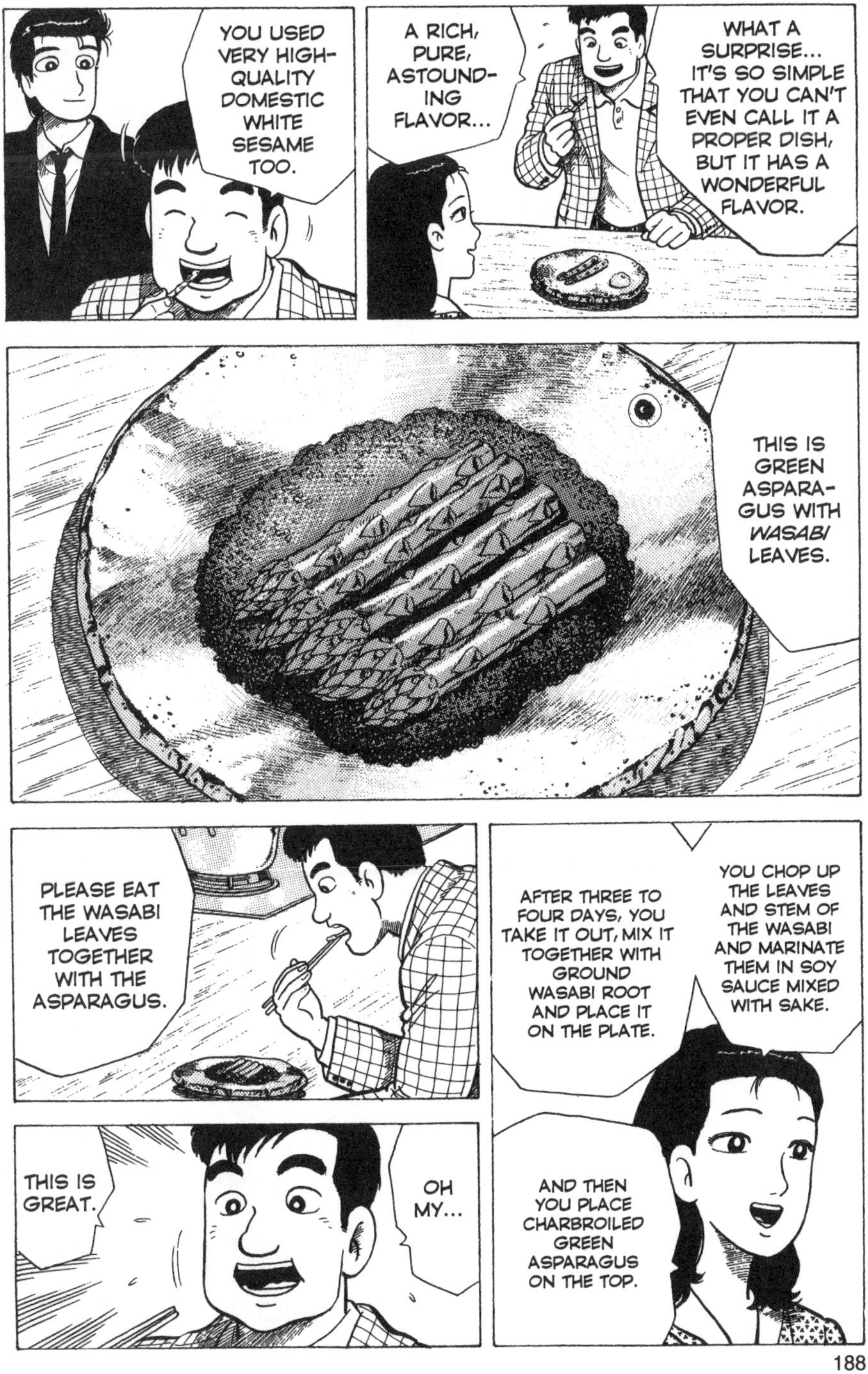
WHAT A SURPRISE... IT'S SO SIMPLE THAT YOU CAN'T EVEN CALL IT A PROPER DISH, BUT IT HAS A WONDERFUL FLAVOR.
A RICH, PURE, ASTOUND-ING FLAVOR...
YOU USED VERY HIGH-QUALITY DOMESTIC WHITE SESAME TOO.
THIS IS GREEN ASPARA-GUS WITH *WASABI* LEAVES.
YOU CHOP UP THE LEAVES AND STEM OF THE WASABI AND MARINATE THEM IN SOY SAUCE MIXED WITH SAKE.
AFTER THREE TO FOUR DAYS, YOU TAKE IT OUT, MIX IT TOGETHER WITH GROUND WASABI ROOT AND PLACE IT ON THE PLATE.
AND THEN YOU PLACE CHARBROILED GREEN ASPARAGUS ON THE TOP.
PLEASE EAT THE WASABI LEAVES TOGETHER WITH THE ASPARAGUS.
OH MY...
THIS IS GREAT.

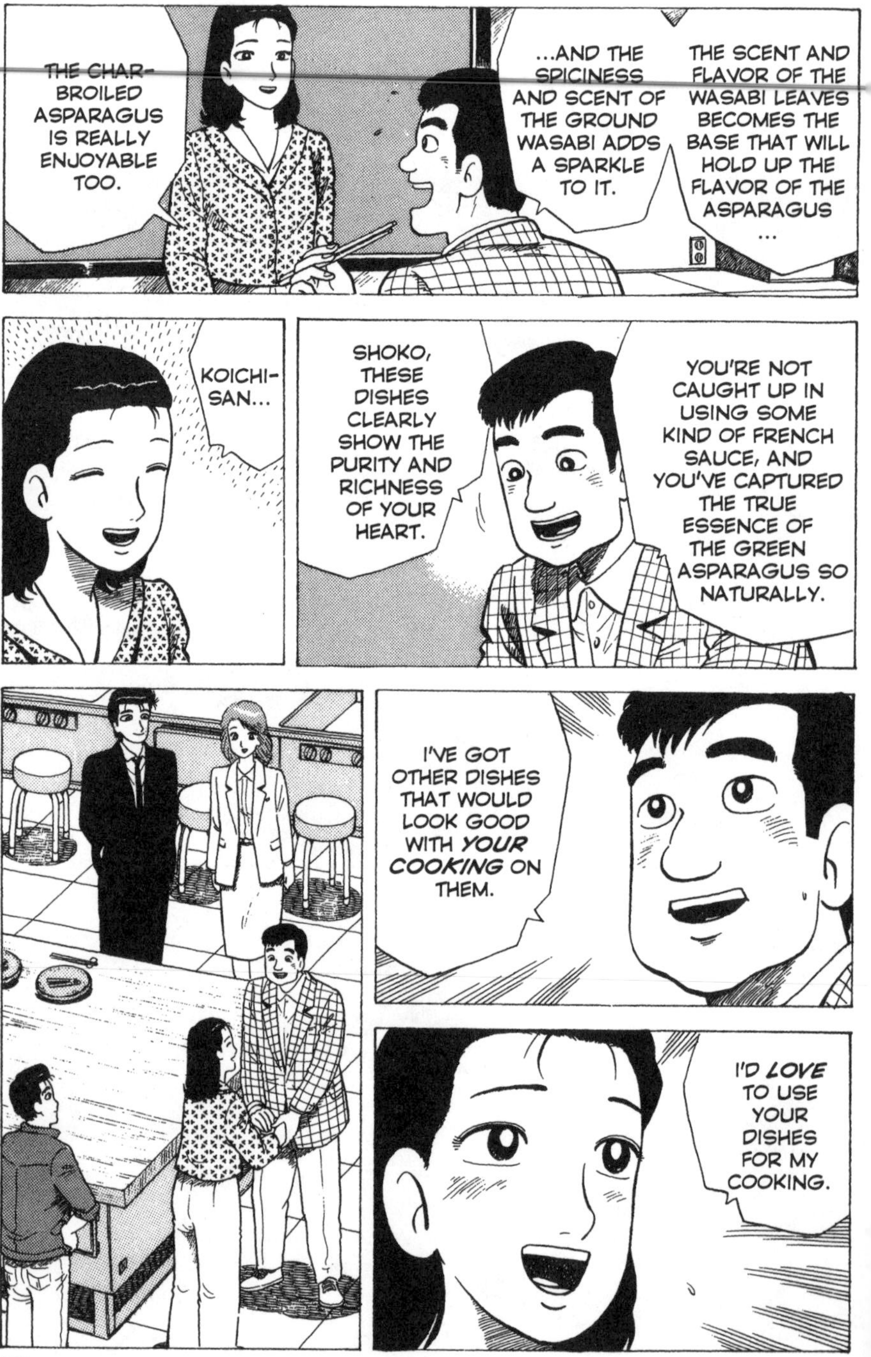
THE SCENT AND FLAVOR OF THE WASABI LEAVES BECOMES THE BASE THAT WILL HOLD UP THE FLAVOR OF THE ASPARAGUS ...
...AND THE SPICINESS AND SCENT OF THE GROUND WASABI ADDS A SPARKLE TO IT.
THE CHAR-BROILED ASPARAGUS IS REALLY ENJOYABLE TOO.
YOU'RE NOT CAUGHT UP IN USING SOME KIND OF FRENCH SAUCE, AND YOU'VE CAPTURED THE TRUE ESSENCE OF THE GREEN ASPARAGUS SO NATURALLY.
SHOKO, THESE DISHES CLEARLY SHOW THE PURITY AND RICHNESS OF YOUR HEART.
KOICHI-SAN...
I'VE GOT OTHER DISHES THAT WOULD LOOK GOOD WITH *YOUR COOKING* ON THEM.
I'D *LOVE* TO USE YOUR DISHES FOR MY COOKING.

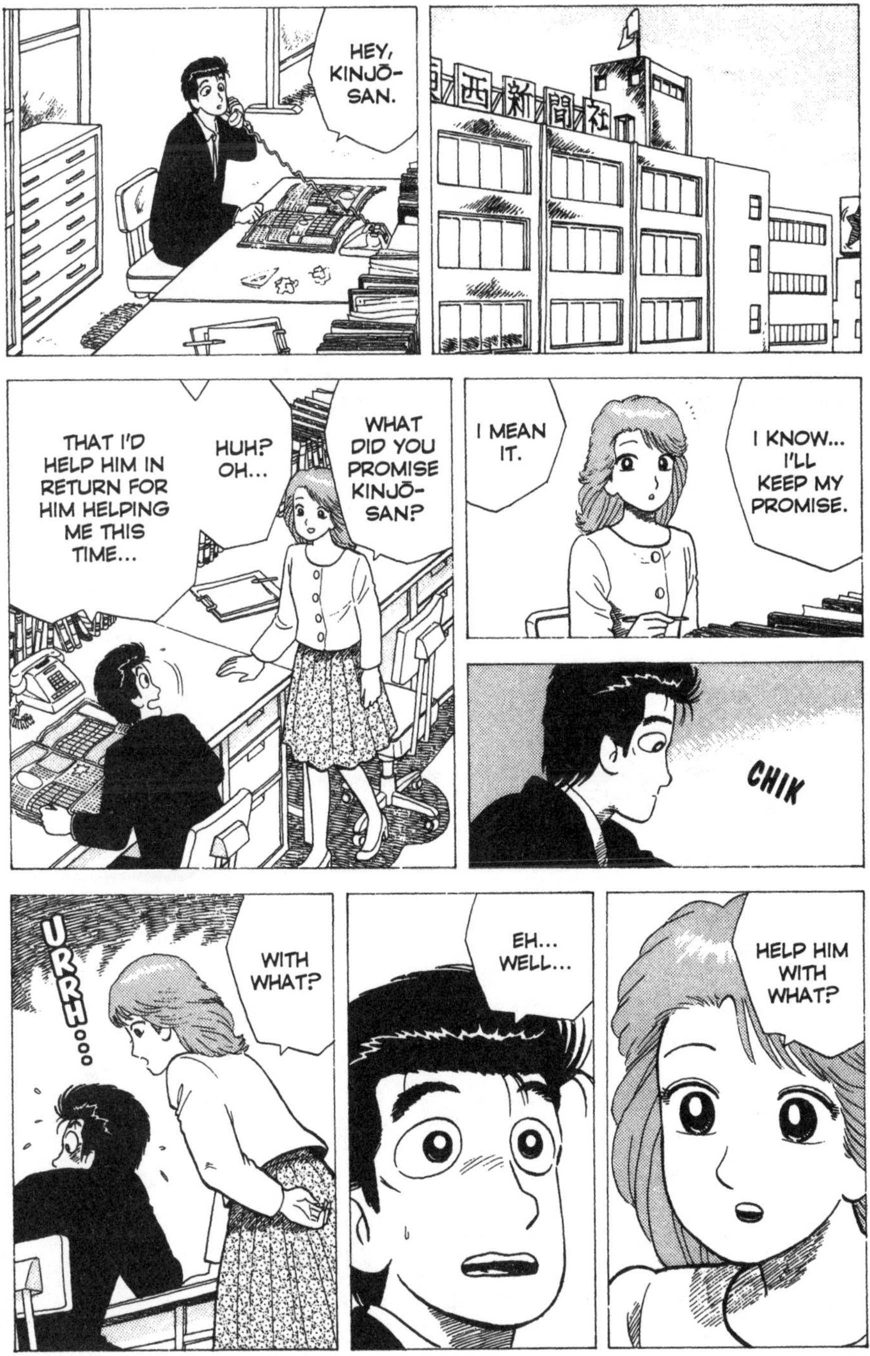

HEY, KINJŌ-SAN.
I KNOW... I'LL KEEP MY PROMISE.
I MEAN IT.
CHIK
WHAT DID YOU PROMISE KINJŌ-SAN?
HUH? OH...
THAT I'D HELP HIM IN RETURN FOR HIM HELPING ME THIS TIME...
HELP HIM WITH WHAT?
EH... WELL...
WITH WHAT?
URRH...

SEVENTH COURSE

A SURPRISING TASTE (PART ONE)

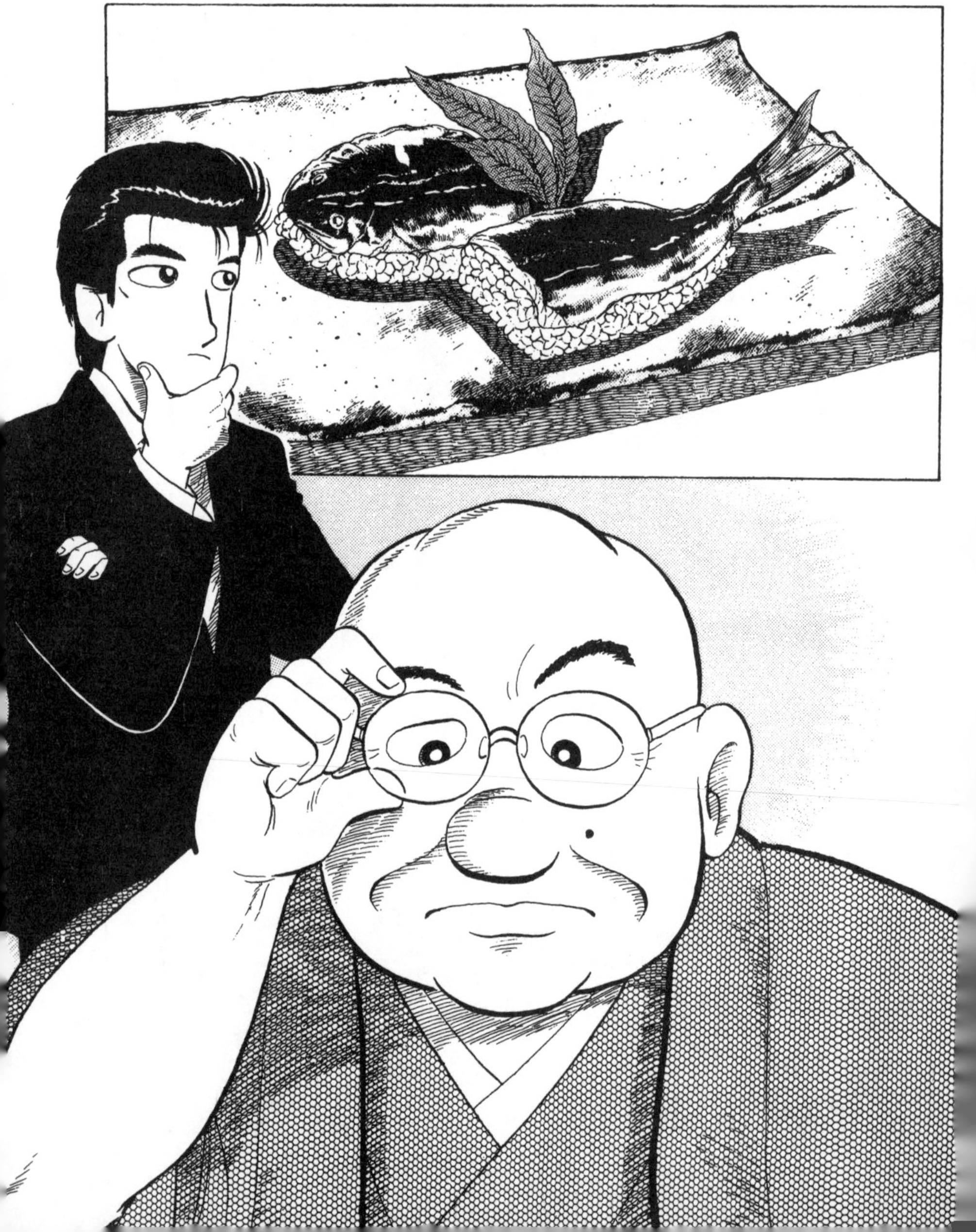

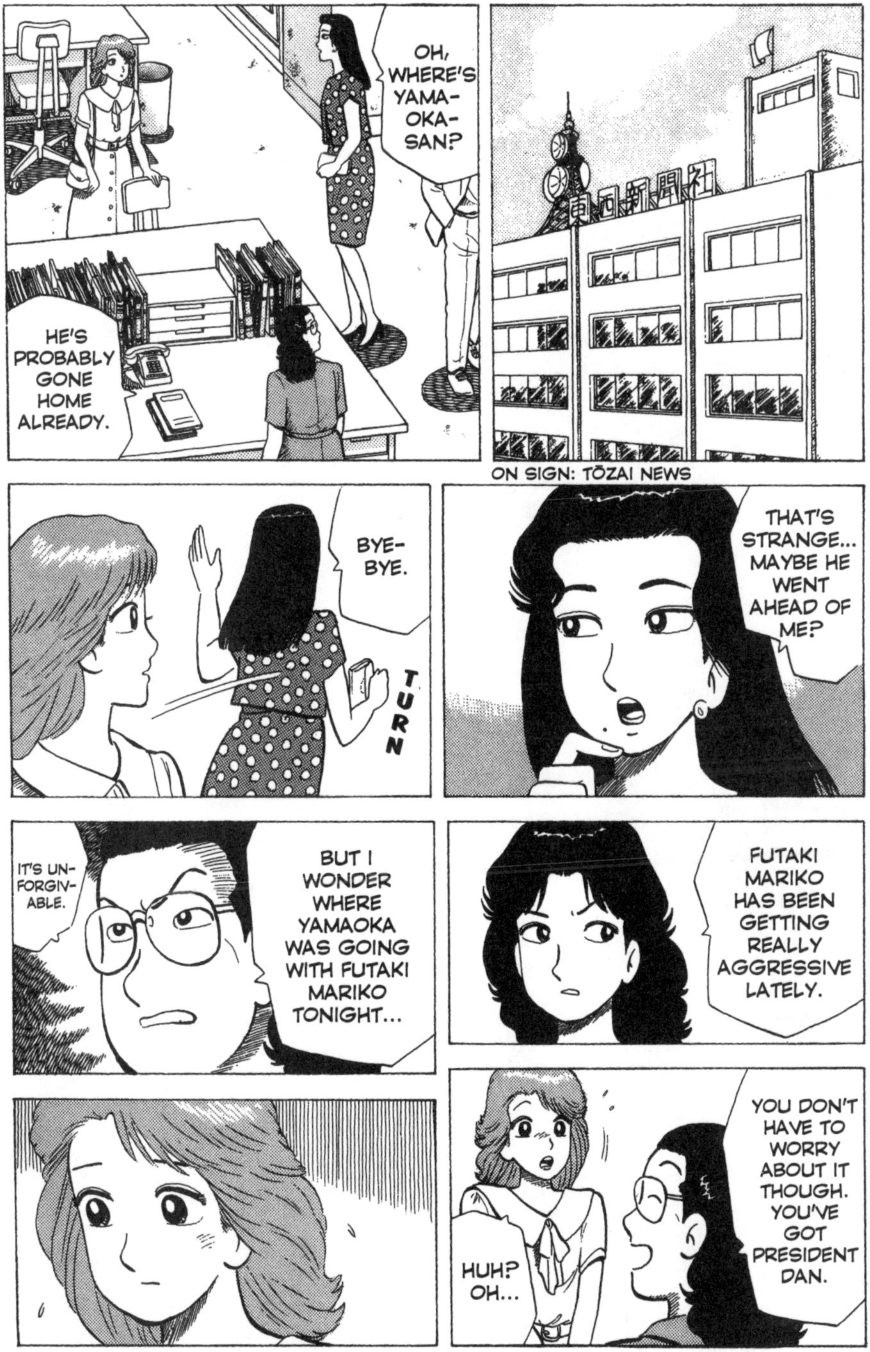
ON SIGN: TŌZAI NEWS
OH, WHERE'S YAMA-OKA-SAN?
HE'S PROBABLY GONE HOME ALREADY.
THAT'S STRANGE... MAYBE HE WENT AHEAD OF ME?
BYE-BYE.
TURN
FUTAKI MARIKO HAS BEEN GETTING REALLY AGGRESSIVE LATELY.
BUT I WONDER WHERE YAMAOKA WAS GOING WITH FUTAKI MARIKO TONIGHT...
IT'S UN-FORGIV-ABLE.
YOU DON'T HAVE TO WORRY ABOUT IT THOUGH. YOU'VE GOT PRESIDENT DAN.
HUH? OH...

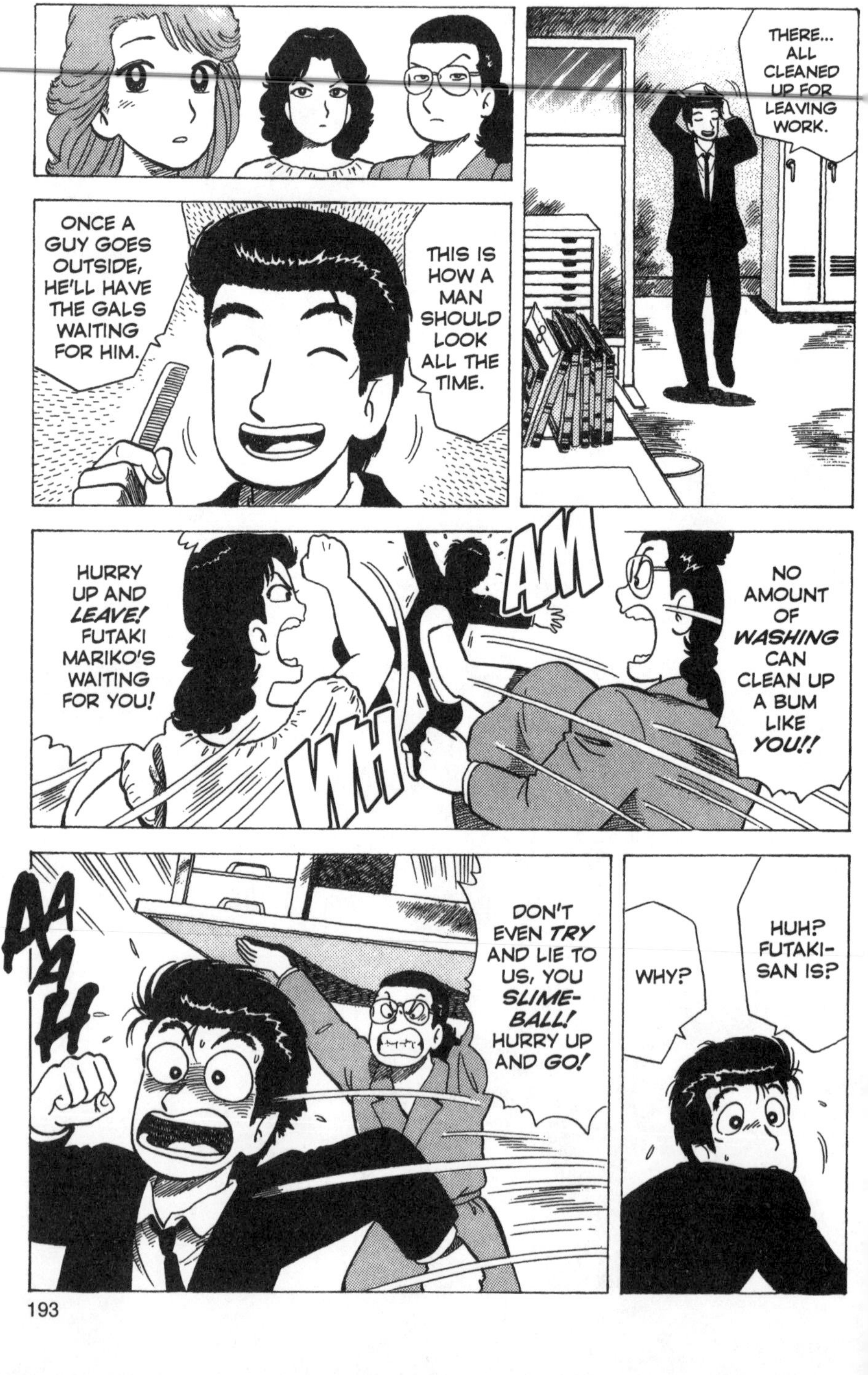
THERE... ALL CLEANED UP FOR LEAVING WORK.
THIS IS HOW A MAN SHOULD LOOK ALL THE TIME.
ONCE A GUY GOES OUTSIDE, HE'LL HAVE THE GALS WAITING FOR HIM.
NO AMOUNT OF *WASHING* CAN CLEAN UP A BUM LIKE *YOU!!*
AM
HURRY UP AND *LEAVE!* FUTAKI MARIKO'S WAITING FOR YOU!
WH
HUH? FUTAKI-SAN IS?
WHY?
DON'T EVEN *TRY* AND LIE TO US, YOU *SLIME-BALL!* HURRY UP AND *GO!*
AAAAH

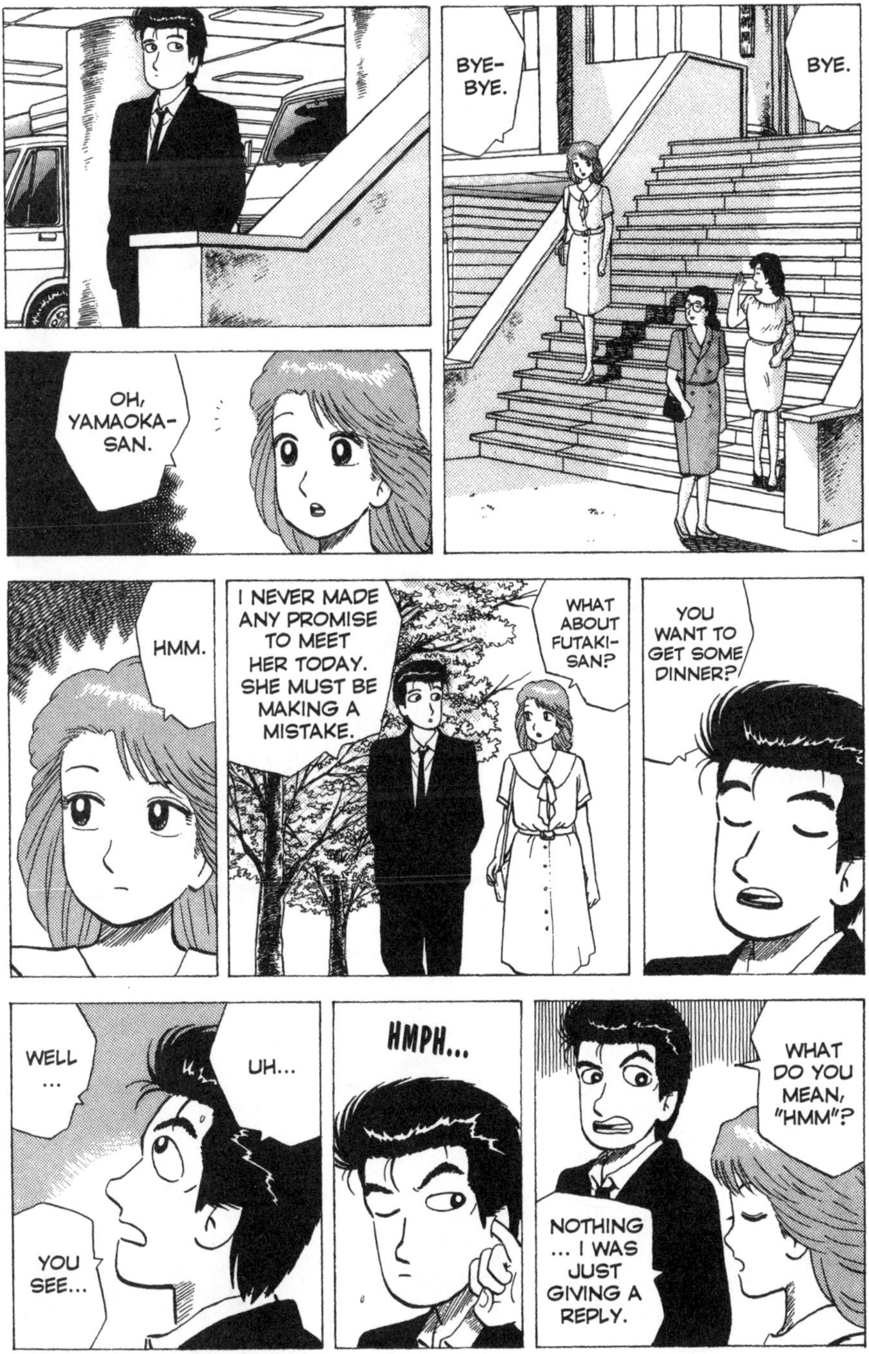
BYE.
BYE-BYE.
OH, YAMAOKA-SAN.
YOU WANT TO GET SOME DINNER?
WHAT ABOUT FUTAKI-SAN?
I NEVER MADE ANY PROMISE TO MEET HER TODAY. SHE MUST BE MAKING A MISTAKE.
HMM.
WHAT DO YOU MEAN, "HMM"?
NOTHING ... I WAS JUST GIVING A REPLY.
HMPH...
UH...
WELL ...
YOU SEE...

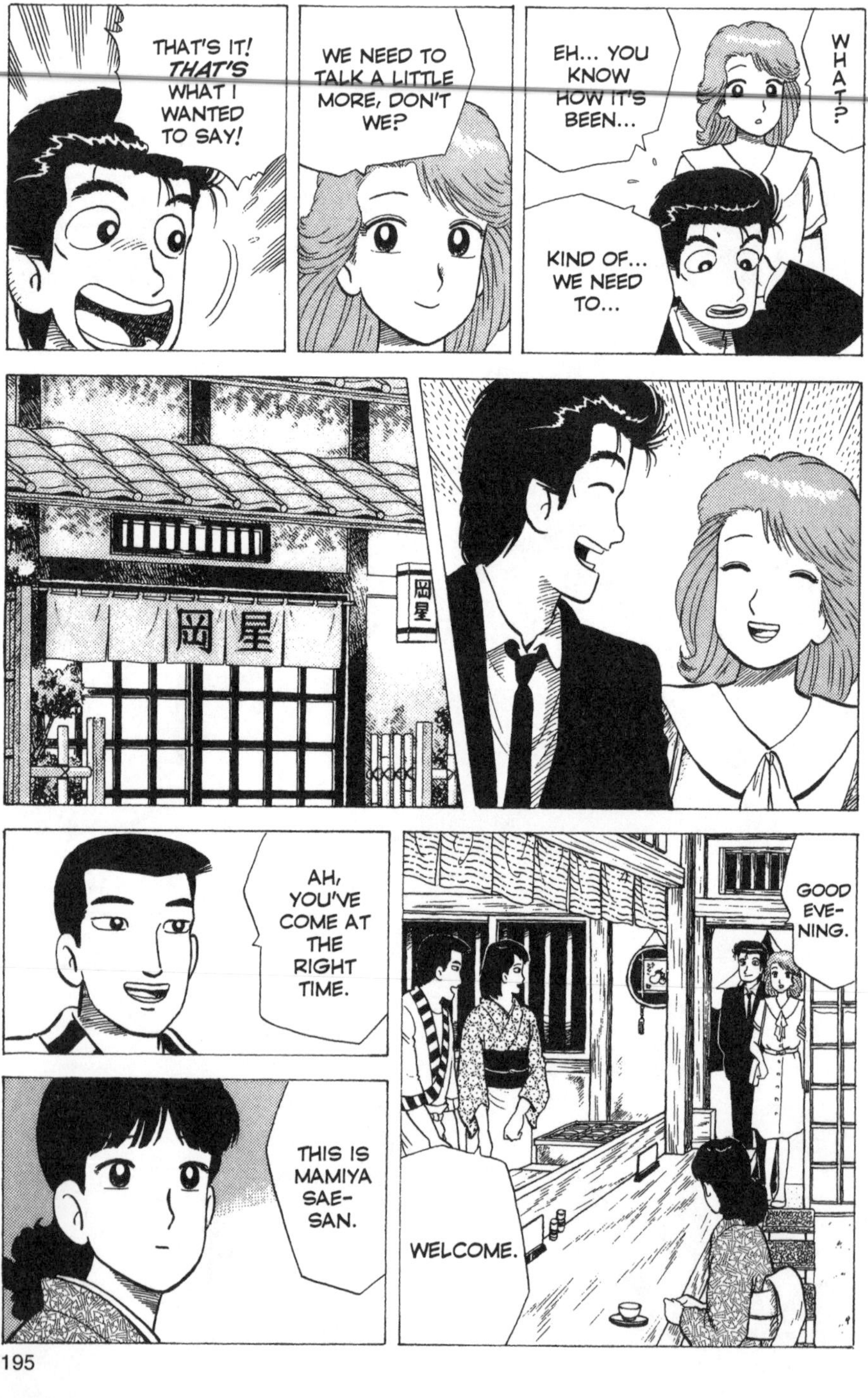
WHAT?
EH... YOU KNOW HOW IT'S BEEN...
KIND OF... WE NEED TO...
WE NEED TO TALK A LITTLE MORE, DON'T WE?
THAT'S IT! *THAT'S* WHAT I WANTED TO SAY!
GOOD EVE-NING.
WELCOME.
AH, YOU'VE COME AT THE RIGHT TIME.
THIS IS MAMIYA SAE-SAN.

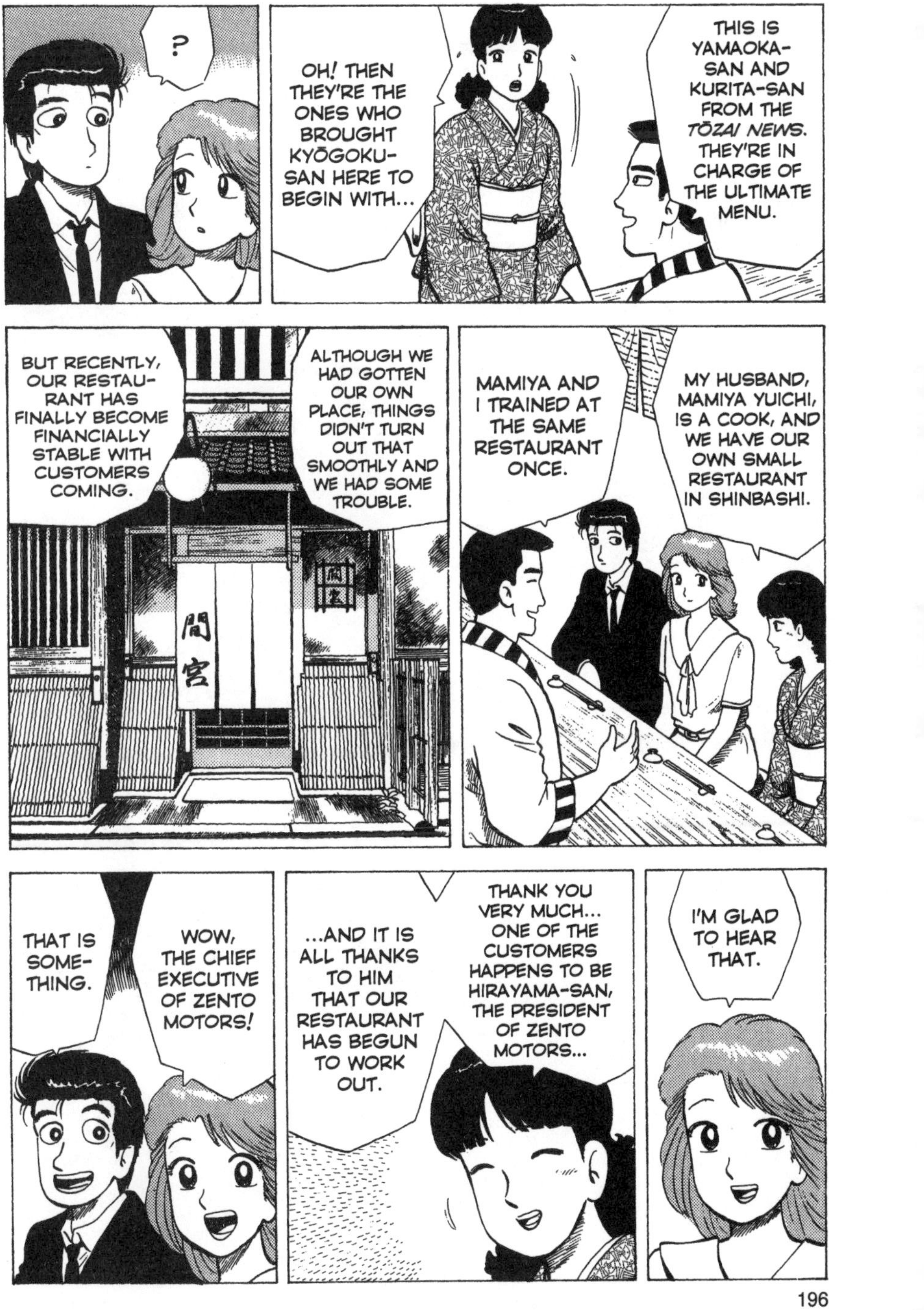
THIS IS YAMAOKA-SAN AND KURITA-SAN FROM THE *TŌZAI NEWS*. THEY'RE IN CHARGE OF THE ULTIMATE MENU.
OH! THEN THEY'RE THE ONES WHO BROUGHT KYŌGOKU-SAN HERE TO BEGIN WITH...
?
MY HUSBAND, MAMIYA YUICHI, IS A COOK, AND WE HAVE OUR OWN SMALL RESTAURANT IN SHINBASHI.
MAMIYA AND I TRAINED AT THE SAME RESTAURANT ONCE.
ALTHOUGH WE HAD GOTTEN OUR OWN PLACE, THINGS DIDN'T TURN OUT THAT SMOOTHLY AND WE HAD SOME TROUBLE.
BUT RECENTLY, OUR RESTAURANT HAS FINALLY BECOME FINANCIALLY STABLE WITH CUSTOMERS COMING.
間宮
I'M GLAD TO HEAR THAT.
THANK YOU VERY MUCH... ONE OF THE CUSTOMERS HAPPENS TO BE HIRAYAMA-SAN, THE PRESIDENT OF ZENTO MOTORS...
...AND IT IS ALL THANKS TO HIM THAT OUR RESTAURANT HAS BEGUN TO WORK OUT.
WOW, THE CHIEF EXECUTIVE OF ZENTO MOTORS!
THAT IS SOMETHING.

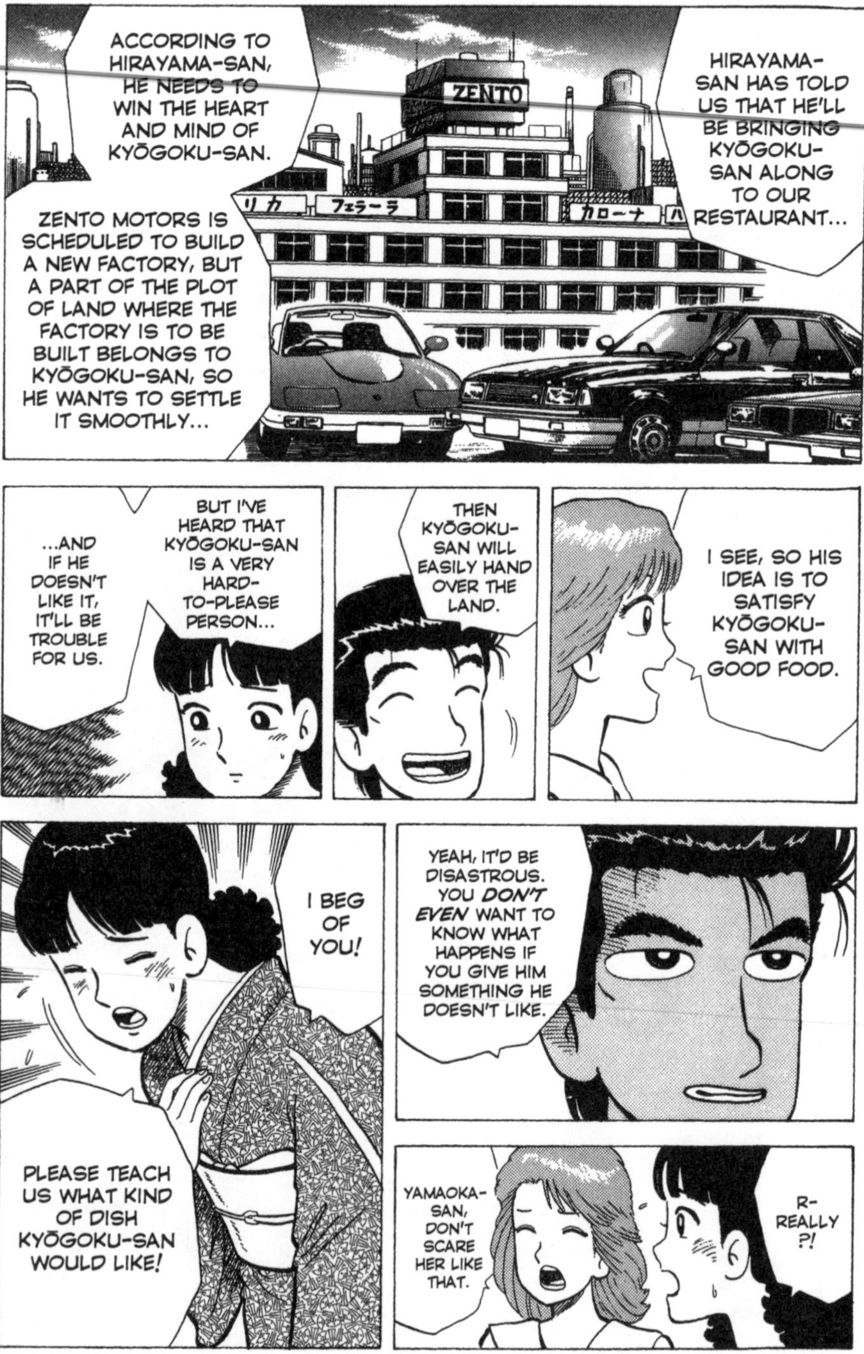
ZENTO
リカ
フェラーラ
カローナ
ハ
HIRAYAMA-SAN HAS TOLD US THAT HE'LL BE BRINGING KYŌGOKU-SAN ALONG TO OUR RESTAURANT...
ACCORDING TO HIRAYAMA-SAN, HE NEEDS TO WIN THE HEART AND MIND OF KYŌGOKU-SAN.
ZENTO MOTORS IS SCHEDULED TO BUILD A NEW FACTORY, BUT A PART OF THE PLOT OF LAND WHERE THE FACTORY IS TO BE BUILT BELONGS TO KYŌGOKU-SAN, SO HE WANTS TO SETTLE IT SMOOTHLY...
I SEE, SO HIS IDEA IS TO SATISFY KYŌGOKU-SAN WITH GOOD FOOD.
THEN KYŌGOKU-SAN WILL EASILY HAND OVER THE LAND.
BUT I'VE HEARD THAT KYŌGOKU-SAN IS A VERY HARD-TO-PLEASE PERSON...
...AND IF HE DOESN'T LIKE IT, IT'LL BE TROUBLE FOR US.
YEAH, IT'D BE DISASTROUS. YOU *DON'T EVEN* WANT TO KNOW WHAT HAPPENS IF YOU GIVE HIM SOMETHING HE DOESN'T LIKE.
R-REALLY?!
YAMAOKA-SAN, DON'T SCARE HER LIKE THAT.
I BEG OF YOU!
PLEASE TEACH US WHAT KIND OF DISH KYŌGOKU-SAN WOULD LIKE!

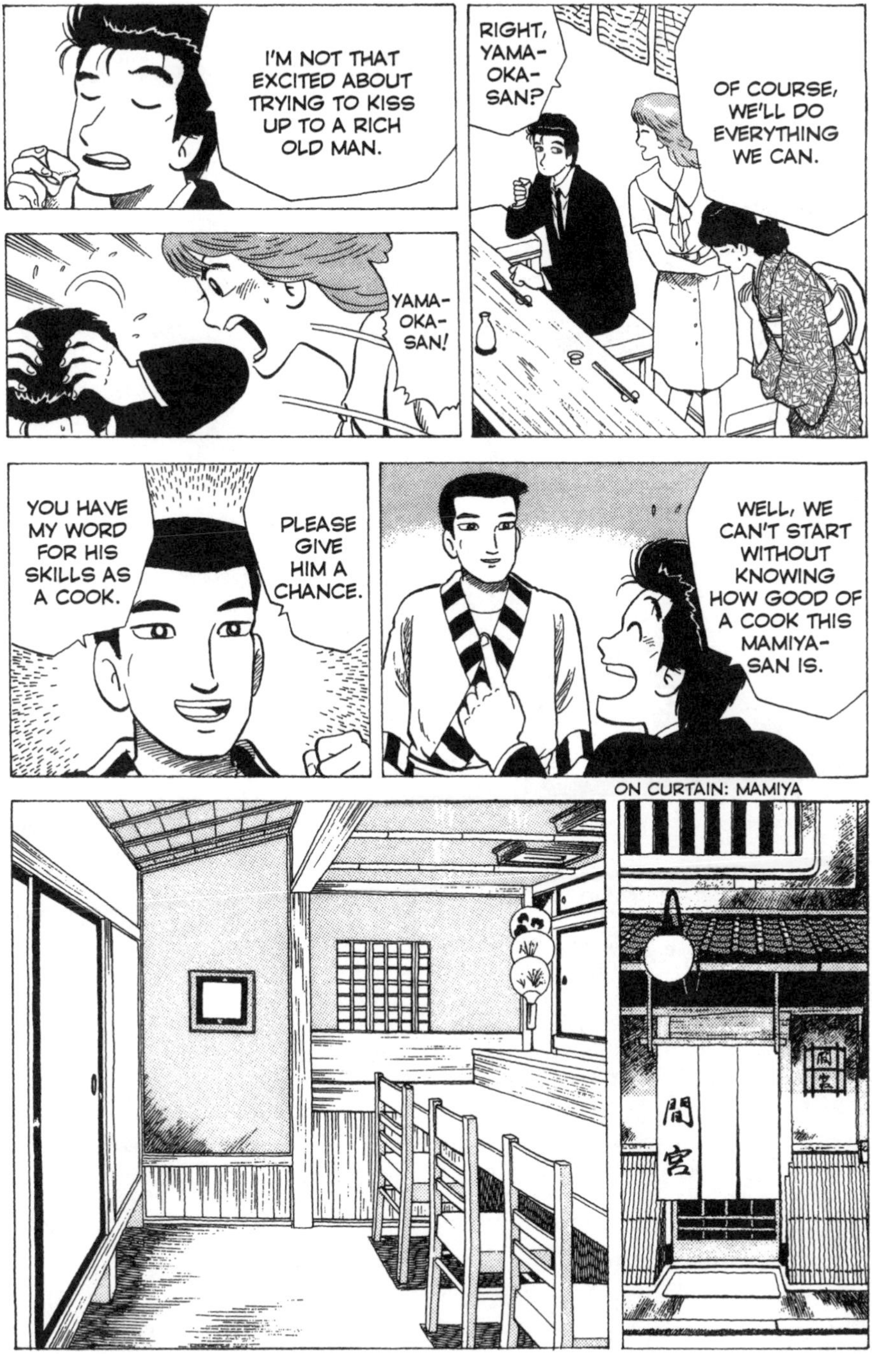
OF COURSE, WE'LL DO EVERYTHING WE CAN.
RIGHT, YAMA-OKA-SAN?
I'M NOT THAT EXCITED ABOUT TRYING TO KISS UP TO A RICH OLD MAN.
YAMA-OKA-SAN!
WELL, WE CAN'T START WITHOUT KNOWING HOW GOOD OF A COOK THIS MAMIYA-SAN IS.
PLEASE GIVE HIM A CHANCE.
YOU HAVE MY WORD FOR HIS SKILLS AS A COOK.
ON CURTAIN: MAMIYA

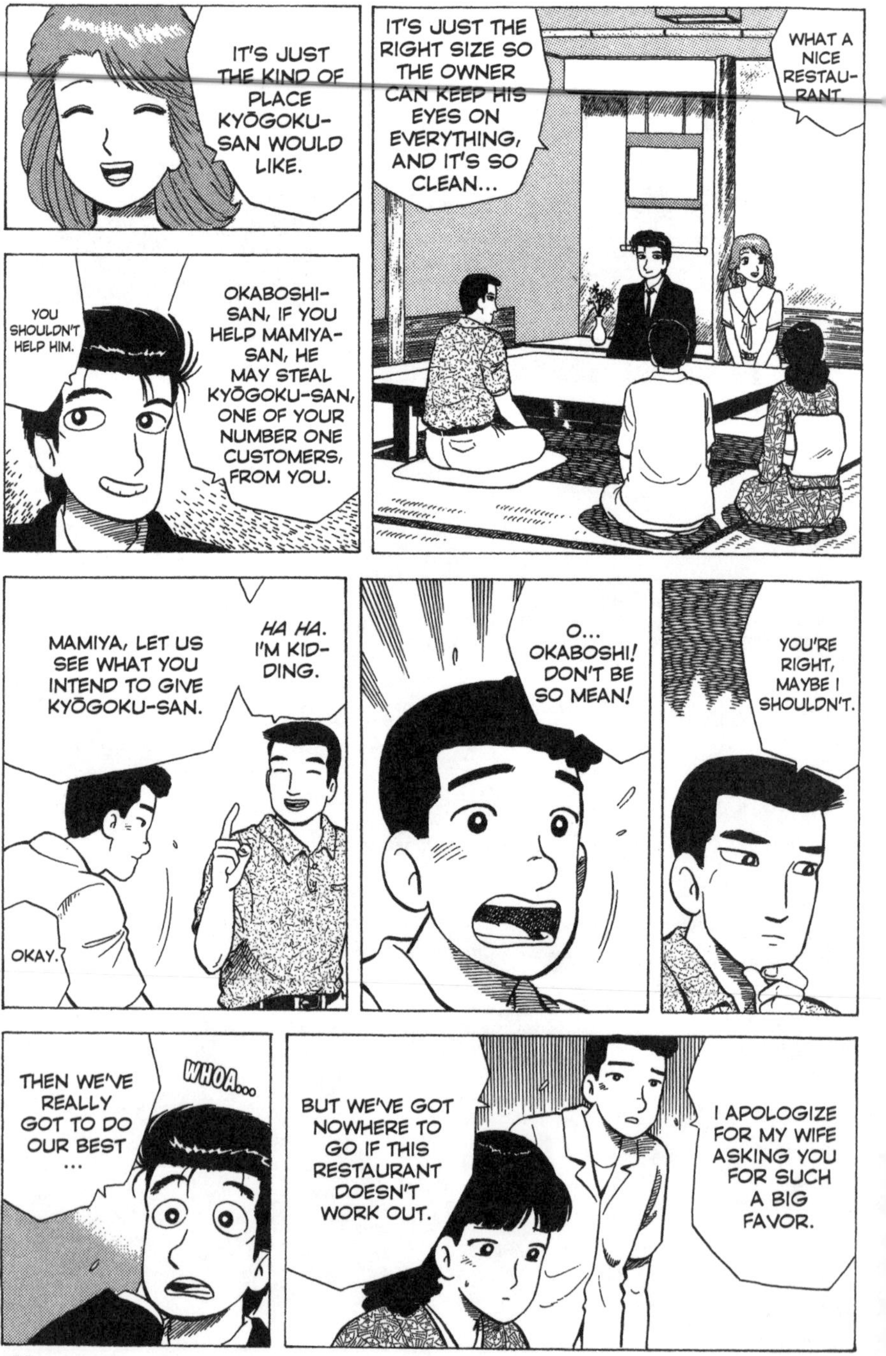
WHAT A NICE RESTAURANT.
IT'S JUST THE RIGHT SIZE SO THE OWNER CAN KEEP HIS EYES ON EVERYTHING, AND IT'S SO CLEAN...
IT'S JUST THE KIND OF PLACE KYŌGOKU-SAN WOULD LIKE.
OKABOSHI-SAN, IF YOU HELP MAMIYA-SAN, HE MAY STEAL KYŌGOKU-SAN, ONE OF YOUR NUMBER ONE CUSTOMERS, FROM YOU.
YOU SHOULDN'T HELP HIM.
YOU'RE RIGHT, MAYBE I SHOULDN'T.
O... OKABOSHI! DON'T BE SO MEAN!
HA HA. I'M KIDDING.
MAMIYA, LET US SEE WHAT YOU INTEND TO GIVE KYŌGOKU-SAN.
OKAY.
I APOLOGIZE FOR MY WIFE ASKING YOU FOR SUCH A BIG FAVOR.
BUT WE'VE GOT NOWHERE TO GO IF THIS RESTAURANT DOESN'T WORK OUT.
WHOA...
THEN WE'VE REALLY GOT TO DO OUR BEST ...

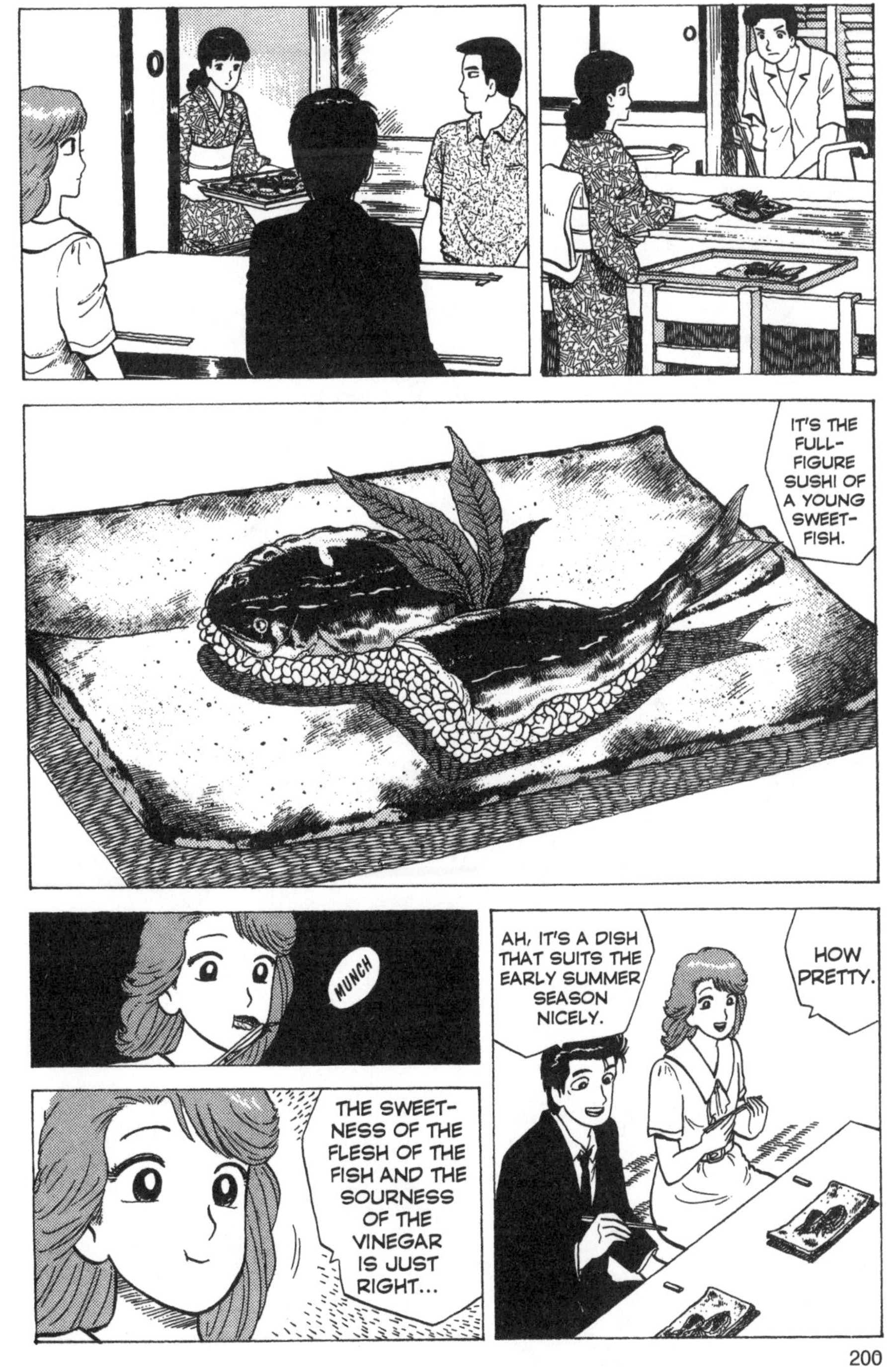
IT'S THE FULL-FIGURE SUSHI OF A YOUNG SWEET-FISH.
HOW PRETTY.
AH, IT'S A DISH THAT SUITS THE EARLY SUMMER SEASON NICELY.
MUNCH
THE SWEET-NESS OF THE FLESH OF THE FISH AND THE SOURNESS OF THE VINEGAR IS JUST RIGHT...

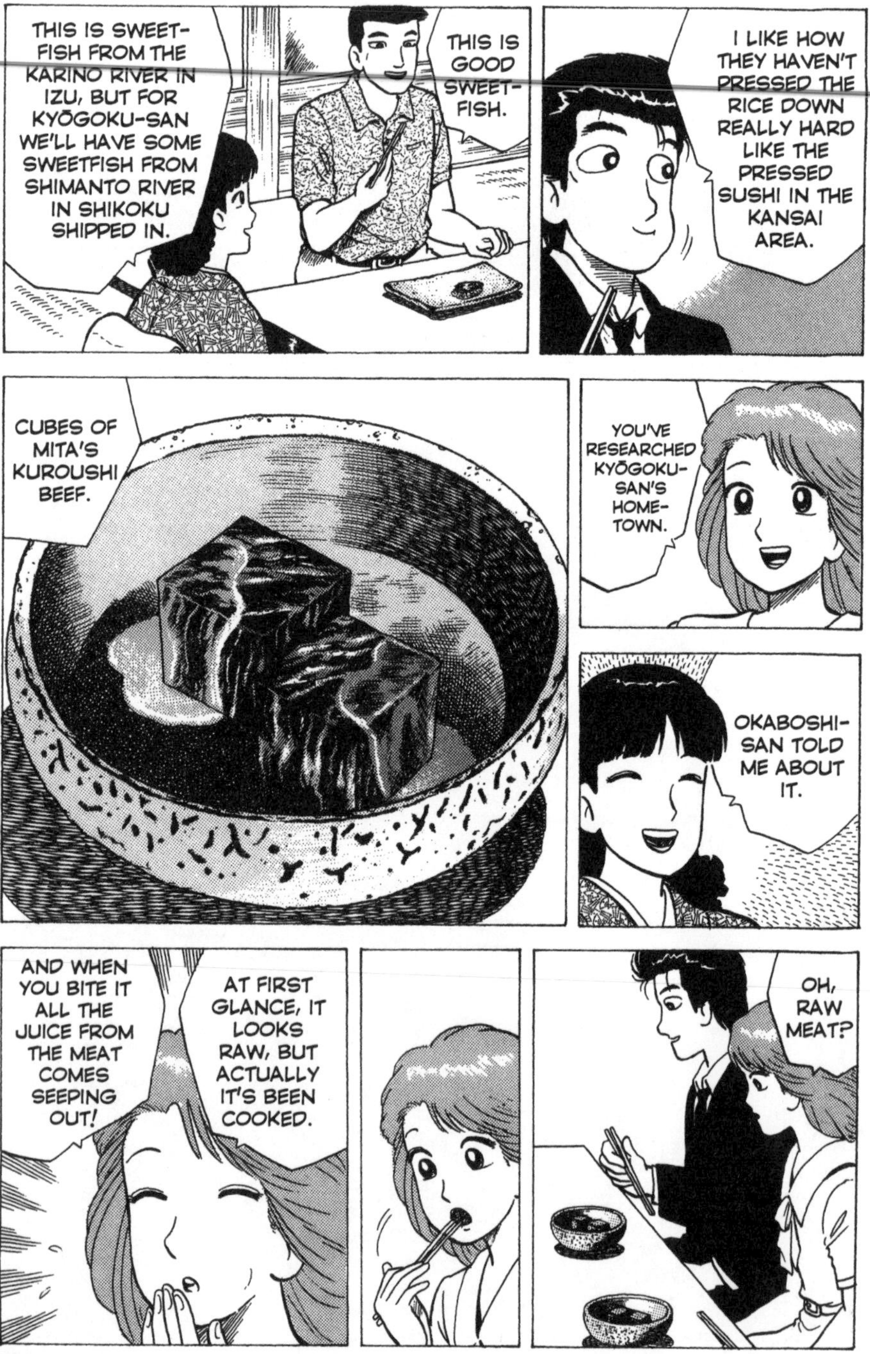
I LIKE HOW THEY HAVEN'T PRESSED THE RICE DOWN REALLY HARD LIKE THE PRESSED SUSHI IN THE KANSAI AREA.
THIS IS GOOD SWEET-FISH.
THIS IS SWEET-FISH FROM THE KARINO RIVER IN IZU, BUT FOR KYŌGOKU-SAN WE'LL HAVE SOME SWEETFISH FROM SHIMANTO RIVER IN SHIKOKU SHIPPED IN.
YOU'VE RESEARCHED KYŌGOKU-SAN'S HOME-TOWN.
OKABOSHI-SAN TOLD ME ABOUT IT.
CUBES OF MITA'S KUROUSHI BEEF.
OH, RAW MEAT?
AT FIRST GLANCE, IT LOOKS RAW, BUT ACTUALLY IT'S BEEN COOKED.
AND WHEN YOU BITE IT ALL THE JUICE FROM THE MEAT COMES SEEPING OUT!

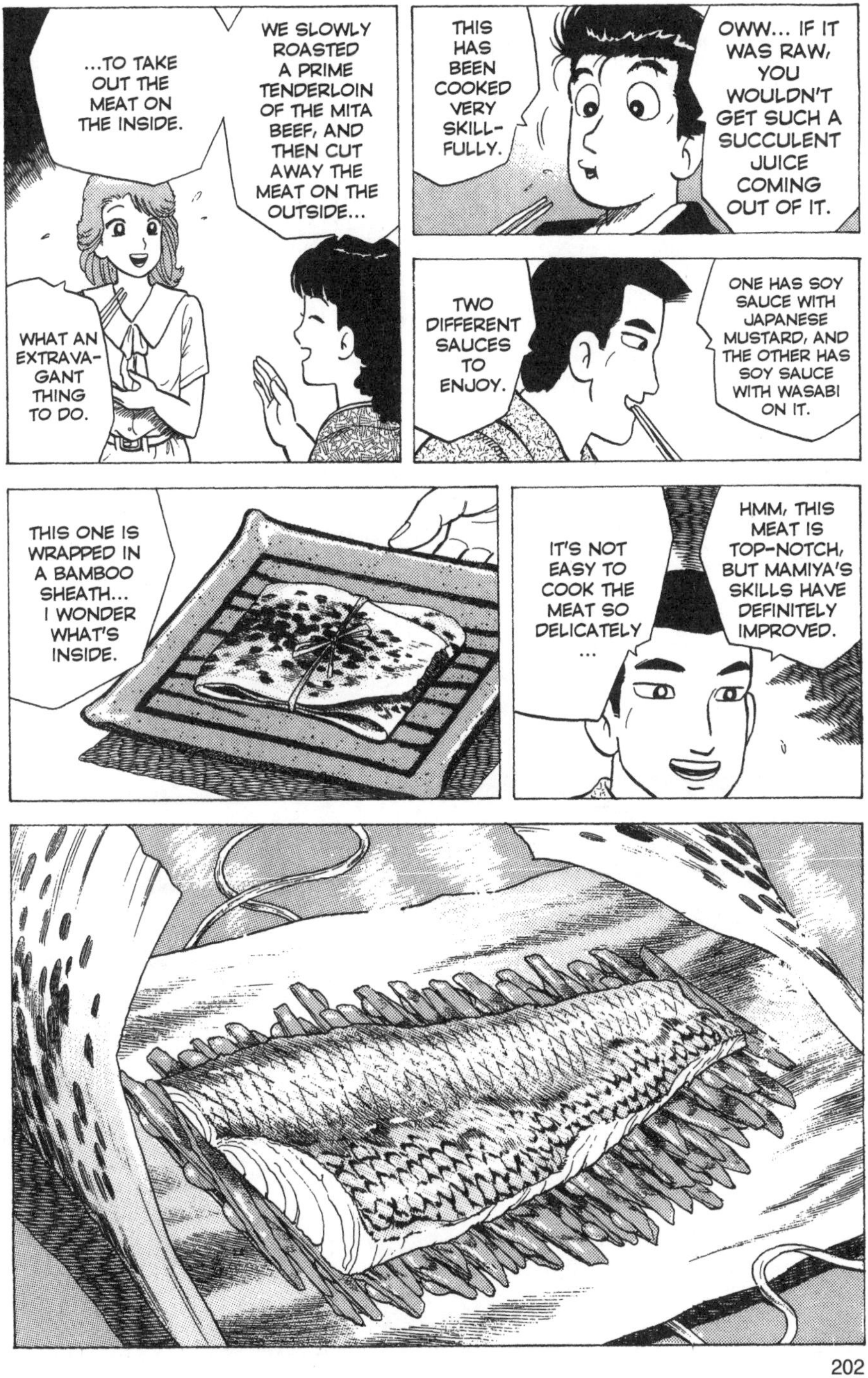
OWW... IF IT WAS RAW, YOU WOULDN'T GET SUCH A SUCCULENT JUICE COMING OUT OF IT.
THIS HAS BEEN COOKED VERY SKILL-FULLY.
ONE HAS SOY SAUCE WITH JAPANESE MUSTARD, AND THE OTHER HAS SOY SAUCE WITH WASABI ON IT.
TWO DIFFERENT SAUCES TO ENJOY.
WE SLOWLY ROASTED A PRIME TENDERLOIN OF THE MITA BEEF, AND THEN CUT AWAY THE MEAT ON THE OUTSIDE...
...TO TAKE OUT THE MEAT ON THE INSIDE.
WHAT AN EXTRAVA-GANT THING TO DO.
HMM, THIS MEAT IS TOP-NOTCH, BUT MAMIYA'S SKILLS HAVE DEFINITELY IMPROVED.
IT'S NOT EASY TO COOK THE MEAT SO DELICATELY ...
THIS ONE IS WRAPPED IN A BAMBOO SHEATH... I WONDER WHAT'S INSIDE.

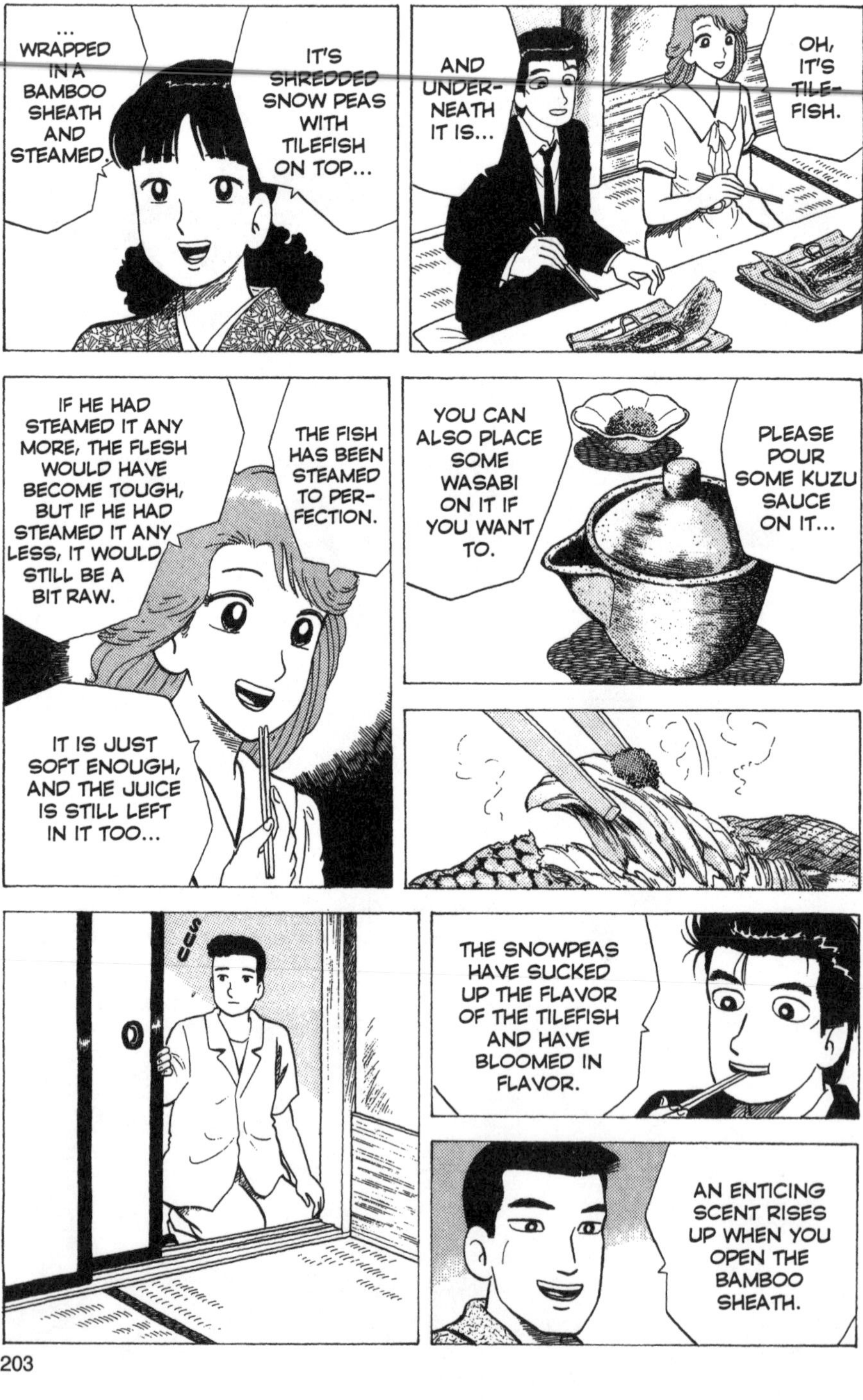
OH, IT'S TILE-FISH.
AND UNDER-NEATH IT IS...
IT'S SHREDDED SNOW PEAS WITH TILEFISH ON TOP...
...WRAPPED IN A BAMBOO SHEATH AND STEAMED.
PLEASE POUR SOME KUZU SAUCE ON IT...
YOU CAN ALSO PLACE SOME WASABI ON IT IF YOU WANT TO.
THE FISH HAS BEEN STEAMED TO PER-FECTION.
IF HE HAD STEAMED IT ANY MORE, THE FLESH WOULD HAVE BECOME TOUGH, BUT IF HE HAD STEAMED IT ANY LESS, IT WOULD STILL BE A BIT RAW.
IT IS JUST SOFT ENOUGH, AND THE JUICE IS STILL LEFT IN IT TOO...
THE SNOWPEAS HAVE SUCKED UP THE FLAVOR OF THE TILEFISH AND HAVE BLOOMED IN FLAVOR.
AN ENTICING SCENT RISES UP WHEN YOU OPEN THE BAMBOO SHEATH.

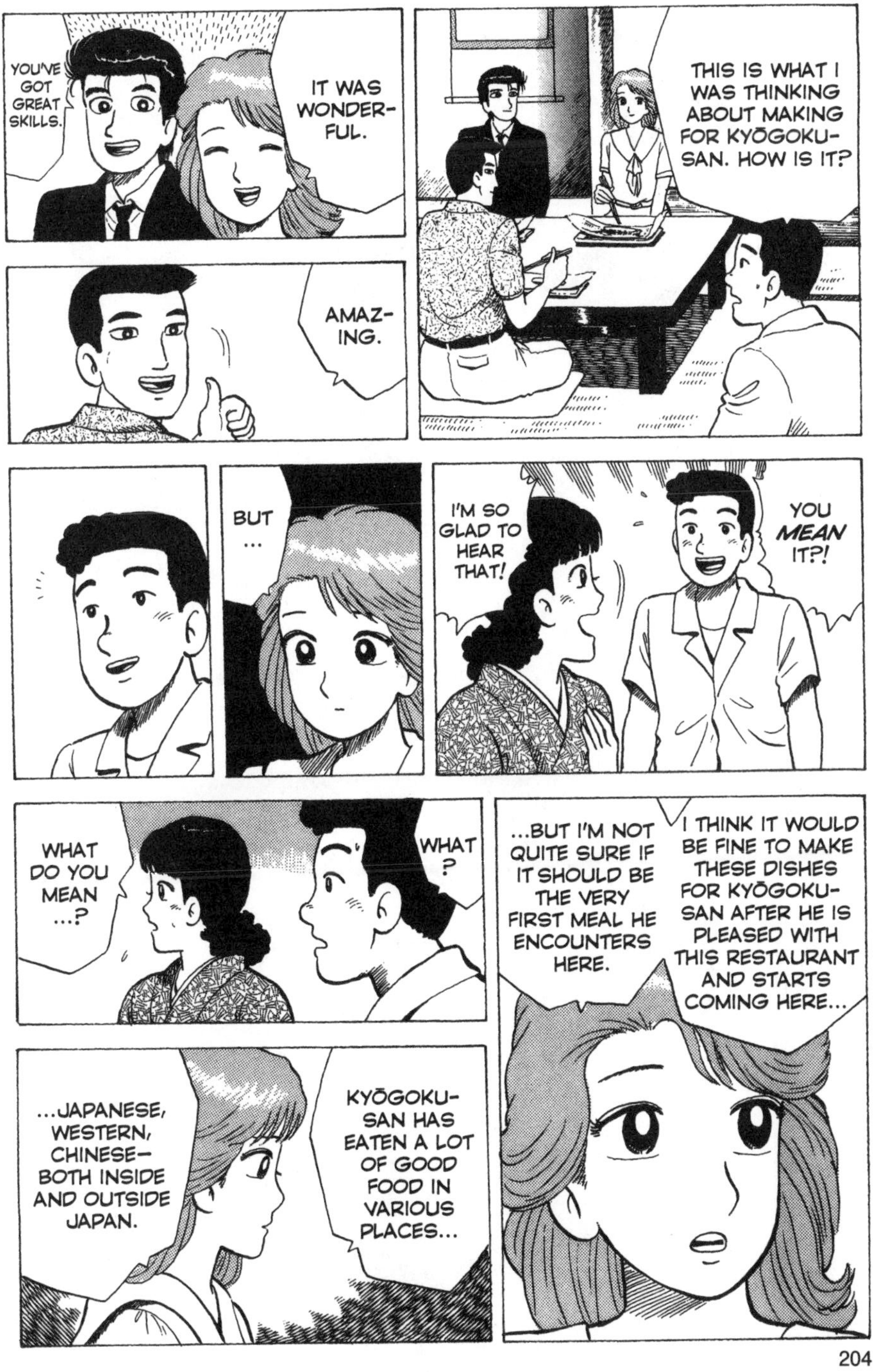
THIS IS WHAT I WAS THINKING ABOUT MAKING FOR KYŌGOKU-SAN. HOW IS IT?
IT WAS WONDERFUL.
YOU'VE GOT GREAT SKILLS.
AMAZING.
YOU *MEAN* IT?!
I'M SO GLAD TO HEAR THAT!
BUT ...
I THINK IT WOULD BE FINE TO MAKE THESE DISHES FOR KYŌGOKU-SAN AFTER HE IS PLEASED WITH THIS RESTAURANT AND STARTS COMING HERE...
...BUT I'M NOT QUITE SURE IF IT SHOULD BE THE VERY FIRST MEAL HE ENCOUNTERS HERE.
WHAT ?
WHAT DO YOU MEAN ...?
KYŌGOKU-SAN HAS EATEN A LOT OF GOOD FOOD IN VARIOUS PLACES...
...JAPANESE, WESTERN, CHINESE—BOTH INSIDE AND OUTSIDE JAPAN.

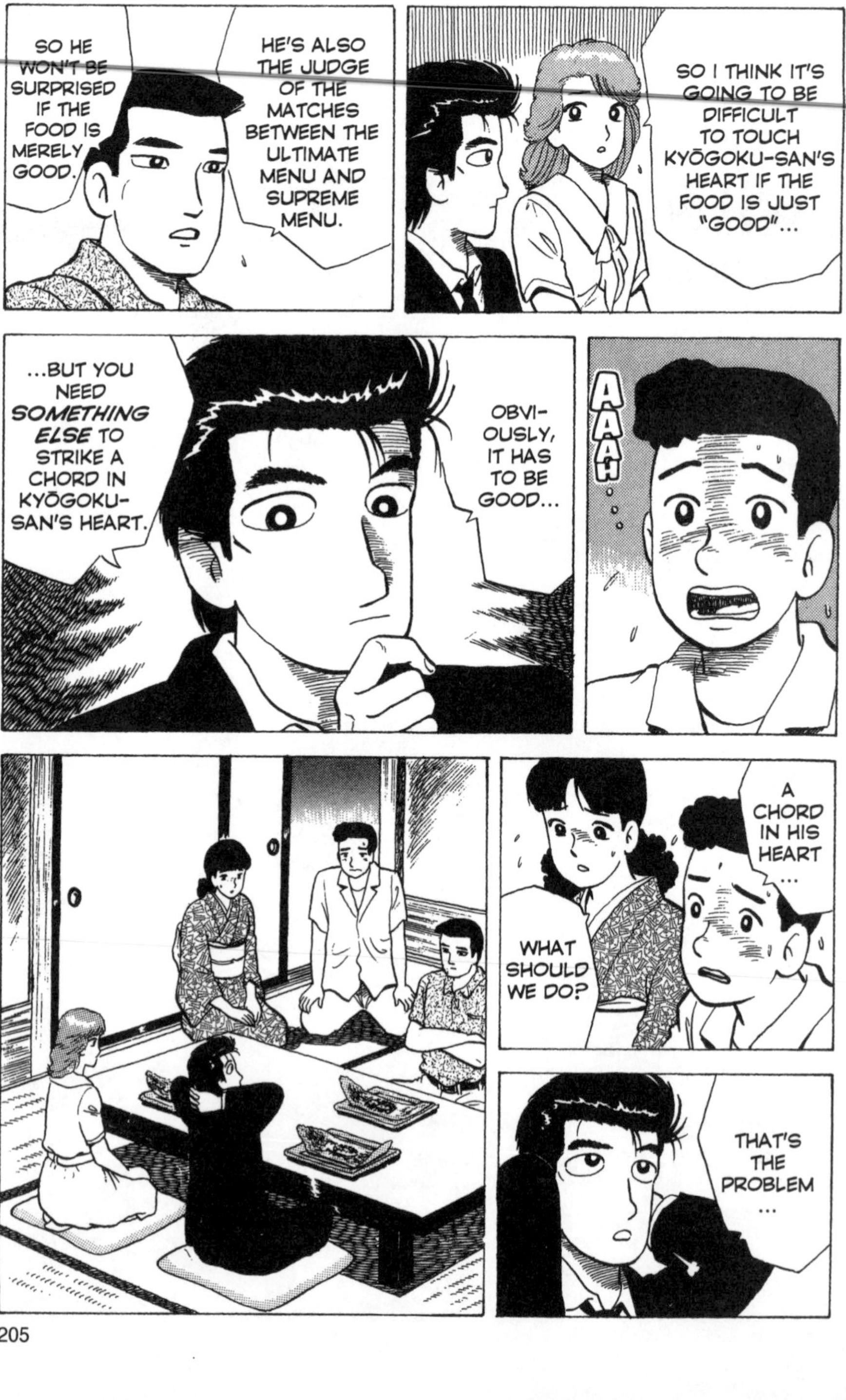
SO I THINK IT'S GOING TO BE DIFFICULT TO TOUCH KYŌGOKU-SAN'S HEART IF THE FOOD IS JUST "GOOD"...
HE'S ALSO THE JUDGE OF THE MATCHES BETWEEN THE ULTIMATE MENU AND SUPREME MENU.
SO HE WON'T BE SURPRISED IF THE FOOD IS MERELY GOOD.
AAAH
OBVIOUSLY, IT HAS TO BE GOOD...
...BUT YOU NEED *SOMETHING ELSE* TO STRIKE A CHORD IN KYŌGOKU-SAN'S HEART.
A CHORD IN HIS HEART...
WHAT SHOULD WE DO?
THAT'S THE PROBLEM...

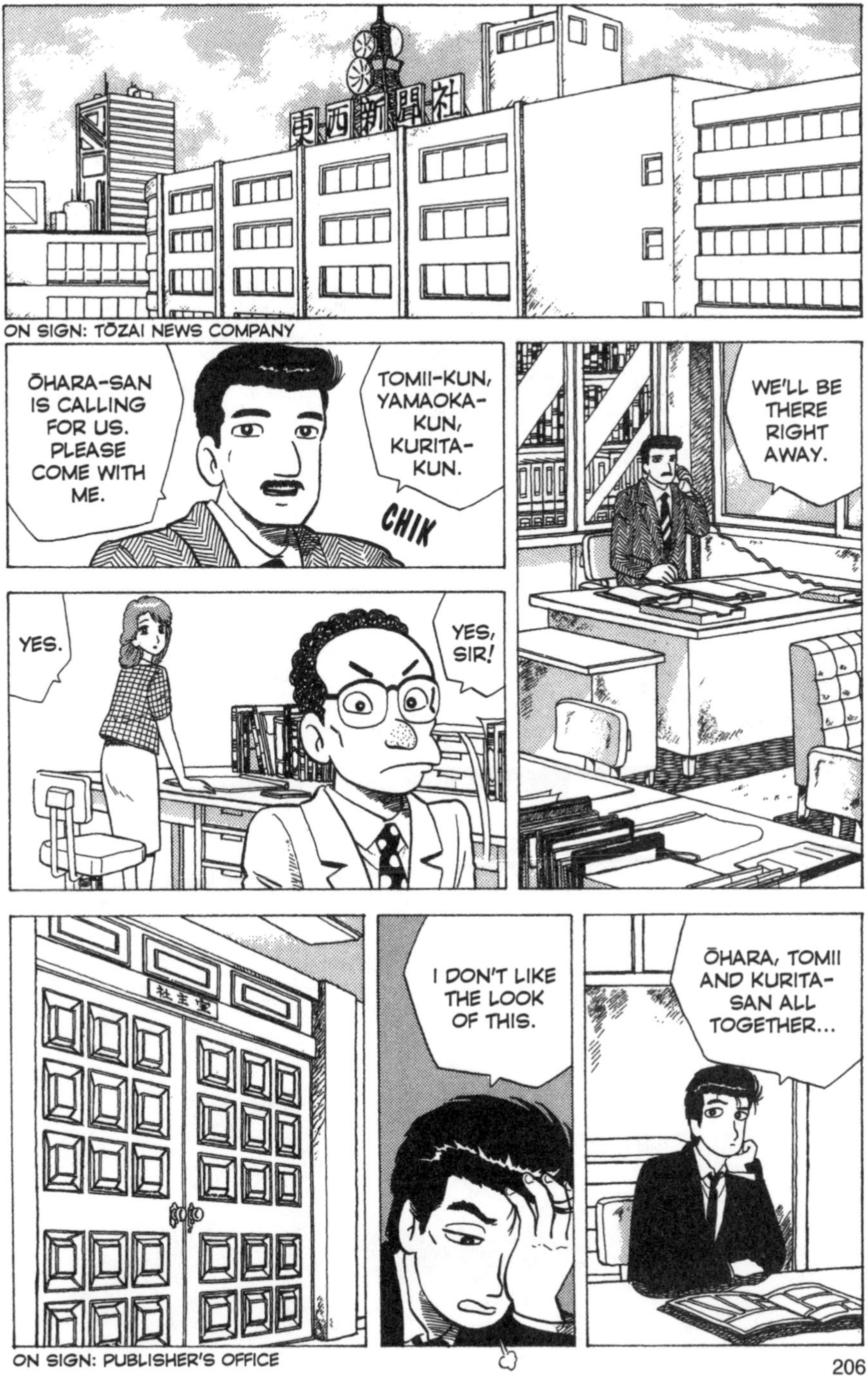
ON SIGN: TŌZAI NEWS COMPANY
WE'LL BE THERE RIGHT AWAY.
TOMII-KUN, YAMAOKA-KUN, KURITA-KUN.
CHIK
ŌHARA-SAN IS CALLING FOR US. PLEASE COME WITH ME.
YES, SIR!
YES.
ŌHARA, TOMII AND KURITA-SAN ALL TOGETHER...
I DON'T LIKE THE LOOK OF THIS.
ON SIGN: PUBLISHER'S OFFICE

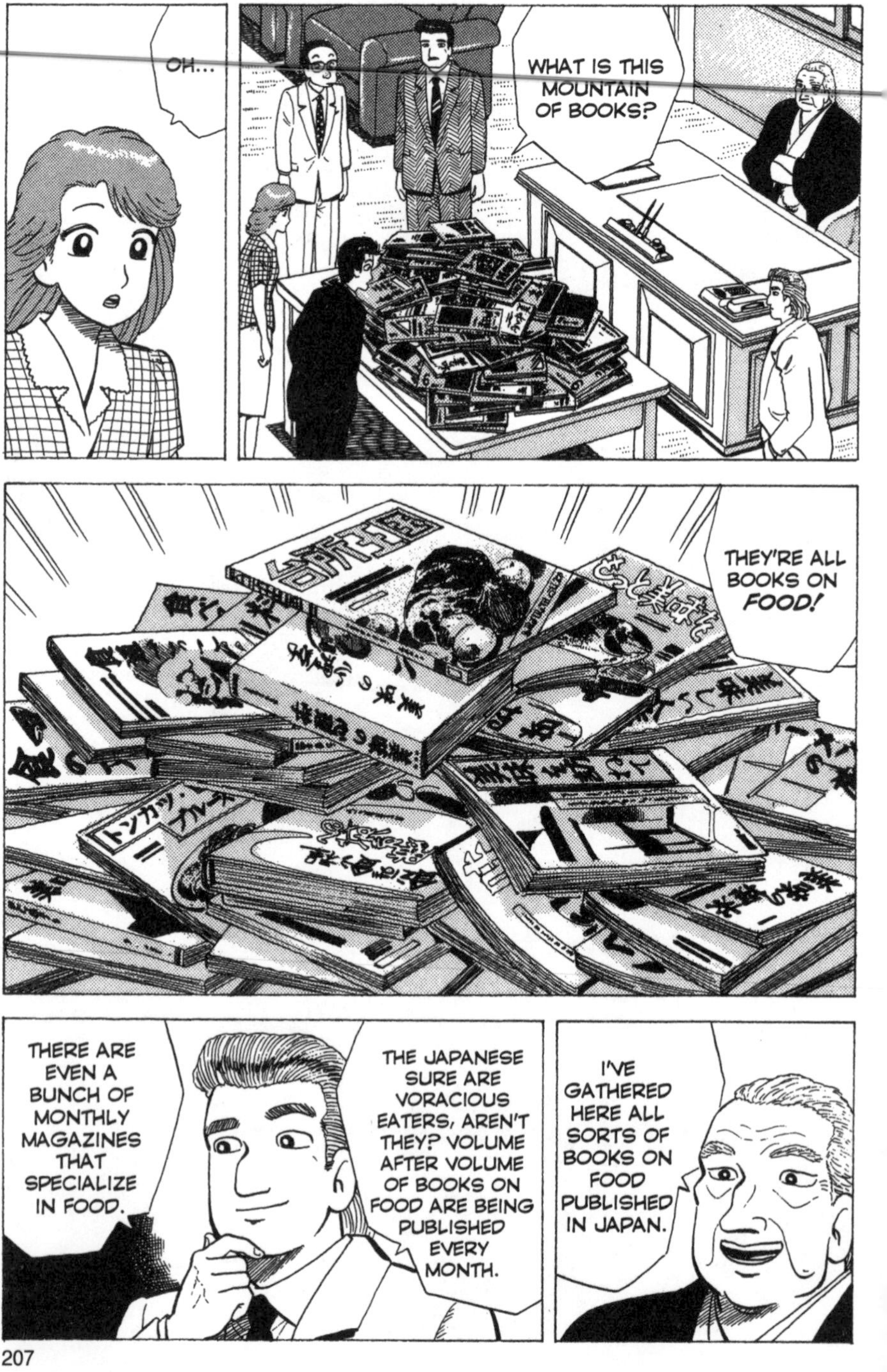
WHAT IS THIS MOUNTAIN OF BOOKS?
OH...
THEY'RE ALL BOOKS ON *FOOD!*
I'VE GATHERED HERE ALL SORTS OF BOOKS ON FOOD PUBLISHED IN JAPAN.
THE JAPANESE SURE ARE VORACIOUS EATERS, AREN'T THEY? VOLUME AFTER VOLUME OF BOOKS ON FOOD ARE BEING PUBLISHED EVERY MONTH.
THERE ARE EVEN A BUNCH OF MONTHLY MAGAZINES THAT SPECIALIZE IN FOOD.

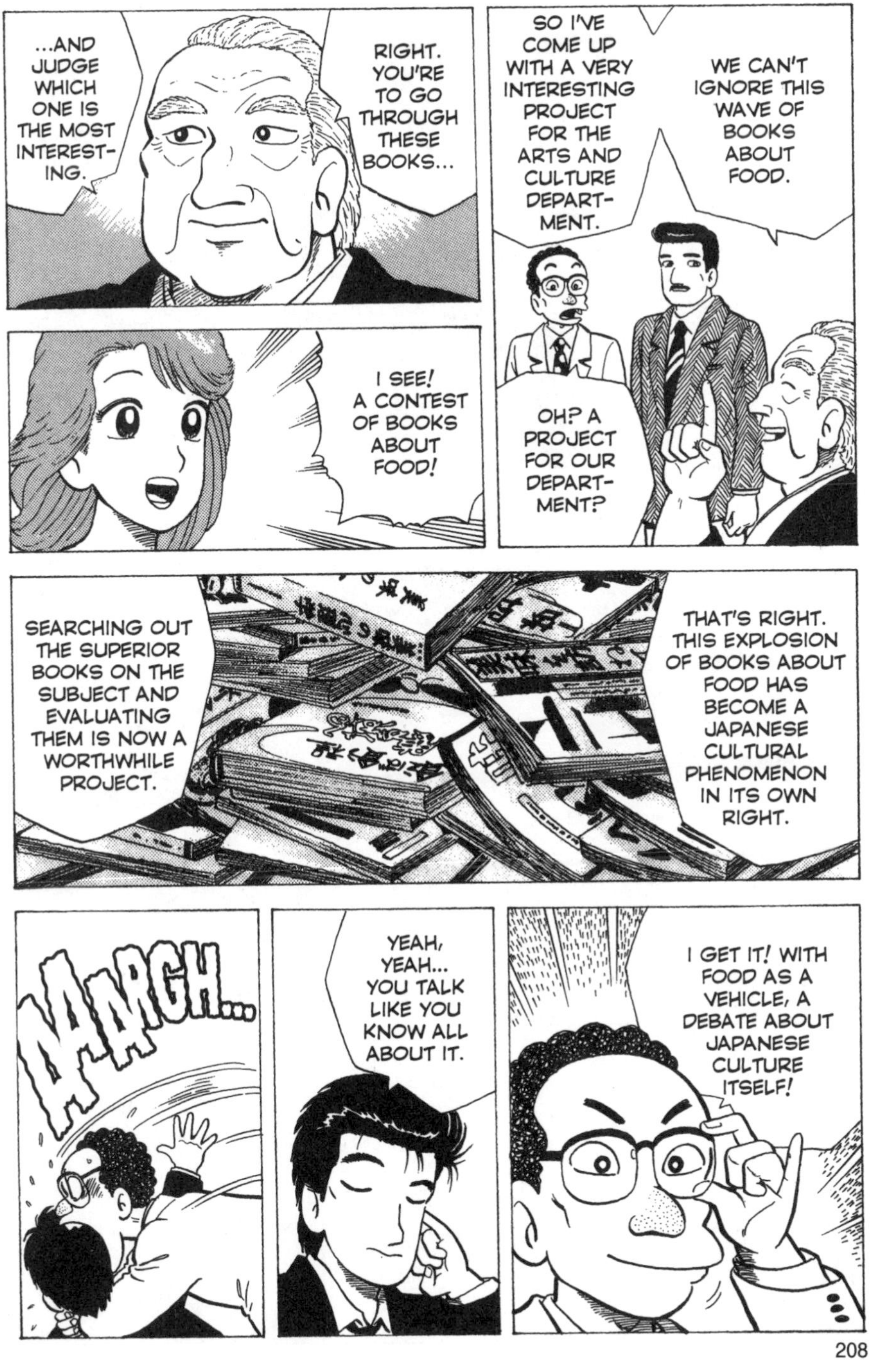
WE CAN'T IGNORE THIS WAVE OF BOOKS ABOUT FOOD.
SO I'VE COME UP WITH A VERY INTERESTING PROJECT FOR THE ARTS AND CULTURE DEPARTMENT.
OH? A PROJECT FOR OUR DEPARTMENT?
RIGHT. YOU'RE TO GO THROUGH THESE BOOKS...
...AND JUDGE WHICH ONE IS THE MOST INTEREST-ING.
I SEE! A CONTEST OF BOOKS ABOUT FOOD!
THAT'S RIGHT. THIS EXPLOSION OF BOOKS ABOUT FOOD HAS BECOME A JAPANESE CULTURAL PHENOMENON IN ITS OWN RIGHT.
SEARCHING OUT THE SUPERIOR BOOKS ON THE SUBJECT AND EVALUATING THEM IS NOW A WORTHWHILE PROJECT.
I GET IT! WITH FOOD AS A VEHICLE, A DEBATE ABOUT JAPANESE CULTURE ITSELF!
YEAH, YEAH... YOU TALK LIKE YOU KNOW ALL ABOUT IT.
AARGH...

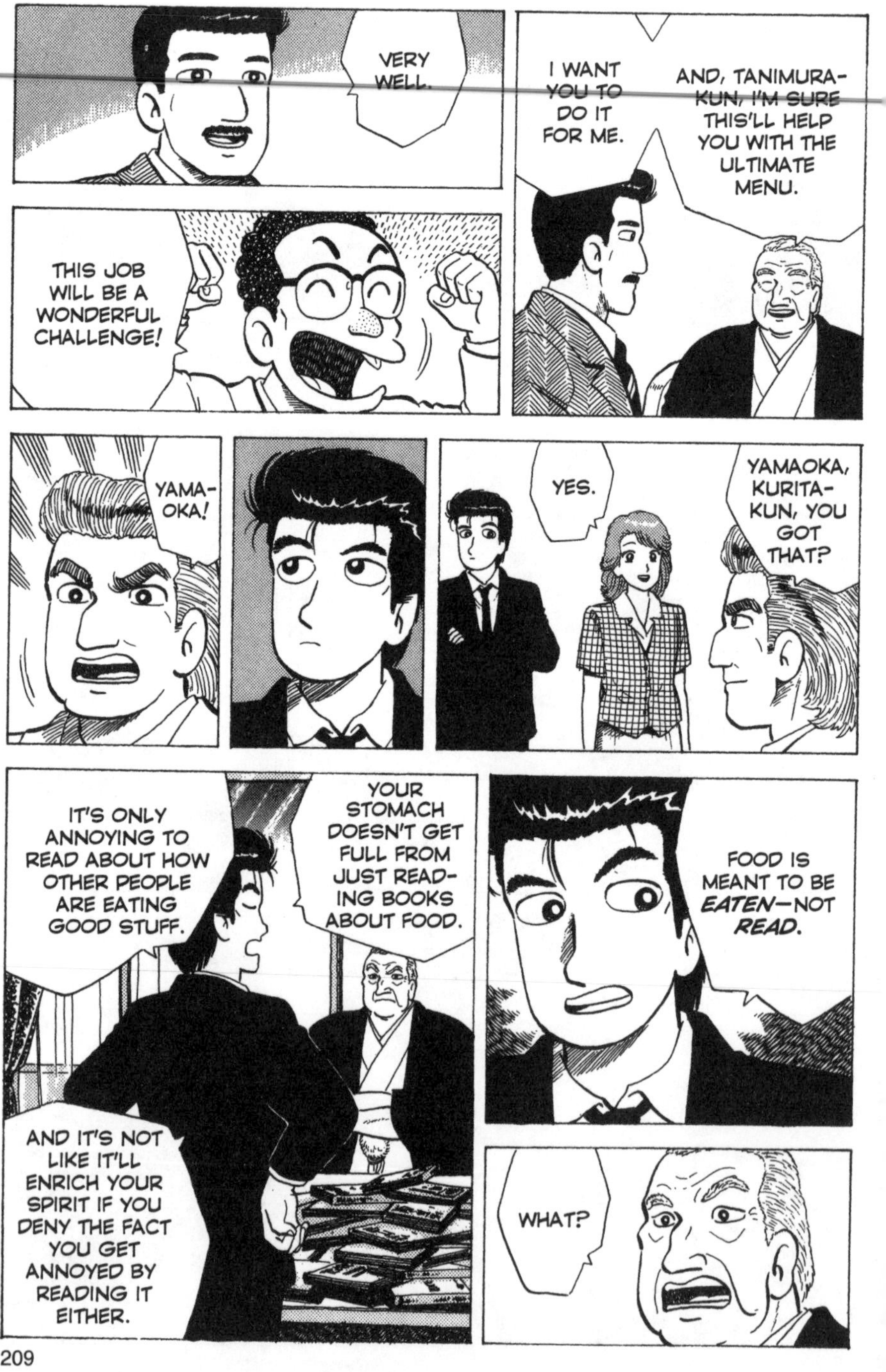
AND, TANIMURA-KUN, I'M SURE THIS'LL HELP YOU WITH THE ULTIMATE MENU.
I WANT YOU TO DO IT FOR ME.
VERY WELL.
THIS JOB WILL BE A WONDERFUL CHALLENGE!
YAMAOKA, KURITA-KUN, YOU GOT THAT?
YES.
YAMA-OKA!
FOOD IS MEANT TO BE *EATEN*—NOT *READ*.
WHAT?
YOUR STOMACH DOESN'T GET FULL FROM JUST READ-ING BOOKS ABOUT FOOD.
IT'S ONLY ANNOYING TO READ ABOUT HOW OTHER PEOPLE ARE EATING GOOD STUFF.
AND IT'S NOT LIKE IT'LL ENRICH YOUR SPIRIT IF YOU DENY THE FACT YOU GET ANNOYED BY READING IT EITHER.

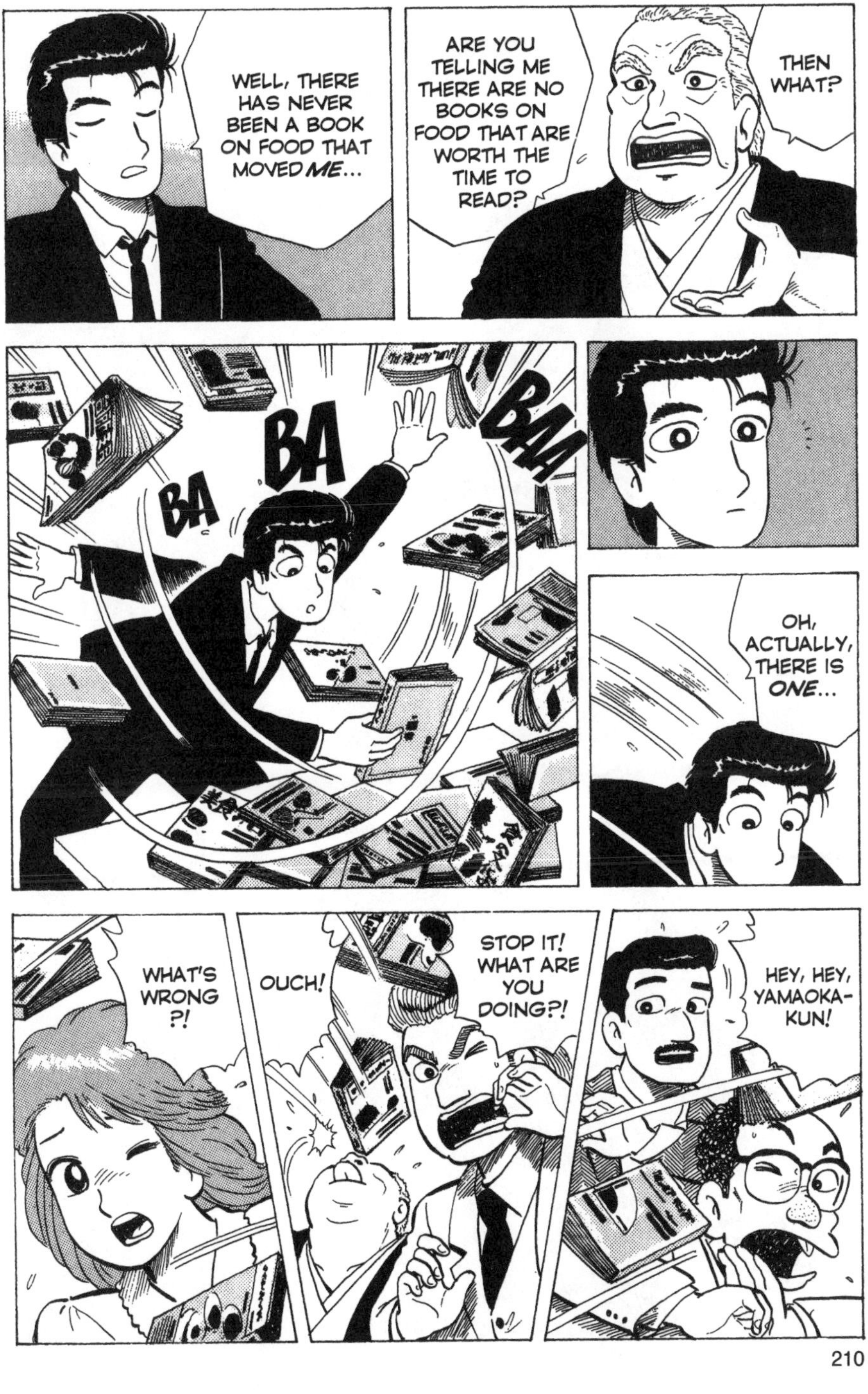
ARE YOU TELLING ME THERE ARE NO BOOKS ON FOOD THAT ARE WORTH THE TIME TO READ?
THEN WHAT?
WELL, THERE HAS NEVER BEEN A BOOK ON FOOD THAT MOVED *ME*...
OH, ACTUALLY, THERE IS *ONE*...
BAA
BA
BA
HEY, HEY, YAMAOKA-KUN!
STOP IT! WHAT ARE YOU DOING?!
OUCH!
WHAT'S WRONG ?!

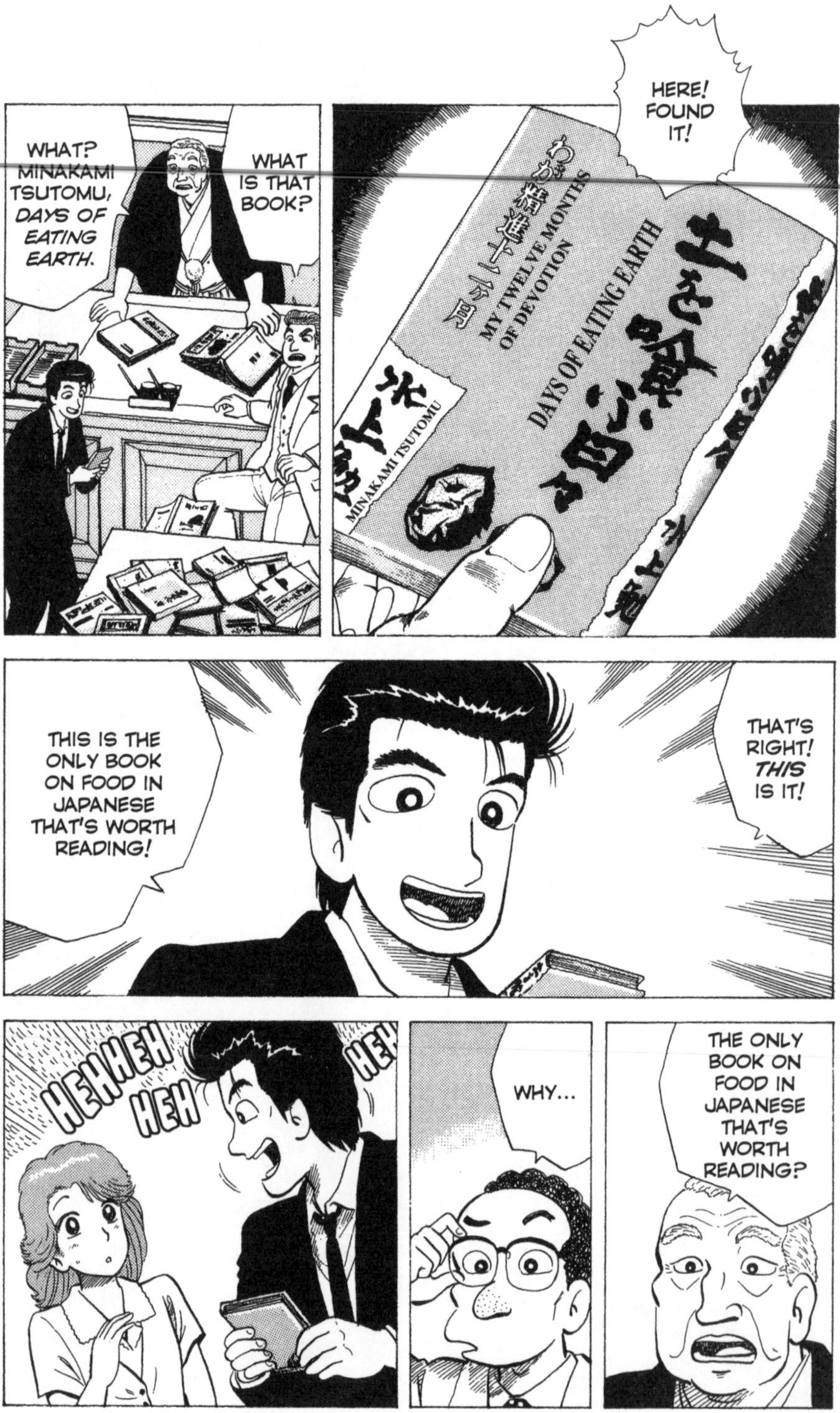
HERE! FOUND IT!
土を喰ふ日々
DAYS OF EATING EARTH
MY TWELVE MONTHS OF DEVOTION
MINAKAMI TSUTOMU
WHAT IS THAT BOOK?
WHAT? MINAKAMI TSUTOMU, *DAYS OF EATING EARTH*.
THAT'S RIGHT! *THIS* IS IT!
THIS IS THE ONLY BOOK ON FOOD IN JAPANESE THAT'S WORTH READING!
THE ONLY BOOK ON FOOD IN JAPANESE THAT'S WORTH READING?
WHY...
HEHHEH HEH HEH

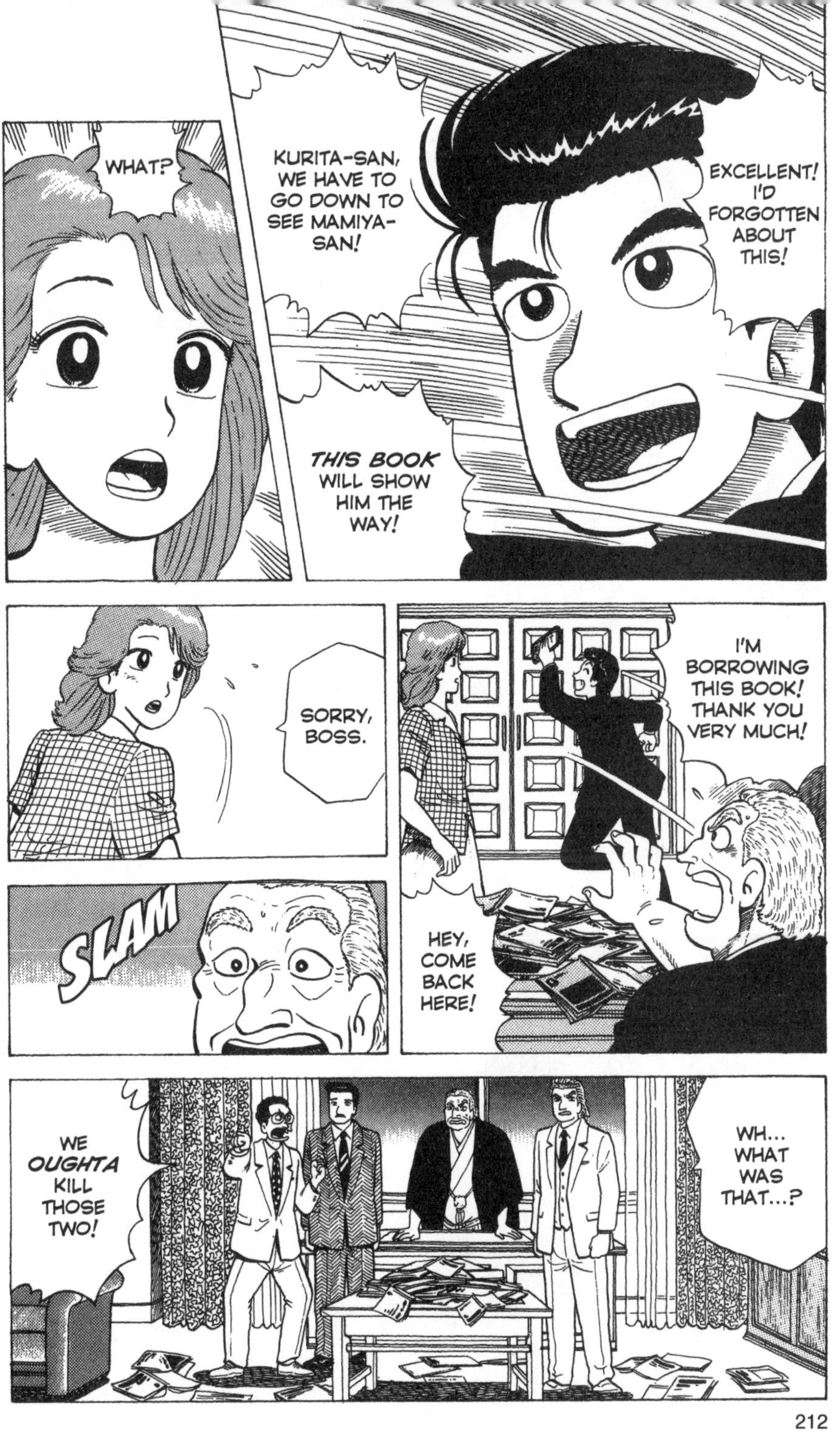
EXCELLENT! I'D FORGOTTEN ABOUT THIS!
KURITA-SAN, WE HAVE TO GO DOWN TO SEE MAMIYA-SAN!
THIS BOOK WILL SHOW HIM THE WAY!
WHAT?
I'M BORROWING THIS BOOK! THANK YOU VERY MUCH!
HEY, COME BACK HERE!
SORRY, BOSS.
SLAM
WH... WHAT WAS THAT...?
WE OUGHTA KILL THOSE TWO!

SEVENTH COURSE

A SURPRISING TASTE (PART TWO)

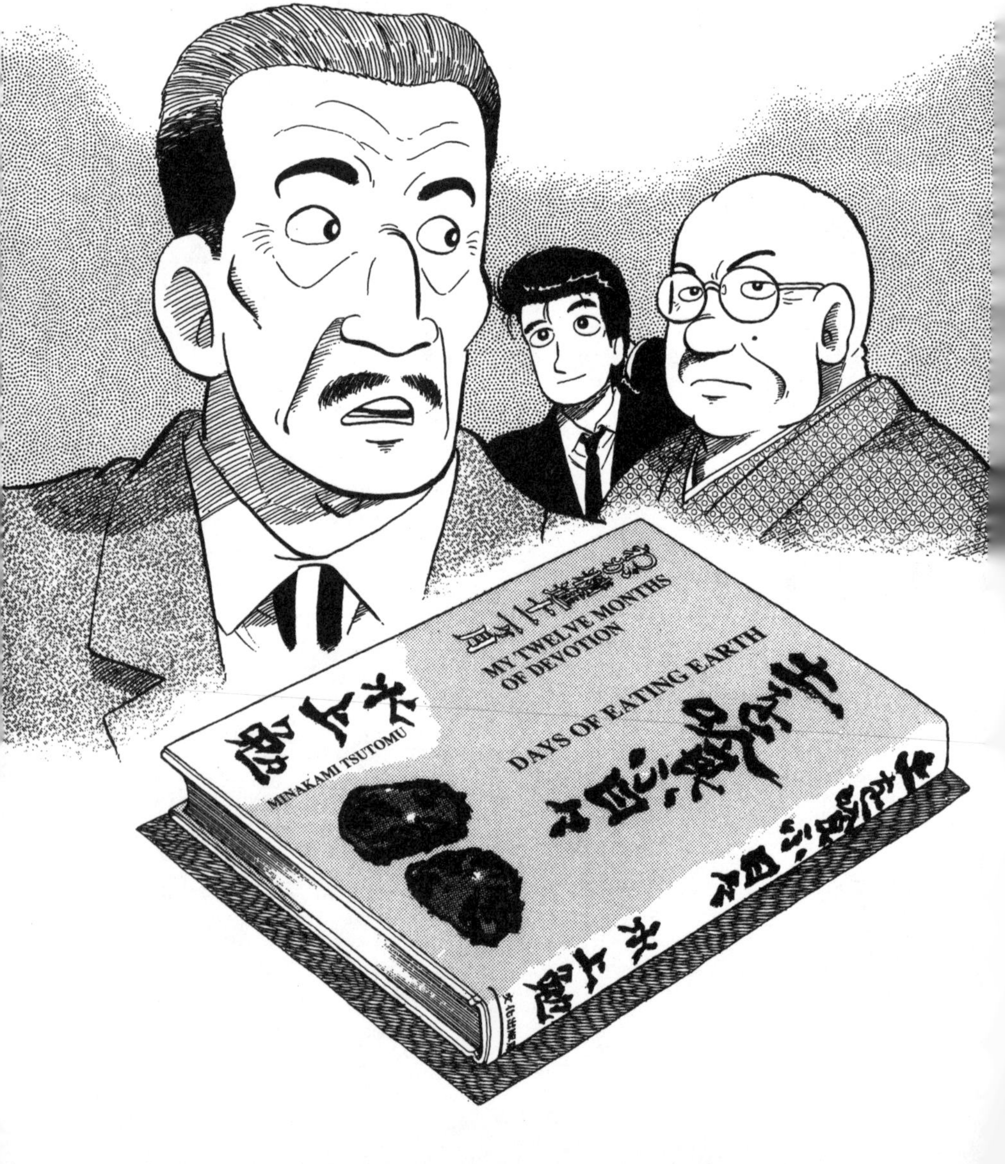
MY TWELVE MONTHS OF DEVOTION
DAYS OF EATING EARTH
MINAKAMI TSUTOMU

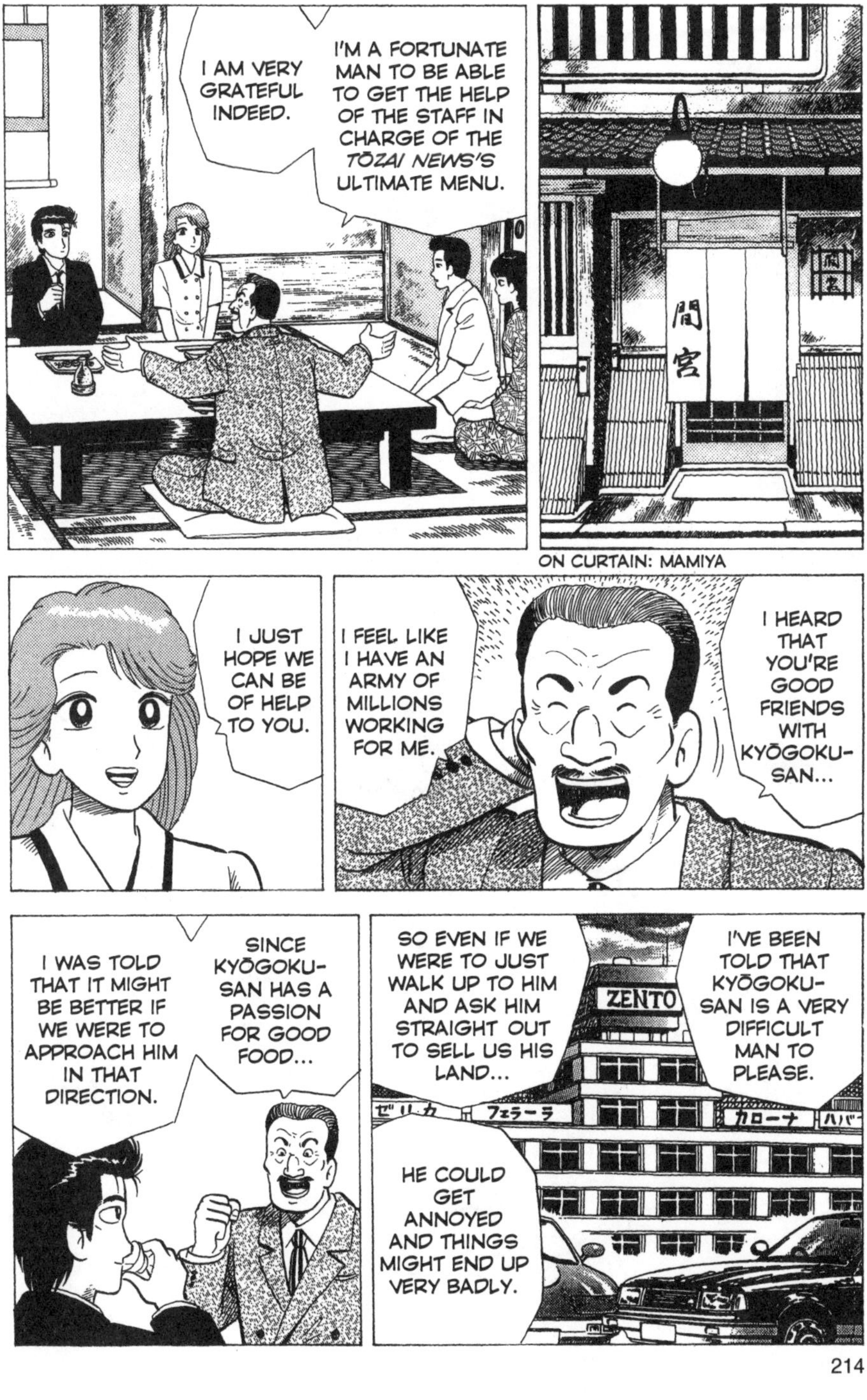
間宮
ON CURTAIN: MAMIYA
I'M A FORTUNATE MAN TO BE ABLE TO GET THE HELP OF THE STAFF IN CHARGE OF THE *TŌZAI NEWS*'S ULTIMATE MENU.
I AM VERY GRATEFUL INDEED.
I HEARD THAT YOU'RE GOOD FRIENDS WITH KYŌGOKU-SAN...
I FEEL LIKE I HAVE AN ARMY OF MILLIONS WORKING FOR ME.
I JUST HOPE WE CAN BE OF HELP TO YOU.
I'VE BEEN TOLD THAT KYŌGOKU-SAN IS A VERY DIFFICULT MAN TO PLEASE.
SO EVEN IF WE WERE TO JUST WALK UP TO HIM AND ASK HIM STRAIGHT OUT TO SELL US HIS LAND...
ZENTO
ゼリカ
フェラーラ
カローナ
HE COULD GET ANNOYED AND THINGS MIGHT END UP VERY BADLY.
SINCE KYŌGOKU-SAN HAS A PASSION FOR GOOD FOOD...
I WAS TOLD THAT IT MIGHT BE BETTER IF WE WERE TO APPROACH HIM IN THAT DIRECTION.

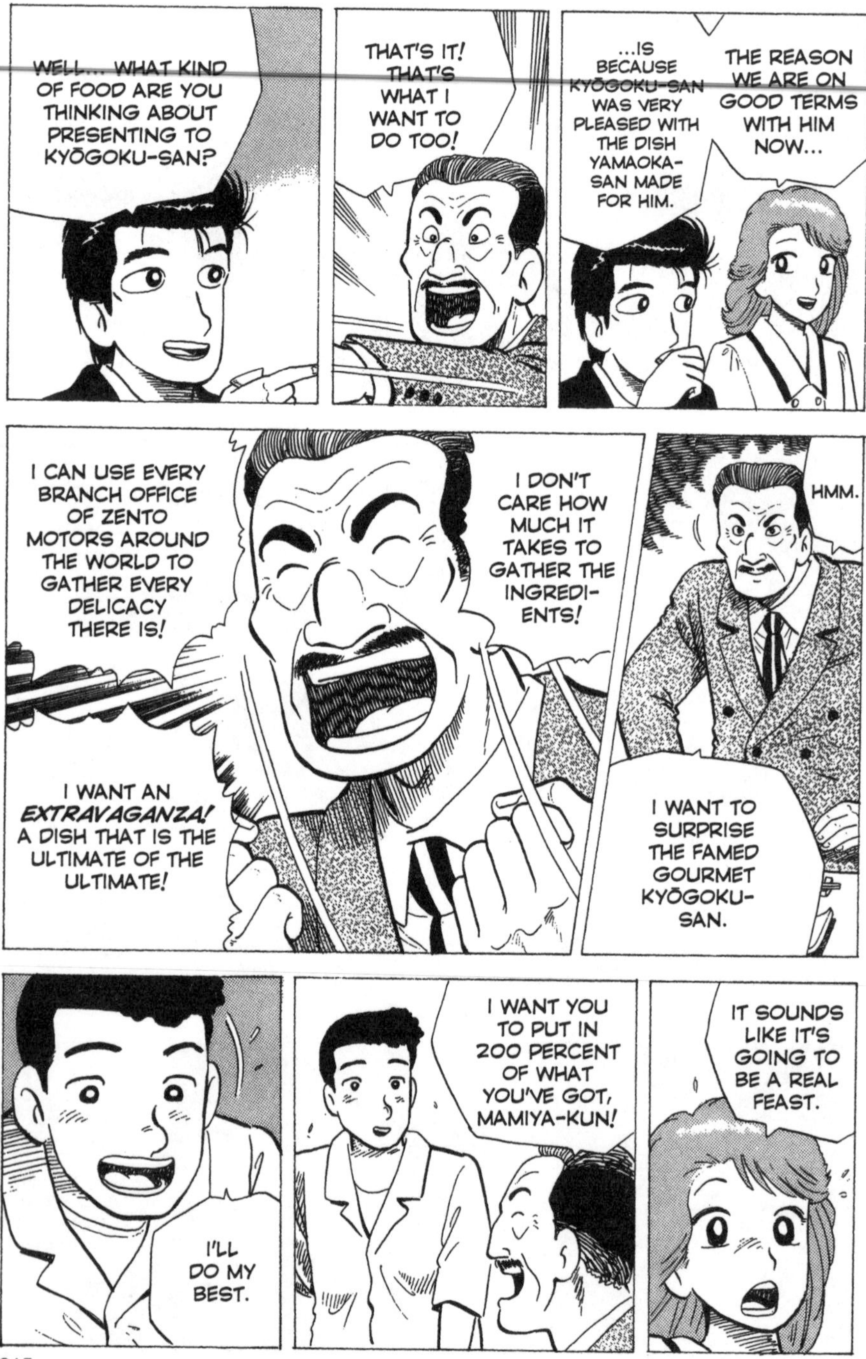
THE REASON WE ARE ON GOOD TERMS WITH HIM NOW...
...IS BECAUSE KYŌGOKU-SAN WAS VERY PLEASED WITH THE DISH YAMAOKA-SAN MADE FOR HIM.
THAT'S IT! THAT'S WHAT I WANT TO DO TOO!
WELL... WHAT KIND OF FOOD ARE YOU THINKING ABOUT PRESENTING TO KYŌGOKU-SAN?
HMM.
I WANT TO SURPRISE THE FAMED GOURMET KYŌGOKU-SAN.
I DON'T CARE HOW MUCH IT TAKES TO GATHER THE INGREDIENTS!
I CAN USE EVERY BRANCH OFFICE OF ZENTO MOTORS AROUND THE WORLD TO GATHER EVERY DELICACY THERE IS!
I WANT AN *EXTRAVAGANZA!* A DISH THAT IS THE ULTIMATE OF THE ULTIMATE!
IT SOUNDS LIKE IT'S GOING TO BE A REAL FEAST.
I WANT YOU TO PUT IN 200 PERCENT OF WHAT YOU'VE GOT, MAMIYA-KUN!
I'LL DO MY BEST.

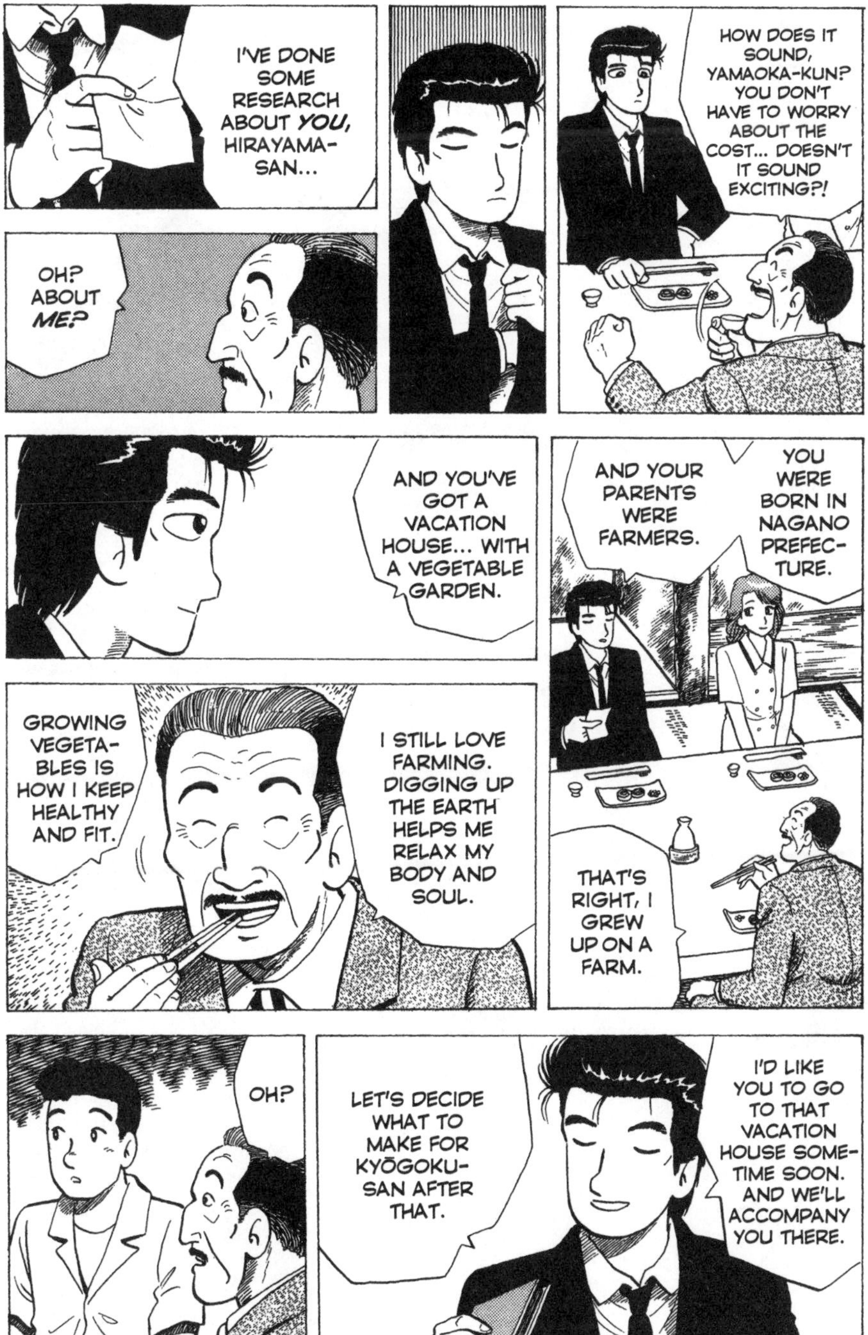
HOW DOES IT SOUND, YAMAOKA-KUN? YOU DON'T HAVE TO WORRY ABOUT THE COST... DOESN'T IT SOUND EXCITING?!
I'VE DONE SOME RESEARCH ABOUT *YOU,* HIRAYAMA-SAN...
OH? ABOUT *ME?*
YOU WERE BORN IN NAGANO PREFECTURE.
AND YOUR PARENTS WERE FARMERS.
THAT'S RIGHT, I GREW UP ON A FARM.
AND YOU'VE GOT A VACATION HOUSE... WITH A VEGETABLE GARDEN.
I STILL LOVE FARMING. DIGGING UP THE EARTH HELPS ME RELAX MY BODY AND SOUL.
GROWING VEGETABLES IS HOW I KEEP HEALTHY AND FIT.
I'D LIKE YOU TO GO TO THAT VACATION HOUSE SOMETIME SOON. AND WE'LL ACCOMPANY YOU THERE.
LET'S DECIDE WHAT TO MAKE FOR KYŌGOKU-SAN AFTER THAT.
OH?

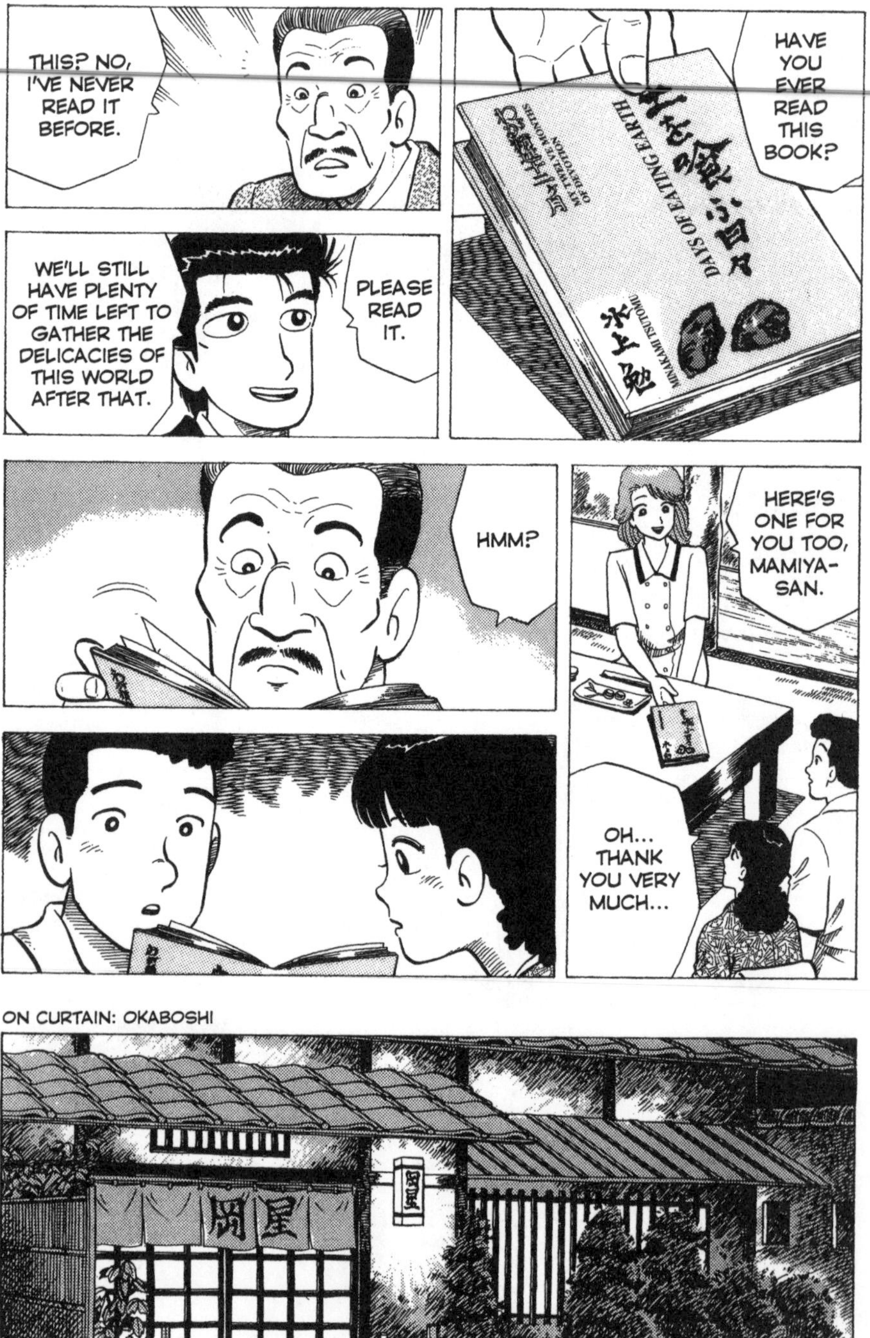
HAVE YOU EVER READ THIS BOOK?
DAYS OF EATING EARTH
MINAKAMI TSUTOMU
THIS? NO, I'VE NEVER READ IT BEFORE.
PLEASE READ IT.
WE'LL STILL HAVE PLENTY OF TIME LEFT TO GATHER THE DELICACIES OF THIS WORLD AFTER THAT.
HERE'S ONE FOR YOU TOO, MAMIYA-SAN.
OH... THANK YOU VERY MUCH...
HMM?
ON CURTAIN: OKABOSHI

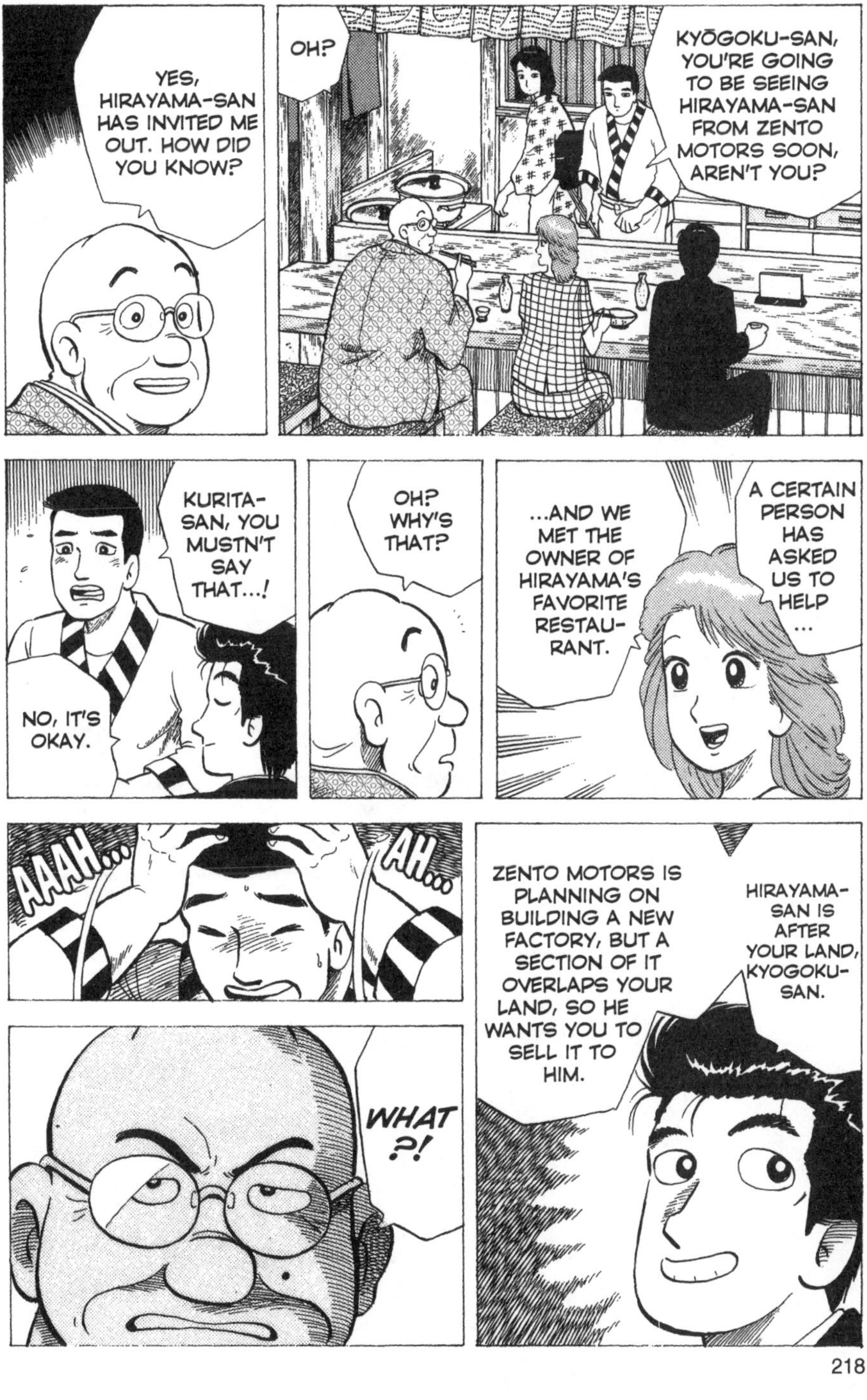
KYŌGOKU-SAN, YOU'RE GOING TO BE SEEING HIRAYAMA-SAN FROM ZENTO MOTORS SOON, AREN'T YOU?
OH?
YES, HIRAYAMA-SAN HAS INVITED ME OUT. HOW DID YOU KNOW?
A CERTAIN PERSON HAS ASKED US TO HELP ...
...AND WE MET THE OWNER OF HIRAYAMA'S FAVORITE RESTAU-RANT.
OH? WHY'S THAT?
KURITA-SAN, YOU MUSTN'T SAY THAT...!
NO, IT'S OKAY.
HIRAYAMA-SAN IS AFTER YOUR LAND, KYOGOKU-SAN.
ZENTO MOTORS IS PLANNING ON BUILDING A NEW FACTORY, BUT A SECTION OF IT OVERLAPS YOUR LAND, SO HE WANTS YOU TO SELL IT TO HIM.
AH...
AAAH...
WHAT ?!

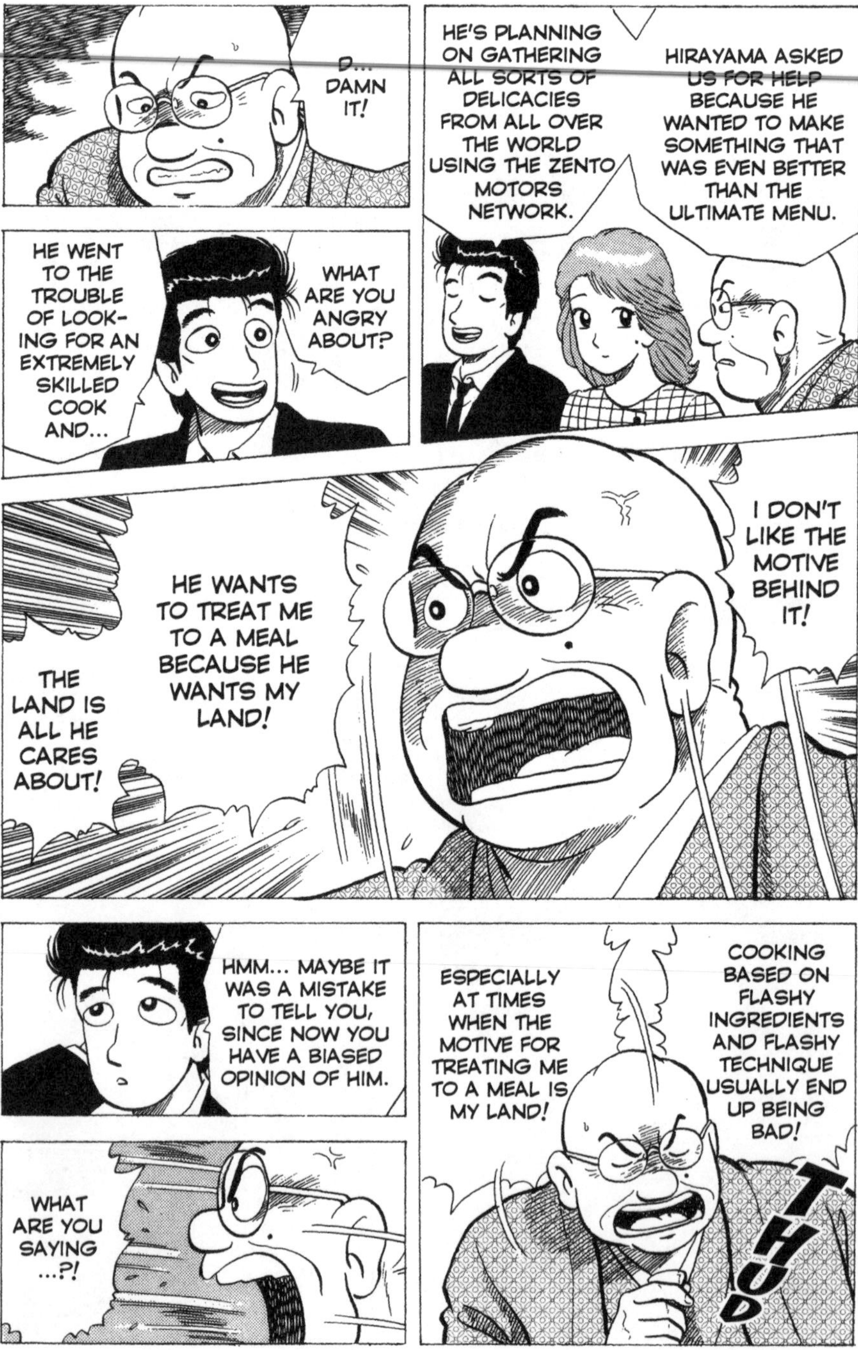
HIRAYAMA ASKED US FOR HELP BECAUSE HE WANTED TO MAKE SOMETHING THAT WAS EVEN BETTER THAN THE ULTIMATE MENU.
HE'S PLANNING ON GATHERING ALL SORTS OF DELICACIES FROM ALL OVER THE WORLD USING THE ZENTO MOTORS NETWORK.
D... DAMN IT!
WHAT ARE YOU ANGRY ABOUT?
HE WENT TO THE TROUBLE OF LOOK-ING FOR AN EXTREMELY SKILLED COOK AND...
I DON'T LIKE THE MOTIVE BEHIND IT!
HE WANTS TO TREAT ME TO A MEAL BECAUSE HE WANTS MY LAND!
THE LAND IS ALL HE CARES ABOUT!
COOKING BASED ON FLASHY INGREDIENTS AND FLASHY TECHNIQUE USUALLY END UP BEING BAD!
ESPECIALLY AT TIMES WHEN THE MOTIVE FOR TREATING ME TO A MEAL IS MY LAND!
THUD
HMM... MAYBE IT WAS A MISTAKE TO TELL YOU, SINCE NOW YOU HAVE A BIASED OPINION OF HIM.
WHAT ARE YOU SAYING ...?!

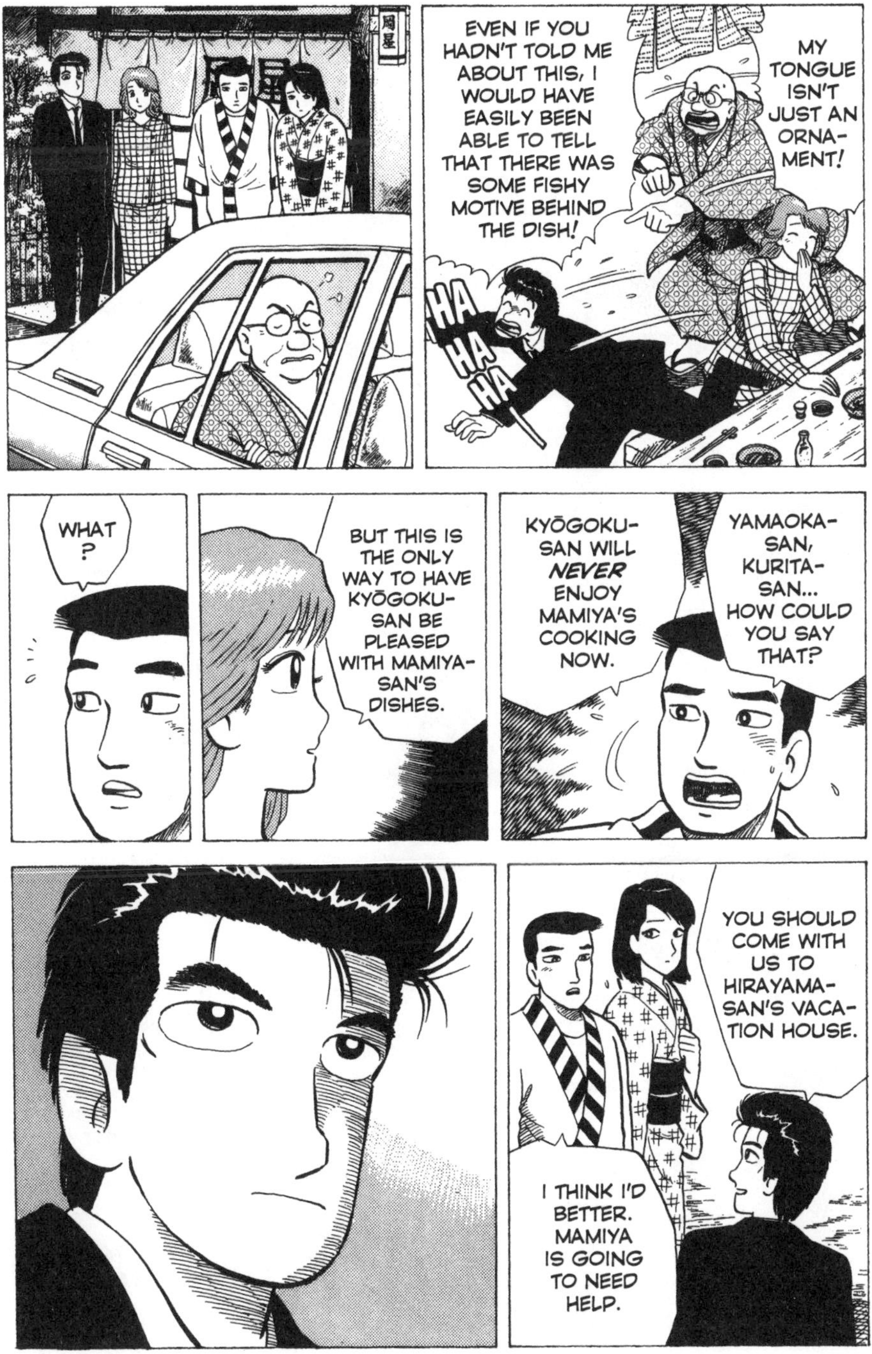
EVEN IF YOU HADN'T TOLD ME ABOUT THIS, I WOULD HAVE EASILY BEEN ABLE TO TELL THAT THERE WAS SOME FISHY MOTIVE BEHIND THE DISH!
MY TONGUE ISN'T JUST AN ORNA-MENT!
HA HA HA
YAMAOKA-SAN, KURITA-SAN... HOW COULD YOU SAY THAT?
KYŌGOKU-SAN WILL ***NEVER*** ENJOY MAMIYA'S COOKING NOW.
BUT THIS IS THE ONLY WAY TO HAVE KYŌGOKU-SAN BE PLEASED WITH MAMIYA-SAN'S DISHES.
WHAT?
YOU SHOULD COME WITH US TO HIRAYAMA-SAN'S VACA-TION HOUSE.
I THINK I'D BETTER. MAMIYA IS GOING TO NEED HELP.

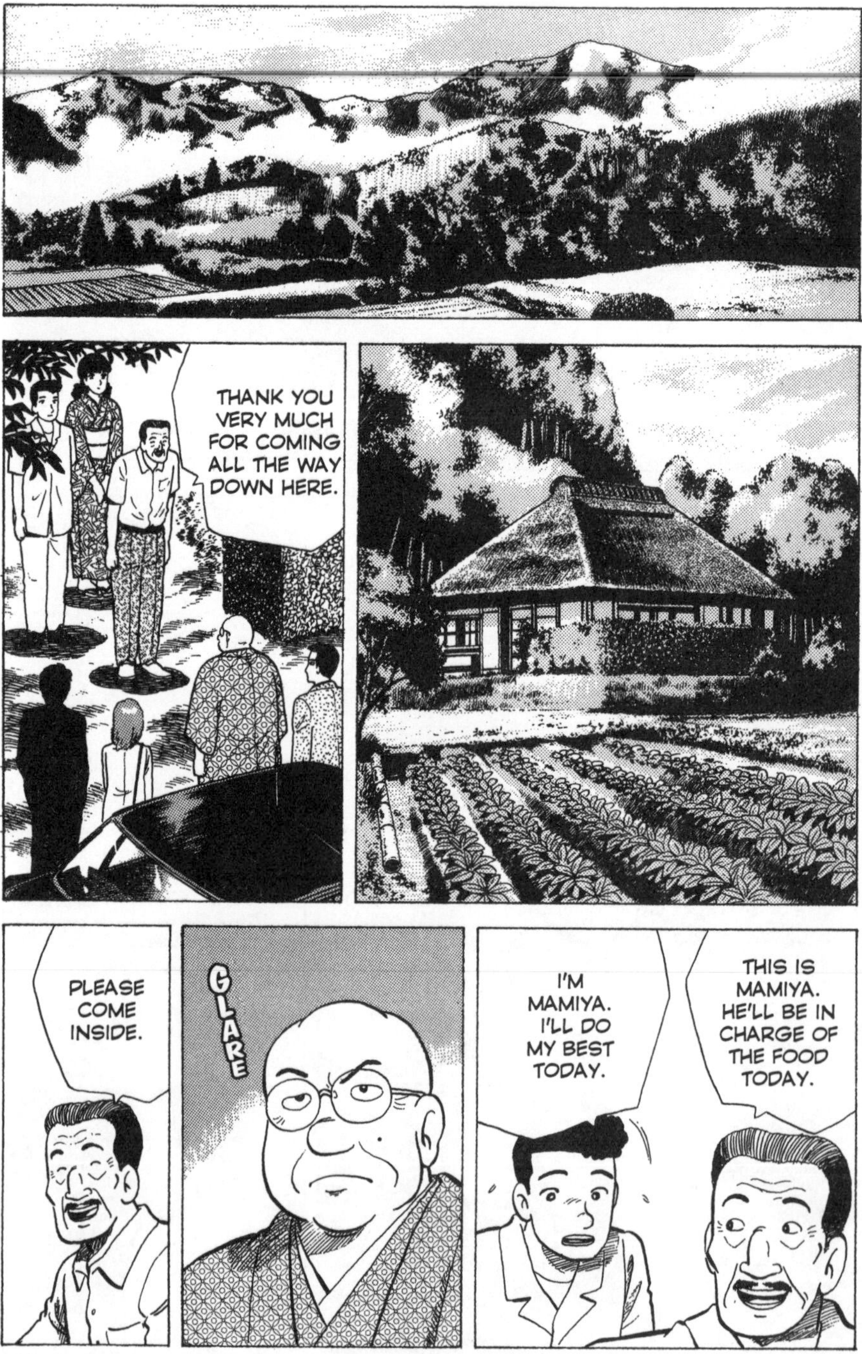
THANK YOU VERY MUCH FOR COMING ALL THE WAY DOWN HERE.
THIS IS MAMIYA. HE'LL BE IN CHARGE OF THE FOOD TODAY.
I'M MAMIYA. I'LL DO MY BEST TODAY.
GLARE
PLEASE COME INSIDE.

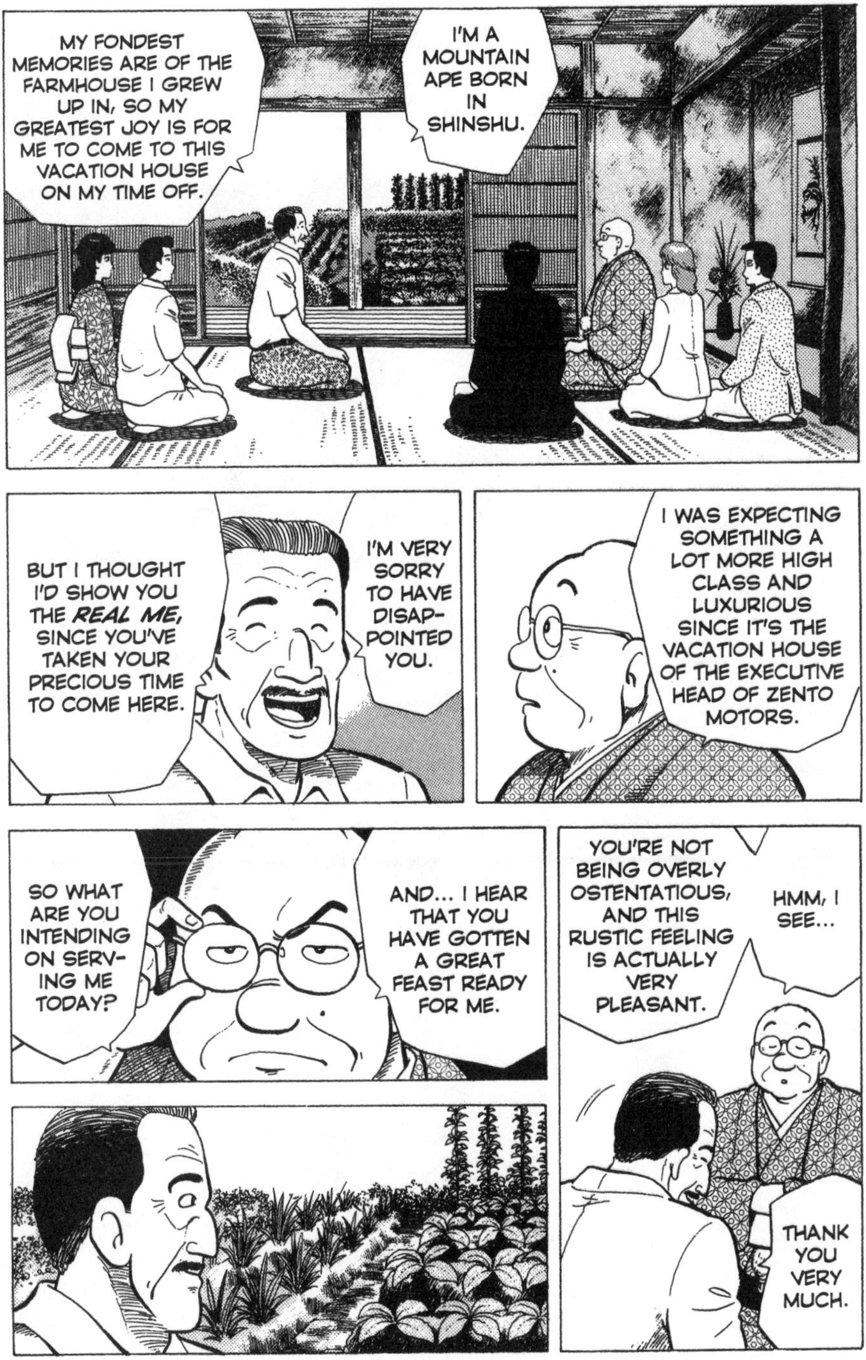
I'M A MOUNTAIN APE BORN IN SHINSHU.
MY FONDEST MEMORIES ARE OF THE FARMHOUSE I GREW UP IN, SO MY GREATEST JOY IS FOR ME TO COME TO THIS VACATION HOUSE ON MY TIME OFF.
I WAS EXPECTING SOMETHING A LOT MORE HIGH CLASS AND LUXURIOUS SINCE IT'S THE VACATION HOUSE OF THE EXECUTIVE HEAD OF ZENTO MOTORS.
I'M VERY SORRY TO HAVE DISAP-POINTED YOU.
BUT I THOUGHT I'D SHOW YOU THE ***REAL ME,*** SINCE YOU'VE TAKEN YOUR PRECIOUS TIME TO COME HERE.
HMM, I SEE...
YOU'RE NOT BEING OVERLY OSTENTATIOUS, AND THIS RUSTIC FEELING IS ACTUALLY VERY PLEASANT.
THANK YOU VERY MUCH.
AND... I HEAR THAT YOU HAVE GOTTEN A GREAT FEAST READY FOR ME.
SO WHAT ARE YOU INTENDING ON SERV-ING ME TODAY?

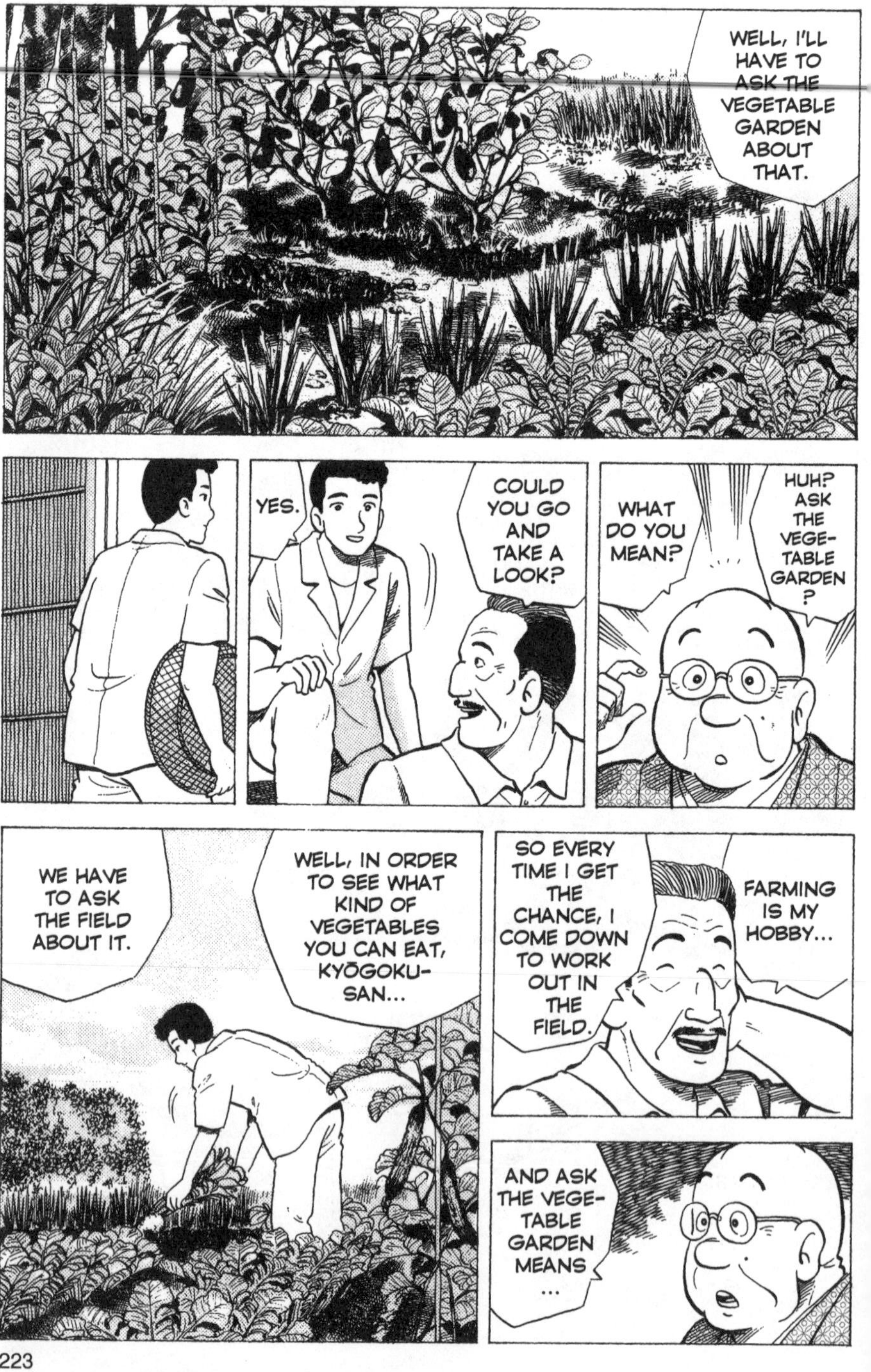
WELL, I'LL HAVE TO ASK THE VEGETABLE GARDEN ABOUT THAT.
HUH? ASK THE VEGE-TABLE GARDEN ?
WHAT DO YOU MEAN?
COULD YOU GO AND TAKE A LOOK?
YES.
FARMING IS MY HOBBY...
SO EVERY TIME I GET THE CHANCE, I COME DOWN TO WORK OUT IN THE FIELD.
AND ASK THE VEGE-TABLE GARDEN MEANS ...
WELL, IN ORDER TO SEE WHAT KIND OF VEGETABLES YOU CAN EAT, KYŌGOKU-SAN...
WE HAVE TO ASK THE FIELD ABOUT IT.

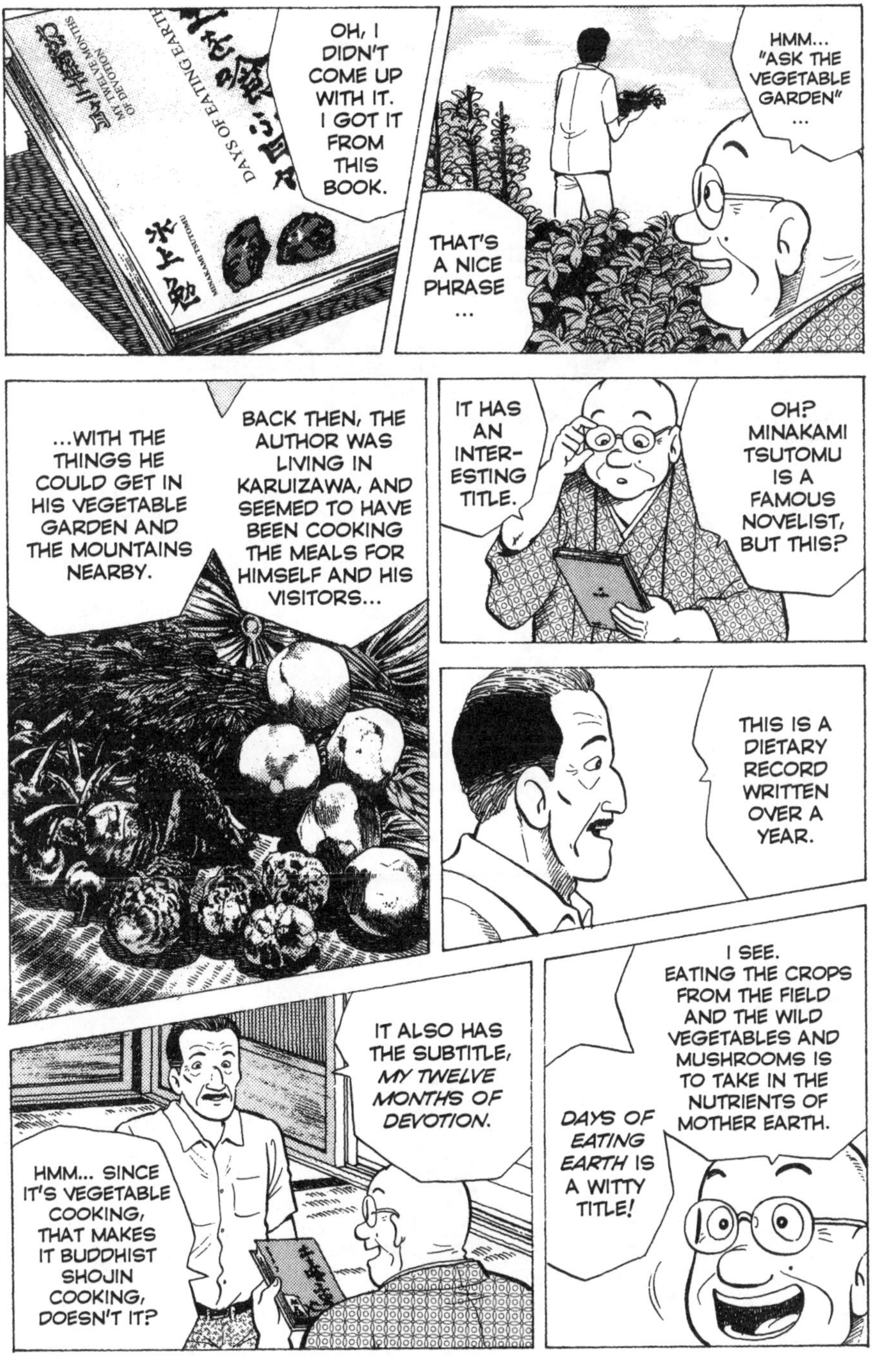
HMM... "ASK THE VEGETABLE GARDEN" ...
THAT'S A NICE PHRASE ...
OH, I DIDN'T COME UP WITH IT. I GOT IT FROM THIS BOOK.
DAYS OF EATING EARTH
MY TWELVE MONTHS OF DEVOTION
OH? MINAKAMI TSUTOMU IS A FAMOUS NOVELIST, BUT THIS?
IT HAS AN INTER-ESTING TITLE.
THIS IS A DIETARY RECORD WRITTEN OVER A YEAR.
BACK THEN, THE AUTHOR WAS LIVING IN KARUIZAWA, AND SEEMED TO HAVE BEEN COOKING THE MEALS FOR HIMSELF AND HIS VISITORS...
...WITH THE THINGS HE COULD GET IN HIS VEGETABLE GARDEN AND THE MOUNTAINS NEARBY.
I SEE. EATING THE CROPS FROM THE FIELD AND THE WILD VEGETABLES AND MUSHROOMS IS TO TAKE IN THE NUTRIENTS OF MOTHER EARTH.
DAYS OF EATING EARTH IS A WITTY TITLE!
IT ALSO HAS THE SUBTITLE, *MY TWELVE MONTHS OF DEVOTION*.
HMM... SINCE IT'S VEGETABLE COOKING, THAT MAKES IT BUDDHIST SHOJIN COOKING, DOESN'T IT?

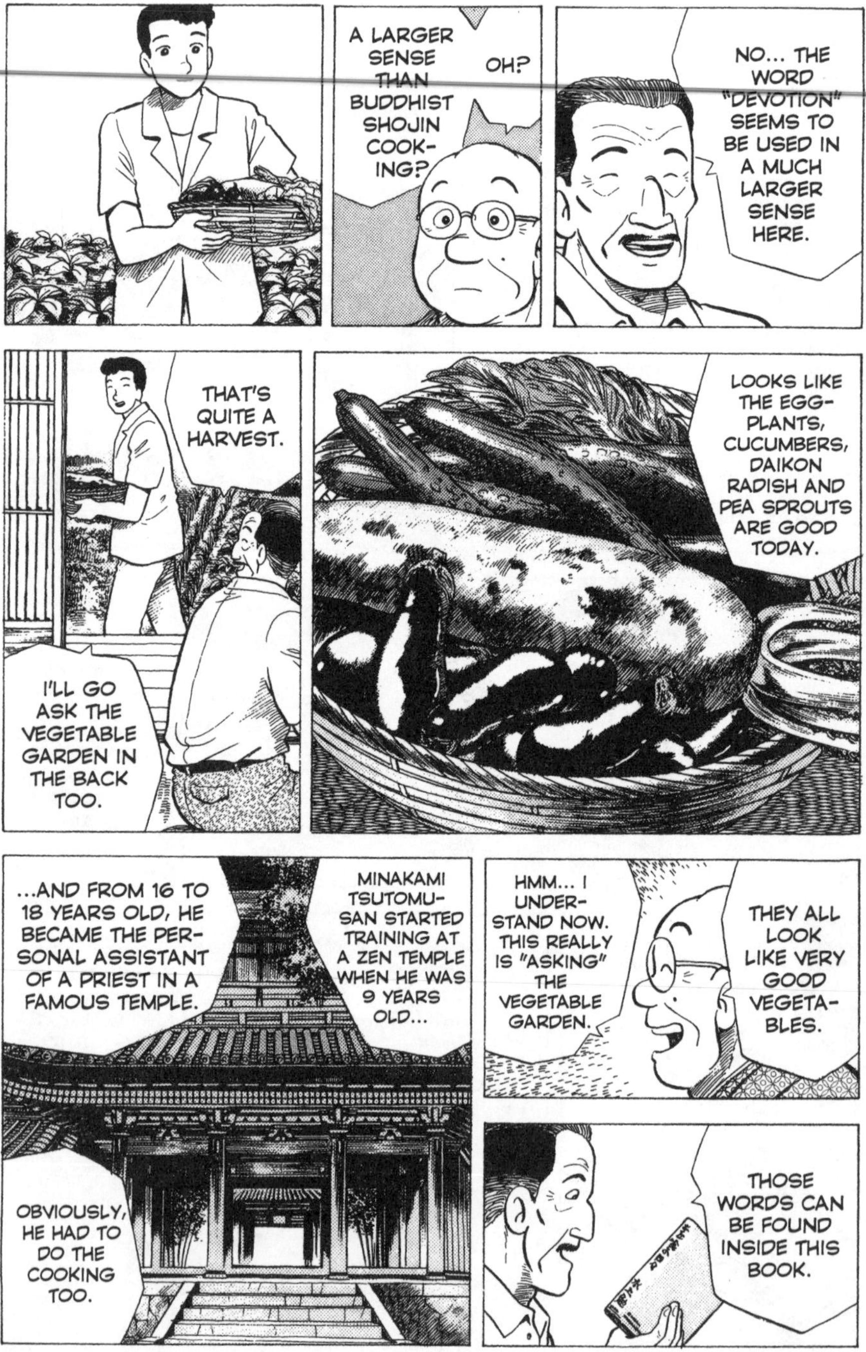
NO... THE WORD "DEVOTION" SEEMS TO BE USED IN A MUCH LARGER SENSE HERE.
OH?
A LARGER SENSE THAN BUDDHIST SHOJIN COOKING?
LOOKS LIKE THE EGGPLANTS, CUCUMBERS, DAIKON RADISH AND PEA SPROUTS ARE GOOD TODAY.
THAT'S QUITE A HARVEST.
I'LL GO ASK THE VEGETABLE GARDEN IN THE BACK TOO.
THEY ALL LOOK LIKE VERY GOOD VEGETABLES.
HMM... I UNDERSTAND NOW. THIS REALLY IS "ASKING" THE VEGETABLE GARDEN.
THOSE WORDS CAN BE FOUND INSIDE THIS BOOK.
MINAKAMI TSUTOMU-SAN STARTED TRAINING AT A ZEN TEMPLE WHEN HE WAS 9 YEARS OLD...
...AND FROM 16 TO 18 YEARS OLD, HE BECAME THE PERSONAL ASSISTANT OF A PRIEST IN A FAMOUS TEMPLE.
OBVIOUSLY, HE HAD TO DO THE COOKING TOO.

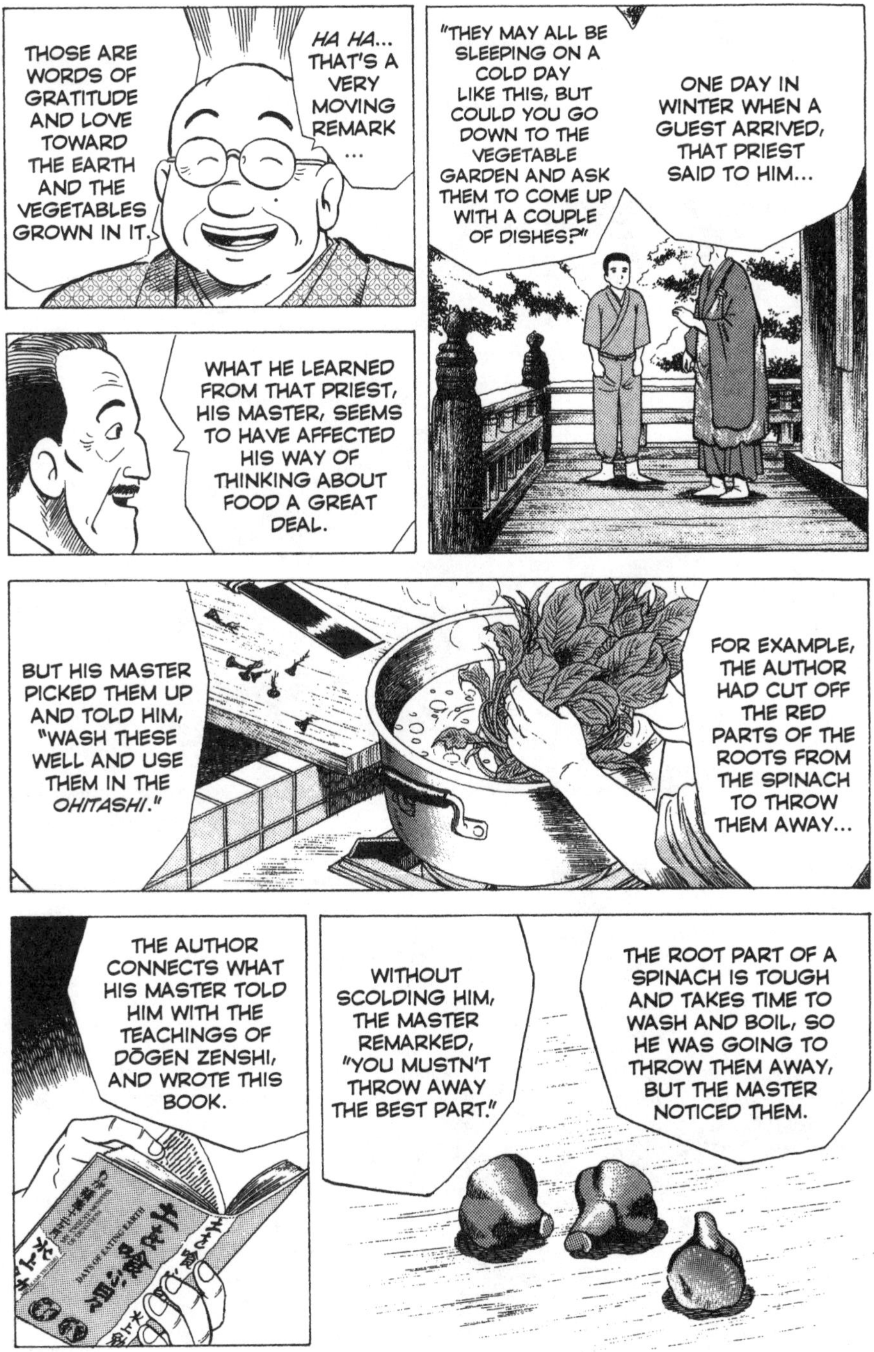
ONE DAY IN WINTER WHEN A GUEST ARRIVED, THAT PRIEST SAID TO HIM...
"THEY MAY ALL BE SLEEPING ON A COLD DAY LIKE THIS, BUT COULD YOU GO DOWN TO THE VEGETABLE GARDEN AND ASK THEM TO COME UP WITH A COUPLE OF DISHES?"
HA HA... THAT'S A VERY MOVING REMARK ...
THOSE ARE WORDS OF GRATITUDE AND LOVE TOWARD THE EARTH AND THE VEGETABLES GROWN IN IT.
WHAT HE LEARNED FROM THAT PRIEST, HIS MASTER, SEEMS TO HAVE AFFECTED HIS WAY OF THINKING ABOUT FOOD A GREAT DEAL.
FOR EXAMPLE, THE AUTHOR HAD CUT OFF THE RED PARTS OF THE ROOTS FROM THE SPINACH TO THROW THEM AWAY...
BUT HIS MASTER PICKED THEM UP AND TOLD HIM, "WASH THESE WELL AND USE THEM IN THE *OHITASHI*."
THE ROOT PART OF A SPINACH IS TOUGH AND TAKES TIME TO WASH AND BOIL, SO HE WAS GOING TO THROW THEM AWAY, BUT THE MASTER NOTICED THEM.
WITHOUT SCOLDING HIM, THE MASTER REMARKED, "YOU MUSTN'T THROW AWAY THE BEST PART."
THE AUTHOR CONNECTS WHAT HIS MASTER TOLD HIM WITH THE TEACHINGS OF DŌGEN ZENSHI, AND WROTE THIS BOOK.

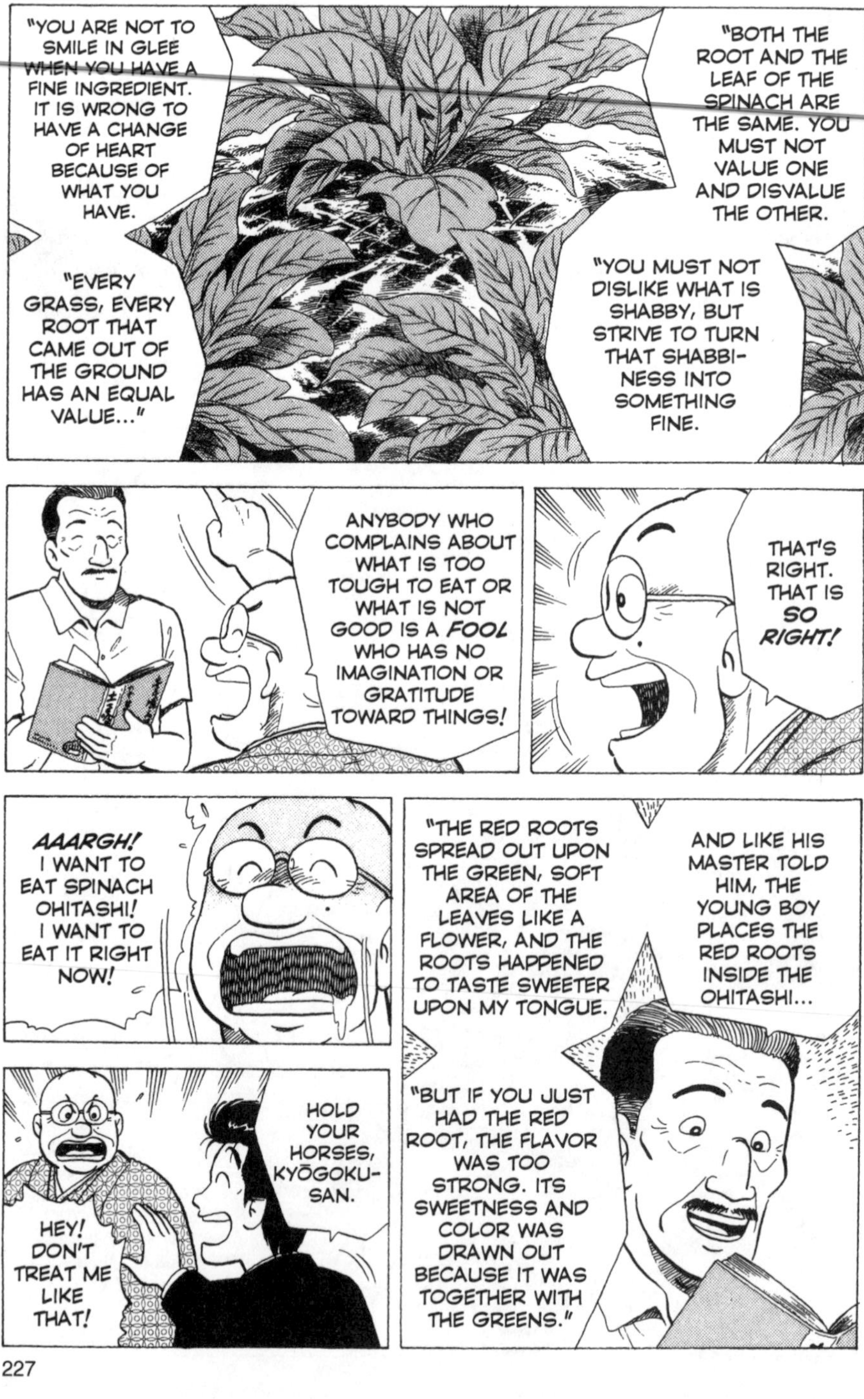
"BOTH THE ROOT AND THE LEAF OF THE SPINACH ARE THE SAME. YOU MUST NOT VALUE ONE AND DISVALUE THE OTHER.
"YOU MUST NOT DISLIKE WHAT IS SHABBY, BUT STRIVE TO TURN THAT SHABBINESS INTO SOMETHING FINE.
"YOU ARE NOT TO SMILE IN GLEE WHEN YOU HAVE A FINE INGREDIENT. IT IS WRONG TO HAVE A CHANGE OF HEART BECAUSE OF WHAT YOU HAVE.
"EVERY GRASS, EVERY ROOT THAT CAME OUT OF THE GROUND HAS AN EQUAL VALUE..."
THAT'S RIGHT. THAT IS *SO RIGHT!*
ANYBODY WHO COMPLAINS ABOUT WHAT IS TOO TOUGH TO EAT OR WHAT IS NOT GOOD IS A *FOOL* WHO HAS NO IMAGINATION OR GRATITUDE TOWARD THINGS!
AND LIKE HIS MASTER TOLD HIM, THE YOUNG BOY PLACES THE RED ROOTS INSIDE THE OHITASHI...
"THE RED ROOTS SPREAD OUT UPON THE GREEN, SOFT AREA OF THE LEAVES LIKE A FLOWER, AND THE ROOTS HAPPENED TO TASTE SWEETER UPON MY TONGUE.
"BUT IF YOU JUST HAD THE RED ROOT, THE FLAVOR WAS TOO STRONG. ITS SWEETNESS AND COLOR WAS DRAWN OUT BECAUSE IT WAS TOGETHER WITH THE GREENS."
AAARGH! I WANT TO EAT SPINACH OHITASHI! I WANT TO EAT IT RIGHT NOW!
HOLD YOUR HORSES, KYŌGOKU-SAN.
HEY! DON'T TREAT ME LIKE THAT!

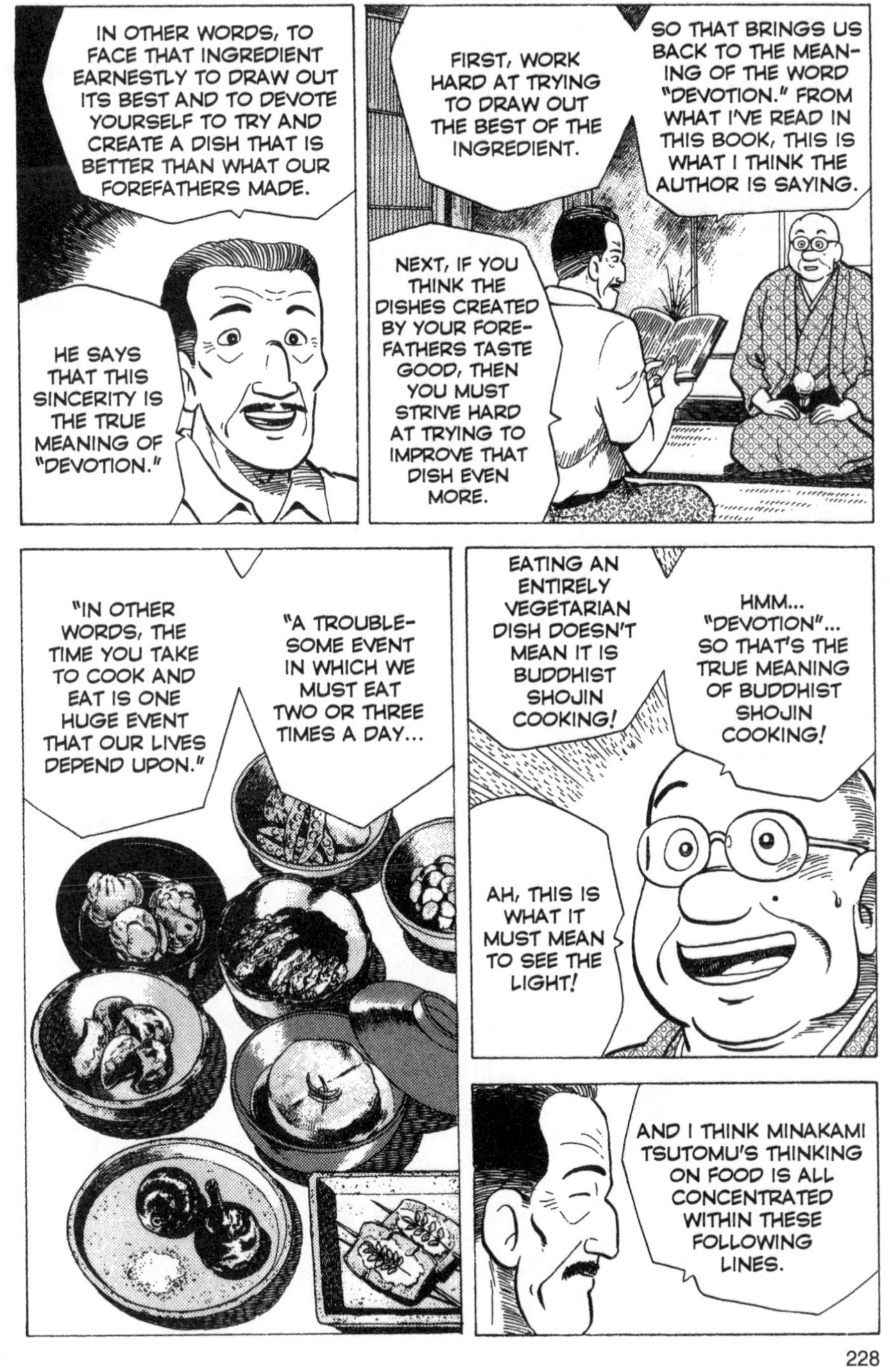
SO THAT BRINGS US BACK TO THE MEAN-ING OF THE WORD "DEVOTION." FROM WHAT I'VE READ IN THIS BOOK, THIS IS WHAT I THINK THE AUTHOR IS SAYING.
FIRST, WORK HARD AT TRYING TO DRAW OUT THE BEST OF THE INGREDIENT.
NEXT, IF YOU THINK THE DISHES CREATED BY YOUR FORE-FATHERS TASTE GOOD, THEN YOU MUST STRIVE HARD AT TRYING TO IMPROVE THAT DISH EVEN MORE.
IN OTHER WORDS, TO FACE THAT INGREDIENT EARNESTLY TO DRAW OUT ITS BEST AND TO DEVOTE YOURSELF TO TRY AND CREATE A DISH THAT IS BETTER THAN WHAT OUR FOREFATHERS MADE.
HE SAYS THAT THIS SINCERITY IS THE TRUE MEANING OF "DEVOTION."
HMM... "DEVOTION"... SO THAT'S THE TRUE MEANING OF BUDDHIST SHOJIN COOKING!
EATING AN ENTIRELY VEGETARIAN DISH DOESN'T MEAN IT IS BUDDHIST SHOJIN COOKING!
AH, THIS IS WHAT IT MUST MEAN TO SEE THE LIGHT!
AND I THINK MINAKAMI TSUTOMU'S THINKING ON FOOD IS ALL CONCENTRATED WITHIN THESE FOLLOWING LINES.
"A TROUBLE-SOME EVENT IN WHICH WE MUST EAT TWO OR THREE TIMES A DAY...
"IN OTHER WORDS, THE TIME YOU TAKE TO COOK AND EAT IS ONE HUGE EVENT THAT OUR LIVES DEPEND UPON."

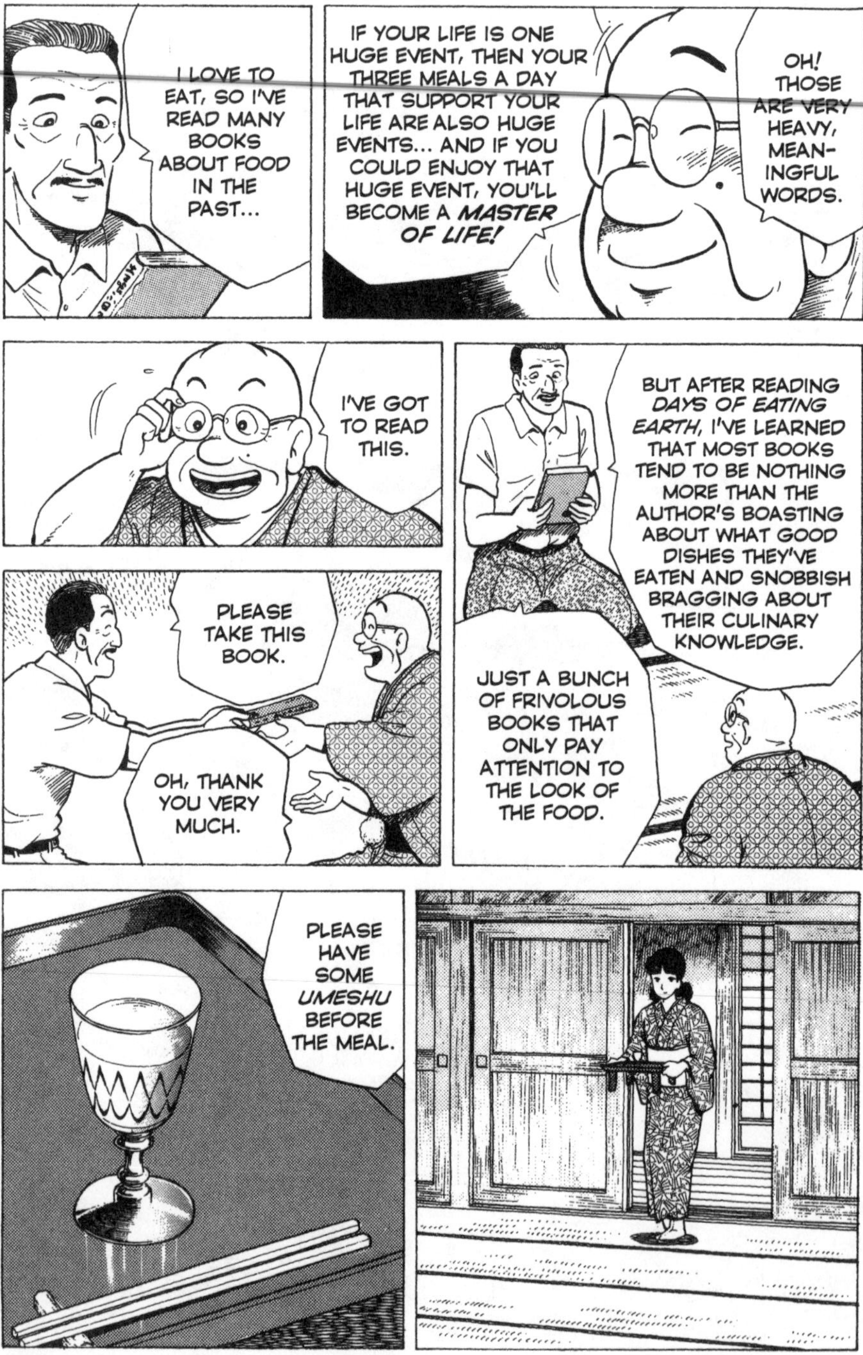

IF YOUR LIFE IS ONE HUGE EVENT, THEN YOUR THREE MEALS A DAY THAT SUPPORT YOUR LIFE ARE ALSO HUGE EVENTS... AND IF YOU COULD ENJOY THAT HUGE EVENT, YOU'LL BECOME A *MASTER OF LIFE!*
OH! THOSE ARE VERY HEAVY, MEAN-INGFUL WORDS.
I LOVE TO EAT, SO I'VE READ MANY BOOKS ABOUT FOOD IN THE PAST...
BUT AFTER READING *DAYS OF EATING EARTH*, I'VE LEARNED THAT MOST BOOKS TEND TO BE NOTHING MORE THAN THE AUTHOR'S BOASTING ABOUT WHAT GOOD DISHES THEY'VE EATEN AND SNOBBISH BRAGGING ABOUT THEIR CULINARY KNOWLEDGE.
JUST A BUNCH OF FRIVOLOUS BOOKS THAT ONLY PAY ATTENTION TO THE LOOK OF THE FOOD.
I'VE GOT TO READ THIS.
PLEASE TAKE THIS BOOK.
OH, THANK YOU VERY MUCH.
PLEASE HAVE SOME *UMESHU* BEFORE THE MEAL.

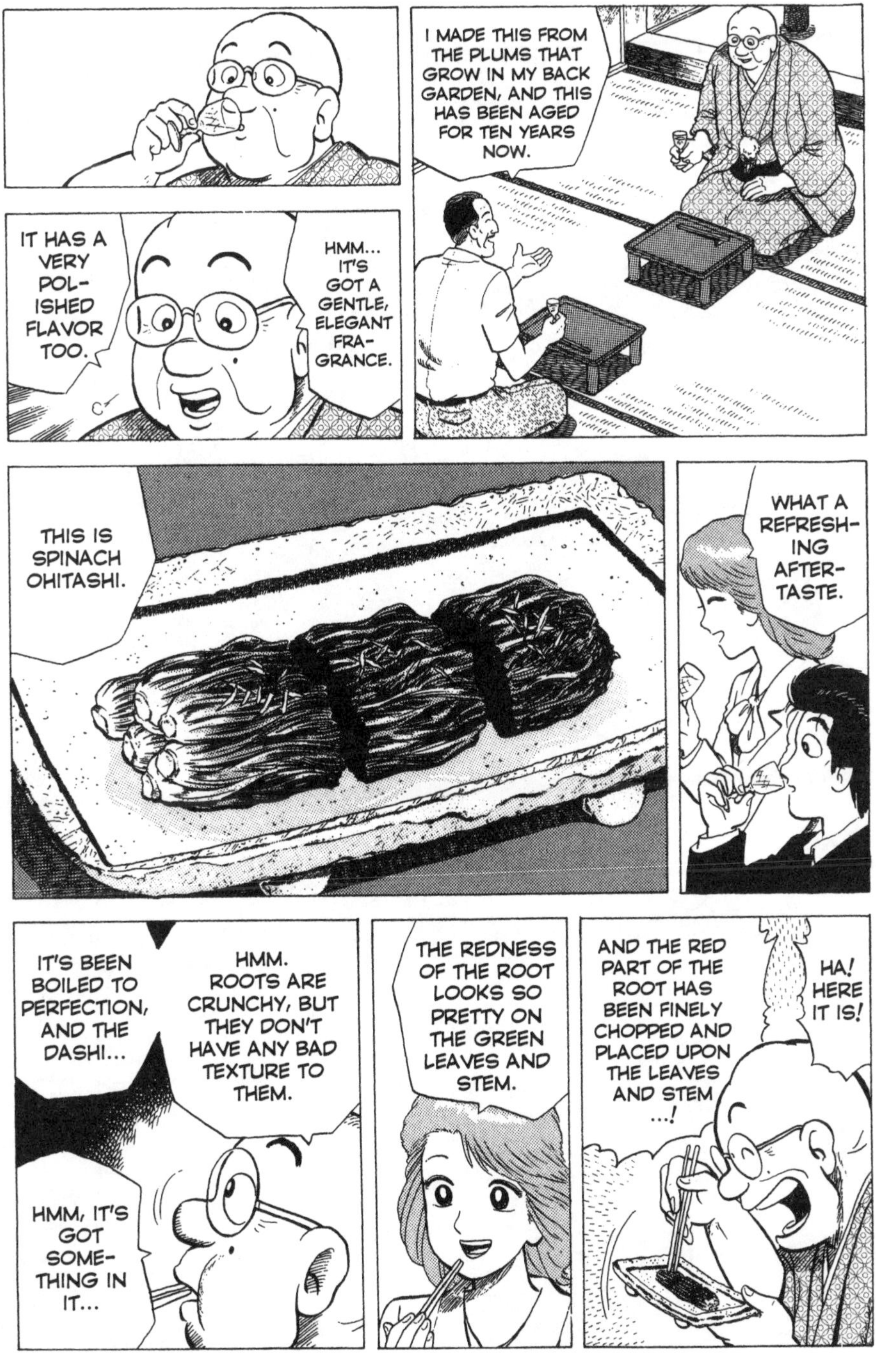

I MADE THIS FROM THE PLUMS THAT GROW IN MY BACK GARDEN, AND THIS HAS BEEN AGED FOR TEN YEARS NOW.
HMM... IT'S GOT A GENTLE, ELEGANT FRAGRANCE.
IT HAS A VERY POLISHED FLAVOR TOO.
WHAT A REFRESHING AFTERTASTE.
THIS IS SPINACH OHITASHI.
HA! HERE IT IS!
AND THE RED PART OF THE ROOT HAS BEEN FINELY CHOPPED AND PLACED UPON THE LEAVES AND STEM ...!
THE REDNESS OF THE ROOT LOOKS SO PRETTY ON THE GREEN LEAVES AND STEM.
HMM. ROOTS ARE CRUNCHY, BUT THEY DON'T HAVE ANY BAD TEXTURE TO THEM.
IT'S BEEN BOILED TO PERFECTION, AND THE DASHI...
HMM, IT'S GOT SOMETHING IN IT...

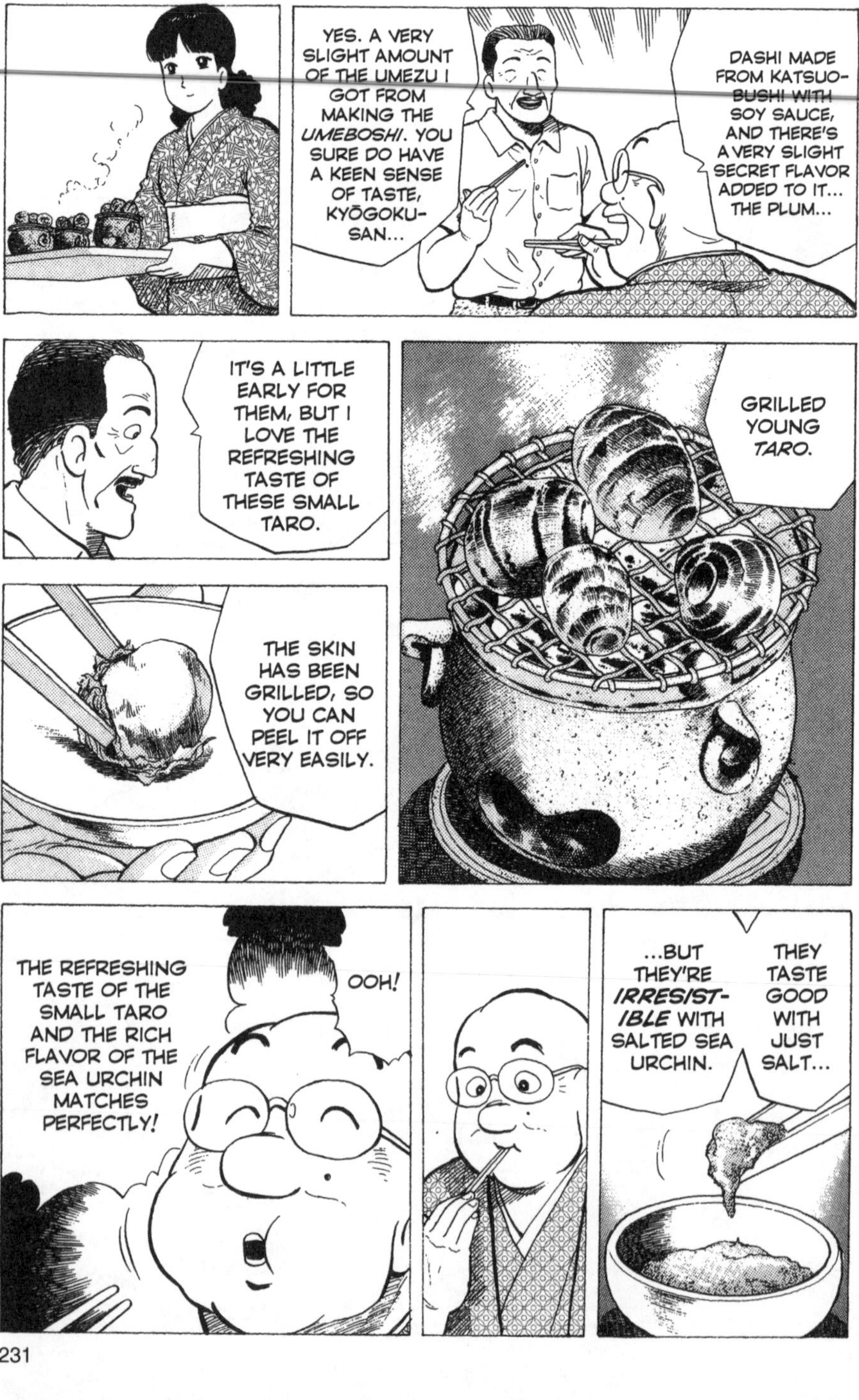
DASHI MADE FROM KATSUO-BUSHI WITH SOY SAUCE, AND THERE'S A VERY SLIGHT SECRET FLAVOR ADDED TO IT... THE PLUM...
YES. A VERY SLIGHT AMOUNT OF THE UMEZU I GOT FROM MAKING THE *UMEBOSHI*. YOU SURE DO HAVE A KEEN SENSE OF TASTE, KYŌGOKU-SAN...
GRILLED YOUNG *TARO*.
IT'S A LITTLE EARLY FOR THEM, BUT I LOVE THE REFRESHING TASTE OF THESE SMALL TARO.
THE SKIN HAS BEEN GRILLED, SO YOU CAN PEEL IT OFF VERY EASILY.
THEY TASTE GOOD WITH JUST SALT...
...BUT THEY'RE *IRRESIST-IBLE* WITH SALTED SEA URCHIN.
OOH!
THE REFRESHING TASTE OF THE SMALL TARO AND THE RICH FLAVOR OF THE SEA URCHIN MATCHES PERFECTLY!

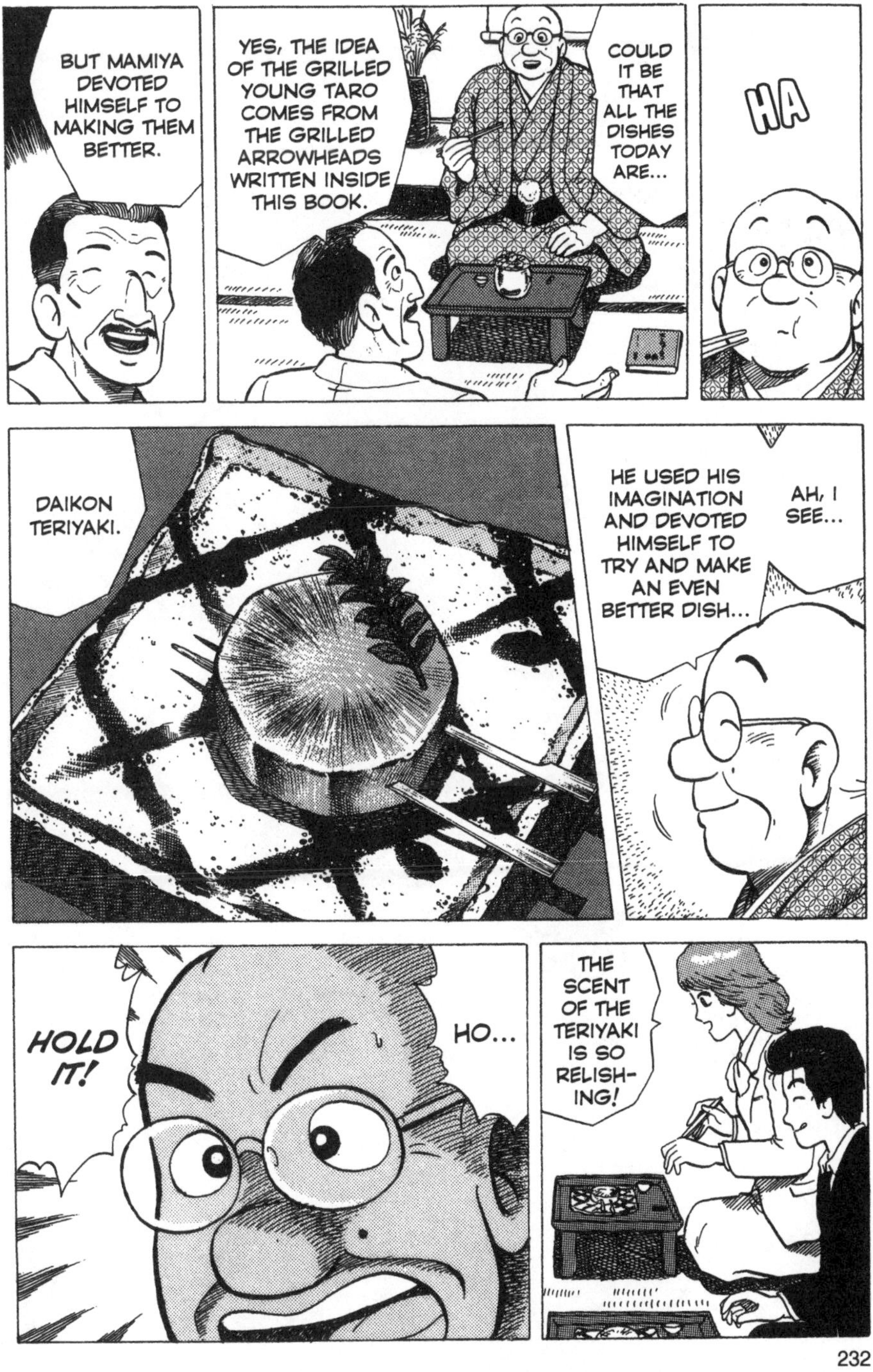
HA
COULD IT BE THAT ALL THE DISHES TODAY ARE...
YES, THE IDEA OF THE GRILLED YOUNG TARO COMES FROM THE GRILLED ARROWHEADS WRITTEN INSIDE THIS BOOK.
BUT MAMIYA DEVOTED HIMSELF TO MAKING THEM BETTER.
AH, I SEE...
HE USED HIS IMAGINATION AND DEVOTED HIMSELF TO TRY AND MAKE AN EVEN BETTER DISH...
DAIKON TERIYAKI.
THE SCENT OF THE TERIYAKI IS SO RELISH-ING!
HO...
HOLD IT!

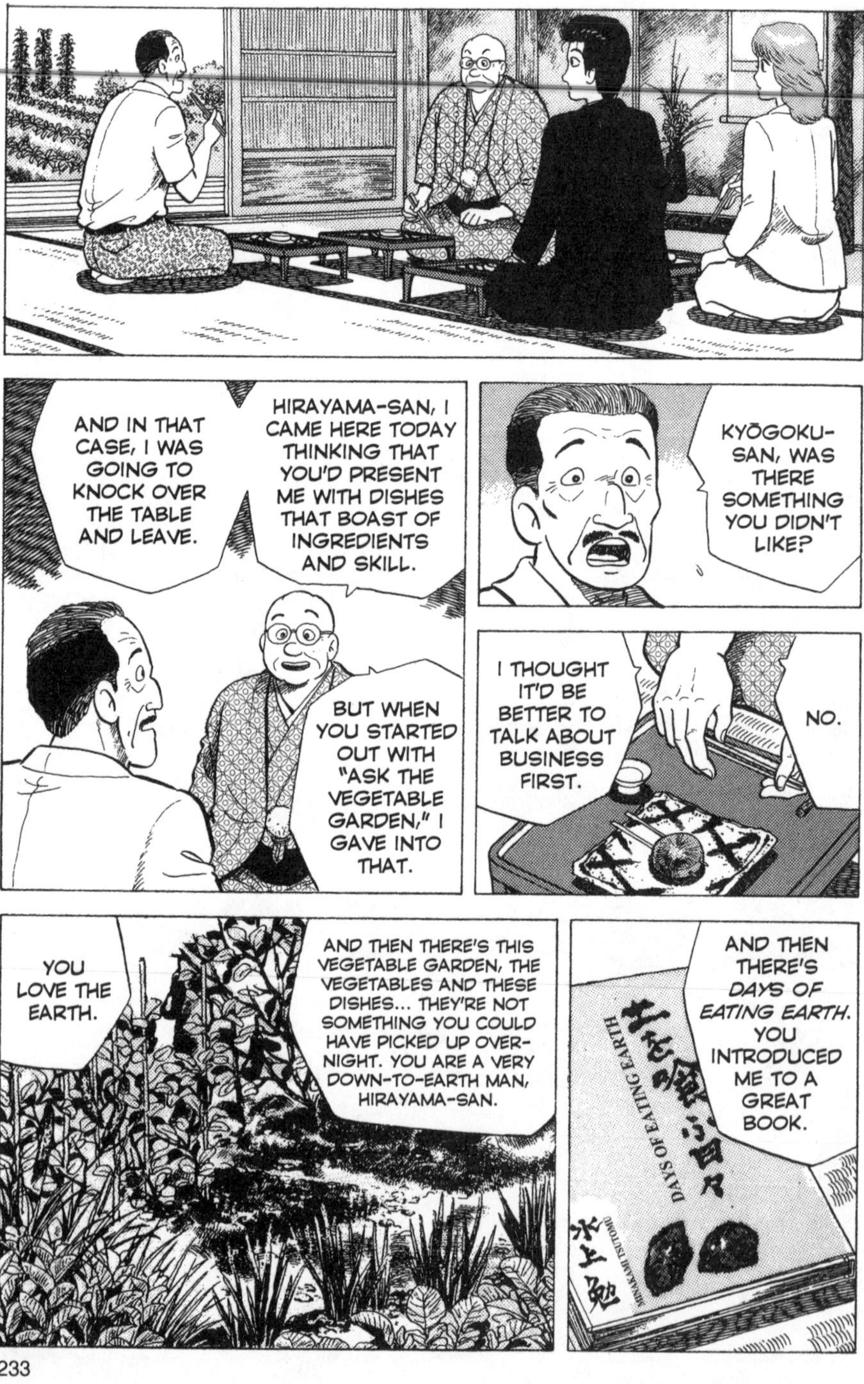
KYŌGOKU-SAN, WAS THERE SOMETHING YOU DIDN'T LIKE?
NO.
I THOUGHT IT'D BE BETTER TO TALK ABOUT BUSINESS FIRST.
HIRAYAMA-SAN, I CAME HERE TODAY THINKING THAT YOU'D PRESENT ME WITH DISHES THAT BOAST OF INGREDIENTS AND SKILL.
AND IN THAT CASE, I WAS GOING TO KNOCK OVER THE TABLE AND LEAVE.
BUT WHEN YOU STARTED OUT WITH "ASK THE VEGETABLE GARDEN," I GAVE INTO THAT.
AND THEN THERE'S *DAYS OF EATING EARTH*. YOU INTRODUCED ME TO A GREAT BOOK.
土を喰う日々
DAYS OF EATING EARTH
水上勉
AND THEN THERE'S THIS VEGETABLE GARDEN, THE VEGETABLES AND THESE DISHES... THEY'RE NOT SOMETHING YOU COULD HAVE PICKED UP OVER-NIGHT. YOU ARE A VERY DOWN-TO-EARTH MAN, HIRAYAMA-SAN.
YOU LOVE THE EARTH.

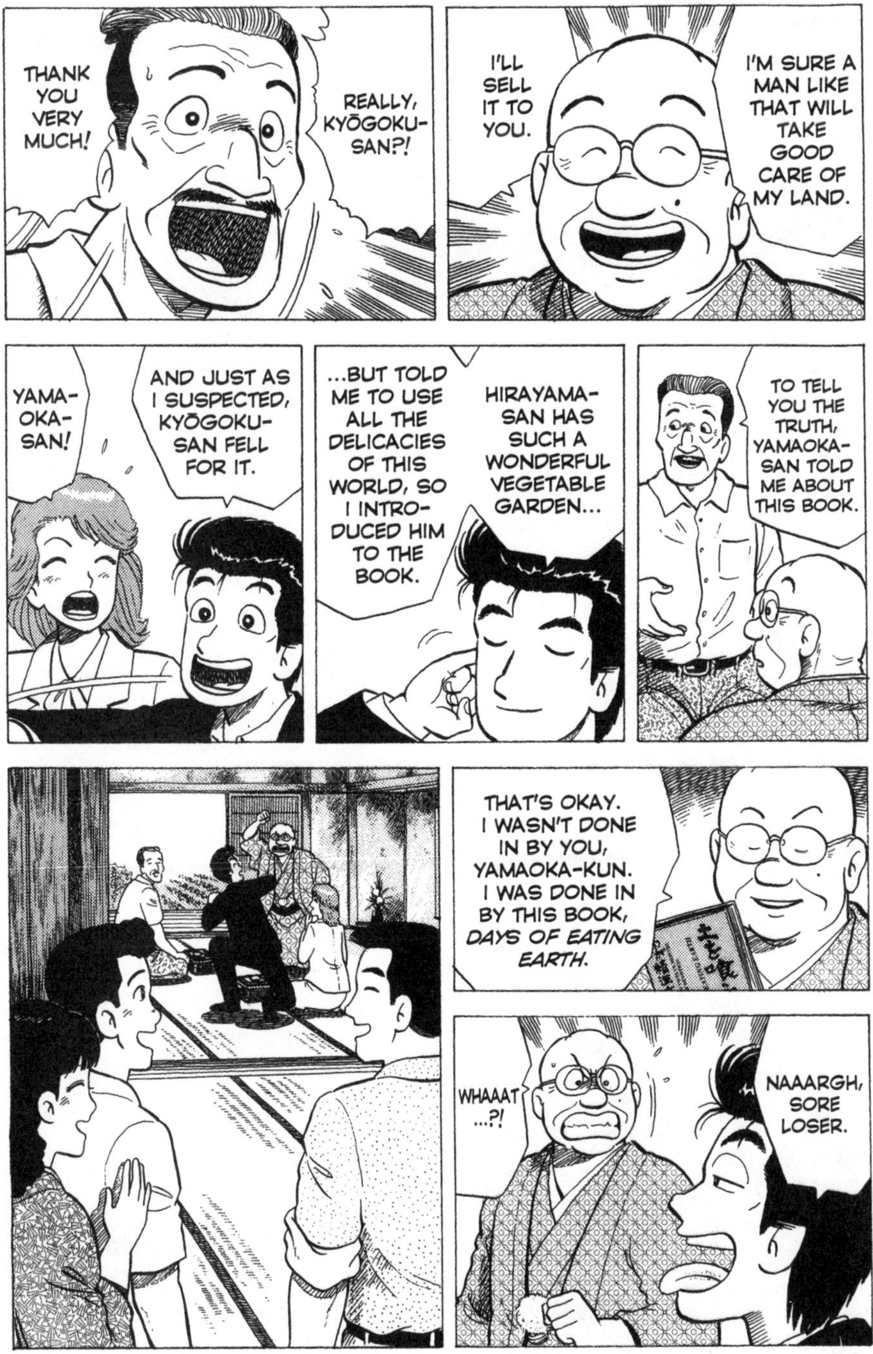
I'M SURE A MAN LIKE THAT WILL TAKE GOOD CARE OF MY LAND.
I'LL SELL IT TO YOU.
REALLY, KYŌGOKU-SAN?!
THANK YOU VERY MUCH!
TO TELL YOU THE TRUTH, YAMAOKA-SAN TOLD ME ABOUT THIS BOOK.
HIRAYAMA-SAN HAS SUCH A WONDERFUL VEGETABLE GARDEN...
...BUT TOLD ME TO USE ALL THE DELICACIES OF THIS WORLD, SO I INTRODUCED HIM TO THE BOOK.
AND JUST AS I SUSPECTED, KYŌGOKU-SAN FELL FOR IT.
YAMAOKA-SAN!
THAT'S OKAY. I WASN'T DONE IN BY YOU, YAMAOKA-KUN. I WAS DONE IN BY THIS BOOK, *DAYS OF EATING EARTH*.
NAAARGH, SORE LOSER.
WHAAAT ...?!

EIGHTH COURSE

THE TASTE OF CHICKEN, THE TASTE OF CARROTS

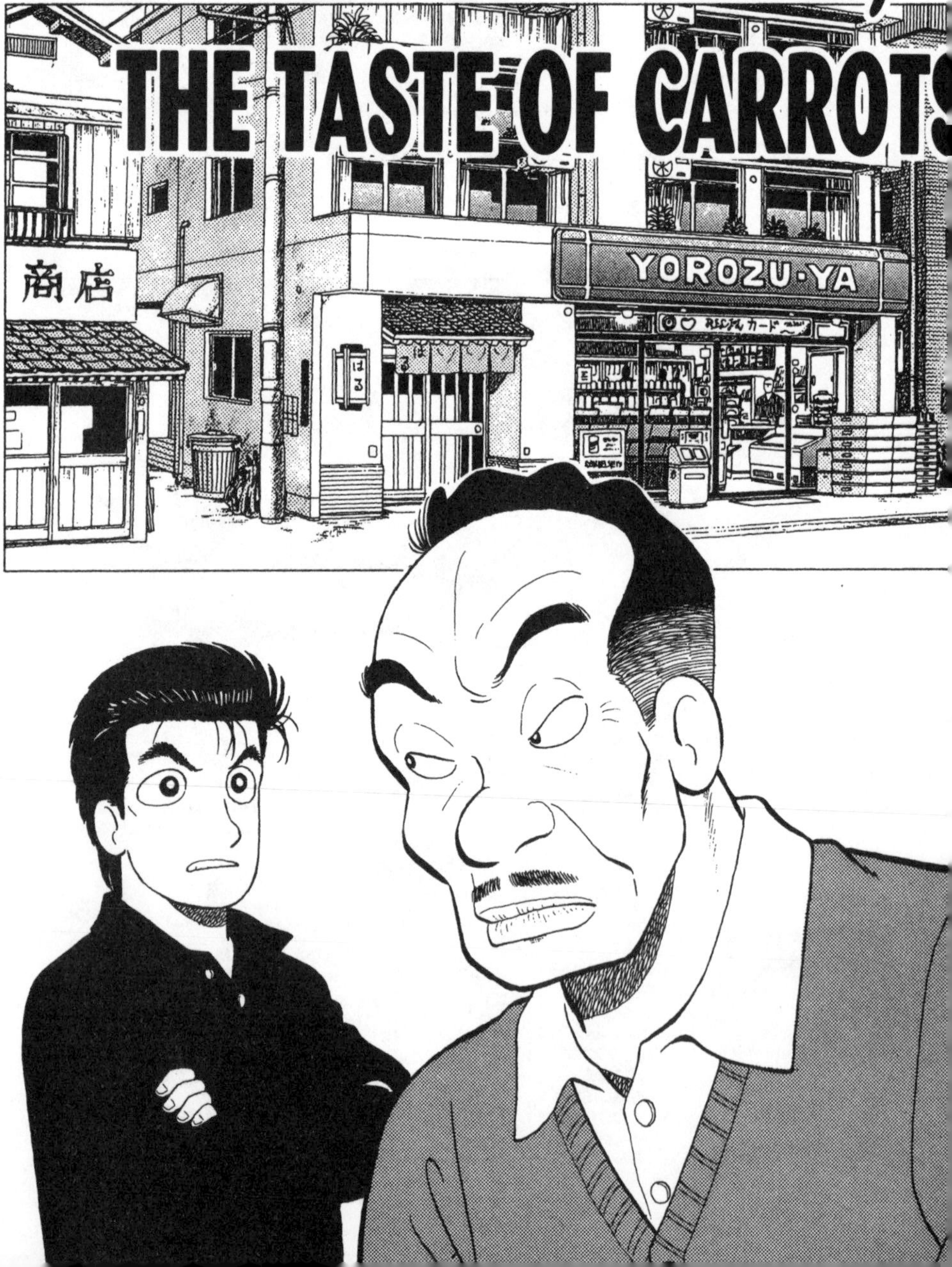
商店
YOROZU-YA

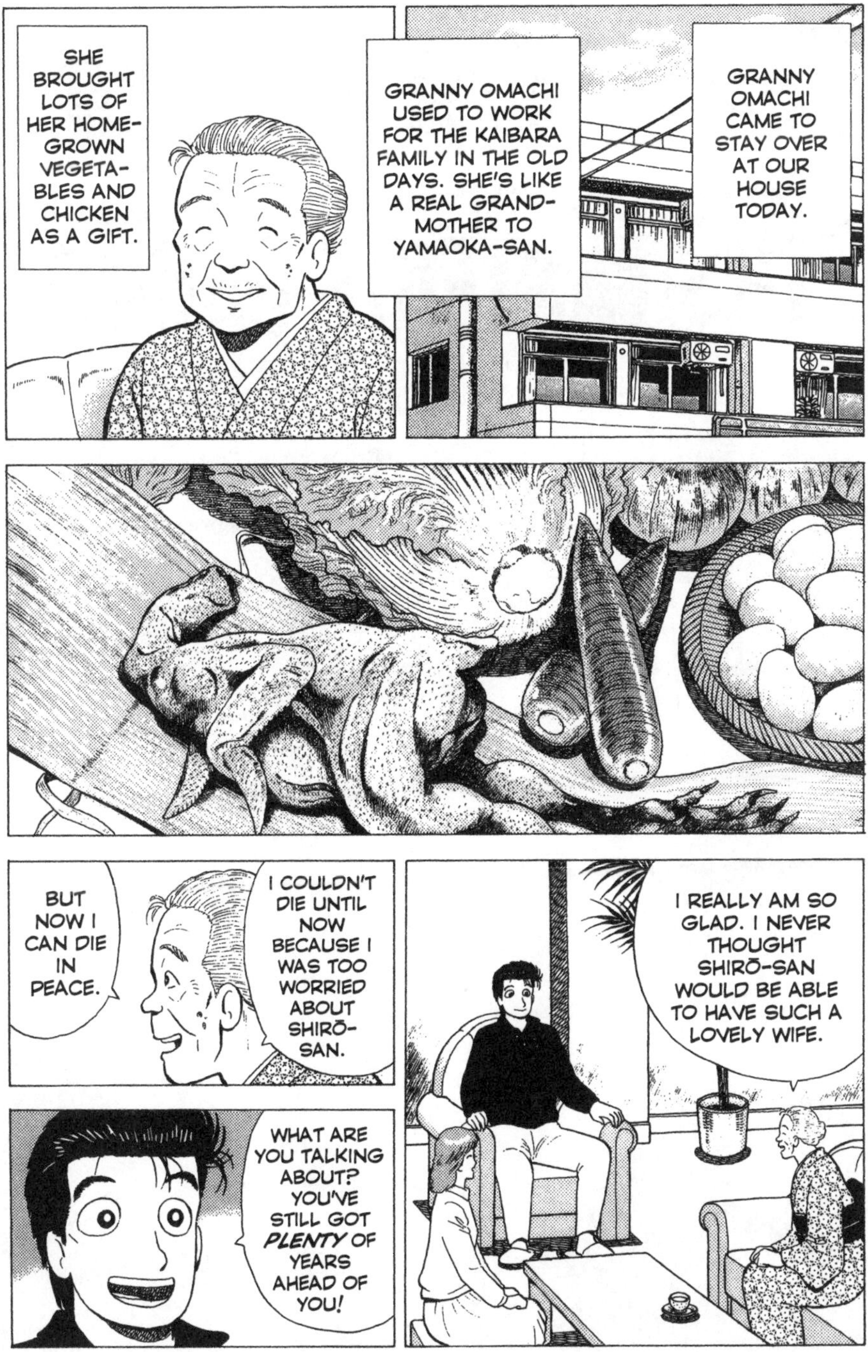
GRANNY OMACHI CAME TO STAY OVER AT OUR HOUSE TODAY.
GRANNY OMACHI USED TO WORK FOR THE KAIBARA FAMILY IN THE OLD DAYS. SHE'S LIKE A REAL GRANDMOTHER TO YAMAOKA-SAN.
SHE BROUGHT LOTS OF HER HOME-GROWN VEGETABLES AND CHICKEN AS A GIFT.
I REALLY AM SO GLAD. I NEVER THOUGHT SHIRŌ-SAN WOULD BE ABLE TO HAVE SUCH A LOVELY WIFE.
I COULDN'T DIE UNTIL NOW BECAUSE I WAS TOO WORRIED ABOUT SHIRŌ-SAN.
BUT NOW I CAN DIE IN PEACE.
WHAT ARE YOU TALKING ABOUT? YOU'VE STILL GOT *PLENTY* OF YEARS AHEAD OF YOU!

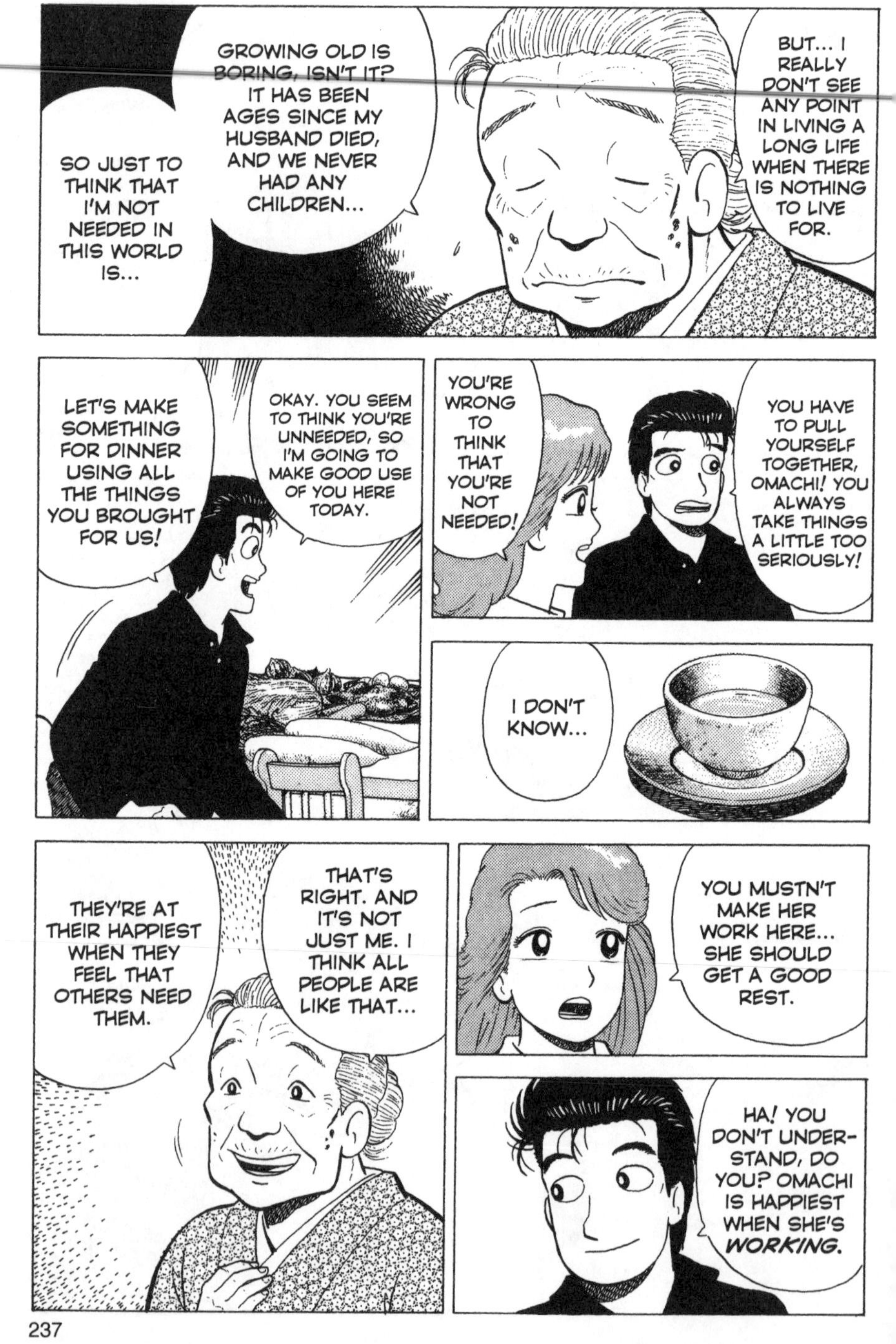
BUT... I REALLY DON'T SEE ANY POINT IN LIVING A LONG LIFE WHEN THERE IS NOTHING TO LIVE FOR.
GROWING OLD IS BORING, ISN'T IT? IT HAS BEEN AGES SINCE MY HUSBAND DIED, AND WE NEVER HAD ANY CHILDREN...
SO JUST TO THINK THAT I'M NOT NEEDED IN THIS WORLD IS...
YOU HAVE TO PULL YOURSELF TOGETHER, OMACHI! YOU ALWAYS TAKE THINGS A LITTLE TOO SERIOUSLY!
YOU'RE WRONG TO THINK THAT YOU'RE NOT NEEDED!
I DON'T KNOW...
OKAY. YOU SEEM TO THINK YOU'RE UNNEEDED, SO I'M GOING TO MAKE GOOD USE OF YOU HERE TODAY.
LET'S MAKE SOMETHING FOR DINNER USING ALL THE THINGS YOU BROUGHT FOR US!
YOU MUSTN'T MAKE HER WORK HERE... SHE SHOULD GET A GOOD REST.
HA! YOU DON'T UNDER-STAND, DO YOU? OMACHI IS HAPPIEST WHEN SHE'S *WORKING*.
THAT'S RIGHT. AND IT'S NOT JUST ME. I THINK ALL PEOPLE ARE LIKE THAT...
THEY'RE AT THEIR HAPPIEST WHEN THEY FEEL THAT OTHERS NEED THEM.

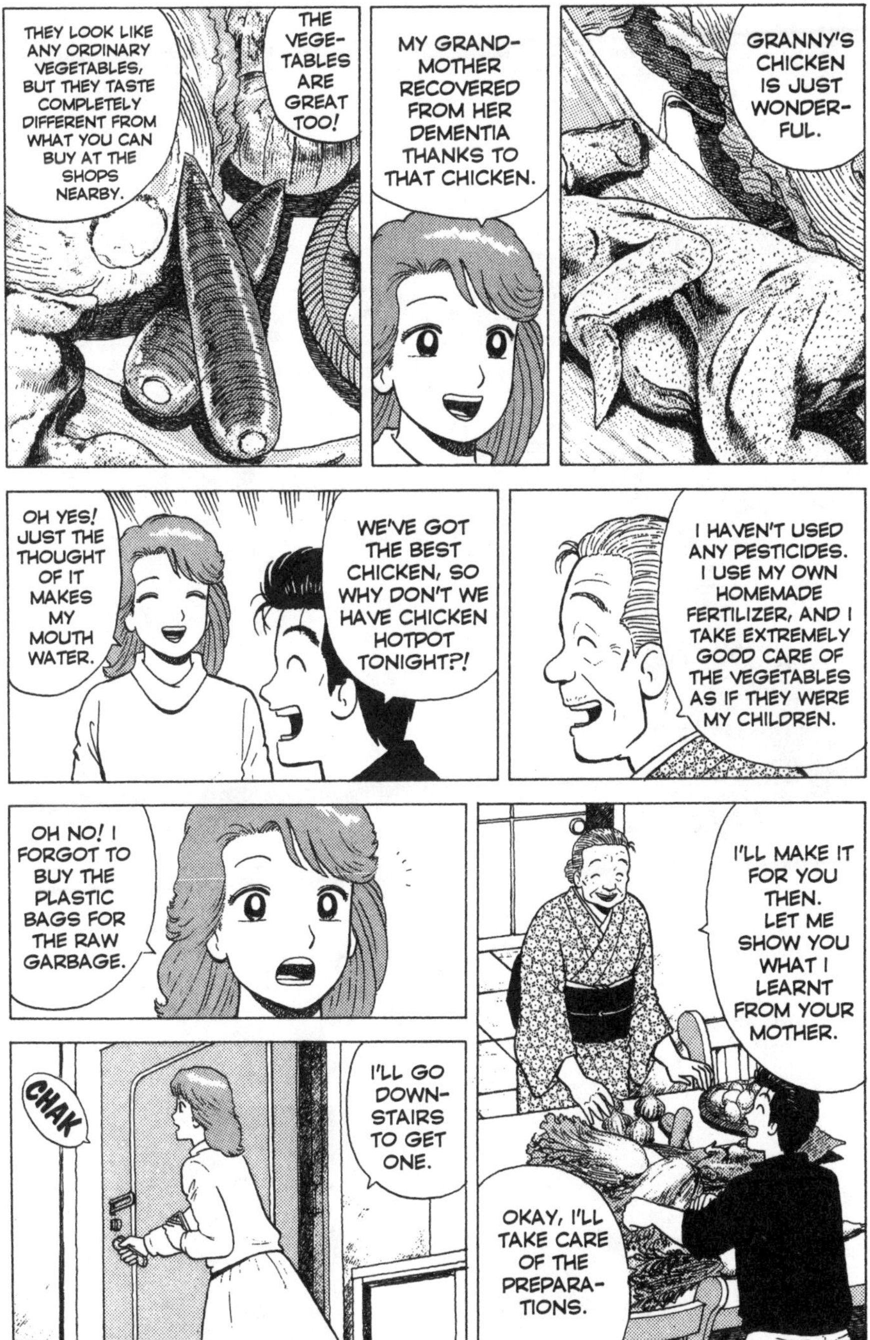
GRANNY'S CHICKEN IS JUST WONDERFUL.
MY GRANDMOTHER RECOVERED FROM HER DEMENTIA THANKS TO THAT CHICKEN.
THE VEGETABLES ARE GREAT TOO!
THEY LOOK LIKE ANY ORDINARY VEGETABLES, BUT THEY TASTE COMPLETELY DIFFERENT FROM WHAT YOU CAN BUY AT THE SHOPS NEARBY.
I HAVEN'T USED ANY PESTICIDES. I USE MY OWN HOMEMADE FERTILIZER, AND I TAKE EXTREMELY GOOD CARE OF THE VEGETABLES AS IF THEY WERE MY CHILDREN.
WE'VE GOT THE BEST CHICKEN, SO WHY DON'T WE HAVE CHICKEN HOTPOT TONIGHT?!
OH YES! JUST THE THOUGHT OF IT MAKES MY MOUTH WATER.
I'LL MAKE IT FOR YOU THEN. LET ME SHOW YOU WHAT I LEARNT FROM YOUR MOTHER.
OKAY, I'LL TAKE CARE OF THE PREPARATIONS.
OH NO! I FORGOT TO BUY THE PLASTIC BAGS FOR THE RAW GARBAGE.
I'LL GO DOWNSTAIRS TO GET ONE.
CHAK

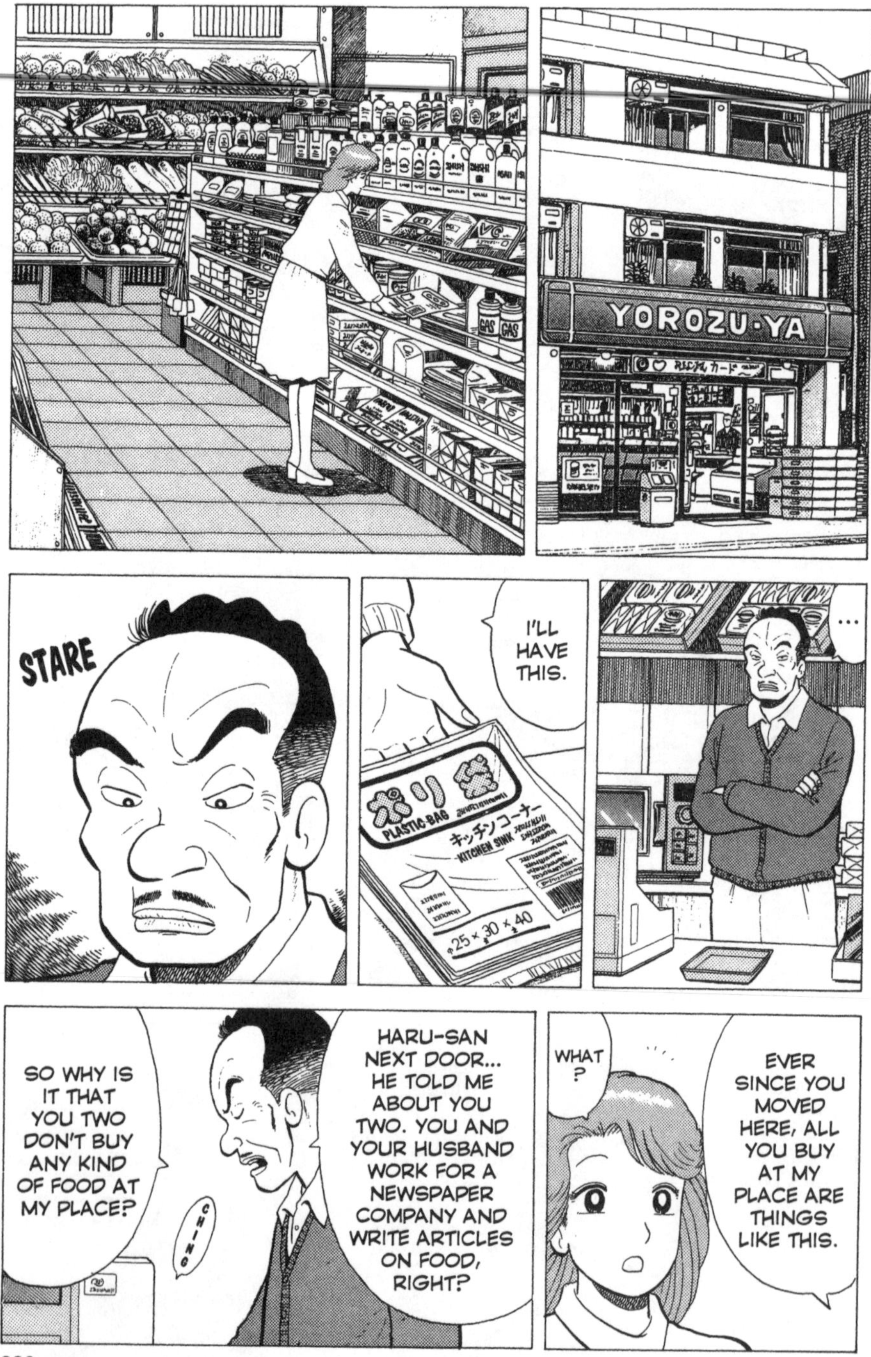
YOROZU-YA
...
I'LL HAVE THIS.
ポリ袋
PLASTIC BAG
キッチンコーナー
KITCHEN SINK
STARE
EVER SINCE YOU MOVED HERE, ALL YOU BUY AT MY PLACE ARE THINGS LIKE THIS.
WHAT?
HARU-SAN NEXT DOOR... HE TOLD ME ABOUT YOU TWO. YOU AND YOUR HUSBAND WORK FOR A NEWSPAPER COMPANY AND WRITE ARTICLES ON FOOD, RIGHT?
CHING
SO WHY IS IT THAT YOU TWO DON'T BUY ANY KIND OF FOOD AT MY PLACE?

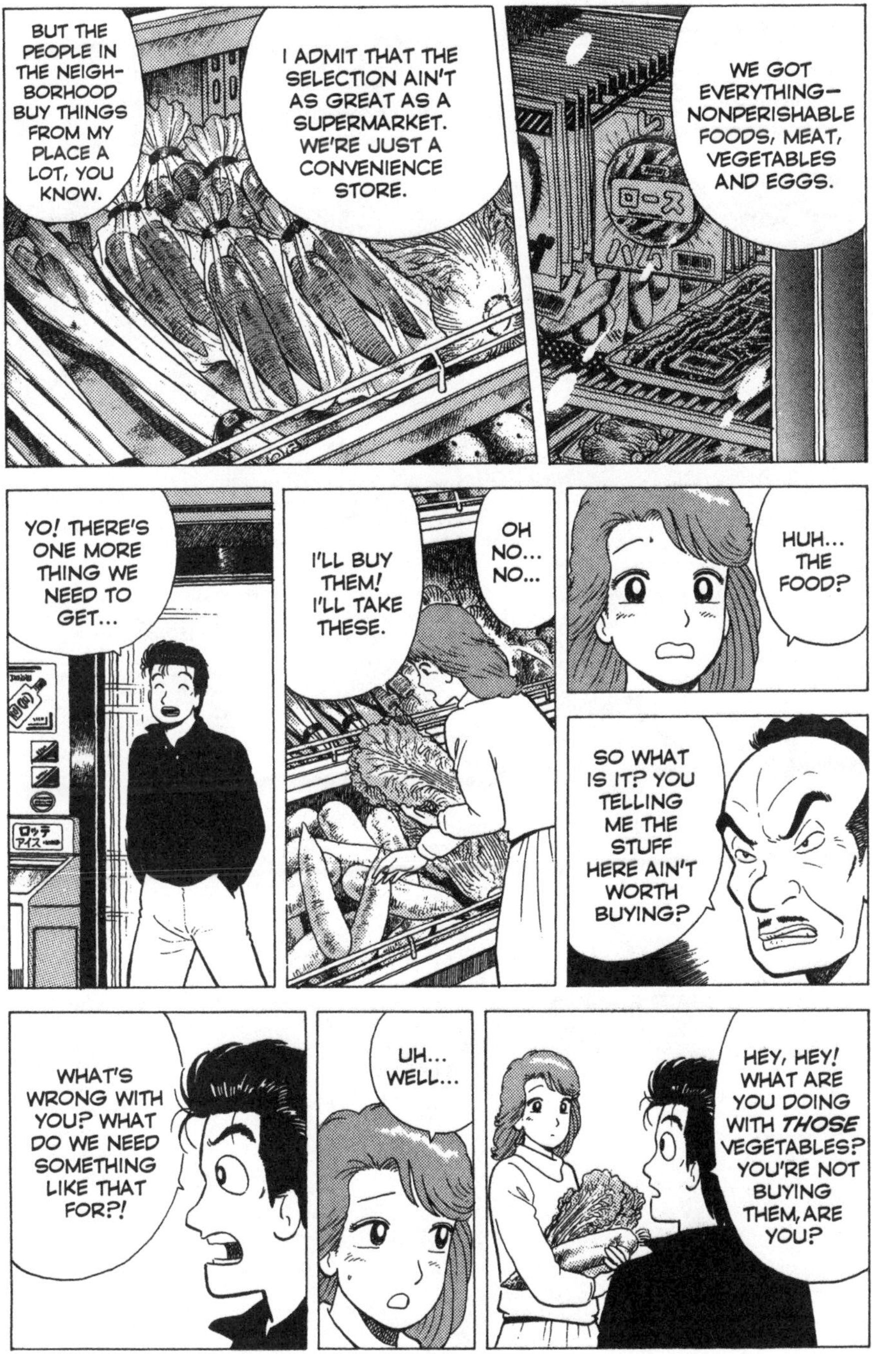
WE GOT EVERYTHING—NONPERISHABLE FOODS, MEAT, VEGETABLES AND EGGS.
ロース
I ADMIT THAT THE SELECTION AIN'T AS GREAT AS A SUPERMARKET. WE'RE JUST A CONVENIENCE STORE.
BUT THE PEOPLE IN THE NEIGH-BORHOOD BUY THINGS FROM MY PLACE A LOT, YOU KNOW.
HUH... THE FOOD?
SO WHAT IS IT? YOU TELLING ME THE STUFF HERE AIN'T WORTH BUYING?
OH NO... NO...
I'LL BUY THEM! I'LL TAKE THESE.
YO! THERE'S ONE MORE THING WE NEED TO GET...
ロッテ アイス
HEY, HEY! WHAT ARE YOU DOING WITH *THOSE* VEGETABLES? YOU'RE NOT BUYING THEM, ARE YOU?
UH... WELL...
WHAT'S WRONG WITH YOU? WHAT DO WE NEED SOMETHING LIKE THAT FOR?!

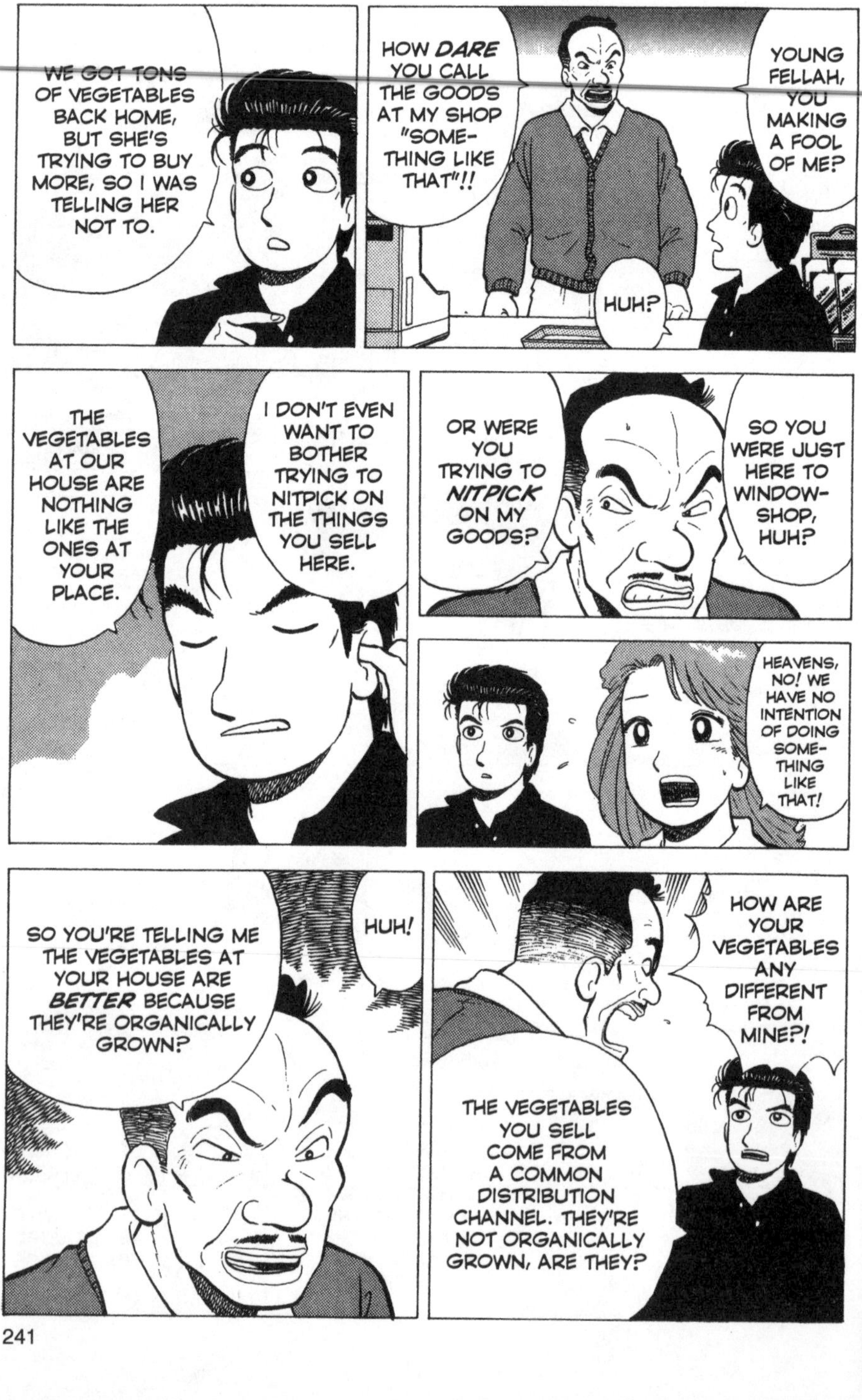
YOUNG FELLAH, YOU MAKING A FOOL OF ME?
HOW DARE YOU CALL THE GOODS AT MY SHOP "SOMETHING LIKE THAT"!!
HUH?
WE GOT TONS OF VEGETABLES BACK HOME, BUT SHE'S TRYING TO BUY MORE, SO I WAS TELLING HER NOT TO.
SO YOU WERE JUST HERE TO WINDOW-SHOP, HUH?
OR WERE YOU TRYING TO NITPICK ON MY GOODS?
HEAVENS, NO! WE HAVE NO INTENTION OF DOING SOMETHING LIKE THAT!
I DON'T EVEN WANT TO BOTHER TRYING TO NITPICK ON THE THINGS YOU SELL HERE.
THE VEGETABLES AT OUR HOUSE ARE NOTHING LIKE THE ONES AT YOUR PLACE.
HOW ARE YOUR VEGETABLES ANY DIFFERENT FROM MINE?!
THE VEGETABLES YOU SELL COME FROM A COMMON DISTRIBUTION CHANNEL. THEY'RE NOT ORGANICALLY GROWN, ARE THEY?
HUH!
SO YOU'RE TELLING ME THE VEGETABLES AT YOUR HOUSE ARE BETTER BECAUSE THEY'RE ORGANICALLY GROWN?

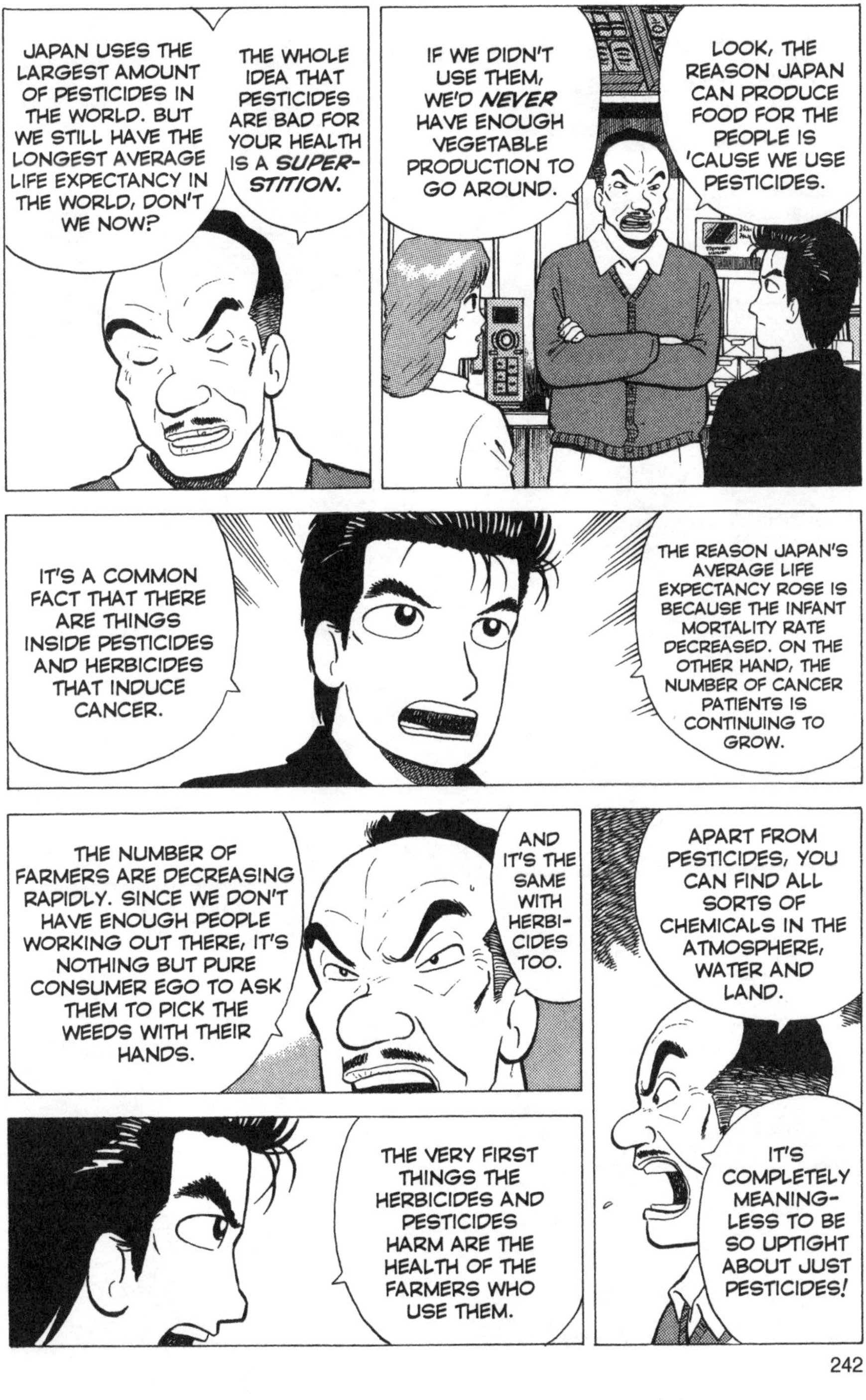
LOOK, THE REASON JAPAN CAN PRODUCE FOOD FOR THE PEOPLE IS 'CAUSE WE USE PESTICIDES.
IF WE DIDN'T USE THEM, WE'D *NEVER* HAVE ENOUGH VEGETABLE PRODUCTION TO GO AROUND.
THE WHOLE IDEA THAT PESTICIDES ARE BAD FOR YOUR HEALTH IS A *SUPERSTITION*.
JAPAN USES THE LARGEST AMOUNT OF PESTICIDES IN THE WORLD. BUT WE STILL HAVE THE LONGEST AVERAGE LIFE EXPECTANCY IN THE WORLD, DON'T WE NOW?
THE REASON JAPAN'S AVERAGE LIFE EXPECTANCY ROSE IS BECAUSE THE INFANT MORTALITY RATE DECREASED. ON THE OTHER HAND, THE NUMBER OF CANCER PATIENTS IS CONTINUING TO GROW.
IT'S A COMMON FACT THAT THERE ARE THINGS INSIDE PESTICIDES AND HERBICIDES THAT INDUCE CANCER.
APART FROM PESTICIDES, YOU CAN FIND ALL SORTS OF CHEMICALS IN THE ATMOSPHERE, WATER AND LAND.
IT'S COMPLETELY MEANINGLESS TO BE SO UPTIGHT ABOUT JUST PESTICIDES!
AND IT'S THE SAME WITH HERBICIDES TOO.
THE NUMBER OF FARMERS ARE DECREASING RAPIDLY. SINCE WE DON'T HAVE ENOUGH PEOPLE WORKING OUT THERE, IT'S NOTHING BUT PURE CONSUMER EGO TO ASK THEM TO PICK THE WEEDS WITH THEIR HANDS.
THE VERY FIRST THINGS THE HERBICIDES AND PESTICIDES HARM ARE THE HEALTH OF THE FARMERS WHO USE THEM.

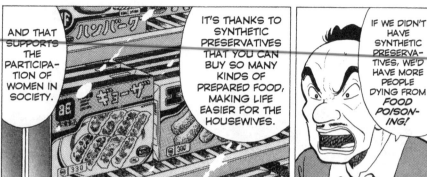

IF WE DIDN'T HAVE SYNTHETIC PRESERVATIVES, WE'D HAVE MORE PEOPLE DYING FROM *FOOD POISONING!*
IT'S THANKS TO SYNTHETIC PRESERVATIVES THAT YOU CAN BUY SO MANY KINDS OF PREPARED FOOD, MAKING LIFE EASIER FOR THE HOUSEWIVES.
AND THAT SUPPORTS THE PARTICIPATION OF WOMEN IN SOCIETY.
ON BOXES: HAMBURG STEAK, DUMPLINGS
THAT'S *NOT* TRUE. THE FOOD COMPANIES USE PRESERVATIVES BECAUSE IT MAKES IT EASIER TO MANAGE THEIR PRODUCTS AND KEEP THEM EDIBLE FOR A LONG TIME.
IT'S THE *DISCRIMINATORY ATTITUDE* OF THE JAPANESE *MEN* THAT IS HINDERING THE PARTICIPATION OF WOMEN IN SOCIETY.
UH...
I AIN'T SELLING YOU ANYTHING! YOU'RE NOT EVEN ALLOWED INSIDE MY SHOP FROM NOW ON!!
I DON'T EVEN WANT TO COME TO A SHOP LIKE THIS!
THIS SHOP HAS NO FUTURE WITH ALL THE PESTICIDE-COVERED VEGETABLES AND PRESERVATIVE-FILLED PREPARED FOOD!
WHAT WAS THAT?! I'LL *KILL* YOU!!
OH YEAH?! TRY IT!
STOP IT!

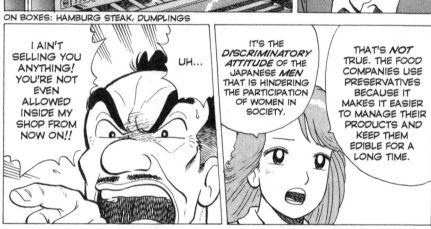

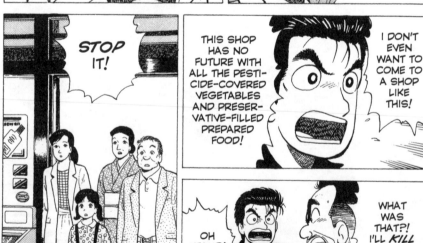

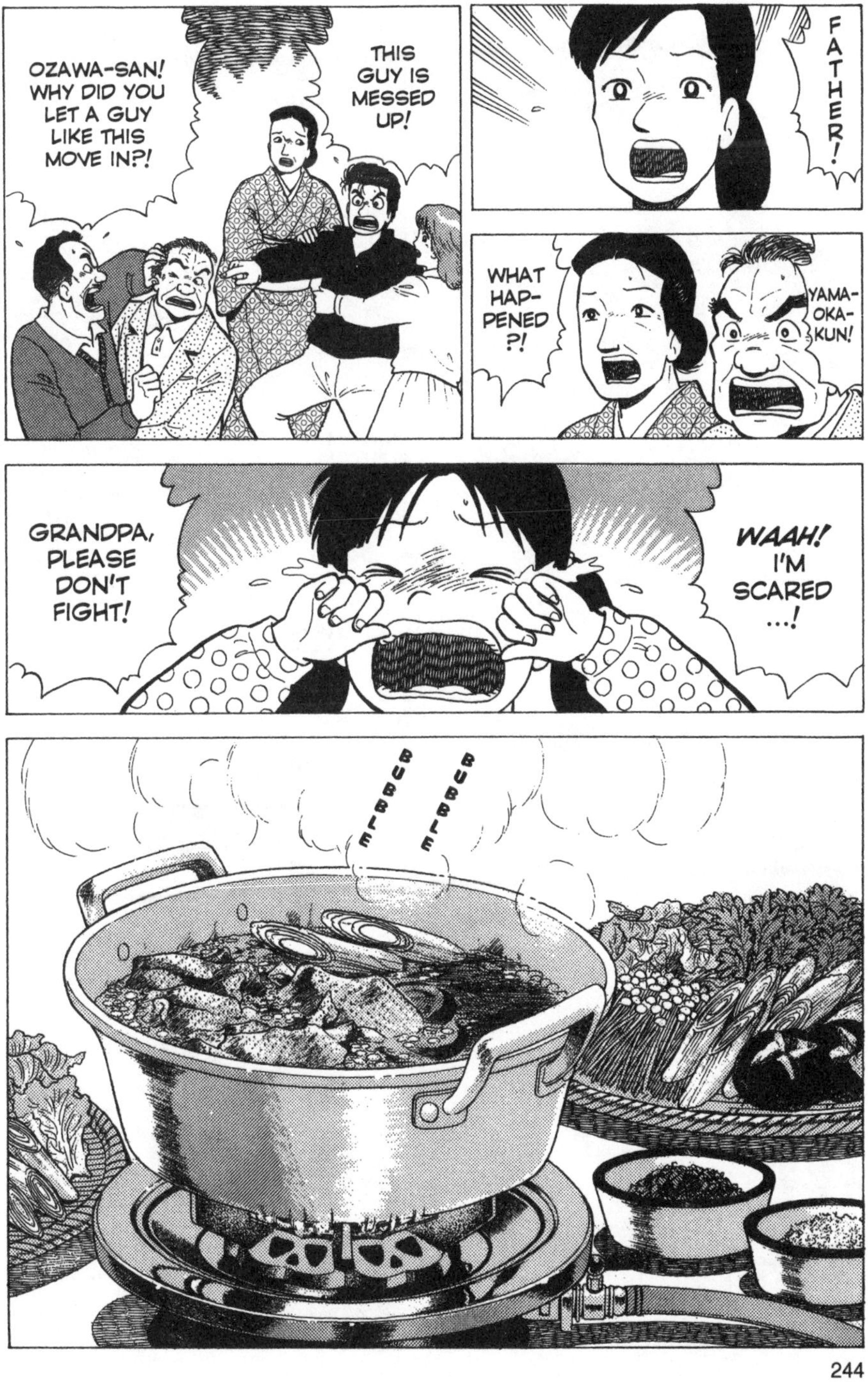
FATHER!
YAMA-OKA-KUN!
WHAT HAP-PENED?!
THIS GUY IS MESSED UP!
OZAWA-SAN! WHY DID YOU LET A GUY LIKE THIS MOVE IN?!
WAAH! I'M SCARED ...!
GRANDPA, PLEASE DON'T FIGHT!
BUBBLE
BUBBLE

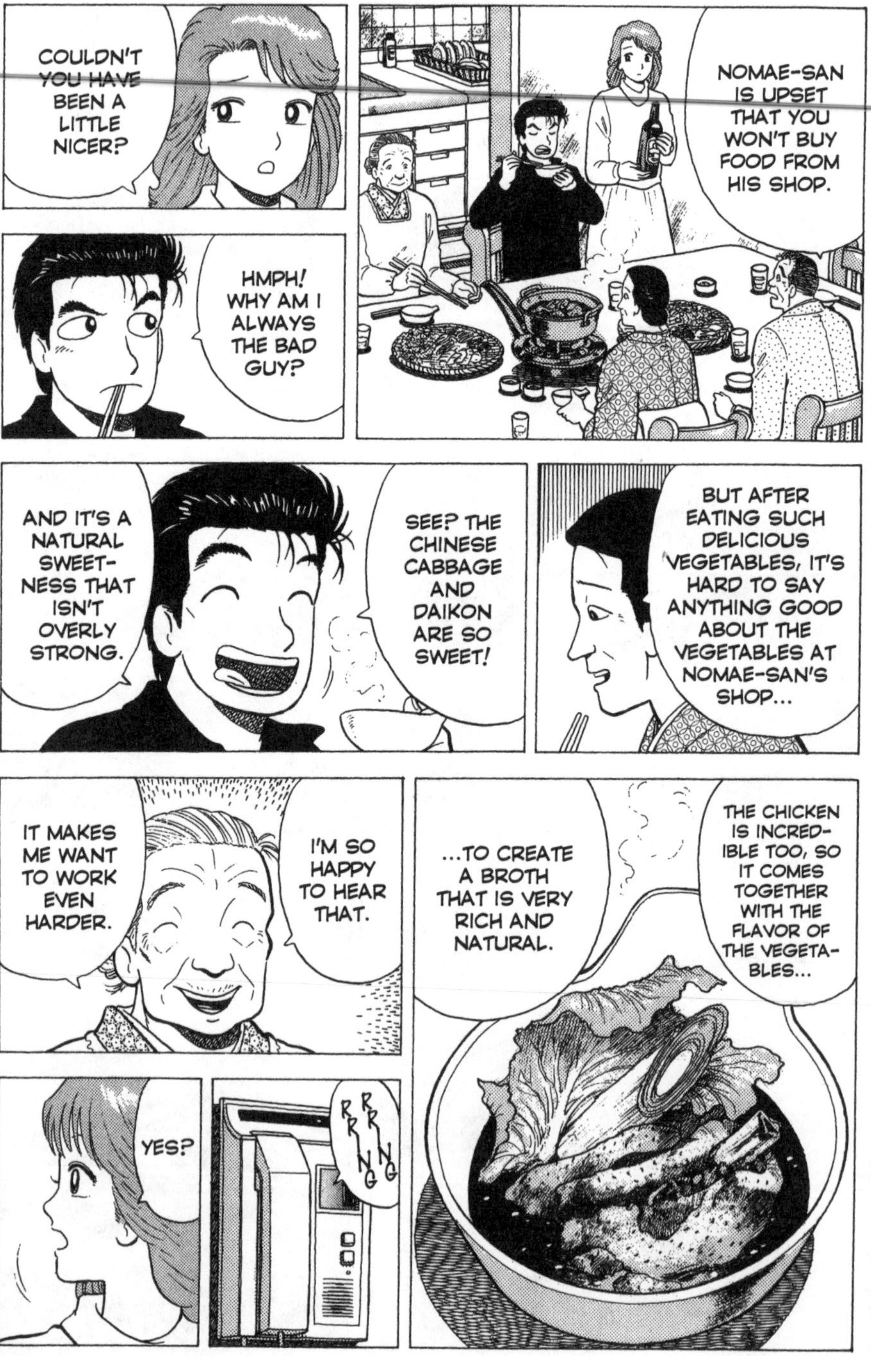
NOMAE-SAN IS UPSET THAT YOU WON'T BUY FOOD FROM HIS SHOP.
COULDN'T YOU HAVE BEEN A LITTLE NICER?
HMPH! WHY AM I ALWAYS THE BAD GUY?
BUT AFTER EATING SUCH DELICIOUS VEGETABLES, IT'S HARD TO SAY ANYTHING GOOD ABOUT THE VEGETABLES AT NOMAE-SAN'S SHOP...
SEE? THE CHINESE CABBAGE AND DAIKON ARE SO SWEET!
AND IT'S A NATURAL SWEET-NESS THAT ISN'T OVERLY STRONG.
THE CHICKEN IS INCRED-IBLE TOO, SO IT COMES TOGETHER WITH THE FLAVOR OF THE VEGETA-BLES...
...TO CREATE A BROTH THAT IS VERY RICH AND NATURAL.
I'M SO HAPPY TO HEAR THAT.
IT MAKES ME WANT TO WORK EVEN HARDER.
RRRING
YES?

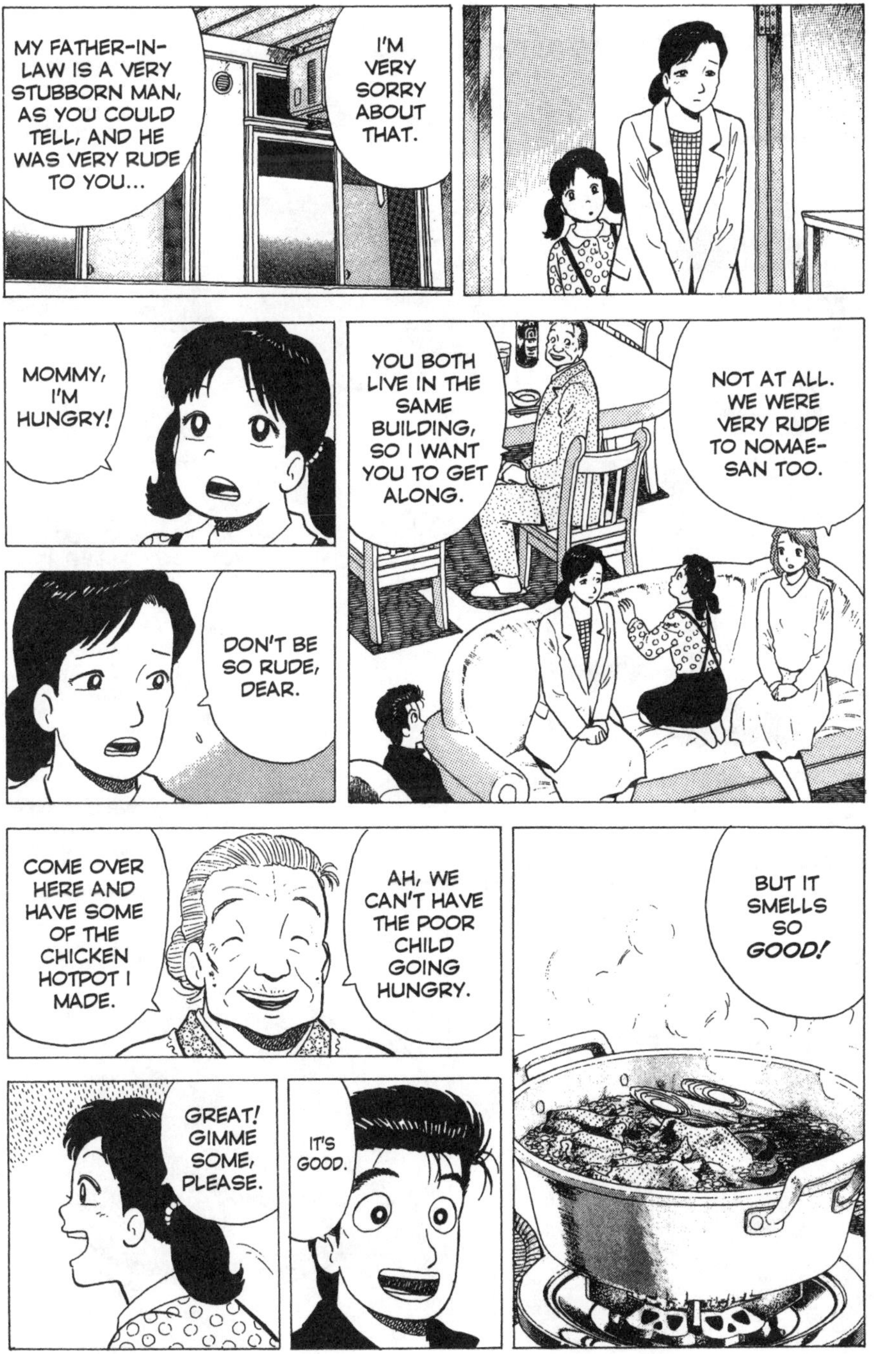
I'M VERY SORRY ABOUT THAT.
MY FATHER-IN-LAW IS A VERY STUBBORN MAN, AS YOU COULD TELL, AND HE WAS VERY RUDE TO YOU...
NOT AT ALL. WE WERE VERY RUDE TO NOMAE-SAN TOO.
YOU BOTH LIVE IN THE SAME BUILDING, SO I WANT YOU TO GET ALONG.
MOMMY, I'M HUNGRY!
DON'T BE SO RUDE, DEAR.
BUT IT SMELLS SO *GOOD!*
AH, WE CAN'T HAVE THE POOR CHILD GOING HUNGRY.
COME OVER HERE AND HAVE SOME OF THE CHICKEN HOTPOT I MADE.
IT'S GOOD.
GREAT! GIMME SOME, PLEASE.

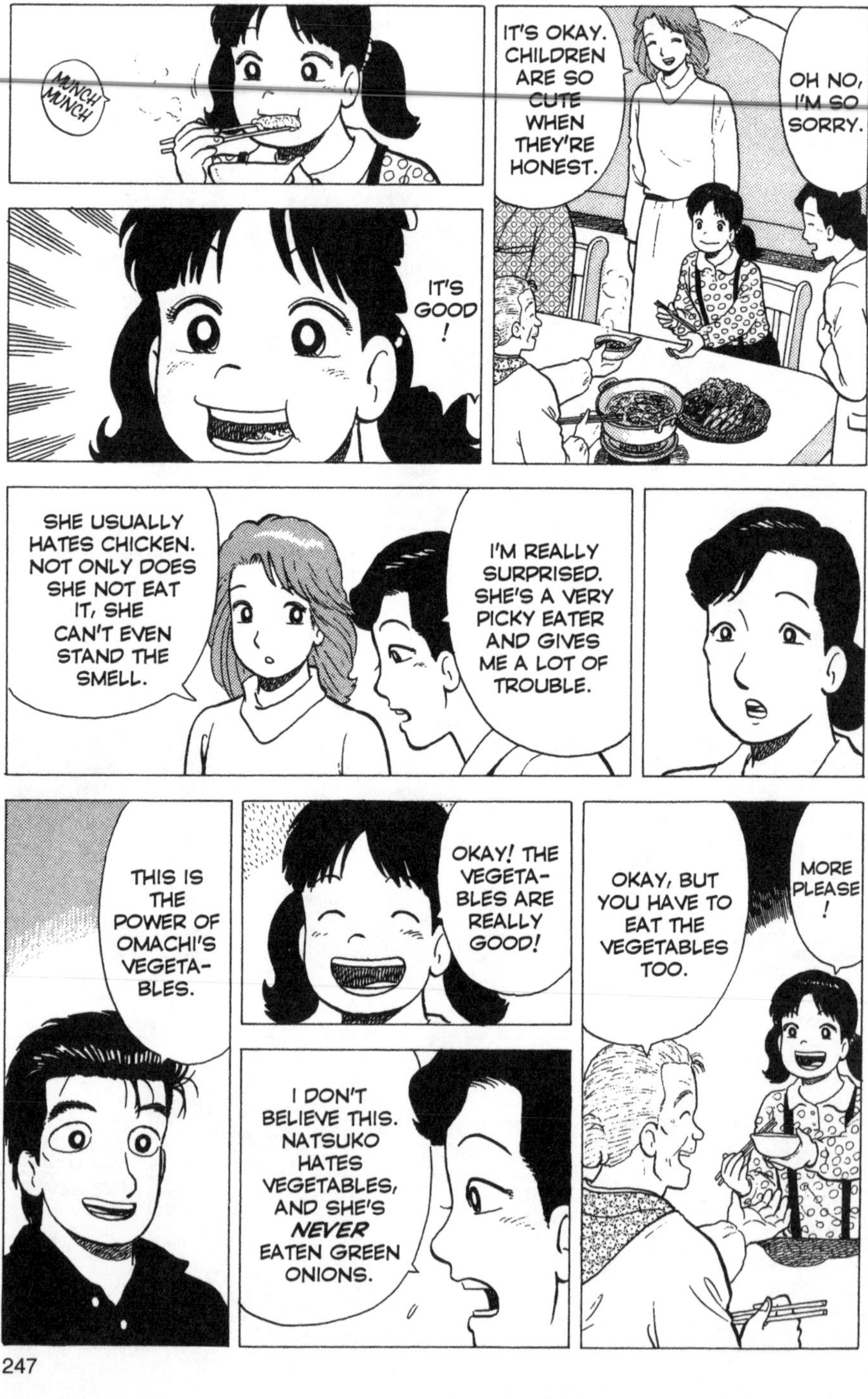
OH NO, I'M SO SORRY.
IT'S OKAY. CHILDREN ARE SO CUTE WHEN THEY'RE HONEST.
MUNCH MUNCH
IT'S GOOD!
I'M REALLY SURPRISED. SHE'S A VERY PICKY EATER AND GIVES ME A LOT OF TROUBLE.
SHE USUALLY HATES CHICKEN. NOT ONLY DOES SHE NOT EAT IT, SHE CAN'T EVEN STAND THE SMELL.
MORE PLEASE!
OKAY, BUT YOU HAVE TO EAT THE VEGETABLES TOO.
OKAY! THE VEGETA-BLES ARE REALLY GOOD!
I DON'T BELIEVE THIS. NATSUKO HATES VEGETABLES, AND SHE'S *NEVER* EATEN GREEN ONIONS.
THIS IS THE POWER OF OMACHI'S VEGETA-BLES.

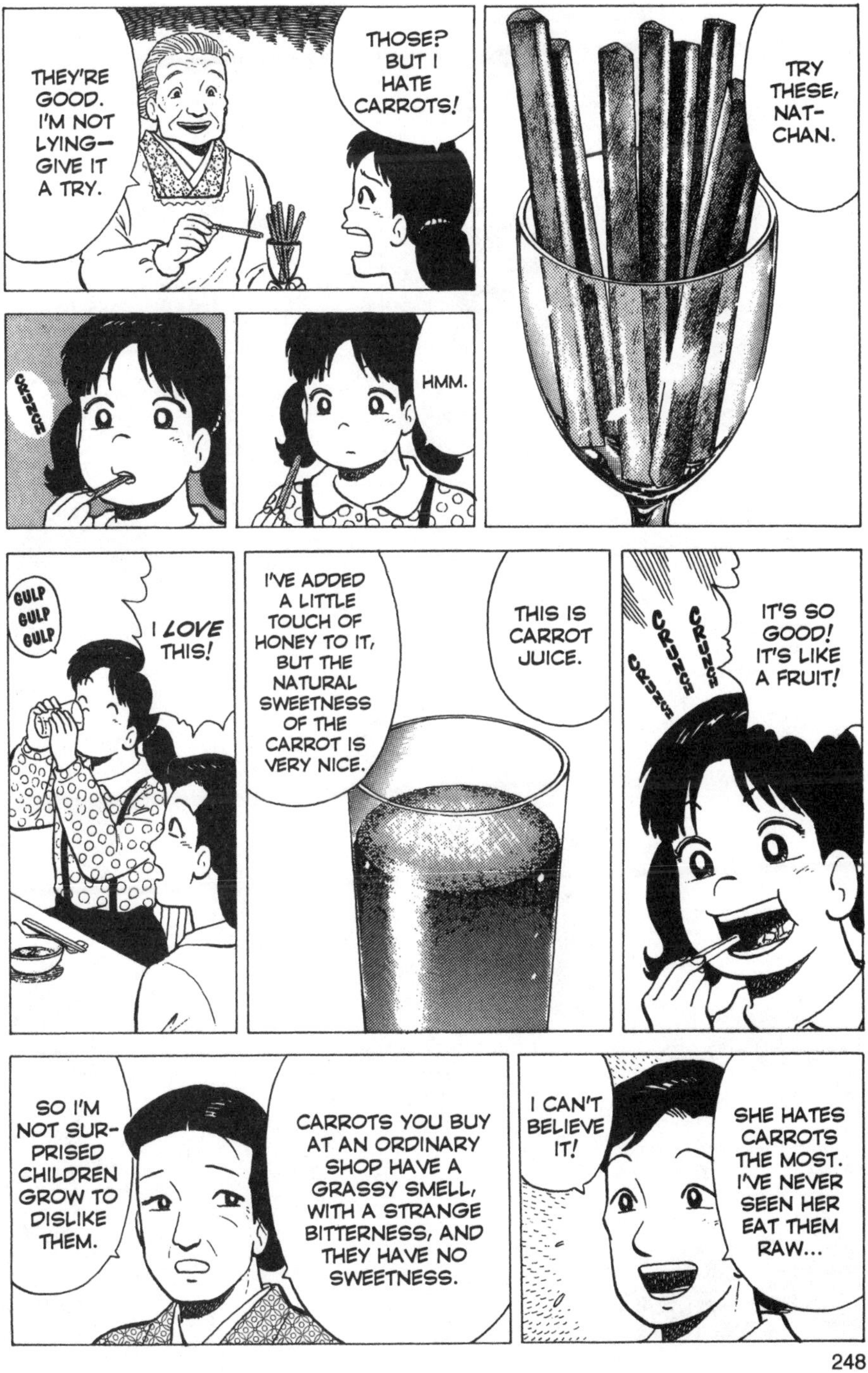
TRY THESE, NAT-CHAN.
THOSE? BUT I HATE CARROTS!
THEY'RE GOOD. I'M NOT LYING— GIVE IT A TRY.
HMM.
CRUNCH
IT'S SO GOOD! IT'S LIKE A FRUIT!
CRUNCH CRUNCH CRUNCH
THIS IS CARROT JUICE.
I'VE ADDED A LITTLE TOUCH OF HONEY TO IT, BUT THE NATURAL SWEETNESS OF THE CARROT IS VERY NICE.
I *LOVE* THIS!
GULP GULP GULP
SHE HATES CARROTS THE MOST. I'VE NEVER SEEN HER EAT THEM RAW...
I CAN'T BELIEVE IT!
CARROTS YOU BUY AT AN ORDINARY SHOP HAVE A GRASSY SMELL, WITH A STRANGE BITTERNESS, AND THEY HAVE NO SWEETNESS.
SO I'M NOT SURPRISED CHILDREN GROW TO DISLIKE THEM.

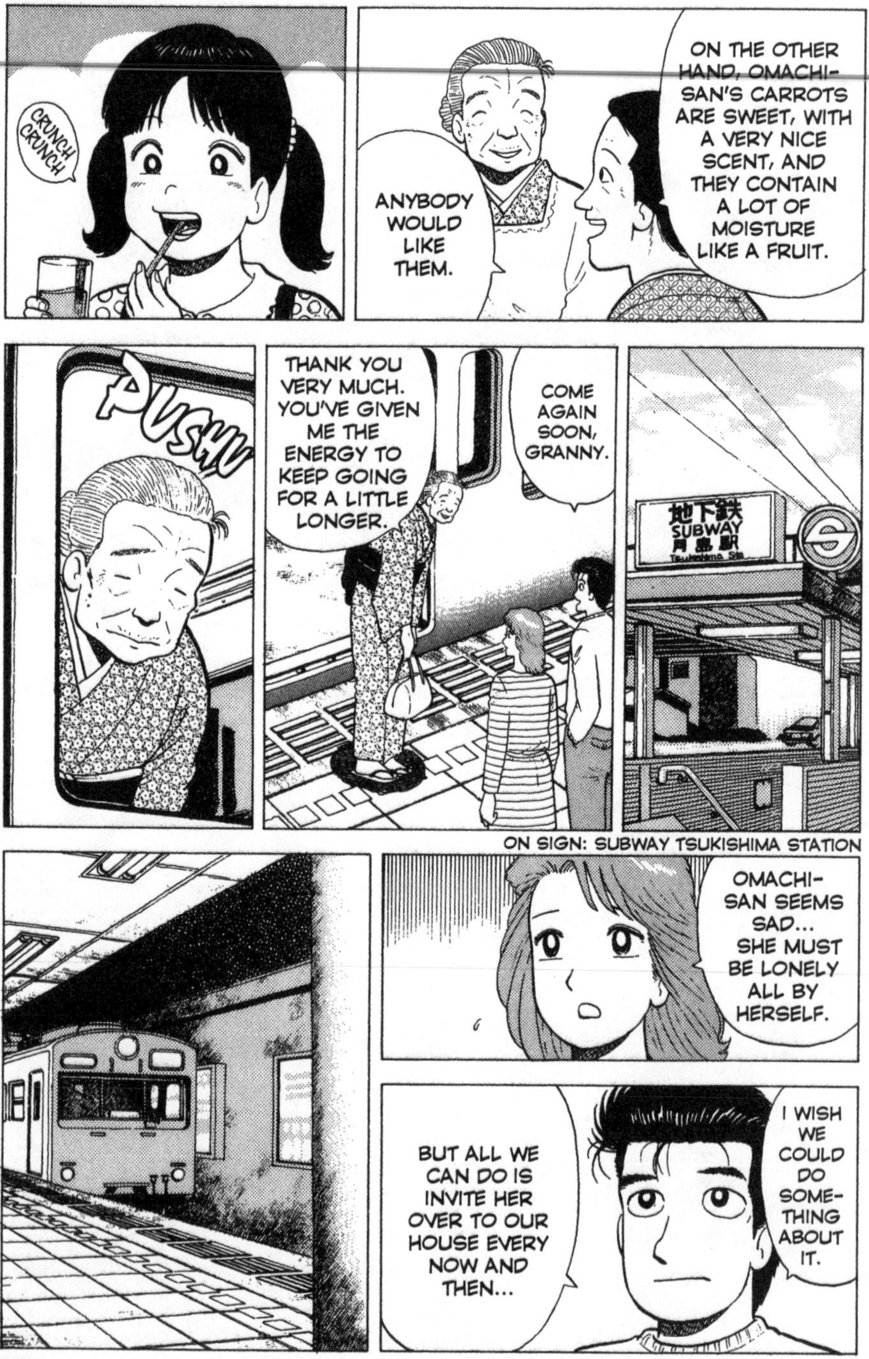
ON THE OTHER HAND, OMACHI-SAN'S CARROTS ARE SWEET, WITH A VERY NICE SCENT, AND THEY CONTAIN A LOT OF MOISTURE LIKE A FRUIT.
ANYBODY WOULD LIKE THEM.
CRUNCH CRUNCH
地下鉄 SUBWAY 月島駅 Tsukishima Sta.
ON SIGN: SUBWAY TSUKISHIMA STATION
COME AGAIN SOON, GRANNY.
THANK YOU VERY MUCH. YOU'VE GIVEN ME THE ENERGY TO KEEP GOING FOR A LITTLE LONGER.
PUSHU
OMACHI-SAN SEEMS SAD... SHE MUST BE LONELY ALL BY HERSELF.
I WISH WE COULD DO SOME-THING ABOUT IT.
BUT ALL WE CAN DO IS INVITE HER OVER TO OUR HOUSE EVERY NOW AND THEN...

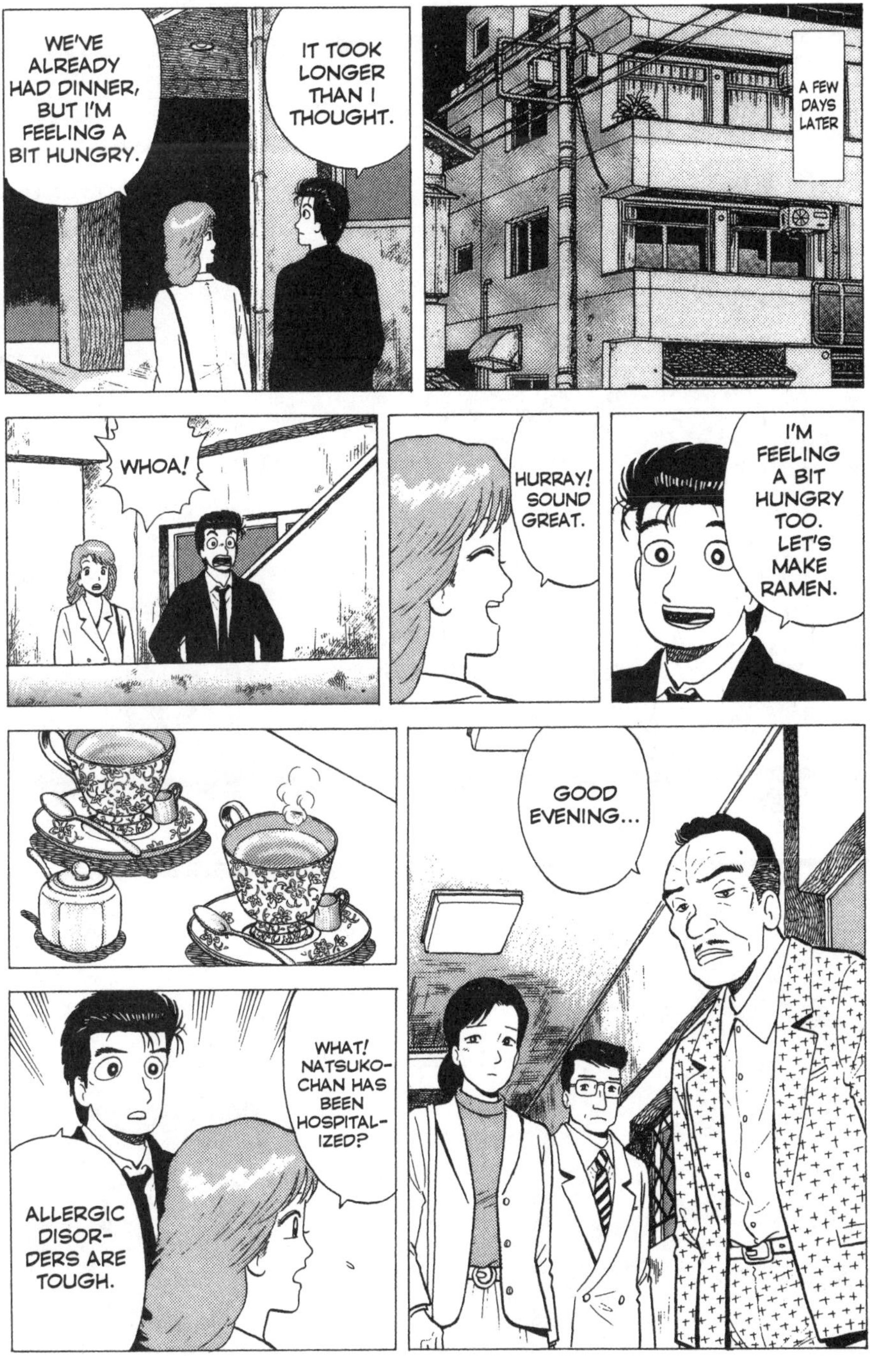
A FEW DAYS LATER
IT TOOK LONGER THAN I THOUGHT.
WE'VE ALREADY HAD DINNER, BUT I'M FEELING A BIT HUNGRY.
I'M FEELING A BIT HUNGRY TOO. LET'S MAKE RAMEN.
HURRAY! SOUND GREAT.
WHOA!
GOOD EVENING...
WHAT! NATSUKO-CHAN HAS BEEN HOSPITAL-IZED?
ALLERGIC DISOR-DERS ARE TOUGH.

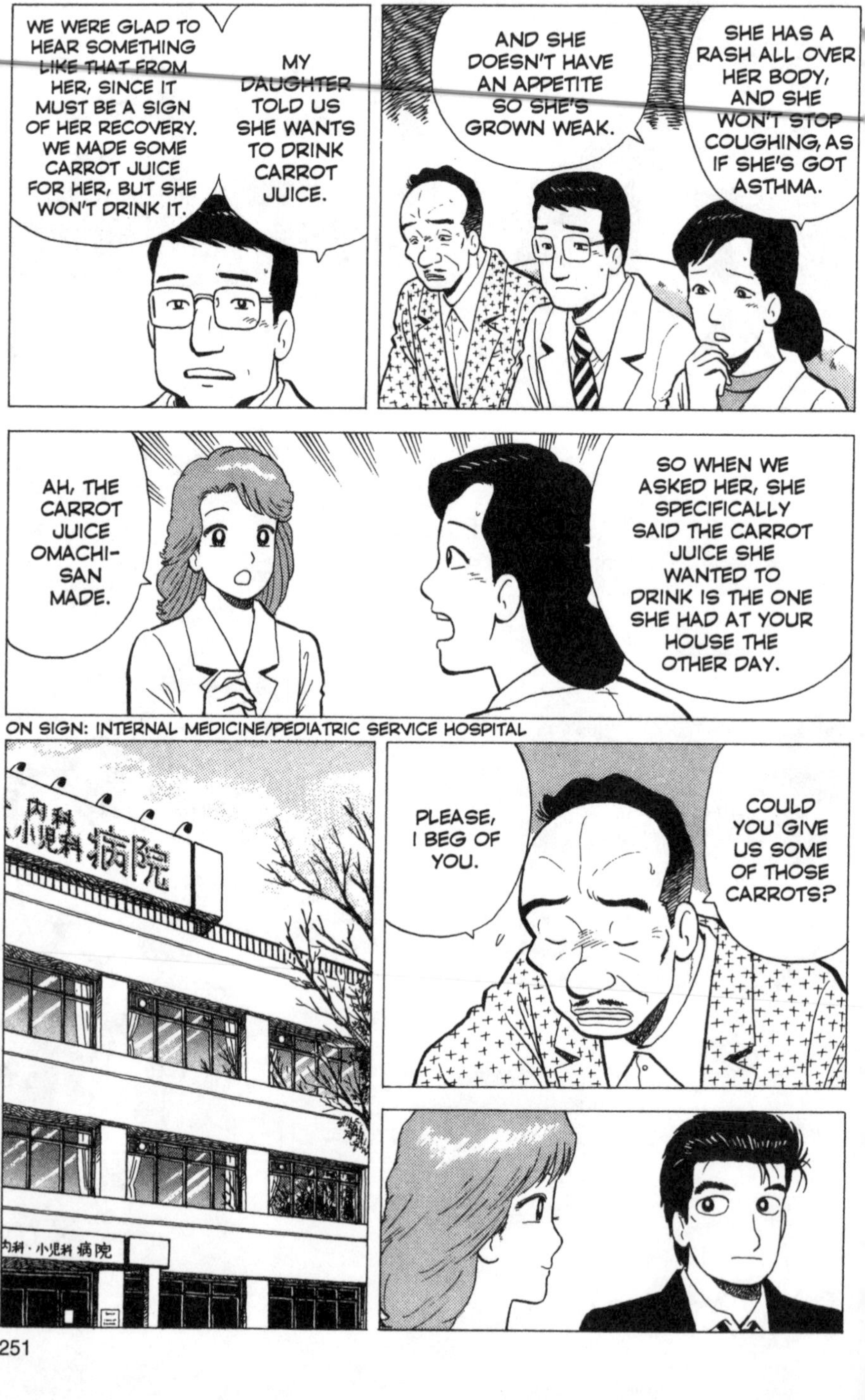
SHE HAS A RASH ALL OVER HER BODY, AND SHE WON'T STOP COUGHING, AS IF SHE'S GOT ASTHMA.
AND SHE DOESN'T HAVE AN APPETITE SO SHE'S GROWN WEAK.
MY DAUGHTER TOLD US SHE WANTS TO DRINK CARROT JUICE.
WE WERE GLAD TO HEAR SOMETHING LIKE THAT FROM HER, SINCE IT MUST BE A SIGN OF HER RECOVERY. WE MADE SOME CARROT JUICE FOR HER, BUT SHE WON'T DRINK IT.
SO WHEN WE ASKED HER, SHE SPECIFICALLY SAID THE CARROT JUICE SHE WANTED TO DRINK IS THE ONE SHE HAD AT YOUR HOUSE THE OTHER DAY.
AH, THE CARROT JUICE OMACHI-SAN MADE.
ON SIGN: INTERNAL MEDICINE/PEDIATRIC SERVICE HOSPITAL
COULD YOU GIVE US SOME OF THOSE CARROTS?
PLEASE, I BEG OF YOU.
内科・小児科病院

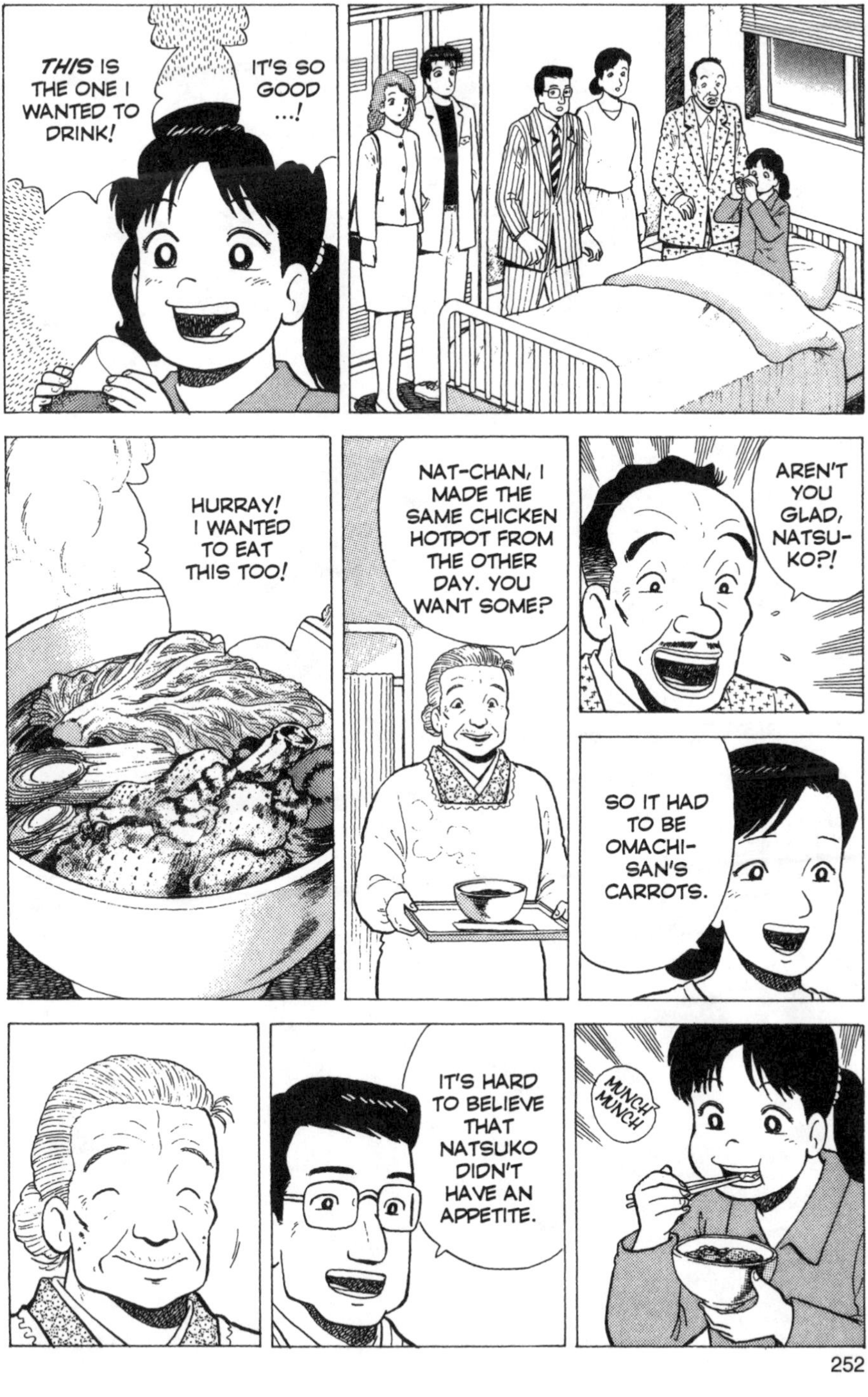
IT'S SO GOOD ...!
THIS IS THE ONE I WANTED TO DRINK!
AREN'T YOU GLAD, NATSUKO?!
SO IT HAD TO BE OMACHI-SAN'S CARROTS.
NAT-CHAN, I MADE THE SAME CHICKEN HOTPOT FROM THE OTHER DAY. YOU WANT SOME?
HURRAY! I WANTED TO EAT THIS TOO!
MUNCH MUNCH
IT'S HARD TO BELIEVE THAT NATSUKO DIDN'T HAVE AN APPETITE.

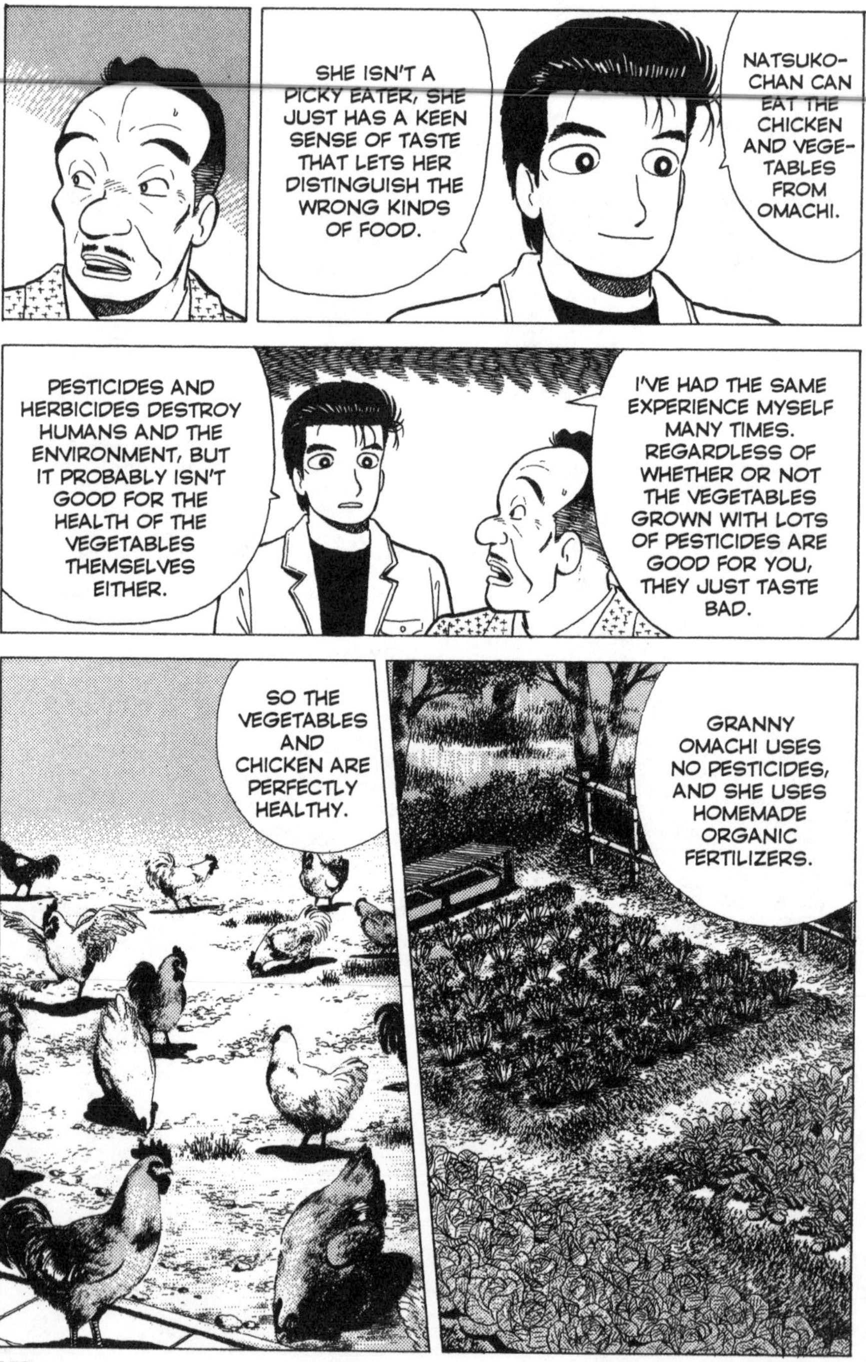
NATSUKO-CHAN CAN EAT THE CHICKEN AND VEGETABLES FROM OMACHI.
SHE ISN'T A PICKY EATER, SHE JUST HAS A KEEN SENSE OF TASTE THAT LETS HER DISTINGUISH THE WRONG KINDS OF FOOD.
I'VE HAD THE SAME EXPERIENCE MYSELF MANY TIMES. REGARDLESS OF WHETHER OR NOT THE VEGETABLES GROWN WITH LOTS OF PESTICIDES ARE GOOD FOR YOU, THEY JUST TASTE BAD.
PESTICIDES AND HERBICIDES DESTROY HUMANS AND THE ENVIRONMENT, BUT IT PROBABLY ISN'T GOOD FOR THE HEALTH OF THE VEGETABLES THEMSELVES EITHER.
GRANNY OMACHI USES NO PESTICIDES, AND SHE USES HOMEMADE ORGANIC FERTILIZERS.
SO THE VEGETABLES AND CHICKEN ARE PERFECTLY HEALTHY.

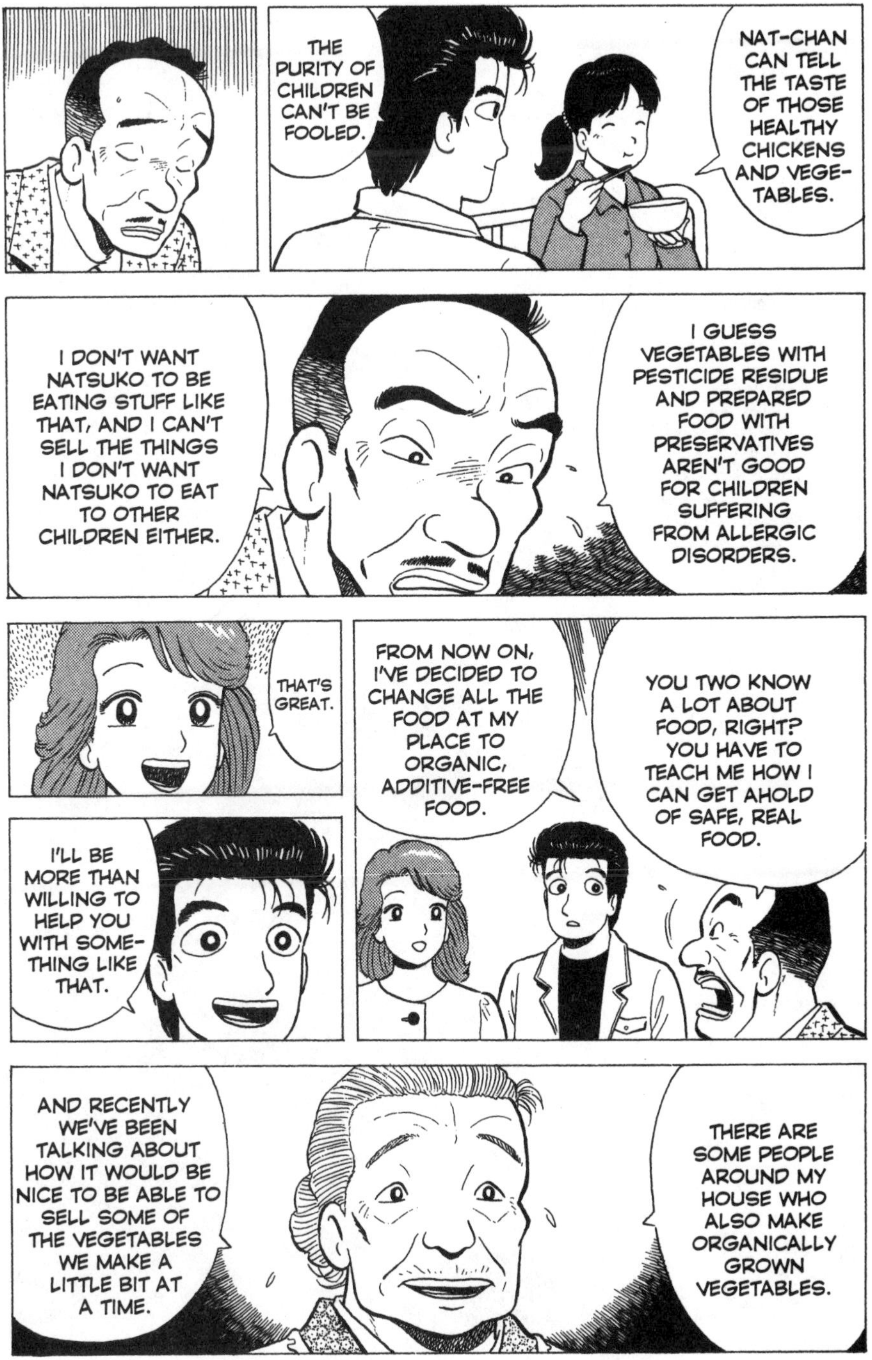
NAT-CHAN CAN TELL THE TASTE OF THOSE HEALTHY CHICKENS AND VEGE-TABLES.
THE PURITY OF CHILDREN CAN'T BE FOOLED.
I GUESS VEGETABLES WITH PESTICIDE RESIDUE AND PREPARED FOOD WITH PRESERVATIVES AREN'T GOOD FOR CHILDREN SUFFERING FROM ALLERGIC DISORDERS.
I DON'T WANT NATSUKO TO BE EATING STUFF LIKE THAT, AND I CAN'T SELL THE THINGS I DON'T WANT NATSUKO TO EAT TO OTHER CHILDREN EITHER.
FROM NOW ON, I'VE DECIDED TO CHANGE ALL THE FOOD AT MY PLACE TO ORGANIC, ADDITIVE-FREE FOOD.
YOU TWO KNOW A LOT ABOUT FOOD, RIGHT? YOU HAVE TO TEACH ME HOW I CAN GET AHOLD OF SAFE, REAL FOOD.
THAT'S GREAT.
I'LL BE MORE THAN WILLING TO HELP YOU WITH SOME-THING LIKE THAT.
THERE ARE SOME PEOPLE AROUND MY HOUSE WHO ALSO MAKE ORGANICALLY GROWN VEGETABLES.
AND RECENTLY WE'VE BEEN TALKING ABOUT HOW IT WOULD BE NICE TO BE ABLE TO SELL SOME OF THE VEGETABLES WE MAKE A LITTLE BIT AT A TIME.

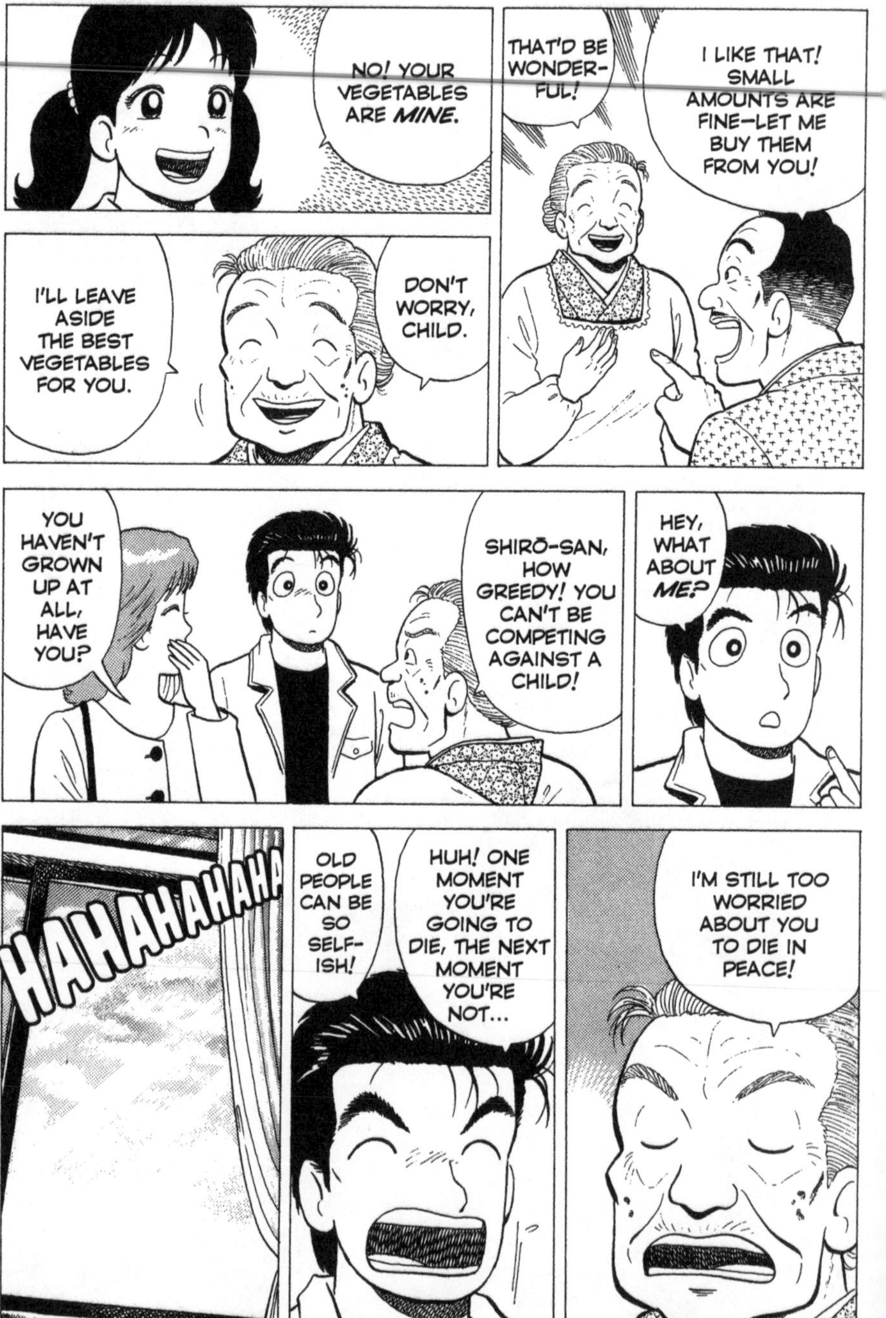
I LIKE THAT! SMALL AMOUNTS ARE FINE—LET ME BUY THEM FROM YOU!
THAT'D BE WONDER-FUL!
NO! YOUR VEGETABLES ARE *MINE*.
DON'T WORRY, CHILD.
I'LL LEAVE ASIDE THE BEST VEGETABLES FOR YOU.
HEY, WHAT ABOUT *ME?*
SHIRŌ-SAN, HOW GREEDY! YOU CAN'T BE COMPETING AGAINST A CHILD!
YOU HAVEN'T GROWN UP AT ALL, HAVE YOU?
I'M STILL TOO WORRIED ABOUT YOU TO DIE IN PEACE!
HUH! ONE MOMENT YOU'RE GOING TO DIE, THE NEXT MOMENT YOU'RE NOT...
OLD PEOPLE CAN BE SO SELF-ISH!
HAHAHAHAHAHA

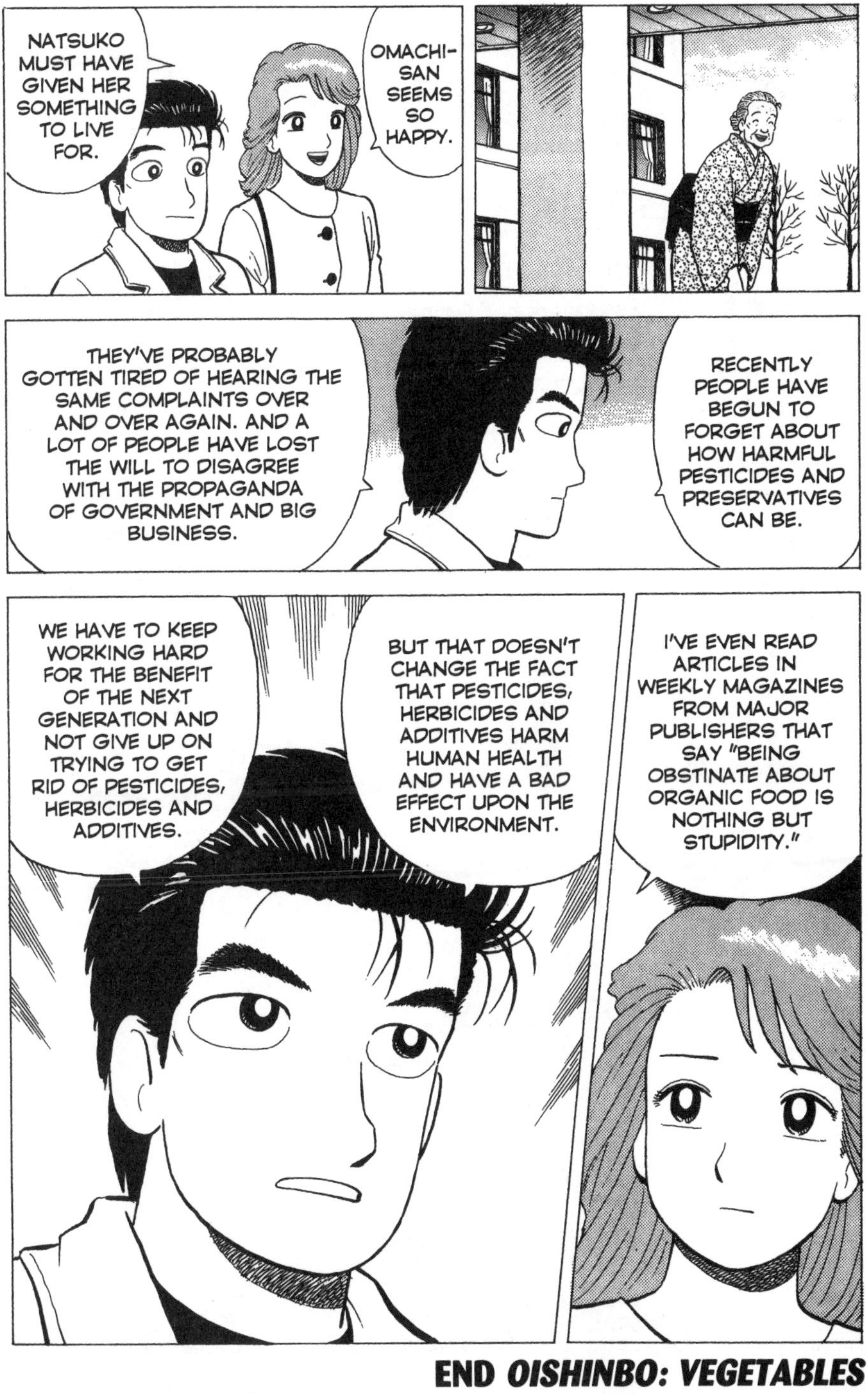
OMACHI-SAN SEEMS SO HAPPY.
NATSUKO MUST HAVE GIVEN HER SOMETHING TO LIVE FOR.
RECENTLY PEOPLE HAVE BEGUN TO FORGET ABOUT HOW HARMFUL PESTICIDES AND PRESERVATIVES CAN BE.
THEY'VE PROBABLY GOTTEN TIRED OF HEARING THE SAME COMPLAINTS OVER AND OVER AGAIN. AND A LOT OF PEOPLE HAVE LOST THE WILL TO DISAGREE WITH THE PROPAGANDA OF GOVERNMENT AND BIG BUSINESS.
I'VE EVEN READ ARTICLES IN WEEKLY MAGAZINES FROM MAJOR PUBLISHERS THAT SAY "BEING OBSTINATE ABOUT ORGANIC FOOD IS NOTHING BUT STUPIDITY."
BUT THAT DOESN'T CHANGE THE FACT THAT PESTICIDES, HERBICIDES AND ADDITIVES HARM HUMAN HEALTH AND HAVE A BAD EFFECT UPON THE ENVIRONMENT.
WE HAVE TO KEEP WORKING HARD FOR THE BENEFIT OF THE NEXT GENERATION AND NOT GIVE UP ON TRYING TO GET RID OF PESTICIDES, HERBICIDES AND ADDITIVES.

END *OISHINBO: VEGETABLES*

Page 8, panel 2

In the previous chapter of the series, Arakawa and Tabata Kinue want to get married, but his mother is against it because of Kinue's inability to cook rice properly. Thanks to Yamaoka's help, Kinue is able to get Mrs. Arakawa's approval. This story appears in Chapter 3 of the VIZ edition of *Oishinbo a la Carte: Rice*.

Page 8, panel 6

Yamabudo, the name on the label of the bottles, means "mountain grapes." The specific species is *Vitis coignetiae pulliat*, a wild grape found throughout Japan and parts of Korea. It can be used to make wine, but here the bottles contain pure unfermented grape juice.

Page 10, panel 1

At this point in the series, there has been only one match between the Ultimate and Supreme menus. No common theme was agreed to beforehand. Kaibara used a very special high-grade egg that Yamaoka objected to.

Page 16, panel 1

The use of herbicides and pesticides is an extremely volatile issue in Japan, as reflected in the stories contained in this volume. Between the pressures of a large population, limited arable land and a shrinking number of farmworkers, the Japanese are trying to balance getting the most from their agricultural industry without destroying their environment.

Page 24, panel 2

Shirako, translated here as "milt," is fish sperm. It's obtained from the reproductive glands of the male fish.

Page 24, panel 3

Kuzu (*Pueraria lobata*), known in America as "kudzu," is a pea vine indigenous to Japan. It is an edible plant and is used as an ingredient in Chinese medicine. Its root contains a lot of starch, and it is often used in traditional Japanese cooking to add thickness to sauces and jellies.

Page 26, panel 4
The tomato and farming process referred to here comes from volume 3 of the complete *Oishinbo* series. The Ryokuken farming method, otherwise and more commonly known as the Nagata farming method, was created by Nagata Terukichi. It is a unique method of growing vegetables, characterized by minimal use of water and fertilizer. The idea is to draw out the full energy of the vegetable itself—"coercing" it to grow strong by driving it to a state of near starvation.

First Course, Part 2

Page 35, panel 6
Dashi is the basic Japanese word for soup stock. *Ichiban-dashi* (literally "first dashi") is made by dropping *konbu* in a pot and bringing it to a light boil. As soon as the konbu floats to the surface, it is removed. Just before the liquid comes to a boil, shaved *katsuobushi* is added. It is allowed to boil for a few seconds, and then the heat is turned off. When the katsuobushi sinks and the liquid cools slightly, the dashi is poured through a strainer to remove the katsuobushi, leaving only the broth, ichiban-dashi.

All the same ingredients are recycled for the *niban-dashi* (second dashi). The used konbu and katsuobushi are placed in a pot and heated. When it starts to boil, another piece of konbu is added. The stock is then simmered for ten minutes and strained to remove the ingredients, leaving the niban-dashi broth.

Page 37, panel 1
When you get miso soup in a restaurant in the West, it's almost always made with white, or *shiro*, miso. However, there are actually many different kinds of miso, ranging from the smooth and sweet white miso to robust and hearty varieties. *Hatchō* miso is dark brown in color and has an intense, rich flavor that makes it a good choice for marinating meat. Red miso, or *aka* miso, is somewhere between white and hatchō miso in strength and taste. It is a specialty of Sendai, a town in northern Honshū, and is sometimes called Sendai miso.

Page 43, panel 4

Katsuobushi is dried bonito, or skipjack tuna (*Katsuwonus pelamis*), a staple of the Japanese kitchen. Chunks of the fish are smoked and dried into hard blocks, which keep for several months. In the past people would shave off flakes of the fish by hand, but these days *katsuobushi* flakes are sold by the bag. (It's roughly analogous to how Westerners buy packages of grated cheese instead of doing it by hand.)

Page 43, panel 7

Sweetfish is the English name for *ayu* (*Plecoglossus altivelis*), which lives only in the rivers, lakes and coastal waters of Japan and East Asia. The name "sweetfish" refers to the sweetness of its meat.

First Course, Part 3

Page 54, panel 1

Yakiboshi means any fish that is broiled and dried. It is a very common way of preparing fish ingredients for use in dashi.

Page 57, panel 4

At this point in the story, Yūko and Yamaoka aren't yet romantically involved. Yūko is interested in Yamaoka, but he hasn't figured this out yet.

Page 62, panel 4

Arakawa's mother speaks with a very strong Iwate accent. In the English version, she is given a very old-fashioned and countrified speech pattern.

Page 63, panel 6

Zenmai is the Japanese royal fern (*Osmunda japonica*), a plant native to Asia that is eaten as a wild vegetable. That Arakawa's mother uses this in her cooking implies that she lives in the countryside where such plants are available.

Page 63, panel 7

Kogomi is the Ostrich fern (*Matteuccia struthiopteris*), another edible wild plant considered a delicacy in Japan.

Page 65, panel 5

The *oni-gurumi* (demon walnut) is a particular species native to Japan, with nuts that ripen in the autumn.

Page 69, panel 2

Umezu, sometimes translated as "plum vinegar," is the juice that accumulates in the jar when making *umeboshi* (pickled plums). It can be used for flavoring dishes in the way Westerners use regular vinegar.

Page 69, panel 4

Kaibara is shocked at Yamaoka's stupidity because he believes the dish in front of him is turnips pickled in umezu, which is an extremely ordinary dish. But we are about to find out that Kaibara is wrong.

Page 71, panel 5

The text on the upper right is the first two lines of a famous Japanese song called "*Furusato*" (Homeland) written by Takano Tatsuyuki. It evokes images of a childhood spent in the countryside, echoed by the background art in this panel.

Second Course

Page 76, panel 1

In a previous story, Yamaoka and the Ultimate Menu team traveled to Korea to do a story for the World Taste Tour. Pyon is a Japanese-speaking Korean journalist who came to their aid by helping them understand Korean cooking.

The World Taste Tour is a promotional gimmick for the *Tōzai News*. It allows Yamaoka and Kurita to travel to various locations in Japan and around the world to cover stories while continuing to do research for the Ultimate Menu.

Page 77, panel 1
The sweet soup here is *oshiruko,* made with *azuki* red beans. It's a traditional Japanese dessert, but similar dishes can be found all over Asia.

Page 78, panel 6
Here Kinjo calls Yamaoka *danna,* which literally means something like "my lord Yamaoka" or "Sir Yamaoka." Nakamatsu also calls Yamaoka the same thing.

Page 79, panel 4
The rank *shachō* means "chief executive" or "president" of a company.

Page 87, panel 7
Potatoes (*jagaimo* or *jaga* in Japanese) were introduced to Japan in the 17th century but did not go into widespread cultivation until the 19th century, when the Meiji government promoted Western-style agriculture in Hokkaido.

Page 88, panel 1
Beef stew, or *niku-jaga,* is one of the basic dishes of Japanese home cooking. It has an interesting (and possibly apocryphal) backstory. A naval officer who had eaten stew while he was studying in England—and with hopes of eating it again in Japan—ordered his cook to make it for him. Not surprisingly, the cook had no idea what "stew" was, and so after placing the meat and potatoes in the pot, he used his own familiar Japanese ingredients (e.g. soy sauce, dashi, *mirin*) instead of Western ones (e.g. salt, meat stock, red wine). The result was niku-jaga. In western Japan, it is common to use beef in this dish, whereas pork is more often used in eastern Japan.

Third Course

Page 102, panel 7
Sports Day is a national holiday in Japan celebrated on the second Monday in October. On the previous Sunday, many schools have a Sports Festival, where members of each class are chosen (often unwillingly) to represent the class in various sporting events. Parents of the students are also expected to attend and participate. The school is divided into a Red Team and a White Team, with points from each event being tallied to see which team is the winner.

Page 106, panel 7
The stacking lunch box depicted here is an *oju*, make of lacquered wood boxes that stack together to make it portable. Mariko's box and its contents are quite luxurious and clearly meant to outshine Yūko's simple wicker lunch box.

Fourth Course

Page 124, panel 1
Utako runs an ice cream shop frequented by Yamaoka and his friends. She is engaged to Police Inspector Nakamatsu.

Page 126, panel 6
In Japanese schools, each class elects a representative to represent them in the student council. Student council in Japan is much more important and influential than in American schools.

Page 130, panel 8
Sticking chopsticks into eggplants to make animal shapes and throwing them into the river is an ancient custom associated with the *Obon* festival of the dead. There are varying accounts of where this tradition started, but it is commonly assumed that the spirits of the dead would use the animals as transportation to and from the other world.

Page 132, panel 7

Nuka-zuke are a kind of Japanese pickle, make by fermenting vegetables in rice bran (*nuka*). Eggplant, carrot and cucumber are the most common ingredients.

Page 142, panel 2

The cooking method described here is *abura-doshi*, where the meat or vegetable is briefly passed quickly through hot oil as a pretreatment to cooking.

Page 142, panel 2

Yuba is usually translated in English as "tofu skin." A common item in Japanese, Chinese and other East Asian cuisines, *yuba* is a versatile, neutral-tasting sheet made from the fats and proteins that float to the top when soy milk is boiled. (It's like the skin that forms on top when you make yourself a cup of hot milk.)

Page 144, panel 7

In the last line, Yamaoka says "*Otankonasu*" to call Tomii an idiot. It is a pun on the word *nasu*, Japanese for eggplant.

Fifth Course

Page 148, panel 6

Ryōtei is the term used for extremely fine Japanese restaurants (which are also usually quite costly).

Page 152, panel 1

Waribashi and *rikyu-bashi* are disposable wooden chopsticks, meant to be used once and thrown away, as opposed to durable chopsticks. There is a great debate in Japan over whether waribashi are a major waste of natural resources or an efficient use of otherwise useless scrap lumber. A lot of environmentalists pride themselves on carrying their own non-disposable chopsticks.

Page 152, panel 7

Temari-zushi (literally "handball sushi") is a small, round, ball-like sushi.

Page 152, panel 7

Shiso is an herb in the mint family that is used in a variety of Japanese dishes, especially sushi and sashimi. The most common variants are *aojiso* (green shiso) and *akajiso* (red shiso).

Page 162, panel 3

Kabosu is a Chinese citrus fruit closely related to *yuzu*. It has the sharpness of a lemon and is used as a substitute for vinegar in Japanese cooking.

Sixth Course

Page 180, panel 1

Yamaoka is still in denial about his feelings for Yūko and her feelings for him. When Kinjo pursues Yūko, it forces Yamaoka to confront his real feelings.

Page 183, panel 2

Kabayaki-style means brushed with sauce, skewered on sticks, and then grilled over charcoal.

Page 186, panel 1

Kohiki refers to the silky white color of the dish. *Maruzara* literally means "round plate."

Seventh Course, Part 1

Page 200, panel 3

Sugata-zushi (full-figure/whole shape sushi) is sushi where the entire shape of the fish is preserved in the presentation, as opposed to just a slice of the meat being served.

Page 201, panel 1

Oshi-zushi or "pressed sushi" is a type of sushi where usually a fish that has been marinated in vinegar is placed inside a wooden case along with rice and then pressed from the top to create a square block of sushi.

Page 201, panel 2

Kyōgoku-san was born and raised in the Shimanto area and has a strong preference for the fish from that area.

Page 201, panel 5

Kuroushi beef literally means "black beef," but it actually functions more as a brand name than a species of cow.

Page 211, panel 1

Minakami Tsutomu is an actual author who wrote novels and nonfiction often on the subjects of food and simple living. He gained much of his inspiration from his early days working in a temple kitchen as a Zen disciple. The book mentioned here has not yet been published in English.

Seventh Course, Part 2

Page 224, panel 5

Karuizawa, a town in Nagano Prefecture, is a popular resort area. Due to its elevation, it is cool in the summer. For that reason, it has long been a place for wealthy Tokyoites to escape the summer heat. The area contains many summer homes nestled in mountains.

Page 224, panel 7

The word in the title translated as "devotion" is *shojin*, a term that does not translate directly into English. It can mean diligent striving, devotion and Buddhist monastic discipline. *Shojin ryōri* is the term for Buddhist monastic vegetarian cooking.

Page 226, panel 4

Ohitashi is a dish in which the vegetable is lightly boiled and then placed in dashi. In modern usage, it can also mean boiled leaf vegetables with soy sauce poured on top.

Page 226, panel 6

Dōgen Zenshi is a historical Japanese Zen priest, the founder of the Soto School of Zen, which is one of the two major Japanese sects of Zen Buddhism.

Page 229, panel 7

Umeshu, often translated as "plum wine," is spirit made from steeping ume plums in *shochu* with sugar.

Page 231, panel 6

Uni no shiokara is roughly translated "salted sea urchin." It is a mixture of fresh *uni* shellfish, salt and sake.

Eighth Course

Page 238, panel 5

The word translated here as "hotpot" is *nabe*, which literally means pot or pan. Nabe is also a style of cooking where all the ingredients are cooked together in a pot, often right atop the dinner table.

Page 244, panel 3

Ozawa is the landlord who owns the building that Yamaoka and Yūko live in. Nomae's home and shop are also in the same building.

In the next volume of *Oishinbo*, Yamaoka must show his skills with the cornerstone of the Japanese diet—rice. The issues are weighty and the points contentious: brown rice versus white rice, the importation of foreign grains, the side dishes most suited to a bowl of rice, and—most important—the proper way to cook rice itself. When the subject is so closely connected to the heart of Japanese culture, will the Ultimate Menu be able to meet the challenge?

Available Now

OISHI

Vegetab.

VIZ Signature Edition

Story by Tetsu Kariya
Art by Akira Hanasaki

Translation/Tetsuichiro Miyaki
Touch-up & Lettering/Kelle Han
Cover & Graphic Design/Hidemi Dunn
Editors/Leyla Aker, Jonathan Tarbox

Recipe Credits:
Food Photography/Hideo Sawai (Assistant: Kunihiro Yokoi)
Food Styling/Yuko Tanaka – Le Treat (Assistant: Yoko Ito)
Recipe Composition/Yoko Yasui – The Tracks

OISHINBO A LA CARTE 19 by Tetsu KARIYA and Akira HANASAKI
© 2006 Tetsu KARIYA and Akira HANASAKI
All rights reserved. Original Japanese edition published in 2006 by Shogakukan Inc., Tokyo.
English translation rights in the United States of America, Canada, Australia and New
Zealand arranged with SHOGAKUKAN.

Printed in Canada

Published by VIZ Media, LLC
P.O. Box 77010
San Francisco, CA 94107

10 9 8 7 6 5
First printing, September 2009
Fifth printing, November 2020

www.viz.com